THE JOURNALS OF
Samuel R. Delany

IN SEARCH OF SILENCE:

VOLUME 1, 1957–1969

ALSO BY SAMUEL R. DELANY

FICTION

The Jewels of Aptor (1962)

The Fall of the Towers

Out of the Dead City (1963)

The Towers of Toron (1964)

City of a Thousand Suns (1965)

The Ballad of Beta-2 (1965)

Babel-17 (1966)

Empire Star (1966)

The Einstein Intersection (1967)

Nova (1968)

Driftglass (1969)

Equinox (1973)

Dhalgren (1975)

Trouble on Triton (1976)

Return to Nevèrÿon

Tales of Nevèrÿon (1979)

Neveryóna (1982)

Flight from Nevèrÿon (1985)

Return to Nevèrÿon (1987)

Distant Stars (1981)

Stars in My Pocket Like
    Grains of Sand (1984)

Driftglass/Starshards
    (collected stories, 1993)

They Fly at Çiron (1993)

The Mad Man (1994)

Hogg (1995)

Atlantis: Three Tales (1995)

Aye, and Gomorrah
    (*and other stories*, 2004)

Phallos (2004)

Dark Reflections (2007)

Through the Valley of the
    Nest of Spiders (2012)

A, B, C: Three Short Novels (2015)

GRAPHIC NOVELS

Empire
    (artist, Howard Chaynkin, 1980)

Bread & Wine
    (artist, Mia Wolff, 1999)

NONFICTION

The Jewel-Hinged Jaw (1977;
    revised, 2008)

The American Shore (1978)

Heavenly Breakfast (1979)

Starboard Wine (1978; revised, 2008)

The Motion of Light in Water (1988)

Wagner/Artaud (1988)

The Straits of Messina (1990)

Silent Interviews (1994)

Longer Views (1996)

Times Square Red,
    Times Square Blue (1999)

Shorter Views (1999)

1984: Selected Letters (2000)

About Writing (2005)

publication of this book is funded by the

BEATRICE FOX AUERBACH FOUNDATION FUND

at the Hartford Foundation for Public Giving

THE JOURNALS OF SAMUEL R. DELANY

In Search of Silence: Volume 1, 1957–1969

THE JOURNALS OF
SAMUEL R. DELANY

IN SEARCH OF SILENCE

VOLUME 1, 1957–1969

EDITED BY KENNETH R. JAMES

WESLEYAN UNIVERSITY PRESS

Middletown, Connecticut

Wesleyan University Press
Middletown CT 06459
www.wesleyan.edu/wespress
© 2017 Samuel R. Delany; Editor's Introduction © 2017 Kenneth R. James
All rights reserved
Manufactured in the United States of America
Typeset in Linoletter and Aller by Tseng Information Systems, Inc.

publication of this book is funded by the
BEATRICE FOX AUERBACH FOUNDATION FUND
at the Hartford Foundation for Public Giving

Permissions information appears on the last page of the book.

Library of Congress Cataloging-in-Publication Data
Names: Delany, Samuel R., author. | James, Kenneth R., editor.
Title: In search of silence: the journals of Samuel R. Delany. Volume 1, 1957–1969 /
    edited by Kenneth R. James.
Description: Middletown, Connecticut: Wesleyan University Press, [2016] | Includes
    bibliographical references and index.
Identifiers: LCCN 2015044546 | (print) | LCCN 2016002218 (ebook) | ISBN 9780819570895
    (cloth: alk. paper) | ISBN 9780819576934 (ebook)
Subjects: LCSH: Delany, Samuel R. | Authors, American—20th century—Biography. |
    Science fiction—Authorship.
Classification: LCC PS3554. E437 Z46 2016 | DDC 813/.54—dc23
LC record available at http://lccn.loc.gov/2015044546

5 4 3 2 1

CONTENTS

Editor's Introduction   xi

1. BRONX SCIENCE AND OTHER NEW YORK SCENES   1
Notebook 1—January–February 1958   3
Notebook 3—January 1959   5
Notebook 7—1959 [March–April 1959]   7
Notebook 6—1959 [April 1959]   11
Notebook 4—April–May 1959   13
Notebook 5—1959 [Summer–Autumn 1959]   26

2. *IN SEARCH OF SILENCE*   29
Notebook 2—January 1959 [January–February 1960]   31
Notebook 8—March 1960   59
Notebook 11—Spring 1960 [Spring–Summer 1960]   63

3. *JOURNAUX D'ORPHÉE*   67
Notebook 12—Inclusive to July 1960   69

4. CITY COLLEGE   95
Notebook 13—September 1960   99
Notebook 14—Autumn 1960   103
Notebook 9—Winter 1960   107
Notebook 10—Spring 1960 [Spring 1961]   115
Notebook 16—Spring, Summer 1961   119
Notebook 17—Summer 1961   136

5. MARRIED LIFE IN THE EAST VILLAGE   143
Notebook 18—August 1961   145
Notebook 15—September–October 1961
    [October 1960 / September–October 1961]   162
Notebook 19—November 1961–June 1962   167
Notebook 21—Spring 1962 [January 1962]   178
Notebook 20—Spring 1962 [March 1962]   179

6. *THE FALL OF THE TOWERS* AND *VOYAGE, ORESTES*   181
Notebook 22—Summer 1962   183
Notebook 23—November 1962 [October–
   November 1962]   189
Notebook 25—Inclusive through March 1963
   [Autumn 1962–Spring 1963]   195
Notebook 24—Inclusive to January–February 1963   202
Notebook 75—[Spring–Summer 1963]   207
Notebook 68—[October 1963]   226
Notebook 71—[Winter 1963]   239
Notebook 92—[Spring 1964]   252

7. *BABEL-17* AND BEYOND   255
Notebook 26—June–July 1964   259
Notebook 27—August 15, 1964   273
Notebook 28—September 1964–January 1965   294
Notebook 87—[Early Spring 1965]   298
Notebook 82—[Summer 1964–Spring 1965]   304
Notebook 81—[Late Spring 1965]   313
Notebook 29—June–July 1965   317

8. TRAVELS IN EUROPE   335
Notebook 67—[Autumn 1965–Summer 1966]   337
Notebook 96—[Autumn 1965]   343
Notebook 31—March 1966 [February–March 1966]   346
Notebook 30—December 1965 [Spring 1966]   360

9. CHANGING SCENES   377
Notebook 80—[Spring 1966]   379
Notebook 91—[Fall 1966]   386
Notebook 83—[December 1966–January 1967]   391
Notebook 84—[February–April 1967]   402
Notebook 76—[Spring–Summer 1967]   417
Notebook 69—[Summer 1967]   424

10. *PRISM, MIRROR, LENS* AND OTHER PROJECTS   427
Notebook 86—[Summer 1967]   429
Notebook 32—July–October 1967   432
Notebook 88—[Autumn 1967]   455

Notebook 33—December 1967 [December 1967–
    January 1968] 464
Notebook 35—1968 [Early Spring 1968] 483
Notebook 77—[Early Spring 1968] 491
Notebook 85—[Spring–Summer 1968] 496
Notebook 90—[Summer 1968] 507
Notebook 78—[Summer–Autumn 1968] 508
Notebook 34—August 1968 [August–September 1968] 522
Notebook 79—[Winter 1968] 532

11. TO SAN FRANCISCO 537
Notebook 36—January–February 1969 539
Notebook 37—April 1969 [February–April 1969] 550

12. APPENDIXES 555
Appendix 1. Notebook 89 [Winter 1957–January 1958] 557
Appendix 2. Notebook 1—January–February 1958 569
Appendix 3. Three Short Works from 1959–1960 587

Acknowledgments 605
Notes 607
Bibliography 645
Index 649

Illustrations follow pages 312 and 536

EDITOR'S INTRODUCTION

I

In late 1957, at age fifteen, Samuel Ray Delany Jr. began using spiral-bound notebooks to record personal journal entries and produce working notes and drafts for creative projects.[1] He made it a regular practice to carry a notebook with him when he traveled from his family's middle-class home in Harlem up to his classes at the Bronx High School of Science, down to Upper West Side apartments where he participated in fiction and poetry readings, and farther downtown to East Village cafés where he performed as a folksinger. Delany filled his notebooks at a rapid clip and saved them assiduously. By the end of the '60s, at which point Delany had published nine science fiction novels and several short stories to plaudits that included three Nebula Awards (followed later by a fourth Nebula, as well as two Hugo Awards), the number of notebooks he had filled had passed sixty. By the end of the '90s, at which point he had produced work in other genres and earned still more honors, such as inclusion in the *Norton Anthology of African American Literature* and reception of the Bill Whitehead Memorial Award for Lifetime Achievement as a contributor to LGBT literature, the number of notebooks had passed three hundred. Today, Delany's notebooks, along with manuscripts, memorabilia, and other artifacts of his extraordinary career as a novelist and critic, are stored at the Howard Gotlieb Archival Research Center at Boston University. But when Delany wrote the earliest of the entries collected in this book, the beginning of that career still lay over the horizon.

This is the first of a projected series of volumes presenting Delany's personal journals as well as other items of interest from his notebooks. Each volume in the series will contain roughly a decade's worth of material; the entries collected here date from winter 1957 to spring 1969. The first half of the volume covers the period Delany examines in his autobiography *The Motion of Light in Water: Sex and Science Fiction Writing in the East Village* (1987/2004), and may be read in profitable dialogue with it. During this time Delany attended and graduated from Bronx Science, attended City College sporadically before devoting his energy entirely to freelance writing, married fellow Bronx Science graduate and poet Marilyn Hacker, and eventually departed for Europe—meanwhile writing the science fiction novels by which he would first become known to readers, as well as a good deal of unpublished work in other genres. The second half of the volume carries the story forward from where *Motion* leaves off, covering Delany's travels in Europe and return to New York City, his increasing involvement in the science fiction community and reception of major SF awards, his separation from Hacker and involvement with a rock band / commune—an experience he describes in his extended essay on urban communes, *Heavenly Breakfast* (1979)—and finally his move to San Francisco to reunite with Hacker. The volume ends with Delany on the verge of drastically reconceiving what would become arguably the pivotal novel of his career, *Dhalgren* (1975).

In the selections that follow, the richness and multiplicity characteristic of Delany's fiction, essays, and memoirs are fully evident, and evident in multiple senses. First, the early entries indicate that well before he had graduated from high school, Delany was already producing work in a variety of genres and displaying a sophisticated historical understanding of all of them. This combination of creative range and erudition exemplifies one of the more remarkable qualities of the early entries: the degree to which Delany's mature voice is already recognizable in them. Not only are the tones and cadences of his later prose readily apparent, but so are his characteristic themes: sexuality and gender, race and class, identity and difference, precociousness, mythopoesis, and the role of the artist as a catalyst for social change.

Also present at the outset is a portrayal of urban diversity that has been central to Delany's published work. From the earliest entries, Delany responds, with an articulateness remarkable for a teenager, to both his immediate family in Harlem and his extended family with its impressive history of professional achievement and political activism in the black community; to his extremely gifted, and predominantly white, peers at the Bronx Science; to the gay population of the city, pre-Stonewall; and to the community of performers in the city's folk music scene, in which Delany participated enthusiastically through much of the '60s. As the years pass and Delany's career as a writer advances, we see him navigate new social circles—and cities—as he engages with both well-established and newly ascendant literary communities.

Finally, the multiplicity characteristic of Delany's work and life is reflected in the eclectic and multiform quality of the journals themselves. Because Delany used his notebooks as repositories for both private entries and creative working notes, in their pages personal meditations and aphoristic *pensées* jostle with outlines and drafts of fiction, poetry, plays, song lyrics, and other creative work—not to mention letter drafts, school notes, and to-do lists. And since Delany did not take a systematic approach to journal keeping, the personal entries themselves follow no set form and are often fragmentary, sometimes trailing off in mid-sentence. As a result, the experience of perusing Delany's notebooks in their unedited form is less like reading the journals of, say, André Gide—an important literary model for Delany, both as novelist and diarist—and more like navigating the *Arcades Project*, Walter Benjamin's massive and fragmentary collage of found texts and critical commentary, with each entry engaged in complex dialogue with its neighbors.

In this collection I have attempted to preserve the dialogical quality of Delany's notebooks by including, alongside the personal entries, a substantial selection of the surrounding material, such as story outlines, working notes, drafts of correspondence, and the like. I have also included less readily categorizable writing born of various kinds of desire, such as pornographic fantasies, hypothetical book blurbs anticipating fame and renown, and writerly experiments whose main purpose seems to have been to propel other pieces of writing into being. The entries selected for this volume thus reflect multiple intentions on Delany's part and speak in a variety of registers. They encompass both polished, finely wrought private musings and relatively unpolished, inchoate or incipient writing—a kind of infra-writing, to use a Barthesian turn of phrase.

The reader will note that even the more polished entries in this volume tend to take for granted, or respond only indirectly or belatedly to, circumstances or events that someone familiar with Delany's life might consider very important. For example: while this volume covers the period of Delany's stay in the Heavenly Breakfast commune, the entries that date from that period treat the experience only in a glancing or tacit way. It was not until later, after moving to San Francisco—during a period just outside the range of this volume—that Delany began to discuss the experience at length in his journals. Readers of *Dhalgren* may recall, in one of the journal entries written by the novel's protagonist, Kid, a meditation on this sort of pattern of representation:

> The falsification of this journal: first off, it doesn't reflect my daily life. Most of what happens hour by hour here is quiet and dull. We sit most of the time, watch the dull sky slipping. Frankly, that is too stupid to

write about. When something really involving, violent, or important happens, it occupies too much of my time, my physical energy, and my thought to be *able* to write about. I can think of four things that have happened in the nest I would like to have described when they occurred, but they so completed themselves in the happening that even to refer to them seems superfluous.

What is down, then, is a chronicle of incidents with a potential for wholeness they did not have when they occurred; a false picture, again, because they show neither the general spread of our life's fabric, nor the most significant pattern points.[2]

I submit that many, if not most, of the situations and events covered in this volume are present in its pages in just the manner described above, and further that this quality of obliqueness and partialness, of falling somewhere between the momentous and the everyday, is a key ingredient of the pleasure and meaning of the text.

The dual project of selecting and presenting the entries in this volume presented many challenges. In regard to selection, the sheer quantity of material to be considered was immense, encompassing sixty notebooks and thousands of pages. Moreover, the diversity of material meant that even well-defined criteria for inclusion and exclusion still entailed countless difficult decisions. Additionally, Delany's own writing habits created ambiguities in the internal chronologies of individual notebooks, which necessitated further interpretive choices. Finally, the archives in which the notebooks are stored frequently presented situations in which the job of editor shaded over into that of literary sleuth. Meanwhile, in regard to presentation, the volume needed to balance two somewhat divergent goals. On the one hand, I wanted to make explanatory information on individual entries easily accessible to the reader. On the other hand, I wanted to keep the entries relatively free of scholarly encumbrances in order to preserve a sense of their original appearance and impact on the notebook page. Overall, the challenges of both selection and presentation in this volume tended to reflect both the complexity of the material and my own sense of the diverse ways the material might be read.

Part of my solution to the challenges of clear presentation has been to provide contextual signposts for the reader at strategic points in the text. The remainder of this introduction will supply three such signposts. The first is a fuller account of the social circles Delany inhabited and navigated during the decade-plus covered in this volume. The second is a description of the many projects on which Delany embarked during this period; this account will be brief and informal, as the purpose of this volume is to prompt, not preempt, critical discussion. The third is a fuller discussion of the criteria and procedures used in selecting and presenting the material. Taken together, these signposts, along with others supplied in the main body of the text, should facilitate the reader's trip through what is, after all, a thrilling narrative: that of an exceptionally gifted young writer beginning to formulate a response to his race, his sexuality, his historical moment, his city, his language.

II

As the journals begin, Delany, at fifteen, is already navigating several disparate social worlds. The reader may think of these worlds as a collection of intersecting sets in a Venn diagram, with Delany inhabiting their overlapping center. Naturally such a conception can only be provisional, since upon closer inspection each set either quickly breaks down into contradictory particulars or ramifies new, and equally provisional, sets. This is a dynamic that Delany's writing dramatizes repeatedly. In a passage from his novel *The Mad Man* (1994/2002), the protagonist John Marr observes that the inevitable outcome of any attempt to produce a "general" description of any given community or constituency is for the description to explode into complexity and contradiction, leading to the recognition that "the pattern you first intuited is only a reduction—or taming—of a vast number of exceptions to itself."[3] Construing Delany's social worlds as clean and closed sets, then, might best be interpreted as a first step toward opening those sets up.

One such social world is that of Delany's family. His father, Samuel Ray Delany Sr., owned and directed a successful funeral establishment in Harlem; the business was located on the ground floor of the Delany family's three-story house, with the family occupying the floors above. His mother, Margaret Carey Boyd Delany, was a clerk for the New York City public library system. Beyond the immediate household was Delany's extended family, both the paternal and maternal sides of which had distinguished histories. Delany's paternal grandfather, Henry Beard Delany, had been born into slavery, and after Emancipation had gone on to become the first African American bishop of the Episcopal Church, as well as vice principal of St. Augustine's College, a black college in North Carolina.[4] Henry Beard Delany's children were similarly accomplished, as well as politically active. One of his sons, Hubert T. Delany, became a judge and was an important civil rights advocate in postwar New York.[5] Two of his daughters, Sadie and Bessie, were a public school teacher and a dentist, respectively; Bessie was the second black woman in the state of New York to be licensed to practice. Both women were active in civil rights causes, and both achieved national prominence late in their long lives upon publishing their 1993 memoir *Having Our Say*.[6] Meanwhile—as Martha Biondi notes in her illuminating historical account *To Stand and Fight: The Struggle for Civil Rights in Postwar New York*—Delany's maternal uncle, Myles Paige, was the first African American judge for a New York State criminal court, as well as a civic leader in New York City.[7]

In the entries to follow, Delany seldom discusses his immediate household or the general atmosphere of high achievement in the extended family. He makes a few direct mentions when responding to very important events, such as the death of his father from lung cancer in the fall of 1960. But more often such references take the form of passing details that imply, rather than state, his family's domestic and social circumstances. In Notebook 15, for instance, Delany mentions visiting the summer home of his uncle Myles at Greenwood Lake, an area that served as a summer enclave for well-connected black families, intellectuals, and artists in the New York City area. And in Notebook 4, Delany mentions several childhood friends who had, like young Delany, participated in Jack and Jill of America, a social networking club for the children of middle-class black families.[8] Delany has said in conversation that while such contextual details do imply social sophistication, they don't entail structurally entrenched wealth in the pattern of the white bourgeoisie: many of Delany's immediate neighbors in Harlem lived in poverty.[9] In general, these details convey that Delany's family circumstances placed him in the milieu of the black professional middle class, with all the complexity and dissonance that that milieu implies—given the larger context of an America for which *Brown v. Board of Education* was a very recent ruling, and for which the great civil rights acts of the time, which were proceeding through the work of black folk like Delany's own uncles, had only just begun clearing Congress.

One index of the situation of (relative) privilege into which Delany was born was the high quality of his primary and secondary education. During his primary school years Delany attended the progressive, private Dalton School on the Upper East Side. (Here again, though, the ambiguity

of Delany's class position manifests itself: it was only through a financial need–based scholarship that he was able to attend Dalton.[10]) As the
journals begin, Delany has recently moved on from Dalton to the very
selective and prestigious public school, the Bronx High School of Science.
Delany's gifted peer group at Bronx Science, or "Science" as it's called by
its students, is another major social circle in which Delany moved during the earliest years covered in this volume. In *The Motion of Light in
Water*, Delany conveys the flavor of the environment at Bronx Science by
listing participants in the school's creative writing classes either during
or close to Delany's stint there; these included "future journalists Todd
Gitlin, Sheldon [*sic*] Novick, Stewart Byron, and Michael Goodwin ... and
SF/fantasy writers Peter Beagle and Norman Spinrad," as well as the poet
and future editor and fiction writer Lewis Warsh, and the very precocious
poet Marilyn Hacker, who became Delany's close friend and, shortly after
graduation, his wife.[11]

Hacker is a powerful presence in these journals. As Delany's friend, literary confidante, lover, and—eventually—spouse, Hacker is not only the
most prominent individual represented in this volume besides Delany
himself, but she also periodically contributes to its pages in the form of
commentary written on the margins of Delany's entries. (I have used bold
type to indicate passages in Hacker's own handwriting and plain type to
indicate material originating with Hacker and transcribed by Delany; the
few passages where Delany doesn't make an explicit attribution I have
pointed out in the notes at the end of the volume.) Hacker's voice counter-
points and challenges Delany's, undercutting his teenaged rhetoric with
the same wit and incisiveness characteristic of the poetry she would produce over the course of her own very distinguished career. (Her work
would eventually garner a National Book Award, the Lenore Marshall
Poetry Prize, and many other accolades.) Through her presence in these
pages as a figure of great affection and fascination for Delany, as well as
through her own direct commentary, Hacker makes a salutary contribution to the dialogical quality of these journals. Moreover, her own precociousness, in a roundabout way, adds another group to Delany's circle
of peers during the period covered in these pages. Though eight months
younger than Delany, Hacker was already a year ahead of him when he
entered Science, and in her junior year, at age fifteen, received early ad-
mission to NYU. As a result, shortly after the volume begins we observe
Delany adding Hacker's circle of college friends and acquaintances to his
own immediate circle at Science.

The juncture between Delany's home and school life was not smooth and unproblematic. As Delany recounts in *Motion*, his father was a chronically anxious and argumentative man, at constant loggerheads with his wife, with Delany himself, and with Delany's younger sister, Peggy.[12] Until his father's death, Delany coped with the general atmosphere of anxiety and volatility at home by periodically running away to stay with friends or by skipping school.[13] Thus, at least one relevant context for Delany's accounts in this volume of his peripatetic journeys around the city in the company of friends was his uncomfortable life at home. (Hacker's home life was also difficult; Delany has commented that one attraction of early marriage for both Hacker and himself was the chance it afforded them to escape from their respective households.[14]) But there is also a racial context to the relationship between Delany's home life and peer group: the elite education to which his family's professional and social success had given him access meant that the majority of his immediate peers were white. According to Delany, his youthful experience of traveling from Harlem to the Dalton School and back was "in social terms a journey of near ballistic violence, carried out each day in more or less indifferent silence."[15] This violent traversing of social boundaries as a routine part of life indelibly marked Delany's writing after Dalton; as he has said, "I have written about nothing *but* the trip through such socio-psychological barriers ever since."[16]

Two additional, and closely related, circles Delany navigated during this period suggest a kind of counterpoint to the schismatic qualities of home and school. The first consisted of friends Delany had made at Camp Woodland, which he had attended from age ten to fifteen.[17] The second consisted of participants in the downtown folk scene, in which Delany became deeply engaged as a direct result of his time at Woodland. From his accounts of the camp in *The Motion of Light in Water*, as well as his extended essays "Shadows" (1974/75), "To Read *The Dispossessed*" (1977), and "Coming/Out" (1997), it is clear that Woodland was a very positive formative experience for Delany. "My five summers there," he writes in *Motion*, "were an astonishing lesson in humanity, tolerance, and the workings of the social world as truly caring men and women tried to envision them."[18] Central to everyday life at Woodland was music, and specifically an experience of music shaped by the then-burgeoning American folk revival. One activity of the Woodland campers, as Delany relates in *Motion*, was the recording of traditional music and stories of the upstate population displaced by the Lackawack Reservoir;[19] in the present volume (Notebook

19) Delany mentions the camp's involvement in gathering folklore for the Catskill Folk Museum. This sort of fieldwork had been foundational for the folk revival and was central to its musical vision. Additionally, much of the music performed at Woodland—by campers, counselors, and visiting performers alike—expressed the progressive ethos of the revival. In *Motion*, Delany recalls fellow campers presenting the premiere performance of a choral piece based on the life and sayings of Sojourner Truth, written by Woodland's music director, Robert DeCormier, as well as performances given at the camp by Pete Seeger.[20]

Delany's experiences at Woodland spurred his involvement in the folk revival. A fellow camper, Mike Michaels, had taught Delany to play the guitar; armed with this instrument Delany sang in cafés in downtown New York City and supported himself by performing during his travels abroad. While still in high school Delany cofounded a folk group called the Harbor Singers, whose members were friends from Bronx Science and Delany's Harlem neighborhood.[21] (In a draft of an article on folk music in Notebook 19, Delany presents a vivid picture of a Harbor Singers performance.) Delany's single most exhaustive attempt at extended journal keeping in this volume is an account, in Notebook 12, of a trip to the Second Annual Newport Folk Festival in 1960 with another Woodland alumnus, Peter Horn. Surprising at it may seem in light of his subsequent literary career, a pressing question for Delany throughout the '60s, which he directly addresses in an entry in Notebook 25, was whether to forgo fiction writing altogether and throw his artistic energies over to music and performance.

Camp Woodland also influenced Delany's social life in ways not directly related to music. During Delany's final summer at the camp, his family moved from the floors above the family business to the Morningside Gardens cooperative apartment complex.[22] Shortly after he returned from Woodland, Delany began fostering social connections between the young people of Morningside and those associated with the community center of the nearby General Grant Houses.[23] In conversation Delany has affirmed that these community-building efforts, which included Delany's teaching of remedial reading classes to some of the General Grant youths, were inspired in part by his experiences with similar outreach activities at Woodland. In retrospect it seems fitting that it was at Woodland that Delany, in effect, named himself, choosing the nickname "Chip," by which he would be known for the rest of his life: at Woodland Delany saw and seized a social ethos that would stay with him forever.[24]

Another community Delany had begun to negotiate during this period was New York City's homosexual population and its enclaves. And here the oblique representation of circumstances and events that characterizes much of the material in this volume acquires a certain political accent. On the one hand, in these pages Delany is often quite frank about sexuality in general and homosexuality in particular; see, for example, his comments on his relationship with the actor Ron Bowman, his poetic accounts of cruising, his descriptions of his life with Hacker, and his spectacularly uninhibited exercises in pornographic fantasy. But on the other hand, in these same entries—written, we recall, during the decade before Stonewall—Delany is cautious about exactly what information he will provide and how he will provide it. For example: from these pages the reader cannot directly discern that the artist Simon Kestenbaum, whom Delany discusses at length in Notebook 25, was gay, had slept with Delany, and had informed him about the cruising area on the Christopher Street waterfront that Delany describes in *Motion*.[25] Similarly, in Notebook 4 Delany does not explicitly state that the piece of writing he mentions having inscribed in his friend Gale's notebook had been an account of an early cruising experience. (Delany discusses this experience, as well as his botched attempt to describe it accurately to Gale, in the essay "Coming/Out."[26]) And anything like explicit sexual content in these pages appears strictly in the mode of fantasy, of pornographic fiction. Even in his own journals, then, Delany partitions his writings on sexuality into separate rhetorical zones, presenting a kind of exploded view of the situation that the reader must bring into synthesis. In a sense, the mode of reading demanded by these portions of the journals—a queer reading, requiring sensitivity to coded language and strategic reticence, in which circumstances are implied rather than spelled out—is the exemplar, the type, of the sort of reading required by the journals as a whole.

At both the Dalton School and Camp Woodland, Delany had tried his hand at writing fiction and nonfiction.[27] But it was at Science, under the influence of gifted peers, creative writing classes, and his own precocious talent, that Delany burst into literary activity, producing a variety of accomplished work. This work quickly propelled Delany into new social circles. Before he had graduated from high school, his writing began to earn national awards and other forms of serious recognition: his short story "The Gravedigger" and his essay "Portrait of the Artist as Six Characters in Search of Tea and Sympathy" netted him first and second place in the nationwide Scholastic Writing Awards competition.[28] In the summer of 1960 Delany received a work-study scholarship to attend the Bread Loaf Writers' Conference, where he met Robert Frost, John Ciardi, Allen Drury, X. J. Kennedy, Edward Lewis Wallant, and the black novelist John A. Williams.[29] In just a few years his science fiction would bring him into the company of several American SF communities, indicated in these pages by mentions of SF conventions, the Milford Writers' Conference, and the Clarion Workshop, as well as by drafts of correspondence with editors and writers such as Donald Wollheim, Damon Knight, Judith Merril, and Roger Zelazny. Delany's travels in Europe in 1965 introduced him to the circle of British and American writers associated with the SF magazine *New Worlds*, which, under the editorship of Michael Moorcock, had become the epicenter of what came to be called New Wave science fiction.[30] Once Delany returned from Europe, he befriended writers and artists who had recently migrated to New York from San Francisco, where they had been part of the circle associated with the poet Jack Spicer; these artists, like the aforementioned SF writers, increasingly occupy Delany's attention in later entries in this volume. They include Russell Fitzgerald, Helen Adam, William McNeill, and Link Martin (Luther Thomas Cupp)—the last of whom Hacker would eventually join upon his return to San Francisco, the city to which Delany himself would relocate near the decade's end, as recounted in the closing entries of the volume.[31]

Part of what these journals portray, then, is a set of partially overlapping social circles, pinwheeling about one another as they advance forward in time—with a young Chip Delany tracing a complex helical path through them all. It is within and in response to this rich set of social contexts that Delany wrote.

III

The public component of Delany's literary production in the '60s is well known. In the first half of the decade Delany published five journeyman works of science fiction: the two stand-alone novels *The Jewels of Aptor* (1962) and *The Ballad of Beta-2* (1965) and the trilogy collectively titled *The Fall of the Towers* (1963–65). In the second half of the decade Delany produced a quartet of SF novels that showed significant artistic growth, the first and third of them winning Nebula Awards as the best novels of their respective years: *Babel-17* (1966), *Empire Star* (1966), *The Einstein Intersection* (1967), and *Nova* (1968). Delany also wrote the award-winning short stories that would eventually be collected in *Driftglass* (1971) and several of the essays that would be gathered in his classic first collection of SF criticism, *The Jewel-Hinged Jaw* (1977). He also completed two works that would be published later: an early version of the short fantasy novel *They Fly at Çiron* (1993), written in 1962, and the first of several pornographic novels, *Equinox* (1973), written in 1968. Working notes for all these projects can be found in the pages to follow.

Other entries in this volume reveal the degree to which Delany's published output of the '60s was matched by his production of a very substantial counter-oeuvre, the majority of it not science fiction, which has not been published. Delany mentions this counter-oeuvre—which includes nine novels and numerous short stories, plays, poems, translations, and more—in *The Motion of Light in Water*. There the work serves mainly as part of the narrative background. In his journals, however, it moves strongly to the fore as a major part of Delany's ongoing creative life. Its scope is suggested in Notebook 16, where Delany lists the works from that corpus (or at least the portion he had completed before *The Jewels of Aptor*) that he considered significant, in the form of a table of contents and blurb material for a projected omnibus titled *Portraits from the Immature Mind*. The list suggests that in volume alone this body of work easily matches, if not surpasses, Delany's published work from the same period.

A few words on the culminating project from this counter-oeuvre will clarify the meaning of some of the entries to come. At certain points the notebooks refer to the writings of one "Geo Keller." As the reader will infer from various entries, Geo is a major character in *Voyage, Orestes*, a massive novel Delany began developing around the time of his visit to Bread Loaf and worked on intensively while he was completing the three volumes of *The Fall of the Towers*.[32] A brilliant and charismatic young writer, Geo is Delany's alter ego; another major character from the novel, the poet Edna Silem, is a fictive counterpart to Marilyn Hacker. (Edna Silem is an inversion of "Mélisande," from the Debussy opera *Pelléas et Mélisande* and the Maurice Maeterlinck play from which it was drawn; Hacker had come up with the name herself. Delany eventually used the name for a character, herself based on Helen Adam, in his Nebula- and Hugo-winning short story "Time Considered as a Helix of Semi-precious Stones."[33]) Several entries suggest that Delany allowed a certain fluidity to exist between works he wrote under his own name and those he included in *Voyage, Orestes* and attributed to Geo. An entry in Notebook 25, for instance, reveals that Delany conceived the entire text of his first published SF novel, *The Jewels of Aptor* (1962), as a text-within-the-text of *Voyage, Orestes*, where it would be presented as Geo's work; among other things, this gives new significance to the fact that the protagonist of *Aptor* is himself named Geo. (Similarly, in entries unrelated to *Voyage, Orestes*, Delany sometimes refers to Hacker as Edna Silem—his other fanciful nickname for her, as well as for other female friends, being "Eurydice."[34])

In addition to his artistic productivity, Delany was driven by a powerful impulse toward analysis and synthesis. Throughout the pages to follow, alongside notes for creative projects we find numerous critical passages in which Delany grapples with the meaning of both his own writing and the works dominating the American and English literary scene of the time. Delany interrogates the icons of modernism—Joyce, Pound, Eliot, and others—as well as prominent critical-scholarly work associated with them, including that of the New Critics (I. A. Richards) and the myth scholars (Frazer and Graves especially; Delany's letter to John Brunner in Notebook 85 sheds some light on the attitude he brought to the subject of myth in his science fiction works of the '60s). He also comes to grips with a more personal and idiosyncratic pantheon of writers. This pantheon includes the Symbolist poets, preeminent among them Arthur Rimbaud, who for both Delany and Hacker stood as a kind of icon for the precocious, homosexual outsider-artist. Precociousness as such is important in the pantheon, as suggested by Delany's frequent mentions of Raymond Radiguet, Thomas Chatterton, Samuel Greenberg, and others. Delany also engages with the work of homosexual writers (Crane, Cocteau, Auden, Rechy, Baldwin) and writers of science fiction (Sturgeon and Bester, and in a more contestatory relation, Herbert and Heinlein). Delany's sense of the possibilities of the form of the author's journal itself is influenced by André Gide, whom Delany mentions several times in these pages and whose journals had been published in a Vintage paperback edition that Delany had read as a teenager.[35] (Also important for Delany were Gide's novels. The structure of *Les faux-monnayeurs*, with its cast of young people and its intricate interplay of novelistic sequences and fictive journal entries, would inform two of Delany's major projects from the '60s that never saw publication: *Voyage, Orestes* and the unfinished SF series collectively titled *Prism, Mirror, Lens*. The working notes for these projects included in this volume suggest that Delany's 1975 novel *Dhalgren* can be read as a development and synthesis of elements from both.)

The earliest literary-critical meditations in this volume clearly show a very young man assaying the voice of the critic as he has inherited it, much as the youthful aliens who populate the far future Earth of *The Ein-stein Intersection* try on the masks of human myth. In what I feel is both a classic indicator of precociousness in general and an early expression of what will become a perennial theme, Delany mimics not just the rhetoric of the critic but that of the entire semiotic environment of mid-century lit-erary production and reception: see, for example, in Notebook 16, Delany's imaginary blurbs for his own as-yet-unpublished novels, as well as similar texts scattered throughout these pages, all written from a kind of imagi-nary utopian future of writerly wish-fulfillment. In these passages, with both adolescent grandiosity and precocious wit, Delany rehearses his own subsequent literary reputation. (The reader may discover, as I did, that a frequent, if disorienting, pleasure in reading Delany's early journals is the accuracy with which they anticipate the reader's own responses to them.) In a sense these passages perform the same sort of work of self-mythicization as does Delany's conjuring up of fictive alter egos for him-self and Hacker in *Voyage, Orestes*. They give us a glimpse of what Delany, discussing the writings of his later critical alter ego K. Leslie Steiner—a direct descendant of the imaginary writers of these imaginary blurbs—has called "the dreams a writer must dream in order to write at all."[36]

More mundanely, such passages also remind us that we are, after all, dealing with a teenager—who, besides being smart, was also, as Delany himself has remarked subsequently, a "smart-ass."[37] As Delany's bibliog-raphers, Michael Peplow and Robert S. Bravard, have called to our atten-tion, Delany's urge to show off, to perform his own erudition, once moved his junior year creative writing teacher, Jacob Luria, to remind him in an evaluation, "you need impress no one—we know the breadth of your read-ing and the depth of your intellect."[38] What is striking is what happens to Delany's writing when his own youthful ego has less at stake, when he turns his energy away from projecting a certain kind of authority and attends closely to the object confronting him, whether it be aesthetic or otherwise. For example, in his analysis of Satyajit Ray's "Apu" film trilogy in Notebook 23, Delany drops the mask of authority in favor of the crisp, incisive, and humane voice characteristic of his best critical work. (His strikingly focused and specific discussion of the character of Aparna and her marriage with Apu suggests that the review was at least partly in-formed by his own experience of marriage, as well as by his growing femi-nist consciousness at a time when second-wave feminism was still nearly a decade from organized public articulation.[39]) Similarly, in Delany's early account, in Notebook 2, of a boy in the throes of illness on a city bus, we recognize not just the extraordinary descriptive precision characteristic of his later work, but also something like a thematic primal scene: we're presented with a densely populated social space into which intrudes a leaking or exploding body, whose abject presence polarizes the inhabitants of the space, sending some into denial and flight, and others into empathetic recognition and communion. In such accounts as these—with their precision, empathy, and deep feeling—we observe Delany cutting past rhetorical distractions and excesses, seizing the language he has inherited and giving voice to his vision.

From all this material the reader will be able to construct an image of Delany's literary output over the course of the '60s, an output that, like the circumstances of his life during this time, is now a direct, now an indirect referent of the entries. Moreover, as the text advances, both his writing and his life can be seen to progress steadily from the private realm into the public: hypothetical book blurbs give way to drafts for real ones, and personal musings are joined by drafts of letters to professional colleagues. Ultimately, the entries come to engage in an intricate dance of private and public contexts, with each entry serving as the backdrop, the negative space, for the next. It is this interplay of writerly contexts that the collection as a whole invites us to read.

IV

The importance of context in relation to the act of reading has long been a major concern for Delany, and his formulations on the topic are fascinatingly pertinent not only to considerations of how this volume might be read, but also to my own experience of compiling and editing it. One such formulation can be found in correspondence from Delany cited in an article by Scott McLemee for the *Chronicle of Higher Education*, written on the occasion of the death of Jacques Derrida, whose presence can be strongly felt in Delany's work from the late '70s onward: "'[Derrida] made us recontextualize what we read, because he saw that context expands infinitely, until, when we are exhausted by that expansion's velocity and inclusiveness, we erect some fiction of intention, completed and in place, to justify our failure to go on.'"[40] Such a fiction, as Delany has repeatedly dramatized in his work, is part of the control structure of discourse. Discourse, in the Foucauldian sense Delany is interested in, is the constellation of conventions, procedures, and institutions governing the production and circulation of statements, rhetoric, and texts, as well as of their privileged (and deprivileged) producers and recipients. Foucault has noted that within the discourse of literary analysis, one such convention is the concept of the "author," which provides a foundation for the various unities we posit in order to navigate a text: those of style, argument, and, as Delany indicates above, intention.[41] Another such conventional concept is that of an author's "work."[42] Both, Foucault says, are important in guiding the literary scholar through the process of winnowing and selecting for publication the "millions of traces" left by a writer.[43]

In Delany's fiction, the workings of discourse are often represented by a villainous, or at least unreliable, editor or redactor. Think, for example, of the editors of the "Anathēmata" chapter of *Dhalgren*, the off-stage publisher mentioned by K. Leslie Steiner in her introduction to *Tales of Nevèrÿon* (1979), the unnamed schoolmaster-historian in *Flight from Nevèrÿon* (1985)—Delany's best villain, in my opinion—and the academic Irving Mossman in *The Mad Man*. In a more sympathetic vein, consider K. Leslie Steiner herself, the graduate student John Marr in *The Mad Man*, and Randy Pedarson in *Phallos* (2004). In the working notes for *Voyage, Orestes* included in this volume, we find a major prototype for these characters in the literary biographer O'Donnells. And in Notebook 34 we find a faux-scholarly introduction to the private notebooks of Ian Scorda (the futuristic hero of *Prism, Mirror, Lens*), which directly states what will be major thematic concerns in both *Dhalgren* and much of the work that followed it: the interplay between journalistic re-creation and fictional dramatization, the dialogue between conflicting historical accounts, and, especially, the discursive pressures operating on the procedures of textual inclusion and exclusion—as suggested by the fictive editor's all-too-self-revealing comments.

At this uncomfortable point I now turn to a discussion of my own editorial choices for this volume. The chronological range of the project—just over a decade's worth of material—played a large role in these choices. The criterion for selecting personal entries was simply to be as exhaustive as the legibility of the notebooks themselves would allow, within the given chronological range; once these entries were collected, the bulk of the text was accounted for. Also selected for inclusion were drafts of unpublished poems and stories that commented directly on the biographical context of the surrounding entries; hence, for example, the reader will find in these pages a poem Delany wrote on the occasion of the death of his father, a collaborative novella jointly written by Delany and Hacker during their bus trip to Detroit to be married, and humorous verse written between Delany and Hacker in the early years of their marriage. In a similar vein I have included drafts of letters and commercial blurbs that point to significant circumstances or developments in Delany's life and thought at the time he wrote them. On the other hand, drafts of unpublished creative work that lacked direct biographical relevance were, with certain exceptions, excluded, with the justification that any attempt at systematic inclusion would have swamped the volume and occluded the biographical narrative.

While I have been sparing with drafts of or excerpts from creative projects, I have tried to include, wherever possible, notes and outlines for them. However, to avoid burdening the text with multiple outlines showing only minor variations, I have selected such material on the basis of typicality, not exhaustiveness. Thus, while the reader will find notes for most of Delany's early SF novels and several of his short stories here, in almost every case at least some material has been excluded, with the rationale that what has been included already conveys the most pertinent information about Delany's approach to a given project.[44] Some favor was shown to notes and outlines for unfinished stories if they showed an organic connection to other published work; one selection from Notebook 29, for instance, is an outline of a novel featuring story elements that would eventually appear in Delany's novel *The Einstein Intersection* (1967). Particular favor was shown to notes and outlines for unpublished work if that work constituted an important and ongoing part of Delany's creative output at the time, as with *Voyage, Orestes* in the early '60s, *Prism, Mirror, Lens* in the late '60s, and the "Faust" project to which Delany returned throughout the decade.

I have also included notes and drafts for critical writings that did not ultimately see publication. Since Delany often frames personal entries in literary-critical terms, the exact status of some of this critical material is hard to pinpoint; certain entries seem to hover between strictly private musings and drafts intended for eventual publication. An interesting example of this is Delany's extended meditation on matriarchal and patriarchal cultures in Notebook 27. While inventive and provocative, the piece has the feel of a personal exercise rather than an attempt to work through an early draft of something seriously intended for later public consumption. Like much of the critical work included here, it has a hypothetical quality about it: "*If* I were to write a work in the vein of Graves's *The White Goddess*, it would be *like* this, though not precisely this."

Finally, I have included a significant amount of Delany's pornographic writing, which weaves like an electric wire around the other entries in the notebooks. As Delany indicates in Notebook 27, this writing was produced for its own sake, as private masturbatory fantasy—and is, following Cecily's logic in *The Importance of Being Earnest*, "consequently meant for publication." The pornographic writing in the notebooks tends to take fragmentary form: often a passage will commence, be interrupted in mid-sentence by a new and unrelated entry, and then pick up where it left off. It is not always clear, at such break-points, whether the writing of the passage halted in favor of a new thought and recommenced afterward, or whether the writing process was continuous, hopping over a previously existing passage and continuing forward from there. Though tempted to join the segments together, I have preserved their fragmentary presentation, as this captures—in the face of other material that has been excluded—a sense of what reading the notebooks in their raw form is actually like, and conveys a sense of the multiplicity, even incommensurability, of discourses Delany is navigating in writing such passages.

My decisions about how to present the entries, both in terms of their appearance on the page and their overall organization in the volume, have been guided by the desire to supply the reader with useful contextual information without unduly interfering with the reading experience. Making the physical notebooks the primary units of the text was an obvious choice (but not, it turns out, a wholly unproblematic one; see appendix 2 for details). The notebooks have in turn been grouped into chapters whose divisions correspond to major changes in Delany's life situation or artistic focus. Each chapter opens with a brief synopsis of the circumstances and events of the period it covers. Detailed contextual information on individual entries is supplied by an independent section of notes at the end of the volume, also grouped by chapter and notebook. (At an earlier stage of this project footnotes were tried, but I found that when juxtaposed with the already fragmentary entries, footnotes tended both to clutter the page and obscure the distinction between entry and commentary. Contrariwise, an independent section of notes at the end of the volume kept the main text clean, which I felt on balance improved the reading experience.) Given the overall organization of the volume into chapters-with-synopses, individual notebooks, and a final section of notes, I recommend that the reader initially tackle the text by making two passes through it: the first a relatively loose and open reading using the chapter synopses as the main contextual guides, the second a more systematic reading connecting individual entries with information supplied in the notes.

In some of the entries to follow, Delany indicates gaps in time, topic, or

occasion with asterisks (*   *   *) or straight lines (———). I have reproduced these in the passages in question. All the remaining text breaks,
signaled with +   +   +, are my own. The reader should be mindful that
these latter breaks might signal the presence of a poem, a story, a fragment of a longer work, or, for that matter, a grocery list—or they might indicate a simple gap in the notebook, leading without any intervening text
to the next entry. Many entries break off in mid-sentence; I have let these
full stops stand without comment. In the few cases where entries are not
presented in full—generally because they are parts of much longer drafts
of work—I signal this with a note in brackets. Where Delany has crossed
out words, phrases, or passages in the drafting of a given text, I have presented the clean text toward which Delany was revising. Punctuation
errors have been corrected without comment, while punctuation eccentricities have been retained. Anomalous or missing words or phrases have
been indicated by or supplied within editorial brackets; illegible words or
inadvertent repetitions of words or phrases have both been indicated by
bracketed ellipses: [. . .]. Delany's irregular spelling, stemming from his
dyslexia, has been corrected here without comment. In another critical
context, the faithful reproduction of all editorial cross-outs, punctuation
errors, unintentional repetitions, and spelling mistakes would undoubt-
edly constitute useful information. In the current context, I feel that such
exhaustive reproduction would constitute noise. But in matters of interpretation the context does not automatically justify interpretive decisions.
Susan Sontag, in her own private journals, remarks that the situation may
be the contrary: "Interpretation is the medium by which we justify context."[45] Whether my choices are adequate to the context of the conventional discourse of the "author's journal," to say nothing of justifying that
context, or even challenging it, is for the reader to decide.

The archives in which the notebooks are stored also influenced some
of the editorial decisions for this volume. Although the cataloging procedures at the Gotlieb Center are extremely meticulous and thorough, unavoidable ambiguities have crept into the archival record. For instance,
while Delany usually inscribed dates on the covers of his notebooks before passing them on to the archive, he did not always do this; it would
then fall to an archivist to assess the date using internal evidence. Sometimes this evidence was simply not present, or if it was, would be discern-
ible only to an expert on Delany's work and life. Moreover, since the notebook collection spans decades, its catalog represents the work of more
than one archivist, thus adding another variable to the mix. As a result of

such complexities, upon examining the notebooks I learned that a good half of them had, appropriately, been given either very broad and approximate dates or no date at all—or had, in fact, been dated incorrectly. Determining the proper order of presentation for the notebooks in this volume thus required a reexamination of every notebook in an exhaustive procedure of internal dating and cross-checking.

In carrying out this investigation, I found that the multiplicity of the notebooks' contents could often be counted on to save the day. For instance: the personal entries in a given notebook might lack dates of inscription, but the content of the entries would allow the chronological position of the notebook to be pinpointed. Or a notebook might lack personal entries altogether, but contain a portion of a creative project that would enable me to determine a position. Or it might contain a story outline that by itself suggested only a broad and approximate time frame, but would also contain, say, a school assignment with a specific due date. (Apropos of this last example, the reader should note that while the reason for a notebook's chronological position will usually be clear upon inspection, not all the material that helped pinpoint a position—like the aforementioned school assignment, or a poem with an inscription date—was selected for inclusion.) In general, different threads of information in the notebooks tended to clarify and reinforce one another.

In addition to the information contained in the notebooks themselves, I made extensive use of Delany's published output as well as several unpublished biographical chronologies by him. I also consulted previous scholarship—especially Michael W. Peplow and Robert S. Bravard's pioneering bio-bibliographical study of Delany's work—and other material stored at the Gotlieb archives, including manuscripts, memorabilia, and more. But the richest source of information to which I had access during the editing process was Samuel Delany himself, who answered my countless queries with his characteristic combination of engagement, graciousness, and patience. While any oversights or errors are my responsibility, I remain grateful to Chip for his generous time and assistance. To borrow an image from the science historian Peter Galison (who in turn borrowed it from Charles Sanders Peirce and Ludwig Wittgenstein): ultimately, notebook contents, supplementary sources, and Delany's own testimony threaded together into a kind of historical "cable" that enabled the notebooks to be arranged into a coherent timeline.[46]

In regard to the presentation of material in this volume, I designate individual notebooks by their archival numbers and dates (when they have dates) as given in the Gotlieb catalog. When I have ascertained a date for a previously undated notebook, or determined a more precise or correct date for an already dated one, I have presented the alternative date in brackets. (And rather than refer to a notebook as a "Journal," as the catalog does, I have stuck with "Notebook.") The reader should also note that I have placed what is likely the earliest extant notebook—Notebook 89, which has no archival date—near the end of the volume, in the first appendix. As I explain there, this placement is intended to accomplish several things. First, it clarifies the somewhat complicated structural relationship between that notebook and Notebook 1. Second, because the material in Notebook 89 connects with earlier entries in the volume in diverse ways, it invites the reader to reread the text, to travel the hermeneutic circle once more. Third and finally, it highlights the distinction between the archive's chronological claims and my own. (Needless to say, further research might suggest revisions of my chronology as well.) Delany has said that "history begins only when we do *not* know what happened—when there is disagreement over what happened."[47] This dialogical view of history has been central to Delany's project at least since *Dhalgren*, and some of my editorial decisions are intended to call attention to this sort of dialogue.

Although the contents of the notebooks usually supplied the information necessary to determine their order of presentation, those same contents sometimes presented challenges to making such a determination. For instance, two or more notebooks might have been used during the same period, or contrariwise, a single notebook might contain entries produced at widely separated dates. An example of the former situation is the chronological overlap among the notebooks Delany kept while traveling in Europe, and an example of the latter is Delany's account of his trip to Detroit with Hacker, which he wrote in the margins of a notebook he had completed a full year earlier. Situations like these complicated the process of establishing a proper order of presentation.

Moreover, the notebooks sometimes presented editorial puzzles with no solution. One of Delany's consistent work habits was to fill his notebooks from two directions at once: front to back and back to front. This often made it impossible to determine whether a given passage had been written before or after a neighboring one. Several times in the editing process, for instance, I was confronted with multiple outlines for stories or novels with no way of discerning, either from internal evidence or order of appearance, which outline came earlier and which later. Similarly, while dated entries might display a proper chronological relationship to each other when read in conventional order, this would not clarify their relationship to surrounding undated entries. All of this implies that many of the undated entries may not have been written in the front-to-back order in which they appear. Because problems like this mark a kind of limit point for interpretation, I have chosen—in all cases but one, to be discussed in the notes at the end of the volume—not to reorder any entries in a given notebook according to internal dates and evidence, but rather to let them stand in their front-to-back order of appearance in the notebook, with a reminder to the reader that each notebook is a material artifact, a situation, with inherent uncertainties and ambiguities.

v

All the complexities discussed above will be hauntingly familiar to readers of Delany's work. Both the confusion of chronologies and the writing of later entries on the margins of earlier ones have formal parallels in the final chapter of *Dhalgren*. Numerous conundrums of historical-textual reconstruction can be found in Delany's earliest SF novels (such as *The Jewels of Aptor* and *The Ballad of Beta-2*), throughout the Return to Nevèrÿon tetralogy, and in *The Mad Man* and *Phallos*. The interplay between private journal and public fiction is given dramatic expression in *The Einstein Intersection* and *Flight from Nevèrÿon*. And the conflict between official and marginal knowledge plays out in essentially every novel from *Dhalgren* onward—not to mention several earlier ones.

One particular formal and thematic parallel between the notebooks and Delany's published work bears further discussion. The comments inscribed by Hacker on the margins of Delany's entries, as well as the pornographic passages that unfold alongside other material, recall the formal device of the "double column" of text Delany deploys in *Dhalgren*, *Atlantis: Model 1924* (1995), and the essays "On the Unspeakable" (1987) and ". . . Three, Two, One, Contact: Times Square Red" (1999). The double column serves in these works as a figure for the dialectical dance between conflicting histories or discourses, as well as for the split and discordant nature of the human subject. Delany argues that histories, discourses, and subjects are intrinsically split, never to be recuperated or homogenized into some single, pure, self-identical order. In the afterword to the second paperback reprint of his science fiction novel *Stars in My Pocket Like Grains of Sand* (1984), Delany claims that any notion of such an order is an "ideological mirage" in the name of which voices of critique, contestation, or protest have historically been marginalized and silenced; what must be affirmed in confronting such mirages is the heterogeneity, the polyvocality, of the human situation.[48]

Although Delany does not directly deploy the form of the double column of text in *The Motion of Light in Water*, he repeatedly considers the idea of such a form when he pauses to assess his own autobiographical project. In one passage, Delany considers two discourses of "literature," which he characterizes in psychoanalytic and Marxist terms:

> The parallel column containing the discourse of repetition, of desire, whether satisfied or unrequited (but always purveying its trope of truth), forever runs beside one of positive, commercial, material analysis. Many of us, raised on literature, have learned to supply the absent column when the material is presented alone. And a few of us have begun to ask, at least, for the column of objects, actions, economics, and material forces when presented only with, in whatever figurative form, desire.[49]

Delany goes on to note that these two seemingly distinct discourses do share one arena of action: what holds the "columns" both together and apart, he says, is the material context of writing itself, a context "never constituted of anything more meaningful than blue lines (cut by red marginal indicator) over white paper—or the motion of light in water."[50] But this is nothing other than an image of a page from a notebook, which we see Delany carrying with him in several scenes and sequences in *Motion*. The connection Delany makes between notebook and title suggests that at least one way to read the memoir is as a critical meditation on the meaning and form of the notebooks, and especially on those passages in them—like Hacker's comments and the pornographic fantasies—that seem to speak from the margins. (Conversely, the reader may find, as I have, that a familiarity with the contents of the notebooks can greatly facilitate and stabilize a reading of *Motion*. For all the complexities I've described, the agreement between notebooks and autobiography is startlingly close, down to very fine details.) More generally, the correspondences between the situations Delany dramatizes in his published writing and the internal dynamics of the notebooks suggests that he has been carefully scrutinizing those dynamics from the very beginning. Actually negotiating them as an editor has repeatedly produced a sense not simply of *déjà vu* but of *quod erat demonstrandum*; it has been a singular privilege indeed to experience, through a direct encounter with Delany's notebooks, the hermeneutic drama that has so captured my imagination as a lifelong reader of his work.

In an interview in *Camera Obscura* (later collected in *Silent Interviews* [1994]) Delany describes this hermeneutic drama in terms of the "inadequation" of language, experience, and desire to one another. Such mutual inadequation, he says, creates the "field," or stage, on which such dramas play out.[51] Delany illustrates his notion through an account of an early childhood episode, or rather a series of intricately entailed episodes, involving a night-lamp he had received as a Christmas gift. In concluding the account, Delany notes that none of the episodes had actually made it into the pages of *The Motion of Light in Water*:

> The reason the tapestry of individual perception remains external to history is that, whatever [*Motion*] may be to the reader, for me it is— today—only the absence of any mention of that lamp. That is what invalidates it. That is what makes it merely a mention of some happenstance occurrences in a life only a fool might seriously think more than marginally congruent with my own, certainly not central, certainly not with like historical import. And if (and certainly you already know this), somehow, in some ideal future edition, I added this account to complete it, to correct it, to revise and rewrite it, to bring it in line with history, the process of inadequation would only repeat itself, as I fixed on some other, absent object, and the tale I might tell about its complex of sensory reductions.[52]

Again, context expands infinitely—and the vacuum in its wake is desire. Or, as Delany's partner Dennis Rickett puts it in plainer language, quoting Delany's own words back at him in the afterword to Delany's graphic novel memoir *Bread & Wine* (1997): "If you tell one story, that means there are always lots of others that you don't tell."[53]

For me, the entries in this volume are very much "about" the drafts of novels, stories, scenes, poems, songs, and even school notes that are not reproduced here. As rich as this maze of entries is, what has been left out constitutes, for this editor, its dark reflection. To suggest to the reader the magnitude and range of the material being held offstage by my selections, I have included a second appendix, which presents a more complete, though still not exhaustive, collection of the material from Notebook 1. By showing the larger textual landscape from which the entries selected for this volume have been extracted, the appendix offers what I hope is a tantalizing glimpse of the infinitely expanding context of these journals. In a passage from the pages to follow—part of a longer account of his experiences before and after playing at a hootenanny at the Newport Folk Festival, which he is visiting with his friend from Woodland, Peter Horn— Delany, eighteen, describes his own sense of this offstage context, this unvoiced infinity, the epistemological, political, sexual, and aesthetic meanings of which will reflect and refract throughout his work in the future:

> Something I remember brings me to the point of all this. While I was walking to the hoot, I reached back to adjust the capo on the guitar. I pricked my thumb on a loose string, and sucking it, a drop of blood, when I looked, glazed thin through saliva over the whirls of my thumb print. I sucked it, and then it stopped. For a moment then, I wondered [if] I would be able to play if I was called. But [it] didn't hurt, so I forgot about it, until just a few moments ago. I didn't record it—almost. But these journals are not to remember the things I record, but for all the things that pass un-written, and forgotten. That is [by] far the majority of the trip. For all the single drops of blood at Newport, or anyplace. For shadow configurations on the sand, to Pete's wet hair, dark and filamental, to all the things—the million un-recorded thoughts I have over Eurydice. That's what these journals are for.

Kenneth R. James

NOTES

1. Samuel R. Delany, *The Motion of Light in Water: Sex and Science Fiction Writing in the East Village* (1988; reprint, Minneapolis: University of Minnesota Press, 2004), 84.

2. Samuel R. Delany, *Dhalgren* (1975; reprint, New York: Vintage Books, 2001), 734.

3. Samuel R. Delany, *The Mad Man* (1994; reprint, Rutherford, NJ: Voyant Publishing, 2002), 307.

4. Gene Andrew Jarrett, ed., *The Wiley Blackwell Anthology of African American Literature*, vol. 2, *1920 to the Present* (Chichester, West Sussex, UK: Wiley-Blackwell, 2014), 715.

5. Michael S. Peplow and Robert S. Bravard, eds., *Samuel R. Delany: A Primary and Secondary Bibliography, 1962–1979* (Boston: G. K. Hall & Co., 1980), 3–4; Biondi, *To Stand and Fight*, 39–40, 87–88, 107, 179.

6. Jarrett, *Wiley Blackwell Anthology*, 715.

7. Martha Biondi, *To Stand and Fight: The Struggle for Postwar Civil Rights in New York City* (Cambridge, MA: Harvard University Press, 2003), 40, 216–17, 253.

8. Delany, *Motion*, 87–88.

9. See E. Franklin Frazier's *Black Bourgeoisie* (New York: Free Press, 1957), whose publication, according to Delany, occasioned a good deal of discussion in the Delany family. (Samuel R. Delany, interview with Kenneth James, August 9, 2014.)

10. Peplow and Bravard, *Samuel R. Delany*, 5.

11. Delany, *Motion*, 197. "Sheldon Novick" is an error; the person in question is Julius Novick, who became a theater critic for the *Village Voice*. Delany has said in correspondence that while these two Novicks were not related to one another, both were campers at Woodland (Delany, interview with James, August 9, 2014).

12. Ibid., 49.

13. Delany, *Motion*, 107–8; Peplow and Bravard, *Samuel R. Delany*, 18.

14. Delany, *Motion*, 95, 109–10; Peplow and Bravard, *Samuel R. Delany*, 21.

15. Delany, *Motion*, 34.

16. Peplow and Bravard, *Samuel R. Delany*, 5.

17. Ibid., 11.

18. Delany, *Motion*, 60.

19. Ibid., 44.

20. Ibid., 44–45.

21. Ibid., 10, 94. Delany's involvement in creative writing at Science and folk music downtown hardly exhausts his artistic activities during this period. As a child Delany had received six years of violin instruction and played in the Dalton School orchestra, and at Science he composed a violin concerto (for Peter Salaff; see appendix 1), electronic pieces, and a chamber symphony (see *Motion*, 49, 92). In the realm of performance, beyond participating in the Hunter College Dramatic Program for Young People, Delany also participated in the Chamber Theater and the New York Repertory Company and took ballet lessons at Ballet Theater (*Motion*, 99).

22. Ibid., 80.

23. Ibid., 81.

24. Ibid., 336–37.

25. Ibid., 215–16, 225–27.

26. Samuel R. Delany, "Coming/Out," in *Shorter Views: Thoughts and the Politics of the Paraliterary* (Middletown, CT: Wesleyan University Press, 1999), 83–84.

27. Peplow and Bravard, *Samuel R. Delany*, 12–13.

28. Ibid., 16.

29. Ibid., 17–18.

30. John Clute and Peter Nicholls, *The Encyclopedia of Science Fiction* (New York: St. Martin's Griffin, 1995), 867–68.

31. Lewis Ellingham and Kevin Killian, *Poet Be Like God: Jack Spicer and the San Francisco Renaissance* (Middletown, CT: Wesleyan University Press, 1998), 118, 179, 272, 352.

32. In *The Motion of Light in Water*, Delany refers to the novel as *Voyage, Orestes!*, which was the title under which he submitted the finished manuscript to publishers. However, in the working notes collected here, with a few exceptions, Delany consistently refers to the novel as *Voyage, Orestes*—without the exclamation mark. To maintain clarity and consistency within these pages we will also refer to it by the latter title.

33. Delany, interview with James, August 9, 2014.

34. Ibid.

35. Ibid.

36. Samuel R. Delany, preface to *The Straits of Messina* (Seattle: Serconia Press, 1989), x.

37. Peplow and Bravard, *Samuel R. Delany*, 6.

38. Ibid., 17.

39. Delany, *Motion*, 126–27, 189–91.

40. Delany, quoted in Scott McLemee, "Derrida, a Pioneer of Literary Theory, Dies," *Chronicle of Higher Education* 51, no. 9 (2004): par. 11, http://chronicle.com.gate .lib.buffalo.edu/article/Derrida-a-Pioneer-of-Literary/30791/.

41. Michel Foucault, "What Is an Author?," in *Aesthetics, Method, and Epistemology: Essential Works of Foucault, 1954–1984*, ed. James Faubion (London: Penguin Books, 2000), 214–15.

42. Ibid., 207–8.

43. Ibid., 207.

44. The relative sparseness of working notes for short stories in this volume reflects the actual paucity of such notes in the original notebooks. For many of these shorter works Delany appears to have passed from initial conception to typewritten draft with very little intervening development.

45. Susan Sontag, *Reborn: Journals & Notebooks: 1947–1963*, ed. David Rieff (New York: Picador, 2008), 98.

46. Peter Galison, "Trading Zone: Coordinating Actions and Belief," in *The Science Studies Reader* (New York: Routledge, 1999), 137–57.

47. Samuel R. Delany, "Sword & Sorcery, S/M, and the Economics of Inadequation," in *Silent Interviews* (Middletown, CT: Wesleyan University Press, 1994), 147.

48. Samuel R. Delany, afterword to *Stars in My Pocket Like Grains of Sand* (1984; reprint, Middletown, CT: Wesleyan University Press, 2004), 355–56.

49. Delany, *Motion*, 228.

50. Ibid.

51. Delany, "Sword & Sorcery," 162–63.

52. Ibid., 151.

53. Delany, afterword to *Bread & Wine* (1997; reprint, Seattle: Fantagraphics Books, 2013), 49.

IN SEARCH OF SILENCE

1

···

Bronx Science and Other
New York Scenes

···

As of the first entry of Notebook 1, Samuel Delany—born April 1, 1942—
is a fifteen-year-old sophomore at the Bronx High School of Science. Most
of the young people Delany mentions in this and the entries to follow are
either fellow students at Science or, after Notebook 1, part of Marilyn
Hacker's social circle at NYU.

With the exception of an extended sequence in Notebook 4, most of the
private journal entries from this period are brief and fragmentary. However, the notebooks in which the entries appear are far from empty; many
of their pages hold class notes and homework assignments, with most of
the remainder devoted to drafts of stories, poems, play scripts, and more.
By the time of his writing of the first entry of Notebook 1, Delany had already completed two novels, *Lost Stars* and *Scavengers*—the first of which
he had written while still at the Dalton School—and was working on a
third, *Those Spared by Fire*.[1] By Notebook 3 he had moved on to his fourth,
Cycle for Toby.

As various entries indicate, during this period Delany contributed to
his school's literary magazine, *Dynamo*, and participated in the Hunter
College Dramatic Program for Young People. His fiction and nonfiction
had already begun receiving significant recognition: in Notebook 4 Delany
mentions receiving prizes from the nationwide Scholastic Writers Awards
for the short story "The Gravedigger" and the essay "Portrait of the Artist
as Six Characters in Search of Tea and Sympathy."

Although the entries from this period present a picture of a talented
and ambitious young artist, they also hint at a teenager in flux and responding to a number of pressures. In an autobiographical fragment in
Notebook 4, Delany states that while his strengths are in the arts, his
professional interests are still "diversified" and that he is "fascinated" by

nuclear physics. In a private entry in the same notebook, he ponders an account he had written in the notebook of a friend of Hacker's describing a cruising experience. And in the closing entry from this period, Delany mentions staying with friends for several days: a hint of the uneasy atmosphere at home.

The first three of the four entries from Notebook 1 are written on pages that have come loose from their spiral binding; see appendixes 1 and 2 for a fuller discussion of these pages. Notebooks 3 and 4 contain the first of the marginal comments by Hacker, indicated in bold type.

NOTE

1. Samuel R. Delany, *The Motion of Light in Water: Sex and Science Fiction Writing in the East Village* (1988; reprint, Minneapolis: University of Minnesota Press, 2004), 88–89.

to every thing. That's it: my writing—at times—captures the intangible. Good for me! (Conceited bastard that you are!) And it is almost always when I write about Ellen! I must stop being so analytical when I read; and be more so when I write. I have lost more effect from the greatest works of literature than anybody in the world!—I bet. That's it! I'm too chemical. I know too much about what is being done with the words and themes. Although I can whip the words into place myself; I can see the scars on the backs of the words whipped by other writers. That analytical frame of mind is hell. I write creatively as though I were writing a math textbook, and damn it, it comes out just as good. I know what humor is, I know what suspense is. Someday I will know what tragedy is. I do not want to know; then I will be static completely. The hell of it is; when I don't understand the construction, I don't get the effect; or rather, I block out the effect. Oddly, in my contemporaries this is not true; I can read their writing and achieve the effect and not be so scathingly analytical. I hope it continues.

+   +   +

R.U.R.

+   +   +

Dickens
George [Eliot]—*The Mill on the Floss*
Hawthorne
Thackeray
Victor Hugo—*Les Misérables*
Cooper
Melville

+   +   +

Try to think up a situation involving kids. What types of characters: Ellen; a shy girl. Reserved: Vinni; Shy as hell. Tito; he is an all around type of person. Other; confused. Vivian, all around. Phyllis is out & out glamour girl type. Ruben; he will do whatever is demanded of him. Paul is an inhibited younger brother type. Whom should I pair Ellen up with? Not Paul. Who's taller then Ellen? Joe! Not for Ellen. Tito! That's who! All right. How? Vinni & Butch. Ruben with Vivian. What about Mildred? Mildred is indispensable as a character. Analyze Mildred: Nice. Shy. Likes to pretend. No! That is not right for Ellen. Characters: A Dreamer! That's right, a crazy mixed up kid. That is Ellen. Punchinello! That's Butch. But that's cruel. So what. Forget about the actors. That's hard. Let's see. I like the dreamer. And I like Ellen in the C.M.K. role. What about the boys. I like the juvenile delinquent kick. What to do with it. Tito is the hero type, he is more dynamic then Vinni. Vinni is tragic type. Vinni, he can be the juvenile delinquent with his friend. Tito wants to grow up. Growing up. There is a conflict, man—or boy, against society. What will be the symbol for adulthood. The dreamer, her symbol is the tree. The tree! That's it. It's all falling into place. Good. Tito and Mildred are brother & sister. The tree— I see her throwing herself at the tree. Ellen makes a play for him. Vinni is sort of in love with Ellen. Vinni kills Paul. Oh, that's fun. Butch, what & where is she? She wants to help Mildred. What is her problem. Vinni! That's her problem. Vinni & Tito are friends. (What about Other? Forget about him!) So far so good. What to do about Paul. I don't know! Where do we stick him in. I have this feeling we should start off with Paul. No. Yes, I don't know. I have to get a first scene. How I like the back alley. All right. The back alley. What do we do with it? I've got to get—I've got it. Mildred & Paul. Mildred to see the tree. And Paul teases her. Then Tito to chase Paul away with Vinni. Mildred—

Write it, stupid. Don't just talk about it. Write it out!

NOTEBOOK 3—JANUARY 1959

Journal of 5 Minutes in Park.

I feel a discouraging lack of creativity at the present.

Music—when poems become things that are forced and can not sing.

Marilyn is sitting beside me reading my manuscripts. The creativity—we are in the park—is coming back.

This is one of those shaded bowers that grace good old Central. There is shade dappling among the sun spots on the white paper, and a leaf has fallen onto Marilyn's lap where she has picked it up and fingers it as she reads with her pretension of enrapture. The cars sound behind me on a highway. There are no birds here.

I just stopped to title these. Marilyn has turned another page; a boy passed and has turned off the path 20 feet away to stare at the horses on the bridle path. Now he has gone away.

Poetic Dialogue

—José, what is a word ending in "ry" that is the opposite of "mandatory."

—Are you writing creative material?

—Yes.

—Then I can't tell you. You are a craftsman incompetent in your field. You are writing prose?

—Yes. José, I am a craftsman who is asking another to lend me one of his tools momentarily, for one of mine has dulled. Oh José, I know the word, I just can't think of it.

—If you were writing poetry, I could tell you, but prose is out of my domain; you have not justified yourself in that. Poetry is music and I could easily tell you upon what line a certain note which you had sung, must fall. But that is poetry and poetry (as I said) is music.

—Then tell me the word, José, prose is poetry.

—TRUE, BUT I DON'T *KNOW* THE WORD.

+ + +

Experiment in Alexandrine

The chest I saw put out.

Out the *chest* now *cast*
off—*she* did *hang* them *high* up.
So much for that.

+ + +

When one loses $20, one gets such a horribly mortal feeling—I mean
like *one could die.*
And saying that, doesn't make me feel a damn bit better.

+ + +

If my collected works
    ever be published
Let them be called
    "Womb of Shadows"

+ + +

—Bruitto half drowsily nuzzles his face in Cain's naked groin; Cain's
fingers play Bruitto's hair in his sleep, the silent sleeping hand upon
Bruitto's hair and head which moves occasionally under its burden across
pulsing genitals.

He placed his hands on her cheeks and pulled her down, sliding his
hands down her shoulders and then under her arms, so that his thumbs
played across her breasts and finally completely covering them and moving together beneath her blouse which opened and then she was shrug-
ging out of it and the nipples beneath his fingers, pulling her down, until
she was full upon his own naked chest and his hands going into her skirt
caressing softly and then he stretched his hands apart tightening his
shoulders so that the snaps [tore] and he moved around her whole pelvic
area in lingering frantic rhythm at her cunt and then he was twisting until
he had worked himself naked and home and in that struggle was born that
rhythm with which he now poured himself into her, her body beneath his
own his face happy against her neck, Bruitto lay—

Why
Are there
No fragments
Of
            My soul
            In this
            Record
Of
Disintegration
            —April 19, '59

+   +   +

LION CUBS

Brown bodies
Slender, heads whirl
and crowns of black
        fly loose
        Brown pupils in yellow ivory
        Slender faces open
"Chinga tu madre—"
        Hands flash against each other in
High contrapuntal laughter comes
the answer
"Chinga te—"
Running, they separate, and one,
Sneakers carry him in a wide arc
across the city asphalt

+   +   +

To a woman getting on the subway with a pot containing three tall lilies
who took a seat behind another woman—who had her back to me so I
couldn't see her head.

I want to pen a terse and
   Turgid rhyme
To insulate this thing from
World and time;
But how may I hope to escape
A woman with 3 heads
   Who're trumpet shaped.

+   +   +

THE TALKING INVERTED BLUES

I consider it one of life's great joys
that boys like girls and girls like boys
but it sometimes happens as the old globe whirls
that boys like boys and girls like girls.

Thus we are faced with the reality
of homosexuality
which causes lots of righteous anger
and very bad business for Margaret Sanger.

Now Sodomy falls into three different classes
There're sodomists, inverts, and pederasts,
But as Paul Verlaine said one fine night
I'm not a Sodomist, man. I'm a Sodomite.

Now some folks who make up the nomenclature
Say one kind's sin and the other kind's nature,
But I can't see why it's a sin
Because of what entrance you go in
(As long as it isn't the fire exit.)

There are some folks under the impression
that Sodomy's just an ethics session:
to you I say who thus surmise
Just open your mouth and close your eyes.

You'll see that the moment often starts
in urban life or in the Arts

And that is why in this fair city
The girls are so handsome and the boys so pretty.

On this theme the movies have been just a mite slow;
Said the censors, "Perversion just won't go."
But up we pop like hands from gloves
With *The Third Sex*, and *Three Strange Loves*.

I saw a man dressed in rather bad taste
With Revlon and Avon all over his face
Said he, "Son you may not like the way I dress,
But I'm a member of the S.O.S.
          Sons of Sodom."

I mean it rather sets you back to hear:

Oh, George, I really do love you
When your voice goes up an octave or two,
And you walk with such grace and refinement,
With your hip swing ten inches out of alignment.

Now John likes Jane and Jane likes Jim
And Jim likes someone who doesn't like him,
And it's easy to see how this can annoy
Since the one Jim likes is a boy
(And so is Jane for that matter).

In France the movement took the lead
With Marcel Proust and André Gide
And the loving couple we all know
As Paul Verlaine and A. Rimbaud.

Gide's pleasantly pederastic essence
Was in his love for adolescence
And it was said—and it be truth
He loved that old sweet bird of youth.
(Even went to bed with the damn thing)

Proust, dabbling with more subtlety
Perverted even Sodomy
And it was said at certain scenes
'twas Albert and not Albertine
(that the man loved).
(Did I say man?)

Simone de Beauvoir had her fun
till they kicked her out of the Sorbonne
for starting little innovations
in student-faculty relations.

Something I've noticed from all of these
the eternal triangle's gone isosceles
two men at the base all setting up home
Some girl at the vertex all alone.

No matter what it's all about
they always kick the odd one out
But the question—when you get it down to old home Sod—
is just who is what, and what is odd.

My story's over; I've no more to tell
So I'll bid my love a fond farewell
So if I want to win that Nobel Prize
I guess I'll have to transvestize—
(Besides, he's a boy and too flat chested anyway.)

+ + +

I know a [centered] man
    Whom Jove begot
Before remorse began
    And lust forgot.

So let your vaulted thunders roar
    In caverns deep
I have no hiding but my circled soul
    And that asleep.

NOTEBOOK 6 — 1959

[April 1959]

This is the problem: two ethical systems clash. The stronger one wins out.

+ + +

H.P. continued from Vol. I

hand of which whisked up and down the stem of his cock. The nigger, with his own hand, grabbed his own penis and his black hand flew up and down like a piston. Erect, the prick was huge, like [a] tree standing out between his spread legs, black and tall, curving smoothly from the crinkly black bush. The great low hanging black balls swung back and forth as the ebony hand pumped, the fingers flying in furious ecstasy. The nail bitten fingers that closed about Larry's stiff prick kept the same rhythm. The black sex scepter would have taken both Larry's and Bastos's hand to cover. Larry reached out and grappled the aching bitch stick, it was like caressing a hot water pipe. Basto reached around with both hands and lent his power. The four hands, like a single enclosing column, swept rhythmically up and down the ebon obelisk. There was still six thick inches of night standing beyond their fingers.

Larry leaned over and put his mouth around the vibrating head of the black flower, [reaching] his warm wet tongue over & beneath the salty foreskin. The three of them were in ecstasy. They were straining so hard — the black body about to explode with energy — that he collapsed in the hay, still beating his black meat. Larry saw the shit eater had arisen. The gigantic white man pulled apart his fly and the crazy pinnacle jutted forth. The shit eater stepped to the ground. The nigger's head leaped forward and thick lips closed over his juicy cock. Larry felt something wet between his buttocks. The S.E. tongued violently Larry's rectum. The shit eater grabbed Larry's free hand, and Larry tumbled to stub nailed fingers, in themselves like vast phalli. The shit eater had jammed his other hand into Basto's ass. Now the combined energy as they tongued, fingered, and assed each other beat like a huge sea among them.

+ + +

[*inscription on inner back cover of notebook*:]
    Return this to
    Bruno Callabro

NOTEBOOK 4—APRIL–MAY 1959

April 28, 1959

Illuminations in the night ululant—the small voices in the back of the brain; my mind crawls across the floor. "Step on it quickly." The ice is black. When the image crashes on the tiles; shattering, isn't it? It is inebriated—the drunken babbling of the soft voices pierces up behind the surface of existence. When I wonder what they say, they lisp out, inaudible.

Where am I headed for; the surface of things about me is dark and love is hideous against my flesh—and love is hideous.

I'm writing a letter now:

Don't you remember, Ellen, when we cut down the green of fresh grass with our laughter; you had red hair and I could never touch you—and there were three of us, Ruben and I and you; the corridors of the Metropolitan Museum are dark and the walls, where they are not plastered with artifacts, are black slabs of ice. I pressed my face against the marble, and I said—

Oh god how I would love a conversation; I want to say what we said; I want to tell you on paper. The futility of mere syllables; and anyway, it would be meaningless, for Ruben first came in and then he put his hand up and rubbed his mouth, watching; you stood with your red hair in the black hall, and we were silent for a while.

Then we went on among the tombs.

+ + +

April 29,

Isn't that a nice date?

Quotes

M—Where the hell is he?
J—He's taking a shit for himself, which he'll write in his notebook when he gets back.
  (half hour later)
M—Either constipation or diarrhea. I don't know which one.
J—You can look in his notebook tomorrow and find out.

**It's getting colder. I can't lie down and absorb the warm light any-
more. The rock has made a ruin of my stockings. Judy asks me how
long you've been gone. She is making strange hieroglyphs in her
notebook. I say about half an hour. She says it's not as long as that.
She lies down and I hold the book so she cannot see it. I'll see it anyway. He must have gotten lost she says, turning over. He got lost.**

+ + +

—It is now 11:30 at night; shall we record the day? 'Twas a weird one. How
does one record a day?

   —Oh, i have novels in my eyes; quick quick, the glint of glass—

When i left, it was a fine morning; it was spring weather, or rather the
sky said it would be spring weather by noon. When i walked between the
buildings, it was nearly cold.

   I went through the swath of free form cement walks that wind between
the projects; the houses are like one huge twenty story pink brick horror
reflected in a dozen faces. Because it was a Jewish holiday, only about one
hundred (out of 3,000) kids would be in school, so I went down to NYU—
besides, i had told Marilyn i was going. I took the A train and stood with
my back to the door—the train was packed—and read the dance section
over the shoulder of a young trench coat.

   I got off at W. 4th St and went up and out Waverly Place. I trotted along
8th Street until I came to the square; the first place i went when i came into
the NYU building was the cafeteria.

   It is a huge room that is checkered with somewhat dull tables. I didn't
think i would meet anyone i knew, but i did. Paul and Polly—aren't those
names comical? I mean in combination; and they always act like two
people named Paul and Polly too; they look like they should be called
Herbert and Melissa, but they act like Paul and Polly—anyway, they were
laughing sweetly at one another and holding hands.

   I sort of eased in gently, asked if i was unwanted, and was ignored for
the most part. Paul is a big, grinning faced boy who wears dark rimmed
glasses, thick clothing like heavy sweaters etc, and always gives one the
impression that he needs a bath. And he always tries to be sophisticated while never be[ing] able to stop grinning at his *suavité* which is all
but nonexistent. He is disgustingly innocent and doesn't know it; which
makes him rather refreshing. He's the type of person who entertains—not
seriously, at any rate; or at least doesn't appear to be serious—delusions
that he will eventually get somewhere by scribbling poetry on the back

of paper napkins, theatre programs—wherever he happens to be, and on whatever paper is handy; i haven't seen any of his men's room sonnets—i wonder if there are any? Oh well.

Polly is just willowy—like a Melissa should be. She's innocent too, which makes them quite nice and compatible.

They directed me to the Waverly building where i was to meet Marilyn—in Psychology; how appropriate.

In front of the elevator—I had to go to the tenth floor—i saw someone squinting through at me. That is Judy.

Conversation:

"What . . . what . . . what are you doing here?" Small hand across the mouth. She stumbles forward. "You're here to see Marilyn?"

"Um-huh."

Hand comes away from mouth. "Oh, my god. Oh, my god, oh my go—do you know?"

"What?"

"I saw a bomb last night. It was terrible." Terrific giggle; we step on the elevator. We are the only ones talking. "Freddy was magnificent, but then he always is. This is so stupid—the play, i mean. And Tom Poston—dead! Absolutely dead. You know how a comedian is when he's trying to play a dramatic—well, serious role? Absolutely dead."—(incidentally, Freddy is a chorus boy who is in Judy's ballet class and who is in the chorus of the play—which is why she saw it)—"It's being financed by some Texas millionaire or something—no, don't laugh, I'm serious. Doesn't know anything about the theatre. They're paying them fabulous prices, and it's equity no less. It's so funny: in the middle of rehearsal one day, Freddy told them he was a dance captain now; so they're giving him $10 a week more."

"What the hell is a dance captain."

"They didn't know either; that's why they gave him the raise. Actually it's a dancer who sort of keeps everyone in line. But Fred doesn't know his part anyway; my god, none of the dancers knows his part. They cut out all the good dances anyway."

"When they cut, the dances are always the first to go."

"Yes," she said. "Yeah," and made a face. "I hope they learn the damn thing by Friday."

Psychology was a bore. Marilyn came 20 minutes late and slipped me a note asking if i had brought the Nietzsche—which i had forgotten. When i couldn't take it any longer, i started an argument—well not quite—with the professor all about repression, inhibitions, disorganized viscera, and other tasty tidbits. NYU is afflicted with a plethora of professors who do not know how not to take their little charges seriously. Some girl in the front row wanted to know whether her predilections and adversities to holding the hands of various boys was a purely mental or physical action. Well, I mean, can't she figure it out? I later learned that this charming young thing was in the process of translating some short stories from the Persian and was generally—or at least by Judy; Marilyn liked her—considered rather funny—"No, not funny/peculiar; that's me. I just mean funny."

We went back down to the cafeteria, cut Classics, and Pierre came along who proceeded to draw angels for me. That might really have turned into something interesting had not Paul and a girl named Joan popped up. But they were both innocent—too bad, hah! hah!

Besides, Pierre had to go to German or something.

The next class—incidentally, as of this paragraph, I am on the D train uptown and it is the morning of April 30—was Ethics. Marilyn didn't want to cut, but Judy, as we got up to leave, grabbed our coat sleeves as we stood up and implored us to stay. I stayed, Marilyn went. Someone suggested that we all go out to the square—José had just stopped by the table and had put everybody in a good mood; Hildy, his wife, has a cold; José had a haircut.

Judy, myself, and Joan ended up walking toward the square.

Joan is very nice, but insufferable. The conversation went something like—"Well, I know you write, and so I really want to read some of your work. Victor was so impressed—I believe in encouraging talent you know. Now if it's bad, I'm the first to say so. I never believe in finishing a bad book. But then I suppose you literary people do, just on a matter of principle. And oh—have you read *The Castle*—by Kafka, you know—"

"Yes."

"And wasn't that a wonderful book. Oh my God, what a book. I'm reading *Moby-Dick* now—that's by Melville. But I'm prejudiced; last year we read *Billy Budd* in school you see and our professor kept on talking about 'the beautiful blond barbarian'—'the noble savage' and all that. My professor's name was Benda and keep on getting them all mixed up—or at any rate, I put them all together: 'big beautiful blond barbarian Billy Budd Benda'—the alliteration is stifling. Now *Moby-Dick*—there is a wonderful book. I've only read a hundred pages; but what a book. You've read Nathanael West, haven't you?"

"Some."

"What a writer. What a wonderful writer. *Lonelyhearts*—a small masterpiece. Didn't you think so?"

"Yes."

"And then *The Day of the Locust*. I love Fitzgerald. What a writer. But *Lonelyhearts*, what a book. It's the skeleton of a masterpiece, don't you think? Just like *Gatsby* is the skeleton of a world. Gatsby is Fitzgerald, you know—"

"I know."

"—Remember those letters at the beginning of *Lonelyhearts*, the girl with no nose—My god. Oh, and have you read—"

This went on until we reach[ed] the empty fountain—a large dry pan of concrete it seemed now. We sat down on the edge. There was a girl beside us—she lay near the edge of the rim, talking to a boy in a green sweater. I got up and talked to her for a few seconds, hoping to break the momentum of Joan's babbling. I give you what she said in toto because i am feeling a mite sadistic right now. I hadn't seen Linda—the girl to whom I was talking—for over two years. The strain of time brought us smiling embarrassedly away from each other—her sister, Jane, she told me, was in Australia, or did she say Austria?

Joan would not stop. "*The Day of the Locust*—my god—"

"The only things I have read by West is *Lonelyhearts* and that thing about the adventures of some flea along the guts of some horse. They were both very good."

"Flea?—intestines?—"

"I have to be going back," said Judy.

Judy and I left Joan in the fountain.

"My lord," I said to Judy. "That girl sounds like she just discovered literature last week and hasn't gotten over the initial shock."

Judy laughed, defended Joan for a while, and then we went up to Calculus where I met Marilyn. The professor tried to throw me out, but Marilyn let out a piercing ululation of agony, so I was allowed to stay. The class was reviewing some puerile example which I could have done in the seventh grade. Afterwards, we went down to the cafeteria again after having met Gale, picked up an application for NYU, picked up Pierre.

Pierre had records, but they were over at the French house. We sat around at the Chuck Wagon for about an hour and then went over to get the records. The floors were being waxed, however, and M. Squires would not let him in. Finally he took off his shoes and tiptoed in, retrieved his discs, and came out again, albums in one hand, shoes in the other.

Have been riding the D train now since quarter to 9, and now at 10:20.
Slept some. Must get around to writing
"Passacaglia
With
Death
in
the
Higher
Voices"

(10:25) So anyway, then we went up on the Fifth Avenue bus and made
grade-A asses of ourselves. There were two women beside us who kept up
with a conversation that would have put Ionesco to shame:

"And may all your troubles be . . . small pointed ones . . . with white
gloves, high heels . . . and slanted woman." What one can do with an ellip-
sis, my, my!

We got off, Pierre went to work, Marilyn, Judy, and I went to the park. I
wasted an hour looking for a men's room—which explains those interesting quotes in Marilyn's handwriting about 8 pages ago. Later Pierre took
us on a tour of those lesser known—to a few—areas of the park. It was fascinating and a little frightening too.

We are at the last stop in Coney Island. Someone has written "Young
Sinners" on the wall.

The man up the car blows his nose on his hands, whistles and says, "—
You know it takes a long time to get started too—" The doors close, open,
close. We sit and the trains around us move. We are still.

"Shit," mumbles the man.

A guy in blue pants and a white cloth jacket has come in and propped
up his foot on the seat before him. Around outside there is the web of
tracks. We are moving. Once beside the tracks there were three old drums.
One was filled with fire. The skeletons of the Coney pierce up into the
grayness. We are in and out of the next stop, curving around with the
metal plates of the train crashing. And I can't see the web of steel that is
the roller coaster anymore.

I hope it gets nicer. The sky is an even cold dirty white, and oddly
enough it is spring.

Who speaks of stabbing memories of childhood is wrong. They come and touch various parts of the face like gauze hands and then are gone.

———

We ride in the elevated train over an immense grave[yard]. You can see nothing—oh my god, nothing but tombs.

———

Today is a day without shadows. The light is gray—bright, but gray, and diffuse. When you look, everything is significant; because we can never record everything, perhaps it is better to write nothing. I do not believe that—but it hurts, oh lord, it hurts—

———

When one rides over the city, one sees what a wreck it is. When one walks into the city, one sees just what wreckage is. We are going underground now.

———

A black man sits across from me and reads a paperback—"Look not upon me, ye, though I am black and comely oh ye daughters of Jerusalem." The boy in the white jacket rests his cheek on his fist, by the windowsill. The train has filled now. What is black? Children—we are in the last car— have come to stare out the back window. Everyone doesn't smile at children, but the one or two that do make you think everybody should. This afternoon I went to Forty-Second Street—

—when I was sketching the children, the mother came over and watched, and then we talked and I nearly missed my stop.

"My god, my god, why have you forsaken me—"

What does this mean. Are there any nuances of meaning in such details, missing significances? Take letters, a G [and] an R; connect them to numbers, 7—8—o—4—o, and do they spell anything beyond themselves— I don't know.

———

May i write an autobiography tonight? I must do one for school. Is there protection from the soul in words? Is there protection from anything. Tonight i feel that i have ceased to grow. There, I've said it.

What have i done with life—i must call Judy to call Marilyn. Bob wants us to go to an all Cocteau night at the theatre.

Today I finally have felt, and am feeling the "depression of metaphysical negation." And besides being hideously uncomfortable, it is a lie.

* * * I was born in New York City. I have had, in some respects, a most provincial life, and in many others, a variety of experience which is amazing.

My interests are in literature, art, and science. My enjoyment of prose, poetry, and drama come from exposure. I can't say that any piece of work has influenced me too much more than any other. I was fortunate enough to get involved with a forthcoming literary magazine about 2 months ago. This group put out the *Florida Review* a year ago. Besides having a story of mine published, i am also getting a chance to learn something about publishing.

+   +   +

When I first started school, my father—or Dr. Allen—would drive myself and his son, Farrow, to school. Then something happened and I had to change schools; the time I cried one day when my father left us one morning without saying good bye—standing by the gate with a little girl named Karin and saying, "It's big here—I don't like it," and her saying "I want to have fun here—I like it very much," and my saying, "Well then, all right, I like it too"—and there was a boy in my class with his birthday the same day as my own; all this suddenly wasn't any more, and I never saw Dr. Allen and Farrow anymore. My father drove me to school all the time now. It was a nice drive because we lived uptown, and the school, a private school named Dalton, was downtown.

I remember very distinctly someone saying to me, "My mother says that you're a Negro. Why are you here?"

I probably said something such as, "I don't know."

In a school whose total enrollment from kindergarten, primary, elementary, and [high school] was not 500, it seems odd that we should have over ten teachers who specialized in the arts. I received a grounding in music which was quite thorough; it has sometimes surprised people that I write music without ever having taken lessons on any instrument. But from the first, these were things we were taught.

My art teacher, Miss Gwendolyn Davis, said to me once: "What painting is [is] very simple. There are only shape, line, and color to worry about. But how you do [it]—there are so many things to learn!"

This has been my feeling toward all the arts.

I seem to behave passably in most of the arts. I dance with a group at the community center and I did some of the choreography for one of its productions. I have always enjoyed drama and for the past three years I have attended Hunter College Dramatic Workshop for Young People.

Drawing and painting have always been fun for me. Writing, however, is the only art which I take seriously for myself.

I am now in a "creative writing" class in school and I managed to win first and second prize in the National Scholastic writing competition this year. I am also going to have a novelette published in a forthcoming magazine, *The New Ark*, in September.

My summer experiences have been summer camp up until last year. I attended Camp Woodland up until two years ago, and then I went to Camp Rising Sun for a year, an international scholarship camp sponsored by the George Jonas foundation. Last summer I worked in the New York Public Library as a page.

My interests as far as a profession is concerned lie in physics. That is why I wanted to go to the Bronx High School of Science. Nuclear physics in particular has always fascinated me. The questions which the field poses appear to be like half completed mathematical equations; the perfection which is found in math coupled with the enigmas of the workings of the universe seem to be the basic characteristics of the field. But my interests at the present are so diversified that [I] would like to go into them all a little further until I found the one that was the most rewarding.

———

Love is a lie, and our bodies are betrayers—Why did I write what I did in Gale's notebook? Why? (May 9, 1959) I did it at Judy's party—and I sweated when I wrote it; but I had to tell her because perhaps she would understand—oh God—

Joe—

Joe—

That probably isn't even his real name. I know it isn't.

———

(May 10th)

> I doubt if there
> Is any more than half a world
> And all the day
> Is only dust
> And only half a world away

———

(May 10th)

> You see,
> There is no truth
> There is no certainty

And we
Are merely ambiguous statements
Of
A nonexistent lie.

———

My sex
Dissects itself
In the gray, diffused, & shadowless
Light of a
denuded
dawn.

———

May 11, 6½ minutes to twelve: there is something rather graceless about splattering your guts all over all the available paper in the house. Trust is man's greatest virtue. With it, innocence is maintained.

———

(8:45)

What has happened? Marilyn has run off again. Why the hell doesn't she call me? i called everyone, Gale, Judy—no one knows where she is. Her mother blubbered into the phone for an hour to Gale.

When i called Judy, she said that Gale had been bitchy to her this morning & that she had missed an appointment with Judy at one. Where the hell does Marilyn get the idea that i even look at Judy? Judy kept on saying that Marilyn was jealous, only she never said it outright—what is wrong with her. If anything happens to Marilyn i think i'd go crazy.

And then what Judy said has been going on between Gale and Marilyn—i don't care what they did; how could i care!

And then what i wrote in Gale's note-book. Why am i such an idiot? That was probably what Marilyn & Gale were arguing about.

Can't she trust me [on] this one thing? i had to tell someone, what could i do? The fact that she would trust me would mean that it was unimportant and i could tell her—that is, if i had need to i could. Even then it would hurt her very much, but if she trusted me, everything would be fine.

She wonders why i don't go to bed with her. She hasn't ever slept with anyone before and so she doesn't know what trouble she could get into. She hasn't had the close calls i have. She really doesn't know how to take care of herself. Any girl who acts like Marilyn does about it is not ready to go to bed with anyone. If she would stop throwing her body at me, i could go to bed with her when there was an opportunity. It's hard enough to re-frain from it as it is.

She is one of these girls who still thinks that sleeping with someone is just a matter of going to bed and praying that nothing serious goes wrong. She doesn't realize that the universe swings in its arc about the act. If i didn't feel the way i do about her, I'd sit her on her ass with a very rude jolt.

But she is innocent—and i—unfortunately or fortunately—am not. i love her more than anyone in the world—perhaps this is only the one true thing i have ever said. Why doesn't she call? What the hell am i here for if not to help. I've run to her enough times—please, if she'd just call.

And with the note i wrote: my god, why did I? And yet i couldn't do anything else. i told her once the day Pierre made a pass at me that she was innocent. She never did understand that—she wonders why i always quote her "shattering plains" or "dividing plains"—she doesn't know that the plain is cracked up in the middle and blasted into fragments. i hope she never finds out. If i could only say i would cease to love her if she did? But i couldn't.

Won't she call?

Truth is a lie.

God damn it—i can't get out, and my hands are bleeding, and the ink from my veins drips down into the crevices of my fingernails.

———

Dynamo came out today; after all that correction, there were still three typographical errors in "Silent Monologue For ..." that I have found so far.

———

My soul is a lying fragment
On the tongues of a thousand
People.

———

I received my Sheaffer pen—which I am using now—in Math class this morning. Everyone wanted to see what it was, read the congratulatory let-ters on my prizes in the Scholastic contest.

And I, who half the creative writing class thinks of as sort of out of the realm of human beings, am no more than a prostitute. Why don't you go back to him, you bastard. Why don't you bleed him for every penny he has—go OH YOU STUPID FUCK, GO ON,

Stop me, please. Why the hell won't she call me? Huh—why?

———

When i told Murray, he said, "I just see all the shit; you go and plunge right into it, don't you."

His flesh was like lard.

———

(May 11) I received Gale's letter today. She told me it was coming.

———

Pierre must have been living there without his shirt. Marilyn was there, and she told me. Gale said: *Turn over, I don't want to hit you in the face,* and then she raised the belt in her hand. Pierre turned, and then she hit him—hard.
He screamed.

———

(My God, it was my line: she said to him what i had said in my novel, and that is wonder. The horror engulfs me.) When I read her letter, I cried—for the first time over words on paper; not because of what they would say to anybody else, but to me.
She is the only person who could illustrate my novel—now i think i understand why.
There is no love—
And yet she knows that—
Oh lord, what does she know?
Marilyn says she has almost finished "3 voices." That's wonderful.
It's funny, the instant in which i learned what shit and filth were, i also learned what respect was—and that respect was merely the lie which enables us to cover up love without destroying ourselves.

———

In Gore Vidal's critique of Friedrich Dürrenmatt's *The Pledge* he says the literary scene of today is obsessed with love. He lauds Dürrenmatt for bringing justice to the fore. From Vidal's novels one should gather that the man knows neither love nor justice exist as anything more than facets of—of what?
The review was in *The Reporter,* which reminds me; i must thank the Ascolis for the subscription of *S.A.* which Peter gave me. That is long overdue.

———

I have left my watch at home but it is about 8:30.
Marilyn had an extra ticket so i am on the way to the Bolshoi again. It is May 12. I am sitting on the A Train in my suit and trench coat. It is driz-

zling outside and the heat turns everything into warm fog. My clothes
stick to me.

+ + +

We pull into 59th Street. I have *Dynamo* for Marilyn since her poem appeared in it. My opera glasses are uncomfortable against my thigh through
the coat. They are new
—off again.
We will see the Bolshois at Madison Square Garden this time from the
top balcony.
Ulanova is dancing—

+ + +

Deathless Lines at the
Bolshoi

But why *can't* they have a 3-ring ballet

Excuse me madam, but you can't be too sure with whom you're playing footsie.

Oh look, there go two girls who look as if they come from *Sylphide*—
without the binoculars
You mean the one [with] the sort of beige-ish peach and the one in
sickly saffron—
Yeah—
They're too fat.
Did you see the cow in the blue dress
Yes
Well that's me. Shut up.

No, she only speaks Russian

Will you be here? I'm going out to take a—refreshment (this with
heavy Russian accent)

Oh, isn't that Vasiliev?
The conductor? I would have known if it was the conductor

What is the matter
With writing out patter
When one wonders just how to pass

The time of the day
In unusual ways
In a long boring S.S. class

+ + +

Pay High the Piper ...

"*Agon*, a ballet composed by Igor Stravinsky, choreographed by George Balanchine and danced by the New York City Center Ballet ... was given an enormous ovation ... The balcony stood up shouting and whistling ... people came out into the lobby, their eyes bright as if the piece had been champagne."

". . . today the world's leading ballet country is unquestionably the United States. In vigor, variety, artistic eminence and perfection of performance, American ballet stands at the top of the ladder—outranked nowhere on earth."

"The modern dance reached its peak in America ... Martha Graham, Doris Humphrey, Charles Weidman, and Hanya Holm danced, composed, taught, and traveled. In a very short time they spread the new dance across the country."

These three quotes might appear to some people in turn pointless, pretentious, and slightly mystifying. This article is directed toward the mystified.

In a year during [which] we have been pummeled with the Bolshoi—still not having completely recovered from the Royal Covent Garden's (Sadler's Wells) Ballet two years ago—those people to whom dance is a mystery have been inundated in a sea of superlatives which have all been directed out of the country. This, coupled with a general myth that America is culturally defunct as a nation, makes a great many raise an eyebrow at the possibility that the US has a foot in the top rung of the international cultural ladder. America can afford to be generous with its praise.

If one wished to start dropping names that command international respect, the list would fill up pages. The tragedy is that because none of our ballet companies are subsidized by the government [. . .] they cannot get one tenth the publicity they deserve. They have their following—sufficiently large to keep them from folding up—that is, in the case of the N.Y.C. Ballet, to keep the N.Y. City Center fairly filled to the rafters eight times a week for three ten week seasons a year. That's a lot of people. But it also means that because of lack of publicity there are people who know that there is a dance in America, and the rest simply haven't heard of it.

This is a shame because of the very reason that the American ballet has achieved the place it has in the world of dance: with all due respect for the classics of ballet, the American ballet is not a museum in which the classics are taken out to be aired. It is a living thing which is constantly growing. The ballet mentioned at the beginning of this article, *Agon*, makes a challenge that anyone would be foolish not to accept. It says in so many words, or movements as the case may be: "I will take four boys and eight girls without scenery and with only practice costumes and dance them for twenty minutes and keep you on the edge of your seat for the entire duration of the dance; I will make you laugh, scare you with my daring, and enchant you with a pas de deux which has been labeled the pas de deux to end all pas de deux." Are you more mystified? Good.

The American dance has come from a mongrelized heritage that is staggering. The modern dance, the old Diaghilev company of Paris from which we get such names as Nijinsky, Pavlova, and Fokine, American folk elements, all this is part of the parents of the American dance. The term Ballet for some people brings up painful experiences with bad performances of *Les Sylphides*, wet geese in the middle of *Swan Lake*, and this is enough to discourage anybody. But this, fortunately, is not representative of the dance in America, although too often it has alienated people who might have received a great deal of pleasure from good dancing.

But most of these same people can connect names like Jerome Robbins, Michael Kidd, and Gene Kelly with exciting evenings in the musical comedy theatre; these choreographers are also among [those who] helped make the Ballet what it is in America today. Even more mystifying?

The mystery is simply this. People want to [be] entertained. Culture is merely good entertainment. Dance has always been one of the most vigorous forms [of] entertainment there was. In America, this vigor, coupled with innovation and general excitement, has given us some of which we can really be proud.

+ + +

Another trilogy of short stories coming up, folks!

I   "An Empty Stretch of Beach"
II   "Pomegranate"
III   "Salt"

In December, Coney Island is only the gaunt skeleton of a fantasy.

Call the whole thing "An Empty Stretch of Beach"

I   "Quicksilver"
II   "Pomegranate"
III   "Salt"

+ + +

Tuesday—2nd week of July. I have left home again. Spent last night and will spend the rest of tonight at what is left of Victor's—Victor is in England, and what is left of Victor is three roommates who seem to spend all their time walking around in either blue suits, or the all-together.

Tomorrow—out I go for a job—I hope.

The only thing I got done today was a hell of a lot of reading and 6 pages of the Coal Creek saga.

Great novels:

The Faulkner Pentology—(which I consider one book): *Sartoris, Light in August, Absalom, Absalom!, The Sound and the Fury, As I Lay Dying.*

Proust: *Remembrance of Things Past.*

Joyce: *Finnegans Wake.* (Don't ask me why—but my God, what a book when it hits you.)

2

....

In Search of Silence

....

The three notebooks in this chapter cover Delany's final year at Science. The bulk of the first notebook, Notebook 2, consists of *In Search of Silence*, Delany's first exercise in exhaustive journal keeping. With its epigraphs, references to the journals of Gide, mentions of precocious writers like Chatterton and Radiguet, and interweaving of critical analysis and memoir, *Silence* displays the erudition characteristic of Delany's later published work. *In Search of Silence* and the two notebooks that follow contain outline material for the novels *Cycle for Toby*, *Those Spared by Fire*, and *Afterlon*, as well as notes and drafts for, and discussions of, other literary projects.

In 1959 Delany's father had been diagnosed with cancer and had had one lung removed.[1] As his condition worsened, tensions grew between him and the rest of the family, and young Delany increasingly sought refuge in the company of friends.[2] In section III of *Silence* Delany mentions "leaving home again," and in several passages describes time spent in the apartments of friends from both Science and NYU. Delany also filled his social time with artistic pursuits, participating in poetry readings at friends' apartments on the Upper West Side and in coffee shops downtown, as well as performing with the folk group he had cofounded, the Harbor Singers. Several times he visited the poet Marie Ponsot, whom he had met through Hacker at a Halloween party at NYU.[3] Ponsot became a mentor figure for Delany, and the two continued to meet through the early years of Delany's marriage.

In the summer following graduation, Delany attended the Bread Loaf Writers' Conference, where he met William Sloane, John Ciardi, John A. Williams, Edward Lewis Wallant, Allen Drury, and Robert Frost.[4] It was probably at Bread Loaf that Delany wrote the passages in Notebook 11 under the title "Studies"; these are the opening lines of the prologue to what would become Delany's major project of the early '60s, the long novel *Voyage, Orestes.*

NOTES

1. Samuel R. Delany, *The Motion of Light in Water: Sex and Science Fiction Writing in the East Village* (1988; reprint, Minneapolis: University of Minnesota Press, 2004), *Motion,* 3.

2. Ibid., 107–8.

3. Ibid., 8–9, 96.

4. Ibid., 7–8.

NOTEBOOK 2—JANUARY 1959

[January–February 1960]

Journal:

In Search of
Silence

> I want to declare that I am a traitor to the human race.
> —Henry Miller

> Make me a mandrake, so I may groan here,
> Or a stone fountain weeping out my year.
> —John Donne

> ... that strange craving for sea-sickness children have ... But certainly I
> felt this strange need even more than they. I liked to feel my heart beat
> irregularly and fast. The spectacle before me, so rich in poetry, satisfied
> me more.
> —Raymond Radiguet

I

In the search for the things I can not say I move through the crevices in the city, the streets, the littered alley-ways of winter. I was born in
autumn, though my birthday is in April, and my road travels through an
icy, January sun. I want to prologue what I have seen with something that
opens me up, something that tears apart my face and lets you look behind
my eyes. They say that thought is an inversion of experience; what is experience, then: an extroversion of thought?

I am strangled with words, suddenly, and the things which need to be
said—I don't even know what they are. That's why I cry so poignantly at
times; and the poignance is not because my situation calls so much for
pity, but because something locked in my gut screams for love, and so this
something makes me affect poignance; for pathos is a subject I am well
studied in. There was brilliance I once wanted to achieve, an ebullience of
style and subject, but I don't have it—it was never mine to exercise. Why

does language suddenly burst forth for some—sometimes for me—and rocket the hearer and the heard so far that—that—and here the metaphor fails, language fails, words become depleted bags of breath and sighs, and I can find no semblance of meaning in any thing.

This incalculable emptiness that is as much inside me as out—

—When I had worked my way to the back of the bus—No!

It was hot with people, and in the bus you have to strain to reach over [the] old lady's shoulders so that you can grab the strap, and when you finally get back where there are not enough people to be uncomfortably crowded and too many to feel free (and my coat was for the brittle winter air outside, not the effluvia of body heat that bloats up a crowded bus) you can reach a fair sort of balance between agony and simple displeasure. The back seat of the bus runs from one side to the other. The rest are placed either in rows along the side or (in those places just over the wheels) with the seat backs to the wall so that the people in them must stare straight across the aisle into the dull faces of those people perched above the other wheel who are staring back.

There was a boy in the back seat, with a blue zipper jacket on—he was near fourteen. He had good hands; I remember that's what first made me look at him. Then suddenly he turned away behind the shoulder of a bigger boy who was sitting next to him and spit up a handful of brownish fluid into his palm. He must have been trying to hold it in, but he couldn't, and he vomited again, this time all over the shoulder of the boy next to him. He got out his handkerchief and tried to wipe his hand, and wipe off the boy's shoulder. The boy turned around and saw what was happening, and gave the kid another handkerchief. Then he tapped the knee of a young guy who was sitting on the other side of the kid. The guy was probably asleep, and the boy had to hit him hard, but when he woke up, he looked and then moved to a seat in front of the back seat, and he tried to tell the poor kid to relax. The kid sat there with his hands filthy and all wrapped up in the dirty handkerchiefs. He was embarrassed as hell, and when he had to spit up again, he looked around and tried to do it in the seat behind the first boy, only it ran all down his blue zippered jacket. The first boy had moved forward in his seat and now he rested his arms on the back of the chair [before] him and put his head down on his arms. The guy who had moved was now patting the kid on the knee and telling him to relax and there were tears streaked across the kid's face, not from crying but from the effort of trying to keep it back. The kid just sat there with his jacket streaked and his hands and pants messy. I could smell it now.

One middle-aged man in a brown coat, clutching a *New York Times* to his breast, got up and changed seats so he wouldn't have to look at it.

I wanted to say to him, "You stupid ass, why don't you give the kid your paper and let him clean himself off instead of running away from it." There were at least two other people with newspapers who just looked in the other direction. I would have even given the man the nickel for the paper if he had given it to the kid. There was a young woman in a black coat who was sitting next to where I was standing and she had on a black knitted hood. I could tell that she wanted to help as much as I did; because it wasn't disgusting; it just made you feel bad that nobody would help, or that the kid was too embarrassed just to spread his legs, lean forward and puke on the floor. I would have said something to that guy who changed his seat if I had stayed on the bus another thirty seconds. But it was my stop.

I felt so much for the kid because once, when I was a lot younger, I had been going to school on the bus in the rush hour, standing up, and all of a sudden I got a bloody nose. It was a bad one and it didn't stop and I didn't even have a handkerchief and I had to hold my coat sleeve against my nose, but it kept leaking. All the people did was move away from me. Not one tissue was forthcoming, not one handkerchief, not even a news-paper. I remember when I finally got off the bus, a huge clot of red mucus exploded from my nostril and the blood stopped, but my face was a mess.

I remember another kid I saw throw up, once; in the subway station one morning, a train had come on and since I was at the front of the station, the beginning of the train was about twenty feet down. Suddenly this kid walked over to the edge, leaned over and heaved his breakfast into the tracks, but as he started, the train did too, so that he had to jerk his head back again, and he finished by splashing all over the platform. I was with a girl at the time and we both thought it was sort of embarrassingly funny. But at least the kid was O.K.

When I got out of the bus, I suddenly felt an emptiness, a false empti-ness, however. It was next to the little park right across from Grant's Tomb and beside Riverside Church. The streets were wet and there were shelves of melting ice in the drop from the curb to the street, and there were sheets of ice on the sidewalk and patches of old dirty impacted snow—most of the pavement was wet. The emptiness was a façade, as if it were hiding an inferno behind it, like the magician who flashes both sides of a silk ker-chief and says, "See, nothing at all," while all the time you know that he will produce from behind that kerchief something mysterious and even a little horrible.

Only it wasn't a little horrible, it was a great big horror that had nothing to do with the puking kid in the bus or the subway—more to do with a little kid with a bloody nose in a bus years ago, and a beautiful tongueless monster who haunted so many deserts—

(I had a notebook in my hand. Why didn't I tear some pages out and give them to the kid. I thought about it in the bus, but the notebook was writing paper which isn't absorbent like newspaper. I felt guilty about it, though—)

—and yet not quite about anything I can say. I wanted to run—I stood there, feeling for the impulse, trying to find out what it was, where it was, trying to find how to work it through. On another day I would have never realized that I wanted to run, but I was trying now to feel myself out, and I saw—felt what I wanted to do and was slightly shocked, and yet I kept on trying to work that horror through. Even now I want to externalize the feeling, say that it lurked beneath the filthy snow, behind the wall of the park, hissed in the crackle of dead leaves that still rattle in breeze, hanging like a [...] of slaughtered criminals among the branches of the trees behind the wall, sounding like the clatter of hollow locust shells, dried insects battering among the foliage, but the horror was inside me.

They say that when a child is scolded and in turn the child scolds her doll, she is healing the wound of her chastisement. This is a healthy cycle. And yet I was never able to do this. And so, perhaps, the wounds were never healed, and the festering still goes on someplace where I can't hear it, see it, smell the rot inside; I could never use dolls for scapegoats, nor could I even use people for dolls. This isn't a justification, it's just a fact. Gide says somewhere in his journals in a reference to Radiguet and *Le Diable au corps*, that young Radiguet has destroyed Madeleine on the roof. In the book, that fantastic mad woman on the roof of the house of Marechaud's has no name. But knowing how close Gide, and Cocteau (and consequently Radiguet) were at the time, I wonder just what did go into the creation of the incident. It is by far the best single section of the book.

I want to run in the dark; my soul is a madwoman, terrified of the slightest sound, the least movement. The most minute change in the direction of the breeze sends her howling upon the roof—Radiguet's creature talked with a frighteningly gentle voice. I once said that night was stitched across the streets and stitched onto the roofs of the buildings. I walked in the cold winter beneath the canopy of night. That will do.

I must tell next of the Ionean Horse, and there are other fragments, too, which get lost in the telling.

The questions concerning tragedy are ridiculous in this modern time when we are presented with a genesis of [the] artist whose individual works are not only enhanced by comparison with the whole output, but are completely pointless when looked at as individual works of art. William Faulkner, even perverted and metaphorical Tennessee Williams with his brilliant but meaningless theatre, less so Eugene O'Neill, but even the minor cross-references in Camus suddenly illuminate whole series of works. The phenomen[on] is probably because society has given permission to the artist to present half consummated works as art. No seventeenth-century poet would even think of using one metaphor throughout a whole string of poems without knowing exactly what it signified—today a writer suddenly understands what it was he was trying to say ten, fifteen, twenty years ago and immediately writes a poem, short story or novel, or even an essay explaining all; and a host of biographers and critics are sent scurrying. It is always good to keep the critics scurrying; it prevents them from getting in your hair. Perhaps this entire situation was merely a collaborated defense on the part of the Gestaltic Personality of the Collective Artist.

Ian and I came over to L.M.'s two evenings ago when everybody was stoned out of his head; but Ian didn't know what was going on.

So here I am, this Friday morning in January, seventeen years and nine months old, the age when Thomas Chatterton committed suicide. How depressing, to say something arch. Gale & Stuey are always sober and yet they are perhaps the most incessantly high without recourse to anything but life. I am back at L.M.'s and the phono is playing Scarlatti harpsichord sonatas. There are sixty of them and I am only in the middle of the second side of the first record.

L.M., cylindrical with a great little beard, looking like a frustrated but happy Mephistopheles—"Why do you have this fucking harpsichord on." Then he emits a high falsetto bubble like a harpsichord.

Shall we do a dream analysis of Paul?

He sits in the chair in his underwear. Marty is lying back on the couch. L.M. has gone back to get the phone, and it is silent now, except for the weird counterpoint of L.M.'s laughter in the next room with the harpsichord—And slow occasional comments to each other by Paul and Granny (Marty).

What the hell is tragedy?

Am I a deaf mute, or a slightly retarded kid who walks barefoot around the city. When I came here this morning I took off my shoes and walked up to the roof, and the rain was beating on the roof, but I couldn't get out. Then I went down, out into the air shaft, down the metal steps and moved in the rain on the January pavement, and there was snow on the pavement where the rain hadn't melted it.

Then I went back up the stairs near the roof, sat down in the corner of the stairwell and went half to sleep. I didn't want to wake anybody in the apartment up, so I hung around on the stairs in my bare feet, trying to catch some early morning January sleep, hoping that no janitor would come along and kick me out. The thing is the way janitors' faces don't know how to be anything but hard and grimy.

Janitors should understand people because they know so much about garbage, but they handle so much crap that they resent it, they resent it in people. Anybody who resents crap in people is going to be disappointed.

Jennifer just came in and the conversation oscillates madly from "How many Contracts would there be in the telephone book?"

Then to dinner—"Steak? Lloyd, are you gonna bake a steak."

They decide against it. Jazz has replaced the Scarlatti, and occasionally Lloyd comes in and burbles like a harpsichord.

"Paul, like before you go like down to the bar, would you like empty the garbage."

"Is that my assignment?"

"No, it's a request."

They argue.

Lloyd:

"Take out the fucking garbage!"

Now they want to make Lloyd the maid but he still burbles like a harpsichord. They keep on joking. There is an ebullience that fascinates me.

"Lé sure?"

"Lêsure!"

"That one's preferred."

"Then I gotta say Lesure?"—Does Elly have a home. Everything goes on, but Elly is a tragedy—looking wasted.

"She looks like she ran through the defense line of the N.Y. Giants with no equipment on."

"She looks like she came to the village on a football scholarship."

"The wit?"

"She has a face like—"

"Nice body—"

"What." Each word, a fragment in Elly's tragedy.

Castration complex now, and before—"Did you drop ashes on the rug?"

Paul and Lloyd are starting to horse around. Granny has his head in Jennifer's lap. Paul was 97 lbs when he was in the 3rd grade, and Lloyd is in a dream world. Paul fell into a big pan of blueberries in a white summer suit when he was a little boy in his grandmother's bakery, & he is always eating. They talk, sometimes to me—Oh God, I can't hold everything. The jazz goes too fast and suddenly it stops and the voices go on.

Elly is a tragedy. God, Elly.

Marty has no money for his tuition & his aunt won't give it to him. Now they're playing Billie Holiday.

I wish I could stop the voices and just hear Billie and understand the tragedy of Elly whom everyone has forgotten now but me.

If this goes on, the insane double level on which I function, experiencing & recording, commenting and committing and never able to fulfill my purpose in either one. My life is an eternal story which I am constantly telling myself. The trumpet is sloppy, but impassioned, and Holiday's voice is back again and cooling everything. I don't like jazz, I like music and Art maybe justifies anything—that is the myth the society functions under, only the artist knows differently. Society must have something untouchable, sacred, magnificent, which justifies everything. Something they can't touch, the people; Holiday, under her unjustifiable curse.

Words are completely fictional, lies—Holiday—why her? Why not Washington, Bessie Smith, Fitzgerald, Peggy Lee, or anyone else. All narrative is false because it imparts value to certain actions, things, thoughts—and that editing is an imposition that creates adventure. I am feeling the same sickness that is even more prevalent in Sartre than in *La Nausée*, and this was the real sickness that Sartre felt—Camus is dead.

I am waiting to see his progress up through the realms of the Gods. I saw the beginnings of it in the village the other night (a week ago?) when I was talking with J. P. Schachter. He mentioned Camus' deification (the man had only passed away days before) jokingly, but beneath the joke was the vague terror of truth that is beneath so much humor.

The myth of adventure, that is what the artist strives for. José is an ass when he says philosophers are a ruttish bunch. He has confused the philosophers with the philosophy professors. He laughs and says yes, perhaps he has—and the ephemeral terror again.

What are artists—they are dogs. Watch them bark, hunkering after the bitch-goddess—

"Marty—which Goddess was the Bitch-Goddess?"

"In the *Iliad*. I think it was Athena—no, Aphrodite, I've got it here if you want to look it up."

"No, that's O.K."—Jennifer gets up to change the record. Marty is wrong, but the whole thing is unimportant.

Oh God, Elly whom I have never seen before in my life, what a joke. Oh Elly, what a huge joke. And I can't even laugh.

*   *   *

I am going to leave in a few minutes because it is after four o'clock.

*   *   *

I rode the bus home through the fog. (It is frightening and reassuring to know how few people are competent in any field—heaven protect me from this poetry reading tonight. I am reading "Silent Monologue for Lefty" (nobody I have talked to yet gets the pun of Silent Monologue and Monologue Interieuse) and also the verbal part of "Trio for two dancers and a voice." We were going to have the dancers, but we didn't really have time so we decided against that.)

After finishing the last long section, I suddenly realize how journal writing became so obsessive with Gide, Miller, and Reinstein. I wonder if Cary's journals will ever be published. They would probably become another child terrible classic. Too bad the volume devoted to Marilyn was burned. That's the only one of the twelve volumes no longer extant. Thus she is denied a small measure of immortality.

But I must get ready for this evening.

+   +   +

The great battle as [to] who was to be Milena to Cary's Kafka between Louise and Marilyn. Marilyn, the greater of the two, so that Cary had to destroy those parts of himself that were her—Louise, less great than Cary, and subsequently and consequently destroyed herself and was destroyed by him.

*   *   *

It is now 1:40 in the morning. I just got in from the reading. It went well. I did "Lefty," "Love-Tide" & "Time-Tide" plus the trio. I received a number of compliments. Afterwards, things began to go slightly haywire. Lew, Vikki & I listened to T. S. Eliot for a while, and then there was a wild wrestling thing in which I carried Lew all over the house. Then I carried Vikki.

The quality of the poetry was surprising. As long as Erik Felderman reads his own stuff, the meaning flies across with a force that is surprising, but without him behind it, everything falls through—at least for me.

Lew—by far the best poet there, with the possible exception of Johnny Lipsky when he is being serious—does not know how to read. Besides, Lew looks too much like a poet to be appreciated. With very few exceptions, they are all people who are aware of poetic concepts, aware of music and meaning and the delicate interplay between the two—they are not always able to put it across, but they have it. There were a plethora of those finely competent little gems which, had [they] been written by "major" poets, people would point to as examples of great men dealing with simplicity upon humble subjects. Time will wear away most, if not all of them—Lew is far too deeply caught within himself to let time touch him—and that is somewhat a shame. One of the reasons why there are so many incompetent writers around is because some people are so caught up in themselves that they were never touched by either time or talent. To have talent you must be able to see and feel things about you, and it is this seeing and this feeling that winnows through the greatest number of truly talented people by the time they are twenty. And seldom is the talent great enough to warrant us watching it closely before then.

Society only allows a very few artists to get through—compared with the ones that start out—and then it Lauds and Magnifies those people who have defied it.

III

> We that are human cannot hope.
> —James Agee

I have just been reading Elizabeth Drew's book on poetry. She has done a fine, though sometimes pretentious job. But then, art is the ultimate pretension.

The world shatters around me. I am filled with the ineffable fear and emptiness. "Silver"—the replacement for "Coin" which Vikki lost for me (along with the first version of "Sand" and "Salt") sits four pages finished in the typewriter.

I am leaving home again tomorrow, & nobody knows. I had such an ordinary conversation with Ian on the phone a little while ago. I told him I would meet him in the morning, yes, and I would bring the girl's rubbers, yes, and I would be expecting the notes, yes, I will bring those papers if I can find them—knowing all along that I am leaving; it's this ludicrous hypocrisy that I am running away from.

The filled feeling, up to the throat, it is both anger and fear. I really want to hide. If I go to school tomorrow, nothing will happen to me. I don't have a paper, or homework! Yet nothing will happen—and that's why I'm not going because all this importance is attached to a paper or a homework [assignment], and yet it actually does not affect a single thing in the running of the universe. Education is a farce as it is conducted in this society. We are taught to read, all well and good. Even now I am still learning new things in Mathematics. That is why Mr. Glicksman likes me, not because I am doing well, which I am not doing, but because I am honestly learning from him. But Dr. Gordon finds me frustrating because A) I think far more clearly than she does, though I have far less information at hand than she, and B) if she allowed me to follow my thoughts completely through, I would be teaching the class. Now, a vast contradiction exists here. She is supposed to be teaching, but I can teach better than she can. Since I happen to know more than most of the students in the class with the possible exception of Mike O'Hare who, unfortunately, does not think visually, and therefore will never write anything but prose, the only people I can learn from are Dr. Gordon, and Mike upon occasion. This is not to say that the others do not know things which I don't know—the law of averages says that they must. But they really have no conception of the process of analysis. Shakespeare says that, among other things, "art, tongue-tied with authority" makes him wish for death. That trussed up art is the essence of our education, and because, almost against my will it seems, I am being made part of art, my everything, intellect to id, demands release.

Anger, fear, "filled up to here"; analysis is the process of creating fiction from experience. Even psychoanalysis. I am consciously aware of editing what I say to Dr. Krim. The mind that does not have the discipline of art does this editing poorly and automatically, and through the psycho-deterministic nature of the mind, we can figure out what makes the man tick. But my editing is almost completely conscious. Since I am "orally regressed" (a humorous phrase) I think pictorially. In my verbal recount of an image, no matter how complete I make it I am always aware of having left out some detail. A square inch of white porcelain has details enough to occupy the alert mind for hours. A human action is inconceivable!

I am completely snowed under with details when I think, as if, under scrutiny, the image is constantly falling to pieces. The world falls to pieces as I look at it; and that's why I am leaving tomorrow morning. My family, school, familiar things in general, have just decomposed under my eyes, without becoming any more familiar, and they no longer, in this decomposed state, possess authority to demand the responsibility from me which they did before. A paper on "Can Contemporary Tragedy Truly Be

Written?," make up my bed when I come home, or keep the blinds closed when you undress for bed. This just doesn't mean anything to me anymore. I cherish the illusion that nobody is particularly concerned with my disrobing but me—and if they were, so what?—and if contemporary tragedy can be written and someone wants to write it badly enough, then it will be written no matter what my opinion on the subject may be.

Now I shall be told that I am missing the point. But the point gets lost just as quickly when you try to pin it under your finger. I might have easily been a madman, but I never had the energy, or even the inclination to try and convince other people of my delusions.

Edited forms of the constant commentary that I make upon my life constitute my art. What conceit to think that someone else might be interested in this commentary. And yet the editing is done strictly with that in mind.

Poetry is called "concentrated" because editing the commentary, the poet tries to imply what was left out by the shape of the resulting hole. He then picks up the strings, gives a pull, and Lo! the pieces are pulled in to form—Poem!

Prose suffers from the illusion that it parallels, or is capable of paralleling all of thought.

An experience—like a poem—must be half inside and half outside you. And to that extent, a poem is an experience.

I have become lost in the Macmillan abridgement of *The Golden Bough*. I am not the same person when I come through another hundred pages as I was when I began them. Whole patterns of nightmares of sleep and seeing-time become immense with significance and reality; so far, I wonder if Frazer comprehends the reality behind his collection of fantastics. On the aspect of reality to which I refer he has made no comment. In '22, the Authority of Freud was not around to help him. Jung must have felt conniptions of ecstasy over this book.

I somehow think of each new book I read as though I was the first person to read, or, in many cases, to write it. (A book is written by many people. The non-fictionist knows this well; the fictionist knows it better. Perhaps this knowledge kills some of them.) This is a charming naiveté, I suppose, but accursedly boring to others.

I have been buried all today and yesterday in "Song of My Hands." The melody of the thing is epic. Propaganda in which you believe is so much fun—if it's well done. The layout of the Hart Crane book of poems is beautiful. If anyone ever wanted a lesson on Poetic Compression, one simply had to take an evening's glide through *The Complete Poems of H.C.* They contain an entire life. He is not a great poet because you must read him too closely for them to burst forth as poetry. This has nothing to do with esoterica, it is merely the poetic texture, which in Crane's case becomes the texture of prose if they are read any faster than 200 words a minute.

His juxtaposition of images reminds me of me. Although he could have learned more in sustaining poetic energy from Pound. Then again, more than likely, if he had, he would have been imitating Pound. Best be his poems as they are. Marie has this same problem of compression (not to be confused with concentration—perhaps the distinction is only in my mind:
"When I say a word, it means what I want it to mean."
—Humpty Dumpty) as Crane. But I have no authority to criticize. That is exactly the reason I can. T. S. Eliot can write such brilliant books of criticism because he knows (and covers it up by proclaiming it loudly every couple of books and then promptly forgetting it) just how little, how nothing, how negative is know[ledge] about poetry, or art in general. We accept the fact that he knows this because he has written some pretty good poems. (The incongruity of that colloquialism impresses me as masterfully intentional. Nobody, except perhaps a robot, could read that line out loud and make it say what it means on paper. That's one example of the fact that written and spoken language are two different things. Slowly but surely, it is becoming the actor's job to translate one into the other.) When Johnny told me that the greatest authority in the world on Emily Dickinson was teaching at his school, I had to smile. The greatest authority on Emily Dickinson is probably some fairly intelligent fourteen-year-old girl living some place in the mid-west who once wrote a fairly good poem, but lost it, and can't quite remember the way the words went. Perhaps she one day came across a Dickinson poem in a school text, and reading it, she suddenly felt a kinship with something which she did not quite know but understood completely—she is, perhaps, a far greater authority than John Kronenberger's teacher. And if I could be sure (and one can never be sure, which is the hinge of the fantasy) I would take her word quite well above the tomes produced by this teacher. There is a vast confusion in this world between information and authority. Read two authorities on the same subject, and it suddenly comes home to you how little authority there is in the world. Poets have the authority of their ignorance. A young, budding Ph.D. in psychology told me that one very concrete argument against the Freudian view was that none of Freud's works would have gotten him his Doctorate in psychology. This is a magnificent

example of the confusion which toddles along with most things that we do in this world (my "we" is never editorial).

Authority has become, with abuse, a method of surreptitiously pointing [out] what you don't know. Authority has left the domain of the monarch and become sole property of the academician. This is neither good nor bad in itself because the reason for both the monarch's being a monarch and the academician's being an academician is ultimately entangled in a quest for authority. Like most goals men set for themselves, these goals of gaining authority are set because the authority is not already possessed. As a temporary replacement for the goal, the monarch substitutes power; the academician substitutes information, and both have magnificently missed the point. To define authority is difficult, if not impossible, but its essence is this. "I exist, and I have the authority to say so. (*Cogito, ergo sum.*) You exist, that is you are not a figment of my imagination, and I have the authority to say so, because if I am wrong, then it really doesn't make too much difference what I say, after all." Authority, from one point of view, is merely pointing out to people the obviousness of the obvious. The teacher who tells her students (as Dr. Gordon invariably does), "Take any side of the argument you wish as long as you prove your point," is an ass (unless she is being sarcastic). If two conflicting opinions arise in which there is an element of truth in both (I am not referring to semantic paradoxes or scientific observations—God bless the "wavicle theory"), it is a maxim that one opinion can be formed embodying the truth of both points. And I have the authority to say this because if what I say is not true, then what is the point of having an opinion in the first place. Authority is far more common sense than information. In fact, I would say that authority is common sense working with information.

While "Authority" rested with the monarch, the academician was free to rave and rant like a spoiled child. But being an intelligent spoiled child, in his raving and ranting he pointed out that might doesn't comprise the *sine qua non* of right. Ergo, the monarch turned around and said "Shut up," and he backed his statement with some Grand Inquisitions, a bit of witch hunting and other sundry elements. When Democracy rolled around, the monarch found himself in danger of extinction, so instead of being so forceful, he smiled and whispered, "All right, you may have the 'Authority' but as long as you don't get in my way. I'll give you a subsidy so that you can eat while you criticize me, provided you stop at criticism and don't do anything. Collect your statistics which prove how inefficient I am, but just keep quiet." And the academician, having gotten information and authority confused, accepted the offer, and so far, has been playing along. The only trouble is that while the monarch had authority, there was someone to complain, but now that it is in the hands of the teacher there is no one to point out that he is clutching air. The monarch just isn't interested, which is the basic difference in character between one who goes in for political economy one, two, and three, and one who goes into politics.

I doubt whether there will ever be a study of the psychology of the teacher, or at any rate, it will not be conducted by a Ph.D. in psychiatry who has spent a few years teaching in order to make ends meet. Anyone who has the stomach for tongue-tied art, or science, or philosophy, has more than a stomach for it. He has a need for it, perhaps a neurotic need. (The useless courses that get on the required list for Ph.D.'s are fantastic. 3 Credits for Cultural Attractions of NY, for a Ph.D. in psychology at Columbia!) But people take the courses. You don't go through this kind of torture unless you're a masochist.

But since the psychologist has charge of determining what's healthy, and since the Ph.D. has more "charge" than anybody else, he blindly states: "I did it, therefore since I have charge of determining what's healthy, this, above all things, is what's healthy."

This is not a new situation. The painter and the sculptor will always have charge of setting up the beauty standards in society. Pimply skin will never become a criterion for beauty because smooth skin is far easier to draw or sculpt.

Poets and writers have charge of setting up the rules for our thinking and feeling. Scientists let us know what we are allowed to be certain that we know.

In regard to poets and writers (seeing that it is sort of my field like sort of): it has always been contested whether or not the time produces the philosophy or the philosophy the time. Again, there is a discouraging lack of common sense shown by taking either [side]. A writer writes about what he sees, and in that respect what he sees produces what he writes. But a writer is an editor. He edits according to the way he feels. But what is the nature of art? I am surprised that I have never seen it pointed out that in very small tribes, nomadic or otherwise, there is very little visual art. When you have an idea which you want to tell to more than one person individually, [and] you start thinking out how you are going to say [it], whether your thoughts take the turn of how to say it most clearly or most effectively, you are doing what the writer does. Art is communication, but is a special kind of communication; it is a method of individual communication with more people than one individual can communicate with without the use of some artistic medium. You cannot just have something to say. You must have some way to say it, whether with words, pictures, movement, or statuary. Social values cannot be set up, revised, or updated without communication, and art, science, and criticism form the basis on which the ablest minds can communicate with the most people. And from this, when that elusive "authority" is pointed out concerning a certain subject during the interplay, it becomes accepted by society when this "authority" has been communicated to enough people. In that the artist, especially the writer, communicates this authority, he influences the time.

The artist and the philosopher have charge of the value system of society. They record the existing value system and they perpetuate the growth of the new one that is constantly replacing the old. Each is a Janus-faced performer and critic. The fiction writer in particular is in charge, so to speak, of the moral values of philosophy. In his story he presents characters which either conform or do not conform to the philosopher's view of life and they either succeed or fail. Thus he performs and criticizes at the same time. The philosopher, in turn, uses social criticism to form his view of life, and he uses literary criticism, or art criticism in general, to comment on whether or not the artist is being honest, logical, competent, and so forth. And in this interplay the system of values is set up, re-examined, thrown out, and a new revised one substituted. This interplay touches, in one respect, very few people, and in another, far more people than one might think. It works indirectly in its mightiest effects: Nobody considers TV Westerns as serious literature, but the fact is that their maudlin plots are so markedly Existentialistic that one could do a wild study of the subject. That is not odd, when we look closely. These Westerns, which really do influence the moral growth of thousands upon thousands, are written by a handful of men who probably, in the majority of cases, saw at least three years of college. Maybe they had, or not had read Sartre, in greater or lesser amounts, but they had teachers who either had read him or read his sources. And these people, all down the line, have been influenced, sometimes by the things that Sartre saw—the war, corruption: one verbalization of the thoughts that were forming inside them, and they were ready to re-verbalize, and so an idea or a concept, very much like a joke, travels, spreads to all levels and influences. Unfortunately, the instant you try to trace the influence of one idea or set of ideas from one man, the example becomes more and more ludicrous the further it goes. Only with the perspective of time can we say, yes, this or that idea certainly took hold in that society. The process of seepage is the process of communication through individuals, and it is impossible to trace so many individuals in something the size of a society. And so we sit and argue who affects who, completely forgetting to look at society as a thing which is here now, obviously has certain needs, has always behaved in such and such a manner in the past, seems to be behaving the same way now, has and has had artists, philosophers, painters and poets, did and does value them, so let's see why—

This is not speculation, and is based on that authority of common sense.

But artists are human. And as academicians have justified the "little quirks" which make them what they are, so do the artists, as social value setters, set immediately the value [that] art justifies any personal eccentricity.

You may be sick, crazy, priest, prophet, or politician, murderer or thief, but if you produce art, you are completely vindicated. I do not know whether this is right or wrong, and I have thought about the subject a great deal. Something that has not made the problem any easier is the current myth that the truly great artists were all really very mature, well adjusted type people. This is absolute nonsense. I won't go so far as to say the greater they were, the screwier they were, but it comes out something very much like that. Alcoholism, compulsive gambling, and homosexuality seem to take top priority as minor eccentricities that various great artists engaged in (sometimes discouraging combinations of two or more) with sadism, masochism, and acedia running close seconds.

It's not very hard to see why, either. Very few great artists have not publicly acknowledged the responsibility that they had. Shakespeare, in a score of lines, tells us that he believes his words to be everlasting, outliving marble and monument.

Around 600 B.C. Sappho let us know in no uncertain terms that she would be remembered.

Although they are
Only breath, words
That I command
Are immortal.

And I'll be danged if she wasn't right.

People argue whether or not Sappho was a lesbian. She may not have been, but she wrote as if she wanted to be, which to my mind indicates something.

As to good old W.S., the only reason we have any biographical information about him at all is because he behaved so strangely. And three quarters of those sonnets we are always reading about were written to a beautiful young man—not a woman. They say that Homer was a blind man led by a young boy. I don't know about you, but when I was a young boy, I was warned to stay away from strange old men.

Of course if Dostoyevsky popped up today, Random House would probably be just as willing to pay off his impossible gambling debts as it currently is to take care of Faulkner's liquor bill—as long as they write. You can get away with anything if you have either money or talent.

The responsibility involved in knowing that you are affecting—even creating, or even helping to create the value system of a society is terrific. And it is not only the responsibility which sets the artist a little wacky—and I am not saying that one must be crazy to be an artist; on the contrary, one must be afflicted with sanity, which produces the same problem eventually, i.e. that reality occasionally becomes unbearable. Why? Because the artist must be sensitive, or sick enough, to have incidents, pictures, scenes, people and feelings, embed themselves into his very being. He must be masochist enough to approach his suffering with the objectivity of a craftsman, taking this from one experience, that from another. He must see the same meanings and symbols in everything that happens to him as [does] the raging paranoiac behind bars. He must be egomaniac enough to feel that what he is doing is important. He must be sadist enough to bleed those closest to him of their every emotion. Then he creates from these things his art.

The simple life that Poets lead, whether it is the simplicity of the hermit or the complete hedonist, is not maturity at all, but an escape into simplicity. When life gets too complicated, or when the absurdity of the arbitrary order of society becomes too oppressively ludicrous—which amounts to the same thing—the Poet has to get out! Things begin to decompose when he looks at them, things fall to pieces in his hands.

True, this is a neurotic sensitivity, but it goes hand in hand with sensitivity in general.

The masochistic element of the Poetic makeup constantly makes the Poet place himself in "complicated situations" from which he is eventually forced to flee. But since the Poet has the measuring rod in his hand, he compensates for it by saying, art is of the first importance.

And isn't it? Even Leon Trotsky and Lenin agreed upon this point to the extent that they both acknowledged that in any culture, the vigor and health of that society was mirrored and directed by the vigor and health of the art of that culture.

Actually to debate whether or not this sensitivity is justified or not is skirting a very pertinent fact of common sense: since it is a question [of] which is more important, the art or the artist, it is a question of value. Since society has handed over the rule book to the artist to revise, we must seek the answer there. So, I suppose this question can only be settled by each individual artist for himself. In that respect, the artist is free and above the law, since he has made the law exempt himself. It's a sort of Nietzschean concept, but it works: the artist may be punished for what he does, but he will always be forgiven. So what shall I do?

I leave tomorrow, I take another step further in my systematic self destruction. I take my unfinished manuscripts because I must, and because they explicate me, and, Oh God, this endless ratiocination!

* * *

All is fiction: I have stayed up to 3:30 in the morning writing this essay for the sole purpose of exhausting myself so that I could not possibly go to school tomorrow, for I will be too tired. The energy involved in producing this thing is fantastic. Rilke found out in his *Notebooks of Malte Laurids Brigge* what I am discovering now: there can be no honesty.

The harping on Psychiatry and Ph.D.'s and Psychology is obviously a product of my hostility toward Dr. Krim & Dr. Gordon. Yet does that hostility vitiate the logic? That is the antithetical question I asked as to whether the art justifies the artist.

There are even ulterior motives behind this, only I do not know what they are yet. The horror of psychological determinism. That is the knowledge which every artist is born with. And it is the examination of this knowledge that causes the "falling to pieces" I spoke of, and eventually to an extreme and terrific contemplation of the whirligig of death and meaninglessness.

This is an effective place to stop. That is the only reason I stop here.

* * *

Every action I take has been built up over such an immense time. Christ, the wonder of it! It is quarter to four on Monday morning in January, and I have just numbered the pages.

* * *

The essence of journal writing (as opposed to journalism) is ultimate mendacity. In fiction, you make no pretense of telling the truth; in these pages I have tried [so] hard and failed so miserably.

*   *   *

There is a character with whom I have become obsessed down into my bowels. He is the strange, black-haired hero of "The Gryphon Has Two Heads." I saw him on the bus going to Lloyd's one morning lots & lots of weeks ago. (Why do I say obsessed; nothing obsesses me.)

The frustrated Demon face, the destructor of silence—

He is a strange interest, a strange symbol for a strange fantasy. (The accepted duplicity of the artist's fantasy world and reality—odd how readily it is taken as natural by the public.) To become an artist is to be completely seduced by a word, an idea, a thing, or the remembrance of a person, even to the point of physical orgasm. Civilized society will never understand this because it is such a basically primitive process. It is more complex than becoming inextricably enmeshed in fantasy—that can happen to any mad man. It is becoming chained in reality. This is rhetoric, but it expresses what I mean.

IV

It is the dull morning—not quite seven thirty—and I am sitting on the bus with stiff fingers from last night's writing spree.

I have a theory—that a man only has a limited amount of creative energy, let's say 18 hours' worth which he can use in a day. After this is expended, he just vegetates. Like Freud's psychic energy theory.

Of course I do not believe this. It is only an analogy. Any attempt to explain a process in terms of anything but: you start off with A and you get B relies on using an analogy of greater or lesser applicability: the atom is planetary; the atom is composed of energy shells; to satisfy thirst you drink water; if you start here and travel for three miles you will end up there—each one has its degree of inexactness.

I watch this—and things decompose.

The bus is filling up and we [ride] all the way down to 103rd Street. How inexact for while I write—Lo!—we have passed 102nd.

*   *   *

Henry Miller would be ecstatic now if he were I. Where I write of inexactness, he would be describing the pain in my crotch. My underpants are too tight!

*   *   *

I came across the quiet valley of Seventy-Fourth Street: it was a morning dark dull street, sided widely with brownstones. It made me feel quiet and active at the same time. Men were finishing loading a truck, yet the guy walked past me with vigor and silence. Further on there was a little wrinkled oriental, maybe Filipino, in a green army-jacket parka, pulling at a police dog that was barely as big as he was—the dog was trying to nose down into the gutter, and the man was trying to pull back.

Then there was a guy delivering papers with a stock bicycle which hardly had any paint left. He was a big heavy man, a sort of old sloppy thirty-eight; you think of boys delivering papers on bikes, but this guy in a greasy cap, sweatshirt with a blue windbreaker over it, creaseless grey khakis and a face that had somehow gotten lost inside itself was coming down the porch stairs and taking his bike and moving on.

On another porch, over the cars I saw a grandmother type woman in a black dress staring up into the sky like she expected God to be there— wispy white hair and still full of years more scrubbing and dish washing and house cleaning and grandchildren raising—and maybe He was.

When I got to the door, there were two typically friendly, tender, healthy looking teenagers sitting in the lobby taking to each other. I knocked on the door and the girl came and opened it and we smiled at each other so bigly and warmly that it was slightly farcical.

I went upstairs on the elevator and now I am sitting in front of the al- cove before 2B and wondering when Gale will come out and go to work, with vague thoughts in the back of my mind that she might have moved already and that I will be sitting out here forever and ever, because I will not have energy to look at my watch.

I don't feel like taking my shoes off and going out to sit on the back steps because, for one thing, I might not catch her if she is still here. The last time it was pure chance that I came back when I did and she was just going out in her black coat, without makeup and looking fantastically fresh and sleepy at the same time.

So I'll just sit and scribble away. Besides, Lloyd gets home at four thirty and it can't be too much past eight o'clock now. (That was meant to sound ridiculous.)

Paul is a real phenomenon. Right now he is working as a combination short order cook and barkeep at the College of Complexes.

Just now someone opened the door down the hall and I jumped like a fox. The doors around here really make a loud thing when they open. Be- cause I am in the alcove, he can't see me, but he is still moving around. I got up to make myself less conspicuous. After all, strange people sitting in front of apts. scribbling ecstatically do present a problem.

I think he's gone now. There is a woman talking unintelligibly on this floor or the one below, and occasionally a man sneezes. The elevator relays in this building hammer wildly.

Here I sit on the red tile floor, with too stiff fingers, searching for just a little bit [of] silence, a little way out of fear, some peaceful sleep—but I doubt I will ever find it.

Someone else has come out into the hall and left down the stairs. The sounds are hollow and reverberating in the hall. There is another apt. door that opens onto this alcove beside Lloyd's. I'm just a little afraid of what will happen when the own[er] come[s] out.

As I wrote, someone did come out of another door—a young lady in a peach scarf. I said Hello and smiled, she did too, but I won't be surprised if the janitor is up here in a minute.

Another person just echoed out of sight and off to work—or someplace.

It is surprising how scared I am of the people who come by, sitting here in perfect innocence, waiting to be let in because I don't want to wake anyone up, yet I manage to feel guilty of their every thought (so far "they" is only one) but it is discouraging.

I think that girl had a nice face. Funny, I remember that peach (apricot?) scarf and the tweed coat, but I couldn't tell you if she wore glasses, and she looked right at me.

I wonder how much she remembers of me, now.

Women steps are clicking in the hall. I feel well protected, and yet completely vulnerable.

(I just changed pencils.) Writing gives me some feeling of permanence.

Somebody has scribbled on the paint of Lloyd's door
<u>Knock</u>

This is the first time I ever noticed it. There are lots of breakfast sounds coming from one of the two apartments, but I can't tell which. If I had to bet though, [I'd] say it was the wrong one.

The sound of one person getting breakfast and two people getting breakfast, even if nobody talks, is completely different.

I always have wondered just who lives in the other apartment.

Perhaps I should take off my shoes. Would it make me look more or less harmless? I am so completely harmless anyway that it is rather pathetic.

What about Paul.

Paul is strange, big, gross, impossibly intelligent in a frustratingly slow way. Paul said:

"I am nothing; I am waste; I am weeds; I am nothing."

Which, in context, was really rather brilliant. Paul's is the conception of the line stander. He believes that there are certain people whose sole function is to make lines long, subways crowded, and traffic heavy. He got this idea from the Navy, where, he said, there were a great many people who merely hung around on the ends of lines. Paul is going to make an excellent bartender.

But he needs a father. That's why he is at Lloyd's. Lloyd is sort of a community father. He was "The Animal" in "The Gryphon Has Two Heads." I conceived—

Kids in the hall. Parents, "bye honey"—weird sounds.

—that story as sort of a present to Lloyd, but it got out of hand somehow.

The telephone rang in Lloyd's apt. It was answered. Dare I ring the bell. It's quarter to nine. I dare. Gale must not be here.

* * *

I did, mainly because somebody was about to come out of the other door.

Paul opened the door.

"Don't curse," I said.

"Oh man, why don't you get a fuckin' key, Chip." It was a rhetorical question, and he lumbered back off to bed.

This place is a wreck. Newspapers on the floor, girls' coats and a pocketbook on the couch; a liquor bottle props up the window, but that's usually there. For some inexplicable reason the light over the reading chair is on. So I sit down and continue scribbling. I wonder who's here. I think I'm going to explore, clean up a bit, and go to sleep.

* * *

I'm trying to figure out what sort of orgy went on here: matches, cards, an UNSMOKED pipe full of shit. Girls' coats, boys' pants—

—it's a real thing. Well, I'm sleepy. (Oh, and a yachting catalogue. That must be Lloyd's.)

* * *

Albert Mouangue and his African Ensemble on the phono, and a very lovely girl picking up clothes in the bedroom. Oh, well.

* * *

Stuey just left for work, and the young lady is Jennifer—without her glasses.

* * *

Lloyd with his great beard:

"Portrait of Jesus Christ as a young head."

D. Ephraim—who has just come in.

* * *

Jesus Christ and this divine idiot are blowing shit beneath a green blanket to the tune of the Lambeth Singers.

Lloyd's bare legs stick out of the blanket—strange sounds coming from beneath the green [...] cover.

Stuey looks out of it—aren't we all. There the heavy odor of marijuana with—

Lloyd claps his feet together—this [is] sort of like a wild orgy of communication in which nobody learns too much.

I:

"At least it keeps the smell in."

Stu:

"Yeah."

Lloyd:

"Dig the shadow."

Dave:

"You've also got a bellow around you. We're in trouble."

They lie there right in the middle of the living room floor under the blanket.

Now they emerge in an inverted panic. Soon we will be going down to 42nd St.

I wonder how long this baroque immersion goes on: the counterpoint of sounds, voices, thoughts and things is like a mad Bach impromptu of all the senses at once.

They notice me writing—

They notice nothing and everything, this wildness of fear and horror involuted among the rifts of constant humor create an oppressive gothic atmosphere.

Lloyd is walking around with a towel around his middle. Dave still retains his tie in complete disarray.

Stuey is so involved with vacuum. I am trapped in vacuum too.

"Billie Holiday might depress me."

Negro Prisoner Songs—that comes on with a rhythm and order that is incongruous with the rest of the scene. The clash between this order and disorder creates silence—starkly confused silence.

Lloyd is dressing now.

And the search for order in tortured voices goes on.

Dave:

"I can't take this record. I'm dead."

IN SEARCH OF SILENCE [53]

Stuey types behind it [all]. The rhythm of the typewriter is the antithesis of the rhythm of speech.

I am being hounded by both Dave and Lloyd.

* * *

It is twelve o'clock and the day has destroyed itself.

Lloyd, Stu, D. Ephraim went down to 42nd. Between these two entries, Boyd, my well-meaning cousin, came over. We discussed, of all things, my novel. He had some good points.

In Grant's—

An aluminum slaughterhouse for fairies and prostitutes. 25¢ for lima bean soup and 15¢ for a frank.

The place is frightening; it has its own verbal jazz which is completely different from any other section of the city because it has no words, only a vocabulary of sound, the sound of the stifled rebellion against its huge assembly-line mechanization.

There was an inebriated electrician who struck up a conversation with me. I usually like to listen to people talk, but this man was too angry, and his drunkenness only afforded him a shield from behind which he could lash out. Lloyd took over the conversation from me. The man was apparently a one-time pimp. He said that Lloyd's beard reminded him of what was between his woman's legs. He was funny, but every once in a while he would lash out.

Afterwards, a man came over to Lloyd and told him, "You have a nucleus of a mind; why don't you shave off your beard and begin to think." He was really being humorous in an uncommunicable way and we all laughed. Poor lost Dave left, looking broke.

I watched a long-haired, dirty, but fairly passable fag pounce upon a good looking [hustler] at the edge [of] the great frank counter.

(All the franks on the tray, looking like raw or fried penises—abandoned phalli of all the castrated fags who nurse-mother 42nd Street—bite her great breasts and spit silver.)

They left together, each one hard on the destruction of himself and the other.

There was an ancient prostitute next to Lloyd with no teeth. She spooned up all the liquid from her lima-bean soup and left the beans, soggy at the bottom of the bowl. Then she became furious at Lloyd for ignoring her; I really don't think he saw her. She went over to the counter and glared back at Lloyd for fifteen minutes.

"I just watched two masterful pick-ups," I said. One was the two twilight boys, and the other was the furiously failing attempt by the prostitute to get Lloyd.

"I must be facing in the wrong direction."

At one of the tables, sat a fantastic dyke, a man save for her pulled back hair and the red of its mouth and nails. It wore a blue sailor's jacket and had a paper bag of food.

I went out and scouted for a movie. It's a very strange feeling to be walking up and down 42nd Street really looking for a movie. One feels unique.

When I get back, two girls have arrived who Stuey knows. We finally leave and get into a real hysterical hassle over what movie to see. I had forgotten all the titles. Lloyd and I go see *Goliath and the Barbarians* eventually. Stuey and the girls? I don't know.

In this movie is a girl who has a body like I have never seen before, but my God, the movie is so hideous that I have to shake my head to clear it occasionally. The combination of this Goddess and this film is ludicrous. I have never seen a woman built or moving or emoting like this one. And it is so impossibly effortless.

I sit here, thinking, wondering what I am doing. It is as if I am being dragged down by every element of the life I am constantly running away from, as if I am sinking beneath its decomposing surface.

When I try to act out what I feel, I struggle like a dog trying to get out of a muzzle. I plant my heels on the wall-to-wall carpeting and crouch like an animal, balking back. Pell shaking off the hands of the strange hero— that's what I was trying to express in that scene.

v

It is Tuesday, and Jennifer sits at the blue table studying, while my stomach rumbles over the remnants of a tuna-fish sandwich.

My eating is too irregular. It is 2:30, and I just got up.

I finally called Harcourt, Brace to find out just what was going on. They said call back in about an hour.

There is a story that has been brewing subconsciously for a long time now;

"Half of Blindness"

Notes: Acrobat and circus motif: witch and priest—Dishwasher from *Figaro* along with the girl. (Karl type thing.)

—But first I must finish "Silver" and rewrite "Salt."

[VI]
How many days later is it?

+ + +

4) The boat house
5) Barbara and Johnny getting fish
6) Zan & Toby getting lobster
7) The party—at which Toby kisses Zan
8) On the beach—Zan & Toby

1) Beach—4 pgs.
2) Snack joint—Beach
3) Zan's house—Beach

The Beach—6
The Snack B—10
Zan's—6
Jane's—6
B & J—2-3
Party—5
Rd—2-3

+ + +

I refuse to be absorbed in philosophizing.

I refuse to be lost in words. Words engulf me. I feel in the mood for a dissertation on the language. Once I begin to write I am obsessed with a wish to orient myself—to say here I am! I am sitting in thus and such a place and this or that is going on about me:
Study Hall
February first.
My schedule has been completely messed up.
Otto is sitting behind me and reading "The Gryphon Has Two Heads." He quotes occasionally. It is most disconcerting. Last evening, José said that I should wait, be more patient, must not jump to the typewriter with such alacrity.
Yet I have to finish the hexology. "Pomegranate" is one of the worst things I have ever written.
When I finish this series I will hibernate for a while. How can I hiber-

nate with "Half of Blindness" (not to mention "A Walk in the Country") burning holes in my brain.

The jar of "Bosco" just sent Otto and J. Rivers (Erik) into paroxysms. Oh well—?

I will finish the sea stories and stop for a year—or perhaps I will write "Half of Blindness"—I could not possibly do "A Walk in the Country" unless I wanted to turn out another *Atlas Shrugged*.

Otto just looked at the word count on the front of "Passacaglia" and found it quite amusing.

I must have a limited sense of humor.

Bridgette Bardot is sitting across the auditorium from me.

Otto spotted the same thing José did in the "Gryphon"—the incongruity of the woman's attitude after having been raped.

This beautiful auditorium—it turns my hypersensitive stomach. Without malice, merely curiosity, I wonder why I give my things so easily to be read. Well, they shall not get unfinished "Pomegranate" bad as it is.

I just handed "Pomegranate" to Otto. Oh well. Otto is giggling again. This [is] fantastic.

Otto just blew his nose. He says I have sort of let down endings—true. J.R.—Ridiculous, is his loving comment.

I made the mistake of telling Otto that "Pomegranate" was funny. Oh well, this is just one of my bad days.

J. Rivers is pretty damned profound.

Otto—Absolutely nothing happens!

Why don't you write something real wild. (I listen to some of these things simply because they are so unbelievable!)

+ + +

80 LaSalle Street
New York 27, New York
Thursday, February 4, 1960

Cambridge Book Company, Inc.
Bronxville, New York

Dear Sir,

I have seen a number of your paperback books in such stores as The Eighth Street Book Shop, The Paperback Gallery, and The Brick Floor

Book Store. I have been much impressed by your selection and would like to have a complete list of your soft-cover publications.

In the introduction to your books, you asked for comments and suggestions for future publications. My comments on the books of yours I have read [are] unreservedly complimentary; you fill the need for inexpensive editions of the lesser known works of important thinkers of our time, and all time, and you fill it most competently. As to future publications, I would like to see more of your collections of articles, such as your collections of Whitehead's articles, and the publication of the collection of Proust's criticisms (published along with *Pleasures and Days*). Thank you for your interest, and for the job you have done.

Yours truly,

Samuel Delany

+ + +

Dynamo represents the creative organ of a school whose production in the humanities is no less outstanding than its achievement in the sciences.

We have included in this issue

We have excl
This year *Dynamo* has

+ + +

Trouble in Mind
East Virginia [Blues]
Song of my Hands
Bells of Rhymney
Kumbaya
12 Gates to the City
Ana's Version of Traveling
Delia's Gone
Good Morning Captain
Cotton Mill Blues
Ox Driver's Song
Si Me Quieres Escribir

Is this language capable of Gidean simplicity, of mastering a beauty that is founded on perfection? Have we any author who has shown such high consistency by stylistic elegance in presentation of the soul? Perhaps we pick out Thomas Wolfe for such an honorary post; his style is to perfection as assonance is to rhyme. And yet his share of greatness is doled out in half merits; his work is a long, delightful, lovely letter to himself. And what more are *Les Journaux*; yet Wolfe so far below them stands, succeeding somehow merely to defend his place in adolescent favor.

Words divested of the savage unexpected streaming equably along to make some wondrous new goat-song: is this great style?

Words raging on the printed pages with some elemental candor which strives, it seems, to crack the rhythm of the thoughts which they support, destroy the brevity of lucid declaration, crassly hauling their explosive cerebrations through the mire of obscurity—and out again? Is this any style at all?

The French tradition holds it that literature's perfection roots its eloquence in competence and therefore can be found in one certain *clear* direction.

The American tradition, its plethora of esoteric balderdash, its [. . .] clattertrap, its obscuring ugly phrase, runs rampant through fine arts like some harpy on a mission to complete the rank degradation of the very spoken word.

I seek not any vile or ugly prostituted muse to whip for this despicable condition. The French perfection mounted for comparison marks me not for some evangelistic garbage man who's taken on the equally crass mission of sweeping the arts free of refuse.

Analysis of what exists may prove more fruitful. France cracks apart "respectable" tradition with Beckett, Ionesco, Robbe-Grillet—

In America tradition never even had its day as such, save in its expatriated products, James, Eliot, Pound; setting or breaking some propriety which they construed, from things they saw around, should be, though it was not necessarily so.

They have marked the chart as writers.

Someplace in this degenerate heap, America, some Christ is buried; the Artist plunges his shovel in the muck and throws up poetry while digging for holy flesh.

+ + +

[*The lines in brackets below are brief excerpts from a draft of a long erotic poem by Delany titled "Flesh and Roses." The excerpts are presented with accompanying marginal comments by Hacker. The limerick immediately below signals the beginning of Hacker's commentary.*]

I KNOW A YOUNG MAN CALLED DELANY
WHOSE VERSE ISN'T OVERLY BRAINY
   WHEN YOU START TO GET WITH HIM
   HE COMPLETELY DROPS THE CONCEPT OF RHYTHM
AND EVENTUALLY DOESN'T BOTHER RHYMING, EITHER
WHICH WOULD BE ALL RIGHT IF
HE DIDN'T START OUT
WITH IT.

["... The homosexual rhythm of the sea— / The heterosexual rhythm of the sea—"]
   CAN'T YOU MAKE UP YOUR MIND?

["... Two spits combined to make / one single froth ..."]
   OH COME ON

["... His key swung wide / a door on some weird cubicle / Where there was nought but bed / space and some floor ..."]
   ALSO, TO MY SURPRISE, A NAKED WHORE.
   MY MOUTH FELL OPEN, AND MY HANDS WENT LIMP
   "GOOD LORD!" I SAID "YOU'RE JUST A GODDAM PIMP!"

["His body hesitates within the darkness / And suddenly the blinding searing starkness / Of his presence descends upon me there / My fingers reach out and they close on air ..."]
   HONEY-O, QUIT THIS RHYMING JAZZ

["... He got one thick nail bitten finger up / my asshole ..."]
   (WHICH, ALL IN ALL, WOULD BE A GOOD PLACE FOR CERTAIN MANUSCRIPTS)

["... And that which falls / From my dick at which he sucks my barren balls / clean ..."]
I AM NAUSEOUS

["... I lay on top of him, his head between my legs ...]
IS THIS WHAT'S REFERRED TO AS "SOIXANTE-NEUF" (TECHNICAL QUERY)

["His tongue shot out and wrapped around my prick ..."]
I'M BORED

[*poem interrupted by a homework assignment on the life of Galileo*]
THIS IS THE BEST PASSAGE

+ + +

"This Place, Rumoured to Have Been Sodom—"

First section, 5–10, Analysis of guilt, crime, etc, without literary reference; set up the scene of Paul Bherens on screen. Second section, 8–18, the plot, the trio, the two [...], and the study of the woman and the child. Section three—20–30, Analysis of

The vulnerability to evil of those who lack identity

Through the eyes of P.B. who walks in the city. The lack of guilt in an evil society; the lack of any absolutes. Marital systems which pervert themselves.

Section four—Paragraph to five pages, the death of the child, and [...] wife goes insane

Bruno flees, and Paul Bherens comes to the river and we must insinuate previously that he does not—or rather that it is unimportant whether or not he jumps—included in Section 3, an italicized conversation between Bruno and Paul, that is broken up and analyzed.

+ + +

How People React to Various Emotions.

She was standing by the sink in the kitchen when I told her. I could only see her back. But when I said it, she jumped a little with a sharp indrawn breath, and put her arm up over her forehead and stood there for a second.

"Do you wanna sit down?" I asked.

"No," she said. "No. I'll be all right." In a few minutes she started to wash dishes.

My sister screwed up her face. Then she asked Grandma if she wanted her to wash the dishes for her.

"No," said Grandma—"No."

I felt very afraid, but for Grandma, not for myself.

+   +   +

Logic is an imposition of experience. The child does not think in syllogisms.

+   +   +

I lived the first 14 years of my life above a funeral parlor; my father was the proprietor. I remember we lived with [Gramp's] cousin, a huge woman who occupied the back rooms and used to feed me shad roe upon occasions. There was also a dog named Butch; the only thing I remember of Butch was that he was small and black—I have a picture of my uncle scratching the dog's stomach and every one around was laughing except me. There are also vague dreamlike impressions of large rooms strung with clothesline—rooms with blue tiling on the floors. I never knew that there was a war on. I remember one night I was sitting on the toilet and then suddenly the lights went out all over the world. So I sat there and then I got up and went out, and faces moved around above candles.

There were always many more people in my house than just my father and mother. They all had similar sounding names.

The romantic image

The image of the Yeats poem presents a hero about to act, with a positive outlook that he will complete his task; he will arrive at Innisfree. This arrival represents an arrival at tradition, that mystic past. The "carpenter's son" shows the romantic figure not as an Odysseus but as a crucified Christ figure. His romanticism is saint-criminal, destroyed by his efforts which have been a-social in their manifestations as he looks for his Innisfree, which is death.

Housman's life view is death.

Yeats finds his life's meaning in a mysticism, but in an optimistic plane, acknowledging life.

+ + +

Epigraph for *Afterlon*

> If you are squeamish
> Do not prod
> At the beach rubble.
> —Sappho

pg. 59—

Part Two: Washed up from Atlantis
Lon controls.
Rona made Lon kill, eat.
Considered herself dangerous for a while.

———

Man's going to die out by starvation (instead of A-bomb)
Mr. Jones comes down with Leukemia
which is preventable by hypnotism

School trips through abandoned BHSS.

Grass matting floor—Mr. Cotter & custodian & old woman stay and are burned alive.

Everybody is told to get out. We stay too long. Peggy goes back for a doll. She runs out.

Then the old woman is seen and the house goes.

Trying to [...]

+ + +

Nation and Rebirth

Studies

I

I have gone up to Maine, and then come down. Scenes in which the beauty ached are all compressed now into single details: a dull green leaf, hung from a twig, its underside suddenly sheen-silvered with shadows from the forest; a large half-wet rock in the mud by the side of a rain-washed road; or the shattered prism of a dragonfly wing shafted out from the thin black body against a bending fern growing at the edge of an afternoon stream.

In Vermont I came through a meadow of chest-high goldenrod. The path went down the sloped pasture toward a pine wood. Each time I put my foot down on the mat of yellowing grasses, ten or fifteen locusts would leap up ahead of me, like flipped pieces of gray bark. Yet all that meadow is caught for me in one sandsized grain of yellow shivering at the end of a stem of goldenrod—amid sestillions of others!

2

I wound through rock-bound New Hampshire, and into Massachusetts, and below the Cape, there. I found the sea as something I had lost; down from the rocks where I stood, a dark green glass shield, the edges rippled into the sand with white froth.

(the boy on the beach)

* * *

My only memory of the second W.W. has no victory or anything. I was too young for that. I remember a blackout once when I was in the bathroom, sitting on the toilet. And then it was dark, and people held candles.

* * *

Fran asked me, "Have you ever read any of the poems of Edna Silem?"

"I've never even heard of her," I said.

+ + +

The "Song of Songs" was almost definitely not written by Solomon himself, but was ascribed to him by its anonymous author perhaps two hundred years after Solomon's reign (c. 950 BC).

3

Journaux d'Orphée

After graduating from Science and attending the Bread Loaf conference, Delany traveled to the Second Annual Newport Folk Festival with fellow Camp Woodland alumnus Peter Horn. At the festival Delany participated in seminars, played at hootenannies, and watched performances by major figures of the folk revival. His notes on the experience, headed with the title *Journaux d'Orphée*, take up the bulk of Notebook 12.

A draft of a letter near the end of Notebook 12 requires more explanation. Delany's short story "Salt," originally the third chapter of his novel *Cycle for Toby*, had won him a creative writing scholarship to NYU—the same scholarship that had been awarded to Hacker a year before—and was published in the university's annual literary journal, *Good Themes*.[1] However, on the basis of Hacker's reports of her dissatisfaction with the school, Delany chose not to attend; the penultimate entry in Notebook 12 is a draft of the letter he sent to NYU declining the scholarship.

As Delany recounts in the closing pages of the notebook, upon returning home from the festival he typed a polished prose account of the trip.[2] However, in 1963, during his and Hacker's move from Paul Caruso and Joe Soley's apartment, the typescript was lost, along with the original uncut typescript of the novelette "We, in Some Strange Power's Employ, Move on a Rigorous Line" and many letters from James Sallis and to and from Hacker.[3] The following notebook entries are all that remain of the *Journaux*.

NOTES

1. Michael S. Peplow and Robert S. Bravard, eds., *Samuel R. Delany: A Primary and Secondary Bibliography, 1962–1979* (Boston: G. K. Hall & Co., 1980), 18; Samuel R. Delany, interview with Kenneth James, August 9, 2014.

2. Samuel R. Delany, *The Motion of Light in Water: Sex and Science Fiction Writing in the East Village* (1988; reprint, Minneapolis: University of Minnesota Press, 2004), 7.

3. Delany, interview with James, August 9, 2014.

NOTEBOOK 12—INCLUSIVE TO JULY 1960

Journaux d'Orphée

11:40–11:55

We start in the gray mist of late morning. Pete sits next to me in the car. We have just set the clock. "You better make it go to 12:00. The clock is fast." Then he does.

"Oh boy," says Pete. "I bet when we get home, a home-cooked meal will really taste good."

"I'm looking forward to it right now," I say, laughing. "Before we have reason."

We drive through the gray of afternoon Harlem. Storefronts, filth, and great confusion, slow motion confusion under gray.

The whole world lies between me and Pete: encased in the paper folds of maps, blue, yellow lines. We finally go beneath the railroad station that hovers blackly over—

"What avenue is this? 4th?"

"No," look[ing] up to the windshield. "Lex; no, Park."

"That's Fourth up here, Park further down."

—Park avenue.

Noises, constant, soft, and obtusely incommunicative. Motors, voices here, and a man in the car next to us, smoking; he bites his nails, unshaven, and black haired. He is gone; and Pete winds the clock (and bites at his nail: strange symphony of image and counter image). I suddenly become conscious of myself, feeling the present: back against seat, maps against thigh. A red head man has marched across the street: a garbage attendant, I think.

Pete looks occasionally at what I write.

"What's the confessions of a driver, driving to Newport?"

"Look at the road," I say.

Into the steel maze of the Triborough Bridge. We have erupted momentarily from the city, into the sky & now we descend again.

* * *

It is raining and the train running above our heads ceases—another train, this time in the Bronx. Minutes, fears, and relief have elapsed. But I will not tell you of those. Brick walls, not yet shiny with the new rain, and wet leafy foliage slip back by the open windows as Pete and I discuss the route we will take.

A woman with an umbrella, and one without, pass, change places and race across the highway. Small houses, wide streets, and gray gone clean and transparent with rain-washed light. Theaters, stores: this woman crosses before us on a single crutch. One man yells to us, "Which way Gunhill road is?"

"No," we shake our perplexed heads, slipping off into frightening motion. Beneath the black skeleton of the Webster Avenue train, have I seen a man in a brown suit?

"Which way is east?" Pete asks.

There are tombstones along the side of the road. A man pulls up and asks, "Are we going to the George Washington Bridge? Or are you stuck too?"

Grinning, "Yes." What is this embarrassment.

"We can't both be right," says Pete.

Later, their voices, asking a policeman, fade away before the answer comes in the rain.

Trying to turn around, we are held up by a woman driver.

"If she can't make it now, she stinks," says Pete.

*   *   *

"How long have we come?"

"144 miles."

And I emerge onto the gray rubber of the thruway from the light-land of closed eyes, lapped with shadows.

You can—

Peter is (167 miles) slender, not quite as tall as I am. From where I sit now, across the seat from me, I see his khakied leg go across the seat, bend at the knee and lower past a white sock with a blue design on it into a scuffed white tennis shoe on the gas-pedal. His shirt is a dull, maroon red, bunched high on his arm. I see the hand with the thumb extend[ed] for support arc along the wheel. His arm is flesh light and the forearm is lightly haired.

His head is small, the features small, the eyes gray, and the hair blown stiff and brown. One arm rests, elbow out, hand hung slightly down, on the open window.

This car has a personality (it hugs me into its rough covered front seat width of the sway and jog of the road). The dashboard is paint-chipped, a line of colorless dull rust shows here and there. It is green.

(My hand rests on the open window. The wind slips cold along my arm and in between my fingers, slaps my sleeve about my wrist.)

The thruway has given out now into a two lane highway.

"It's just about five," Pete says. He has been talking while I wrote.

The sun has just begun to puncture through the sky behind us. 20 miles or less to Providence.

With all this writing, we have stopped twice, eaten, urinated, I have slept and awoken with an erection, and even sung a few songs—between entries. Orpheus is retro-active: I am lost in the name.

The Rhode Island State Police house is white, has a porch, and roses grow beside the steps.

We are in a town now.

Pete saw the word "erection" and told me, laughing, he wouldn't be able to drive if I wrote like that. I told him I'd read it to him. Being in Rhode Island, it is easy to joke about its size.

A car passes us which has a distinctive flutter in its engine. Pete recognizes it from when we stopped about 20 minutes ago to get milk to drink.

*   *   *

We have passed two beautiful lakes, one on either side of the road within 5 minutes of each other. The water splashes out through the trees, catching and melding the sky into even sheets of the rippling blue gray.

"Entering Providence," I said thirty seconds ago.

Suburban streets grown dirty, and too cramped. A car filled with green [...] (I think) goes ahead, and a yellow bus comes back from Hartford past us. Gray, bleak, L-shaped city housing facing suburban wrecks.

A little boy in a gray sweatshirt frantically wheels an empty baby carriage about a lawn.

An elevated highway takes us up into gray sheets of concrete, following Route Six.

Curve, and then back to stop—"Sun's out," says Pete—with shadows distinct for the first time across the page.

"I'd like to ask [a] cop if there is a kosher delicatessen here."

"Why?" I asked. "To make him mad?"

"No, to find out if there is," with laughter—and the cop is past, and houses are more sedate (a sign we followed said "Downtown Providence"), and carhop, and a kid wrestling with a coil of hose back at a filling station.

Another bus slips back past.

The Citizens Savings Bank veers around our right window and a large, blank red brick building marches a parade of thin windows by.

"Egads, a star of David"—on a synagogue [...] to the right.

Providence drivers are lousy. We lurch behind a gray, dull '47 Cadillac for minutes.

We pass the bus marked "Southern Jubilee Singers"; they are probably heading for Newport too. But the bus was empty and veering off in a lot.

"The signs aren't too bad."

Here the earth is pitted with construction of some type, and then the highway swells under us again. For an instant the skyline made me say, "Hey, you'd almost think we were in N.Y.," but then incongruities—houses with bleak Cape Cod facades, break through the picture.

6
Keep
Left

A fly crawls on Peter's leg. The smallness of the fly makes me see the rocking movement of Pete's hip more clearly as he switches from gas to break, or simply rocks with the car's motion.

I brush it off, after I am finished writing. It lands on the towel and disappears beneath my thigh.

We are on the thruway again, and suddenly, out of Providence.

"Do you realize I have been writing through all of Providence? It has taken me all of three pages."

*   *   *

Fall River 12 miles.

We're getting into hysterical territory, wondering how much I shall be disappointed in the lack of nightmares.

"What say we bring home some watermelon?"

"O.K." I say, preoccupied with my scribbling.

"What time is it?"

"20 to 6. We won't have much time to eat and get to the show."

The highway fans into nothingness ahead.

*   *   *

Because of a sign in the road, Pete has decided to bypass Fall River, and save about 10 miles.

* * *

The Bridge into Newport is green, straight, soaring and far slimmer than any other suspension bridge I have ever seen (201 miles). We come off—Route 114.

At the beginning of the bridge, a torn cardboard sign tied up with string, "Welcome Odd Fellows. Newport Chamber of Commerce." And another sign on the other side telling about the Folk Festival.

"I wonder if the Odd Fellows means the Folk Festival."

* * *

The road has crept back into the fog.

"Don't you get an impending feeling of the sea."

"Yes," I say. "We're back on I-8. Is that OK."

"Yeah. That's what it should be."

We turn right at Portsmouth down Newport Island. (6:05)

* * *

(Eurydice has water through her window; glass, then air, and then too much rolling water, over the whole area: my lord, memory through the fog.)

The fog, thick-massed about the side of the road, could be the water.

"Do you think the beaches are free."

"I hope at least one of them is," I say, "so we can park and get some sleep."

* * *

Farmland spreads away beneath the mist.

"That bus is going to Fall River," Pete says, pointing.

We do not know whether to go to the beaches, or where. I suggest that if we pass the Viking Hotel, we look for 14-year-old Gerry. He said he might meet me there.

"I just saw a sign that pointed to 'Folk Festival.'"

I have to take a minor shit just now.

"I wonder how many people this town has?"

We pass a sign saying Hotel Viking and after talking continue on.

Another sign says "N.P.F.F. straight ahead."

We wonder about eating.

"I have to go to the bathroom," I say.

We go on.

"We're two and a quarter hours early."

A man [...] is talking to the car in front of us. Then he goes off, his tan raincoat swinging out, yet buttoned up.

"I think I'll sleep on anything tonight," says Pete.

We follow the car the man was talking to.

There are little white signs with red lettering:

No

Parking

Either

Side

"There is a sea down there," I say, pointing along streets.

We turn down.

"Small streets, close houses look vaguely Martha's Vineyard-y," I say.

*   *   *

We wind through the waterfront streets of Newport. Power stations, children, & boats. We ask a kid in a white shirt and thin black tie how to get to the Viking Hotel.

We finally park in front of the green walled stadium.

*   *   *

The morning after. The singers have sung, a night sing upon the blowy beach, watching the dawn fan gray up across the cloud streaked sky, blankets upon a hillock.

And finally at the car, we are taking off into town for breakfast.

*   *   *

We just paused to look for Gerry on beach 2. We finally met our crowd last night before the concert started. Danny & Susan were up and we promised George Auerbach and Johnny Lipsky a ride home. But we lost them right afterwards. The concert was great: lasted from 8:45 to 1:30.

Jumping from seat to seat, we ended up in the reserved section to watch Joan Baez at last transform the stadium into—something that can only be described as her own creation. Without "group singing" the concert became a projection of herself.

*   *   *

It's after the morning seminar (1:30) and Newport, becoming intolerable, we have left and now plow beneath the shadows of New England foliage. We turn towards the bird sanctuary. A motor scooter is ahead of us.

The sky is fluffed sparsely with sheer clouds.

Piled stone walls, small houses, a curving fork in the road and light from weeping willows slips by on our left.

We look for a place to turn, find it, and start back.

A collie dog watches from the top of a brick wall beside a little house where two men fix a lawn roller.

Now we are going back to the sea. The road is chipped gray along the side and grass pushes up unevenly to the tar.

The sea breaks blue between the leaves, fans out, & disappears as we turn off down another road. The air is clear but the leaves are blowy, hissing at us as we pass. And now calm.

We pass two redheaded girls in sweatshirts and black shorts.

Two more girls we pass.

Peter: "I wonder if we should ask them where they're going?"

(The rock at the bird sanctuary [is] high, layered and green laden, forming [a] quiet place. I must get back there.)

Again into Newport. We still haven't really left. We'll get out through Bellevue Avenue. (An [appropriate] name.)

* * *

After getting gas, figuring out money matters, we decide to go to Fall River. We'll get dinner wholesale. (2:35)

* * *

(I have sent Eurydice her picture. I wonder where she—)

The map begins to flap violently in the back seat. I have just closed it. It flapped once again, fell on the floor, & is now silent.

* * *

We are now in Fall River.

I bring the nightmare with me to this small town. Children's wash flutters from a geometrically straight line between two houses.

"Lizzie Borden with an ..."

A boy loads groceries into a car.

"Lizzie Borden ..."

Pete says: "It's only about 20 miles from here to Newport, you know." After passing a Chinese restaurant we decide to park the car. (No causal relation.)

* * *

Sitting in a restaurant in Fall River: good food, cheap, but only the smell is objectionable. Pete reads the newspaper beside me at the counter. In the back, the children string up crepe paper and balloons for a party. The waitress has one hideous tooth that juts straight out of her mouth. The cook, her husband, hardly has any. It is their daughter who is having the party.

"... with an ax."

Scribbling as I walk along the street.

The sun is bright on the streets of Fall River.

Into a fine smelling Bakery. Their display shelves are nearly bare.

We get cupcakes.

Out again—still scribbling. The cupcakes have white icing.

Back in the car (notice, writing is more stable), & by mutual consent, back to Newport. (I chew on my cupcake paper.)

Pete got a pocket knife to cut dinner with, but then we decided not to do it that way.

*   *   *

On the road back to Newport, I note that at the seminar this morning I found Gerry and Johnny (who may come back with us). This leaves George to discover.

I also met the Gittelmans coming up: they walked right in front of where I was sitting, so I got up and went with them. We sat down: finally they left to get something to eat. This was when I saw both Johnny & Gerry. Gerry finally came over and up against me.

(A strange dead yet green treed island Pete points out to me, out in the water.)

Gerry seems to enjoy getting close to me. He's very proud of the fact that even though he's just a kid, he knows what's going on. In Fall River I sent a piece of the nightmare to Eurydice, by way of post card. I have sent her seven post cards (fragments of the past tense dream) today. Six at one time with sketches on them, and one (the Fall River card) simply to send one more. It had the time & the date on it;—to orient me for one moment in infinity.

We are almost back in Newport.

*   *   *

We're both tired. We head down the beach to take a nap before we go to the concert this evening.

*   *   *

Lying in the sun on a red blanket, my shirt & shoes off. The wind falls and plays cool over my back, under my arms, my heels.

I am on the raised & grassy bank of the Reservoir—

(Pete just came back, laughing over a parking ticket, and plops down in tee-shirt and khaki beside me.)

—and my rock [is] down the bank and hand high across the road. Pete keeps reading what I write. He tells me that he read the entire notebook while I was at the seminar.

My head on my arm, I stare at the water-heavy horizon through the flickering grass & clover. The wind, irregular and cool on my back—

I've never gotten burned yet; and the sun breaks warm between the gentle gusts.

Pete's ticket is only a dollar.

I have to piss.

"I'll send 'em 99¢ in pennies," Pete says.

He lies there propped on his elbows. The sleeves of his shirt flap around his upper arm, the yellow envelope in his hand.

Dicky Bellman & girlfriend just came by, & now leave.

The wind & the cars and the waves all blend their sounds. Pete puts his head down, then raises it again. An insect lights on & leaves my shoulder before I can look. The wind comes up again; a nearly microscopic bug crawls over the paper, between the blue lines.

The taller, nearly leaf-high shrubs flail in the slightest gust, and some are broken.

The wind does not whisper: it rumbles gently.

Bugs come, & I blow them away. Pete gets up and goes away a few feet and kneels down, examining his pocketknife. He cuts a stem of grass, looks off at the rock across the road & comes back and lies down beside me on the blanket. (He has looked across the water heavy horizon.)

Dicky and girlfriend are up the bank 20 feet.

Pete slashes at a stem of grass in his hand, and then splits it slowly.

Now on to other grass.

*   *   *

Still have to piss (Pete has a day of stubble), I stick my foot into the grass beside the blanket; when the wind blows, it tickles, even tries to sting. I let my foot fall [...] into the grass [...] crushed beneath my ankles. It is rough and cool and damp. Back to the blanket.

Pete says we sound like mariners. He gets up and goes down; he says maybe over to the beach. Dick and girlfriend upon their blanket lie on their stomachs with feet in the air.

I sit up, annoyed by the vaguely pleasant feeling in my bladder of having to go, but not *having* to go.

I'll put my shirt on. The wind is beginning to outweigh the sea.

*   *   *

(I am now sitting on the top of my rock, the wind catching against me strong & hard. Two other guys are up here too.)

I came down to the car with the blanket. Pete was throwing his knife in the ground. I put the blanket in the car & came across the road. I ducked under the barbwire fence—

"Hey dummy, how are chances of taking a picture into the sun. I want to get to that tower," says one boy.

—and came up between the wind lashed, chest high foliage. I went, and then continued up. It was, of course, larger than it looked. But it was easy climbing. The wind, when I didn't watch out, blew the notebook paper all around, threatening to tear it out.

I sat down near the top, just as the two others came up. The one with a camera just lost his hat. (They are leaving now.) They went closer to the top; so I did too. It is difficult to write in this wind.

The brownish grass, frazzle topped, whips so rapidly as to appear liquid, and down back the way I came is meadow & marsh where the naked water sprays out.

A cloud just came. I will go down.

*   *   *

A quarter down, I stopped to write about the feel of crackling lichen on the bubbly looking rocks, beneath my hand. In the meantime, a boy & girl have come up. I continue further . . .

I am down to the bush level again. The wind is not strong and the sun touches me on my cheek and, through my shirt, my shoulder. The leaves' growl is friendly now—and not so terrible. I have heard the wind lash loud. Why do I stand here with a notebook on my arm, scribbling?

*   *   *

Getting back to the car (Pete's feet were sticking out the window so I wiggled him to wake him up) he tells me, when I get in, "We now have a one bladed knife."

He had broken the big blade off throwing it.

*   *   *

While Pete goes off to piss, I record that we have made music. We sat with both car doors open, Travis picking against Scruggs (I watch Pete urinate at the top of the bank, his back to me); sometimes the counterpoint gets rather out of hand.

He is back, and off into town, the sun hot through the window. (6:40)

*   *   *

Getting back into Newport proper, most of the parking is taken up. The mass of the F. F. has hit the town. Many more people than last evening. The weather is better; the sun is out, & no fog.

*　*　*

I'm sitting in the creamery waiting dinner. Pink wallpaper—too many people—a nice waitress but the feeling of a "pleasant" assembly line. The waitress in front of me is concocting a sundae.

Pete examines his parking ticket. The voices sound like the buzz at the back of your mind just before you go to sleep. We [meet] a boy and girl I knew who directed us here. It is in a shopping center across a huge concrete desert with white-washed stripes here and there in completely meaningless order.

There are glass chandeliers in here; incongruous with the aluminum and Formica sheen of the place. The shadow of the building on the parking lot is farther out than when I looked last.

There are people behind me discussing the stagnation of the world.

My hamburger is here, and I eat: milk, meat, bread, relish, potato chips; waiting for my sundae.

The man next to us complains of the lousy service. (Which is.)

There is anticipation of the concert, oddly ajar with the mood music that wafts through the stark, cool, deodorized air.

I eat another potato chip.

*　*　*

My sundae came. It's good. (I haven't finished it yet.)

Pete seems to be sort of protective over the notes: I dropped a spot of ice cream on them, and he was careful about seeing I wiped it off. He's made a couple of other comments.

"I've done so much in two days," Pete says. "I got a ticket!"

The waitress brings our change.

I mentioned that the way most waitresses bring change, does not facilitate tipping. It's always too big.

Since I am finished, I stand and wait for Pete, to give someone else a chance to eat.

Leaning against the wall, the people move back and forth.

One guy asks me how to get to the men's room, sort of sidles up close like it was a big secret.

"I guess it's in the back," I say, "but I don't know."

The shadow is all the way across the street. Only the faces of the houses opposite, through the trees, are bright with sun.

Pete when leaving asks a man sitting near the windows with a banjo what model it was.

"I don't [know]," he says. "But she run pretty good. About 1934, doesn't need too much oil, motor works well. About 18 miles to the gallon."

"What?" asks Pete.

"He means 18 picks per second," says a man next to him.

* * *

Outside we see a chubby boy playing to a group of boys. It's a boy we sang with last night on the beach. He lost our flashlight. Pete decides not to ask him about it, and we walk away.

* * *

A monogrammed hearse goes by. Miss Joan Baez.

* * *

We've passed, twice now, two old women who sit on their porch and observe everything like benevolent hawks. One wears a red sweater. I have a red shirt.

We come back to the car for sweaters for the last time before the concert.

+ + +

After the concert, driving back to the beach in the dark; the people are swarming down to the second beach; the cars are as thick as bugs; a mass of red lights.

The Weavers ended the concert with some rousing old and new songstry. I am just about reconciled to Erik Darling.

The stars are bright, almost too big; more than pinholes in the blackness, actual rips.

The cop chases us by the second beach. I remember from last night, headlights on the oncoming waves make a frightening sight, magnificent, rhythmic, stately.

The froth is white on the black water. Marching line after line—too slow for marching, actually—waves.

Light, headlights and lines of tail lights are all I see on the road, and the grass by the side, shivering in the breeze. The grass billows off right into the stars.

The big dipper hangs down near the sea, as if to empty itself into the ocean.

A man with a light bobs along the black sand beyond the grass. It is 1:45.

I can now see why the stars are often compared to diamonds. They are all flung so haphazardly across the sky, however.

Or, their pattern is like the sea waves, far too complex to fully fathom in one glance, sweep of blackness, or night.

We have trouble getting on the beach. There are many cars ahead of us.

Pete couldn't find a handkerchief before. Finally he used a pair of underpants: "Same ones I used to wipe my ass with."

He finally found the handkerchief right where it should have been. He flung it down in that mixture of laughter and disgust which is his.

We are in the lot now, and the headlights make a drifting necklace for a mile back along the road.

We pull up to park.

I am walking up to the night sea. It is _____ so really can't see it. Misty white sheets roar and break in the too near distance. Sometimes an extra loud one makes you step back, no matter what.

Only a mist glimmers from the stars. The wet sand is firm beneath my feet. I feel the sea might rise up and engulf me at any moment. Each second I watch it seems to be bigger. It's pretty terrifying. And hypnotizing, each long misty frothy line seeming to roar up toward my eyes. My mind sticks shadows in the water. There is a vague dark band of sand about 3 feet before me and then the thrill of endless water in the dark. The blanket is around my neck, and the whiteness (in the dark) breaks and shifts and swells and the constant roar . . .

People walk by—talk to me. Shock the hell out of me—

And I walk away from the sea—behind me, roaring—and toward the fire, far up the beach. My neck and arm (with which I write) is stiff.

I feel as if I am walking into the sky.

I look down, the forms in the sand come out in the firelight.

There are fires, orange and people shadowed, sparking in the wind—all along the beach.

Songs, and an announcement on the P.A. system over the dark.

I come back to the living. I know what that means now.

I go back to the car. I really can't remember what I've written and it is too dark to see.

I must walk slowly and write too.

*   *   *

We are preparing for sleep.

"I've got so much sand between my toes, it's amazing."

I'm in the front seat. Pete in back. Movements and voices outside.

Flashlights flicker on the window. Pete blows his nose and shows me how to turn the light on.

Pete settles to go to sleep. So will I.

+ + +

Morning, and the car begins to heat up. (8:00) Pete has developed a sniffle, and does about every 15 seconds.

The sun is high & sleep is gone. Things get folded, shirts changed. Pete announces he scummed off last night.

We moved the car once last night & found a quiet spot. Dickie and g.f. just walked hand in hand by & said hello. There is a bottle of (untouched) bourbon on the floor that we have been judiciously abstaining from.

(I am sitting in the open car door on my folded red blanket. The wind is cool and very gentle.)

I'm hungry. Pete's putting last minute things in the car.

We found George Auerbach & Gerry last night in the concert park, but lost them right afterwards. We searched for about 15 minutes and then came on down here.

Off to walk …

* * *

We have walked this morning along the sunlit sea and found her playful. We drank Cokes and I tried to tell Pete about last night.

We pick up a stranger who spent most of the night in jail. (Expanded later)

* * *

Back in the breakfast place of yesterday; the creamery was closed.

Our hitch-hiker seemed to be from Jamestown; friendly enough: got in a fight over some fellow's wife. (Bermuda shorts, blond, sunglasses, & white sneakers.) He went on at great length about losing his party, punctuating it with comments of this bitch or that. He asked me what I was writing, which was why I stopped: I'd rather he talked about himself than this. We let him off by the park, & then walked here.

* * *

Pete takes a nap in the back. I'll go sing.

* * *

I sit on the grass, damp through my black chinos, singing.

No letter from Eurydice. How could she possibly write me anyway. I wish she was here. I could sing to her. On the grass—my guitar case is open before me, like a plush lined coffin. There is a blade of grass on the felt.

I have been practicing songs for the hootenanny this afternoon. I probably won't get a chance to sing at all. They're going to put the names of the people who bring instruments in a barrel and draw out ten or so. The lucky few—out of heaven only knows how many—get a chance to perform.

I've been going over & over about five songs to get them perfect. Why do I waste my time. It will be interesting to see what happens, anyway.

*　*　*

I try to compose a song for Eurydice.

*　*　*

A verse comes to "Ana's Travelin'":
    "I lift a song for all to see,
    And at my voice comes Eurydice."
True, it's Ana's song, but I stick this verse in, and it's Eurydice's.
Second couplet:
    "I lift my voice for every one,
    Yet at my notes, Eurydice comes."
The whole stanza. I write it again so as not to forget.
    "I lift a song for all to see,
    And at my voice, comes Eurydice.
    I lift my voice for every one,
    Yet at my notes, Eurydice comes."
This is the only 4 line verse. The rest have 2. This, then, is special.

*　*　*

I will announce it as "Ana's Travelin'" (which it is) and tell her story. But it has become Eurydice's.

Songs, like men, are fickle. And why not; since men make songs?

It's a lazy, quiet summer Sunday in Newport.

*　*　*

I put the guitar away and go back to the car. The salt air is murder on the rubber capo. It eats into it and makes it rot.

*　*　*

Back in the car. Pete's cold does not seem to be getting better, though the sun is out. His nose when he blows it sounds absolutely liquid.

He asks to take out the guitar; he plays on it while I sit in the front seat and write.

I'm worried as hell about the kid, Gerry. The night before last he got about an hour's sleep, snatched in an abandoned pup tent. And I haven't seen him at all today. I hope he shows up at the hoot.

The Seminar, yesterday, was better than I thought it was going to be. We sat near the front of the stadium & on the stage. The panel discussed "Commercialism of Folk Music."

It was almost an accident we went. That's why I haven't had a chance to talk about [it] till now. Pete didn't want to go, but it was free, & we had nothing to do (Pete's playing Spanish style) so we wandered in.

Ewan MacColl and Fred Hellerman were the best speakers there. These days seem to possess a strange lack of outrage—myself included—and the discussion, although everybody kept saying things like, "Well let me just say this before the discussion really gets heated," went politely and calmly.

Oh well.

Newport, on Sunday, is a dead town, except for the endless flow of cars. I still haven't been to the wharves.

Thinking about climbing the rock yesterday, it may not have come across as such, but it was the scariest thing I've done since I've been here. (Not counting last night at the sea, which I just don't think about.)

Pete plays well, but he remembers Sabicas, who played at the first concert. So do I. The man's fingers must be steel. The notes hail out from his guitar, they clatter through the strings like bullets. His technique is almost too perfect.

Last night we saw Olatunji, & his troupe from Africa. My eyes kept tearing from the bright lit stage, and I kept having to look down.

When I was coming down from the rock, the wind blinded the water up in waves of tears across my eyes, till the tears blew down my cheek.

(I must go and look at the wharf.)

Pete plays blues now.

I stretch.

* * *

Still sitting. I wonder about people in this city: like Larry (whom I described to Eurydice as my "Wednesday Morning Problem"). I never did call him up to tell him I couldn't see him Friday. I hope Benny relayed the message—Pete, reading the above entry, looks over and says, "I'm glad you call it blues."—to him. Gerry was with Eurydice and me when we were playing around at her house; I wonder how much he understood what we were talking about. Then again, I might be surprised. I think that may be one of the reasons I feel so protective toward Gerry. Then, there's always the fact that he seems only to know how to survive, but not do it comfortably.

Absent Eurydice, her voice—

Last night I felt horny as hell: these guys kept trying to make these girls in the car next to us. Finally we moved our car.

The heat this afternoon occasionally gives me a boner. In the city, when Gerry was relaying a description of the Festival, he said something about "Walking among the campfires along the beach at night, an instrument slung over your back, Woody Guthrie style, singing here for a while, then going on: finding a girl and necking for half an hour. Then you go on singing."

Well, it's sort of like that, only the unattached and outgoing girls are at a minimum. I've gotten introduced to more guys' girlfriends (actually, only about three, but that's enough) so I content myself with the memory of Eurydice. I met Carol Simon & her girlfriend who were up by themselves and was thinking of getting a nice little Platonic thing going (Carol is not the type of girl you want to be anything but Platonic with; her girlfriends are all right, though). But we lost them.

The first night, going to the concert, we literally ran into the Seegers: Toshi, Pete, and the little ones. Speaking of the Seegers, Peggy Seeger & Ewan MacColl are great.

Gerry was with us then and called hello to little Tinya; however, Gerry tells me they don't get along too well with each other. At *Sing Out*, where he works, he took the postage machine away from her (after 36¢ worth of stamps), and they haven't really been speaking since.

Pete starts to play "Buck Dancer's Choice" with a note missing in the accompanying arpeggio strum.

The first night on the beach, after the predawn grey had broken over the landside edge of the world, we found a guy in sandals, who played my guitar for fully a half an hour without stopping in a great three finger style. I picked up a few things from him: but this Travis–three finger–Tom Paley style is something I've got to master. I've finally got the "Buck Dancer's Choice" strum down (vaguely) with all the notes (more or less) in the right places.

It's 1:00.

*　*　*

I am sitting in the lavatory of the Sunoco station across from the car attempting to (pause) defecate.

The walls are enameled yellow and free from witty sayings. Too bad.

Outside, the people were already on their way to the hoot. Some (pause) in couples, some in cars—with/without instruments; some even singing along the street.

* * *

I'm finished, wiped, out I go.

* * *

At the hoot; not started (sun hot), but there's a group over there sing-ing "Jimmy Brown."

We're sitting up close in the press section, the guitar resting the back on the ground and the head on my chest.

* * *

I sang Eurydice's song: I also met Mike Michaels, whom I haven't seen in two years. I went up to the stage, he sort of grabbed me; we sit here, lis-tening to the next performer—Mike, Pete, and I.

Oscar Brand may use the material on his program. Oh, well. What a simple climax to an incident. I have sung her song.

I'll tell Ana to listen to it; now that's perfidy. Oh, well.

* * *

The hoot is over. Pete says the song went well. That's luck. I lost a cou-plet of the special verse. Oscar Brand played my guitar while I was wait-ing to go on. Big deal.

We're sitting in a new restaurant. This one is dimmer, cooler, the ser-vice is good—prices: ridiculous.

Pete goes to the men's room.

I sit, waiting. We've verified whom we're taking home. Now, if we can just find them. Orpheus, unlike Homer, was not blind.

There is a poem by Peter Beagle called "Advice to a Guitarist."

There is a line that says

"Do not feed them the minor chords.

They are the wind."

Well, I fed them the wind at the hoot, and they liked it.

Beagle does not say it, but the major chords are the sun; and in this song I put them together.

This restaurant is cool. (3:55)

* * *

A group of the folkniks leave the restaurant: 2 men and a woman. One of the men has no shoes on and has a beard. He grins at us as he leaves. Per-haps he recognizes us from the hoots.

A girl pauses in the door of the ladies room to remove a second sandal and walks barefoot back to her seat. We have finished dinner.

Back in the yellow walled men's room, defecating again. My left foot hurts a little. I'll take my shoe off and massage it. We're going back to the beach until the concert.

In case you wonder, I changed my pants and shirt in the car, driving with Pete to Fall River. I don't know if I'll change them again, though.

Outside I hear a folk song group of men singing with a banjo, a song, "King Judah."

Now they sing, "Angelina."

I have sand in my shoe.

*   *   *

On the grass, waiting for Pete to come out. The first night I pissed on the sand down behind the car in the dark. We met a boy there, who helped us stay away from the—

(Pete's back. Revs the car up for me to come on. I do.)

—fuzz who were kicking people off the beach. We got kicked off anyway and moved to the next one.

*   *   *

Pete makes face masks through the blanket, in the sand.

"Here," he says. "Feel it."

I put my hand in. (His arm is sun dark, but his shoulder is white.)

"You can feel the eyes, the nose, the chin."

We have been in the water & dry now (on a red blanket in the sun).

Something I remember brings me to the point of all this. While I was walking to the hoot, I reached back to adjust the capo on the guitar. I pricked my thumb on a loose string, and sucking it, a drop of blood, when I looked, glazed thin through saliva over the whirls of my thumb print. I sucked it, and then it stopped. For a moment then, I wondered [if] I would be able to play if I was called. But [it] didn't hurt, so I forgot about it, until just a few moments ago. I didn't record it—almost. But these journals are not to remember the things I record, but for all the things that pass un-written, and forgotten. That is [by] far the majority of the trip. For all the single drops of blood at Newport, or anyplace. For shadow configurations on the sand, to Pete's wet hair, dark and filamental, to all the things— the million un-recorded thoughts I have over Eurydice. That's what these journals are for.

Pete digs beside the blanket [and] lifts out handfuls of wet sand, only a few inches down. I relax & watch. (Close to 6:00, Pete says.)

*   *   *

Bongos down the beach.

*　*　*

Recorder replaces bongos.

*　*　*

Pete looks for faces in a stone. Now he tosses rocks at a beer can. The sea sound behind.

*　*　*

An occasional gull: black dots skimming over clear blue glass.

*　*　*

Pete jams a feather into a mound of sand. The gulls aggregate up the beach and scatter.

*　*　*

The recorder plays "This Land is Your Land" & a gull cries.

*　*　*

Back at the car, changing to go to town (6:40) Pete tells me I went to sleep on the beach & he took a walk & came back. I don't remember, though.

We parked on a side road to avoid paying parking fees. The cars all around had tickets, so Pete put yesterday's ticket on the windshield wiper—in case a cop came. Apparently it worked.

Pete sneezes.

*　*　*

We change clothes; a weird family pulls up behind us, yell at each other and leave. The sun is about 10 feet from the horizon and light splashes over the dashboard from the back and left windows. My door is open (front right) & I have to put my sneakers on. No socks; I looked but I guess I forgot them.

*　*　*

(1:00) A church bell rings. We will go back into town now.

Last things in & out of the trunk.

Pete comes, and we throw the *Sunday Times* away. Some kid borrowed half of it when I was sitting in the grass singing, this morning. But he read it right on the grass in front of me, & then returned it.

Pete glances through the magazine, leaning up against the car, beside where I sit. "Come on; what are you reading—oh, on the fight." He tosses it away: "O.K." Comes back. "What did you do with your towel? The green one."

I hand it to him. I feel clean, my skin a little tight. I'm thirsty.

I get out to pick up a *Sing Out!* folder.

"Nothing you want," says Pete.

"No."

He closes the trunk.

We get back in after sweeping out the sand. Finally, he says "Oh yes," reaches across and removes the ticket. Tucks in the sun shade and closes the door. His watch on, my sweater jacket flung into the back seat, & we pull out.

*   *   *

I put the ticket in the glove compartment. "What 2 great things to have in the glove compartment. Half a bottle of bourbon and a ticket."

"Yeah," Pete says.

"How to be arrested. Oh, look. Don't mention the bourbon to George when we pick him up. He won't make any hassle if we say he can't have any, but he'll just go around looking sad eyed for the rest of the evening."

*   *   *

We pass a place that advertises

"Hamburgs
&
Frankfurts"

"Frankfurts," I say. "Sounds like small farts."

We stop but they don't have anything we want. On into town.

*   *   *

We park by the grass. There are shadows on the street and light on the faces of the houses.

*   *   *

Back in the creamery. We got seats at once, this time. Coming here, we saw two kids biking slowly beside a young guy in blue jeans and beard. They were asking him if he was a real beatnik, if he had a pad.

The older kid who was doing most of the talking looked beater than the guy he was talking to. A dirty, wide striped blue & white Italian boat neck shirt, faded light-blue jeans, his arms, face, and too-long hair the same even tan. The guy finally lost them. We asked which way to an ice cream place. They pointed out the creamery, which apparently opens late on Sundays.

Here we sit.

*   *   *

Gerry runs by: we make final arrangements for meeting. Gerry runs off again. My drink (a sophisticated milkshake) cold and awful. Gerry just came back. Mike and his crowd come by. A redheaded guy comes up and says to Mike, "Hey, your girlfriend's about to go to sleep out on the sidewalk." Mike takes his leave, commending his regards to a mutual friend. They're off.

*   *   *

Finished my drink. We had one of these spry waiters, a long legged kid in sneakers; no chin, but friendly.

We may not get to see the wharf.

They are playing "Perfidia" in the background.

We go.

*   *   *

Sitting in the concert park in the early dusk (8:35).

We went (the herald starts) back to the car, sang a bit; we attracted quite a crowd of kids. The M.C. is the inane Dr. of the seminar. He starts the "Talking Dust Bowl," a real twanging guitar: memorial to Woody Guthrie.

We're underway with music.

Now the New Lost City Ramblers. They're a little late in coming.

(They're tuning an autoharp says M.C. He's going to do another Woody song: "The Ladies' Auxiliary.")

I'll comment further in the intermission.

*   *   *

The N.L.C.R. wail a plaintive "Frankie and Johnny"; the crescent of the moon is caught in the trellis supporting the loudspeaker against the full blue sky.

The stage is lit with pastel spotlights that flash off the edges of Paley's banjo. They finish. Applause.

*   *   *

Big-voiced Cisco Houston sings "Stack O'Lee" and "Railroad Bill" beneath blue lights. The violet spots glow too. The top of the music cabin is pocked with spots. The sky gets darker.

*   *   *

Bright lights come up and a talking blues comes up.

He spreads the mule skinner blues out over the whole field, thick with the seventh, and thinning it a high string break.

Odetta:

Her first note is shocking with power. The final timbre of her voice sets the mike ringing.

Softer now, "Waterboy" becomes green velvet over steel.

Again, thunder, and breaths, great and full.

Over!

Thunder of hands.

I can't comment anymore. She is too powerful to think in counterpoint to her voice.

That voice kept me from committing suicide once. (A foghorn, outside the park, honks in tune.)

She has sung a cappella one prison song, and now the velvet and the steel mixes with strange modulations on the guitar.

She acknowledges the bass player.

The light catches in the peg complex of the bass.

But no more from me till intermission.

*   *   *

She leaves to shouts of more.

And the lights come up for intermission.

Pete and I have moved up; blanket is out across our knees.

This is the most acceptably polished evening. The people mill, and in the darkened music shack, the mixers fix the microphones.

Odetta sings from where I stood this afternoon: what conceit! Stray voices leak softly over the mikes. In the distance, someone else plays a guitar among the standing crowd. The first night it drizzled a bit & the blue loudspeakers were covered with what looked like Saran wrap. The stars are dim in the hyper blackness of the night created by the field lights.

Gerry comes down and leaves his duffel & banjo next to us. He'll be sitting here, so that means he won't get lost. He rather dug Odetta.

Intermission is over.

The lights are dark, and the M.C. introduces John Jacob Niles.

*   *   *

Till the next intermission, then.

*   *   *

The dulcimer weaves in through the fabric of the song in his high voice.

"Matty Groves" comes now, with the stranger instrument: a lute I think.

His high notes are clear and cool.

He asks the people backstage to keep quiet.

This is a wild song.

His low notes are wispy at times, but they intimate crystal.

Gerry takes the program to look at it. He has the most naked personality of anyone I've heard here—possible exceptions, the two singers from Louisiana. And he has better presentation.

He sings "Go Away From My Window."

He is responsible for "I Wonder As I Wander," I think.

The people don't appreciate him as much as they should.

(But enough, I say.)

His voice and movement and the modal ring of the dulcimer make the Hangman live, jump out of the stage and vibrate over the audience.

Some people are embarrassed to get so close to an individual without being crucified with power, as with Odetta. There are even a few people who snickered when Odetta went below 20 decibels.

*   *   *

Alan Mills brings Canada with him, a cappella. He's distant, declines closeness, but he does it well.

He has a good fiddler with him, after all.

But *no more* comments. You see the way it's going.

*   *   *

Intermission, again: Gerry has been making perspicacious (but annoying) brilliant 14-year-old comments.

The Abyssinian Baptist Chorus held the stage with varying amounts of strength. I want to get the Bob Gibson things.

I wonder when we'll find George (a rhythmic, tight muscled boy; he reminds me of a dark tree, an animal. He's the original slim, too good looking kid).

Pete decides to miss the last third of the program & go back to the car and sleep. Gerry comes back and looks over my shoulder. (Gerry is a Loki-child, thin and hawk like. Gerry offers me a nickel to change his age to 16.)

Our village folksinger (he performed in the hoot) sings back in the audience.

The M.C. comes out, the lights dim.

With Frank Warner we're on again.

The Gateways exploded with an individual fervor that before I only attributed to the Weavers.

They really didn't have enough time & next to Niles, I regretted this the most.

Theodore Bikel ends up. My only comment is that he was better than I expected. The last concert is drawing to a close; Gerry beside me, Bikel still singing on the stage. For all practical purposes, this whole weekend is over. It's past 12:00.

God, everything is . . .

What is it.

Where and time and come, Eurydice. (There's a constant moth flashing among the spotlights. Gerry asks whether I think he's happy. I say no—but I don't really know.)

Cries of "more, more" have brought Theo back four times up to now. He is now in the middle of "Dodi Li."

I wonder if we'll find Johnny Lipsky. He reminds me of a bear child: he sounds, acts, and sort of looks like a very young bear. He closes (he says) with his own song.

It's all right. He has a personality and it wheedles through the polish and touches you eventually.

We're all tired. Mr. Bikel doesn't realize that some of us have been here three days.

Lights.

It's over!

Back to find George and Johnny.

*　*　*

Back in the car, Johnny & Gerry are with us. George didn't come. His gear was scattered among three vehicles. The sea air blows through the dark window.

Light from the snack shop, and we veer off toward I-38.

The whole trip is over. I'm sleepy.

Gerry and Pete argue in the front seat.

I read as I write to Johnny, who is also interested in "writing."

The sky glows over the land-side hill and the car sways in the gleam of its own headlights. My hand is tired.

*　*　*

Inserts:

1) That final night for one instant, being on the sand in the new morning light, Orpheus for one second realized that when the years turned far enough, he would be—sand. The blanket seemed, for that second, to protect him from dissolving into the beach.

2) On the beach again, he had that same feeling as before, of potentially being a part of the inanimate beach: but this time the thought mere[ly] rested peacefully in his mind. Perhaps the sea at night had told him something that took away the fear.

*　*　*

Dear Sirs,

As first prize winner of the senior division of the NYU prose writers contest I want to thank you for selecting me and for the nomination of your scholarship. However, upon consideration of many factors, too involved to enter into now, I have decided not to attend NYU but rather City College. Again, I thank you for your consideration.

Sincerely,

Samuel Ray Delany

*　*　*

July 5. I finally finished typing *Les Journaux*. Within the period of an hour, I wrote—or better: transcribed—the entire text of "The Glass Negro." This has been knocking around for six months now.

Like Joyce, like Chaucer, like Rimbaud—I wish to do something to my language from which it will never recover: because there will be no need of recovery, because it will be far healthier because of me.

4

....

City College

....

In September 1960 Delany began his first term at City College. Just a few weeks later, on October 6, his father died of lung cancer. (In the opening pages of *The Motion of Light in Water*, Delany describes the circumstances surrounding his father's death.[1]) The following evening Delany wandered barefoot around Grant's Tomb, and, on a bench in front of the mausoleum, wrote an elegy. Shortly afterward he polished and made a fair copy of it, which appears in Notebook 14.

Delany continued with school. His City College notebooks, like the earlier notebooks from his Science years, carry both school notes and creative material. Some of the school notes are for courses in Latin and Greek, the latter of which Delany would put to use during his travels in Greece in '64 and '65. By the end of the spring semester of 1961, however, Delany had dropped out of college.[2]

The notebooks from the City College period contain outline material and scenes for three short novels Delany wrote in quick succession at this time: *The Flames of the Warthog*, *The Lovers*, and *The Assassination*. In Notebook 16 Delany lists and discusses these works, along with his five earlier novels and numerous shorter pieces, as part of an omnibus titled *Portraits from the Immature Mind*. He also discusses a new, as yet untitled novel, which is the evolving *Voyage, Orestes* project.

Other projects Delany mentions in these pages should be noted as well. "Prism & Lens," discussed in Notebook 13, was a projected collection of poems by Hacker, some of which would appear sixteen years later in her second book, *Separations* (1976).[3] The chapter outline from Notebook 13 that begins "Chapter One / To the Ship," as well as the accompanying verse ("By the dark chamber sits its twin"), are notes for Delany's first published novel, *The Jewels of Aptor*. Since the remaining material in both notebooks (classroom notes, outlines for the three short novels, and so on) points to the autumn and winter of 1960 as the primary period of their use, the notes for *Jewels* are likely an example of Delany's revisiting an earlier notebook to record later material. However, the brief mention in Notebook 9 of *Auberon*—the comic novella Delany and Hacker would cowrite during their trip to Detroit in the summer of 1961 to be married—is not out of place, as Delany and Hacker conceived the novella long before writing it.[4]

The title "The Fall of the Towers" in Notebooks 9 and 10 does not yet refer to the SF trilogy he published a few years later under that name. As Delany recounts in *Motion*, the title had originally designated a series of drawings by Hacker and Delany's friend at Science, Cary Reinstein. The drawings were subsequently destroyed by Reinstein's mother, and Delany, appalled at their loss, had wanted to commemorate them by using their title to designate a work of his own.[5] The migration of titles, names, and other story elements from one project to another before finding a home in a published work is a common pattern in the notebooks.

In Notebook 16 Delany makes his first direct mention of an important mentor figure: Bernard Kay, or "Bernie." Kay had been a psychologist at the Payne Whitney Psychiatric Clinic in Manhattan who worked with disturbed young people. He was also a polymath—fluent in several languages, a composer of music, and active in the New York City theater scene as a company organizer, performer, and discoverer of young talent. He had an extensive social circle and, as Delany has said in conversation, seemed to have "met, at least once, everyone in the world."[6] Delany had been introduced to Kay by David Logan, a student in Marilyn's French class at NYU. Delany and Hacker became occasional dinner guests, both together and separately, at the household of Kay and his wife, Iva. Kay was openly gay, but his marriage with Iva was a congenial one. Iva provided much of the financial support for the household through her job as an executive secretary for the Junior League. Kay was, Delany has said in conversation, the "first person" with whom Delany "could talk about things gay."[7] Delany and Kay would become lifelong friends.

During his first semester at City College, Delany lived with his family in Morningside Gardens, the apartment complex to which they had moved while Delany was still attending Bronx Science. Hacker, meanwhile, lived with her mother. In the spring, Delany moved to the apartment of a young Morningside neighbor, Bob Aarenburg.[8] During this time Delany and

Hacker's relationship became sexual; shortly thereafter, Hacker became pregnant, and Hacker and Delany decided to get married.[9]

Meanwhile, through a friend of Marie Ponsot's, Delany had secured an assignment to write an article on folk music for *Seventeen*. After he submitted the article, the editors rejected it as "too informative" and invited Delany to write on a topic about which he didn't know so much.[10] So in July 1961 Delany traveled once again to Newport, this time to cover the Newport Jazz Festival; notes on this trip can be found in Notebook 17, the final notebook of this chapter.[11]

NOTES

1. Samuel R. Delany, *The Motion of Light in Water: Sex and Science Fiction Writing in the East Village* (1988; reprint, Minneapolis: University of Minnesota Press, 2004), 3–5.

2. Ibid., 12.

3. Marilyn Hacker, *Separations* (New York: Alfred A. Knopf, 1976).

4. Delany, interview with James, March 27, 2016.

5. Delany, *Motion*, 197–99.

6. Samuel R. Delany, interview with Kenneth James, October 30, 2011.

7. Ibid.

8. Delany, *Motion*, 8, 108.

9. Ibid., 112.

10. Ibid., 12–13.

11. Ibid., 13.

The most illuminating thing about Gibran is his ability to say—not what you have always known but could never express, but rather his ability to say what you've known, expressed, and then become disillusioned with through invalid reasons. And therefore, reaffirms these ideas.

If you've never gone through his thinking on your own, then he doesn't mean too much.

But *most* intelligent people have.

Disillusion, I admit, isn't the right word.

+   +   +

The Flames of the Warthog

Margo. Steve. Nancy. The Headmistress. The man in the woods. Elizabeth Barrett Browning. The woman with the collapsed face, thin, in her black dress.

Part One

Introduction. Steve and Margo, set up against the Headmistress. Elizabeth Barrett Browning vs. the collapsed woman.

+   +   +

The neurotic (even more so the psychotic) is constantly attempting to have his identity acknowledged (fortunately for writers).

And so if you realize that most of his psychotic actions are done for this purpose, you can usually manipulate the psychotic in[to] a comparatively normal relationship with you.

+   +   +

To navigate undrunkenly when drunk demands a focusing of the senses which is probably what endears the state to most alcoholics; rather than any sense of oblivion, which the psychs. ascribe it to.

+   +   +

Do your silly music paper!

+   +   +

Present and past, they trap time upon the water in between.

+   +   +

The major poem in this collection, "Prism & Lens" perhaps deserves all the comment, not that the others are less good, but that it encompasses so much of the others. Autobiographical data is never necessary to the internal beating of a poem, but often helpful. It is only this that prompts me to say, as one who has been more intimate than many with their genesis, that "I," "You," and "He" of the last poem are all consistent characters; the crumbling sand upon which the characters wake up in Part I is the same "scorching sand" on which the "terrible children" lie in the second poem of the book; the "Terrible Children" themselves are the Protagonists of "Sestina" seen in a mirror, and that the subject of "Poem for Brana Lobel" is the girl in the man's blue flannel shirt of the party scene in "Prism & Lens."

I suppose it is [too] obvious to say that the speakers from the series of poems "The Traitors," as well [as the] seventh-century Irish poetess Liadain, the imagined letter from Rimbaud, Helen's monologue from nearly defeated Troy and the heroine of "To Carthage Then I Came" each define a different facet of the same poetic voice. On a similar level, perhaps, is the fact that the boy drinking beer in the windowsill of P & L is "he" of "He Meets Me on a White Street" or that "Amy ..." is an all too real figment of his imagination.

And for those who enjoy the very rich, "A—" of Part III returned for dinner some weeks after the completion of the poem, and was judiciously not shown the lines he had inspired.

+   +   +

Chapter One
To the Ship

Chapter Two
Explanations

Chapter Three
More Riddles

Chapter Four
Transition—To Aptor

Chapter Five
By the Moon's Light

Chapter Six
The Temple of Hama

Chapter Seven
The City & the Flame

Chapter Eight
   Argo at Aptor—Geo asks about Hama, gets told about volcano. They try
to escape, are prohibited, they are nearly sacrificed, but get away [from]
the volcano after running by the river and missing the jewels.

Chapter Nine
The Mountain and the Flame—117

Chapter Ten
The Birthday of the Infante—130—or thereabout
Introduction—they meet Hama—go with him—The Infante wakes up. […]

Chapter Eleven
To the River—140

Chapter Twelve
To the Ship, again—150

   "By the dark chamber sits its twin,
   Where the body's floods begin
   And the two are twinned again
   Turning out and turning in.

   In the bright chamber runs the line
   of the division, silver, fine,
   diminishing along the lanes
   of memory, an inward sign.

Fear floods in the turning room,
Love breaks in the burning dome."

+   +   +

In Praise of Limestone

   1) Leaves House. (1 page)
   2) At Geo's—Suggest trip to camp, they go out, meet Ann. Suggest Trip
      to Harvard. Find Riva. (15 pp.) (Geo asks him to pick up papers)
   3) Home—Encounter with Mother (5)
   4) Margaret & Jimmy go to pick up papers from Ms. Keller.

+   +   +

But most neurotics leave holes in their mask.
With Bruce.
If there weren't any hole, he wouldn't have asked.
The main place that neurosis affects functioning is in commun. with people (and subsequently in conditions that the neurotic identifies with commun.). And this causes him to build a mask to avoid commun. Because, usually, he has been injured by commun. previously (like parents).

+   +   +

All psychotics are neurotics too.

Suffered through *Bolero* once more this period.

+ + +

Perfection is the myth we invent when our own ability to find flaws is overcast.

+ + +

MARLIN NIGHT-BOUND

"Marlin? Marlin!" (Out of a yellow sea
Of window light her voice washed over him.)
Dulled by starlight, a head shocked and dark blond,
Marlin, tonight cast up from the drumlin,
Stands night-bound in the night. (Chains of darkness—
—Journey to a darkness) Watch Polaris!
Betelgeuse! Arcturus! Rushing Vega
Caught in a still arc on a dark heaven.
This earth child, tho' star-steered is night-hobbled.
And in the darkness by the house he hears
Her at the window call: "Marlin! Marlin!"

2

Caught up from pools of yellow on the ground
From shadow nets hung among stars—he stands
Returned to Earth now. He holds out his hand
To touch her voice. Dreams break across his eyes
Which, star-misted, plummet from the skies. Round
Ripples extinguish them and they are drowned
In window-light. (She says night has chained him.
And she has chained him at her sea to walk
Her shores, endlessly.) She just can't abide
That night is his goal, prison, and his road;
Because of seas how many fish have died.

           —Bread Loaf, 1960

+ + +

On the dying of the poet's
Father by cancer

They told me you were not in any pain
Or anything, father. What strange orders,
Then, place me here? In the September rain
The inner bastions of my crumbling heart
Are flooded through with cool swirling waters.
I want those chambers washed in aseptic
Quicksilver, luminous and grave—
                                        —I start
At the sound of the heels on the pavement. Click—
Click—Click. I press my bare feet hard against
The stone at the foot of the dark park stair.
The unknowing man who passes me, pulls
Me from behind my eyes. Night, draped on air
Covers him now. And he's not my father.
And he is not my—and the word blinks out.
(The uneven cement is wet.) And in
The vacuum of the absent word, there
In the dark hollow of my convoluted
Ear, rife with ancient mumbling whispers, I
Hear all the words you wouldn't, couldn't say.
And sitting here, after the end of day
I keep on thinking, how damn inane that
I cannot weep a tenth as much as rain.
When I let my head drop upon my knee
And crooked forearm, now, all that I can see
Is a stretch of wet cement, my bare foot
On the ground. Which should I finally take:
The wild, wide, ululant coronachs of
Home, or my choicely cadenced hysterics.
This strangeness of pre-mourning that to me
—Means nothing. And that is why, now, I put
My penitent self, shoeless in the night
To ponder all those thoughts you will not leave.
It is my absent grief for which I grieve.

I am silent, father, with the entombed
Passions of my mother. Grieve, grieved, grieven;
God! The pavement is so wet and so uneven!
And my words are too old, wanting pity
And archaic awe; they will not fill with light.
O this gray stone city under the night
In which you have no pain, they say. The rain
Is gray in the dull yellow-washed street light.
Mother, a stone under spilled quicksilver,
Would have you think the water in my heart is tears,
Though you're so within me now with love, I
Find it ludicrous that I cannot cry,
Except a little—that's one answer
We're given; all our urgent, pulsing fears
Are ludicrous again. What must I do?
I will not see the brown ox, the white lamb
As bone, meat, dung and gut, nor also you.
Christ, Order! Or Compassion—here I am.
They keep on saying that you have no pain!
Yet through the dim and seeming cellophane
Of the oxygen tent that holds your flickering
Death, all left-bent, we see each other's drowned eyes,
And I listen to your inarticulate breath.
And when your mind has fled your body's cage
The wildness trapped inside you will still rage
Out in the emptiness. So cold, so cold
This night. And all my aging youth, already old.

+   +   +

WATER-LOGUE

After
Vom ertrunkenen Mädchen
by Bertolt Brecht

When she was drowned, her body was washed down
Among the streams and rivers. The pulsing
White sun gleams in the sky! Why? To appease
Her corpse. The winding weeds looped and bound her

And algae clung to her; under her feet
Dim fishes still flick silver, meet, and swim around.

As night awoke, the sky grew dark as smoke
And the stars chuckled at the brilliant joke.
When they were done, they watched to see where she would come:

As her pale body now began to rot,
It happened, very slowly, God forgot
Her there: first face, then hands—at last her hair.
At last, her liquid flesh: scum on the river's scum.

                              —final version. Oct. 1960

                         +   +   +

Advice to an even younger writer

Remember,
Little brother,
Arthur, when a child,
Won all the Latin prizes.

Nation & Rebirth
      Poems and parts:
          Water-Logue
          The Ballad of Wandering Jo.
          The Fall of the Towers.
*On the Dying of the Poet's Father by Cancer.

+ + +

The Fall of the Towers
Part I
  The Scavengers

+ + +

Society cannot be defined with our languages.

+ + +

The poetry of Marilyn Terry Hacker
  —To gorge a paragraph of verse—a hundred words, perhaps—with as
  much light and music and nightmare—Christ!

+ + +

  This class is tending to verge on the surrealistic. Did he say Out because
I was yawning?

+ + +

The Last Hour of Night

Psychological miniature:
Paulette's family
Jake's family

Lesbianism
Rachel's Lesbianism over Paulette.

Strange reaction to Paul & Jake. Paul & Paulette (both are homosexual symbols)

Only false note is the basic situation of Rachel.

Christian vs. Rachel.
Even to the distractive elements of the cats and the Madam.
Why isn't this the prostitution novel to end all prostitution novels?
The process of miniaturization most apparent in Jake's story p. 135 "No-account brat"—this is what
147 (don't use "stiff" as adjective to describe corpse's feet)
Ambiguity over who's dead for all of one page—also good
"Paul's girl" becomes a contrivance to avoid Paul as a H. figure—especially since you finally give her the name Estelle.
(good musical descriptions—want sense)

+ + +

I asked him about school:

"To go for the degree is as ridiculous as going for an education, anyway, at least in America it is. But I would always advise an intelligent man to go, if he could. One must engage in human disciplines to understand humanity's problems. And that is the only valid end that a university can serve an intelligent man. As far as what is supposed to be taught, it *can* all be gotten out of books, and with far greater thoroughness, along with bull sessions with people in the field as supplementary. But the function of a university is to present an intellectually dynamic system to people in a dynamic relation. And God knows, dynamic does not mean interesting, enthusiastic, or even intelligent. It just means change, and that can be the simple change that comes when hard boring facts are presented by a hard, boring instructor, in a hard, boring way to a living mind."

+ + +

Notes for *Flames of the Warthog*

Part III (The king coon nigger and the burning wart-hog)

First night—
Mr. Blake
strange barefoot prints

First day—
　Fishing, eats, goes down to observe.
　Miss Browning and Mr. Blake: morbid talk, goes back, Wolverine incident, and graveyard. More footprints.
Evening: stringing out gut—meets the gravedigger.
　Fires the lean-to.
　Mr. Blake comes up, and the mountain reflects him.

*

After Chores—
　Next day, goes and observes Mrs. Raider talking with Mr. Butching, about the parties, and how she is not going to any, anymore. (her breakup progresses)
　He goes back up to the woods, climbs in the rocks after Wolverine and gets hurt, gets back to graveyard in the dark.
　Gets suddenly illuminated.

———

"Just wanted to see you, that's all."

———

Goes down, meets Carolin-May and she explains that running away won't help.

Comes back to graveyard and goes for a walk in the woods and sees water down in the mountains.

Two days—
Paragraph of work

Goes down, sees Betty Browning and Wolverine.
　Talks to her. "I see you now."
　And runs back.
Then he comes back, and begins to goof. The mountain is rejecting him. (Or he is rejecting mountain.) The gravedigger tells him this, but Margo won't take it.

He goes down, sees Nancy, she tells him how dirty he is. As he goes away in the evening, he meets Steve, who is worried about him.

———

Mr. Blake starts the forest fire.

The forest fire.
    Margo is driven into the slain falcon.
    Rescues Mrs. Raider who did not go to the party.
    Betty urging him on.
Runs off. Betty calling after him. The wind changes.

———

Part IV

+   +   +

New Songs for "Harbor Singers"
    1) The Escape of Old John Webb
    2) Delia
    3) I'm on my way
    4) No more auction block
    5) Take this hammer
    6) I'm going down that road feeling bad
    7) Come and go with me to that land

    Miriam Makeba
The retreat song
The click song
Olilili
Nomeva
Sanduva
One more dance
Iya Guduza

+   +   +

The Assassination

Notes.

1 The Pale.
Robert—
Saw Dust hill—
Richard & Shit
Johnny & flying
Falling off the jungle gym

Falling down the stairs.
Walnut Dye—
Stealing Jason's toy.

2 Robert and the Dirt
The chicken plucker
The chicken
Going to Robert's, and the ducks.
3
The ducks,
Inviting Robert to Labor Day,
Labor Day,
Robert comes back.
Discover the chicken plucker

Chapter 5
Pollo—the bus

Chapter 6
More Pollo
Robert from Alaska
Gabbie's mother's book
Hawaii
More Pollo

Chapter 7
The Girl—

Part

+ + +

The opening

Pollo's mother
The political section
Barbeque section

Pollo in Washington Square

The opening
Barbeque 6
Grandmother

The political section 4
Polo in Washington Square

Polo's mother 4
Group identities 2

Justine 6
The Blind 2
Closing from Ray's journals 1

+   +   +

What a sick, *atrophied* xi you have.

+   +   +

[*Loose pages from notebook*]

Society cannot be defined with our languages.* This is not society's fault but the language's. Often we mistake our inability to express the meaning of something for a lack of meaning, or an ambiguity of meaning at any rate. We say sometimes that certain meanings, ideas, concepts are vague, or intangible; what has happened when we say this, is either that we do not understand these concepts, or that the words we use are vague and intangible.

The concept of society, though words cannot contain it, is no less tangible than a steak dinner, art, the working of a refrigerator, death, or taxes. Nor is it more so. Words cannot define society because the purpose of words is to communicate and define incidents, ideas, and feelings. And society is a concept, and not an idea, etc. A concept, for the sake of discussion, is a complex of ideas in application, or potentially applicable to a complex of incidents, situations, etc. Words can generate a concept in a sort of oblique way, but they cannot define it logically.

*And yet I shall be using words at least to discuss it. So let me briefly run over the "why" of this unfortunate fact, to keep before some of the resulting limitations. First of all, the inability of language to define logically society

+ + +

1) Languages, or words have a function, and that is the recording and communication of ideas, feelings, meaning and incidents. Straight words cannot communicate (or even record) a concept.

To keep things simple and lucid (which for me is synonymous with comprehensible and v

+ + +

Nietzsche, when he felt like it, could be about as lucid as a two-to-one mixture of horseshit and ink.

+ + +

We carry the seeds of destruction in ourselves. And our guilt at the manifestation of their flowering is only one method of avoiding the responsibility of their harbor.

+ + +

Language must be learned freshly and completely each time thoughts are molded by sound or calligraphy.

+ + +

Auberon will take his place in the equine hall of fame with such other horses of fiction as Black Beauty and National Velvet, embalmed under the gentle hand of Octavia De Clivity, taxidermist.

+ + +

Dylan Thomas achieves some of his most glittering effects through the combination of physiological & mechanical imagery. It is the same thing that the German expressionists did, in a way; however they did it to make man appear more mechanical, whereas Thomas makes his mechanics into plastic, vital adjuncts of man; somewhat in the manner of the metaphysical poets (i.e. like Donne's "Compass" metaphor). Yet Thomas' effects are panaplosive and brilliant, where the metaphysicians' are comparatively stolid and Homeric.

+ + +

Reading, you can determine whether or not the author is really concerned with writing after a page, or two at maximum, but you must not, like our bungling *Intelligencia Publica,* mistake concern for competence.

Lateday sadness
melting madness
to recapture
morning rapture
misty blending
into ending
for the winning
of beginning
skies are strumming
stormy coming
and the yellow
light is mellow
through the hazy
morning daisy
withers soon to
afternoon pre-
serve it yet lest
we forget.

+ + +

The Fall of the Towers
    Prologue
    1) Thanatos
    2) Scavengers
    3) The Elegies
    4) Horrospectus of Civil War
    5) Metricus
    6) Satiricus
    7) Bios

+ + +

Notes on Part IV of *The Flames of the Warthog*

Characters to Resolve
Steve
Carolin-May
Mandy
Mr. Butching
Mr. Blake
Betty Browning
Mrs. Raider

Major:	+ Betty	Minor:	+ Mr. Blake
	– Mrs. Raider		+ Carolin May
	+ Steve		– Mr. Butching
	+ Nancy		

Margo sees Mr. Blake in woods.
Then footprints
Goes down and observes Betty
Steve talks with him.
Goes back into woods: Wolverine incident: love
Come down observes Nancy,
Sees Mr. Blake, talked to by Carolin-May,
Goes back up. Follows footprints.
Incident by grave
Goes down and observes Butching & Raider.
Fire—end of incident by grave.
Gets a chance to save Mrs. Raider.

+   +   +

Carolin-May	Mrs. Butching
Steve	Mrs. Raider
Nancy	Mr. Blake
	Miss Browning

Before Triptych	After Triptych
Nancy	Nancy
Mr. Butching	Miss Browning

Mrs. Raider	Mr. Butching
Steve	Steve
Miss Browning	Mrs. Raider
Mr. Blake	Mr. Blake
Carolin-May	Carolin-May

Nancy made the observation that people grow.

1) Doing things
2) Watching things
3) Thinking things

C-May—love affair with one of the other dishwashers.
Steve—secret places—the graveyard, the lake—now
Nancy—sunset & wants to see sun rise.

+ + +

Preface to *The Assassination*

There are two types of structure in a novel: external and internal. Fixing the external structure of a novel may certainly be a painstaking task, balancing the plot, maneuvering characters, incidents, so that they mesh into the overall shape, emotionally and architecturally envisioned. But building internal structure, that nearly indefinable flow that carries over from passage to passage, the reflection or contrast of phrasing, of arrangement within an incident, the recurrence of themes not in statement, but in development, this is a monumental task that must be done with feeling, with the finger tips, with the weight of a thought, the torque of phrase turned correctly—and it is maddening.

In order to indulge in this sort of writing, a *complete* unity of artist & the materials being written about is necessary. For this reason, the best examples of internal structure have been in autobiographical novels.

The first message that comes to a writer of the autobiographical novel is that the absurdity of life can be redeemed by moral commitment. And the commitment that the great writers have been most unified with is to their art. Thus the redemption of life by art has gone almost as a foregone conclusion as to theme of an autobiographical novel.

This is the theme that is so monumentally stated in *À la recherche du temps perdu,* so blatantly—even a little obviously—in *Of Human Bondage,* and it is the theme drawn with such cameo perfection in *Portrait of the Artist as a Young Man.*

But this need not necessarily be the message of the autobiographical novel.

If the "I" of the novel can be validly distorted to a non-artist, and his commitment to himself (what would be the source of his art had he re-mained—in the novel—a creator), then there is still an end to this novel.

The writer is a distorter. And ideally he must always be conscious of his source and the amount of distortion. And [for] anyone who cares to know, the rule, rather than the exception, [is that] the [more] accurate the writing appears, even when correlated with "autobiographical facts" [then] both cleverer, and greater the distortion

A poet systematically destroys, or better, consumes his subject by means of the poem's form. One ingests the other, assimilates it, makes the two of them one.

+ + +

Any art that is primarily concerned with discipline eventually destroys itself, runs into meaningless formalities, becomes an empty frame on which nothing is supported. The discipline is subservient to the arts; and the primary concern of any art is the human forces of the universe.

+ + +

12:45, Saturday.
On the morning of his death the wind
Made knots in leaf boughs
And the afternoon strew cruel heat
(a cruelty of dust and diamonds)

+ + +

Things to note.

I "let" myself get depressed on the rejection of a manuscript. (How psychology would misinterpret this.)
Sensitivity—condition—not chemical.

———

Golden ages of literature—always dramatic—not only because of communications problems, but also because human understanding is always needed to make great art come to life.

———

Thing to think about:

Why do the doings of artists so fascinate non-artists.
I never worked out any other reason than guilt for being idle. In my case this guilt must have been tremendous, because, if nothing else, I have

been prolific. Society plays a double trick on the artist. It excuses almost any indecency of life in the name of art, and at the same time has condemned so many "indecencies" in life. So that the artist, when he is not being an artist—or at any rate not directly creating—is suddenly borne down under the guilt of acts for which he had complete license, let us say an hour before. And the worst of these acts is idleness. I say society. Usually when I say that, you can be pretty sure I am trying to avoid saying my own damn little neurotic mind.

*　*　*

The sudden desire to kiss one's own reflection on a hot, bronze lampshade. I move and feel the heat, and watch my face distorted in the curve of burning metal, with the bulb's white glow below upon my hands.

*　*　*

My basic awareness of order, humanness, civilization—if you will—did not come from observing it. It came from looking in. Man projects his inward reality on the outside world. The psychologists are just getting around to seeing that: yet the facts [have] been the property of artists since the beginning of history.

The writing of a great novel, for instance, is no less an imitation of life for the contrivance of the plot. We contrive life. In that we can contrive it lies the individual's salvation. In that death is the one thing we cannot contrive—there is the unknown that surrounds ... everything, I guess.

*　*　*

Shyness, hesitation, and most "unexplainable little fears" are only other names for embarrassment. And what's more, most of us know it. Man has been called the thinking animal to distinguish him from the rest—obviously by someone who'd never been on a farm. A far more sensible person called him the laughing animal—but even he had not observed dogs too thoroughly, or chipmunks, or monkeys. But man is the only animal I know of that gets embarrassed—oh, ashamed, or afraid, yes. So do house cats. But to be embarrassed, that's the one human *sine qua non*.

*　*　*

Great talent is great knowledge of one particular area—the area in which the talent lies. And great knowledge in one area—though the critics of our modern day specialization would have us believe otherwise—implies a general wisdom in many. If for no other reason than that it is usually coupled with a respect for how much knowledge is needed in any area to do anything well. Talent is like an iceberg in that most of it stays submerged in the individual—even, unfortunately, when he tries to create.

(It is something else, not discipline either, that brings it up from the sea.) Sometimes it is implied by a few minutes of brilliant conversation or criticism. More rarely, in a brilliant work. And what I would see of his talent used to frighten me. He could urge and coax a group of words into a sentence that would suddenly snap off the page and quiver like a living thing.

*　*　*

Bad writing is a funny thing. At least one meaning can be draped over any combination of words. The careless writer (often the most serious writer) rereads a passage, makes sure that he has said *something*, and goes on. Well it's impossible to put two words together and not say something: blue shit—running beeswax—and so forth. And you still get *lots* of bad writing.

Oscar Wilde was perfectly correct at his trial when he retorted that there were no immoral books, only badly written ones. Of course the prosecutor didn't have sense enough to ask him whether he thought *Dorian Gray* badly written. Had he been able to think along those lines, the trial would have been over much sooner.

*　*　*

Generally speaking, something that appears twice in a story is only a prop, while if it appears three times, it's a symbol. (Expand)

+　+　+

Mr. Durrell, hovering around the age of 40, has written five novels (*The Black Book* and *The Alexandria Quartet*), and I have written eight. I've read three of his, *B.B.*, *Justine*, and *Balthazar*, and as exasperating as the utter sloppiness often is (both in pure writing—the dialogue for instance, which is unbelievably poorly handled from a purely technical point, and comes close to destroying *Justine* as a serious work—and in thinking: the whole structure and execution of the affair between Pursewarden and Justine is impossible), yet they are, taken together at any rate, good. Yet the only thing of real value to any one that I have found (except for occasional sentences here and there—far more occasional than Mr. Durrell might like to hope) is Pursewarden's letter to Clea. Well, as soon as the other two volumes come down to 50¢, we should see what happens now.

The reviews of these books have been unbelievably ridiculous and idiotic.

Final comments about the first half of [the] Alexandria quartet. There is some extremely fine writing in here, along with a great deal that is unbelievably poor. About a ½ ratio.

Who has what?
 April 25 1960

Bernie—*Lost Stars*
   Scavengers
Judy—*Those Spared by Fire*
J. Kronenberger—*Cycle for Toby*
Me (SRD)—*The Lovers*
Marie Ponsot—*The Flames of the Warthog*
   The Assassination

+ + +

 Most artists/authors [...], after a brief flirtation with the technique of rendering either form or experience, discover that true art is composed "of one's tissue, or not at all." Then comes the process of digging in, which continues to death. This is not at all the same thing which compels the avant-garde, experimental (bad always) artist who is trying to "express himself." True artists are always trying to express themselves. But the ones who talk about it all the time are indulging (completely pejorative), not expressing. But what very often happens to the artist is that he (loses sight of technique)
THINK OUT!
That's not what you mean.

+ + +

Portraits from the Immature Mind

Novels:
 Lost Stars
 Scavengers
 Those Spared by Fire
 Cycle for Toby
 Afterlon (with "Lon")
 The Lovers
 The Flames of the Warthog
 The Assassination

Dramatic and Semi-dramatic:
    Small dialogue
    Fire
    The home of the Slain Falcon
    Bright Seven
    Silence
    Wander's song
    A Walk in the City

Fragments:
    A State of Revolution
    Sun Dark
    The Stranger Beast

Long Poems:
    The Song of Songs (Eng. rendition)
    Antigone
    The Ballad of Wandering Jo
    Three Poems for Icarus
    Seven Christmas Sonnets
    Blind Seeds
    Billie from the Tower
    Helen in Mexico
    The Glass Negro—with sketches
    Canticle for Ephesus
    The Raven's Song

Incomplete:
    The Fall of the Towers

Juvenilia:
    First & Last
    The Splendor of Space
    Exercise
    Far off Bells
    The Man Who Smelled of Lion
    The Death of the Phoenix

Short poems:

Brooklyn Bridge (Sestina)
Triolet
Ciudades
Lion Cubs
Trio for Voices and Two Male Dancers
Cinquain—(I will)
Tanka (She whispers in the)
Reflections
The Faith of an Artist
The Faith of a Scientist
Lament
Hokku (I toss a metaphor . . .
      Death can come as sweet . . .)
Microcosmia
The Water Witch
Reflection
"energy sings out with inane music"
Quatrains (Exe(o)rcise in Dada)
Nine Square Inches
Combinations and permutations . . .
The King of Harlem (trans.)
Incident in Greenwich Village
Sonnet for a Sedate Wait for a Late Mate
Fragment from a Chain Gang Song
Atlantis I
Atlantis II
Sarcasm
Marlin Night Bound
Murdered by Heaven (trans.)
Pastiche among the Mushroom Clouds
Frustration
Individuality
Importance
Traveler
Society
My Chromatic Poem
Memory
Jazz, Progressive

Brass Cycle
The Existentialist's Intruder
Epistles
Song
Child's Song
Song of Incest for David
Thought Upon a Box of Soap
A Long Thin Poem
The War Game
Cinquains on an Insurance Class
Hokku (The Wail of Wild Dogs)
Catullus Five (trans)
Sonnet after Rimbaud (adapt.)
Orpheus

From *The Lovers*
    Toccata & Fugue
    The Drunken Ship (trans)

Folk song lyrics, from the Harbor Singers
    The Saddest Thing
    Chaconne
    Ana's Travelin' (parts)
    Fire

Villanelle premature
from *La vida es sueño*
Water-Logue (after *Vom ertrunkenen Mädchen*)
Three Spenserian Stanzas
Traveler
Notebook fragments
Poem on *The Poem* (Incest)
Επιθαλαμια

Short stories—fiction:
    A Wisp of Night
    Tales of the Gestalt
        1) the pigeons
        2) the oxen

3) the wail of wild dogs
A Prose Thing
Portrait of the Artist as Three Characters in Search of Tea and
    Sympathy
Torture Garden
Cerberus Barked
November Evening in the Blood My Hand: Robert
Passacaglia with Death in the Higher Voices
Silent Monologue for Lefty
Payday Don't Come at Coal Creek Nomore ...
Five Men in a Telephone Booth
Night of the Wild Horses
Les Journaux d'Orphée
The Gryphon has Two Heads

+   +   +

Lost Stars
    Portraits from the immature mind. Part I
Scavengers
    Portraits from the immature mind. Part II
Those Spared by Fire
    Portraits from the immature mind. Part III
Cycle for Toby
    Portraits from the immature mind. Part IV
Lon and *Afterlon*
    Portraits from the immature mind. Part V
"Orpheus's Journals" and other stories
    Portraits from the immature mind. Part VI
"Geo's Poems"
    Portraits from the immature mind. Part VII
The Lovers
    Portraits from the immature mind. Part VIII
The Flames of the Warthog
    Portraits from the immature mind. Part IX
The Assassination
    Portraits from the immature mind. Part X
"_____"
Portraits from the immature mind. Part XI
Fragments

Portraits from the immature mind. Part XII

+ + +

Dear Commissioner Wiles,

I would like a permit to film the Brooklyn Bridge, and the areas adjacent. This is an amateur experimental film

+ + +

Fragment for Geo

"Precocity, historically, has been the metaphor through which all greatness has been explored."

+ + +

"I've always abhorred novels that spent ten pages introducing themselves, which is why I so enjoyed *Jude*, *Tess*, and *The Native* of Hardy, Jane Austen, & even Thackeray & Fielding, and Proust, Faulkner, because no matter how slow their movement became, how bad the writing often got, I was always looking at something, feeling, sniffing, hearing a real voice (even the author's), which I could connect with an over condensed life, while so many other books became heaps of words attempting to explain something to me."

+ + +

And then I began to run, the pavement beating up against my feet and battering me toward the sky. As I reached the bridge, the low sun scoured away the suspension cables with hot white-orange light so that the main support seemed to sear off free, without support against the blue sky, and I was running, light with leaving.

+ + +

The trouble with my three novels, the thing that keeps them from

+ + +

I want to let my reader in on worlds that he has never seen before. And make his eyes burst with the fury of my words.

+ + +

That ritualization is the will to poetry is often hard to take, especially for poets. Understand, essentially my medium is prose (which wants a definition, I admit); at any rate, it means I am relieved of a certain dark subjectivity.

+   +   +

The tragic man is a man trapped in a myth
Too often of his own creation: go
From Oedipus to Hamlet, Elektra
To Winterset; each shows a being forced
To travel patterns somehow pre-ordained
By judges, gods, and men (all are the same)

+   +   +

For me a poem was only just a stone
with which to whet the scalpel of my tongue
for prose. Something I discovered early:
the art that takes itself too seriously
dies easily. That art that takes itself
not seriously enough will not be art:
A mirror that reflects imperfectly
is what an artist often strives to do;
And yet the imperfection is the jewel
Which when controlled makes genius out of fault.
But it is imperfection, none the less,
which is the irony of its creation.

+   +   +

Fragment for Geo

"There are two types of analytical novelists: one who keeps saying, 'There was something indefinable, ineffable between this and that character.' And the second is the one who accepts the challenge of defining it."

+   +   +

Blurbs

For first published novel (probably)
The Flames of the Warthog
"Portraits from the Immature Mind" Part IX

By his nineteenth birthday, Delany had left eight completed novels, and had fragments already for a huge ninth. There were also a dozen or so short stories, and a thick sheaf of verse, not to mention three or four plays, two opera libretti, and an orange crate full of fragments, discards, and alternate versions. In one of his journals, Delany had listed the works he considered publishable with the subtitles "Portraits from the Immature Mind." In each one of his works he limns in brilliant language the ambiguities of life he saw in the world as personified in the adolescent: emotional, sexual, intellectual, and racial. Through these ambiguities, Delany's world is often one of terror, but his characters, as Margo does in this story, move through that terror toward maturity and beauty.

Lon and Afterlon
"Portraits from the Immature Mind" Part V

Of his novels, this is the most complete of his longer efforts. There is far more direct analysis in this book than in any of his others, though the story is still told primarily through action. Oddly enough, this book was almost written as a tour-de-force. His third and fourth novels, *Those Spared by Fire*, and *Cycle for Toby*, had aroused a publisher's interests, but also their trepidation. They complained to him of a formlessness, a lack of organization. Although he himself always considered his fourth novel to be his best, and "the tightest 100 pages I've ever seen written by anybody," he did come to say of his third novel, "I see that I substituted structure for form, patterning for shape." At any rate, after a session with his editor, in which he was told "formally" what was "wrong" with *Those Spared by Fire*, he went home and wrote the first fifteen pages of part one of *Afterlon*, the day before his eighteenth birthday.

Afterlon, among other things, is a study in formal unities. It all takes place in one day. The five main characters occupy the stage almost exclusively. Each one interacts with all the others in a symphonically arranged balancing of incidents which achieves gothic symmetricality. As Delany said, "I wanted to show them that I was perfectly capable of writing a novel with a plot that began here and ended there." The book was completed in under four months, just before his publishers sent him to the Bread Loaf Writers' Conference.

Those Spared by Fire
"Portraits from the Immature Mind" Part III

Although the main criticism of this book is that it lacks the form of a novel, it is interesting that its title pages (as it went from publisher to publisher) referred to it respectively as "A Study in Seven Parts," "A Cycle," and eventually, with a sort of cynical irony, "Almost a novel."

The book was the product of a "monster of erudition," as another literary prodigy has been called, of sixteen, and it would take, to completely annotate, a well rounded Ph.D. sitting on top of all twelve volumes of *The Golden Bough* with a Bulfinch in one hand, a Bible in the other, and perhaps a good textbook on abnormal psychology. It was written with all (except the last) quite close at hand.

The book is a pyrotechnical display of writing styles, and also a catalog of violences woven like jewels through the tapestry of myth. It is perhaps the greatest and most effective delineation of the horror that is adolescence ever written, not in a recounting of its ignorances, but through the stark presentation in a hallucinated language of its terrible knowledge.

Cycle for Toby
"Portraits from the Immature Mind" Part IV

This short book was the only one Delany began and completed in his 17th year. (Which, when it is considered that he wrote eight between his 15th and 19th birthdays, is notable.) It was written from start to finish three times (the first time because half the manuscript was lost), and considered by the author to be his best book. It was praised by the publishers for its writing, but rejected because of length and, again, a lack of unity. Length is understandable (it runs less than 100 pages), but that so short a book which covers in such detail so great a time (12 years in Toby's life) could be so dazzlingly cohesive as it is, is a technical feat worth marveling. "I wanted each section to be able to stand alone as a short story, complete, alone." The third section won the 1959 NYU prose writers' contest, securing for Delany a full scholarship (subsequently turned down) at New York University. The theme, a recurring one, is the movement of Toby from terror, through Beauty, to Maturity. Like a small, glittering thing, it is jeweled with a dozen memorable characters besides Toby himself. Jonny, his brother Josh, the summer vacationers, and the children of the small New England fishing island.

Scavengers
"Portraits from the Immature Mind" Part II

This was Delany's first attempt at a controlled book of novel length. Its four-part structure, as *Afterlon*, as *The Flames of the Warthog*, is decidedly symphonic, but in this first effort, perhaps forced. This is one of the two times Delany ever deals directly with an artist, and the only time he deals with him as an artist.

Once we pass through the first movement (a pyrotechnical tour de force which attempts to create, through both stylistic and typographical experiments, the despair of the artistic personality in forty pages of description of his city—the same city which is, perhaps, the dream focus of his novel, *Afterlon*—description never dull, and often spellbinding) we see Delany, for rest of the book as pure storyteller, and though, with perhaps two exceptions, the female characters lack depth, there is a breakneck quality of adventure as these children try to survive in their divorced world. There is also on occasion a shocking tenderness, which he waited through three more novels before he displayed it again with the same power.

Lost Stars
"Portraits from the Immature Mind" Part I

Delany subtitled this a "fragmented narrative incapable of sustaining itself any longer." It is incomplete, though perhaps not "just as well so," as he comments on it. It is a fifteen-year-old['s] novel. But it avoids two things which seem to be the marking traits of the "very young" writer: it makes no attempt at the intolerable blasé sophistication which is so often used to cover up naiveté. Delany, in a remarkably condensed life, had little room for that sort of naiveté. Had he been so, he could not have survived. What naiveté there was, was almost entirely extra-literary: The style lacks the honed precision of his later work, but often captures beauty through the same methods; the weak spots of the book are things such as the dependence on Ibsen, and the occasional pontificating.

As an insight into Delany's works it is invaluable. We meet the neighborhood in which so much of *Those Spared by Fire* takes place. We meet his theme of identity here, along with Snake who is so much of *Afterlon*. And there are the prototypes for half a dozen other easily recognizable characters.

There are things which want to make one say, yes, this is a novel by a fifteen-year-old, but there are other things that keep you from saying it too quickly.

The Journals of Orpheus
"Portraits from the Immature Mind" Part VI

The young novelist is often told to try the tightly constructed short story. Delany started with the short story, approached it as a challenge, and overcame it, before any of his better novels were written. "A Wisp of Night," "Five Men in a Telephone Booth," and "Night of the Wild Horses," will fit anyone's definition of the classical short story, Poe's to Henry James (not to mention the short short stories, "Mike, Jesus, and Me," and "The Gravedigger" (which won the National Scholastic Award for 1958)). But as any truly creative artist, he could not leave the form alone, and with beautiful and moving results, from the stylistic experiments of "A Prose Thing" and the hysterically funny "Pygmalion Complex."

The experimentation in most of the stories, however, is kept completely controlled, with the moving and often grotesquely beautiful results of such pieces as "Torture Garden," the exploration of a healthy and an unhealthy relationship between three boys. "Pay Day at Coal Creek Don't Come No More," the shattering effects of a mining disaster on a town in Tennessee. "The Gryphon Has Two Heads," the results of a sadist loosed on a bunch of already half-lost people, and "Passacaglia with Death in the Higher Voices," a piece which delineates four ways in which a frightened boy runs away from life, and living.

The title piece is in a class by itself, or better, takes in all classes. It is perhaps the most honest and accurate bit of autobiography ever written: it is mostly constructed from notes written over, at, and during the weekend of the 2nd Newport Folk Festival (the weekend before the infamous riots at the Jazz Festival), and we have the beginning of the dichotomous personality that is the focus for *The Assassination*, Delany's eighth novel, and his untitled ninth. It is also an exciting story, and brilliant and lovely writing.

The Lovers
"Portraits from the Immature Mind" Part VIII

The last six months of Delany's 18th year produced three novels, and poetry; no short stories, no other prose pieces. This, the first of the three, is perhaps the most inconsistently written, the most moving, and the most amazing. Inconsistent brings up the wrong picture. The writing is always good, until suddenly it becomes fantastic. This book is filled with a tenderness unusual and unequaled in Delany. Characters whom he usually eschews (the artist, the child prodigy) are suddenly brought in en masse, and are made to perform under his verbal whip perhaps more competently than those with whom we are more familiar. The book also contains the verbal "Toccata and Fugue" (which alone would make it worth reading) plus the complete translation by the character Keller, of Arthur Rimbaud's "*Le Bateau Ivre*," the best I have seen in English. (It need not be mentioned that Delany's age makes his translation doubly interesting: Rimbaud was at the end of his 17th year when he wrote the poem which "has the precarious position of being the most famous poem in the French language" (Henri Pirenne) and Delany did his translation of it when he was just 18.)

And the book is about love. The beautiful 17-year-old pianist, Niva, the sensitive 18-year-old writer Keller, and the 16-year-old delinquent, Jeyo, these are the people who love, and the frighteningly sound psychological resolution to this love will have the head doctors pondering a long time, about things that well could be pondered.

The Assassination
"Portraits from the Immature Mind" Part X

Delany's last three novels, *The Lovers, The Flames of the Warthog*, and *The Assassination*, were, the journals tell us, written as part of a series of six short novels, which he proposed writing before he launched into a huge work for which fragments have been written as far back as his last days at the Bread Loaf Conference. Each, in its way, hits a separate high point in Delany's works. *The Lovers* in sensually lyrical writing, *The Flames of the Warthog* in controlled storytelling, where *The Assassination* is a minor epic achievement in "the study of internal structure," as its preface tells.

The writing is intensely, vividly autobiographical, contains almost no violence, or that "abuse of the terrible" which, in the earlier works, was almost the Delany trademark.

The most interesting part of the work, both as writing and insight into Delany's character, is that part which deals with his relation with the poetess Edna Silem (who becomes the Evelyn in *The Assassination*). It is always dangerous to assign too strict an autobiographical significance to any author's writing, even if it is alleged by the author himself to be so. But this is a relation that lasted the entire length of Delany's creative period. (Two of his novels, the second & third, bear her in the dedication.) Again Delany eschews discussion of the artist directly. Neither Evelyn nor the narrator Ray is presented as an artist. The final section is composed of two sets of journal entries—Evelyn's and Ray's ... The book is made more meaningful in that Miss Silem wrote the beautiful short selections from "Evelyn's Journals" herself.

+   +   +

Reflection on I. A. Richards: there is a certain lack of literary taste involved with being the editor of a "shortened version" of the *Iliad*, or writing a book on "practical" criticism which precludes me from being one of his admirers.

+   +   +

Like good poetry, there's a whole world caught in a good song. I think you can see the industrial revolution influence and hear the 1890 twang to the melody. So far you've had an old old song, a fairly old song, and now let's try one that was composed just a handful of years ago, by a young fellow on Martha's Vineyard named Dave Gould. The melody of the song is a little more complicated than most, but if you have the required octave & a sixth range to get through it, I think you'll find it worth it. It's one of the three or four songs that have become connected almost exclusively with the young folksinger Joan Baez. Her first recording was made of it when she was nineteen. Joan sings in a crystal soprano voice with almost no vocal or rhythmic adornment. Listen to the words closely, and you'll see something interesting.

+   +   +

Geo's Poems

Antigone—long
The Ballad of Wandering Jo—long
The Drunken Ship—trans.
Rebellion—lyr.
Seven Christmas Sonnets—long
Villanelle—tdf.
Epithalamia—lyr.
World—lyr.

Billy From the Tower—long
We also die—med.
Pritchard Bleary—hum
The Betrayed—tdf.
Catullus V—trans
Sestina—tdf.
Song of Songs—trans
Blind Seeds—long
Sonnet after Rimbaud—tdf.
Triptych—tdf.
Love/tide—lyr (med)
Water-logue—trans.
Proem—hum.
The Water Witch—lyr.
Landscapes—tdf.
Hokku—lyr
Tocatta & Fugue—long
Lion Cubs—lyr
Faith of an Artist—lyr
Faith of a Scientist—lyr
Microcosm—lyr
Frustration—hum.
Sarcasm—hum.
Triolet—tdf.
Spencerian—tdf.
Lorca—Back from a walk—trans
Icarus—long

+   +   +

In any man's day is enough to make a myth.

+   +   +

Hemingway is dead.

NOTEBOOK 17—SUMMER 1961

Starting to N.P. and on 6 hour notice, and $20.00 from *Seventeen* Magazine; bus late, but here I am.

Two friends already. Man from New Orleans who's going to tape record the concerts and young sailor from Brooklyn. Man with tape sits beside me, sailor behind. Man plays recorder for me of his plane trip. Conductor is coming round for tickets.

Now, tickets punched, we sit in the stuffy bus, waiting to leave while the little transistor tape recorder rumbles and roars.

Now we rev up, the doors close, and we—start to pull out. Backing from between the other silver-sided buses, and slowly I can see now people moving outside the bus. We're in the street; now we lurch around the corner, & we're off.

*

Just stopped to get something to eat. The late afternoon rolls blue-gray outside the window of the bus. That was Norfolk. And now we are on the thruway again. Next stop, Providence.

*

The sun sits low on my left, warming my cheek through the bus window, as trees flop by between the bright copper light and me. A little while ago, behind the clouds, the light came around the edge as bright as a magnesium flare. Now it is hollow and pulsing gold.

I wonder what sort of Jazz Festival this will be. M. Davis and T. Monk aren't in it; after the riots last year, the prestige of the Festival I would guess has gone down. They can make more money in the city probably.

My friend from N.O. asked the driver how long it would take us into Providence (no signs have I seen yet). The driver responded that he didn't know; it was his first trip. I am plagued by a half a dozen cameo-like nightmares in which we miss Providence in passing, or simply never get there. It's now about 8:00.

The sun on the opposite window becomes a ball of light, flashing with trees; you can look straight at the reflection and your eyes don't hurt.

"We've been traveling four hours," says the man from N.O. "I sure hope we hurry up and get there."

*

Just passed my lake again; so new, like the sky caught in a huge rim of trees; we seem to be on the outskirts of Providence. My friend says: "Skitcherwood. Providence, ten miles," reading from a sign.

Now, the lake on the other side of the road, five minutes later. Yes. I'm coming back. Only more alone, this time, older, and sans Eurydice ... In a way.

Just passed Drive-In movie theater playing *Gone with the Wind*. How corny and ironically significant.

*

We are well into Providence now. I remember these squat low-cost housing projects, the raised ribbons of concrete highway. Through the green & blue tinted bus windows the scattering of mercury lights among the buildings looked like the glowing fragments of a shattered ghost in the thickening evening. Now we are back on the main street. I am resigned that I shall miss most of the first concert. We can't possibly get there by eight thirty. In fact it's eight thirty now. Only light to write by is when the gray page is relieved by neon red or green.

Man from N.O. flashes lights on but I'm almost finished. I tell him to turn it out.

We are pulling into the change terminal. We're here!

*

On the bus to [Newport]. Met another sailor, this one had been to the Jazz Festival last year. According to him, "It got too dangerous, so I went back to the ship. The whole town was drunk."

It's completely dark now. The bus is full. Even a few people standing. All the street lights and outside are green, and so are their spotted reflections on the Narragansett River. New sailor is from Tennessee. Back in the terminal he told me that he had five more months to go. I wished him luck.

*

Robert Green Trio
>   It Don't Mean a Thing—starts tone row
>   Go Down Moses
>   The Journey Man

Some quick figuring: here I am, sitting in the press section of Freebody Park at 3:30 (c) on Sunday afternoon.

I have $12.00 left to last till Tuesday, or even Wednesday.

At $3.00 a day, I can make Wednesday with cab fare left to get home from the bus station to home (back in the city).

At the Navy "Y" I can eat on $2.00 a day, & eat well on $2.50. Oh well.

+   +   +

Impressions:

Tramping (now I get the full onomatopoetic impact of that word) by the sea wall, I feel the burning weight of my pack straps down over my shoulders.

The moon, low and full, has taken its little finger and smeared ivory around the huge folds of clouds like black rags flung on the sky.

Two colors: the low ivory light on the water, a dull creamy pool with orange tint miles away.

A storm has blown out over the water. You can only see it when the lightning flashes: a patch of sky flares orange, cut by yellow streak, & the clouds flicker on & off beneath the moon. The orange, the inverse of the moon on the sea, has an ivory backing.

+   +   +

Later, the moon is higher. The storm is gone, and the [moon] a chalk disk with dirty fingerprints on it. The swell of black water drives a patch of foil before it; shivering silver turns to gray froth under the moon.

High moonlight on the water is bleached, flat, silvery, and far away. The rocks near me are deep wet brown run with velvet laces of shadow.

+   +   +

The cool sea smell; a wet, salty vegetable smell, and the breeze on my arm as I sit here, eight o'clock in the morning on the sea wall; and the sun lines my cheek bone and the people are walking by.

+ + +

People I must get to see shortly:
James Baldwin
Edward Steichen
Robert Frost (re-meet—he needs to be told something)

+ + +

Every once in a while—say once or twice a year—I delve into my orange crate of old manuscripts. It's a frightening experience. I just did so tonight—there are still half a hundred sheets on the floor. These moments are the only ones during which I am ever massively attacked by time.

They date at maximum from five years ago: maybe seven in perhaps three or four cases. Yet each time I wander through their hills of recollection, I come up with half a dozen things which I must read sometimes 400 words before I am even vaguely assured that it is something I wrote, I ever touched. There are about 25 inches of thickly piled manuscript, plus another 3 or 4 inches of music-script. This doesn't include my eight completed novels and my completed short stories. These I keep separate. But judging 175 pages an inch that's—

17500 / 4 = 4375

4375 plus pages. Not counted also are twelve or more spiral notebooks full of journals. I should get a big filing cabinet and fill it all. The last seven years of my life buries me in literally thousands of pages of memories. I don't believe I'll be able to write much more, unless I have a radical change in my being. I'll be lucky if I can finish off "Portraits from the Immature Mind."

The things I have done in my condensed nineteen years; an actor, singer, honor student, classical language student, translator of the Bible, Thomas Chatterton, Rimbaud, Brecht, and at the same time I have run narcotics, lived with and loved a brilliant poetess (also typed up her damn manuscripts) done a bit more than my share of dabbling in perversion, even made pornographic films, been conversation close to Robert Frost, John

Ciardi, Louis Kronenberger, Allen Drury, Bernard Kay, Marie Ponsot; and I am a writer of genius, whether I like it or not.

And I am bound to the world and to the word by these thousand pages.

I have composed music, written operas, sung in church choirs, and have gorged myself on more sin than many in half a lifetime.

+ + +

Wind sent leaves flipping against thousands of leaves in the trees above me as I trudged along the crush of gravel and dried foliage at the edge of the cracked macadam. Across the road from me, the tall grass of the huge meadow swayed away in waves of white sun-light, and the sky was blue.

I was a spring child, born in April; and my summer sheets were always the crispest, my bedspread of the driest and crinkliest material, that, during my earliest years, as I lay under their clicking and crackling, I must have hardly gotten any sleep at all. (Strange, journeys for me have always been times primarily composed of retrospection, even beside such a deeply peaceful wood, or beside so broad a sun washed field. No, not strange; because a journey is not composed primarily of those incidents and stories you later recounted to friends about what happened to you or what you did; it is mostly movement, progression, and peaceful continuity.)

+ + +

Life is a story we tell to ourselves composed of incidents we suspect [have] happened to us, minutes, days, years ago. A day is a thing we review just before going to sleep at night.

+ + +

The Prologue to this silly novel, finished last night, has taken me almost a year. I wrote the first version of the first page either just before or just after I returned from Bread Loaf last year. I have plans, outlines and notes dating from well before that. But I believe that now the work will go much much faster. Prologue over; now we begin the introduction: ha! ha!
—July, 1961

+ + +

James Baldwin
WA9–5921
Call James B. at 11:00 Thursday.

+ + +

A quarter of the way through the letters of J. Keats, it occurs to me that the mildly homosexual effusion of the romantics *was* charming after all.

* * *

Finished the first section in Trilling's selection of Keats letters. The editing job is unbelievably poor. I must get the complete letters some-day and read them. I would have liked to read Keats writing at length on Chatterton as he does on Milton, Shakespeare, and Wordsworth, but I only find two references to him in the letters. I wonder what the situation of the composition of his sonnet to Chatterton was.

+ + +

Marilyn and I went to see *Much Ado About Nothing* this evening. Good direction. This afternoon we read out loud the first four Cantos of *The Faerie Queene* to one another.

—July, 1961

+ + +

Since Lord Byron, most art has been constructed so that the audience identifies with the myth of the artist rather than the body of the artist's work.

+ + +

Blank verse has always been the letter-form of poetry.

+ + +

The "Jo" poems
    and
The Terrible Children

Of the host of literary prodigies, Delany was by far the most prolific. Be-fore the age of twenty he had amassed 4000 odd pages of miscellaneous manuscript which did not even include the finished versions of his nine novels, score of short stories, plays, opera libretti, 12 odd volumes of jour-nals, and [a] sheaf of poetry from which we have selected the "Jo" poems. It is an interesting scholarly problem whether or not the Jo poems deal with the "same" or only similar characters, since we only have names in the longest one, "The Ballad of Wandering Jo," from which the set of three poems have derived their collective name.

Delany was not a poet—or at any rate not [a] fine constructor of lyric poems. (Although he has been rightly called "the lyric genius of English prose.") And one reads the longest of the "Jo" poems with that breakneck sense of adventure and horror, something that might have resulted had Byron's Oriental Tales been written by Poe.

Just a note on where the "Jo" poems fit into Delany's *Magnum Opus*, the "Portraits from the Immature Mind." In the somewhat schizophrenic world that Delany created, [they] belong to Part X of the *Portraits*, Geo's poems—a group of poems supposedly written by Geo Keller, the protagonist of the sixth novel, *The Lovers*, and one of the main characters of the final novel which remained untitled and formed Part XI of the "Portraits."

*   *   *

That Edna Silem and Samuel Delany should have known each other, and so greatly affected each other's work (we have a journal entry describing how Miss Silem sat up with Delany half one spring night while he wrote the last six pages of his novel *The Flames of the Warthog* four times, pretty much at her command until she was satisfied with them) is one of the greatest pieces of literary good fortune we have known. These unbelievably finished pieces of Miss Silem are technically far better wrought than those here included by the young Delany, [and] were written primarily during the five years of their relationship, the same five years that produced Delany's "Portraits."

In the title poem, and probably in many of the others, we get the most searing and vivid pictures imaginable of Delany and that strange ménage of young people who roamed through his life and his novels.

+   +   +

P.S. Tell Bill Sloane that I am still alive, if you see him, and that *The Flames of the Warthog* is finished and has been rejected by Random House already. One down, infinity to go. (Recognize the title?)

+   +   +

In private, every young artist runs after the Child Prodigy myth like death. In public, they battle it—for their lives.

+   +   +

Great writing should release worlds.

5

Married Life in the East Village

In light of Hacker's pregnancy, she and Delany decided to marry. Because of differing miscegenation and age-of-consent laws across the United States (Delany was nineteen, Hacker eighteen), the nearest state in which they could legally wed was Michigan—so in late August the two traveled by bus to Detroit.[1] During the trip they entertained themselves by collaboratively writing a comic novella, *Auberon*, the text of which takes up the bulk of Notebook 18. Various story elements in *Auberon* allude to the circumstances surrounding the Detroit trip. Just preceding the *Auberon* text is a list of authors and topics for a work of literary criticism Delany and Hacker had discussed writing together.

Although most of the material in Notebook 15 dates from the fall of 1960—nearly a year before the trip—the notebook also contains an account of the trip itself, as well as its aftermath. Since this is the most significant biographical material in Notebook 15, I have placed that notebook after Notebook 18 rather than among the notebooks of 1960. The Rimbaud translation and the couplet that follows it—the latter of which was written by Hacker and transcribed by Delany—date from the earlier period.

Notebook 19 contains a short entry anticipating an episode Delany describes in detail in *Motion*: a dinner visit to Delany and Hacker's apartment by W. H. Auden and Chester Kallman.[2] The notebook also describes a performance by Delany's folk group, the Harbor Singers.

Several entries from the notebooks of this period suggest a new role for the notebooks in the early years of Delany and Hacker's open marriage: in addition to personal entries, critical essays, and drafts or fragments of stories and poems, the notebooks contain informal verse written between Delany and Hacker as part of their daily communication with each other. In the notebooks from this period we also observe Delany's increasing interest in the sociocultural situation of the female poet—an interest spurred in part by his now living with one.

During this period Hacker worked as an assistant editor for Ace Books, an important publisher of paperback science fiction that served as a career springboard for many prominent SF writers, including Thomas M. Disch, Ursula K. Le Guin, and Roger Zelazny.[3] Hacker was frustrated by the characterizations of women in the works published by Ace and discussed this with Delany. Around the same time Delany had experienced a series of vivid dreams, which as yet lacked a vehicle for narrative expression.[4] As a gift to Hacker, Delany wrote the science fantasy novel *The Jewels of Aptor*. Hacker submitted it to Ace editor Donald Wollheim, claiming to have found it in the slush pile of unsolicited manuscripts, which it was her job to winnow once a month. (Delany had submitted the manuscript under the pseudonym "Bruno Callabro," the name of a character from his novel *Those Spared by Fire*.) Wollheim accepted the book, at which point Hacker revealed that the writer was her husband. As Delany recounts in *Motion*, Wollheim responded well to this revelation—as he professed to "hate the name Bruno Callabro."[5]

The Jewels of Aptor, Delany's first published novel, appeared on bookstands in late 1962. Delany was twenty years old.

NOTES

1. Samuel R. Delany, *The Motion of Light in Water: Sex and Science Fiction Writing in the East Village* (1988; reprint, Minneapolis: University of Minnesota Press, 2004), 22–24.

2. Ibid., 155–71.

3. John Clute and Peter Nicholls, *The Encyclopedia of Science Fiction* (New York: St. Martin's Griffin, 1995), 3.

4. Samuel R. Delany, interview with Kenneth James, October 30, 2011; *Motion*, 150–51.

5. Delany, *Motion*, 182.

NOTEBOOK 18—AUGUST 1961

The Romantics—English & American

Spenser   Boccaccio
Chaucer   Ariosto & Tasso

→ Walter Savage Landor
→ Villon → the Galliards

The […] 14-year-old poet

Eric Felderman
Paul Elitz
Rimbaud
Chatterton
Radiguet
Byron
Shelley
Mozart
You & I
Natalia Crane, Margery, Mimi, Greenberg, Lautréamont

The novel & how it grew
The epic & why.

———

Henry James. Tennyson & the Brownings. "Dover Beach."

Homosexuality & literature.

The Myth in literature.

Tristan & Isolde.

Hamlet—as first modern man—

—Oedipus
—Medieval
Robert Burns
Blake
Wordsworth. Robert Browning. Swinburne. The Idylls of the King. (Why 19th-century epic didn't work.)

Lots of money—anti-religion for which bloody mess.

What's wrong with most Negro literature:

Poe, Melville, Hawthorne
[Poe] → & the symbolists: Baudelaire

Women in literature

Novelists

Pilgrim's Progress
Fielding, Swift,
Defoe—Butler
Jane Austen
Don Juan
Lady Blessington's novels

What's wrong with *Silas Marner, Daniel Deronda, & Mill on the Floss.*

The eighteenth-century French novel

Jean Christophe
Don Quixote
Hardy as a tail end
& the Poetry
Dickens
Charlotte & Emily

W. H. Auden
Yeats
T. S. Eliot

Graves
Norman Mailer
Laurence Sterne
Virginia Woolf
Aldous Huxley
James Joyce—D. H. Lawrence
Sartre
Gide & Camus
Djuna Barnes

Chapter: She & Her & role reversal

Thomas Wolfe

Drugs
   Naked Lunch—Burroughs
John Ciardi
Proust
Hemingway
Faulkner
Me ← Durrell—Miller
Anaïs Nin

Melville's Poem
Swinburne's novel

Goethe
Dante
Nietzsche
Kafka

Stephen Crane
Katherine Anne Porter
Tennessee Williams
Miller & O'Neill
Carson McCullers

The Gertrude Stein Syndrome
The Imagists

Literary Hoaxes
Ossian
Chatterton
Anne Knish
'Pataphysics & *Ubu Roi*
Dadaism

Great Secretaries
Ezra Pound
Samuel Beckett
Boswell
Rilke

Other 14-year-old poets
The Brontë Children
Heine
Rupert Brooke

+　+　+

My love is like a dead, dead horse
That's newly killed in June.
My love, when having intercourse
does it with a spoon.

+　+　+

Detroit

We sat on the wide shred of stone wall where the men were fishing. In the river, down the wall, a four-foot lip of twisted metal caught the in-rush of rising water and spun it out in double pools. Broken piles disappeared inches beneath the swell, and swirled a green hair of weed. Down the river, beyond the wall, rocks sloped into the falling and rising, the bottom ones wet, Kelly-green.

"What's that over there," I asked a fat man fishing, pointing to the hedge of buildings across the river. "Is that still Detroit?"

"That's Canada," the man said. He had glasses, small circles of light on his face.

A double branch in the water moved up and down, one arm carrying a hemping of brown, wet grass, a conductor to the river's risings.

"I guess we know where we are," I said. "We've seen the Y, the hospital, the police station and the river." The wall began to whiten beside us; suddenly I had a shadow and there was heat on the back of my neck.

Walking back, on the under streets behind the train-yards, rusty puddles tinted the billowings of reflected sky liquid amber. The street lamps creaked with breezes.

———

Over the river, a moving cloud rolled back gray to reveal the water smoked, algae green. And sunlight advanced up the bank to where we were, and our knees and hands lightened suddenly.

+ + +

Auberon

§ 1

In a field of grain on the outskirts of Detroit, early one Sunday afternoon, a horse died.

§ 2

Miss G. Alice Stein looked across the desk top at the plump face of a girl about twelve, with brown hair the color of sycamore bark.

"I want a room," said the girl.

"Are you alone, dear?" Miss Stein asked.

The girl reached up and took one of the pens from the pen holder and looked at it, hard. "I just got off the bus from New York, and I have no place to stay. Do you have any 'Y' stationery."

"A . . . only picture postcards," Miss Stein said. "I thought you wanted a room, dear?"

"Yes, please," the girl said. "And twelve picture postcards."

"Let me sign you in first. Write your name here."

Miss Stein opened a black ledger and turned it toward the girl, who had begun to chew the end of the pen.

"Right on this line dear," Miss Stein pointed. The girl took the pen from her mouth and printed in large uneven letters, "MESSALINA SCHMIDLAP." Then she turned the book around.

"*What* is your name, dear?"

The girl leaned across the desk toward her. **"My name is Martha**. But I'm traveling incognito."

(Miss Stein had taken the key to room 1066 and placed it on the desk. Then she started to fill out the receipt.)

She picked up the key and went to the elevator, pressed the button, and the door opened.

"What floor, dear?"

"1066," Martha said. "That's my room."

"Well, that's on the 10th floor, dear," explained the elevator operator. The elevator girl had an immense admiration for Miss Stein and called everybody dear with ludicrous results. "You can tell floors from the room numbers by the first number."

"10 please," said Martha.

The elevator was large and walled with creaking, brass doors.

"Are you all alone, dear?" asked the elevator operator.

"For the present," said Martha. "How much do picture postcards cost."

"2 for 5 cents, I believe," said the elevator girl.

They reached ten; the elevator girl pulled the doors open, and pointed down the hall. "That way, dear."

Martha did not say thank you **and walked quickly down the hall in the direction of the pointed finger. The first room number she saw was 1051. The next was 1050. At 1046 Martha stopped and rapped tentatively on the door. It flew open, and she was confronted by a large, ruddy, naked girl with curlers and red pubic hair.**

"Which way is room 1066?" said Martha. "And don't call me 'dear.'"

"I shan't call you anything if I can help it," said the girl, "and I don't think there is a room 1066." The door slammed shut.

Martha went back five paces to 1047 and knocked again, harder this time.

"Can I help you, dear," said a high voice behind her.

"Damn," said Martha, turning around. In front of her was a pillowy woman in a mauve taffeta dressing gown, with a cake of soap in one hand and a towel in the other.

"There's no one in there, dear."

Martha debated between an imperative and the question: "Which way is room 1066?" The question won.

"I'm not sure," said the woman. "Is someone you know staying there?"

"It's my room," said Martha. "I am. Only I can't find it."

"Are you all alone, dear?"

"Look—" said Martha.

The woman suddenly laughed and the towel shook at her wrist. "You know," she said, "I bet you're awfully annoyed at people treating you as if you didn't know anything."

"Hum?" said Martha.

"Here, open the door and come in with me. I have a hot plate in my room and we can have tea. I'm not supposed to, however. And you can't tell Miss Stein. She's the woman at the desk."

"I just want to find [my] room ..."

"After we have some tea, we'll look for it together. Open that door, will you; it isn't locked. I have both hands full."

Martha turned back around and opened the door. Two orange furred Pekinese stood on the dresser, staring at her with black, beady eyes.

"You have *dogs*," said Martha. "Is that allowed at the Y? Do they bite?"

"They don't bite," said the old woman behind her, "and they're allowed because they aren't alive. They're stuffed."

The hot plate sat between a blue eyed Siamese cat and a medium sized goat with a pigeon perched on one horn. The tableau was crowded onto the writing table by the window.

"I do all my own taxidermy," said the woman. She put the soap and towel on the dresser, opened a drawer whose insides glittered with implements and put the soap and towel away in one corner, took two teabags from the other, and then two sets of mis-matched cups and saucers.

"My name is Octavia De Clivity," she said, filling a tea-pot with water from a sink in the corner, above which was a sardine on a wooden plaque.

"My name is Messalina Schmidlap. But you can call me Martha."

"Messalina?" said Miss De Clivity. "How classical. I'm sure we'll get along very well."

She set the teapot on the hot plate and plugged it in.

"Sit down over there and tell me about yourself."

"Messalina isn't really my name at all," said Martha. "But I hope we get along well anyway." She smiled and sat down on the bed, while Miss De Clivity sat down in that chair by the writing table and crossed her legs.

"Do you have any postcards?" Martha said.

"I don't think so," said Miss De Clivity. "I'm sure I could spare you some stationery and stamps, though."

"You see, I have to send out the announcements," said Martha.

Miss De Clivity handed Martha a sheet of pale lavender paper from the writing table. "Will this do?"

"Announcements for what?" she added.

Across the top in deep mauve lettering was engraved:

Octavia De Clivity
— Taxidermist.

"Marriage announcements," Martha said. She looked at the paper for a few seconds and frowned. "I really don't think so," she said. "Although it's very pretty."

"Oh, I understand," said Miss De Clivity. "Not for marriage announcements. Who's getting married?"

"I am," said Martha.

"Oh?" Said Miss De Clivity. "Aren't you a little young?"

Martha looked at her hands. "I have to," she said.

Miss De Clivity raised one eyebrow after the other.

"I just told everybody that I was going to, and they'd laugh at me if I didn't."

"Just whom did you tell," asked Miss De Clivity.

"I left a note for my parents on the table," said Martha.

"I see," said Miss De Clivity. "Were you going to marry anybody in particular, or were you just [...] getting married?"

"Just get[ting] married," Martha said.

"After tea," smiled Miss De Clivity, "why don't we instead of looking for your room, go take a walk to your parents' house and we can all talk this over."

"They live in New York," said Martha, "so we'd have to take a bus."

"You came all the way from New York to Detroit to get married?"

"On the bus," smiled Martha. "It took all night."

"Why did you come to Detroit?" demanded Miss De Clivity.

"Because the wife and the husband both only have to be 18 to do it without parents consent."

"Oh," said Miss De Clivity. "But that still doesn't help you any, does it."

"I know," said Martha. "But at least they don't have a double standard."

"Oh," said Miss De Clivity. "Oh. I see."

"I'm socially conscious," said Martha and sat a little straighter.

Miss De Clivity looked at the plump little girl in blue jeans sitting on her bed, and finally said, "Have some tea."

"Yes ma'am," Martha said. "Thank you for not calling me dear."

"That's perfectly all right," said Miss De Clivity. "After tea, I guess we'll go look for 1066."

"Thank you," Martha said again.

They sipped tea from the mismatched coffee cups and Miss De Clivity gave her a marzipan.

"It tastes funny," said Martha.

"Keep it until you get hungry," Miss De Clivity said.

They went outside, across the 10th floor lobby, and through the lounge.

"Here it is," said Miss De Clivity. "It was on the other side of the building."

Martha put her key in the lock, turned it and stepped inside. "Thank you," she said, turning to Miss De Clivity.

"Anytime," said Miss De Clivity. "And I want you to come and see me very soon. In fact you must drop in this evening. We'll have dinner together and talk some. Remember now."

"Yes ma'am," Martha said.

Just then a bevy of 16/17-year-old girls came down the hall laughing loudly.

"Who are they?" asked Martha.

Miss De Clivity humphed. "I call them the campfire girls," she said. "The most obnoxious bunch of children. They are all practicing to be wayward minors or unmarried mothers or something. Well, I'll see you for dinner."

"Yes *ma*'am," said Martha.

Inside, she waited for Miss De Clivity's footsteps.

§ 3

Martha was sitting on a rock in the middle of a field.

§ 4

Miss G. Alice Stein, on her lunch hour, took long walks through downtown Detroit. She left her desk, called "So long" to the elevator operator, and walked outside & down the steps. Judge Larned, whose great-grandfather had had a street named after him, was coming down the block on a pale green motor scooter.

"Hello, Judge," Miss Stein called.

"Can I give you a lift, ma'am?" asked Judge Larned. He was a rotund man; he took out a red bandana and swabbed his face.

"Not really," said Miss Stein. "But thank you. No, I was just going to walk around some and take in some air."

"Mind if I putter along beside you?" Judge Larned asked. He finished swabbing his face and leaned over to wipe off the windshield.

"Pale green and red," said Miss Stein. "You clash."

The judge grinned. "I know," he said. "It's part of my charm." He sat back in the seat, and the machine began to roll forward with the sound of bicycle spokes on small balloons. Miss Stein walked along the curb and the judge kept more or less abreast of her.

"Sure you wouldn't like to hop up behind me and take a run around the park there?"

"No thank you, Judge," smiled Miss Stein. "Say, how is that sanitation bill coming. You were telling me about it last week."

"Well," mused the judge above the puttering of the motor scooter, "I'd say we'll have it through in a week. Senator Harrington, he really thinks of it as his baby. It would be a real blow to him if it didn't get passed. It's getting so he feels positively paternal to every old garbage can he sees. But Harrington's a good man. I had dinner with him last night. He and his wife were just as pleasant as could be. And we both feel that it will be a real boon to the city."

"What exactly are the provisions of the bill," asked Miss Stein. "I still don't understand it."

"Polychromatic sanitation program."

"Polychromatic?" asked Miss Stein.

"It means," said the judge, "that we shall have three different color garbage cans."

"At last," said Miss Stein, dryly. "What in the world for?"

"To facilitate garbage disposal," rhapsodized Judge Larned, "we shall have garbage cans of three different colors: red, green, and yellow. Red for urgent garbage, green for not so urgent garbage, and yellow for napkins, old newspapers and non-putrifying matter."

"What is urgent garbage?" asked Miss Stein.

"Old, dead things and rotten fruit," said Judge Larned.

"Do we have enough garbage in Detroit to make that sort of plan really practical. I mean, do we have enough *urgent* garbage."

"Oh we did an extensive study, got the best brains from the university. Dr. J. Theotoropolus M'Bwunga, an exchange student from Ghana whose mother was Greek I believe, did a beautiful job on the report. We sent mimeographed copies to just everybody."

"What were the results of the study?"

"I really haven't the slightest idea," said Judge Larned as they went around the corner. "I couldn't read past the first two pages, but it was impressive as hell."

"Do you think it's impressive enough to get the bill passed."

"It better be," said Judge Larned, "it was a $50,000 study."

Miss Stein "tisked" twice and shook her head. "All that on garbage."

"All that on the polychromatic refuse disposal program," Judge Larned corrected. "If this bill goes through, we're going to give the most bang-up luncheon for Dr. M'Bwunga that Detroit has ever seen. Keys to the city, everything."

"I'd like to meet the good Doctor," said Miss Stein.

"Surely," replied the judge. "I could get you a ticket to the luncheon; no trouble at all. Even maybe get you on the dais, representative of Detroit's home for friendless girls."

"That's not what the YWCA is at all," said Miss Stein. "We are a place for young women away from home."

"Well," said Judge Larned. "You know this is the kind of affair where money—real money—gets passed around. You want to make a little speech and maybe get a donation."

"Oh, I couldn't," said Miss Stein.

"Everybody else is making speeches," replied Judge Larned. "You could really do the YW a favor."

"I really don't think I could," said Miss Stein. "What would I say."

"That would be up to you," said the judge. "But I know you could think up something. You're efficient, you're practical—you're a good woman, Miss Stein."

"Oh, thank you Judge."

"Well," said the judge, "I guess I'd better be puttering off downtown. You think about what I said."

"I will," said Miss Stein. "Really I will."

§ 5

Two parties arrived at the warm marble steps of the YWCA at a fifteen second discrepancy. The first was a flustered Englishwoman covered with Pan Am bags and loose, red fox boa, who bustled up the steps, nearly tripping over the top one, and made for the desk with the purposeful stride of a nearsighted moose. The second consisted of a hulking deaf mute, a tall, wispy transvestite, a somewhat pudgy little girl, and a dead horse. Chester was whistling "Goodbye Old Paint."

As they started up the steps, Chester looked back over his shoulder (they were carrying Auberon hind end first) at Martha who was walking between George and Chester in the shade, and said, "Well, here goes nothing. I've always wanted to get into the YWCA."

"Onward," said Martha, and giggled.

In the YWCA lobby, the Englishwoman had *just* dropped two of her Pan Am bags, pounded loudly on the desk and demanded a room, and Miss Stein had just returned from the inner office after putting a refill in the ballpoint pen which chose to run out at the most inopportune times, when Chester, holding Auberon's tail end above his head, came through the door and up the steps. An incoming breeze whipped the skirt of his dress high around his shins.

"I'd like a room with a private bath," said the Englishwoman.

"Certainly," said Miss Stein. She filled out a receipt, turned the ledger around, looked up brightly to hand the woman the pen, and said: "Yahrgaaaablablayahha . . ."

"Come again?" said the Englishwoman.

"Ohhhhha," said Miss Stein. Then she flung the pen across the lobby and sat down hard on the floor behind the desk.

"Here, here," demanded the Englishwoman and leaned across the desk to see where Miss Stein had disappeared to.

"I thought you said there wasn't going to be anybody in the lobby?" Chester said.

Martha frowned. "Well, then we better get it upstairs before anybody sees us."

Chester shrugged and began to whistle "The old gray mare she ain't what she usta be."

"Here, here," demanded the Englishwoman, still leaning over the desk. "I want the key to my room. My good woman, where have you gotten to?"

A bevy of campfire girls suddenly emerged from, and immediately retreated back into, the main television lounge with a rising squeal.

By now, the Englishwoman was standing in a veritable heap of Pan Am bags; once more she began to pound on the desk and look vaguely around the register's office.

"Service," she said. "Here, here, let's have some service. Desk clerk? Desk clerk!"

Miss Stein pulled herself to the edge of the desk, gurgled in the direction of the red ink well, beyond which Chester and George with Auberon above and Martha between were passing toward the elevator.

"Stand up and give me my room key," said the English. "Really." Suddenly the Englishwoman looked down, and, seeing her dropped Pan Am bags, bent down to pick the largest one.

Miss Stein, her field of vision cleared for the moment, gained her footing and managed to call, breathlessly, "You . . . You . . . You can't bring that into the YWCA." She waved her arm vaguely in the direction of George who was supporting Auberon's bulkier half.

"Oh, that's all right—he's a girl too," said Chester, holding his half of Auberon aloft with one hand and doffing his wig with the other.

The Englishwoman finally hefted the Pan Am bag onto the desk.

"You can't bring that into the YWCA," declaimed Miss Stein once more.

"Why on earth not?" demanded the Englishwoman, looking up and panting a little with the effort.

"Because it's a . . ." Then she saw the Englishwoman. "Oh god," she [said], her eyes imploring sympathy.

"*Will* you give me my key."

Martha rang the elevator bell at the other end of the lobby.

"Dead horse," said Miss Stein poignantly.

"You may bloody well curse at me," barked the Englishwoman, "but I think you're acting downright un-Christian. I'll have you know I was on the founding committee of the YWCA in Kenya, and have as much right to be here as you do."

"Dead horse?" ventured Miss Stein, meekly.

"My kingdom for a . . ." echoed Chester with magnificent bravado as they disappeared into the elevator.

"*What* dead horse!" exploded the Englishwoman, rolling her eyes around and losing three more Pan Am bags. "*Will* you give me my key."

The elevator girl had remarkable presence of mind. She did not begin to scream until they passed the third floor. By the seventh, the scream had turned into hiccoughs, and when they left the car on the tenth, she was cowering in the corner and waving her arm futilely after them, accompanying her gesticulations with a sound in between the gulp of a thirsty wildebeest and a chihuahua in heat.

In the tenth-floor lounge, a large ruddy girl in blue toreador pants was playing Baptist hymns on the piano for the spiritual edification of 5 sixteen-year-old girls who clustered about her like pale, quivering rosebuds.

"My room is on the other side of the lounge," Martha said to Chester. "This way."

"Do you know the limerick," said Chester, as they entered the lounge, "that begins,

'There once was a hermit named Dave,
Who kept a dead horse in his cave ...'"

"That's not the way I've learned it," said Martha.

"Knowing little girl, aren't you," said Chester.

"The way I've learned it, it went, 'There once was a hermit ...'"

"My god," screamed one of the campfire girls. "What is that ..."

"His soul goes marching on," concluded the ruddy girl and turned around on the piano stool. "Yahrgaaaablablayahha ..." she added, in an amazingly accurate imitation of Miss Stein.

"Doesn't that sound like the county in Faulkner?" asked Chester.

"You've read Faulkner too?" Asked Martha.

"You know," Chester went on, "I can't understand why everyone says 'My god, what's that,' when they can see perfectly well what it is."

Three campfire girls had become hopelessly entangled with the pedal apparatus beneath the piano.

"Hey," said Martha, "Chester! That girl has pubic hair the same color as your wig."

"Do tell," said Chester, looking back over his shoulder as they left the lounge. "Which way to your room. This thing is heavy."

"This way," said Martha.

"It's a dead horse," cried one of the campfire girls at last and then broke down completely.

Martha swung back into the room around the doorjamb. "No it isn't," she said. "It's a live cow; but it's asleep." She darted back down the hall after George, Chester, and Auberon.

"Hey Chester," she called. "That limerick, it goes: 'There once ...'"

"I know, I know," called Chester, "'... there once was a little girl named Martha, who kept a dead horse at the YWCA.' Where the hell do we put this damn thing."

"Right here," called Martha, skipping in front of them. She put her key in the lock, looked back at Chester and frowned. "That's not the way it goes at all."

"Watch out," said Chester, and he and George barged into the room.

"One, two, three," said Chester, "heave." The mirror on the desk shook with the crash. "Well, that's a relief," said Chester, rubbing his arms. He sat down on the bed and arranged his skirt about him across the bedspread.

George, using Auberon as a doorstep, hoisted himself on top of the dresser, turned around and sat down; he blinked his quiet brown eyes at Chester, Auberon, and Martha and let his heels thud against the lower drawer.

"What do we do with it now?" asked Martha, innocently.

"*You're* asking *me*?" said Chester. "You were the one who wanted it up here."

"I know," said Martha. You wait right here. I'll be back." She turned, ran down the [hall], went through the lounge skipping ponderously over the legs of prostrated campfire girls, and presently knocked on the door of 1047.

Octavia De Clivity, taxidermist, answered the door in her mauve dressing gown, looking pillowier than ever. "Oh, hello there," she said. "How are you coming along."

"Fine thank you," said Martha. "I have something for you to taxiderm."

"Really?" smiled Miss De Clivity. "Did you kill it yourself?"

"No ma'am," said Martha. "Come and see it." She started Miss De Clivity down the hall. "What is it?"

"You'll see," said Martha.

"Did you hear all that racket out here a few minutes ago?" asked Miss De Clivity. "I wonder what it was."

"Let's go around the lounge," said Martha. "All those silly girls are in there."

"Certainly," said Miss De Clivity.

When they reached Martha's door, Chester was still sitting on the bed.

"You can't stuff that," Miss De Clivity said. "It's alive."

"Not Chester," said Martha impatiently. "Auberon!"

Miss De Clivity looked across the room to where George sat on top of the dresser drawer, blinking.

"But dear, you can't stuff a human being. I mean a live one."

"Auberon," said Martha, pointing emphatically. "Auberon! Auberon!"

Then Miss De Clivity saw it. She regarded it with the utmost gravity for fully three minutes until Chester began to hum the opening snatches of the William Tell Overture.

Miss De Clivity turned to Martha and said seriously, "Don't you think you're overdoing it a little bit?"

"Hm?" Asked Martha.

"I really don't think I have provisions for stuffing that," said Miss De Clivity.

+ + +

Maxine and Mylum are fraternal twins, age 65, who dwell on East 5th Street where they may be seen at dawn and sunset browsing among the more exotic wildlife. Their mauve brocade and lavender lace coats are legend among the natives. In *Auberon,* their latest book, they return to the familiar territory which so endeared them to readers of their former volumes, *A Child's Book of Home Taxidermy, Coming of Age in East Orange,* and *How to Breed the Okapi in Your Own Home.* Maxine is the author of a volume of devotional poetry entitled: *Compost.*

+ + +

This story has that quality of charm and ingenuousness that one associates with children's books which cop the Newbery Medal.
Yet there is something—how shall we put it—decadent about it all.
Its main characters are
>   A little girl named Martha
>   (alias Messalina Schmidlap)
>   A lady taxidermist
>   A wispy transvestite
>   A deaf mute tentatively known as George
>   And a dead horse.

+ + +

Didn't Richard Eberhart write a poem about a dead ground-hog

Would you believe it—*I* have a dead horse!
"It's mine," said Martha. "You're just carrying it for me."

"A horse, a horse, my kingdom for a horse ..."

Exits, pursued by a dead horse ...

The ride of the Valkyrie

Fragments for Chester

Whistles: Goodbye Old Paint

The old gray mare she ain't what she used to be

You spotted snake with double tongue
Come not near our dead horse

There once was a hermit named Dave,
Who kept a dead horse in his cave ...

Hiyo, Silver

There once was a young girl named Martha
Who kept a dead horse in a room at the YWCA

Strange that I resort to this old journal to record the events of the past several weeks. Except the small notebook, this is all I have, and the entries must be scattered through the following pages in a most un-orderly manner for want of space. However, it is the 12th or 13th of September, 1961. Marilyn is asleep on the other bed and we are at our apartment on Fifth Street. She told me she was pregnant two months ago, no—not quite. And we talked and laughed and cried through those first nights rejoicing, as we walked along the white lit concourse, something which I cannot call youth—because we are still both below 20—but a clarity and alertness as sharp as the edge of broken streetlights and as penetrating as silver wire.

We decided, for parental reasons, to go to Detroit to get married, and we left on a bus the afternoon after I saw Mike and Virginia off to Europe on the *Leonardo da Vinci*. I remember I sat on the top bunk and spirited canapés off the trays as they were carried by during the departure party. The cabin was maddeningly crowded and the upper berth was the only place I could sit.

Oh, we had prepared for this; we had an apartment already, and Bernie had cosigned the lease, and thanks to a loan from David and another from Sharon Rohm we were able to go and come back from Detroit.

We left that night, joking mightily about the work of literary criticism we were to write, and the notes we made are still in the little notebook. We had our traveler's checks; we had planned to hitchhike home and so had bed rolls rather than suitcases, and I sat on the bus, leisurely, half asleep in the rumbling rolling darkness, watching us with bed rolls, striding along 42nd St. looking like two strange children, stopping at Hector's for dinner and getting stared at by also-rans of people who must have thought Marilyn, in her hiking pants, her fresh but make-up-less face, a lesbian.

We stopped in Philadelphia and Toledo, each just long enough to wander around a few blocks of the still cities: I found that waitresses, or at least our waitress, in Toledo, had no idea what Danish pastry was, which was quite surprising, since Danish pastries, paradoxically, I have always considered as American as ham and eggs.

Once in Detroit, we registered at the Y, and descriptions of our first day are in the little notebook. We even took the bus to Canada and wandered through the clean suburban streets of Windsor brushed with an occasional trine leaf from the late August trees. Later, as a companion volume to the literary criticism, we decided to write a joint comic novel during the time we waited for a license which we applied for the second day there. The novel we later (about three days ago) tried out on David Litwin and Randy Mueller who had come down to help us paint, but without too much effect; Marilyn read it to them while I painted the windows. Randy went to sleep on the floor and David just got fidgety. I believe it was mostly due to the reading, because my dear wife would begin to giggle just before each joke or have to stop in the middle of a sentence to switch notebooks or decipher a forgotten word. Oral humor is entirely timing and I must admit, *Auberon* (which is the book's present title) would be far funnier to read to oneself. Or at any rate, authors should never read their own works, unless they have time to prepare the reading. At any rate, though it made the dullest reading imaginable, it was the most enjoyable experience conceivable in the writing. We talked, roved the Greek sections of Detroit, explored our hearts and minds like children looking into closets or old tree trunks with honey coated fingers. Would what we found in the great profundity of love be classed serendipity? We did not look to find, but found anyway, and so much.

We were married in the office of Judge Cartwright at nine o'clock, Thursday morning, August 24, and the court clerk, a small man with hairy and freckled hands, made jokes before and after.

We ran almost straight from the courthouse to the bus, only stopping for a nap and knapsacks.

We found that we really did not have enough money to hitchhike safely home. And so we were back on the bus, a ride full, for me, of the murky sunrise of the next morning seen beyond Cleveland's factories and the steel trellis of some bridge outside the green glass of the bus window. Morbid beauty, the sun hidden yet salmon brilliant in draperies of clouds.

And then at last we were home. Or in New York at any rate. We went up to Bernie's, and with keys from David and Claude, we bathed, loved, and at last came down to the apartment. Paul Elitzik came with us (we called him from Bernie's), and after extracting (how proper a word) some money from the bank we went over and looked at the apartment. It was depressing I must admit.

+ + +

They are playing outside with the fire hydrant; the water makes a white flood over the gleaming asphalt, and all the broken faced buildings, the wet street and the gleaming highlights of wet children's arms and sides are blurred by the mercury vapor street lamps which look so clean, efficient and incongruous in the squalor of this neighborhood. The children, boys mostly, take beer cans with both ends removed and, kneeling behind the hydrant, use the cans as pipes and direct the water into luminous blue white veils up into the night. They have to hold on tight, or the hundred odd pounds of water pressure will tear the can away. They hug that black steel wart so tight they look like they are fucking it. Sometimes a can is torn away and the arc breaks apart into a momentary rainbow as it falls back over the street.

*   *   *

I had gone out to Bernie's to type up the layout for my book of poems. When I got in, Marilyn wasn't here.

(We came back from Detroit, and how well the families took it; my uncle Myles invited us up to Greenwood Lake for the Labor Day weekend and we wandered out one night along the dark mountain roads, bound beneath the bubble of the night, wandering into the lightning that flashed away in the distance over the hill, a silent storm too far away. Sometimes there were great hollowed fields beside us, sloping up to the smooth rhythms of the mountains far and black away; other times, the trees clicked off the great magnitude of the sky into a diminishing V of night above us, and the broad road, a similar lambda below. We were lost together, in the fatigue of three hours walking, and sometime later when we were back at the house, in bed, the breeze through the screen whipped up the odor of the honeysuckle Grandmother and little Karen had picked for us and put in the vase in our room.)

When she came in, she closed the door, looked at me, and her face was broken up into fright. "I went out," she said. "And I got an ice pack from the druggist. I called the doctor, and he said to take these sedatives until the pain goes away ... and you weren't here," and her face was going further and further apart like pieces of broken china in a slow motion picture of a shattered plate.

"Hey, come on," I said. "You better lie down."

"I hurt for the last three hours, and the drugstore man gave me some ice cubes for the icepack, here."

Only she didn't hold out the bag to me.

"Come on," I said again. "Look, what is it."

"I know damn well what it is," she said. I put my arm around her shoulder and we started going to the bedroom. "He put some ice cubes in the ice bag and ... oh, it hurts!"

"Lie down," I said. She sat on the edge of the bed.

"Lie down," I said again. Everything looked hard and brittle. She was wearing the red skirt and the gray and white seersucker shorts, and her brown hair was in a braid, and her face kept breaking apart again and again, now; I lifted her feet up on the bed and she put her head very far back and closed her eyes real tightly. I started unbuttoning her shirt, the red falling back from the pinkish white hue of her skin, only a lot more white than pink. When I looked at her face again, her eyes were open, and she was staring at me, and for a second I wondered if she knew who I was.

"I didn't know when you were coming," she said. "I waited. I kept on waiting. Where are you going—?" And she almost got up on her elbow.

"Just to get a washcloth," I said. I got a washcloth in the kitchen and filled it with warm water; then I brought it back.

"Is it cold?" She asked as I bent down to sponge her face.

"It's warm."

When the dark green cloth touched her, she breathed, in or out, I'm not sure, and closed her eyes again.

We got her shirt off; the shorts were bloody inside the crotch, and her underpants were stained in streaks of the curves of her groin's gulch, like fingers clutching there.

Every time I took off a piece of her clothing, I'd run with it into the other room; the dirty laundry and the suitcase were still open and strewn about the big room.

Finally she asked me again where I was going when I started out of the room again and I realized I was running around like I was crazy.

I stood hard on the ground till my calf muscles hurt. Her bra was a nearly flat slab of white quilted material over her breasts, and the underpants, they were all wet and bloody ...

"Come here?" she asked, and I sat down on the bed and she put her arms around my shoulders. I held her, patting her back like you would a little child. "Keep your hands still," she said. "Just hold me."

I tried to hold her and be still, but my arm was trembling, and when I looked at her, I could tell she could feel it because her face was still going apart and letting the fear leak out the cracks. "The doctor said if I kept on bleeding I should go to the hospital. He says maybe I've already miscarried and I just don't know it yet."

+ + +

The method of art is not "solving the little problems though *still* keeping sight of the whole," but rather keeping sight of the whole *by* solving each little problem as it comes.

+ + +

When my wife says, charmingly, on the phone, "Well, that's nice," you can tell something catastrophic is happening; she said it this evening, and I found out a friend of ours had been smuggling refugees out of East Berlin.

+ + +

SONNET AFTER RIMBAUD
A is onyx, U verdant, ivory E, O blue—
You vowels pierce my heart with darts of lucent silk:
Rouge I. I whirl, tumble, torture, and conquer you
With love, similarities of sound, lulled L's, ilk
Lullabies typed to trip up among themselves
With stuttering cacophonies of consonants.
My song to you oozes smoothly over those shelves
Of my lips where imploded sounds rival the sense.
How cynically abstracted from the realm of sound!
Meaning sours on the high wind, and mounts higher still,
Or drifts, arbitrarily, this way like a leaf, turns round,
Lifts on a breeze, floats the other way. Yet it will
Reach the ground; my quiet will rise up, for then
Sounds cascade down upon one another again.
Oct. 1960

+ + +

For poetry I say to the unwary
Is passion with a dash of dictionary.

Life is too serious & love's too precarious
And my equilibrium's not what it should be.
My taste's too singular & yours is too various
And I'm sick to death of ambiguity.

My therapist told me while back in analysis
Your life has a pattern that you've got too set
The people who suffer from moral paralysis
Don't get what they want but they want what they get.

Oh love's a delight for a day and a night dear
But everything falls after reaching a peak
I guess that fidelity is bad for virility
Cause you charge your battery at least once a week

You see lots of things when you're rambling and drifting
A bit of the best and a bit of the worst
The one truth I've gleaned out of all of this sifting
Is "Do unto others or they'll do you first."
—M. T. Hacker

"My sexual development has been so ambivalent,"
Replied the young husband, "I cannot see why
That as long as I don't find the both of you equivalent
We'll all muddle through and we'll somehow get by.

Quoth he, "If my background weren't so heterogeneous
We wouldn't be in such a miserable plight
Life would be easier if you were androgynous
Or if I were, perchance, a hermaphrodite

Up spoke the third party of this [*cause*] *célèbre*
"You've done it by ones and by threes and by fives"

Our terms are confused; so that this "Dear John" letter
I can't figure out what it signifies

You'll find that I don't care a fig for society
I'll do what I want and I'll screw whom I please
You'll find it provides a delightful variety
To do it by ones and by twos and by threes

Most people suffer from narrow mentality

+ + +

"The little mice are squeaking under
notebooks of the child of wonder."

> M. T. Hacker
> Midnight, Jan 4, 1962
> while reading Amy Lowell's biography of Keats.

+ + +

Reasons exist only in the mind of man. In nature, things only react to things which are themselves reactions to previous reactions. Man's search for reasons for his *action*[s] (and man is unique [in] that he acts in nature as well as reacts—to be proven by circular reasoning), either to prompt them or explain them, is an attempt to escape his gratuitous position in the universe—an attempt to escape the responsibilities that Camus deduced us to have from the paradox of the absurd which is the paradox of gratuitous man in the ordered universe.

+ + +

Liadain of Corkaguiney, a 7th-century A.D. poet in Ireland, on a political round of poetic visit, met and fell in love with Cuirithir, another poet who had made an ale-feast for her. "Let us marry," said Cuirithir. "A son born to us would certainly be a famous poet." Liadain consented to go with him, but not until she and her entourage of twenty-four poet-pupils had completed the visits to the lords and nobles whom they were scheduled to visit.

After leaving Cuirithir, she began to brood on her passion. Cuirithir had spoken of fame, not love. Why a son, why not a daughter? Did he wish to insult her poetic gift? Would [he] expect her to leave poetry and be only a mother of possible future poets? When Liadain finished her circuit, had exchanged poetic lore with other poets of Ireland, she returned to court to wait for Cuirithir, but took first a vow of chastity that would kill her if broken.

The ending of the tale is that Cuirithir came for her, was overwhelmed with grief, but true to their love, they went together. Cuirithir took a similar vow, and they placed themselves in the monastery of St. Cummine who gave Cuirithir the choice of either speaking with Liadain, but not seeing her, or seeing her though not allowed to talk with her. A poet, he chose speech. Eventually Cuirithir asked that the severity be relaxed, but was banished by the enraged St. Cummine for being unchaste.

+ + +

December 6, 1961

Marilyn went to visit W. H. Auden this afternoon. They discussed her poems. She reports the bed was unmade & Chester's blue kimono (in which he surprised her on the landing a week ago, saying: "Can't you call before you come barging over. It's the *middle* of the night." This at 2:00 in the afternoon) was lying across it. Wystan objected to the off-rhymes in "Cain" because there were only 2; "Rock" & "Struck." How ridiculous! He asked her if it were just because she couldn't find a rhyme for it! This is the statement of a man who rhymes "weak" with "physique." Marilyn says he is agreeably grotesque with deep wrinkles and jowls. He and Chester are coming to dinner after Christmas.

+ + +

Every once in a while, Marilyn gets disgusted with me, and one day, when I was declaiming "Put out the light, and then put out the light," she mumbled, "Moors!" And we laughed. Another phrase slips into our catch box along with "Hey! Hey!" "I can't, you're lying on my head!" "Tired hysterical Jewess that you are!" and "The gold-plated meat-hook"—which reminds me: Pierre, of the "Game of the Angels," and notebooks & years ago, has published a novel. Well, he could write. I can remember all the rhymes in that damned poem but I can't remember what it was about.

+ + +

Lucid thought:

The subtleties of English manifest themselves oddly. Conduct & Behavior mean pretty much the same thing, yet "Human Conduct" is filed under philosophy and "Human Behavior" is obviously a psychology text.

+ + +

Wystan Auden does his best
But Chester Kallman is a pest
And must have done strange things to broaden
The (attitude / apertures / tolerance) of Wystan Auden.

—M. T. Hacker

+ + +

Hate has a much tighter warp & woof than lust.

+ + +

It is strange so few moderns have seen that the bad poetry of great poets—and most of it is bad—lies on the side of technical performance and maudlinity of subject, rather than technically sloppy treatment of a basically sound theme. Emily Dickinson and William Blake implode the mind as first examples—and then follows the host.

Maudlinity is often overlooked in the [...] of a man's poetry when power and sensuality mark his successes. For some reason, however, in this year of circled steel, it flays the reputation of women's poems. Thus one monster of American verse, Amy Lowell, is in danger of having her achievements floundered into the oblivious sea. It seems that the only way a woman can survive a fault ignored in men is by pulling the myth. This was done for Emily Dickinson: the figure of the recluse which we bear of her is a) only superficial, and b) a protection woven from her poetry to protect the personality of the poet by her mirror image. Is the ruse used by Byron, by Baudelaire, by Rimbaud, Sappho, Blake, everybody, now that I think of it.

The reason maudlinity is the slough is because of the subject limitation of poetry. By limitation I don't mean Victorian limitation. Robert Graves almost got it at the end of *The White Goddess*, saying all true poetry concerns love, death, or the changing of the seasons. Had I ever bothered to say it, I would have said sex, death, & the changing of the seasons. Love is a reaction we get from these, & in turn use to probe them.

The sad fact is that anyone can learn, or invent technique. Technique includes frame of mind, as well as word slinging. Read Keats, Byron, Amy Lowell, from one end to the other & watch them learn. Some people, Swinburne, Verlaine, Victor Hugo, Dylan Thomas, were born, or seemed to have been, with mouthfuls of language. But this is training. Natalia Crane had it by ten. This training is more training in listening than in writing. The mouth will talk. You must be trained to listen for the right words.

But genius now. Robert Frost said the best thing about that in terms of the "test of time" on great poets. There ain't no such thing. There is sloppy listening, ignorance, & fear of appearing pretentious.

Some sad truths. Most of T. S. Eliot's poetry is prose. Most of the stuff since *The Waste Land* has been muddy, stuffy, & not particularly interesting prose. Most of the Pound is poetry, or at any rate, verse. Pound writes only two kinds of verse. Good verse, and unintelligible verse. Very, very little of any of it is not interesting.

There is William Butler Yeats.

Referring to a particular period, a friend asked me whom I liked. "Yeats," I said, musing over others.

"That's as safe as you can get," he said. "That's like liking Shakespeare." This is true, and it isn't sad.

It is sad, but these three, Lowell, Pound, and Yeats, are about it, in alphabetical order, and reverse order of their importance. Strange, biographically speaking, they got on so badly. Pound vs. Lowell we needn't go into. Pound scribbling "preposterous" over pages of Yeats' manuscripts, some of us do. Amy Lowell siccing her sheepdogs on Yeats, few of us do. And Yeats didn't like either one very much. All three considered the other two insane. Although Pound was the only one to see the inside of an asylum (for more or less non-psychological reasons at that), Lowell's death over Keats, Yeats' mysticism, and Pound's later prose would hint insanity. Never, incidentally, look for insanity in poetry. It doesn't show—ever! Insanity is a property of prose. Madness, on the other hand, afflicts all poets.

The abhorrence of maudlinity in leading poets has led to a host of female poets who categorically never write poems; led by Louise Bogan, followed by Léonie Adams, Muriel Rukeyser, and, as much as I love her, Marianne Moore. They do not write poetry; they write a hard, crystallized, often brilliant prose. They are intelligent, alert, upright, & square, fine critics, and write brilliantly cogent essays on poetry which are often very useful. Their better efforts are seldom connected to either love, death, [or] season changing, and often, to nothing. I've never read a good poem yet that didn't state or imply a particular character in a particular situation, usually at the cusp or nadir of a sensational curve. The only exception to this rule worth noting is Phyllis McGinley and [she] avoids it by sheer trickery. And I do not sympathize. Now there are male poets of this type, but they usually don't receive recognition. The only reason that these females do is because [...] the males who are trying—usually pretty horribly—will only let these completely innocuous creatures into the panther-castrate-dog brawl for rungs on contemporary fame ladder. The last time a woman poet was let in, 5,700 of her 6,000 lines were mercilessly & methodically lost, stolen, and misplaced, until we were left with about 300 of them, which still holds her in the moon's crescent: Sappho.

The reason the men are so jealous is simple. Technically they are a lot lower than the women. (This means lazier.) And although their emotional content usually [is] better directed, its intensity, facility of expression, and aptness make it even less palatable at times to the at least artful bubbling of

+ + +

Everyone who has ever concerned himself with literature has at one time asked, What is poetry, and then further, What is good poetry. The answers to both questions end for most people as a catalogue of criteria which never all seem to apply to even the greatest poem, & which occasionally all apply to an obviously bad one. Among many others, one on my list is "Good poetry generates worlds."

A poem does not end with itself. From most good poems we can extrapolate a particular character, in a particular situation, reacting in a certain way. And the good poem lets us into this world through the intensity of the situation. Sometimes, as in *The Rime of the Ancient Mariner*, we directly observe character, situation, and reaction, and the extrapolated world is a metaphysical matrix defining man's universe. Sometimes, as in Keats' sonnet on the sea, or Rossetti's "The Woodbine," we know the character & his reactions only through

+ + +

I Come for to Sing

Prologue

> "We have come from the morning
> On the red robin's wing,

We have followed the linnet,
And we come for to sing."

The five of us were singing from the small concrete platform at the center of the amphitheatre. Beyond the rings of faces, beyond the farthest stone steps, only a handful empty, the oak trees rolling on up Mount Grant swayed and rustled beneath the sound of music. Laura stepped forward now and sang into the screened head of the microphone, her alto voice, tripled by the amplifier, billowed like sails up the mountain:

"From the music that's born
In the red robin's throat,
And the roar of the river
We borrowed our notes."

She threw her head back now and her rope of black hair flung back in the breeze:

"Of the words of young lovers
at Dawn's lingering,
and the song of the Bargemen ..."

And here we all stepped up around her and joined in.

"We come for to sing."

Pete came forward now. Holding the round drum head of his banjo close to the mike, he played through [the] chorus once, with me behind him on the guitar. Light flashed from the metal rim of the instrument and the neck jiggled with his tapping foot.

Tony took the next verse. He's a small dark boy with a rough tenor voice that sounds like a mixture of sand, rusty nails, and honey.

"We follow the morning,
We follow the sun,
But we'll sit down together
When daylight is done.
To the top of the mountain
Our voices will ring

So raise your voice with me
We come for to sing."

The mountains made a rim of stone on the horizon. The sway of black wires from speaker to speaker on the poles around the amphitheater fanned up the slope before us, over the heads of the people—
Now Ann, our soprano, joined with Laura, and, a third apart—

"We have called to our brothers
In every land
Come sing along with us
Come hold out your hand.
And voices will rise
In accord, answering
From all the world over
'We come for to sing.'"

And again we all joined, heads back, with Ann & Tony taking the high harmony:

"Well, here in the center of
this bright rocky ring,
like the sun in the dawning,
I come for to sing."

With the applause still bubbling over us, we went back to our seats at the back of the platform and sat down with the other performers. We are at one of the many folk festivals that happen across the country around the year. If you turn to the back of this book, you'll find a listing of the largest ones, and maybe even get a chance to go to some of them if you find any near you. What do you do at them? Well, there's usually a program of concerts, and sometimes a seminar where some of the more scholarly aspects of folk music get an airing. People, listeners & singers alike, come to learn new songs, swap old ones, sit up late with guitars & banjos, old & new friends, singing, listening, & drinking from one of America's—the world's—deepest cultural wells. Tony, Ann, Laura, Pete, and myself—my name is Chip, incidentally—have been singing, well, separately, all our lives; but together, just over a year. But to tell you about ourselves isn't our job here, except when it tells you something about the music. So each of us is going to tell you about some different aspect of it. Pete, our banjoist, will take up instruments, Laura & Tony—the only two of us who've studied folk music at college—will go into the book learning aspect—here Laura prompts me to add, she & Tony will also go into one of the most adventuresome aspects of it, also, Ballad Hunting, while Ann & I fill in the gaps here & there.

If you come to […] folk music completely raw, which is to say deaf, you might need a sort of historical framework to pin some [of] what's coming onto. And even if you're not completely raw, which is to say you've heard truck drivers whistling nonsense melodies, shop vendors haranguing their goods in the streets of the city, kids jumping to skip rope rhymes, or fiddlers and accordionists sawing and wheezing a country square dance, a little of the what-got-there-when, and how, and because of who, won't hurt. This is what Ann's going to do the chapter following this one.

Most folk songs seem to be two types (with a large overlap, of course). There are coming & going songs. And sit down and listen songs. Coming & going songs swing up like a flock of hawks, with the industrial revolution. They swung up naturally enough, with increased transportation, and great migrations of people. Today they often outweigh the sit down & listen songs in popularity. But the great majority of folksongs are of the sit down & listen type: the love song, the ballad, and the humorous story. Since to be historically accurate we're going to have so much to say about the sit down & listen song, let's start off, even before the history, with some coming and going songs. The first song we sang you was a coming & going song. One of the first songs in the English language for which we still have words & music together is also. Did I say something about coming & going songs & the Industrial Revolution? This predates it by a handful of hundred years. There's a woman who sang this song this afternoon, accompanying herself on the dulcimer—a very simple guitar-like instrument with two strings which are plucked with feathers. Everyone had to sit forward, even with the loudspeakers, to hear this quiet song beneath leaf-rustlings:

THE TURTLE DOVE

Fare thee well my dear, I must be gone,
And leave you for a while;

If I roam away, I'll come back again,
Though I roam ten thousand miles, my dear,
Though I roam ten thousand miles.

After singing it through, she hummed it, and then sang it through once more. And that was all.

The modern English composer Ralph Vaughan Williams made a choral setting of this song which is very popular with high school choruses, but I still think it remains most touching when done as a solo. It adds something to this song to realize that when it was written, the explored section of the world was only five thousand miles in breadth.

+ + +

Not too far from here—we are in the Catskill Mountains—used to be an organization which saved an immense amount of the folk-lore of this area, from the Irish immigrants, songs & stories from the old tanning industries & the lumber trade—the Catskill Folk Museum under the auspices of Camp Woodland. One of their finds was an eighty-year-old folksinger named George Edwards who was living in a small cabin up on one of the mountains. George Edwards netted Norman Studer and Norman Casden, the men in charge, an entire basket full of tape recordings, and one of his best songs, "I walk the road again," is often given an airing at the Festivals around this part of the country. Tony sings this one with Pete on the banjo in a sort of light, but very rhythmic, accompaniment.

Does the first verse look familiar? It's straight from Turtledove. This is an example of what's called the "Folk-process," the change, the dynamic effect that one song has upon another, in words & melody, the effect of social economic conditions. This is an example of the thing which gives us the reason for writing a book rather than just making an anthology of folk music. It's a thing whose significance, we hope you'll find by the end of this book, is a great deal wider than the simple borrowing or exchanging of a verse here and there. In formal literature, this would be dismissed as plagiarism and frowned on. Here [it] is something else entirely. It's the thing that lets us into the seeming paradox that the tradition of folk music is often of a much more immediate influence than [the tradition of] "formal literature" and the much tighter matrix of folk literature allows for this type of exchange—in short the tightness & tradition of this basically informal and improvised art are more formal than "formal" literature.

Without getting too far afield into philosophy and metaphysics, this is what we're going to explore here. And we also hope we won't get too far away from either the music itself, or one of the main purposes of the music—that's, tell a good story and have a good tune.

Ann Speaking:

Down in the parking area for the Grant Folk Festival, is Pete's jalopy. He's chauffeur, being the oldest & the only one with a driving license except Laura. The rows of cars bring to my mind

+   +   +

Outline for *The Jewels of Aptor*

Geo, Snake, Urson—Soldier, Adventurer, Sailor.
Poet—Four Armed
  Mutant Mind
  Read[er]

Ghoul
Werewolf
Vampire

  The Nizam of Aptor
The Princess of Aptor
  Get
  They are entrusted the Jewels by

+   +   +

Marilyn H. Delany
23 W 47th St (between 5th & 6th Ave.)
7th Floor

Precocious genius blossoms in childhood's ritual fiction. The Brontë children, distilling on the Heath of Howbridge half a dozen works of genius from the fantasy of Gondal & Angria. Hartley Coleridge; though the body of his work cannot rival his father's, there is still a handful of jewels mined from the labyrinthine jungles of his childhood world. Thomas Chatterton constructed the world of the monk Thomas Rowley, and peopled it with an exchange of letters and poems, masques, and so forth which still, upon occasion, invokes some critic to suggest that perhaps Chatterton did not invent it, but that it was a historical reality.

+ + +

Lucid thought, Jan 11, 1962:

History is the objective presentation of man's significant actions in such a way that the significance is revealed.

+ + +

Tonight: Read—
          Woody Guthrie
          Amy Lowell
          Amy Lowell on Keats
          Maurois on Byron
Revise—The Night Alone
Write—The Beast
          After Carmina Catulli
          The City
Deliver Script to Be Typed

NOTEBOOK 20 — SPRING 1962

[March 1962]

Geo leaned against the rail. Below him water churned in the rocks, thrashed along the river's sides, and then, as he raised his eyes, stretched out along the sunny blade of the beach. The length of sand that rimmed the island dropped away from them, a stately and austere arc gathering in its crescent all the sun's glare, and throwing it back on wave, and on wave. His back hurt, his stomach twisted into a knot, his arm was gone now, and Urson . . .

. . . He flung his eyes upward, and tried in one moment to envelop what he saw, whatever it would. Beneath the waters' sound was a still layer of quiet. The sandway pale along the naked crescent, dull in some depressions, mirror bright at certain rises. At the jungle's edge, leaves and fronds sent multi-textured green ripplings along the branches. Each tiny indistinguishable fragment in that green carpet hung up in the sun was a single leaf with two sides, two colors, an entire system of skeleton and veins, as his hand and arm had been. And would maybe one day drop off, he reflected. The diminishing strip of sand was still. He looked from rock to rock. Each one different, shaped and lined distinctly, that one like a bull's head in the water, those two flat ones like the stretched wings of eagles. And the waves, ordered and magnificent, followed one another onto the sand, like the differing, never duplicated rhythms of a great poem, yet peaceful, measured, and calm. He tried to pour the chaos of Urson drowning onto the waters' swell, and it seemed to flow into each glass green wave's trough, and ride, suddenly quiet, up to the still beach. He tried to spread the pain in his own body over that even web of white foam and dull green shimmer, and was surprised because it seemed to fit, to hang there well, quieted, very much quieted, and somewhere at the bottom of his brain, a very real understanding was beginning to effloresce with the water of the sea, under the heightening sun . . .

+ + +

About The Author—

Before his disappearance at the age of 21, Samuel Delany (1942—?) left a

+ + +

Dear L.H.

It's I of the infantile handwriting here. The reason this isn't being typed is that last night all sorts of unpleasant people broke into our apartment & looted the place—completely.

How's your mononucleosis? (How does one answer a question like that? Oh, well.) I hope Syracuse is cooler than N.Y.C. We're going to Vermont next weekend; last week we were up at Newport R.I. We're having an ambulatory summer.

6

The Fall of the Towers and *Voyage, Orestes*

After Ace Books accepted *The Jewels of Aptor*, Delany collected several stories with a shared science fantasy setting, stitched them together into a novel, and submitted them to Donald Wollheim. Wollheim rejected the manuscript, and Delany, abashed, recognized that if his next novel was to pass muster it would require more careful planning and thought.[1]

Early in the summer of 1962, Delany wrote some notes for an ambitious science fiction trilogy. Shortly thereafter, during a walk across the Brooklyn Bridge, he and Hacker discussed the project, and upon returning home Delany set to work on it. Early outline material for the trilogy—initially called *Cities of the Flames*, then retitled *The Fall of the Towers*—appears in Notebook 22. Notebook 23 contains additional material for the trilogy, as well as Delany's sensitive reading of Satyajit Ray's "Apu" trilogy of films.

Although Notebooks 24 and 25 overlap chronologically, Notebook 25 has been given priority because it commences with Delany's account of the publication of *The Jewels of Aptor* in the winter of 1962, which precedes the other events recounted in the two notebooks. These same notebooks also contain outlines and other notes for *Voyage, Orestes*; throughout this period, notes and drafts for *The Fall of the Towers* and *Voyage, Orestes* appear alongside one another.

In Notebook 25 Delany mentions his difficulty completing the second volume of the trilogy—a struggle he discusses at greater length in *The Motion of Light in Water*.[2] During this time Delany also worked on several other projects, including *The Ballad of Beta-2*, a short SF novel he wrote as a respite from the second *Towers* volume.[3] Possibly the most significant new project Delany worked on during this period, if only because of the extended labor he put into it, was a novel with no fixed title, which we will here designate as "Faust." Delany would revisit this project for years to come; the characters of Dr. Branning, Montesque, Corbelli, and Wolf, along with specific settings and scenarios, repeatedly appear in subsequent notebooks. Elements from the "Faust" project would eventually find their way into Delany's first published pornographic novel, *Equinox* (1973).

In the summer of 1963, Hacker traveled to Mexico for six weeks of art classes.[4] During this time, Delany took up with an ex-convict named Sonny, who is described in detail in *The Motion of Light in Water.*[5] Eventually, Hacker returned—to find Delany bedridden with a severe bout of pneumonia, which, several days later, landed him first in Bellevue, then in Sydenham Hospital.[6] As indicated in the pages of Notebook 75, while recovering in Sydenham Delany pondered what was to become for him a perennial question for the remainder of the '60s: whether to focus his creative energies exclusively on songwriting and performance.

Delany continued to work on *Voyage, Orestes* and the *Fall of the Towers* trilogy through 1963. On the night of November 21, 1963, Delany finished *Voyage, Orestes.* The next day, he delivered the manuscript to the offices of Bobbs-Merrill—learning, while in transit, of the assassination of President Kennedy.[7]

In the spring of 1964, Delany completed the trilogy. Over the course of the first half of that year, in a state of exhaustion after this period of extraordinary productivity, Delany began to suffer increasingly severe bouts of acrophobia, anxiety, and self-destructive thoughts and impulses.[8] Eventually he admitted himself to the "Day/Night" outpatient psychiatric program at Mount Sinai Hospital, where he would participate in intensive group and individual therapy for several weeks.[9]

NOTES

1. Samuel R. Delany, *The Motion of Light in Water: Sex and Science Fiction Writing in the East Village* (1988; reprint, Minneapolis: University of Minnesota Press, 2004), 186–87. Just over thirty years later, Delany published a revised and expanded version of this novel, *They Fly at Çiron* (Seattle: Incunabula, 1993).

2. Ibid., 277–79.

3. Ibid., 300, 319–20.

4. Ibid., 211.

5. Ibid., 218–25, 232–33.

6. Ibid., 230.

7. Ibid., 317–19.

8. Ibid., 330–31, 333.

9. Ibid., 334–36.

Notes [on] trilogy

Streaks of light speared the yellow clouds, pried the billowing rifts apart. Shafts of yellow sank into the lush jungles of Toromon, dropping from the wet green fronds, or caught in the moist cracks of damp rocks. Dawn caught on the silver ribbon that arced above the trees, and shadows from the immense supporting pylons formed first great gutted stretches of volcanic rock as the ribbon passed above the gutted lava fields that dotted the jungle. As dawn slipped across the planet's face, more and more of the ribbon glinted from beneath receding shadows. Now the light was brighter and shimmered on the surface of the Tarnor sea, like crinkled foil, like flung diamonds, and the bright ribbon running above the water was nearly dull by comparison.

A formation of airships flashed through a break in the yellow clouds like a handful of hurled silver chips, and the accompanying buzz of their tetron motors descended below jungle.

Quorl rolled over and dry leaves crushed under his shoulder.

[sequence continues]

+ + +

Outline

One—written
Two—written
Three—Devil's Pot—Tel has run away to the city, and there he falls in with Alter, a girl just a year older than himself, Rara, her aunt, a charlatan, and & Kanna, who is involved in a plot to kidnap the Prince. They get started.

* * *

The party, where Jon makes his presence known to his sister.

Let is returned to the Devil's Pot.

Last summer, when I was 19, I hiked, hitched, and explored for two months the tip of the country which rises above New York. The real reason for my journey I have to tell you later; but by the day before the one I had set for my return, I had convinced myself that basically I had wanted to see, absorb, and assimilate the roughness and rocky obstinacy of the area and thus tighten myself by the cinch of experience to some sort of idealized manhood.

I had been up to Maine; and then, come down. But the scenes that would flood back to me when I recalled my trip, rather than rough and obstinate, were beautiful enough that my eyes would ache with trying to hold them again.

But if I did not, at bottom, want this visual opulence (I had instructed myself to watch for stone-pocked meadow[s] where bony cows grazed on spare grass too thin, or the grey farmhouses leaned toward disuse—many of both), why did I stop to stare at one cluster of sandsized yellow granules shivering at the end of a green stem of goldenrod—amid sestillions of others!—the one detail that brings up waves & waves of green?

With ambiguous melancholy and disappointment at my preference in scenery, I wound through rock bound New Hampshire, into Massachusetts and down to the sea.

I found her rimmed with froth, a green glass shield below me. As I started the steep trail that led from the granite embankment, the bushes grew close and leaves slipped by my cheek and shoulder. Pebbles scattered across the dirt and over the rocks as I came down, and I glimpsed the water only five times through the foliage once I started.

+ + +

Cities of the Flames
A Trilogy

I. *Out of the Dead City*
II. *The City of the Sea*
III. *Cities of the Sun*

+ + +

Out of the Dead City (Part I)

Prologue—Jon Koshar wakes up to catch a glimpse of a city on the desert of a strange planet with a double sun.

Chapter I
Survey of Konor's society by following the transit ribbon—the mines, where prisoner Jon Koshar has just escaped, the Forest, where guard Kobor is just waking, to the shore where the fisherman's son Tel is about to run away from home, to the island where old man Koshar is inspecting his ships, to the airport, where Clea Koshar is coming home from the university, to the palace where the King is waking up.

Chapter II
John arrives by the transit tube at the palace (background information) and Prince Let is being prepared for the coming war (?) by Petra.

Chapter III
Tel arrives at Konor after running away from home and is enlisted in a plot to kidnap the prince which will somehow help prevent the war.

Chapter IV
Clea's party that evening which Jon attends & meets the Duchess Petra who tells them that Let is to be kidnapped. She too controlled by enemy.

Chapter V
Tel & Alter (a girl acrobat whom he has befriended) kidnap the prince. Tel finds out [that] Gobbe has a brother in the forest. Alter & Let & Tel

These chapters are all written and therefore sketchy to detail and direction

Chapter VI (Usk proclaimed villain)
Jon gets rid of clothes, meets children. Reveals mission. Let is spirited away to the forest guard after a few atrocities.

Chapter VII
Chaos in the city ending in Alter's capture & torture for kidnapping.

Chapter VIII
Peaceful interlude in the forest.

Chapter IX
Jon tries to reach Clea. Succeeds, talk about getting father to stop fisheries, or cut down. (She is working in navigation.) The place stormed by marauders.

Chapter X
Suddenly whisked to another planet—explain that they need to consolidate the three people—Jon thinks it's Konna, Petra, and himself.

Chapter XI
Konna thinks himself guilty for the war and the marauders kill him. Tel tries to save Alter, and succeeds. Tomar launches a full scale attack on Telphar & is killed. (Konna dies—Tel flees, Petra arrives, Tobar arrives.)

Chapter XII
Jon gets Petra, they discover Konna is dead. Clea receives news that Tomar has been killed; vows to grow up.
Rara discovers a woman looking for her son, who uses the words of the queen.
Jon discovers that actually Gobbe was the third agent, and after a speech on freedom, this volume ends.

The Chains of Fire (Part II)

Chapter I
Some time after the close of Volume I.
Uske gives a party at which Chargill, the prime minister, is assassinated.

Chapter II
Petra & Jon give a synopsis of volume one and decide it's time to rescue prince Let.

Chapter III

+ + +

The City and the Flame (Volume II of *Cities of the Flame*)

Notes:
    Chapters II, IV, VI, VIII, X, XII
Tel in the army. Basic training, through his death.

Chapter I
The assassination of Chargill—Jon & Petra fill in background information. Tell about the kidnapping, the imperial turn of the war, the three levels of human being, the triple being. (Alter & Clea, Tel & the army.)

Chapter III
(Alter & Clea.)

Chapter V
Gobbe called in, recognizes the lord of the flames in Usk and detects an underground movement against the aristocracy.

Chapter VII
The Duchess talks about the aristocracy. Tells Jon it's time to go get Tel back, about how at its worst it is sniveling and neurotic, at its best it can applaud its own death knell if it is eloquent enough.

Chapter IX
Jon's adventures to get to Let, and his discovery.

Chapter XI
They join a traveling circus, which turns out to be run by Clea, and get back to Konor.

Chapter XIII
Gobbe, Petra, and Jon confront Usk and he collapses before the hall of victory, & they get the queen to back her son. And he is crowned.

+ + +

To produce something even slightly monumental takes an amazing amount of energy and toil!

+ + +

I am sitting on a small island in the middle of a small pond. There is a weeping willow that shades the entire place. Two great dragonflies just collided over the water and flew away. M. & I have come up to Greenwich to visit Baird's parents. The house is silent and enchanting. I left M. inside taking a nap, and Baird downstairs, sitting on the russet living room floor in his flamenco boots, cleaning the pistols in his fire-arm collection. Tiki (I guess that's how you spell it), a tiny mop of a dog, goes wildly running after rocks and apples. Baird is afraid we'll get bored and I have to keep on convincing him that we couldn't possibly tire of the relaxation in just days.

His mother is the most magnificently alive person I've ever met. She was for a long time a very high paid Madison Ave. copywriter. On most people, this is a chain that binds in their minds, but she wears her stay there very well. Up till now, I didn't think it possible to do so.

Bill, Baird's father, is affable and ursine, yet still silent. He apparently has quite a temper, & we have been warned not to cross it, but there has been little sign of it.

Spent the morning marketing with Mrs. Bruning (Hall, Robinson, etc.) and touring the yachting docks, polo fields, & fabulous little meat-markets & vegetable stands of the township.

There are a series of fantasies that partake to an amazing degree [of] the flavor of the cosmos, and each by very different methods; *The Worm Ouroboros*, *House on the Borderland*, *The Mysterious Stranger*, and *The Lord of the Rings*. They do it [in] a way that such attempts as *She*, my own *Jewels of Aptor*, and various others fail. Ponder this.

+ + +

Tonight (Tuesday, November) we went to see the Ray Trilogy of films at that Charles Theatre. At the end, M. got very sick, and had a terrible headache. It was made worse, I'm sure, by the fact that I had worn no socks and only a pair of Japanese rubber sandals. The weather was below forty and we had to rush home, where she had an attack of vomiting.

Now she is sleeping in the little room and I am in the front room writing.

That set of films, *Pather Panchali*, *Aparajito*, and *Apur Sansar*, make up perhaps the greatest film I have ever seen. *Pather Pachali* and *Apur Sansar* I had seen before, having missed the middle one when they were shown separately. I feel that they should all be seen once, with perhaps a week or month in between, and then they should be seen in a continuous showing. The themes that run through it, especially the visual themes are, first water which starts as the stream by the Ray house, later becomes the river, finally the rainstorm in which Durga catches her fatal cold, becomes (in the second film) the River Ganges by Benares, the water spigot in their courtyard, the pool into which young Apu dives (his mother calls him to come out so that he will not catch a cold—as his sister did and died); then commences the third film as rain, becomes the various rivers, and—one of the most phenomenal scenes—then we see Aparna's mother crying over little Kajal, and as a tear falls from her face, it suddenly becomes a crashing wave, and we see Apu standing by the ocean. At last we see the gentle complex of streams and pools that Apu drinks from in his final confrontation with Pulu over the child, Kajal.

The next theme is that of roads. From the Pather Panchali of the first film, the little road in front of the Ray house, a trodden path through the brush, it becomes the road to Benares which the Ray family travels. In the city it is lost for a while, but then emerges as the road Apu must travel to college on. In the last film it has become a monstrous, stony ribbon ripped out of the earth on which Pulu and Apu have their encounter (the widening of the roads can only be sensed if the three are seen together) and at last it becomes a long, peaceful road down which Apu, at last, carries his own son Kajal on his shoulder.

The most obvious of the themes, and the one which might be expected to be handled the worst, are the trains. But it is perhaps the best. It has more pitfalls about it because it is the most concrete, visually the most limited, and the most unoriginal in concept—it represents a certain wanderlust, and had it been handled by a less expert filmmaker, it would have been corny in the extreme. But it is not—if anything, these weak spots are turned completely around and made into great strengths:

Apu and Durga, as children, go to see the trains across the meadow. Then, when Durga is sick, she promises to go with him again, but dies before she can.

Apu takes the train to Calcutta to school. He purposely misses the train to stay with his mother an extra day, even though she and he are not getting along too well.

His mother, sick and dying, waits for the train which he has not taken home for the holidays, but stays and talks with Pulu instead.

He and Pulu have their reunion among the train tracks in the third film. It is the blasting train whistle which Aparna covers her ears against when she and Apu are married in the city. It is the train that takes her away to her mother's when she dies in childbirth.

When he has heard that she is dead, Apu goes to the railroad tracks where a train runs over a pig, almost as if this wanderlust is what killed Aparna. Then at the end, Kajal's grandfather is left holding a small toy train, the present from Apu to Kajal that the boy has left behind.

This is by no means a complete synopsis of even these three themes. And we have not begun to touch on the real content of the film, or any of its meaning, but only outline some of the visual scaffolding on which the meaning hangs. In the first film, for example, the main centers of interest are Durga and her mother. Most filmmakers seem entirely at a loss to present female characters realistically, strongly, and sympathetically, all at once.

The mother's concern over what the other villagers will think of her for the behavior of her daughter who has been stealing fruit is both touching and sympathetic. She is too concerned, however, and this begins a tragic vicious circle where the daughter feels less and less loved by her mother and eventually steals a necklace. Apu is an observer to this, and the touching—and perhaps most violent scene in the whole trilogy—when the mother drags her daughter by the hair and throws her out of the house is probably the direct scene that comes back to Apu when in the third film he keeps the grandfather from striking the boy who has just thrown rocks at them. Apu's marriage (a forced one through a superstition that the bride will be cursed unless she marries at the appointed hour; the intended bridegroom, however, was insane) turns into one of the most touching relationships I have ever seen. It is perhaps treated a trifle in miniature for the results that it has—this is my only criticism of the trilogy—but even this is more than forgivable if we think what most directors would have turned it into.

Aparna is not a terribly intelligent girl—though very pretty—but she has been educated more than most Indian women, which is to say she can read and write Bengali. She knows nothing of her dreamer husband save that he is poor and an orphan, and a substitute. By the end of their relation, when she goes back to her mother to have her child, which kills her, both she and Apu have come to love each other.

Heaven protect us from what the average director would have turned this situation into. It would have been either a case of a poor, submissive, ethereal geisha creature who with eastern intuition knows she *needs a man*; or it would have been Apu conquering by force of never-to-be-defined male will some basically insipid, wishy-washy thing who says only variants of "I hate you," or "don't leave me."

In this beautiful sequence we have two very real people doing what real people would do. She is at first miserable, but her self-pride does not let her show it to Apu.

For some reason, self-pride to most artists today is the thing that must be put down in women at all costs unless it is some overblown matriarch fighting for her husband and children (never herself)—then it's all right.

Aparna does not let him see her suffering, does her work, manages to have a good time with him when they are alone; he is kind to her; and she refuses to let him feel guilty about her; and completely for herself, which Apu enjoys, she gets him to teach her English. And she does it without appearing as though she's about to bite his testicles off any minute. Her concern over him when she leaves and her little girlish letter to him about jealousies and what have you are delightfully endearing. And they are endearing (and this is the thing most artists to date fail miserably to comprehend) precisely because she is not the stereotype mushy female who would be mouthing these more or less trivial sentiments; which is to say, because of her actions, we can take them for what they are, sincere expressions of concern and affection, not symptoms of a hyper-neurotic dependency or a paranoid fear of rejection, which they would be coming from the mouth of most cinematographically created females.

Personally, I would have been happy to see the growth of this relationship gone into as deeply and as long as the mother and daughter one of the first film. It was refreshing.

But for the architecture of the entire work, it had to be kept proportionate. As I leave the subject, let me say that it is nice to come across a work where, even though perhaps the strongest relations are between males and males (Pulu and Apu, Apu and Kajal, which occupy the most sympathetic portions of film two and three), it seems this way because that's what the story happened to be about, rather than the maker was suffering from the by now completely inexcusable set of neuroses that vitiates his ability to either observe or portray women as people—a set of neuroses that has erased so much validity from works of the *nouvelle vague* directors (and I don't care how healthy and heterosexual they claim to be) and etiolated either partially or completely the impact of such potentially good films as *Les Liaisons Dangereuses*, *Rocco and His Brothers*, and *Jules & Jim*, to name a few in which this was the most glaring fault.

I believe all art—even music—works with basically the same materials and strives for similar realization. But each art has one thing it can do better than the others, and just as a rule of thumb, there is a correlation between the greatness of a work of art and how much it utilizes its medium's forte.

The forte of the film I have always felt is that it can build to immediate effects of amazing power and vitality in just a few seconds' time. And Apu is full of them—and they are so skillfully done and blended that one is hardly aware of them until they have already happened.

In the first film there is the lightning on the shaking idol when Durga is ill. Before that is the immense, nearly cosmic joy at the two children chasing each other over the field and at last Durga forgiving Apu with the sugar cane in the field of blowing papyrus stalks by the railroad. The terrible pressure of [Harihar's] discovery that his daughter is dead, an amazing coupling of vision and music without words, is a great scene. Then there is the ominous snake which, at the end, crawls into the house.

Into the second film, the death of the father, followed by the screaming birds is perhaps the most effective scene, but it is the high peak in a Himalaya of peaks.

In the third film I have already mentioned the tear that becomes an ocean.

Throughout the three, the running story is that Apu, a young Indian boy, is bereft of every person he loves—in the first, his sister, and the second, at the beginning his father and at the end his mother, and in the third, his wife.

Through all this he gains wisdom, first by observing his mother and sister, second at formal school and college, and last by wandering through the world; and in the end he must bring this wisdom to reconcile himself with the person whom he considers his worst enemy—his own son, whom he holds responsible for his wife's death. Around this terribly ambitious structure is an amazing support work of Indian society, living habits, customs, characters, meticulous economic and social scrutiny.

If there is a second criticism to be made, it is only at the point where Apu writes a novel, and then destroys it after Aparna has died. Pulu has jeered at the idea, saying that Apu has no experience, especially of love. That novel was written—what there was written—before his marriage, and if its destruction is supposed to mean that, after all, Pulu (who praised highly the one section he did read) was right and he hadn't known about love until Aparna—then all well and good. But, even on second viewing, it had a trace of the pre-set oriental mysticism, of sacrificing things of the flesh to achieve purification—including the first few chapters of an apparently good novel—and without any further explanation, this seems a trifle strange for a film which has been, till then, so amazingly free of eastern stereotypes present[ed] stereotypically.

I do not mind, however, giving Mr. Ray the benefit of the doubt and assuming the first interpretation to be correct, even though the second seems closer.

The only friend Apu does not lose is Pulu, his wife's cousin, whom he meets in the middle of the second film, a sort of portly Horatio to his Hamlet. In all, the films make a tremendously powerful statement about man's situation and his reaction to it. Mr. Ray says that this situation is cruel, unfair, and depriving. And he says too, that however cruel it is, it can be met with bravery, kindness, and love. Whether it's to be the kindness of Durga forgiving her brother for causing her a beating, the bravery of a father taking his family to a new city, that of a mother refusing to call her

son away from his exams, though she is deathly ill and neurotically in-
clined toward possessiveness, or the bravery of the new wife in a strange
city with a strange husband, determined to make life comfortable, or the
bravery, love, and kindness that Apu must use to forgive and accept forgiveness, from his son.

+   +   +

To the president of the U.S.

Negotiate. Don't shoot. Call off blockade. Prevent nuclear war.

The Jewels of Aptor was published yesterday and I bought a copy at a 42nd Street drug-store. Returning home (after going out to Marie Ponsot's to tutor Antoine in Math) I found a note from the postman saying that a package too big for my mailbox was waiting for me. It's probably my twelve author's copies. Must make a list of who gets them:

1 Hilda	Others:
2 Aunt Yetta	John Hetland
3 B. and Evelyn	Rose Marion
4 Mother	Mr. Luria
5 Grandmother	Dr. Gordon
6 Tante	Paul Elitzik
7 Dorothy	Cade Ware
8 W. H. Auden	Mr. Bernheimer
9 Marie Ponsot	Mrs. Bruning
10 William Sloane	Thelma Watson
11 John Ciardi	Jesse Jackson
12 Dick & Alice	

+ + +

Note on Geo—after his death cleared up—attempt

He tried desperately to live out a concrete fantasy because he believed at heart reality was a myth.

Why are people so interested in what writers do? (in fragment)

Jimmy surprised—who's that directed against: "The right thing for the wrong reason."

Later, in Part III, he talks to O'Donnells about the biography.

———

After reading journal entry, Jimmy says—"Yes, she knew the mythos, and as you said she wanted to survive, so with that transformation going on she left you."

———

Geo's new book of poems, the Carmina Catulli—O'Donnells wants to base his biography on that. Jimmy tries to explain it's a novel in verse, and though the characters were real, they have little to do with the period of his life they were written in:

Mark Hetland was a bad poet and a pest. Not his best friend.

Niva he hadn't seen in two years.

Claudia, from her ideas on Women & life was probably his wife.

O'Donnells relegates this to "one opinion" in the actual biography. Hardly mentions his wife at all, other than to imply that Geo was consistently unfaithful to her—very hero, very adventurous.

"We're changing the facts to write a glorious biography."

This is foreshadowed in a speech of Ciceroe's in "Cataline."

*   *   *

Finally talks to Laili about it.

O'Donnells—"If he wasn't married, we could play up his bisexuality, but with a wife, we want to keep it down. It wouldn't look good."

+   +   +

Outline for "The Black Comet" series

Ric Qrawford, hero and operator of "The Black Comet"

Outline of five novels with a possible collection of short stories. Each novel 100 pages, ten chapters, no prologues or epilogues.

Opening sentence:

There were fortunes to be made then, and we made fortunes.

+   +   +

Jan 12 (?)—Friday night

Tonight was the first time I saw the paintings of Simon Kestenbaum. Somehow I feel the occasion merits comment. I had never heard of him before that evening at Mike's house when he walked in—head nearly shaven, the stubble of a new beard curving his chin—and we exchanged a few words, mine on the novel I was working on, his about his painting. He said the only intelligent sentence I had heard that evening and on the strength of that I asked for his address and he responded by saying he should like to see me.

I lost his address promptly I got home. A few nights later I returned to Mike's and met Chris (who had been there before), who informed me he was a typist and I asked him if he would be willing to type up the opening chapters of *Voyage Orestes*, seeing as I have some extra cash. I extracted a promise from Chris and Kestenbaum's address.

Once more I lost the address, and by now, strictly through the strange euphony of the name, the question, "Who is Simon Kestenbaum?" became an hourly one, accompanied by chuckles, chortles, and open laughter.

A third time I acquired Kestenbaum's address. And wandered up to his apartment on Eighth Street. It is on the top floor, with tin door painted white. Kestenbaum was out.

Later, I was going to Sally Feingold's—she is doing the verityping for "Geo's Poems" and "The Terrible Children"—to take Marilyn's notes, when I decided to try once more. After finding Sally not home, I wandered up the misty avenue. Fog from the river beyond the projects had lapped the lighted buildings and wedged into the street. Halfway up the stairs, I was overcome with an incredible abdominal surging. Finally I reached apartment twenty-one (white tin, dirty white hall tile) and whispered or rasped—"Simon ..."

When I was let in I simply asked for the bathroom, was pointed to the way, and collapsed on the white-plastic rim, my colon voiding its entire contents at once.

Ten minutes later, I came out, said hello, and tried to explain myself as best I could. We went into his studio, where I saw Chris.

Artists' studios—I think of them usually as bleak, white; even if cluttered, then an emptiness that is cluttered. Kestenbaum's is warm, and calmly disordered, and the space itself is utilized in the disorder. And the paintings—

The light was dim, and at first a bright, no—magnetic orange canvas in which stands the figure of a young man to one side. Behind him is another figure—no, his mirror image—but it is all wrong, it is someone else, looking at him, in entirely the wrong direction for a reflection.

Another, unfinished, abstracted body of a woman, explosive and delicate; there the sketch of a mechanized [...] mass, a cross hatching of red and green.

Later we sat down and had coffee, tea, and cookies. Chris went through a quick explanation of what the typing situation was. (Chris, anemic kid with broken glasses, faggot thin without being emaciated—or a faggot, either. Hair too long, flat chest, thin feet and tiny head.)

I was mute. This verbal net I have been caught in all week suddenly ripped apart, and after I reiterated to an obscene degree how impressed I was by his paintings, I shut up for the rest of the evening and let Kestenbaum talk.

He was at school (he is 27) and was living next to a six foot, incredible queen (his description) who showed his work to a Marquise from uptown. She bought one, and thus he began. To date he has a waiting list for his paintings, most being sold before completion.

He requested me to come back and sit for him on Wednesday evening, seven o'clock. He wanted to know when it would be convenient for me. God, what date wouldn't I break to sit for the painter of these pictures.

+   +   +

The world is made up of curved surfaces which we must approach tangentially—

—Susan Sholley
(in conversation)

+   +   +

I am nearly finished with chapter IX, Volume II of my SF trilogy. I am amazed and terrified at all it has taken out of me, all it has demanded of invention, thoughtful organization of a complexity that is appalling for a work that is only allowed—or that I have only allowed to have— pretensions to entertainment. Today is March 30, and I promised myself it would be finished by my birthday, April 1. But there are only two days left and nearly forty-five pages to go.

My schedule, so beautifully planned 10 months ago, has been completely abandoned—or, at any rate, left behind. The day I conceived this monstrous trilogy, walking over the Brooklyn Bridge with Edna Silem to visit Dick and Alice, I'd assumed that the whole thing would be completed inside of two months: one week for the first volume, two weeks of rest, one for the second, and so on. I figured quite incidentally to have finished Part I of *Voyage Orestes* by January 1st.

The first volume, which will be out in May, was not finished till the end of October. Here it is, four months into the next year, and the end of the second is just heaving into site. As for *Voyage Orestes*—I am crushed whenever I try to think [about] it. Part One is also unfinished—although there is less than a hundred pages to go, and Chris Terdsis—Simon Kestenbaum's roommate—has typed up the first 300 pages which is now at Appleton-Century-Crofts; Bobs Pinkerton has promised me an answer by the first of next week, which is reassuring.

I have done so little, it seems, in the past year. True, there is the year from 17 to 18 when I produced only *Cycle for Toby* but, unless I misremember, that was all that I projected. Well, spring has always been my best time, and so perhaps I shall get somewhere that I can recognize as a place I once wanted to arrive at. Believe me, there is a satisfaction in that. I am a bit worried as to what A.C.C. will say about the inclusion of the *J. of A.* in *Voyage Orestes*—because it fed me for a year independently, people will refuse to believe that it was written specifically for *V.O.*

I was disappointed, though not surprised at my contemporary friends' reaction to it. They will not tolerate my writing SF, especially SF that is at once so austere, seemingly allegorical, un-humorous, so classical in tone, yet not recognizably molded to any of the *sine qua non* errors that this sort of S-F usually conforms to. If it had first appeared in *V.O.* where its "meaning" is underlined by the previous 600 pages, then I'm sure they would have considered it a masterfully vivid stylistic tour de force.

Now, however, I am forced to rely on impersonal critics—at least for my praise. Donald Wollheim, who quite anonymously thought it magnificent (or so he told Edna before he knew it was I who wrote it), the artist Jack Gaughan who did the cover and sent me such an appreciative letter, and one or two others.

Strange incident, which again only corroborates my feelings. Ian Stogel, perhaps one of the most avid SF readers conceivable who was perfectly appalled at the manuscript, came to me quite calmly and apologetically after publication and said, "You know it really does go *much* better on second reading."

The sad truth is that when one approaches a book by an author whom one doesn't know, automatically one tries to discern what his excellences are within the first few pages. I was attempting—and I think obviously—sensual vividness, incident by incident strung on a rather classical plot.

My friends, however, demand the excellences that they may find in my personality. The extreme artificiality of an artifacted creation such as the

J. of A. puts them off a great deal. Going to the *J. of A.* for its plot or its ideas is as ridiculous as going to Bradbury for the same thing.

After all this, however, it occurs to me that one of these friends paid me the highest compliment she could (though she, I'm sure, was not aware of it; its height is simply that her statement concerning her reaction to it corresponded identically to my intentional effects)—she offered it, however, as a slightly backhanded compliment: Sharon (David Litwin's girlfriend) said—"I read it while I was under peyote. I thought it was great. It was all red and green and blue and purple." And the drug aside, aren't these exactly the words Geo uses to describe the major impressions his dream—of which the *J. of Aptor* is ultimately a recounting—produces?

It is far more intimately, structurally, and obviously connected with the main thread of *V.O.* than either "The Night Alone" or "Cataline"—which allows it to be longer, to occupy the central position. (John Hetland—who is staying with Guy for spring vacation (I finally met Guy—and it turns out the two went to BHS! John must feel surrounded), the tiny (small) redheaded, slightly, though not offensively, swish young man—dismissed the first nine chapters as Intrigue. He enjoys Argo's section the most—idiots who glut themselves on the sauce and throw the meat away!) "The Night Alone" is merely a distorted version of an incident in the past that must be undistorted as the novel progresses, while the *J. of A.* is a distortion of what has already been presented—it defines the "fertile ambiguities" (Sue Sholley's phrase) which must be explored later. Whereas "Cataline," whenever I get around to writing it, will be connected more thematically as is the Hamlet essay. I have committed myself to an overpowering form—to discuss the ambiguities of extra-literary analyses of an author. Therefore I must include his complete works. And I believe myself a technician suitably masterful to succeed. Very few people are.

Yet somehow, I feel assured that "Jo & other Poems," "Carmina Catulli," "The Night Alone," *The Jewels of Aptor*, "On Hamlet," "Cataline," and *The Fall of the Towers* is an impressive catalog of the works of any twenty-one-year-old writer.

There is a dire resemblance to Lermontov's dream-within-a-dream poem that Nabokov quotes at the beginning of *A Hero of Our Time*.

My greatest wish is to be able to escape this double set of mirrors that has been my youth—my life here and my writing there.

V.O. or certainly the fragmented novellette "The Beasts" will be my last novel for a long time. After that I will devote myself to getting published the whole series *Portraits from the Immature Mind*. Or perhaps I shall not—

+ + +

Suggested revision in Table of Contents (after four years) for *Those Spared by Fire*

The Small Ellipse
> Three Sketches
>> 1—Eurydice
>> 2—The Execration
>> 3—Death of an Outsider

Animal in the City
> Tales of the Binomial Expansion
>> 1—Summer
>> 2—A State of Kings
>> 3—Ephesus

The Directrix
> This Place Rumor'd to Have Been Sodom
>> Part I
>> Part II
>> Part III
>> Part IV

Vox Humana, Vox et Preterae Nihil

+ + +

Half of man's problems would be solved if the human body smelled of perspiration, rather than coffee, alcohol, perfumes, and tobacco.

Voyage, Orestes

Containing the complete
works of Geo Keller

Prologue

Concerto minore

The Road
The Bridge
The City

Concerto majore

First movement
1) The Night Alone
2) In Praise of Limestone (leaves Margaret)
3) Oblation from the Shattered Urn
4) Summer (first letter from Margaret)
5) Snake by Moonlight
6) The Scorpion Girt by Fire
7) While I Have Tyme and Space (Snake beats up heroin man)
8) O Elektra (first collection of letters)
9) Les Routes Nocturnes (Jimmy meets Geo's father, asks to be abandoned)
Second movement
1) The Jewels of Aptor—150 pages
2) The Bright Season
3)
4) Taking Gahr in the Night
5) Nor this behooves me (Geo and Jimmy X)
6) At Agamemnon's House (second collection of letters)
7)

8)

9)

+   +   +

"One trouble with men is that they see women through so many theories that nothing gets interpreted as human."

+   +   +

Outline for "Tel" novelette
for *Towers of Toron*

(2) Chapter I—Intro

(4) Chapter II—Basic training

(6) Chapter III—On Ketrall—the scout, the first attack, the sign post

(8) Chapter IV—Talk of truce. The three hunt [a] Ketralese [animal]. The major battle. The scout saves Tel.

(10) Chapter V—Tel gets lost. Finds & observes the scout. Comes back, talks to Ptorn, & gets some explanation. The scout disappears with the animal.

(12) Chapter VI—The talk of truce, it nearly comes, joy, surprise attack, Tel killed.

+   +   +

Chapter Outline for
   "City of a Thousand Suns"

Chapter I
   Under Two Suns
Chapter II
Chapter III
Chapter IV
Chapter V
Chapter VI

Chapter VII
Chapter VIII
Chapter IX
Chapter X
Chapter XI
    The Fall of the Towers.
Chapter XII—A Length of Broken Metal
Epilogue.

Outline of last Chapter.

    The Royal Palace
    The Merchants' Houses
    The Hive House
    Military Ministry
    General Medical
    The Air Field
    The Devil's Pot
    The Wharf
    Past the Aquariums
    University Island
    The Island Estates of the Royal Family
    The Fishing Village
    The Farm
    The Ruined Circus
    The Forest
    The Penal Mines
    Telphar
    The Ancient Ruins where the Neanderthals lived
    The Radiation Barrier

+ + +

January 29 Tuesday 1963

    —Read Thomas Mann's *Dr. Faustus* and have just finished chapter 8. It is an amazing book. Two years ago, at Bread Loaf, Miss Bernheimer gave me quite a compliment that till now I did not understand; she said that the jazz section in *Those Spared by Fire* had moved her like nothing about music since Mann. It may be a bad novel, but it is a wonderful book.

The sketch of the relation between the animate and the inanimate world, through the description of Adrian's father's experiments, is something that I had always known must go into the elementary education, or environment of a true creator, but have never seen it expressed so nicely or so well. And this last Chapter VIII, a symphony in words on music— four movements, monumental and thematically connected.

I would like to give this book to David Litwin (who came to visit us with Sharon earlier this evening, to escape his roommate Randy's narcotic haze—Randy and Donya have apparently been high for three weeks; and this is getting on David's nerves, understandably). David has also just lost his job at Tams-Witmark Music Library, and described a depressing visit to the musicians' union—"dirty old men, young queers, and a few women waiting in an empty hall for their names to be called." Perhaps this might restore some of his perspective. He also mentioned in passing that his March concert may be postponed. He must be in the doldrums indeed, and this is certainly the book to spike him to some creative direction, if not to cheer him up.

+ + +

The Road

Section One
    Travel—Jimmy and father
Section Two
    Travel—Jimmy and his mother
Section Three
    His parents
Section Four
    Travel—Geo and the bells
Section Five
    His family at large
Section Six
    Jimmy & his mother and father
Section Seven
    Time progressing—Geo's home
Section Eight
    At the cloisters
Section Nine
    Travel—and summation of histories

Section Ten
  Travel
Section Eleven
  End

+ + +

Show child by your reaction that sex is a healthy part of the adult world, that it doesn't faze you, & it won't faze child.

+ + +

About the author

Somewhere, in a letter or journal, Flaubert confessed that the impetus for writing *Madame Bovary* was to evoke, at some point during the book, the color of the moldy cornice of a French chateau that harbored termites. As a writer, I was very much struck with a sympathetic ringing when I discovered that statement. My first S-F novel grew around, and completely submerged, the remembrance of sweaty handprints drying on a slab of black onyx. This, my second S-F novel (the first of a trilogy, the whole of which grew from a momentary vision of a protean city at the other end of the universe, changing, changing, reflecting the fears and hopes of life anywhere and everywhere—but its significance is only hinted at [in] this volume) coalesced around the luminous hues of shells polished for three hours with shammy-skin, and the copper hue of the sun seen in a reflection on rippling water through in-rolling fog, as sometimes happens at Gay Head on the tip of Martha's Vineyard, Mass.

But about me? Oh, well let's see. Born 1942, Elementary Education, the Dalton School, where I learned Medieval European and East Indian history, also, transfinite mathematics. Secondary education, the Bronx High School of Science, where I learned English. Further education, the Bread Loaf Writer's Conference, where I learned to wait on tables, and City College, where I learned Greek and counterpoint. At present writing I am 20 years, 9 months, 1 week, and 1 day old.

—January 8, 1963

Outline for Chapter XII of "Towers of Toron"

Illu putting up sign-post
Tel asks Ptorn why the scout sacrificed his life for them?
The Truce—king crowned
Talks to Lug about language
Lug talks about the flap-flip
Talks to Curly about Toron
Lug balks, gets excited. Tel saves him and dies.
Perhaps bring in the stranger (How?)

+ + +

Notes on "What Dreams May Come"

Prologue
... Like Grains of Sand

Book One
Andromeda

Book Two
The Home Spiral

Book Three
Beta-2

Book Four
The Crab

Book Five
Brutus

Book Six
Little Caesar

Book Seven
The Black Nebula

Epilogue
… What Dreams May Come

+ + +

Outline for the historical novel:

Secondary Characters:

2   Two street urchins, one brave & curious, the other shy and frightened.

4   Two guards, one boastful & brash, one even-tempered and level-headed.

6   Prostitute & barmaid, one flighty & excitable, one business minded and hard headed.

8   Two Barbarian soldiers: one superstitious & close minded, the other eager to learn.

10   Two witches: one knows her superstition masks knowledge, the [other] more interested in promoting superstition.

12   Two servants, one loyal and trusted, the other scheming to get ahead.

14   Two ladies in waiting, one interested [in] promoting beauty & art, the other dawdling in making ridiculous political speculations.

16   Two understatesmen. One bored and uninterested, the other passionately concerned about the fate of the country.

18   Two merchants of the town, one honest, concerned with the town's welfare, the other dishonest & scheming.

20   A nun and a hired assassin, religious vs. moral.

22   Priest & artist: religious vs. passive amorality.

24   Archbishop vs. prime minister: prime minister politically. Archbishop knows how much his authority rests on superstition.

26   The spy, & the torturer.

————

Main characters

Young Philip Dwayin, educated, traveled, lusty, and adventurous, returning from the barbaric lands.

The Duke of Laslaud, warring against the barbarians, defending the honor, etc.

His daughter, the Duchess Fulvia, beautiful, witty, spunky, virginal, etc.

Her companion Emelia, interested in art, religion, and superstition, and can distinguish between them.

Tertiary characters

Inn keeper
The diplomat
The African
The chief of the Barbarians
The hermit
The Jester
Old Cassandra
The Warlock
The village maid
The idiot
The Old Duchess
The Court poet

+ + +

Small comment [on] *The Ballad of Beta-2* which is pushing p. 50 (Chapter 5 has been launched into some 75 words):

Discovery of the executioner's records, with short, half illiterate comments.

Some explanation of duplicate, back to Beta-2 and the discovery of Leela's diary, and the final untangling of the Ballad.

+ + +

Reorganization of "While I Have Space and Tyme"

Introduction—satisfactory
From Laile to first *Jewels of Aptor* dream—satisfactory.
1–10 equally satisfactory with minor adjustments (70 c.p.).

11—Geo feels guilty about house.

12—Jimmy goes to post office.

13—Jimmy (and Geo) meet "Cley."

14—Positive relation between Ann & Snake witnessed through gate.

15—Build positive relation between Jimmy & Ann.

Ann recounts "particularly feminine" experience and then the cloister episode—the unicorn.

16—Jimmy sees the strange agate.

17—Buys scarf for Ann.

18—The concert that evening.

19—The middle search for Laile.

20—"Cley" & Jimmy have a night on the bars.

Cley recounts incidents of his past knowledge of Snake—the Dynamo.

21—On the beach at dawn—Jimmy alone.

22—Meets Geo, and they talk briefly.

—Night—

23—Morning, Jimmy gives Ann the scarf: #4

24—"Cley" comes in. Reacts to Snake negatively . . .

25—. . . and breaks Ann's guitar.

26—Spilt's reaction to the broken guitar.

27—Intimations of Snake having stolen something.

28—Talk to Geo & Ann before concert.

—Night—

29—Geo's second *Jewels of Aptor* dream.

30—Jimmy goes for a walk—meets Karry. They talk. Recounting of cross country journey, clearing up the Rimbaud speech in "The Night Alone."

31—Meets Ann. The talk about Geo's problem. & hers and his.

32—Snake gives Ann the twelve string he has stolen. & reaction.

33—Ann and Jimmy screw again.

34—Ann plays and sings. (very brief necking)

35—#5 Ann and Geo's farewell.

36—Jimmy sees Geo talking to a girl on the beach—he runs down: confronts Geo with Karry's revelation.

37—Mrs. Portine comes by for the key. Goodbye. They're about to leave.

—Coda—

a—Departures, pick up Snake. Geo doesn't remember Cloisters incident.
b—Post office to pick up "next chapter."
c—See Spilt and Ann.
d—Discuss sanitarium.

+ + +

The state of the literary world today is disgracefully depressing. I have just finished reading the *Saturday Review*'s memorial issue to Robert Frost.

For vitality there must be opposing forces; but though our literary world is divided into two more or less opposed camps (Henry Miller and his followers, the "beats" and the Bread Loaf clique which had Frost at its head, which place

+ + +

Volume III of Cities of the Flames

The retroactive destruction of Toromon. Catham and Nonik (poet and historian) contrasted over the relationship of Jon and Alter.

After introduction, the death of Nonik's girlfriend by a Mali group. Ends, the last chapter, with Nonik at the end traveling the length of the Transit Ribbon—over the length of first chapter with the insertion of the Hive houses, and the ruined circus.

The epilogue.

+ + +

"... If there be a God, then wherefore should He not perform a miracle, so that two times two may be not four, but five, in response to the prayer of the faithful, and to the ignominy of the godless atheists—such as you and I?"
—Merejkowski in *Leonardo da Vinci*

The answer to this, of course—and it should be obvious to anyone who has passed through the wild night and tottered in the ambiguities of human experience—is that the miracle is simply that two times two remains four, no matter what; similarly does steam always rise and rain always fall.

Regardless of the existence of God, that there should be any laws immutable in this chaotic world is the greatest miracle, and it is—to put it mildly—missing the point to demand that these laws waver, fail and become subject to mortal sorts of vacillation before we admit of their divinity.

+   +   +

Ending of O Elektra

I have looked through all these notes and pages, and I have cut them up and re-pasted them into something like a letter. For you to understand them, I feel they must follow some pattern. If I rewrote this all nice and legibly, it would take so long that it would never get to you in time before you left Newcove. But the pattern I have put them in, Jimmy, any computer could have done. All the paragraphs dealing with [the] same subject are together, with one or two hints of what's coming scotch-taped here and there. But it's not the order they were written, and it's a logical pattern that has nothing to do with me. Because we want people to understand us, we present these strange oversimplifications. But it's not my pattern, Jimmy. Jimmy, it's not my pattern.

+   +   +

"My own revisions are usually the result of impatience with un-kempt diction and lapses in logic; together with an awareness that for most defects, to delete is the instantaneous cure."

—Marianne Moore

"… one should be as clear as one's natural reticence allows one to be."

+   +   +

Correlation of notes for "City of a Thousand Suns"

Twelve Chapters & Epilogue

Chapter I
Introduction of the "City of a Thousand Suns."
The death of Renna Nonik—Rara reintroduced.
The Mirage of Clea and Catham—Old Koshar & Cithon.
Conclusion to Chapter: back at the "City of a Thousand Suns."

Chapter II
Arkor and the Duchess—Jon and Alter

Chapter III—Jon, characterization

Chapter IV

    Arkor traitor

Chapter V—Jon characterizations

Chapter VI—Interlude at "C of 1S."

    Duchess traitor

Chapter VII—Jon characterization

Chapter VIII—The Duchess and King Let, death

Chapter IX—Jon characterization

Chapter X

    Jon traitor

Chapter XI—Interlude & C of T. S.
    The whole thing comes out. The discovery of the three.
    Jon characterization
    —ends with interlude at C of T. S.

Chapter XII
Vol Nonik witnesses the destruction of Toron, and wanders to the rim of
Toromon, similar to first chapter of the Trilogy.

Epilogue
    Jon and Alter reach the "City of a Thousand Suns."

+   +   +

Possible Introduction for "Journals of Orpheus"

These are the fragments of a precocious and terribly irregular literary education. It would be presumptuous to go into what bearing these fragments have on the whole scheme of *Portraits from the Immature Mind*. That is for whatever reader who is concerned to decipher.

A general comment on the *Portraits* however. It is a strange work, in that nearly a fourth of its value is in its faults—or in its faults corrected. It is not only the story of an education, but the delineation of one.

It was not until the middle of my third novel, *Those Spared by Fire*, that the realization struck that all these characters, and ideas, that had been in my fragmentary first effort, and strange second, existed in the same matrix. This realization was one of the things that shattered the unity of that third book, it is one of the things I tried to flee in my fourth, *Cycle for Toby*. It is the thing that I tried to return tentatively to in some of the stories of this collection, notably "The Wail of Wild Dogs" and "Five Men in a Telephone Booth." And when I at last turned to it fully in *Afterlon*, I was through with fragments for good. The little sketch "Lon" is the last piece I ever completed that might be called a short story.

Afterlon was begun a day before my 18th birthday, and completed four furious months later. That is to say that all of these stories date previous to the age of 18. "Journals of Orpheus" was written more as an experiment in essay than in fiction about a month before the completion of *Afterlon*, when I took a weekend off with Peter Horn to visit the Second Annual Newport Folk Festival. It is a landmark to me, in that a fault that was growing, here became so acute that I simply had to deal with it: that was the tendency to romanticize the hysterical actions of women and completely ignore any others.

+ + +

For God's sake, the STRUCTURE of O Electra, if you please.

Must contain reference to Jimmy and his father in the opening incident. Perhaps the incident about the race-track.

2

Conversation—Paul & Geo, negative & white

Margaret's first apology

Mother talks about pattern of censorship. Mother's family, father's family.

Incident of the bells, & belief in God.

3

Incident with the destroyed cube

4

Second apology for false emotions.
Three versions. Intimations of the elect. plant.
The beginning.
Paul & Margaret discuss Gide—the emotions invented by novelists.
Judith & mother—get out and do something.
Paul and Margaret on violence: His gratuitous interest in her. They go to the plant. (His relation to the rackets?) Adventure. She comes home—her reaction? from this into what should be a reaction. Finally, afraid of all of them and the contradictions implied.

5

Talks with mother, mother recounts love for children. Incident with Father and Jimmy, conflict between them. But father successful.

————

Conclusion of Margaret story implied in epilogue—you can only be saved by exposing yourself to the wild and the dangerous with the hope of finding what your emotions are.
—Mother and Jimmy in end.

+   +   +

Dear Don,

I got the contracts this morning and here they are now.
Agreed, this is weaker than *Captives*. I guess it just suffers from "Middle-Volume-of-Trilogy-itis." (Then there is just the possibility that I have bitten off too much: an entire society at war with itself.)
In the last volume, Jon actively becomes the hero again. (Alter is the heroine.) And it stays pretty closely with their personal adventures, and the finale of the War of Toromon.

+   +   +

August 10th (I think)

I am on page 10 of "The Roads of Night." Yet I feel vaguely—no, not at all vaguely—as if I am quite pointedly losing my mind. I refused to go to N.J. with Sonny's family today in order to stay home and get some work done. Ana spent the night & in the morning I made her breakfast. I got some work done, and finally—(this great haze, as if I see everything with one eye only, or more, as if I were having some paranoiac reaction to a strange drug I'd taken too much of, but can't remember what it was or when)— went up to visit Nan & Walter.

Nan was very pregnant and we talked about the weird murder of Norma Jean's mother (which was probably a bit unsettling) and they invited me up to Mt. Vernon this evening. I realize I should work. But I also know that I must get rid of this feeling of unreality, and well might that do it. However I also want to see Bernie tomorrow. I feel he could be of more help than they (or maybe that's an excuse); at least with him I feel I could present my excuses to have them knocked down.

+   +   +

Random thought:

Intellect is what we use to compensate for the emotional death we begin to die as soon as we leave childhood.

+   +   +

I have just made a monumental change in the structure of *Voyage, Orestes*, and I wish Marilyn were here to discuss it with me. These past weeks I have felt more lost than at any time in my life. Sonny, for all his violent leanings, has been quite a [stabilizing] force. He cleaned up the apartment with me from one end to the other, washing windows, mopping the foully discolored floors. And today, while I was up at Appleton, doing a bit of rewriting in Cade's office while the moving men were changing the desks around, Sonny cleaned the stove, sink, and ice-box.

In the two years I've lived with Marilyn never did I come home and find such an amazingly positive physical change in the apartment. He said it took him four hours, and the stove, I remember, was frighteningly filthy.

I had been planning to take a nap when I got home, but (Sonny had gone out) when I came in, I was so surprised, pleased, and frightened, that

I scrubbed out the toilet and cleaned off the tank so as not to be taken for a squelcher.

The change in *Voyage, Orestes* has left me shaken. First of all, it involves cutting nearly a third of its projected length, and the structural devices of the inclusion of the poems and the prose and dialogue works [have] been abandoned. Since only one more remains to be written, I will write out "Cataline" anyway, and along with "The Night Alone," *The Jewels of Aptor* in its full 200 page version, and the poems, they will form a strangely surrealistic countersymphony to the work, each a sort of formal saraband to accompany the work.

To plot out part III:

Focus, horror of "the City" understood and realized. Remember Marie and avoid the "abuse of the terrible." Return to the "City." Jimmy afraid to go home.

Geo sinks into a flurry of creative activity producing simultaneously *The Jewels of Aptor* and "Cataline" along with more work on the "Fall." Also protecting Snake.

Jake Lewin and Niva vignettes.

(In "The Road" and in "Limestone," make inserts about Geo's father. The parallelism is much too much and the thing begins to fall apart à la *Les faux-monnayeurs*)

And is attacked by the Syndicate *for producing* "Cataline" supposedly. Is eventually killed, & a biographical article ensues.

Now, chapter by chapter:

Part III

I   Nor This Behooves Me
       House broken into, Jimmy & Geo screw, Jimmy afraid to go home, Geo leaves.
II   Night Studies I
       Snake, Margaret, Louper, Martha, Joe
III   Taking Gaha
       The publishing news, readying production of Cataline, & further mysteries which Jimmy doesn't understand.
IV   Night studies
       Snake, Geo, Ann, Helen, Mr. Keller

V   The Bright Season
             News that Laile is coming to play, that O'Donnells will do
             article and cover the opening with threat.
VI   Night Studies
             Snake, Mrs. Keller, O'Donnells, Margaret, Oona
VII   The High Halls of Night
             The Syndicate breaks up the play, chase to the electric
             plant, death of Geo.
VIII   Night Studies
             Paul
IX   World and Wide
             Conversations with Laile, O'Donnells, the next morning,
             then Ann.
X   Night studies
             Snake, Edna Silem, Mr. Sloan
XI   This Then My Voice
             Ann, Mr. Sloan, final Rimbaud twist.

—Epilogue

+ + +

Tomorrow:

Sleep sufficiently, pick up NYU application, and read *The Corn King and the Spring Queen*

+ + +

"Why is it that we must confuse the terrible manifestations of our inability to realize our emotions with the emotions themselves?"

+ + +

Let's see if I can order a couple of events in the last few days of my existence. To start with, I made a couple of huge structural changes in *Voyage, Orestes*, among other things, cutting out over a hundred thousand words. I wrote all my changes neatly down in a letter to Bobs and then went quietly and quickly up to the office. Bobs was ecstatic over my suggestion (since they incorporated several she had made to me)—she has the really astounding ability to read a scene and see the focus, direction, and intent with an immediacy that grabs me in the stomach (and makes me very happy as well to have her working with me)—and she wanted to know if I needed money. Bless her!

I do not like to take loans, but I am at that odd & strange point where I don't know if I'm coming or going. So we went down, in a taxi, at which conversation began to embroil itself delightedly around and around.

+ + +

List of Epigraphs for *Voyage, Orestes!*

> ... But there is also another kind of life that is not so much living as a miscellaneous tasting of life. One gets hit by some unusual transverse force, one is jerked out of one's stratum and lives cross-wise for the rest of the time, and, as it were, in a succession of samples. That has been my lot, and that is what has set me at last writing something in the nature of a novel ...
> —H. G. Wells

Prologue:

   No epigraph

The Road:

   No epigraph

The Bridge:

   No epigraph

The City:

> If you are angle, I am complement.
> If you are circle, I am circumscribed.
> If my hands mold, yours is the form described.
> Your voice is my familiar instrument.
> I sound a note and you complete the chord;
> Your song breaks through the sounding of my word.
> Your eyes are an inscription in my hand

That reads my face and tells me what I am.
A move completes a move; as games are played,
If I betray, you are the one betrayed.
—M. T. Hacker

In Praise of Limestone:

No epigraph

Oblation from the Shattered Urn:

Here in this night-stillness spread in wings
We turn in the center of all turning things.
—Eric Silberman

Summer:

Not yet in full but in some
abstracted part, order
the façade of the listless summer.
—James Agee

Snake by moonlight:

No epigraph

The Scorpion Girt by Fire:

No epigraph

While I have Tyme and Space:

Enough is maturity
—Theodore Sturgeon

O Elektra:

... I leave off, therefore,
since in a net I seek to hold the wind ...

The Roads of Night:

+   +   +

Then came one to the city
over sand with her bright hair wild
with her eye coal black and her feet sole sore
and under her arms a green eyed child.

Three men stood on the city wall
one was short and the other tall
one had a golden trumpet clear
that he shouted through so all would hear
                                        (that)

A woman stood by a market stall
The tears like diamonds on her cheek
One eye was blind, she could not speak
but she heard the guards of the city call
                                        (out)

One man stood by the courthouse door
to judge again as he'd judged before
When he heard the guards on the stone cry
he said, "She's come back to the city to die."
                                        (yes)

Another man stood on death's head hill
his eyes were masked & his hands were still
On his shoulder he carried a rope,
And he stood stock quiet on death's head slope.

Three on the city wall cried, "go way,
come back to the city on another day,"

But down at the bottom the woman stood,
"I came back like I said I would."

(yes)

A week you gave to travel far
and find the green eyed one who made you what you are,
Well I've searched the desert & I've searched the dune
And I found no man who caused our ruin.

(so)

She walked through the gates and the children cried,
She walked through the market and the voices died.
She walked past the courthouse and the judge so still,
She walked to the slope of death's head hill.

Down from the hill came the man with the rope,
Met her at the bottom of death's head slope.
She looked at the City & she turned & smiled.
A one eyed woman held her green eyed child.

Fire and blood, meat, dung and bone,
down on your knees, steel, stone, & wood,
today are dust, and the City's gone,
But she came back like she said she would.

+ + +

Thought for the day:

"Beauty is the implied perfection of our own imperfect senses of reality."

+ + +

Shirley Jackson, in "The Sundial," comes out as a sort of mystical, atomic-age Jane Austen.

+ + +

No matter what density *Voyage, Orestes* achieves, it is a sketch for a novel. Even if I were to revert to my original full plan, I realize now that even the addition of such extraneous material as my original plan included was to hide from myself that it was just such a sketch. Even certain sentences in it, that must stand unchanged, are only outlines for ideal sentences that I can never write.

How well, then, it fits into the whole scheme of "The Portraits" which I have not considered wholly for two or three months. Actually, I am beginning to realize, there are works of mine that do not rightly belong to the series: *The Warthog*, *The Assassination*, *Captives of the Flames*, *The Towers of* [*Toron*], along with a handful of short stories and "The Journals of Orpheus."

Pieces that definitely do belong are the trilogy of short plays: "Fire," "The Home of the Slain Falcon," and "Small Dialogue," but then, that would pull *The Warthog* back in. I have never known exactly what to do with either *Lost Stars*, or *Scavengers*. Perhaps I never shall.

The Beasts, if I ever write it, will be an amazing little work. The whole thing begins to achieve some sort of density as a world, but, with the exception of *Afterlon*, is there a novel in the bunch? And it is a novel only through structure. Great stretches of it—nay, its entire texture is riddled with clots and snatches of embarrassingly bad writing.

+ + +

First attempt to write, two days after entering Bellevue hospital with what was at first diagnosed as double bronchial pneumonia; as of last night they decided it was some other sort of infection. (Knock on wood.)

I arrived here two days after M's arrival home from Mexico. She had a magnificent array of jewelry and earthenware. I had a temperature of c. 103 (*circa*, not *centigrade*). It had passed 104 when we got to the hospital 12:30 Sat. evening and I was admitted pretty quickly and x-rayed. The lower quarters of both my lungs look as if someone has been ice-skating on them—with a vengeance.

Drop-by-drop, 3 & a fraction pints of dextrose water was pumped into me (the doctor commented what lovely veins I had) and all sorts [of] penicillin was squished through new and interesting holes in my buttocks.

The place is terribly understaffed with nurses and aides. The ones they have, so far, have been as sweet as fabled angels and patient as stones.

There is one poor creature suffering from DTs two beds away from me. He was originally only one bed away, but when he tried to climb in with me (after once disappearing noisily up the fire escape), they isolated him as best they could. He was quite noisy, his fantasy having mostly to do with a car, or car wreck he was in (perhaps trapped in). For a while, our nurse (very pretty, and engaged) kept him occupied by letting him help her push the thermometer wagon (I suppose that's what you call it), but when there was nothing else to do, he became obstreperous again.

(Recollection: when the previous nurse guessed at his condition yesterday afternoon, she began to ask what I assume are certain questions to determine how far gone the patient is: "Where are you?" "What's your first name?" "What is this place?" etc. Yet oddly her tone had a certain edge of belligerence, as if she somehow felt her tenure on reality was morally superior to his—this, incidentally, was the same nurse who blithely forgot to record one change in my sugar water—my only complaint. And that is amazing, considering how understaffed the place is.)

Spent the night swimming in puddles of perspiration. Finally the bedding was changed at about five-thirty. It has just become light outside the window. I was wakened about once every two hours to be handed, by flashlight beam, a greasy rectal thermometer which I dutifully shoved below the sheets and up my ass. I'm supposed to be drinking lots of liquids, but they keep on taking my water away. Oh, well.

* * *

All this reminds me of Cocteau's description of St. Cloud in *Opium*. Just finished breakfast. I ate all my cereal, my egg, and drank a cup of milk. I couldn't eat the bread, but I carried my tray back to the cart by myself. At this point, "myself" is exhausted, the whole business strikes me as rather heroic. Oh, to be truly hungry again!

* * *

The 2 poems that Marilyn wrote while in Mexico possess her usual elegances and excellences. 2 lines particularly struck me in relation to my own poetry:

Having no occupation and no child
she gambles, and her mangy dogs run wild.

Out of context there perhaps seems very little outstanding. They are metrically conservative, if not regular, very unornamented, ending in a phrase that, were it not to be taken literally might almost be considered a cliché.

Yet this is the sort of thing that I can never do! Two lines, and the whole character of the action is caught. Trying to do something similar, I would have six stanzas describing her going to a gambling house, her dogs, etc., with none of the incisive compression that makes M's poetry so much better than mine.

+   +   +

As novel stands now, the aim of Part II should be a steady, but dense picture of 1) Geo's counterfeit search for Laile, 2) for Jimmy, a steady realization of the reality of his own emotions—for 3) Snake, as vehicle for the slow discovery of a surrealistic world of physical horror lurking on another level.

Therefore, are the following necessary?

Frost?

Karry's return?

Dr. Branning's? Once yes, twice, no?

Question for B.P. Is objection to Cley? Or to Cley's connection with the syndicate?

+   +   +

Here, at twenty-one, bedridden with numerous infections of the throat in Sydenham Hospital, it becomes imperative for me to finally codify the picture of myself that I must proceed to live up to. An immediate choice must be made and answered for. Does my life lie with music, or with literature. I think the answer is with music. This means, finish *Voyage, Orestes!*, the SF trilogy, and work desultorily on any poetry around, and then just concentrate on your music: that means singing lessons, lots of work on banjo and guitar, the acquisition of a tape recorder, record player, library, etc.

Well, the decision is made.

This book is more or less reserved for notes on the Historical Novel. See previous notebook for [preliminary] notes. Here we will have a chance to see Sturgeon's rule for characterization and story rolled out like dice to the last combination and permutation.

Set, a number of secondary character conflicts.

Time still to go. Should take about a year, begin in autumn, and end in autumn.

Slight prologue, 6–8 hundred words long, description of witches' sabbath, attendants: witches, Archbishop, Barbarians, court attendants, street urchins.

Part I

Spy has been caught—Phillip returns and meets Fulvia, they fall in love, and Phillip puts himself in her father's service.

Part II

Phillip is in and out among the people to find where their sympathies lie; discovers plot against the duke, and stops one attempt, with meetings with Fulvia.

Part III

Plot thwarted, Barbarians make a full invasion, and Phillip repels it but they have been occupied for a day. (The chief & Emelia)

Part IV

Phillip flees with Fulvia outside the walls, Barbarian country, but safe, Fulvia stays with witches.

Part V

Her father is assassinated. There is a struggle for both Christians and Goddess worshipers to take over. Assassin in the pay of both, it is revealed.

Part VI

Christians win. Fulvia captured, threatened with burning as a witch. Goddess worshipers will not save her. Phillip at last performs daring rescue with help of urchins, & Emelia.

Part VII

Phillip and Fulvia prepare to flee, discover that Emelia has been sent away to marry the Barbarian chief. As they flee, the fortress castle is burned down in a repeat of the witches' sabbath.

Try for each part, approximately 60–70 pages long. Each section should have three 2-page sections, presented as diplomatic speeches, court records, etc. of pure historical balderdash, to establish a feel of historical accuracy and density. These will result in some 7 × 6 pages—42 pages— perhaps make them only one page long—21 pages instead, which will do the same thing. That is all the historical padding the book will allow.

*   *   *

Remember, background shmackground; the background will become quite apparent in the minuets of the characters, secondary, tertiary, & primary.

Costuming: with the exception of pyrotechnical characters, where a special effect is desired—the magician's cloak for example—keep costuming down to three sentences. Three sentences is a general good point for any block of description in this sort of thing.

Landscape—keep it firmly in your mind, the physical diorama of a scene, but describe it only as it comes into play. (Sturgeon's advice again)

Characterization: once again it is time to mull over everything Dick Entin has said. What about—avoid internal character lines unless they are witty. Or play it by ear? I think, so many of my characters are defined by contrasting characteristics, I had best take advantage of them and do them by brief action vignettes and dialogue.

Anathema: Sir Walter Scott.

The element of tour de force here is, like *Red Badge of Courage*, to strive for vividness and reality *without* research. The historical padding mentioned before is totally illusion. The whole purpose of this historical novel is to be able to say, "I have done absolutely no delving save into the file of useless information I carry in my head."

This entire novel must be an exercise in facility. This is a crafted novel of theme, diametric to the garnered process of *Voyage, Orestes*.

In purpose, this is exactly the opposite of the science fiction. There, ideally, research (of a sort) is a priori. For it to "come off" one must keep a certain ready familiarity with a whole complex of ideas, and remain—even in the most fantastic S-F, such as *The Jewels of Aptor*—consistently within.

But in the historical novel (my historical novel) one must only remain true to form and structure on the aesthetic side, and sensation and emotion on the material. Ideas have nothing to do with it, and—though certainly the book will appear to have ideas—are generated only in the ambiguity of emotion relations.

To retrace my minuets of Primary, Secondary, and Tertiary characters.

Primary characters: loosely defined as the main focus of interest and sympathy in the story. More precisely defined as those characters who support several relationships among themselves and among the secondary characters.

They are:

Dwayn, the hero (referred to as Phillip up till now)
Fulvia, the heroine (princess, of course)
Emelia, Fulvia's companion
The Baron, Fulvia's father, warring on the barbarians.

Secondary characters: those who support only relationships of contrast among themselves, limited to one or 2 relations with primary characters.

Tertiary characters: individual characters, perhaps foils, but never contrasting in emotional characteristics, never paired in relationships.

They are:

1   The Barkeeper
2   The Village Maid
3   The Idiot
4   Old Cassandra
5   The Alchemist

6	The Hermit
7	The Court Jester
8	The Old Duchess
9	The Court Poet
10	The Diplomat
11	The Visiting Moor
12	The Abbess
13	The Barbarian Leader

The Secondary Characters, who come in pairs are:
Two street urchins:

+   +   +

Generalizations are attractive falsities. They differ only in their attractiveness. Their truth values are all equal.

+   +   +

I am a Rat Fink.
I shall write a novel.

+   +   +

The essential difference between James Baldwin and Norman Mailer is that Norman Mailer is sure all Negroes screw better than all whites while James Baldwin is sure that all the Negroes screw better than all whites except him.
(Surreal despair vs. prune-like pessimism.)
> —M. Hacker, on seeing a review of Mary McCarthy's "The Group" by N. Mailer

+   +   +

The Bright Season

Section 2, symmetrical with section 4, rotated about section 3.
1) Geo at Randle's.
2) Jimmy discovers Snake hurt
3) Geo discovers Snake and Jimmy
4) O'Donnells arrives with proposition.
5) Geo's reaction to O'Donnells
6) Geo's reaction after O'Donnells leaves

7) Jimmy leaves work to attend rehearsal
8) Briefly speaks to Ann. Disagree on Geo's directing abilities, but then Jimmy comes around.
9) First encounter with Laile, outside the theatre the next day.
10) Snake beaten up again, Jimmy finds him.
11) Theatre broken into, Geo comes back reporting it.
12) Jimmy asks what this is all about
13) Geo avoids the subject, and Jimmy finds the letter from Laile, brief, wishing good luck on the play, surprised by coldness & lack of emotion.
14) They go to the theatre the next day, Randle is there, and O'Donnells comes, and guarantees cash to rebuild the theatre. Guaranteeing safety.
15) That Sunday, the translations come out and get reviewed. They comment that it was awfully fast work for the paper & wonder why.

+ + +

Black pants—the paint stained ones she wears to the League every day.

Bear dance—M & I used to joke about the stage direction in Shakespeare: "exit pursued by a bear" which for years I had thought was from *Coriolanus*, but in truth was, I believe, from *A Winter's Tale*.

Blonde boy—he had short hair, wore a blue work shirt, dark pants, but is no one I could place in real life.

Joel Nance—a half Negro boy I met first at Camp, very neurotic, very sweet, whom I was intermittently sexually interested in. He eventually went to BHSS where for some reason we were never very close. After I was married, I once heard a tale about him, that things were not going well, and tried very hard to find him, calling people, etc. Quite mysteriously, his name and picture were not in the yearbook.

(The two boys seemed to represent a single thing in the dream, although I was more interested in Joel, I did most of my talking to the blonde boy about arranging to meet.)

Acrophobia—I suffer from it not as a fear of falling, but from a desire to jump, and if my mind is otherwise occupied, it doesn't bother me so much. I noted just yesterday that it seems to be improving (I didn't want to jump under the subway).

+ + +

Dream—Wednesday night–Thursday morning, mid-Oct.

I dreamed I went to a funeral at my father's place, for some important Negro official. Marilyn and I were sitting in the back row. Marilyn had to get up and leave for some reason (we were both wearing black pants, however they didn't strike me as out of place) but I could sense she was afraid I would leave. After she got up, I saw a better seat closer to the front. I went to it, but didn't sit down. I stood there with my hand raised so she would see me when she came in. When she did, she looked about at first not seeing me, and then becoming a little upset. But at last she saw me however, and came down beside me. I felt a trifle annoyed that she was so afraid I had deserted her, that I had to stand up with my hand raised & miss some of the funeral, and that she had not simply looked around at first and seen me. But when she had come at last to sit beside me, I saw she was still a little annoyed and partially suspected (which wasn't completely untrue) that a minor purpose for my moving might have been to annoy her.

Anyway, we sat down to enjoy the funeral. An immense stage had replaced the coffin where the rehearsal of some opera was in progress. We were sitting such that an American flag hanging from the ceiling hid the center of the stage, and the whole auditorium had become as big as Madison Square Garden. A loudspeaker explained that we were witnessing a comparison between "the Metropolitan Opera Method," and something that sounded like "the Bauhaus Method." The chorus was so big it needed four conductors who wore red shorts and danced about the stage together. (I pointed out the conductors, I remember, to Marilyn.) Then the "Met" stage was replaced with the "Bauhaus" stage, but the differences were very minor and the conductors wore blue pants instead of red. Then we were shown the difference in the staging of "the Bear Dance from *Coriolanus*" (!). Here the dissimilarities were more in evidence, for in the "Met" version, the lumbering animals attempted some vaguely Victorian imitation of ballet, while in the following "Bauhaus" version, they ran around the stage in patterns leaping over one another's backs, far more gracefully & well within the function of bears.

The lights came on now, and I was sitting in an immense balcony, vaguely reminiscent of the balcony in the "old building" of BHSS. Marilyn was not beside me, and everyone was getting up to go. Near me was a blonde boy about my age whom I knew and who was hailing me toward someone else. I turned in my seat and saw that Joel Nance was making his way through people & seats toward me. But the same time I turned, I felt a terrible pain in my right buttock. And as Joel & the other boy came up to me, I realized that a loose sliver of plywood on the ancient wooden folding seat had speared me as I turned. I tried to explain as best I could to both of them, and at first there was confusion. At last I got myself unhooked and we began to go up the balcony.

I had vague attacks of acrophobia on the way, but the pain kept me from really worrying about it. I told both boys that I wanted to see them and talk to them and they said something about meeting me, and at last about meeting me at home—by now we were in the upstairs lobby of the theatre—which surprised me because I expected them to come home with me on the train. But they had something they had to do before they came, and so I agreed they would meet me at my house at four-thirty.

Still in pain, and even bleeding a little, I began to wander through the building which was very like a school, and at last reached the basement and some sort of white tiled shower & locker room.

As I stood there the other boys went out and a girl in a white smock came in, telling me she was on the first aid squad. She had black hair and was very pretty. I told her she probably couldn't help me, and she said to let her take a look anyway. I pulled down my pants and could just see the cut. It was far worse than I thought it was, being nearly eight inches long. And we removed a piece of sharp wood nearly an inch wide. Then she produced a spray of some sort of red antiseptic. I was wary of it for fear it would burn. But it didn't and she had a way of getting it into the cut without hurting a bit. I felt much better and we began to joke, the joking at last became sexual, and she kept making odd sarcastic remarks about herself being only a female and an incomplete one at that.

Finally I said half jokingly, "You mean you've never had a vaginal orgasm?"

To which she looked quite surprised, & nodded.

"Don't you know there isn't such a thing?" I told her, and went on to tell her all about the vaginal orgasm myth, for which she looked in turns unbelieving and relieved. I told her about the clitoris, which she wasn't even sure where it was, and feeling much better, as if I repaid her for fixing my wound, I woke up.

* * *

Prologue to this dream, remembered only when I was halfway through writing this. Bernie called us up and wanted to introduce us to a young Puerto Rican friend of his about our age who had just arrived here and knew nobody. So Marilyn and I made arrangements to go visit him for dinner. He was staying in two furnished rooms, neither one with a full kitchen, but was preparing something very elegant involving chicken and roasted almonds on a hot plate, and the dish full of almonds much resembled the pie-plate of filbert nuts at our new apartment.

He was a nice-looking boy with a close cut hair, conservatively dressed, and just a trifle supercilious. We sat only in one room, though the door to the other was open.

With our host was another boy, also Puerto Rican, in blue jeans and a black shirt, a small handsomely chiseled face, and as much hair as head.

Our host, though in everything else the essence of politeness, made no attempt to introduce us, and kept the other boy with him at all times. Knowing Bernie's taste in friends, Marilyn and I exchanged a couple of knowing looks, but made no comment. Yet through all this there was something oddly out of place, a tension between the two. Though our guest always had a hand on the other boy's thigh or shoulder, the looks they exchanged were cold and almost malicious.

Suddenly, as if on a signal, just before dinner, our host pushed the other boy into the back room, and M. & I watched amazed, while two other people, at least one of them Spanish American as well, jumped out and the three of them pushed the other boy into a green armchair, pulled his pants down and off, turned his legs over his head, and our host first kicked off his shoe and stuck his big toe into the boy's rectum as if to loosen it, and then grabbed the immense penis of one of the other assailants and guided it into the boy's rectum.

With a switch like a film cut, we were suddenly eating dinner and our host was carving the chicken. I sat watching the thin knife move in and out of the crisp browned meat, still with the violent vision of the penis of the other man moving in and out of the boy's behind. Only Marilyn, myself, and our host were at table.

My interest in the boys was only one quarter sexual, and I was aware of it
    in the dream, and also aware that I really wanted to talk to them.
Spearing my buttock—almost identical to the experience when Marilyn
    & I had a double bed. Marilyn left for the League one morning, while
    I was still in bed. She kissed me good-bye, and as I turned over to say

goodbye to her, I skewered my cheek on a broken spring. I was so surprised, I didn't even cry out. It took me five seconds (M had blithely walked out the door) to get unhooked.

Four-thirty—the time I used to get home from Dalton. Though I expected to take the train home, as from Science, rather than the bus, as from Dalton.

The girl in the locker room—physically she resembled a girl from Dalton—Jill Newman—but she was terribly sweet, and understanding, while J.M. tended to be somewhat of a hellion.

V.O.T.—no feeling—and I looked for it—that I was making speech to avoid having sex. At the time we were just talking & having fun; it could have easily become physical after that. Or maybe I'm rationalizing?

*　*　*

This dream came, as noted, before the other one. We could have easily left dinner at our host's house to go to the funeral. Only Marilyn was definitely wearing a skirt when we went visiting, and was on her best behavior.

Situation—Bernie has done this, but the boy (Julio?) came to our house for dinner, and the evening, though not unpleasant, was not a resounding success, because guests kept dropping in, and stories were told in which nobody bothered to explain the difficult words, for Julio's English was not good.

Our host—he was a boy I saw on the train yesterday morning coming home from Peter Hutchinson's. He was riding between the cars, and I was wondering what my "acrophobia" would do if I did too? (Might I stick a foot between the cars on purpose?) However, the boy on the train had none of the effete manners of our host—in that our host was more like Julio.

Other boy—he resembled Jesus Quiñones whom I taught reading to back when I lived at Morningside, and for a while I thought it was him. But it wasn't.

Hot plate—I have already commented on the almonds—the hot plate could easily have been the electric frying pan M. & I found in our new apartment and cooked dinner on just this evening.

Green armchair—it is the one also left in our apartment, now sitting in the bedroom.

Situation—Puerto Rican in the furnished room, told to me by Bernie . . .
Bernie told me that he had moved Tony Calon on into a furnished room. Perhaps we were symbolically going to visit Tony, though he was not in the dream.

+   +   +

Just for the hell of it, let's transfer my historical novel from medieval central Europe to pre-Christian Asia Minor.

+   +   +

The Ballad of Beta-2

Notes for last section

> Captain Lee, Judge Cartwright
> Blind Billy & his wife Jann
> Sales Clerk Keth of the market
> News of first destruction—Judge
> The Executioner & the One-eyes
> The Green Eyed destroyer
> The call from the other captain.

+   +   +

Saturday—late October.

M not feeling well and stayed in bed all day. I spent a few hours this evening ordering her manuscripts and notebooks.

———

For vivid action: purposeful, habitual, gratuitous. Conflicts,

+   +   +

To Marilyn (in conversation):
If André Gide been a Jew,
He very likely might be you.

(Her answer)
If André Gide had been a she
He very likely might be me
(And that is why I feel no need
To start becoming André Gide.)

+   +   +

Things not to forget as we wind up—at last!—*Voyage, Orestes.*

Snake again—
  —Karry gets Jimmy job—make explicit Karry's relation to Geo.
Ann sings. *The Jewels of Aptor* comes out!
The growth of a legend
Laile is publishing them in her magazine.

+   +   +

55   Prologue

85   The Road (Ann introduced)
43   The Bridge
4   Margaret Mourning
<u>73</u>   The City (Ann reappears)
204

45   Limestone (Ann arrives)
51   Oblation (Ann is identified)
39   Summer
4   Snake
55   Scorpion
150   Tyme and Space (Ann appears and acts)
45   Elektra
<u>30</u>   The Roads
420

35   Behooves me
101   The Bright Season (Ann returns)
35   Halls of Night
9   Margaret at Dawn

<u>50</u>   This Then My Voice (Ann witnesses)

230

10   Epilogue

259

240

<u>420</u>

919

+   +   +

Nothin' conjures up the jism
like a little onanism

Nothing else is half so nice as
childish solitary vices

What's your favorite occupation
Have you heard of masturbation

Hurry up, I think I'm comin'
set a bowl to save the scum in
—M.T.H.—1963

Got some energy to work off
Lock the bathroom door and jerk off

Metaphysic, rather mystic
deep inside I'm narcissistic.

Open your mouth & close your eyes,
then grab your dick and fantasize

Will you get out of here you bum
can't you see I'm about to come

Hope nobody asks me why
that I've got come tracks on my fly.

+ + +

A bit of journalizing—last night I finished the climactic chapter of *Voyage, Orestes*, "The High Halls of Night," and this morning I went on and finished "Margaret at Dawn"—I have no idea if any of it is satisfactory or not. The book has assumed a strange, over-real weight. At once, I am terribly anxious for it to be done and finished with; something I have been working on for almost three years, to suddenly raise its termination; what shall I do next—

—I have another novel in mind, but whether I have faith in it or not is still an odd question to consider at this point (I am sure I will do it, but . . .)—

—and as well, there is the coming job of cutting, revising, etc. that must be done—Bobs, my editor, seems to feel it will be more painful than I do—or am I perhaps so numbed by the act of creation that the prospect of the pain means very little.

But on to the last chapter: at least in notes: "This Then My Voice."

1

Ann and Jimmy—dismissing the question of the guards at the plant. They go back to Geo's to get some stuff.

2

Laile is there, gathering the poems. A moment later, Mark Hetland comes

+ + +

Tomorrow—Monday

Get copy of "Prism & Glass" to Bernie
Retrieved M.S. from David Litwin
Get Play to Bernie
Get "What Dreams May Come" down from your mother.
Call Miss Kale at Appleton Cen. Crofts, about P. & G, and say hello to Bobs

NOTEBOOK 71—[WINTER 1963]

The Assassination

Notes now—I am almost finished with *Voyage Orestes* (22 pages into the High Halls of Night) and the melange of a new novel is a pressing necessity. I would like this book to take place both in and out of society.

Try to avoid appearing like the *Counterfeiters*. It is the secondary characters of my "Historical" novel moving around two sets of principal characters. Keep the homosexuality down to a passing mention.

You will need settings:

One or two upper-middle bourgeois homes for main characters. Church, or church school. Lots of lower-class homes & vicinity.

The school for children, contrasted with the school for assassins. Three principal groups for the assassination: the criminals, the family, the school.

+ + +

Geo's death per se

Jimmy & Bunny come out on the little balcony. Geo & Snake. March arrives, Geo balks, Edna calls from the catwalk, they drop the net, then Laile runs up.

Loupo runs out for the body, but the other net falls. They scream, and distract them from Snake, who runs and disappears.

Outside there's a siren. They converge in the cellar on the

—handfuls of white light flung like water against our faces

+ + +

The Assassination

Short chapters, five to ten pages long, titled. The writer's name is Ramsy.

Primary Characters

Ramsy—SF writer who lives in the village.
Mr. Michaels, the senator

Open three chapters are set in Thommy's family.

Author comments, to be used, but formally and set apart from the action.
Division of styles:
    Actions—direct thoughts of characters, situational analysis—author
    comment upon structure of book.

<u>Action and description</u>
    Usual style

Direct thoughts of characters
Stream of consciousness modified grammatically

Situational analysis
Academic prose stripped as clean as possible

Author comment

+   +   +

<u>Growth of Legend</u>

The publicity, magazine use, etc.

Was he really a hero, just walk[ed] into it.

Need of child prodigy.
    Greenberg

* * *

Old poems vs. new work

Homosexual or not

Prediction of his own death

* * *

I knew him when (borrowed a typewriter from me)

Literary demotic presence, golden ages of literature always dramatic

Running symbolism, characters from Carmina Catulli in play
who was Claudia

Last poem was [worst] vs. best

Hanky-panky with wife & with syndicate; he lived his life for his biographers.

Wonder when the O'Donnells biography should come out, his wife doesn't want him to do it. What's she doing now anyway. Went to that warehouse. There isn't any warehouse

+ + +

Page 78 insert. (?)

From our own encounters, I had somehow assumed that all Geo's sex with men was masochistic, or at least violent. But Snake (his shirt slipped to the floor) turned toward Geo who with his hands on the boy's face, pressed his cheek against the mute face; and firmly his hands moved over the taut small muscles of the back, darker than his fingers. And a steady, quiet rhythm took their two bodies. I went into the kitchen.

+ + +

Let us calm down and take stock:
What is left to do?

Phaedra	−2	HA!
Beta-2	−1	
City of a Thousand Suns	−3	HA!
The Tribal Novel	−4	
The Assassination	−6	HA!
The Beasts	−5	

"Dork and Carmina Catulli"
The Fall of the Towers

+ + +

Conversation

"But don't you ever feel that women are castrating you? They just want to cut your balls off and lock them up in the linen closet?"
"Well, I remember once when a group of Asian cannibals were literally

after my balls. They used to cut them from their enemy and hang them over the doors of their huts. Nearly had me there, too. But somehow, after that, one just doesn't mind what you fellows call a castrating woman. At best I just wonder what your balls are stuck on with. They always seem to be about to come off so easily. Basically, what it seems like, is that whenever you're unhappy, or have done something

+ + +

Another Country

After talking about this book for a couple of years, reading at it, having gone through three quarters of it as many as six or seven times, and having never laid eyes on one quarter, I finally read the whole thing from first page to last, and suddenly reversed my opinion. I have been considering it a bad book with a few very powerful scenes and some fairly exciting writing. I now find that it is a good book with several very weak points.

Structurally what it seems to be about is three relations, two of which, by the end, will live and produce something worthwhile for the people involved, primarily because they have the element of danger, in one case an interracial affair, in the other, homosexuality, while the third relation, which has the safety of marriage, children, & a fair amount of social success, is destroyed because it has made no provision for precisely that danger.

One of the main faults of the book is in the opening chapter which seems to be meant to serve as a sort of catalyst for the development of the other relationships.

I take the brother of one of the women involved through his memories on the night of his suicide. The flashbacks within flashbacks are downright clumsy. Also, the character is presented as such a despicable specimen that it is very hard to have too much sympathy with those who protest that they love him. The power in the writing is there, however. Also, one of those flashbacks could have well been devoted to establishing the character as an individual affected by society. His cry is so constantly against this society that after a while we almost cease to believe it because it is never shown in any magnitude.

+ + +

Dear Bobs,

Having at last re-read my magnum opus, I have quite independently arrived at many of the things you've been hinting at for so long, and I have been feebly responding. My feeling right now is that you have something like a shadow of a novel on your hands—or rather a very heavily shadowed novel.

Onward to see if we can hack away some of the shadows. In the copy I have, I have been quietly trying to tie up some of the loose ends, which has primarily been cutting out their beginnings. There are a lot of discrepancies, loose ends, etc. For what it's worth, the answer to all but one has been

+ + +

In my next novel, a man and a woman must rise from one end of society to the other and a man and a woman must fall.

+ + +

—diachronic
—synchronic
de Saussure
syntagmatic

+ + +

Check Bernie for address on *Those Spared by Fire*
Check Ace for royalty check due.

+ + +

Winter, and I am twenty-one. I'm preparing to strike Christmas with all the strength I can muster. Times Square will explode on Christmas day and the colored pieces will fly so far they will never be able to get it back together for the new year's mob. Today is December 13, a Friday to boot. That seems propitious. Less than a month ago a madman smashed the figurehead of the whole country which doused the world & his wife with blood. A weekend of hysteria and lies ended when the smashed was smashed. Kennedy, Oswald, & Ruby, father, son, & holy ghost. Two generations from now, as many people will know Oswald's name as know the name of the mad slayer of President Garfield. I don't know who shot Garfield. Death in the bloody lap of the nation's mother, Jacqueline. Is that another name of the Goddess, Ananstha, Anatha, Rhea, Sheol, Demeter, Ishtar, Jacqueline, Thetis? Perhaps.

Somebody else is slouching toward Christmas to be born. It will be me, this time. I'll strike so deep to centers the pack will scatter. Even now I have been searching the rim of various mystical insanities, deciding which to put on. I will wear them all, perhaps, and loaded with maniacal splendor, my myth will ride through the shattered world. If I must go mad in order to live, I will go mad.

I have searched the skulls of many young men. The women were harder, for being a wounded male, I found their blood both bright and soothing, their minds too electric. It is my failing, not theirs.

Imagine a combination of *Mansfield Park* & *Naked Lunch*. Miss Austen's amoral prudishness, and Mr. Burroughs' prudish amorality. Perhaps they would cancel the shadows and reveal art.

In the image of the long grey river, between bare December bushes, I seek a merging of the spinning diametricacies of poetry and life. Poetry separate from art is a bastard turn used till now by the undisciplined divine lunatics of romanticism. Lunatic and divine, their definition will serve.

I am looking for a pack, a herd of wolves racing in the city's winter with ice glittering on their coats. For twenty-one years I have been trying to create my own.

I swear with the coming of Christmas, I will fix my blade in the thrusting flood of time and then my metaphysic death will cease, and I shall rage congruent with the river.

I have just given a watch as a Chanukah present. Time fixed with the coming of light. It is square, gold, with thin hands and numbers, and a black suede band. It is very beautiful and very terrible. It will be interesting to see if the watch can stand the strain. It may well explode, because my journey in time will be so erratic, sideways, up, down, but never backwards. The chronic angularity will be terrific, and beautiful.

Very well, then, I am almost prepared for birth.

+ + +

The Darkeys are Happy and Gay

There are three books that should be talked about in light of each other, because in the triple illumination they give, both in bright spots and shadows, something particularly American: William Gaddis' *The Recognitions*, James Baldwin's *Another Country*, and John Rechy's *City of Night*. They are all very exciting works on the various levels that they work on. They are also all very flawed works, so much so that in all three cases the critics have seen fit to say that the flaws destroy the validity of the works. They are three widely different books on the surface. *City of Night* is a work whose power depends primarily on a sort of catastrophic energy. It uses hastily discarded symbols instead of characters, but its overriding metaphor is a sort of mythified vision of homosexual prostitution (it should be so glamorous) and it suffers basically from the same limitations as the romantic prostitutes of the fairer sex have suffered—salvation is accomplished in a blaze of religious glory that rings about as true as a glass dollar.

+ + +

Blues Jumped the Rabbit
Hard Rain
Keep On Keeping On
Roll Down the Line
Nottamun Town
Blues On the Ceiling
Vandy
She Moved Through the Fair
Well, Well, Well
Alabama
Greenland Fishery
[The Song of] Wandering Aengus
Bells of Rhymney
Railroad Bill
In the Pines
When I was a Young Girl
Wants to Get to Heaven
Pretty Horses
Go Away From My Window
Ain't No More Cane on this Brazos
Good Old Wagon

+ + +

Opening Scene for Novel

Inside a shop—young apprentice and old craftsman.

Contemplate: is the essence of the Faust myth the story of a man who sells his soul for wealth, fame, or (à la Thomas Mann) achievement in great art—the soul's sacrifice represented by the sacrifice of pure and true love. Or is it something more subtle?

Hero—Luke Faust—great name—music crafter—

Faust—sixteen—comes under influence of "violin maker" through violence. Their relation is terminated by violence as well.

Part (organic, not paginatory) I, under the influence of museum curate, Leonie (perhaps).

Part II   Under the influence of the Bear

part III
Social structuring

Notes for *Faust* or *Young Faustus*

Faust's second encounter with the devil—in circus.

Dr. Branning

The School (the town)

The City

The Town (the school)

The Country

+   +   +

I have reached a point in writing, where it appears that the only way to go on is to throw over all I have learned about constructing scene, sentence, conflict, or drama, and relearn it in terms of a new single work, each effect controlled as subjugated to the total power of the work.

To create this work, I must survey life as it strikes me through literature *checked carefully* against observation (let us avoid such totally unsalvageable monstrosities as *Afterlon*).

There is Love—self-destructive fearful love, there is healthy love, there is casual boring love.

Art—There is involved, effective but false art, there is powerful, conscious, constructive art, there is casual commercial art.

Religion, deep and moving response to a religious tradition.
Hypocritical belief for social gain.
Casual religion, neither good nor bad.

Manners—Genuine social propitiousness.
Affectation to impress.
Casual good breeding common to all classes.

Political action—sincerely for society.
For personal gain.
Momentum in which vice and virtue struggle through as best they can.

Craftsmanship—honest pride in the work.
False pride to impress.
Competence through repetition.

+   +   +

"City of a Thousand Suns"

Chapter IV
    Alter & Jon, talks about father, her aunt. (Information about Nonik) Go out, she swipes apples. Jon and she discuss the moral dichotomy. She agrees. Mentions Tel. At inn, she meets her aunt. Jon watches & realizes similarities. He stays and talks to psych-officer. Leaves with Alter. Aunt wanted her to stay, and she couldn't.

Chapter V
    Jeof alone
    Renna's mother and Dr. Wental.
    The Duchess and King Let.
    Arkor alone

Chapter VI
    —interlude at the City of a Thousand Suns.

Chapter ?

Jon maneuvers Alter through a social evening at palace Ball.

Chapter VII

All that is aristocracy is gone

End chapter with Jon and Alter running to kiss. In the middle, person looking runs away ("can't you do something decent")

Chapter VIII

Opens with discussion of Kino who overheard, its effect (in terms of random configuration of events)—doesn't recognize Jon.

King's statement, All that is human is gone—ends chapter with death.

Chapter IX

Begins with the kiss completed, and the discovery of the temple, the people doing good, Jon discouraged—asks Alter if any of this worth anything; does it mean anything to anybody. Meets man who was in the mine—how Jon's escape gave him hope.

The priests lecture on random spread of violence and hate. They marry.

Meets the character who turns out to be Nonik

Chapter X

Further adventures with Jon & Alter—1) Guards, 2) the penal mine, 3) Getting into Telphar, saved by the young man of Chapter IX, who after fighting the Computer's deviousness—finally issues them into the Chamber of the Stars where they meet Catham & Clea.

Chapter XI

Clea & Catham & Nonik explain why they have come to Telphar—the creative individual must commit himself to his individual product, not with the betterment of society in mind. Not that the present society is good. This is government censorship. Nor does it mean one pay lip [service] through one's commitment that the present society is improving. But it does mean bearing constantly in mind a concept that man, throughout all his elements, bestial to godlike, as individual or group, can order the random chaos into a meaning[ful] and significant form.

+   +   +

Note on *Faust*

Two of the most difficult ways to make a lasting friendship is from a casual sexual encounter, or from a brief exposure to a person's work, artistic or otherwise, but an ability to do this is a mark of a truly civilized man or woman.

+ + +

Synopsis of Faust Myth

Faust, having gotten all the worldly wisdom possible, turns to the supernatural for solace. He must make a deal with the Devil, the irrational, which means, eventually, destruction during which he loses a true, rational loved one. She dies.

With her death, Faust gains control over the irrational, and can create his own love, classical Helen and the Homunculus.

Eventually he decides he must assume full responsibility for his irrational actions.

The Devil—the minister of the irrational—Leo? Corbelli? Both. A rational man.

Faust—a total homosexual? Dry as homunculus? Possibly.

Synopsis of *Faust* Symbols.

The Devil as a Black Dog, for the patriarchal religions
The Devil as a white wolf for the Goddess.

Perhaps I can use Russell for Faust.

Nuclear physicist, slightly gay, under the influence of Leo, Corbelli, accepts Catherine, remakes Drey only to discover is relation to the irrational which destroys him. Destroys him—perhaps use the opening chapter as the first *Walpurgisnacht*, the last, a drugged foray through the museum where Corbelli has stolen something. Why the intrigue from Leo's point of view, with Corbelli and Leo left whole at the end.

Now, for a plot summary.

Faust equals Russell. He meets Leo at the Museum, and from there, he gets involved with Catherine. Leo, mythologically irrational, Catherine too rational. Catherine dies under his influence. Goes to Corbelli, worldly rational. From there he mints Drey, mythologically irrational, destructive, and eventually he, Leo, and Drey try to destroy Corbelli, and fail in the museum, drugged. Corbelli's dog and the white wolf.

Opening chapter, the white wolf.

Part One
>   The White Wolf

Part Two
>   Catherine

Part Three
>   Neggra

Part Four
>   Drey

Part Five
>   Night

+   +   +

Two Murders
Three Lesbian Sequences
Two Homosexual   "
An Attempted Rape
Three Fully Described Heterosexual Sequences
And Several Minor Ones
An Excruciatingly Bloody Miscarriage

Greenwich Village
The Newport Folk Festival
And the Eternal Road
Religious Ecstasy and Revelation
The Mafia
Folk Singers
Poets
The Negro question

+   +   +

City of a Thousand Suns
Dénouement
>   Any act of coming together invalidates the war
>   A war is running away

+   +   +

Detailed Plan of Entire Faust novel
    Hey! Hey!

Chapter (Part, Section, Book ...) one.
    Faust, student of engineering, receives news of his parents' death. Two professors discussing in terms of whether to pass him or fail him—original work, but standard work is inadequate—interrupted by Faust who somewhat embarrassedly comes in and announces he's leaving. Faust and the academic art teacher—nothing to teach him. A world without artistic values has driven him into the university.
    Faust sets up an apartment in the lower east side.

+ + +

Dr. Gabriel de la Vega
12 E. 72nd St.
LE5—8060

211 East 43rd St.
Room 1107

"Those spared by fire ..."

1   The Small Ellipse—Paul, and Kim in the theater with the nameless boy
2   Three Sketches—Paul and Fern in their Eurydice myth
3   Animal in the City—Simon and the Jewish boys
4   Tales of Binomial—Jimmy & His Family
5   Sodom—Paul, Bruno, & the Sodom-house
6   Vox Humana—Paul, and the Christ Episode
7   The New Directrix: Barbara, Bruno, & Paul, in a thrill kill.

The Small Ellipse   Kim
Animal in the City   Barbara
Three Sketches   Fern
The Directrix   Barbara
Sodom
The Binomial Expansion
Vox Humana   Barbara

+ + +

Possible front matter for the third volume of the trilogy:—they have been reduced to cutting down the old stuff, and that will never do.

Here is the third book in Samuel R. Delany's trilogy of the war of Toromon, "City of a Thousand Suns." Through these three volumes roam soldiers, scientists, kings, duchesses, acrobats, innkeepers, thieves, street urchins, poets, historians, mind readers, idiots, acrobats, the young adventurer Jon Koshar, plus a gallery of intergalactic allies and adversaries.

A gory political assassination, a daring escape from the penal mines by a radiation soaked desert, survival in jungle peopled by mutants and giant telepaths, murder at the hands of a Neanderthal brute, a citywide epidemic of poison food, a royal kidnapping, an interrupted coronation, people who can appear and vanish, magnificent balls, mass plunder and destruction, a search through a deadly, irradiated city, a gigantic computer gone insane, a ribbon of metal hundreds of miles long that can transmit matter in an instant, as well as magnificent flights across the universe, go to make these three books a colorful, vivid, and enthralling panoramic portrait of a nation at war in the thirty-fifth century.

+ + +

Structure for the rest of "City of a Thousand Suns"
—we are now just nearing the end of chapter five.

Six & Seven—Alter & Jon, adventuring toward Telphar.

Eight—The capture of the Royal Palace and the murder of the King and Duchess

Nine & Ten—further adventures of Tel & Alter.

Eleven—The discovery of Clea, Catham, & Nonik at Telphar.

Interlude at the City of a Thousand Suns. Clea & Catham send Nonik to Toron & Alter & Jon to the City of a Thousand Suns.

Twelve—The Fall of the Towers.

+ + +

Plot structure for New Novel, "Faust Metamorphosized"

First of all, a heroine rather than a hero: plucky young girl. Must range from the City to the Town to the Castle.

Vaughn & Laila, middle thirties, rich, sophisticated, and a whole retinue about them, pick up with young Catherine, plucky, bright, artistic. Three affairs: with friendly sexual brute—with sadistic, rich doctor—with invalid mystic. Her friends—S. S. Burke—Sue Sholley type, bright, educated, a bit dykey ("Don't you wish you were a Lesbian.") Pat, totally "feminine type," however, will drop everything at a moment's notice to come to the aid of her friend. Malicious children—Karan and Ralf, the twins—terrible were moving to destroy Vaughn and Laila.

+ + +

New York Psychoanalytic Institute
Columbia Psycho-analytic   "
Post Graduate Center

7

··································

Babel-17 and Beyond

··································

Notebook 26 contains entries treating Delany's time at Mount Sinai Hospital. A key figure in these entries is Dr. Grossman, Delany's primary therapist at Mount Sinai, with whom Delany continued private treatment after his stint at the hospital.[1] Also mentioned in these entries are patients in Delany's therapy group, several of whom appear in *The Motion of Light in Water*. Especially important among them is Deirdre, whose suicide, described in the entry of July 6, 1964, would, forty years later, provide the model for a major episode in Delany's novel *Dark Reflections*.[2] Note that there is a discrepancy between the dates of inscription of the entries in Notebook 26 and Delany's account of his time at Mount Sinai in *Motion*: the entries date from the summer of 1964, whereas in *Motion* Delany represents the same period as beginning a few months later, in autumn.[3]

A different sort of chronological ambiguity in the notebooks from this period requires some explanation. In the summer of 1961, shortly before traveling to Detroit to be married, Delany and Hacker took a camping trip to Bear Mountain, north of New York City among the Hudson Highlands. During the trip, they developed a grammar and lexicon for a syntactically and semantically compressed artificial language. Delany's notes on this linguistic experiment can be found in Notebook 26. Shortly afterward, during their bus ride to Detroit, Delany and Hacker worked further on the language; Delany's notes on that work can be found in Notebook 27. Notebooks 26 and 27, then, contain material written in 1961. The remaining entries in these notebooks, which date from 1964, were written around this older material.[4] Thus, the date named in the title of the entry from Notebook 26, "Camping on Bear Mountain / Summer evening 1964," designates the time of inscription rather than of the camping trip itself; in this entry Delany is presumably responding, in 1964, to his notes from 1961 on the artificial language and the occasion of his writing them.

Following his time in Mount Sinai, Delany decided to re-enroll in City College for the spring semester of 1965.[5] Among the projects he began to develop shortly before returning to school was *Babel-17*, a space opera that takes the notion of a compressed artificial language as its central science-fictional premise. Like the notebooks dating from Delany's time at Bronx Science and his previous stint at City College, the notebooks from this period contain both creative work and school notes. This juxtaposition expresses, as it had in the earlier notebooks, the tension Delany felt between the worlds of school and art; in several entries from this period Delany discusses this tension directly.

Three drafts of correspondence from this period warrant further discussion. The first, in Notebook 87, is a letter to a Mr. Wright. Wright was an acquaintance of Delany's mother who worked at City College and had promised to facilitate Delany's return to school.[6] The second, in Notebook 29, is a draft of a letter to Henry Morrison, who had recently formed his own literary agency and was representing both mainstream and genre writers. In anticipation of his trip to Europe, Delany decided that the time had come to secure an agent who could represent him during his travels.[7] When Morrison took on Delany as a client, it was the beginning of a life-long professional relationship.

The third piece of correspondence, a note from Delany to Hacker near the end of Notebook 29, concerns Bob Folsom. Folsom was a young man from Florida whom Delany had met through Bernie Kay. Delany invited Folsom back to his and Hacker's home for dinner, and the three soon began a ménage à trois, which Delany describes in detail in *Motion*.[8] This period, which appears to have been happy for all three, came to an end when Folsom invited his estranged wife, a half–Native American woman three years his senior, to New York City with the intention of bringing his relationship with her to a close.[9] However, this created new tensions between her and Folsom, and in the spring of 1965, to escape the volatile situation, Folsom decided to hitchhike to Texas. Delany accompanied him, and over the ensuing summer, both together and separately, the two worked on shrimp boats off the Texas coast.[10]

Although Delany discusses the ménage à trois and the Texas trip extensively in *Motion*, the notebooks seem hardly to mention them. Delany did in fact write at length about the Texas trip in the notebooks, but in the form of longhand letters to Hacker, which he then tore from the notebooks and sent. These letters were, in turn, among those lost, with *Journaux d'Orphée* and other material, during the move from Joe Soley and Paul Caruso's apartment.[11]

The Texas trip appears to have galvanized Delany creatively. Notebook 29, which Delany began immediately after his return, contains not just outline notes and extensive sequences from *Babel-17*—the writing of which had been on hold during the Texas trip—but also early outlines, miscellaneous notes, and sequences for his next two novels, *Empire Star* and *The Einstein Intersection*, as well as the novella "The Star-Pit."

Shortly after Delany's return to New York City, Folsom, still in Texas, was arrested for disorderly conduct, and toward the end of Notebook 29 we find the note from Delany to Hacker discussing the incident.[12] Folsom briefly returned to New York, then headed back to Florida, where he ultimately ended up serving a long jail sentence.[13]

Having secured Morrison's representation and finished *Babel-17*, Delany departed for Europe on October 18, 1965. He funded the trip partly through the sale of *Empire Star*, which he drafted over the course of two weeks and edited and typed over two more.[14] He was accompanied by Ron Helstrom, a friend he had made while working the Texas shrimp boats.[15] On the plane ride over, the two picked up a third traveling companion, a young Canadian named Bill Balousiak.[16] The end of Notebook 29 marks the conclusion of the period of Delany's life covered in *The Motion of Light in Water*.

NOTES

1. Samuel R. Delany, *The Motion of Light in Water: Sex and Science Fiction Writing in the East Village* (1988; reprint, Minneapolis: University of Minnesota Press, 2004), 336.

2. Samuel R. Delany, *Dark Reflections* (New York: Carroll & Graf, 2007), 171–72.

3. Delany, *Motion*, 335.

4. Samuel R. Delany, interview with Kenneth James, March 27, 2016.

5. Ibid., 415.

6. Ibid.

7. Ibid., 553.

8. Ibid., 415–74.

9. Delany, interview with James, August 9, 2014; Delany, *Motion*, 463.

10. Delany, *Motion*, 474.

11. Delany, interview with James, August 9, 2014.

12. Delany, *Motion*, 543.

13. Ibid., 549.

14. Delany, interview with James, October 30, 2011.

15. Delany, *Motion*, 508–10.

16. Ibid., 570.

Synopsis of Geography & locality, with contrasts

The City
    The Lower East Side, market & melting pot
    The Brannings, Midtown
    Harlem & Lyontine's home
    The Museum

—the World's Fair Interlude—

The Country
    The Stables
    The Mountains
    The Deserted Town
    The Pagans

The Town
    The School
    The Convent
    The Bridge Trestle

The book should be a progression from scene and counter scene, character and contrasting character, conflicts of a broad, adventurous nature, contemporary, the major characters:

Dr. & Dr. Branning
Du Lac Branning
    Vrest Dorton

+   +   +

Insight about anger → sex.
    Anger at Dr. Grossman—trying to reach same, on subway the beginning of the stomach cramps, which turned into sexual desire: decide to put my

penis in my pants where visible, in this neighborhood (homosexual and P.R.) an almost socially acceptable way of displaying "manhood"—sexual desire in me very sadistic—usually masochistic—continued until I was cruised by a squirt of a faggot—both fear, desire, and anger mounted—then went away, along with anxiety; replaced by a vague, pleasant desire to masturbate or perhaps have sex.

Insight:

What is "homosexual" about this society is not having gotten over the concern with the "father's role." Focus is all patriarchal. I had distinguished between my positive and negative feelings about Dr. Grossman (how, in this situation, he was like and not like my father). Love-hate tensions resolve into sexual desire.

Pattern of homosexual: hates father, desires a son, instead of mother. This holds the explanation of the "buddy" mania this country suffers from.

+ + +

Let's see if we can take the pornography a little further than usual.

I

At four I got on the subway, my lungs full of night and my eyes heavy and my mouth wet. I haven't found anything all night and my stomach was sort of curled up like it gets then. The car was nearly empty; three people at the other end, a beefy motherfucker in scuffed work boots, black pants, a canvas jacket with frayed cuffs. He was shorter than me by an inch, maybe, with a sun burned face and dusty blond hair. His eyes were like gray engines—why I say engines I don't know—working in his face that was broad and heavy boned. His hands were big, his nails chewed way the hell back from his broad nubs. One hand was on his thigh, the other absently scratching his crotch.

I thought, maybe he'll let me suck him, in the part of my head reserved for fantasies. But he looked up, and kept on looking when I sat down and didn't look away. He prodded his plums with his spatulate stud of his thumb, and just on a hunch I scratched my crotch. He grinned and rubbed harder: then he drawls, grinning, "Cocksucker, I'm hot as a bitch."

He was a little drunk, I guess, but what the hell. I got up and sat down next to him with my leg against his. The muscles shifted against mine.

The silence is long and what would be embarrassing if I hadn't been here so many times before. All the stock come-ons like, "That's a handful of cock you got there," etc., etc. are repulsive, but they give the guys trying to come on this butch an entrance into the role they'll be playing; so I say, at last, "I wanna suck cock."

"I wanna get sucked, man," he says. "I guess that means we're sort of looking for each other," and smiles, which is sort of surprising. Most guys like this are pretty nice if they'll let themselves be. But usually it's too much trouble—for both. He looks at me a moment, rubs his hand hard over his meat and says, "That'll fill your face up." Then, almost as though he realizes he's coming on too strong, he says, "You wanna work on my stud?"

So I lick my lips, and he turns his hips up, squeezing his pecker again. "Give you a few fingers in your face, too," he says, a little quickly. "You don't like my fuckin' hands, do you, sucker?"

Belligerently he puts his hand on my thigh, squeezing a little. I hesitate—my neck feels cold—then pick his hand up and run his middle finger into my mouth, sucking and tonguing that broken nail. I glance at him: he looks a little funny. "I guess you do like it." Then he says, "I like that, sucker." Grinning, he puts another finger in my mouth, rubbing them over my tongue. "You wanna suck it here?" he asks, and we are both suddenly aware that there are special things.

I glance at the other people in the car. He looks over. "You don't care about those motherfuckers, they won't even see. Do 'em good if they do."

He takes his hand out of my mouth and puts it behind my neck and pulls my face into his and his tongue works deep in my throat, spurting his urgent saliva in a flood into my mouth. He pulls away, bright. "See, I ain't pullin' no shit with you. But I wanna see you down there working that stud over." I reach for his hand, rub his finger, the big hard wedge of his dick.

"Go down, sucker," he says, and then, "I wanna push your face down on my prick."

The smile just touches the muscles behind my face, but he catches it, grins, grabs my head and pulls it down. I slip around to the floor, my knees scraping on the gray flooring. I grabbed his leg to steady me, and my face goes into his crotch, tonguing the back of his hand, ligaments and the cross-roping of veins, his fingers and the rough cloth of his pants over the hard nozzle of his dick.

He rubbed, squirmed, and I licked; he said, "Man, I gotta piss," and suddenly there was a wet salty blotch spreading under my mouth.

The excitement rang like a plucked wire from my tongue, down through my stomach to the base of my balls. "Take it out and drink it, sucker," he said.

He had thumbed his fly halfway down, and I nuzzled the sweaty golden rose that pushed through. I open his fly the rest of the way and pull out thick, tan cock, that bounces up, quivering from the gold brush. He moves his hands to the side, pissing in my face, while I dig out his big heavy ball bag. I jam my face down on his spurting pecker, and he shoves it into my face. The piss is warm in my mouth, strong, and bitter. With one hand he reaches down and squeezes his balls, while with the other, runs his fingers through my hair.

He squirms into my face saying, "Drink my fuckin' piss, sucker, drink it!"

It slides down my throat, all eight stocky inches. He's put one of his legs between mine and I'm rubbin' on him like a dog.

Now he starts to jerk off, beating me in the face with his fist, drawling obscenities down over me, "Love my pecker, you bastard. Oh, love it, baby. Drink it, you sweet cocksucker." He shoots, I feel him quiver like a struck staff in my face, a hammered stake vibrating. Then he falls back grabbing my hair. After a couple of gasped breaths, he pulls me slowly off his pecker and grins down. "Don't swallow," he says. "Give it to me." And he opens his mouth over mine. I give it to him; and we spritz it back & forth a couple of times, and he starts to jerk off again. It runs down our chins.

He takes it all at last, and pushes me upright. I know what he wants now. I shove my dick—which has been out—into his slimy face, and his tongue loves it like his fingers love my ass and balls. I shoot into that big face and he loves it. It comes up from my knees and he hugs my ass. He keeps it in, and I notice his stud is up again. Slowly he comes off, grinning up at me. "You'll never guess what's behind you," he says.

I frown.

"You want to sit on my stud piece,

+ + +

Outline for yet another science-fiction novelette.

Rahm, the Barbarians' conquest of Marinor.

1

Rahm and Lororq the pirate duel on the raging spit at night. Lororq begging for his life, gives him a ring and a few minutes later is killed, implying a secret.

2

Sketch of oppression by the people of Marinor, the beginning of a rebellion by Tark blacksmith, quelled, but observed by Naä.

3

The King and Princess Alizar plot to milk the people further and get arms for Owlmhia and conquer Calvicon, with reference to ring.

4

Rahm is washed ashore. Sees oppression, meets Naä, Tark, hears of Klikit. If they can only get the other ring—myth of the old King & Queenship.

5

Pulls Klikit away from beautiful girls, to steal ring from Princess Alizar.

6

Rahm is set upon by men [who] steal the other ring.

7

Klikit steals ring.

8

Rahm meets beautiful green-eyed woman who tries to find out plans
Seduction culminating
Naä and Tark begin plans to free country and fall in love.

9

Klikit returns, with ring, hears the other has been lost, is disgusted.

10

Naä has been captured. Rahm and Tark rescue her. Discover green-eyed woman is a spy.

11

Drowns his sorrows in further freeing of Marinorians. Meets a woman who tells him where the second ring [is].

12

Calls Klikit away from beautiful women to come steal ring. This time, Klikit needs his help. Steals ring, but discovers Woman—

13

—discovers Woman in the King's arms. For her sake spares the prince, but drowns his sorrows in freeing more Marinorians.

14

Gives the rings to Naä & Tark who tell how well the revolution is coming. And how his myth is growing. Is summoned by Princess Alizar. Mad love and passion. Princess makes it possible for rebels to win.

15

King calls Klikit away from beautiful women to steal ring from Naä and Tark. But he hesitates to give them to the King. The revolution starts without the jewels. Klikit is killed, Rahm & the Princess get the rings, lead the revolution to victory.

16

The king is dead, Rahm presents the rings of Kingship to Naä and Tark, but the people want him and Princess Alizar. He consents.

Naä sings.

+ + +

Outline of psychology

1—Physical warmth and presence continuing the pre-birth state—food; first volitional action, perception. Babies as absolute psychotics.

2—The religious urge, its psychology and its manifestation, individually— attempt to deal with the "absurd." The dichotomy between the healthy dependence upon parent and the world independence.

3—The sexual transference—begins in infancy, crystallizes only when the personality crystallizes.

4—Mythological and sociological and politico-historical backgrounds for sexual differentiation. All sexual differentiation is post natally determined.

5—The psychology of interpersonal relations.
A) Lesbian
B) Homosexual

6—The psychology of heterosexual relationships.

+ + +

Basic theme—the communication of consciousness.

+ + +

Feelings on Leaving the Group—in simple prose.

I wanted to cry at the end of group when Terry mentioned human dignity. Dick just got around to mentioning his stomach, his obsession with it—I think about how I used to worry about my ass in the same way when I was thirteen or fourteen, the same concern about where to wear my penis, either showing or not.

Mike Kraft finally expressed—his voice shaking, breath quivering in the back of his throat—his hostility.

+ + +

Started to write S-F, when there was feeling of weakness in arms, tingling in jaws—vague "am I going to die." Bus driver bites his nails. All broken up about Mrs. Gilbert.

Feeling of fear, compulsion to hurry—know it's mental, arm aches slightly from scribbling so fast.

Like first time I went to the dentist from hospital. The fear. Thought I was going to cry.

Arm aches so much I never want to write again. Second level feeling I know un-true.

Why couldn't I keep a journal of the time in the hospital—owe it to myself—my doctor.

The time slips. It can only be held by words. Proust, and me during the Newport weekend. That time, written and recorded, is happy. Woodland—place where I was happiest—is unwritten and lost.

No author who kept a journal ever had a nervous breakdown, says Dick, though he might have been hopelessly neurotic.

Is that the answer? Then I would do nothing else. The drive to record is too strong.

Die and Cry rhyme, is thought on rereading.

———

Thoughts developed on the way to the dentist's office. Have I, as an artist, purposely kept my ego so vulnerable as to absorb the characters around me in order to express them better (admitted, a strong psychological tendency in this direction), but the *things* I've submitted myself to in order to learn from them!—and I have learned, and use them—: Marilyn, as a poet, has the same vulnerable ego, but has constructed so many shells to keep people out, so she can work on herself. Perhaps her work suffers—as she complains, lacking in energy, scope, humanity and output—but she comes off in the long run better as a person—she can screw her friends and still be friends with them.

Question: the old symptoms, subway fear, reclusiveness, out of touchness with emotions, developed pretty much on their own. Aren't the new ones directly assumed from the people around me now?

Should I (second question) spend as much time defining my real world in journals and diaries as I do defining the fictitious world of my books. Would both suffer, or benefit.

Certainly—at least at the beginning—there would be less confusion between the two.

I rebel against keeping a diary because I feel that if I started, I would do nothing else.

But writing out reality in the past has always been therapeutic for me.

There's a great deal in Dick's statement about diaries re: nervous breakdowns.

"These are merely the innermost thoughts of a simple girl," says Cecily in *The Importance of Being Earnest*, "and consequently meant for publication."

What about ideas; would I so constantly feel them getting away from me as I do, or would it be even worse, a mad race to write everything out like Newport and *Les Journaux d'Orphée?*

Maybe it's time to get back to the S-F. I don't feel afraid now, but there is the bloated feeling of a fever dream about the dentist's office—about me in the office—magazines scattered on the brown table to my left, the plant rising from the pot and dropping on the black squares of the floor. Actually these are the two most real things I see. As I write about them, reality spreads from them, touching the ashtray stand with blue enamel basin, the Danish modern chairs, the palm plant near me in the octagonal wooden brass-bound pot.

For the first time I see a third plant, Jack-in-the-pulpit I think—it is gnarled, scrawny, dying perhaps. If maybe I've been react[ing] to that here, as the thing un-seen. Feel vague chills.

But the plant is very much alive, with waxy, spatulate leaves. Its irregular, inter-twisted stems, that at first suggest death, now seem only its individual character.

+   +   +

Furious with Dr. Grossman—started to write Esterson—I worked at top intellectual capacity during session. Normal pattern for me—panic should result.

Trying to argue him into not putting me in hospital. I feel the first twinges in stomach—but he is not my father (line from old poem) and I can convince this man intellectually, as well as display my emotions. That is the point—not only display—have my emotions. But, also, I will have to work for this father substitute.

+   +   +

cock-sucker?"

"Sure," I say.

"'Cause man I wanna fuck you."

I grin and unzip the fly in the back of my jeans I put there for emergencies. And Stud—that's what I call him—turns me around.

And I see the policeman.

He's a tall, lanky, blond, cowboy type and he's standing there, groping and grinning.

Stud pulls me down on his stick, and at first I'm scared, but then I realize the policeman is hip, so I let that fucker-rod just slide into me, and suck it up my ass. "Jesus," Stud whispers, "that's a sweet hole."

"You bet," I say.

He watches us fuck, then glances around and takes his pecker out, jerking off for us. It's a long and thin red pecker and it disappears in and out of his jerking fist. I lick my lips for him to give it to me, but he shoots—a lot, and [a] good three feet—on the floor. It would have tasted good.

+   +   +

Camping on Bear Mountain
SUMMER EVENING 1964
In a circle of light crowned trees
Perfect and gnat flecked
Breeze strikes branch
To move forward into branch
To the hiss of leaves
The dance of flickering branch
Before branch.
Thought progresses through the glittering
Obstacles of the mind, hissing.

———

Note: in vast stretches of forest, the leaves and branches give the wind a shape

Bird notes like a happy madman running around in miniature chimes.

+ + +

m   (inclusive = t / exclusive = l)
s   st
n   nt

nouns = begin with vowels   ø x
verbs = end in vowels   k
q = kw

abstract = ø

na = walk

nam
nas
nan
nat—nal
nast
nant

ek = writer

mek

sek

nek

tek—lek

stek

ntek

a = at the beginning [equals] imperfect

a = at the end equals perfect

o = at the beginning equals future

o = at the end equals future perfect

interrogative words

    Qe = what

    Qa = when

    Qo = where

    Qi = who

    Qy = why

relative pronouns

    Qer = the what—which

    Qar = the when—the time when

    Qor = the place where

    Qir = who—the one who-whom

    Qyr = the reason why

    r = nominal ending = gerundive end for verbs

    t = plural

vocabulary list

nouns

    ek = water

    om = person

    oh = house, home

    ex = chair

    at = table

    omp = parent

    ep = pen

verbs

> na = walk
> ke = write
> po = make, do
> do = sleep
> ru = run

adjectives

+ + +

Passing thoughts on Deirdre's suicide.

The skinny little girl with the constant headaches hung herself in the bathroom from the shower-rack yesterday morning. She apparently told several patients—among them Mary-Jane, the twenty-year-old commercial artist—that she was going to do it. After my first session with Dr. Reis this afternoon, in which the anxiety I felt about it poured out in a flood of words, I realized that my feeling was one of fright—Please don't let the same thing happen to me. I think this expresses the feelings of a good deal of the hospital's patients.

—July 6, '64

+ + +

One would think, with so much volume to one's name, writing came easily. Yet it is the most painful—as well as the most rewarding—thing I do. I can feel the constriction in my throat as my hand moves over the paper or my fingers move on the typewriter keys. If all the time were put together when I felt positive I would never have the strength, mental and moral, to put down another word, I would have months of vacation for my rehabilitation. The tension of crafting a sentence into some semblance of congruity with pure thought cramps the wrist and the mind.

Would I could craft my life as well as my words.

+ + +

What are my thoughts right now? Strong feeling that I should enter P.I. Wondering how to tell Marilyn: definite feeling that if I could continue with school, it would be the best possible thing for me. If school couldn't be included, then private treatment with Dr. Grossman it will be, but I do feel that P.I. is a good idea, and I do need something. All that Bernie says about psychiatry notwithstanding, something will have to be done, and it will have to be pretty intensive. But—not only as a way of maintaining my individuality, but because I need it as a live situation—I feel I need the school situation. I think I can say pretty strongly—definitely, that if school can be included in the program, then I should avail myself of it.

Wonder what M's reaction will be. But rather than predict it, I think I would do best to wait until she has. After all, she is a reasonable person.

—at the other table several doctors are discussing Mt. Sinai, mentioning that they average 10 residents. Dr. McKenzie certainly seems a lot more competent than anyone—even than Dr. Grossman—I've seen at Sinai—or is he just older?—My first thought was that he must have had some or a good deal of homosexual experience—experience (accident that I wrote the word twice)—especially his statement that "—New York is a big city."—a very in way of saying what he was trying to say. I also have the feeling that I was more honest with him than with any one I have seen yet—including Dr. Grossman—or have I just advanced in having emotional reactions to people, and so feel more at ease.

+ + +

Characters for a novel

1

Young medical student—perhaps psychiatric resident, middle-class, fairly adventurous, good-humored—one or two really upsetting things in his past which have indirectly caused him to go in for psychiatry. Still a sort of protected life.

2

Heshy, Hungarian illegitimate child from the Lower East Side, very worldly, an odd background of reading developed in prison, very physical young man.

3

The Jewish novelist suffering from writer's block, the beginnings of a reputation established, her own worries about what it will go on as, especially if she can't write.

4

Dr. Branning—male—writer of established reputation, eccentric, upper-class, paternal, archaeological mystic, reserved, much the genius, of great help to the novelist.

5

Dr. Branning—female—archaeologist, Negro upper-class, friendly with her husband, in competition with him. Close and in conflict with family.

6

Du Lac Branning, slightly psychotic son, mathematician, awed by both parents, hates both, just wants approval of both, his own work was violent and brilliant.

[7]

Catherine—musician, passive, gentle, regarded by Du Lac as to pure evil, by Dr. Branning as pure good.

NOTEBOOK 27—AUGUST 15, 1964

Samuel Delany

Passing thoughts & poetic effusions of an x-writer, present human, with an objective knowledge of all past accomplishments, verbal, plastic, musical.

—Aug. 15 or thereabouts, 1964

+ + +

Masturbation fantasy number one hundred and umpty-nine.

I

I was hitchhiking one hot summer with nowhere to go when this big, hulking farm-boy picks me up in a pick up truck. Maybe twenty-eight or nine, blue jeans, blond hair and brick red skin, barefoot, big hands, one around the steering wheel, the other in his crotch, scratchin'. Name's Luke.

"Drivin' down to see Daddy and the kids. Then headin' up north."

We get real friendly and he agrees to take me along. Once he catches me lookin' at his crotch where he keeps scratchin'.

"What you starin' at?" he asks, grinnin'.

"Your big cock," I say.

"Kid like you better watch out," he says.

"What for?" I ask.

"For my big cock," he says, still grinnin'.

After a moment, I ask, "Whatcha wanna do?"

He smiles and shakes his head. "What I wanna do is piss all over you." He looks at me to see how I take it.

I grin and he keeps rubbing inside his pants, slow and twisting it hard. Then he reaches over and feels my pecker, and whistles. "Well, I

+ + +

Things to bear in mind: the character of "Flame," tentative name for the red-headed Negro homosexual young man who walks in on the scene and can out-do everybody. Paint better than the artist, has written, and is still unhappy, tortured, etc.

+ + +

Verb Endings
m mt—lt
s st
n nt

Verbs end in vowels:
na = to walk

Nouns begin with vowels:
ek = writer

ø = abstract article

subject—object—verb—dative

Relatives

Qa = what
Qi = who
Qo = where
Qe = when
Qu = why
Qy = how

t = plural

ə = connecting vowel

a on front of verb = simple future
a on back of verb = future perfect
o on front of verb = simple past
o on back of verb = perfect

ø in predicate equals repeated action (abstracted)

adjectives agree with noun & plurality

H = masculine
R = feminine

Ĥ = himself
Ŕ = herself
ḿ = myself
ś = yourself

ń = negative

na = walk
ke = write
po = see
mo = make-do
lu = hear
cu = run
ga = speak
fo = float
su = screw
te = eat
ši = shit
pi = piss
da = think
do = sleep
de = dream
fi = fight
om = parent, creator
ru = teach
le = learn
ka = sing
re = act, do
wa = want
fe = to be hungry
gre = rain
la = read
foge = forget

ku = come
pe = to be able, can
pé = to be permitted to
pê = to have to, must

I am learning to sing
lem ø ka

There's no business like show business
ń ə n er cy tet er

He wants to eat lunch now, but the children are not hungry.
y wan ke ul, s yit n'fent

We are going to make fools of ourselves singing off key.
amtom m̋t oft ky ø

amomt m̋t oft ky ø komt kok

d ə renh'a

Nouns

om = parent, creator
ok = writer
ak = singer
er = business, thing, matter
l = lunch
et = meal, dinner
eb = breakfast
orm = room
el = pupil
ip = child
af = fool
en = money
oc = cock
uk = cunt
ej = knee
ef = leaf

erg = rain, storm, shower
ob = book
ur = teacher
oho = oho
   rnur = she is a teacher
   hnur = he is a teacher
erd = earth, land, ground

Pronouns

of, from = dy
like = cy
to = ay
with = wy
over = oy
un[der] = uy
in = ny
by means of = ky
but = s
and = d
or = v
then = sec
again = mas
nim = never
always = im

Adjectives

bon = good
tet = theatrical
kok = off-key, fumbling
wod = wooden
gel = yellow

sí = here—isí (here are)
isi = this
ilí = there (there are)
ili = that are

This book is theatrical, off-key and wooden
isi nob tek kok d wod

ul won ke y s
y ul won ke, s yot n'fent
y ul won
y won ke ul, s yit n'fent
He sucks cock for wooden nickels

I want to read this book, but I must not forget to go out
isi wam ob la, s n'pênfoge gra

ten ø ə c fy wodt ent
He sucks cock for wooden nickels.

And on my knees, a shower of yellow leaves.
D'erg û gelbt eft ont oyûm ejt.

I have gone up to Maine and then come down again.
Opunoum ay Maine dsucoglukun, mas.

Parts of the Body

ej = knee
op = eyes
ul = ear
oc = cock
uc = cunt
eh = head
ah = hand
ar = arm
uf = foot
es = stomach
aj = leg
as = ass
at = breast
um = mouth
ut = tongue

en = neck
od = back
in = nose
ish = hair
if = face
id = finger, toe, number
olb = ball

Colors

gel = yellow
red = red
bul = blue
wit = white
bak = black
gen = green
mau = mauve

verb prefixes

ge = out
gu = up
du = down
je = in

apunam d'ajlnisfree anam
na y'apunam d'ay inisfree anam.

There are eight rooms in the house.
ont eight ormt ny ohs.

We are climbing Jacob's ladder, but you are down on the ground.
Punalt Jakobû anup s'du ə st oy erd

anup = ladder
erd = earth, ground, land

er tan pes re, pem re

d = comparative
d′ = superlative

s′ man r, yh, yh, yh

vy am y am, sus n′.

On our way to Vt. we spent hours trying to invent a language. We were surprised how many words you need to say the simplest things. But we can say this much.

Oy aneg oy Vt., spent abt try mo ø Vt. Qy mas oyt tam nest a si und′ ert deren m′t spest. S pemt tu isi.

+ + +

Liam's adventures: conversation between Corbelli & Branning. Liam goes home, has dream, gets up, meets "Flame," the gratuitous in love with death.

+ + +

guess it's true when they say little guys are all cock." He grinned, reached up, & pulled my head down in his lap. His dick was like a floating log in his pants' leg. "Chew on it," he said.

I chewed and he pissed, wetting his jeans all up and laughing & rubbing my face in it. Then he let me take it out and suck it, his ball bouncing all over the seat. His huge, hot dick

+ + +

Niger had bounded to Jon who had rubbed his ears affectionately and twisted his ruff till the dog barked. Now it scampered to a claw scraping halt before the other figure, jaw dropped, breathy panting.

+ + +

slipping in and out of my mouth while he squirmed. He made me suck his fingers too, running them in & out of my mouth with his dick. Finally he popped his thick sticky gism down my mouth, pulled me off, and said, "We're at Daddy's farm. Come on & visit a spell." We got out the truck and were in front of an old rickety barn. Luke

+ + +

wiggled his toes in the dust. His prick is back in but he only buttons one stud on his fly.

Daddy is sittin' in boots & undershirt rarin' back in his chair, scratchin' away with his big hands. "Hi there, Luke," he hails. "Ya' brought along company?"

"That's right," and he pushes me forward.

He shakes my hand and hefts his

+ + +

Notes on *Voyage, Orestes*

Cut out mention of *The Counterfeiters* in "Scorpion."

+ + +

balls with his other. "I'll go scare up one o' the little bitches for him to fuck."

"That's o.k." Luke says. "He's my cocksucker."

"Oh," Daddy says. "Ain't that sumpin. Son, when I was about 14, I decided the one thing I wanted to do in all the world was fuck. An' I been doin it three or four times a day ever since."

A little barefaced girl about 7 years old came down the porch. He grinned and sat her on his knee. She giggled.

"Give your Gramps a kiss." He stuck out his tongue, and the little girl smiled and drew it into her mouth. He had his hand under her dress, while he worked

+ + +

Possible Epigraphs:

> The deepest thing in a man is his skin.
> —Valéry

The poem itself
Valéry, "La Dormeuse"

Charles Reade:
"Look into your own heart & write" says Herr Cant … etc.

Chapter VI, The Cloister and the Hearth

"The modern artist needs giant assimilative capacities …"

Hart Crane
Biography—p. 146

+   +   +

his tongue deep into his grandchild's throat. The skirt was bunched up, so that Luke and I could see him working his finger in the hairless cunt. He reared back on his boots, his pecker was pushing up in his pants legs. He pulled it out, thin, dark, and hooded. Then he lifted the little girl up and sat her down on his dick. She squealed with pleasure, and

+   +   +

Check the stay at Niva's for reference to Geo's poems external to the book.

+   +   +

he stopped her cry by plunging his tongue in her throat again. Luke put his arm around my shoulder and slipped his middle finger in my mouth so I'd have something to suck. While he was humping in the chair,

+   +   +

Bruce

Eyes hidden in glass and white lids thick as dough
Hair wire stiff, yellow white as hemp
Hands manicured, yet capable of blows
To suit [...] those rock like bulging shoulder bumps.

+   +   +

he pulled out his balls. They were red, hairy, and hung down eight inches and were the size of plums. Luke tapped me on the

+   +   +

establish they are exceptional students
(Bx H.S. of Science)

Some of [the] kids had planned to be at the Cloisters

How do the kids meet

+   +   +

shoulder. "Go suck," he grinned. "He likes that." I sprinted to the porch, crawled between his heaving legs and got the sweaty nuts in my mouth. I really gave them what for. Finally he pulled the little girl off and shoo'd her away, chuckled and patted my head. "Hey, Luke, you picked a good one." He pulled me up. "Clean it up for me, son." His prick was up and slimy. As I sucked it off, it throbbed in my throat. "Ah, boy, I remember some of them niggers I used to have round

+ + +

O'Donnells
Lael
Kurt—Curt = Cary
John Howells = William Sloan

—ask Mom about the Roosevelt story.

Check reactions in both versions of *V.O.* of L. & M. in "Limestone" to Mrs. Keller

+ + +

here, son. I remember, right after I got my first woman, Luke's momma, all knocked up

+ + +

As T.S. said—reflecting on the open[ing] of Plotinus on beauty—beauty lies in the tensions created between an object and its environment.

A work of art is an object that exists in the "environment" of the beholder's experience.

But a work of art also tries to create beauty by presenting objects—often characters—in the environment of setting or plot to create tension that partakes of beauty.

—Rather, beauty is *one* of the tensions that can arise between an object & its environment.

+ + +

For The Dynamic Moment

The conflict model is sexual but the conflict is not necessarily so.
The efficacy of therapy is on broadening the self-view—therapy does

not resolve conflicts, it creates a matrix of information which will contain the conflicts and allow the patient a firm position from which the conflicting elements

II

Directive therapy—active therapy—if the patient holds a clear cut distinction between his world-view and self-view, directive techniques can be used to enlarge his world view, but they are wasted, for the most part, on his self-view.

III

The overlap of the world-view and self-view, is the place where most neurotic action takes place.

+   +   +

Why do we take the myths of Electra and Oedipus for our model conflicts? To understand this we must look at these stories and the rituals they contain historically and comparatively with other religions—and I use religion in the broadest sense: man's attempt to integrate his view of himself with his view of the world—and lastly see what tensions and illuminations rise between these myths and the dynamic moment. I reiterate, my reason for using these myths is that they function—they work.

Anthropologically the major factor in the self-view of man and mankind arose comparatively recently in man's history, and is still not settled in his psyche.

Man has been on earth for more or less 3 million years [...], but it was not until seven or eight thousand years ago that what has come to be called the Neolithic Revolution took place.

In that time, man all over the earth changed. As far as [we] can trace, the change began near what is now Lake Geneva, and spread east and west and south through Asia, Europe, and Africa.

At any rate, man [...] for 2 and ⅘ million years had existed with *no* control of his environment. He homed where he found caves. He picked fruit from trees he passed, fled before the season, followed the herds.

Then—and the change caused political, economic, religious, and psychological explosions whose reverberations still shake us today—he discovered how to grow his own food. Grain; the cyclic rhythm of the seasons ceased to be a gratuitous flow of snow, sun, rain and wind, and was apprehended as an order[ed] progression and repetition. Animals; they became domesticated, and [the] cycle of birth, growth and death became more than chance happenings. Where there was no order, man perceived order, and as it was perceived it was controlled. Man's view of himself was transformed from that of a victim, to a master. Man could produce his own food; when he could do this, he could make clothes and live in one spot. Before, man viewed the world as divided into those things that were safe, and those that were dangerous. Now the division shifted entirely, and the world became those things he could control and those things that could control him.

I speak of man up to this point, meaning the generic name of the species, with an overtone of the male. It would be more accurate to say woman. The bias of modern mankind is to define itself in terms of "male." Anthropologically speaking this is very new. Mankind, [which] up till the neolithic revolution, for all practical purposes hadn't defined itself at all, chose the most obvious figure for its definition. The race was propagated through the woman, from appearances, and so the woman became the figure of the human being.

It is difficult for us, in such a masculinely oriented society, to understand the ramifications of the matriarchal society. We envision either a complete reversal of our present role orientation, or a sort of romantic matriarchy which in all its practical, economic applications is a patriarchy.

The information extant is extremely sketchy, and the sexual bias of the researchers is at its best amusing, at its worst, obscuring.

We can assume with just a little common sense, that the society was generally far more egalitarian than ours. Inheritance was through the mother. The chances for the ruler to be a queen or a king were slightly in favor of a queen. Priestesses were more important than priests; poetry, even narrative and war poetry, seemed to be the province of women, though the positions of responsibility in the developing societies seemed to be equally divided. A single general religion covered the whole world, in which the chief figure was a many faced goddess who was both the earth and chaos, life and death.

The earliest pictures of sexual intercourse, which date from the late Neolithic period, show the man on the bottom and the woman on top. In the earliest surviving fertility rites extant, which come from this period, the field is plowed, and the man lies down on his back in each furrow. Then the women, in the full midsummer eve moon, would run about the field coupling with as many men as possible during the night.

The moon was the most important heavenly body in this religion; its swelling and waning was equated with the swelling and waning of pregnancy. She was the moon goddess as well as the earth goddess, the forerunner of Diana and Venus in the Greek and Roman Pantheon, the Great Goddess Rhea of Crete, and Ishtar of Babylon.

The mythology of this period was of an extremely sophisticated nature. The Pelasgian creation myth, probably closest to the neolithic creation story, bears retelling:

The Great Goddess awoke from chaos and breathed out a sigh. This sigh was the north wind. She caught the wind and rolled it into a great snake. The snake coiled about her body and from this coupling she laid a great egg from which the world was hatched. This religion, whose rituals have been transmitted to us—the eucharist, the death of a young god on a tree, the sacredness of twins, the divinity of virgin births, are all survivals from these times—flourished as a politically and economically functional world religion up until 1 thousand B.C.

At this point, two things occurred which were of minor importance compared to the neolithic revolution itself, but of great note nevertheless. Writing was invented in Sumeria, and progressed west toward Egypt and Phoenicia, carrying with it the Indo European language. Up until this time, the world was not crowded enough for major competition between areas. There was a surprising amount of industry but it was local. War, in short, had not been invented.

Compared with the pre-neolithic era, the complexity and subtlety of this society was astounding. Gold and silver and semi-precious stones had gained established value the world around. The great rivers of the world, the Nile, the Indus, the Yellow River, and the Tigris and Euphrates had been irrigated extensively. Karnak and Stonehenge had been built, as well as the amazing moon pyramid of the Teotihuacan. Yet there was no distinction between politics and religion. Though the major gods were women, there were male consort gods a-plenty, and when competition, through the development aroused by writing, the wheel, reached the stage of war, the rebellious, and often barbaric forces rallied under the banner of the lesser male consort gods. The knowledge of what part men played in reproduction was at best a shadowy thing, and although the more sophisticated societies knew of it, it was not even considered an important fact. Where role separation became distinct, the men (as opposed to the women) began to develop a feeling of psychological uselessness, similar to what many women feel today.

The picture of the family as a father dominated unit is a modern projection. If it was a patriarchy, it was a patriarchy in the sense that many Jewish and Negro families today are "matriarchies."

When the Neolithic civilization was beginning to break up, there was a sudden appearance of bi-sexual gods. The whole pantheon began [to] upset. Several male gods drew quite a following, and the society underwent corresponding changes. Here and there, as in the middle-ages, flagellant groups arose, some groups of women relinquished all their power and wealth and had themselves beaten by men. Others formed exclusively female societies, practicing cannibalism on men, the Bacchantes and Amazons of legend.

Male groups segregated themselves from society, as the societies themselves grew decadent; along with economic pressures, there was a definite split between the matriarchal and patriarchal religions. The matriarchal religion made the mistake of incorporating into its ritual the annual killing of a sacred king to keep the patriarchy in place.

The patriarchy did not even try [to] "kill" the woman but either cut her totally out of the religion, or kept her in total subjugation. Patriarchy finally gained ascendance in Greece, India, China, and later in Egypt. The rest of Europe remained matriarchal well into the middle ages.

Judaism was one of the more violent suppressions of the matriarchy. The settlement had been reached with the decision "Yahweh has no dominion over the realms of Sheol." Yahweh was the father god and Sheol was the Sumerian name for the Mother, who was left the province of the dead. The Jews, as an absolute expression of the patriarchy: the women pray; "Thank you Lord for making me what I am," while the men pray, "Thank you Lord for not making me a woman."

Most of the mythology that we have today details in a sort of political shorthand this conflict between matriarchy and patriarchy. The story of the Trojan war and the subsequent tale of the fall of the House of Atreus dates from this conflict. The resolution of the conflict fixed this self-view that began with the Neolithic revolution firmly and historically in the minds of the Greeks; once this self view, as man in control, subject to his limits, yet responsible for his limits, was fixed, a civilization arose that came as close to the perpetual achievement of the creative moment as any before or since.

A historical note: up till now, I have been, historically speaking, guilty of monstrous oversimplifications. I have made no attempt to give either a clear chronological or geographical picture of just what sprang up where or when. Part of this is because there is little agreement. Archaeology, until the First World War, was dominated by the church, and was carried on not to see what was there, but to see if certain things predicted by the Bible were or were not there, and the bulk of material that did not pertain one way or the other to sacred Judeo-Christian writing, was ignored.

In interpreting these myths, we must remember two axioms. When one religion takes over another, the god of the old religion becomes the devil of the new one. Also, history is written by the victors.

The Jews, for example, took over the Pelasgian creation myth almost intact, simply changing the emphases and the order of things. In this version, man comes first, and woman is born from his side. In the Pelasgian myth, a woman and the serpent are the symbols of creativity, fertility, the good. No, says the Judean myth, they were evil; Eve and the serpent. The story of Eve and the apple is contained in an ancient proto-Latin pun. "*Eva est mala*," runs the inscription: *est* is New Latin for the verb "to be"—and is proto-Latin for the verb, "to eat." Mala is the feminine form of the adjective "evil," and in the accusative plural for the noun apple. "Eve is evil" is the same sentence as, "Eve eats apples." How do these symbols get transformed from the generation of all order and good to the bringer of all evil?

The night before she is murdered by her children, Clytemnestra, high priestess of the goddess in Argos, has a dream. She dreams that she sits upon the throne of the Goddess, giving suck to a serpent. Suddenly the snake bites into her breast [and] draws blood. In short, the serpent, or male component of the matriarchy, turns against the mother, and because they war, the forces of the "patriarchy" can defeat them both.

Where does the Oedipus story fit in? Historically, according to Velikovsky, it is a mythical retelling of the reign of the Pharaoh Akhnaten of Egypt. Many of the elements are Egyptian; from the sphinx which opens the story, to the city, Thebes, in which it occurs: Akhnaten's capital in Egypt was Thebes. Akhnaten effected a religious revolution in Egypt which was not approved of by the priests. Finally he had several children by his mother, was thrown into prison by his priests, blinded, and at last escaped to wander the desert with his daughter-sister. During his reign, Egyptian art became suddenly realistic—the striking bust of Akhnaten's wife Nefertiti comes from this time.

Maternal incest was probably common during the period of deistic conflict in Greece, though Egypt was at this time far in advance of Greece. When the story reached the Peloponnesus, it was interpreted as part [of] the prevailing conflict. The bisexual figure of Tiresias the prophet was added as a mediator between God and Goddess, and in this version the story that reaches us today.

Starting with the Trojan War, let us look at the tales closely. In the primitive mind, the distinction between priest, king, and God (or priestess, Queen, and Goddess) was non-existent.

The opening tale of the judgment of Paris and the apple of discord we must take as highly romanticized. About the only thing we can say for sure is that Troy was under the protection of the Goddess, and that the apple came from the same tree, figuratively speaking, as Eve's apple.

To destroy the power of an enemy, one kidnapped his god or goddess, which amounted to kidnapping the king or the queen.

In Greece, the forces of the God or Goddess had reached a fair equilibrium.

Twins were considered Gods, and the twin brothers Agamemnon and Menelaus ruled their respective countries. Their wives, who shared the rule equally with them, were also twins: Clytemnestra and Helen and their twin brothers, Castor and Pollux, ruled in the north. Their mother, the princess Leda—so the rewritten legend goes—was vi[si]ted by Zeus as an eagle.

Recall the Virgin Mary visited by God as a dove. In short, they too sprung of Virgin births.

It was customary that any children conceived in the mid-summer orgies I recounted a while ago, be considered Virgin births, and any twins that resulted were extremely propitious. When the patriarchy took over, the Virgin birth was retained, but the woman was reduced to the vessel to hold the divine seed of the father. Symbolically a bird was introduced as the patriarchal male sex symbol—possibly because of the antipathy of many birds for snakes.

(The mythological tale of the battle between eagles and serpents range from Indian and Mexican lore, to the sophisticated treatment of the theme in Shelley's poem, "The Revolt of Islam." Christianity, needless to say, was an attempt to establish a patriarchal religion that would wipe out all traces of the matriarchy once and for all, taking for its basis a modification of Judaism, which was till then a minor but tenaciously adamant patriarchy. Incidentally, the two reported kidnappings of Abraham's wife Sarah by the enemies of the Jews bears the same significance as the kidnapping of

Helen. Very possibly the Jews instituted their patriarchy to avoid the annual slaughter of the young king—thus the significance of Abraham's and Isaac's story. When Judaism became Christianity, in order to spread the religion, the sacrifice was reinstituted as the crucifixion to make the religion palatable, with the stipulation that this particular sacrifice, however, would do once and for all time to come. In Jesus' own words, "I have come to destroy the works of the Woman.")

At any rate, with Helen kidnapped, the crops of Sparta could not grow, babies might be deformed, rivers might flood. Half the king's power was gone, and the rituals could not proceed. It was essential to get her back. Menelaus called on brother Agamemnon to help him return her.

Agamemnon agreed, but before he went, he realized that if the priest went, the matriarchy might gain complete control in his absence. So, before he sailed, he allowed Clytemnestra to rule from the chair of the Goddess, but caused her heir, Iphigenia, to be sacrificed, so that the line would cease with Clytemnestra. The queen was furious, but as of yet there was nothing she could do.

Menelaus, to pacify the people when Helen was kidnapped, spread the rumor that the queen-goddess had not really been stolen, but was safely in Egypt. Clytemnestra, to avoid public humiliation, spread a similar rumor that her daughter had been miraculously transported, a moment before the fatal blow, to Tauris, where she was safe. Neither ruse, however, had more than a momentary calming effect.

Yet Agamemnon's action hastened what he had feared. The queen sought out Agamemnon's enemies, particularly Aegisthus. Aegisthus' family bore a long grudge against Atreus (Agamemnon's house), for Atreus had murdered Aegisthus' mother and brothers and served them in a pie to Aegisthus' unsuspecting father.

The significance of this story is not quite clear, but it belongs to a whole line of Greek myths dealing with incestuous cannibalism, the most popular of which is the story of Procne and Itys. The general element of all of them seems to be forcing a parent to eat of the flesh of his or her children. This is probably an anthropological survival of some form of human sacrifice.

Under the earliest form of the Matriarchy, only men suffered capital punishment for the crime of murder; the logic running something along this line: If a woman destroys a member of society, within a year's time she can make a replacement for that member. This became associated with the seasonal death and rebirth of plants and crops, upon which discovery this whole neolithic religion stood. This was eventually refined into the annual sacrifice of the king. But when the government became too complex to lop off one of its heads every year, a substitute was often found—at first another man, eventually an animal, usually a bull or a horse. During the human sacrifice stage, cannibalism might well have been involved, and the families involved could have born a grudge for a generation or two.

Aegisthus agreed to support the matriarchy wholeheartedly, even to the reinstatement of the ritual murder, especially since the agreement was that Agamemnon, on his return, would be the first sacrifice.

Meanwhile, Agamemnon at Troy, after all sorts of problems with contending factions, was more or less successful. Troy was sacked, Helen was returned, and the homeward journey begun.

Either Agamemnon had received word of what the situation was at Argos, or his common sense suggested what might have happened. At any rate, he knew that after an absence of ten years there might be difficulty in reestablishing his position as co-ruler with Clytemnestra.

He had left with a grandiloquent gesture by which he had cut away the power of the Mother. He decided that his return would be equally grandiloquent. He brought with him Cassandra, the kidnapped high priestess of the Goddess at Ilium, a woman with reputation of great intelligence, as well as prophecy. He planned to set her up as equal ruler with Clytemnestra. The power of the Mother divided between the two women would give him a good chance to conquer all.

However, his plan did not succeed. The Queen had welcomed him back, heard his decree concerning Cassandra, with comparative equanimity. Then, the moment that Agamemnon's guard was relaxed, she murdered Cassandra, and then, when Agamemnon was in the Bath, she and Aegisthus slew him. The details of Cassandra's murder vary, but the death of Agamemnon is well fixed. The Bath House was in a separate wing of the palace. As Agamemnon stepped into the bath, Clytemnestra caught him in a net, and Aegisthus, wielding the double-headed axe, cleaved open his skull. In short, Agamemnon was killed in a state: "Neither foul nor clean, neither bound nor free, neither clothed nor naked, neither in his home nor away from it, neither on water nor on land." His body was then flung outside the wall without ritual or even a handful of lime to repel vultures.

Three children were left now with pretensions to the throne: in order of age, Chrysothemus, the eldest; Electra, the middle child; and Orestes, the youngest.

Orestes, the male heir, was in the most danger, and the remaining forces of the Patriarchy spirited him away. Clytemnestra expected both girls to go along with her; however, somewhat to her surprise, though Chrysothemus went along with her mother, Electra rebelled against the queen, cherishing the childhood memory of her father and brother.

The exact details of Electra's suppression are not clear. Whether the girl rebelled first and was treated harshly as punishment, or whether the queen instituted the suppression in anticipation of rebellion, we don't know. The succession to the throne of the Mother went to the youngest daughter, and perhaps Clytemnestra feared her daughters as competition. The final humiliation came when Clytemnestra ordered her daughter to marry a common farmer under a patriarchal, monogamous marriage. This was a double irony, and double insult to the girl, though the farmer—according to the legend—had enough fear of the Mother not to consummate the marriage.

The rumors went around of Orestes' doings, and Electra waited for her brother's return, by now openly declaring that she would fight with him to destroy the matriarchy and establish a patriarchal system. That the heir to the throne of the mother should openly avow herself in favor of the patriarchy was quite a reversal.

Orestes return[s]; brother and sister confer and join forces, and the plan is devised: Matricide. Clytemnestra must be killed.

However this killing must be according to ritual. When patriarchy takes over a matriarchy, certain stipulations must be met; the ritual killing of the king either by his wife or within her sight must be replaced by a death and rebirth of the male in which the woman plays no part; in short, a resurrection must take place.

This is the night of Clytemnestra's dream of the serpent. The next day Orestes arrives at the palace bearing an urn of ashes, claiming that these are the ashes of Orestes who is dead. When the Queen, unbelieving, runs up to him to read the inscription on the urn, Orestes wrests the double headed sacred ax from her hand and cleaves her head in two, crying out that he is Orestes.

In another version Electra sends word to the Queen that she has had a child by the farmer she had been forced to marry, and begs the queen to bestow the proper blessings and rituals upon it. The Queen comes, and the two women enter the farm house together. "Where is the child?" asks the Queen.

Orestes steps from the shadows with his sword raised, and as his mother recognizes him, he strikes her dead. The resurrection is still implied.

The Murder of Aegisthus, Clytemnestra's lover, presents special considerations: it was probably carried out before the murder of Clytemnestra. The detail that is important, that comes through the thin mask of the Sophocles version, in which he is killed at an all male wine festival, Orestes surprises him while he is [in] a drunken stupor.

The wine festival is probably a fertility festival, and when Orestes kills him, he gains the power of the sacred king.

In one version, Orestes hamstrings Aegisthus in one leg and lets him limp about before he delivers the final blow.

Let us go a moment to the Oedipus myth. Oedipus means swell-foot or goat-footed, and according to legend, Oedipus was lamed by his father as a child (his father, at any rate, was responsible for the lameness, having given the order for him to be hung from the branch of a tree by his heel). The sacred king, in order to make him easier to kill, was often crippled.

The folk picture of the Devil as a lame old man, Slew-Foot, comes from this picture—when the Mother and her consorts were relegated to the position of Demons under the Patriarchy.

The Mother was dead, the Patriarchy was established politically, but by now the country itself was in chaos.

The Brother and Sister rulers found themselves extremely unpopular with the people—especially Orestes. He was regarded as a foreigner, and at last Electra was left to rule alone, a woman ruling in the name of the father. Orestes, pursued by Furies (very possibly priestesses sacred to the Mother in a sort of assassins society), was forced into exile.

After many years of wandering, Orestes finally made peace with the Mother and was allowed to set up his Patriarchy, in which it was ordained by law: "Woman hath no part in the conception of a child. She is merely a vessel in which the seed of man is implanted."

The pendulum, taking tragic toll during its journey, had reached the other end of the swing.

The point of concentrating on these times is that the whole modern conception of roles of men and women spring from this particular

Form for an S-F novel

5 × 30 = 150 =
five thirty-page sections of different locations, adventures in each under a
general situation with the same hero with 10–20 pages' worth of prologue,
epilogue, and continuity.

Overall situation: Earth has been invaded by completely alien creatures a
little after spaceflight has started.

Part One: In the slums, growing up.
Part Two: The underworld.
Part Three: The space patrol.
Part Four: The High Society of the moon.
Part Five: The caves of the overlord, the world of illusion and reality.

+   +   +

Thoughts of Time & Death

A week before he was discharged, a girl hung herself from the shower-
rod. The kid from Harvard who slept all the time told him at breakfast.
He asked, surprised, "Did she die?"
"Un-huh."

+   +   +

The instructor is a platinum blond woman of about thirty-thirty-five. A
little vague but extremely reassuring. Attractively dressed with a copper
pendant gleaming on a beige dress, she speaks to us very much as though
we were human.

+   +   +

Chemistry J3 Prof. McKelvie

In place of a blackboard projected notes are used. Will wonders never ... etc.

How much more homey and informal this end of the campus seems, as well as serious. Reminds me of the "old building" at Science. Lots of wood in the construction. More beards & jeans on the students. Professor McKelvie is a pleasant, lopsided man (I think) and a trifle arch from the conversation I can pick up from the front of the room.

—he's British

My seat—25

+ + +

Schwartz 1–5—p. 13   Professor Robinson

Well, you can't always pick a winner. Robinson is vague and old.

+ + +

Hostility day

Changes in body state—lower and upper

Fear of being alone

Critique of Dual Session

Ambivalence about me—name misremembered twice, after all that talk about not setting up competition, immediately show the poem to M. who is a professional poet. Speaking about destroying ego after smudge on Dr. (Warning me, perhaps.)

Lack the basic tools for finding out who the person in front of you is.

+ + +

Jan. 1965.

T. S. Eliot died today. The shock, the feeling of supports pulled loose. The radio explained precursorily, yet with great pretentiousness, how he had suffered a heart attack in 1956, married his 22-year-old secretary, had been in failing health.

My mind grips memories of the slim gray volume of his poems that I first read, "Prufrock," *The Waste Land.*

I remember the endless discussions with Sue Sholley, two years ago: she said, "I can see the young professors waiting for him to die, waiting to get their hands on his papers."

I remember no shock like this since Camus' death in the car-crash. But this is more solid.

I called Dick to tell him. He was quite struck. "Who is left, except Pound," he said many times.

Now that the man is ended, we wait for the myth's turning.

* * *

Later memories of Dolly, the middle aged Lesbian recounting Eliot's childish behavior with his young wife right after their marriage

+ + +

How tell, single-tongued, tongues moving to palate, teeth, lips? How tell, double sexed and dead? Tell how they came from Norn to Alik in autumn, rocks glazed then with copper from the low sun, as the rocks glaze now. Or time. How give you history/time, myriad minds moving between stars, afraid, and [cold]. War we fought, and fought around us, anxious, dangerous, dying. How give you man/time, one and two and three minds moving together and seeing and feeling, laughing, knowing, screaming, making and destroying, what is the story, what you would call the story. Or give individual/time, where a year-ago sight, a year-ago sound changes what I see now, say now. How sing, as She taught to sing, time and rock, memory and prophecy, the broken plains where the Gray Ones came from Norn to Alik, silver hair blown golden in the low sun? How I to how you? Answer, simple, and begin: autumn, on Earth in the plains of Pennsylvania, in the 3rd year of the Star War, and from Norn to Alik the Gray Ones came.

+ + +

Babel Seventeen
   —SF novel about communication and tri-sexual society.

Cantos of Mutability
   —homosexual novel to end all homosexual novels
   —the change of a homosexual to a heterosexual

Labyrinths
   —Tommy, Marsha, and the Hunnicut microcosm

Henry Calvin
   —American historical novel on "Negroes"

+ + +

January 21, 1965
   —Woke up this morning (M out at K. Sassel's, Steve spent the night) hawking blood from my chest cold. How mythic can you get.
   And I have a history exam in an hour.

Dear Mr. Wright,

Tuesday, strolling the edge of the upper lake in Central Park, I watched the cygnets that the park department lets home there, try to climb the rock banks from the water to the shore: their backs and wings ruffled and beat like small white seas. But their feet were black, clumsy, and scrabbled in the wet leaves.

In my preparation in English I resemble the swan. By profession I am a writer. I have published three science fiction novels. A fourth is scheduled for November and I am also waiting for decisions [on] the serious novel. By practice I have learned much about dramatic structuring of incident & characterization; I have clipped from my style as many adjectives and adverbs as I can; my ideal is clarity, simplicity, and visual and sonorous intensity (you say vigor). My working theory is that all writing—from a scientist's observations to poetry—is the presentation of information—objective, subjective, or metaphorical. There are my white feathers.

But see my feet!

I never had the intuitive grammatical sense many verbal people have. In elementary school I learned grammar thoroughly but as a fascinating science, something to correct writing other than my own. Today I am fine doctoring other people's writing, scotch taping dangling modifiers to their antecedents, pasting split infinitives back together, unmixing metaphors and nudging violated parallel structure back into alignment, but my own work still glitters with missing commas, perfectly unrelated tenses follow each other in sequence like lame elephants grasping for tails, and the little Saxon words repeat and repeat through my prose. I cannot spell. My agent tells me neither could Nathanael West or F. Scott Fitzgerald. But this excuses neither the carelessness (I am always writing "wont" for "want") nor the absurd ignorances (until two months ago I spelled twelve, "dousin"). It is embarrassing when you are told—after staying up till five meticulously hunting and pecking the last chapter of a 200 page manuscript—"It's fine. We'll take it. But, Jesus Christ, teach your secretary to spell."

My wife, also a writer (the one who fortunately can turn out scholastically perfect prose in three languages) puts up and proofreads with and for me; but my goal is independence. She says, however, my spelling is ruining hers. And [while] her own prose is pure technically, she doesn't know an apposition from a passive periphrastic, and can't correct a sentence other than by "feel."

(An editor once patted me on the shoulder and said, "I think your attempt to change the language is admirable. It takes bravery for a writer to do that." I blushed.)

This summer, partly to correct our mutual failings—but mostly for fun—we invented a language. We began it on the way back from a camping trip, our shoulders raw from sweaty pack straps, hungry from a half-dozen meals of burnt hamburger, undone eggs, and cocoa made from condensed milk. Among the mosquitoes and gnats—raccoons had gotten into the food knapsack the night before and covered everything with butter—I cried out, "Can't we do something civilized?"

So we sat down and began to make up a language from scratch; it has its own grammar, vocabulary, and semantic development. It is very compact; it takes only half as much space to write. A brief example:

"... and on my knees, a shower of yellow leaves."

becomes

"... D'erg û gelbt eft ont oy ûm egt."

Although this may help my wife's theoretical grammar, it won't help my spelling.

That a man makes his living by the English language does not make him an expert. Nevertheless the vocationist assumes the eccentricities of the master. An eccentricity of mine is that when asked a simple question, I may write a book for an answer. (Three of my novels, a trilogy called *The Fall of the Towers*, were so written.) "What is your preparation for English?" you asked.

"Chapter one," I mused, "my progressive school education, pro and con. Chapter two; the reading of the English Romantics and what it did to shake up my language. Chapter three: transcribing the manuscripts of Samuel Greenberg and what that did to settle me again. Chapter four; teaching remedial speech and reading to Puerto Rican youngsters (Subtitle, 'Say what you mean, man. Say what you mean.') Chapter five: the French and wouldn't it be nice if we could do it in English but we can't and why ..." But here I am, back at school after a four year absence, and a chemistry major. There is other homework ...

Sincerely,

Samuel Delany

+ + +

This has been one hell of a depressing day. Don rescheduled *City of a Thousand Suns* from November till February. Apparently, the Dean's office tells me, I am not on the exemption list for English One. Ben Laforge informs me that there is "a lot of unfavorable" reaction to *Voyage, Orestes* at N.A.L. The world seems to be conspiring to turn me into an ordinary man. Plus Bernie was not in with *Ballad of Beta-Two*.

So much to be done with it, says N.A.L of *Voyage, Orestes*. Christ, what do they want from it.

Bless Bobs Pinkerton's professionalism. It makes me respect Ben for him to be honest with me, but my ego shatters every time I speak to him. Wish there was someone to buck me up.

+ + +

Last night Steve called, wanted to know if he could come over and talk. Frimi, his girlfriend, had come over the night before, stayed over, and then tried to commit suicide by taking all her tranquilizers.

+ + +

Pat definitions.

Neuroses rise from contradictions in the ego picture.

Psychoses are what happen when certain sections of the ego picture have been completely destroyed.

Frimi is a highly depressive personality. For all practical purposes, she has no ego picture. Frimi's is the sit-in-the-corner-and-cry-for-hours syndrome. Steve, interestingly, cited all the evidence, but refused to look at it. If Steve could really separate the concept of himself and Frimi, he would burst out crying, because then he could afford to feel sorry for her, and not feel so threatened by the feelings as to misinterpret the times they are in abeyance as "not caring a shit."

The conflicts in the ego picture create tension and anxiety for the neurotic.

When the pathic (to coin a term) wanders into one of the areas where there is no picture, the result is fear, hysteria, and anger. The particular combination and what their manifestation is depends on the particular person and also the particular segment of the ego that is wounded.

+ + +

I am depressed over the news from N.A.L. Ben Laforge tells me that there has been "a great deal of unfavorable reaction" to *Voyage, Orestes*. He is trying to get a third reading. The combination of length, "and so much needs to be done with it" that it more or less looks like that that is that. I wonder what "so much" means; and certainly what is there to do that can't be done by cutting? For a week or more I've been walking around singing "The Times They are A-Changing," caught up in the second verse;

"Come writers and critics who prophesize with your pen ..."
Thinking that at last something was coming through for me. By now I know that one shouldn't hope for anything—remember Joyce & his seventeen publishers—but one hopes nevertheless.

Someone said that Pandora could be forgiven all the sins in her box, but she should be killed and tortured for releasing "hope" to the world. That is the one thing that makes the others intolerable.

School has created an odd situation: for the first time in four years, I would like to take off four years and just write. Marilyn thinks this is very funny. I suppose it is.

Don's postponement of *City of a Thousand Suns* to February seems part of a vast world plot to erase the fact that I'm a writer from the scrolls of Ma'at.

+ + +

Notes on a novel

Hero, a young man returning to school after a few years' absence

Meets and falls in love with Montesque, the young wife of Dr. Arthur Branning.

Leontyne Branning, first wife. Negro anthropologist still hovers in the background.

Outline

1— Dr. Branning, author and anthropologist, is going to speak at school. Kip, a dropout, comes and tells his father, a lawyer, and learns about Leontyne Branning, a relation of his mother.

2— Goes to the lecture, meets Montesque, they run away together. Idyll.

3— At his apartment we meet Edna and Heshy (his "buddy")—and are shown Dr. Branning's novel by novelist, Edna.

4— Montesque and Kip at the gang fight.

5— Edna and Kip & Heshy meet Leontyne Branning at the museum.

6— At Montesque's home, the party, Dr. Branning begins to be threatening, also threat of Leontyne whose presence lingers.

7— Heshy returns to the museum at night.

8— Montesque & Heshy adventure.

9— Edna and Kip exploring the Branning house.

10— The return of the Brannings & working up of the *Walpurgisnacht*.

11— Montesque and Heshy arrive—*Walpurgisnacht* the drunken ending.

12— Kip returns to father, Heshy, & Edna.

+ + +

Most speech comes from the anxiety we feel about a subject. Poetry is the speech which clothes the subject itself. Speech that clothes a subject becomes rhythmic of itself, because it is quiet and catches the heart.

> Poetry should be at least as well written as prose.
> —Ezra Pound

I know a good knowledge of psychology is essential to writing poetry (or prose); I have always suspected that a knowledge of poetry is essential for psychology.

> Prose is words in the best order. Poetry is the best words in the best order.
> —Coleridge

Attic Greek produced a concatenation of great poetry that is almost unbelievable; one could speak of killing ten men in Attic Greek; but if one talked of "annihilating a numerically insignificant popular segment," one would be laughed out of the room, not as amoral, but as illiterate.

The responsibility of everyone who writes—especially poets—is to purify the language, which means keeping it transparent enough so that we can see what we are talking about.

The average man or woman is afraid to undress in public. One remembers William Blake and his wife naked on their lawn, scandalizing the town, as they read their favorite selections of *Paradise Lost* to one another.

Or Shelley marching naked into the meeting of his editors at his home in Geneva. Neurotic behavior, no doubt. (I also recall David Chote, [a] 19-year-old Indian boy, fleeing across 5th Avenue and 85th St. at noon, to dress in Central Park.)

But they have *experienced* the fear of being naked in public, and could probably (all three, as they are (were) intelligent men) could tell you about the working of that particular fear more than you who are afraid, and have never done it.

To learn the mechanics of falling asleep, each shift and slip of consciousness from awareness, through hypnagogy to slumber, one questions the insomniac, who has agonized over each stage—not the lout who is unconscious the moment his head strikes the pillow.

The actual process of going to sleep is the same for both, but given unemotional reports from each the [former] is going to be more informative. This is the whole story of the neurotic impulse behind art. Proust, an incurable insomniac, was the first person to point this out for me.

The opening movement of *À la recherche du temps perdu* is the most accurate evocation of falling asleep in any language.

In Greek the word for "word," the word for "meaning" and the word for "study" are the same. A word was its meaning.

+ + +

Society is the excuse the common man is given to avoid being an artist.

NOTEBOOK 82—[SUMMER 1964–
SPRING 1965]

Notes for Dr. Branning's novel

Setting—Mansions, Slums, Cathedrals, Convents
          Forests, Caves, Beaches

Catherine—light and active innocence
Helen—self-torturing confusion
The Artist—active expression of emotion, immature

The hero works repairing instruments

The idea for the novel should be:

The time was an ambiguous one. The distinct forces moving through society were blurred by the existence of oblique and opposite ones. The meeting of such opposites, many have noted, make violence. But it also leads to resolution.

Delicate questions—what to do with them.

+ + +

Dreams—

Dreamt I was in a car and Dick from the hospital was lying on top of me—the car had just arrived. Dick disappeared and M. came & took me out of the car and began to lead me barefoot over gravel. I couldn't see where we were going. Finally she left me for a minute, and I woke up.

Day before, I dreamed I was three quarters of the way through a large novel, and I was lying in bed thinking about how I would continue it, and about getting up and going to the type-writer. As I got up, I awoke, was lying in bed again, and no book, of course, had been written.
Also dream of going to Peter Ascoli's summer mansion, Peter very ill,

driving there, then walking up to the door—barefoot over gravel—Mrs. Ascoli very saintly about her son's illness. Walking through the inside of her home when it was turned into a museum.

+ + +

Agon
Tentative Outline

I—Introductory paragraph on the effect of opposite forces, followed by a description of the Lower East Side as a place where opposites are to be found all in conflict. Description of Corbelli's music shop.

Dr. Branning comes and there is an interchange, ending with his mention of a boy who has been placed in his charge, whom he cannot keep with him. Corbelli and Dr. Branning conversation, giving information about both.

Dr. Branning brings the boy down who is quiet, morose, but amenable. There is the beginning of [a] music lesson as well as a lesson on how to repair instruments. Dr. Branning leaves, as it is discovered that the boy can play.

+ + +

It is now August, and this accursed book has refused to crystallize since November when I finished *Voyage, Orestes*. Notes pile up—several hundred pages worth—perhaps I exaggerate—anyway, a hundred and fifty—obviously I have been going about it the wrong way. The first thing to do is to relax and let the book germinate in its own method. I should include in my notes the scenes I would like, and not try to falsify the structuring around it. If it takes years, then it will take years. Let them come, when they come, polish them.

What so far is definite, completely certain?

1)   The scene with the artist in bed, struggling over his work, and the girl who convinces him to make love, therefore resolving his problem.

     Comment: but this artist is not the main character.

2)   Dr. Branning, anthropologist and novelist, successful, happy—with problems—but working on a major mature work.

3)   The old, barefoot Italian music repairer with the black dog—Satin
     loose in the city—
         Comment: it is totally false to try and transform Corbelli into
         Ramsy, the mayor of Avilar. This is Satin.

4)   The Negro anthropologist reconstructing the white wolf of stone.
     Older, extremely sophisticated woman.
         Comment: isn't making her Dr. Branning's wife a bit much. Fits
         in better with your conception if she's unmarried.

5)   Catherine, the young girl with red blonde hair who is interested in
art and religion, as an intelligent agnostic.

6)   Helen, the dark young lady interested in science and magic, self tor-
turing, doubting, vicious and vindictive.
         Comment: which of the two girls would the hero be most likely to
         plan to commit a murder with? For intensity, it would be Helen, for
         irony it would be Catherine.

7)   Heshy, the odd combination of the physical and the ascetic, violent,
but does not drink or screw women or men, adventurer
         Comment: might it not be a good idea to pair him with the artist,
         who is quiet, intellectual, yet totally amoral?

8)   Location, first thought is concerned with vividness and scope of
locations, especially in their economic tones, from lower to upper, urban
and rural—though probably more urban—religious and secular.
         Specific locations:
             A) The rural school in the old mansion which Dr. Branning
             runs.
             B) At least a couple of night scenes in the museum, either
             Heshy & the murder, and Dr. Leonie Adams, or the hero and
             the murderer, or perhaps Leonie and a totally new character,
             the young, destructive J.D.—or, perhaps, the Artist, bent on de-
             stroying classical works of art—maybe Heshy, finally drunk and
             vicious, wants to pillage the museum because he doesn't under-
             stand it or art, or its meaning.
             Comparable scene is the artist in the convent, and the father, or
             the sister dissuade him from disparaging religion.

9) The person whom the hero & heroine are planning to murder is torn apart by a wild dog or wolf on a moonlit road. The hero is contrasted to the murderer. The murder's reasons are always economically clear, yet psychologically ambiguous to him.

+ + +

I must make sure my book does not lack the language gouged from the mouth and heaped on the subject, tongue sprung and magnificent. There is much to be said for white classicism, but those of us who can make black explosions glitter in the eye had best release the facility on our aesthetic frames. Mine—my book—can hold torrents.

+ + +

In *Voyage, Orestes*:

Cut the section with the truck driver, & the organic sentence; insert Jimmy's reaction to being abandoned.

Cut the discussion of Herman Melville, insert a discussion about:

All moral & social values are relative, they are the outcome of previous values, and they are constantly transforming into new ones. Inability to recognize the dynamic aspect of morality killed American literature, because it took all its moral presentiments as absolutes. Any assumption made from an absolute morality is a myth. Failure to recognize what its values are kills a society. When a man says he has no values, it means he has the values that are most common, & therefore un-named.

Geo inserts incident about girl who suggested he write something with no ideas, which means it would have everyone's ideas, everyone's myths.

+ + +

"Where are you going?" said Wystan to Chester
"The boys in the park are a very bad lot.
The sore on your cock is beginning to fester
And what can they give you—that I haven't got."

Critic do not beat your breast
Though Chester Kallman is a pest
And must have done strange things to broaden
The attitudes of Wystan Auden

+ + +

Well, writer, where am I now? Rejected from New American Library, I find, after a week, myself still in confusion, and developing a bad stomach. Let me think and order.

Four years ago, I left school with the distinct image of myself writing. I wrote. Other people have probably left school to write and found themselves not writing: but I wrote. I had publishing and critical success with science-fiction. My major effort, however, brooks no gross acceptance. But for 4 years I was in a world where actions condemned me to my way of life and free choice was a real thing, alone in the important world. Through writing I learned an amazing number of things about action, freedom, commitment—majorly that they exist. At last I decided [to] return to school, discovered my reputation had preceded me, and was smack in the center of the college "Literary Life." It was like a buoyant bath in warm cereal. They see me as the man returned from outside, and so I wield a certain respect. They haven't quite yet realized that my return, in a way, was a method of coming to terms with outside defeat.

All right. What happened there?

First, I discovered the whole raft of people who "had once had talent," who "used to write!" like warning statues along the road to my goal. What basilisk had struck them there I don't know. But they were flocked all around.

+ + +

Autumn struck the city and demanded, "Who are you?"

"Kip Railly." His breath trapped before the chasm of perception, tears silvering his retina, the opening of his ears at his unspoken name, and his tongue muscling the roof of his mouth, falling away and testing the blade of air.

Leaves chuckled by the park fence below the hammered spot of the sun. Words wanted to leap teeth at the asphalt and gnaw the gilded street. He opened his hands to stroke the damp. Then convulsion thrust his hips forward, his shoulders back, and he howled. The sound broke like crockery into laughter. He shook. Stub rubbed yellow grass caped the rocks over the fence; blocks away the buildings of the college, gray & white, fungoid.

The pause passed, and Kip jammed his fingers under his belt and pulled out the book wedged between buckle and skin. Its black cover flipped back as he flung it into the air, punched it, falling—it shot thirty feet up the street. Running up the street, chasing the flickering pages unfallen; then, paper and his Wellington cracked concrete at the same spot and he spun his free foot staggering as below the panting in his ear, laughter.

She stood by the stone newel, cradling notebooks, the laugh slowing to puzzlement. "What are you doing?"

He bit his astonishment in two and tongued the rim of his inner gum. "It's my book."

Her head tilted. "What?"

The grin surged tidewise across his face. "My book ... I just got my book last night."

"You wrote a book?" she asked slowly.

The grin broke, pride and the ebullience like flame burning her clear, hair curling on her forehead, the ligaments of her neck holding her face to his.

"It's my book," he repeated, nodding.

"Then what are you standing on it for?"

"Because ..." obvious enough through her bewilderment, "... because there are other copies now!"

Her face blanking with either understanding or bafflement.

"It doesn't matter, because [there're] more copies!"

Then the affection. He ducked, picked up the book—a pamphlet really, sixty-four pages—salvered on both hands he delivered toward her. "You can have this one."

She stared at the heel print, then reached tentative fingers to turn the cover.

"Poems?"

"My poems," he said. "For you!" And turned, pulling his hands from under the book. It flopped behind him.

He walked another six, seven, eight steps. Curiosity, aching in an arc around his back, stopped him, and he turned, apprehensive.

But she had stooped down, and was turning a page.

Triumphant, he loped off.

[sequence continues]

+ + +

Notes for Space Opera.

1)   Ideas—the compressed language enabling man to think faster. The solving of the problem.

2)   he, she, phe, him, her, phem, his, hers, phes
       All things learned.
       The three sexes.
3)   The Meaningless Invasion.

———

Characters—settings & scenes.

The spaceport, slums, and tenements. The swaggering hero, brown skinned, green eyed, red-headed.
       The blonde kid he befriends.

The Psychological Anthropologist.

The Aristocracy of the Moon.
       Three women: the neurotic, helpless, witty, hysterical Negro aristocrat.
       The practical, hardheaded poetess—blonde with Chinese eyes.

+ + +

Three dreams: Monday nite after standing on the waterfront, looking at Jersey. Leaving my country house to go on a hike with a bunch of people— I was always on a different trail than everyone else.

Sitting around with Steve Johnson in the living room of 2250, while parents are there reading newspapers and at last we go into a corner & I masturbate him after he makes me put my head on his hand—I am writing, and though sexually aroused, not really interested.

Miss Newby's classroom at Dalton where there is a different teacher & a different blackboard. I came in in the middle of class & didn't know what was going on. Some equations concerning radar & something akin to the Michelson-Morley experiments—Johnny Nields was there. The rest of the class was totally confused & whispering back and forth; I thought I might help if I could just find out what was going on.

Sig: the next day planned to go to museums with J.L.B. from Dalton, & last night thinking about him had reminded me of Priscilla, whom mother had mentioned. (Priscilla was in my math class.)

I was telling you about some dreams, in which there [were] some portraits, in frames, and you asked me "Why frames?" and I became very angry & threw a pencil at you, and cried out loud & woke up.

Portraits, my mother-in-law discussing the portrait framing place discovered by Evelyn.

Some picture had been incorrectly framed, "Only about this wide ..."

My wife's pictures are unframed, I noticed David's picture was unframed in Bernie's living room.

(Called Bernie: Yes, he mentioned picture frames: in this context he had been in a little church in Puerto Rico where a picture of David's was hung.

David anxiously asked, "Was it framed?"

"Yes."

"How?"

"In a frame as wide as the middle part of the frame we were looking at."
—Bernie seemed to think it was a desire to do something violent to him and protested how hard he'd been trying to reach people. (Jokingly))

———

The dream about group therapy, just before I left the hospital, the doctor turned out to be the druggist. I had given him copies of my book, he'd demanded them, and I never found out if he'd read them or not.

Also, I remember fear starting—near the beginning, and I called out, "No I'm angry. I want to be angry myself." And I'd get the feeling which would mount, then suddenly go away.

———

Long & complexed dream, starting off with Dr. Grossman, knew it was a dream, talking about dream. Banging in my head like a jackhammer, very un-restful—my heart again?—getting up and walking outside bare footed in the street, coming back and lying down, once or twice crying out "help" to wake me up, and M. rolling against me, once clasping me in her arms & saying, "My New Born Babe, I will have to leave you know." She gets up and I flee after her, down a white concrete tunnel. She is not there & the tunnel is sealed at both ends, getting lower & lower. I thought: I can't stay here, because Dr. Grossman will think this means I am feeling trapped by my marriage. So I get out of the tunnel again. In bed, M. gets up a couple more times. As I wake up a voice says to me, that at first thought was Dr. Grossman—"You need a voice to analyze your dreams, even if it's only in your head."

Dr. Grossman was in a great fancy house, working as a psychiatrist, and there was a boy in this house whom he was analyzing, and I had to come there & remember starting to tell my feelings about this boy, wondering if I had any sexual feelings, when Dr. Grossman interrupted and said, let me tell you about him, and advised me to carry a gun. Then he took a gun out of his desk & gave it to me. The next thing I knew I was running through the house in the dark with the gun as waves of terror swept over me. There was a light to the side and a gong—my heart—kept ringing. I remember saying, If I only knew where I was, and I drifted half awake to discover that I was lying with my arms around M. We had just had sex. Drifted back into the dream a few seconds (minutes?) more. Then woke up & wrote it down now in the dark.

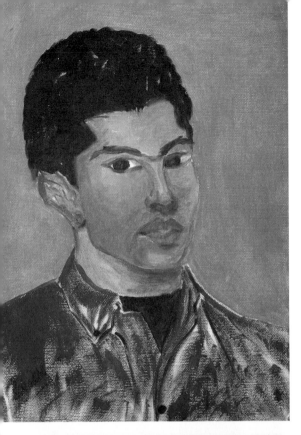

Portrait of Samuel Delany in Claudi and David Logan's apartment, New York City, 1960. Painting by Claudi Logan.

Samuel Delany in Bernard Kay's apartment, New York City, 1960. Photograph by Bernard Kay.

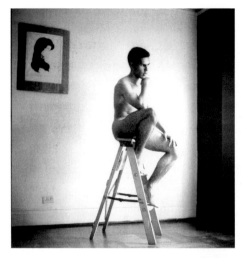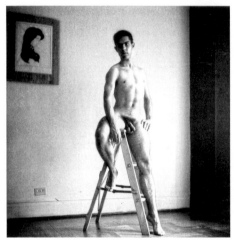

Samuel Delany in Kay's apartment, New York City, 1960.
Photographs by Bernard Kay.

Delany on the rooftop of Joe Soley and Paul Caruso's apartment building, circa 1966. The man with Delany in the bottom photograph is Paul Caruso. Photographs by Ed McCabe.

Marilyn Hacker,
circa 1964.
Photographs by
Ed McCabe.

Delany
in Caruso
and Soley's
apartment.
Photograph by
Ed McCabe.

Marilyn Hacker
in Hacker
and Delany's
apartment, New
York City, circa
1964. Photograph
by Ed McCabe.

In the downstairs supers' changing room of the Metropolitan Opera at Lincoln Center, Samuel Delany wears his merchant's costume for the second scene of Samuel Barber's opera *Antony and Cleopatra*, starring Leontyne Price, directed by Franco Zeffirelli, choreographer and assistant director, Alvin Ailey, summer 1966. Photograph by Ed McCabe.

Marilyn in Gasmask and Polyethylene, circa 1965. Photograph by Peter Reinstorff. Hacker had met Reinstorff through Bill McNeill. Photo © 1967 by Peter Reinstorff. Used here by permission of Henry Morrison, Inc., as agents for the Estate of Peter Reinstorff.

Samuel R. Delany, summer 1966.
Photograph by Ed McCabe.

Delany at the 1966 World Science Fiction Convention.
Standing at right are science fiction editor Terry Carr and his
wife, Carol Carr. Photo: copyright © 2015 Andrew I. Porter.

*Samuel R. Delany Writing
"We, in Some Strange
Power's Employ, Move on
a Rigorous Line."* Painting
by Jack Gaughan, Rifton,
New York, November 1967.
Currently owned by David
Hartwell.

NOTEBOOK 81—[LATE SPRING 1965]

Plot of S-F novel

Cancer Axis is at war with the Gamma Alliance. One of the Cancer Axis's weapons was a secret agent jazzed up from birth and sent across to the Gamma Alliance. They forgot about him. A few years later a strange figure comes back and starts damaging the Cancer Axis troops. Radio interference, a code. Ex-cryptographer who went on to become a great poet is put on the case. Discovers it's a language. Chases him around, finally finds him and determines the flaws in the language.

Things you want to include.

Archetypal experiences: break with parents.
    First taste of love
        ″   ″   ″ war
        ″   ″   ″ art

Locations: rocky plain and desert—emotional scene.
Port City—slums and tenements
Aristocratic Mansion
Inside a space ship.

I have the annoying feeling that all this will not correlate.

*   *   *

A situation here that I have to strike. I am in conflict with school: I don't want to go, I want to write; I am also afraid I can't write. I want to travel. I am afraid I can't travel. I feel totally fucked up and depressed; it is not the feeling I associate with other people's depressions. It is a physical thing, like too much coffee in the belly (which I have) and a faint pressure on the back of my neck, my throat slightly clogged. I will call Marie and talk to her.

+ + +

Science-Fiction Novel

12 chapters again—that's a good steady number—isn't that what they all are when I write them?

Early recollections of the invasion; death of parents. Languages. Work with cryptography.

The structure of the story—is it an adventure story? Or is it a panoramic life of young man/woman during a catastrophic future time.

Becomes court poet to a great feudal star-ship. (The court jester.)

Battle wild monster

Escape from Dungeon

Rescue Princess.

First taste of love

   "   "   " war

+   +   +

The gathering of the Crew

—The Port City

—The Three Sex Aristocracy of Vega

—The Physical World of Oceans Caves and Deserts

—The World of Illusion

—The Traveling Space Castile

—The War Arsenal

—Port City

1 Port City

2 War Arsenal

3 The Aristocracy

4 The Desert

5 Traveling Castile

6 The Illusion

7 Port City

+   +   +

It's a port city.

Fumes have rusted the sky here, the General thought. Layers of industrial gases flushed the evening with oranges, salmons, purples that were too red. West, the descending and ascending transports shuttling cargo from the Stellar-Centers and the inner satellites lacerated the clouds again and again. It's a rotten-poor city, thought the General, turning the corner by a garbage-strewn curb. Since the invasion there had been six ruinous embargoes, which for months apiece had strangled this metropolis whose life line must pulse with interstellar commerce to survive. How could a city like this, sequestered, exist? Six times in twenty years he had asked himself that question, each time with increasing panic. After the first time, the answer was obvious. It can't.

[sequence continues]

+ + +

Exegesis of the Structure of *The Fall of the Towers*

The three books are a meticulous tapestry of a beautifully detailed future society, physically, socially, and psychologically believable. Many characters perform to demonstrate theme and counter theme; but the central story is this: a young man at the beginning of the story escapes from prison. At the end, he gains some understanding of what freedom is. But to do this

+ + +

Outline—Part One

1

Rydra translating when the ship gets in an accident[;] the ship is sealed. Solved by Rydra [...] by translating the language. Great circle—orbit. Discovers when they get out of it that it was on purpose.

2

They arrive at the war yards. Rydra is checking through the secret weapons. (Bombs, big for equipping ships. Spy weapons, poisons, cords, etc. Spies, born and bred.)
Discover the brigade sent 16 years ago, led by the aristocratic Baron Rhill.

3

At the Baron's house, a feast in which he reveals he has stolen one of the children. Who attack Rydra, but she talks her way out. They escape.

4

Circle through the war yard dodging [...] while the accident occurs. Over-hearing Babel-17, she gets more of code.

5

Peace—internal discovery that one of the platoon kids is a supper-kid and doesn't know it. Off through the stars.

NOTEBOOK 29—JUNE–JULY 1965

Having returned from Texas, brown and lean, it is time for me to strike at the world. Let me record effort and reverberation here in this book, begun June 14, 1965.

Notes for *Babel 17*:

Hunger metaphor for the Baron: opening chapter 3, part II
"Yon Cassius has a lean and hungry look."
Also think of appropriate quotes as epigraphs to each part

Transcription of the remaining outline of Part II
—One—completed
—Two—opening completed. Conclusion:
    Rydra is taken on a tour of the weapons and discovers the supper kids.
—Three—dinner at the Baron's; discovery that the Baron has kidnapped a supper kid.
    Again Rydra escapes with the help of Babel-17. She exits with crew and
    escapes to spaceship.
—Four—being chased through the war yards, the accident occurs, sabotage, and more
    Babel-17. They escape.
—Five—she discovers one of eight supper kids is among the platoon.

Part III

The Medieval Space Pirate Ship. She now knows where the next accident will occur. They fight the Invaders.
They fight the Invaders, Rydra is in an actual skirmish of the war, then encounters more Babel-17.

Weapons for use against the Invaders. The lump of metal with stress tension
The poisons

orbis—Latin
'o kuklog—Gr.
il cerchio—It.
ratas—Lithuan[ian]
kruh—Czech

Greek—sphaira—sphere
σφαιρα—Greek
de kring—Dutch
il globo—It.
Gumlas—Lithuanian
Kule—Czech
Kuglet—Norwegian & Danish

+ + +

Chip [Samuel] Delany   Muels Aranlyde
Bob Folsom
Yoml Fol
   Bo Fobs
Oml Boofs
Lomb Fobbo   Fobo Lombs

+ + +

Notes for *Babel-17*

The Story of Language
Quipuca mayocuna—keeper of the knots
13—in Peru—interpreters of knot code
16—Gamblers sign language
36-23—"Marius made me for Numerius"—oldest Latin inscription on a belt buckle.
Old words—p. 23
Lingua latina
40—Lingua Romana rustica—Charlemagne's acknowledgment of the new language
   Decipherment of Linear B
   The Story of Language

The Loom of Language
The Origin of Language
Name and symbol—difference
Jebel Tarik—the Pillars of Hercules
—Greetings: 84 backwards
Ndw-ntr—Egyptian word for writing.
Speech of the gods.
Boustrophedon—as the ox plows—a writing method.
Oldest grammar—Panini Sutras.
Fifteen cases in Finnish

+ + +

Things to explain in the opening conversation between Brass and Rydra:

The saboteur obviously doesn't want to kill her, or else she would be dead. The Spy missed the Baron. The flight orders were broadcast. If he could broadcast Babel-17, he could broadcast English as well; what about the spy on the ship who might also speak B-17, may be responsible for the surprise take-off.

Why did she get everyone back to the ship […] because she didn't know if the whole place was gonna explode or not.

+ + +

Notes on *Babel-17*

Loose ends—
Stellar men.

Paragraphs of character build up on her desire to find out the answer to Babel 17.

Page 24—on her tenacious desire for success, and that she goes after what she wants.
Page 69—anticipation of what will happen at the war yard, her reaction to same.
Page 70—reaction to the Baron, her hauteur, etc.
Page 74—her reaction to her reactions.
Page 101—her reaction to the Baron's assassination.
Page 104—relief at escaping the mayhem.

+ + +

Babel-17

Part I
   Wong
Part II
   Ver Dorco
Part III
   Jebel Tarik
Part IV
   Come Thou Down from High Babel
Part V
   T'mwarba

+ + +

1
Audience with Jebel
They are on a guerrilla fighting ship.
Jebel's respect for poetry, it's important, makes her the ship's bard.
Battle commences; she directs them out of danger with Babel-17. 1st schiz-note.

2
The Butcher—the terrible things he does, executing prisoners.
They explore the ship. Find out the Babel-17 next destination. H.Q. come back.
Try to convince Jebel.
Butcher returns, does something nice, that intrigues her, then convinces Jebel to follow Rydra's instructions.

3
Rydra discusses Butcher with Brass
Battle, in which Rydra foils an assassination attempt on Jebel; he is grateful.
She gets Jebel aside, tells him about aliens, communication, et al.
She witnesses execution, and gets sick.

4

Talks this time with platoon kid.

Watches him, sees, learns.

Goes back to Butcher. It starts to get physical.

The feast. There are almost to Headquarters.

5

The surprise battle; which Rydra directs with Babel-17 and Jebel gets killed. They follow her. The battle is a success. […] A sudden premonition that the traitor has somehow distorted her translation of Babel-17, that all her translations up till now have been wrong. Collapses in Butcher's arms.

+   +   +

Babel-17

Part V

Dr. T'mwarba and the crew. They have to tell him about the Butcher not saying I. Ver Dorco's weapons, the baby he saved.

Rydra has introduced them to new worlds—Callie, new ideas, Ron said Mollya, she made me alive.

+   +   +

Epigraphs—all from M.H.

Part I

> Here is the hub of ambiguity … etc.
>
> —Prism & Lens

Part II

> If words are paramount I am afraid
>
> That words are all my hands have ever seen.
>
> —Quartet

Part III

> You have imposed upon me … etc.
>
> —Nightingale, Falcon and Crow
>
> > —The Song of Liadan

Park IV
> The dark twin
> —The Dark Twin

Part V
> Dawn Passage

+   +   +

Empire Star

Off a primitive planet with a circus
A musician
A murderer
A circus
Across a Pleasure Planet
Across a hell

A "lemming farmer"
A military troop
A group of traveling poets and philosophers
An insane Rimbaud
A traveling brothel
He must conquer a nation
Die, and be reborn

Being set on the idea
Of getting to Atlantis,
You have discovered of course
Only the Ship of Fools is
Making the voyage this year
As gales of abnormal force
Are predicted. And that you
Must therefore be ready to
Behave absurdly enough
To pass for one of the boys

+   +   +

Simplex
Complex
Multiplex

+ + +

⅓ with San Severina
Ron and Elmer
The slaves of Lll
The Brooklyn bridge

+ + +

Now where are we. Marilyn seems to have half moved out (with Bobby
Riccioti).

+ + +

Dear Sir,

I am 23 and have published five science fiction novels. Two more are due
for release this winter. This assures you only of a certain energy and minimal craft. I am enclosing two reviews from *Analog* magazine by P. Schuyler
Miller which will give you a surface idea of my craft's scope and texture.

I have several novel length manuscripts, two of which I feel are publishable. I will be traveling starting at the end of August a year or so (though
still writing). It is imperative I have an agent, a service I have fulfilled for
myself till now.

I am sure of my writing; therefore re-writing, cutting, the various editorial operations occasionally necessary are easy for me to perform, either
working with someone, or alone. I am firm when I am right, but never
temperamental. There are two books which will probably deserve your
primary attention. One is a 200-odd page novel called *Those Spared by
Fire*. It concerns a brilliant psychotic adolescent who moves in a world of
juvenile delinquents, and other youngsters disturbed by the ambiguities
caused by our society's view of adolescents. He maneuvers those around
him, destroying or creating apparently gratuitously. The question of the
book is whether he is redeemable. The book speaks in varied voices with
varied concepts of chronology, and might be classed as experimental.

Its history: it was first written in 1958. Harcourt, Brace thought enough
of it to send me at their expense to the Bread Loaf Writers Conference
that summer, but it was not taken. In 1964, with perhaps 20% rewritten, it
went to Grove Press. We reached the luncheon and martini stage on the
strength of a nonagented submission, however nothing materialized. This
spring both the new and old material was completely rewritten and submitted to New American Library. Again, a luncheon or two, but nothing

was concluded. Two editors took a particular interest in the manuscript and asked my permission to pass it on to Arthur Cohen at Henry Holt, where it is currently.

Voyage, Orestes, the other book, is large, leisurely, and much more conventional than the first. It was first written between '60 and '63. It would make a 600+ page novel. It takes a young man, 19, through a series of interlocking adventures the subject of which is the conflict between the myths of society concerning Negroes, Artists, and Women. The myths dealt with, however, are not the nineteenth century ones which have been poked and punched to death. But rather the contemporary ones that I had to come to terms with to deal with the world. The treatment is not satiric, except in the Kafkaesque sense of a great mythical world all individuals build around themselves.

It has had a jinxed career.

First it was at Appleton-Century-Crofts, who had their fiction department sliced out of existence by their Des Moines Office and my manuscript went toppling. Then it was sent personally to William Raney at Bobbs-Merrill by an editor at Appleton who took an interest in it, two weeks before his suicide. It went to Grove Press, but it is simply not their sort of book and jumps up and down on the toes of the monsters off whom they make their living—with track shoes.

Since then, no one has seen it in entirety.

The first and last third have been completely rewritten. Similar work could easily be done on the middle third, but, with such a lengthy work, I hesitate to jump into such work with no prospect of publication.

I also have a children's book, *Prism*, with Margaret Macaulay at Harcourt, Brace, about which I have heard nothing for over a month.

I also have a half dozen or so short novels and novelettes, which I have no idea what to do with. I feel very cramped by the short story and have not written any in the past three years.

If we reach a constructive agreement, I would like you [to] handle all my work, if you are willing. My reputation in the SF field is such that just about anything I do is assured immediate sale, which guarantees you something.

Could we get together for drinks some afternoon or evening during the next two weeks.

I work at home seven days a week between 6:00 AM and 4:00 PM where you can phone me at 475–5463.

Since I am leaving during the third week in August, it might be wise to meet as soon as possible.

Thanking you in advance,

Samuel R. Delany

+ + +

Discover wounded Golden.
Take him to Allegra's
Allegra projects for Teehalt
Incident with two Golden in front of Sandy (meanness illustrated)
Allegra discovers she's a golden
Golden going to take her away
Teehalt kills her (deprives her of drug).
Goes with golden.
Sandy—clairvoyant— ... recount Teehalt's death to Vyme.

+ + +

How much of your impression of someone is the person himself, and how much is the person in his environment. Red hair on a spade shaped head, skin once freckled but evened out by sun till they were ghosts on his knotted brown shoulders. A mist of gold hair on his forearms and belly. A snarl of brass wire at his groin.

He was standing naked on the rainy deck when I saw him like this, laughing, one hand on the whip line, feet grimy to the ankles, long toe-nail tar-rimmed, his hands with knob knuckled fingers and wide nails wrecked on the nub with gnawing. The barge was in dock for three days during which time he hadn't worn a stitch. Dawn fog hid the harbor and half the city behind the piers.

Hefting his balls, he swaggered over to me. "Nigger," he said. "You gonna tell 'em how I made you *suck* my *dick?*" He fingered his wrinkled sack in my face. The thick tube of his prick, as long as my foot, soft, with a loose foreskin and netted in veins flopped in his fingers. I caught it in my mouth and it curled up warm and raunchy on my tongue, then began to straighten out, pushing me away. "Nigger, you're gonna *make* me drop another load in your face—" but he'd begun to rub his fingers through my hair, gently, like he always did. He began to ease in and out. "Come on, Nigger, jerk yourself. Let me *see* you beat your meat."

I opened the jean fly and began to rub my shaft. He bent down and got one

+ + +

The thing that frightens the general public today is change. No picture of ourselves shocks us. There is little that is alien that is upsetting. The one might be transforming into the other is what terrifies.

+ + +

under my balls. "I'm gonna *fuck* you, you black bastard. *Fuck!*" He pulled me up, slipped his hands down my pants, fingered my hole, and turned me around pushing my jeans down. He bent me over the wet rail and I heard him spitting on his dick. Only one other guy had ever fucked me, a drunken Puerto Rican who made a bloody mess out of my ass. Rivets was incredibly gentle, for all his mean talk. "Oh, shit, shit, shit—" he whispered. "Easing my big red pecker around in all that black nigger-shit. *Man*—" he licked my hair with his warm wet tongue, holding me around the chest. He quivered and panted, going slowly in and out. "You cocksucker, you dirty-nigger motherfuck, you piss-ass, two bit shit-licker." Then he shot. Like a little hammer blow to the base of his spine translated into my ass. Without dismounting, he dragged me back toward the cabin. Rivets liked to play around and he always came three times in a balling. Inside on the gray floor, the corners caked with greasy dirt, there was a mattress. Finally he pulled his dick out, pulled me down; the mattress was damp with piss. Whenever Rivets came in drunk, he wet the bed. He liked the smell, though, and a lot of times he just came in and peed on it. Or times like now.

He kneeled over me, trying to fumble his dick into my face, only I was laughing.

Then Rivets laughed. It was a big sound that clanged around inside him, like an I-beam crashing behind the

+ + +

Empire Star

The seemingly Simplex singer trying to get back to Empire Star.
The light that flashes by them
Her name: Lara

hairy chest. Still laughing, he began to pee on me.

There was a shadow in the doorway, and a drawling voice said, "Piss all over the black bastard."

Rags stood in the door, hefting his nuts and hose already out of the flap of his dirty white jeans.

Rivets rose over me, a-straddle, spurting in my face. Rags was a brass-haired, cable armed Texan. He had a large, loose-lipped mouth, a large, loose-foreskinned dick. He had a thin nose, cheekbones so sharp they looked like they were cutting from under his ice-chip eyes. He came over on his wide bare feet, pavement blackened. He stood, jerking over Rivet's shoulder, his red dick winking the pulsing knot of his dirty fist. Rivets started mouthing for it, drooling into Rags' golden snarling crotch. Rags was laughing and teasing Rivets with his pecker. It ended up with Rivets on his back on the wet mattress. Rags, his clothes in a heap on the floor, astride Rivets' dick (Rivets ended up fucking everybody) his urine hosing from his thick peter through the hair on

+ + +

Have you spoken to Bob

He's at stockade

What about the $200 fine

Have you spoken to Bob?

What is Bob's feeling in all this

+ + +

Rivets' belly. I stood over them while Rags made wet love with tongue and lips and dripping hands to my pecker. That big Texan could really suck and when he was getting it from both ends, it just made him wilder. He caressed my balls, tongued my belly button, then let me fuck his fist into his face. He pulled my load from me twice, once like honey, once like brine. Then he grabbed me and pulled me down on Rivets' belly and made me suck his dick while his fist jerked in my face. He stuck his big wide fingers in my mouth with their round gnawed nails. He started to come—the undertube swelling on my tongue—and began to pee, then shoved the raunchy sack of his balls, salty and strong, into my mouth, prodding to get them both in, the size of peaches in a shammy sack.

Rags slipped on his jeans and we left Rivets curled up naked in the piss. I got on my pants and we went out and sat on the rail. Rags put his bare feet apart and opened his shirt, then began to massage and mangle his pecker. He grinned at me. "Got my motor-cycle here, boy. Thought you might be around here. Let me see that black meat." I lay my black hose across his callused hand. He closed his hand around it and whistled. "Nigger, you got all that down my face?"

+ + +

Origin of golden
Particularly about the viciousness
There's no solution to the golden

Golden influenced the kids' development

The nature of the isolation
The nature of the desire

More about the world

+ + +

Space-boy

Pollo—ugly, strong, ribald young man, semi-orphan status, wanderer in space.

L-Dok—dragon Baron in the Hercules cluster, going on the biggest drive.

Rivets—redheaded, strong man.

Star—L-Dok's daughter who goes in the drive.

Nike—a ball of energy who accompanies them.

Leehan—cook, doctor, computer, telepath.

Kid-death
Myer-wier
Cartou-waro

Divide up into 18 chapters.

Chapter one
Rivets hires Pollo

Chapter two
Pollo and L-Dok and Branning

Chapter three
Pollo meets the rest of the crew and they go off on the range, to round up the cysto forms.

Chapter four
The long haul between, empty space, and Pollo's thoughts alone. They get started, dinner that evening, and Star sings.

Chapter five
Kid-death begins cutting out the dragons, and Nike spots him and there is a battle.

Chapter six
The plague starts among the dragons.
Pollo nurses one back to health—who telepaths him and makes him understand L-Dok.

Chapter seven
Big battle before they put down on Jangle-Hall, to graze.
Star & Pollo.

Chapter eight
Liftoff from Jangle-Hall, into the winds of Myer-wier. Myer-wier wounds Rivets. Debate leaving him behind.

Chapter nine
They encounter the Warriors, who try to take their herd for food.

Chapter ten
Escape from Warriors with the help of Kid-death.

Chapter eleven
Put down on Branning, and Branning doesn't want to pay them, the slaughter and freezing goes on. And finally Kid-death walks in and says you better pay.

Chapter twelve
A glorious drunk, in the middle of which Kid-death is gunned down and they all separate, Pollo on to better things
L-Dok back to do another drive
Emerald who takes Kid-death's place

+ + +

I lead fine dragons
for a fine dragon lord,
a lord of fine dragons
and his dragon horde.

+ + +

Dear Heart,

Spoke to the ingenuous Mr. Folsom late this afternoon—calling from jail. Seems he should have been released yesterday, thanks to the efforts of Mr. Flood, but apparently two more checks were found and there are two more warrants out which were read to him today. He called Mr. Flood, and spoke to his secretary: her dreadfully appropriate comment was, "Oh, my goodness!"

He's mildly petulant about why we haven't been writing him. Darlene has been. She was gonna get him a lawyer an' everything, but then he hasn't heard from her since.

Seems if these last two checks could be paid up (total $50) then everything might be all right—unless some more come in.

At which point I asked, "Do you have any idea how many more are out?"

"About a half a dozen. But I don't really remember." Then he had the good something or other to say, rather reprovingly, "If you pay up *all* these checks, that's going to be a lot of money."

I have the feeling what probably happened was that the entire $300 he came to N.Y. with was gained by misdemeanor-sized bad checks.

Could we send him a couple of bucks for stamps and cigs? He's borrowing stamps from fellow prisoners, and they're getting edgy.

He's digging grass out of the bottom of "shit-ditches"—drainage troughs where the water varies in depth between thigh-deep and head-deep.

He weighs "—at least a hundred and fifty pounds—" and he says he's good n' sunburned and his arms "... are at least ways as big around as they were ..."

Oh, well. My cooking never did that. Told you that's where he would be in his element. Also told you he would contrive to get your first week's salary.

I'll even throw in my ten from tonight.

Oh yes, he wrote us a letter last night, but we are not to take it too seriously because he was "pretty disgusted."

I was friendly, warm, and hung up the phone feeling sorry for the poor bastard. Really.

That's all for now, folks!
Chip

Didn't he get my letter last week? Who's he been cadging stamps to write to—I sent postage. Will have mailed letter when you see this. Oh well, no new bikini.

Happy anniversary

M

I told Bernie the other night it cost about $200 an inch

+ + +

Comet Jo's slang

drop final t, ing, middle t becomes d
no verb to be
most articles gone.

+ + +

Lusp, Lucp, Lump

+ + +

Time to make lists:

Salable

Babel-17
Star-Pit
They Fly at Çiron
"In the Ruins"
Empire Star
Prairies of Space
Prism & Lens

+   +   +

Actions derive their value from the world they take place in.

Bester
> *Demolished Man*
> *The Stars My Destination*

Sturgeon
> *Synthetic Man*
> *More Than Human*

Bradbury
> *Fahrenheit 451*
> *Something Wicked This Way Comes*

Horty—becoming a girl.

Murder in a corrupt but non-evil society.

Read in a world which says you can't read.

Everyday bourgeois actions in a world of supercharged sensitivity.

Olivia's crime in the super Victorian world jaunting has created.

Super actions in the everyday world.
> Jeannie & her mother's house.
> Kids upsetting Alicia's house.

Cantos of Mutability

Notes on a Novel

The basic story must be in terms of a conflict. A young man from the lower middle class, through this conflict, rises over a period of about a year till he is comfortable in the lower upper class. Having first plummeted to the depths, and risen into the upper.

Branning—author
Corbelli—musician
Leontyne—anthropologist

Corbelli—Catherine
Branning—Rags
Leontyne—Helene

Corbelli (Slum) ← → Catherine (solid M.C.) fishing port—slum—field and forest
Branning (Upper Class) ← → Rags (L.C.) nunnery—slum—country school
Leontyne (Déclassé) ← → Helena (U.C.) museum—slum—city mansion

Locations: slums, museum, the fishing port, the field and forest, the country school, the nunnery, the city mansion
Slums

+ + +

Outline
For
Cantos of
Mutability

Characters and relations	mentor & class	location
Vrest—L.M.	Corbelli—L.C.	Slum
Catherine–S.U.M.		Port slum
		Woods
		Slum
Vrest	Branning—S.U.	Country School

Regs—déclassé

Woods
Nunnery
Slum

Vrest

Leontyne—déclassé

Museum

Helene, U.C.

Slum
City Mansion
Woods

Arthur Branning

Minor characters

8

....

Travels in Europe

....

Upon arriving in Luxembourg in October 1965, Delany, Helstrom, and Balousiak spent approximately one week in that country, followed by two weeks each in Paris and Venice. Next they explored the islands of Greece— Milos, then Mykonos, and eventually Crete, with brief stop-offs in Syros, Sifnos, Tinos, and Corfu—and then went on to Athens, where they stayed for an extended period before Delany eventually departed for London.[1] (Note that the entries in the first notebook from this period, Notebook 67, skip back and forth in time and cover the entire period from Venice to London, while entries in subsequent notebooks cover episodes occurring within this same period; there is a good deal of chronological overlap among these notebooks.) During his travels Delany worked intermittently on *The Einstein Intersection*, which he refers to here by its original working title, "A Fabulous, Formless Darkness," and several other stories, including "Dog in a Fisherman's Net" (which, like *The Einstein Intersection*, makes creative use of the Greek landscape) and the ongoing "Faust" project.[2] Delany also began to develop his next science fiction novel, *Nova*. As various entries indicate, this novel went through considerable changes before settling into its final form.

Delany's experiences in Greece eventually found their way into several essay-memoirs: "A Fictional Architecture That Manages Only with Great Difficulty Not Once to Mention Harlan Ellison" (1967), "A Bend in the Road" (1994), and "Citre et Trans" (1995). In various entries in the notebooks to follow we encounter individuals who play important roles in those later works: DeLys Robinson, John Witten-Doris, and Heidi Mueller.

During his travels, Delany supplemented his income with solo folk performances. In early 1966, however, he was arrested by Greek authorities for performing without a permit, resulting in his brief deportation. Delany went to Budapest, crossed back to Thessaloniki shortly thereafter, then spent twelve days in Istanbul before returning to Athens.[3] In the spring of 1966 he traveled to London, where he met a number of British writers associated with the SF magazine *New Worlds*, including Michael Moorcock and John Brunner, as well as the American SF writer and editor Judith Merril.[4] In Notebook 30—which covers the end of Delany's stay in London and his return, two weeks after his twenty-fourth birthday, to New York City—we see the beginning of Delany's discussions of and correspondence with these writers, which will carry forward into future journals. In this notebook we also find a draft of "New Wor(l)ds / Many Inventions," which, appearing in truncated form in *New Worlds* under the title "Sketch for Two-Part Invention," would become Delany's first piece of published SF criticism.[5] After Delany returned to New York on April 15, he completed *The Einstein Intersection* and "The Star-Pit" and continued to work on *Nova*.[6]

NOTES

1. K. Leslie Steiner, "Anatomy of a Nova" (unpublished essay, 1997), 11. "K. Leslie Steiner" is a pseudonym used by Delany.

2. Ibid., 13–15.

3. Ibid., 15.

4. Samuel R. Delany, "Chronology" (unpublished personal document, 2014), 12.

5. Steiner [Delany], "Anatomy of a Nova," 17–18.

6. Delany, "Chronology," 12.

NOTEBOOK 67—[AUTUMN 1965– SUMMER 1966]

Here in the highest spot in Athens, I stare at this immense jeweled carpet lapping toward black metal horizons under a half moon.

—Athens, Colline de Lykavittos, Nov 3rd

+ + +

I just realized how much even my tastes had changed when I caught myself this afternoon making a sandwich: bread slathered with olive oil, four cloves of garlic finely chopped, salt and pepper. That's all. And my tastes are western because I dice my garlic whereas the local people just slice theirs. Oh well. (O tempora, o mores)

—Milos, Nov 27

+ + +

As I struggle with modern Greek pronunciation: the simple word for "week"—spelled bdomada, and pronounced vthomatha, I have to remember that this is the language that gave English such tongue twisters as diphtheria and phthisic.

Go into the local bar and get a "fix." A rizogalo.

Radio station playing Greek, French and English rock an' roll.

Κύων, ancient word for dog.

Σκύλος, modern. Occasionally uses the dative.

The old stories of Delos. The necropolis.

+ + +

Slipped from the night waters of the Adriatic and now skirt down the straits towards Athens. It is lovely. Breezy but warm. What monstrously beautiful mountains gnaw the sky on both sides of the ship. The clouds and the rocks want to chomp closed around us as if we were inside a god's mouth. The ship's speaker gives up Rock and Roll. Vast improvement over the mush from the Orchestra in the Piazza San Marco. We came over with deck-passage. Ron and I snuck into a 2nd-class cabin, however, and got 12 hours beautiful sleep. We were worn out after the all-night ride on the Italian train. (Standing in the hall, sleeping on the floor. I found it an experience, met all the people on both sides of me and got a three hour Italian lesson from the chemist next to me. He spoke French and German.) A boy beside me with a sword length pinky nail had just been discharged from the Army. Ron was just p.o.'d though.

The sun silvers the hosed deck. The Rock 'n roll goes from English, French, to Greek. Met a strange pair of English kids who were going to Corfu to pick up a truck they left there. Skinny, unkempt, witty in an underspoken way; we finally asked what they did: "Sort of unclassifiable." Very good answer. They wanted to know if we liked Bob Dylan.

It is 8:30 in the morning and behind me the Israeli students returning [to Haifa] cluster and whisper happily. The sun above the smoke stack burns away everything before it.

Has the lump under my chin started to swell? That would be sad if it had.

Gulls, like twitching mouths, kiss the sky behind the boat.

I will finish *A Fabulous Formless Darkness* in Greece. It is a perfect place for it, not only because of the myths, but because the world, in its incredibly violent disarray, the chaos calmed before such beauty, has been discovered to me in the past few weeks as such a perfect place for the book.

Recent R. n' R. is such an incredibly appropriate popular art form for this world. I was only aware how well it fitted the capsulated life of N.Y. Even more congruent it is with the rest of the world. Thus its popularity. This incredible time of youth.

The music keeps casting me back to the shrimp boat where I worked for the summer. The boat, the hammered out water 3 thousand miles away are the same. The [nostalgia], without sentimentality is at moments overpowering.

Re-read *The Navigators* just now. Came to some insights about art. The poem is perfectly congruent with everything I have learned since I left N.Y. That is the value of artistically valid constructions. The world extrapolated through the intuitive laws of art always holds together. Thus a Dutch journalist can be moved by the works of a New England recluse. (Discussed Emily Dickinson with Jacques Sitter at dinner in Paris, and other poets. That was only 2 weeks ago!)

* * *

Wandered up to the Αποθηκη ναυκληρου—the forepeak. Slept in same in Texas. Rags and paint just like Texas. A basket of beer bottles behind a huge winch.

* * *

4:00 (Greek time) Ron and Bill play "football"—coins across the table. I sit, soused on wine, beside the table. The weather ranges from pleasant to hot, by the hour.

I have met three young Greek ναυτικι; they've taken a liking to me, and I think we will have friends in Αθήνα.

+   +   +

St. Mark's Square
October 28, 1965,
10:00 at night

Fog over the square; I am sitting on the base of the flagpole, second from the left (facing the Basilica), contemplating the Venetian section of "Wolf." The band is playing Russian music—for which everyone applauds more loudly than for the American standards. There were several scattered Japanese tourists, for which they played that Japanese Rock 'n Roll song that was so internationally popular a few years back. Now they play "Granada." I would prefer Mozart. Oh, well.

———

Wolf in Venice. He is being hunted by Arthur Branning, Catherine's half brother. Roger, his red headed "lieutenant" who runs a gang of juvenile delinquents, among them boys from the Murano glass factory, the helpers with the boats, the Chinese students. The two faces of Montesque. Catherine, Kairn, help "Wolf" but are always disappearing. Here "Wolf" meets Arthur's mother Leontyne Branning in the museum. Kairn takes him to the palazzo for dinner, and he meets Catherine socially unexpectedly. This is where the chase begins (perhaps). Ends in the glass factory, smashes the showrooms.

+   +   +

Outline

Prologue
  New York

Wolf is fired from printing job. Goes to see the Venetian instrument repair man, Corbelli, who has the black dog, Niger. He meets Catherine Branning; mysterious comments on the black and white Wolf. She leaves hurriedly when a dark man appears. He walks in the city by himself: is struck with the confusion of it, the loneliness, his own chaotic perception that seems at once so beautiful and yet confused. He meets Arthur Branning and Montesque in the shop. He stays in the shop that night, Corbelli offers it to him because he is so lonely. That night delinquents break into the shop and he is powerless to stop their vandalism. Next day, Corbelli's reaction, distrust, suspicion. He meets Catherine, tells her about it, how upset he is. She is at first more upset, then becomes interested in "Wolf's" reaction. They ride on the subway—the abandoned station, the men playing bocce: she is fascinated by his method of perception. She explains she cannot see things that way, but she would like to learn. She can teach him things also. She suggests taking a trip with her. Just as they wander back to the scene of the shop, Wolf reveals that Montesque was there. Catherine reacts. They see mad Corbelli, with the black dog barking after him. She suggests the journey again.

Where?

To see her father in Martha's Vineyard. She doesn't like New York, her brother, or Montesque.

––––––

Part One

They hitch to the Vineyard. Wolf assumes Catherine poor. They arrive at the Gay Head school. He assumes her rich. They discuss the business. He meets Kairn, the writer. The discussion between Kairn & Branning; Branning & Wolf. Wolf & Kairn drunk. Kairn declares himself homosexual. Arthur is received warmly, sans Montesque. Wolf discovers he is responsible for the breaking up of the shop. Wolf observes the scene between Catherine and Arthur. Catherine comes to him for comfort. Incest? That doesn't bother her. Wolf and Arthur.

They decide to go to Venice—where Arthur's mother is.

Wolf: You just pick up and go?

Why not. It will give you some more insight into things.

––––––

Part Two:

Venice

(Somewhere: a conversation with Arthur: you are the dangerous one. You are the one who is changing her way of looking at things. I declare war on you.)

Main incidents. Meets Leontyne Branning—brilliant retired Negro artist and archaeologist. Where she is sculpting the White Wolf. The Branning palazzo in Venice. The delinquents break into the museum. She doesn't let them break anything. Fight there. How could I have stopped them from breaking up Corbelli's shop? That's how. Now I know. Fight in the Glass works. Ends up at the Guggenheim dinner. Then to the cemetery. (Here in this dead city you are learning about life.) Let's get away from Arthur. Back to the states.

+ + +

Modern SF might be the only practical
Mainstream does not bring a clearer focus to people about the changes taking place in their world.
SF examines the human possibilities in these new environments.
Mainstream fiction ignores for
                    is the only fiction
Social environmental factors are becoming vastly complicated.

+ + +

Blair Faust

Port City, a gray, dreary center of trade. Map. The space port. The warehouses to the left, the river running by, and the entertainment to the right. Slums and dives. Hospital to the back.
Three characters: Buddy (24), Vaughan (15), and Bellinda (70).

+ + +

Mainstream fiction today is onanistic and defeatist.
SF is the literature that posits man is changing.
Mainstream is the literature that posits he cannot change.
Science fiction is the only heroic fiction left today; it's the only fiction today that admits there is a solution to its problems.
Mainstream fiction is like looking in a mirror; SF is like looking through a door.
SF has liberated the content of fiction the way Proust and Joyce liberated language.

+ + +

More notes on *Nova* (having been in shuttley London for a bit over a week now)

(3 areas to be dealt with: the common working-class, the aristocracy, the underworld)

+ + +

A few ideas on *Nova*, since leaving Athens on the first of June.

Basically make it a Prometheus story. Lorq, as he has been conceived of and written about today, is Prometheus. Characters as conceived:

Lorq/Black/White—Three giants who, throughout the story, must be in league, in conflict alternately.

Lith—the light frail woman whom they destroy, one and then two together, she's a beautiful, helpless, cold bitch.

Araan—the strong woman who kills one of the men. And equal to them all.

Knife—the sense harpist, libertine artist.

Ratt—the little gamin who ultimately effects the freeing of Prometheus.

There has to be a lot of things happening in the real world. I want to contrast the romantic and gorgeous with the suburban mundane. The home life banal with the violent.

———

These are the emotional centers that come naturally. To be filled in artificially: the Titan enemy: what about Izingar, as he began to be postulated. The whole town in which Ratt is dropped.

+ + +

Things—*pragmata* in ancient Greek, a word that had given a dozen other languages their words for practical and pragmatic—things were different—things in the demotic Greek of the late twentieth century had become *periptise*, while *pragma* had degenerated into a word used for luggage and maybe junk under your desk in the dormitory of the Scholi Techniki at Athens—things were a lot different on paper than they were in practice—the current word for things in Greek was *rea*. Crowning irony: it came with the last migration from the little enclave of Vlachs from Epirus, a tight little enclave who spoke, there in southern Macedonia, an early Romanian dialect that was closer to classical Latin than Italian. They had taken over the flea market at Monastiraki Square, under the chunky rocks and tan walls of the Acropolis, pushed out the gypsies, and *things* were not what they used to be.

Minor interruption of "Shadows"

Thoughts on Syros

Its main waterfront city seems immense after two weeks in Milos beside Plaka and Adamas. In area, it is probably ⅔ the size of Venice, which Bill insists on comparing it to. The city, definitely a sea town, with (as one leaves the central length of hill-embraced waterfront and reaches the outskirts) barefoot fishermen, nets stretched between hands and feet, mending the yellow webs. The city carpets two mountains, joining together in the saddle, with small houses spilling to the waterfront where cafés line the stone apron of the harbor, a few cheap hotels (we're staying at the Xios) and the palatial Eppes. The big boats, freighters and inter-island ferries, use the left arm of the harbor, the fishing boats and dinghies use the shallow right arm (facing the sea). Climbed to the top of the right hand mountains, where, from the church yard, you can see the whole city. This morning walked along a high road with private houses on one side and the sea at the cliff's bottom to my right. Followed the road beyond the city where it clung to the mountain till after a hairpin turn it left me at a stone, crosscrowned gate with rusted grill doors. There was a church and below, on three sides, was a stone park overlooking the sea. From the wall, watched two fishermen lay out a net across the warp of water below. Got a motorcycle ride back. Earlier, I walked out toward the beaches, passed a burned out building with one arched wall still standing, through which you could see the whole town while chickens ran among the blackened foundations. The day was almost too hot for suit jackets. I watched dawn along the waterfront come up through my hotel window. An exciting gathering of fishermen, dock hands, freighter workers. Trade and the sea give even the smallest town a cosmopolitan atmosphere. Talked briefly to two French boys who had sailed a boat here from France. I am sitting on the sidewalk chairs in front of a café. To my right the last of the crew boards a squat square black freighter. Ron, who has been ill since we left Milos, sleeps on my left. Bill (I don't believe this kid, really!) is reading *The King Must Die*.

We passed a ship building place this morning, and later a hedge of paddle shaped cactuses; many green woolen soldiers here last night, though none today. Cars and motorcycles galore, and an extremely picturesque market street with butchers, tomatoes, oranges, olives, and barefoot boy on the corner selling fish. Incongruous jukebox in one café which was obligingly silent on our first visit, but raucously present on our second. Boat leaves for Mykonos at (c.) 6:00.

[Our] boat "left" Milos at 5:00 in the morning. We didn't pull out till after 9:00. And we were there a few minutes early.

+ + +

—Spyros asks Dr. Gautier about his Greek.
—Combani likens himself to a fisherman and the relations among them all to a net.
—Cathy talks to Christian and Liza and Spyros about Combani's strange love for the young.
—Spyros thinks they are all beautiful and wants to go where they come from.
—Cathy talks to Dr. Gautier about Spyros's Greek and discovers his age.
—Dinner toward the site, and the dive.

+ + +

BIRTHDAY PRESENT

All right, stranger, as on
these looping thousands we
lick new foods and languages
and you circle your twenty-third year;
as you come up from under illness in the Greek
rain and the Greek sun, it is time
for a pledge and a present.
These new articulations
we are learning may
spiral us together to the loop's end
without fray. Still, here at the catenary's bottom
I know, now, you feel
the lack (without fear, but still,
the lack): why
am I here? Why

did he bring me here (or worse),
once he discovers the reason, will he find
it lacks. This pledge then:
we are equal.
Where you surpass, I will get no envy in the gap
For the rest, here are my eyes and my tongue.

13 April
1 May—on our way, or know how we're going.
15—in New York, with completed draft of at least one S–f novel.
Until July 15, performing and working together on songs.
July 15 to August 15, polishing—whatever that entails.
August 15: on—jobs

Jimmy's at the Door
Black Train
My Shoes are by the Door
Good Days are All Gone
Five Dollar Bill
Adios
My Gal's Fat & Lazy
I had a Feelin'
Play With Fire
Hold My Right Hand

+ + +

DeLys, loves to cook, octopus curry.
Down to Marrakech for the Moroccan folk festival, and the tapes are erased.

+ + +

Athens?
This evening a peacock rattled its hundred eyes at me while the peahen in her green bib, shamed by his blue-brilliant throat, pecked at her husband's scaly feet, and a swan honked from the lake as I hurried beneath pines and cypress.

Minutes later I was walking through carnival raucous streets where herds of masked boys bleated horns while streamers scarred the sky and an angry girl flung a handful of red confetti in my face then fled after her date beneath blue and orange balloons. One minute and thirty seconds later, night clubs, tavernas, and packed streets were echoes below me: stone steps perhaps eighteen inches wide rose between the walls, tiled roofs sloped below, and tiny huts, built into the mountainside, on streets that had basically run in this same pattern not two, not three, but over four thousand years. Less than thirty feet above me, the back porch of the Erectheum jutted above the cactus and the Acropolis wall. On the other side of the agora in the fenced field below, the temple of Hephaestus faced me, where Lord Byron, more Greek than Englishman, had carved an epitaph for Watson. And not a half an hour later I was searching the moon lit marble chips, the broken columns, through the roofless Parthenon for a marvelous girl.

I found her sitting on the south porch, staring out across the night city to the sea. Lycabettus Mountain to the east, the monastery at the top like a lighted bone. Further mountains west and north gnawed like black teeth on the pale sky. She's a New Orleans aristocrat, painting abroad. When she saw me, she jumped. "Pigeon! You scared me to death, coming out of the shadow. How did you know I was back?"

"Had a feeling. Also, your door was open. How was Morocco?"

"Lovely. I have the most incredible tapes to play you. Though I broke my recorder coming back. You should have come."

"I was slaving away at the Prison."

"The tape recorder," she said. "I was hitchhiking across the Moroccan desert, see, out of Marrakech, in fact I was just outside of Mahmid."

"Mach-ha'mynidhe, you mean."

"It's spelled Mahmid, although when anybody there said it, it sounds more like you. Anyway, I was getting some songs down from a group of Arab truck drivers, and something went wrong, so I took it apart right there." She smiled sheepishly. "Well, I think I put all the parts back in the case, but ..." She shuddered. "At least I've got the tapes."

"I'll get John that English engineer up to take a look at it. If you can't fix it, I don't think I can."

"I feel so silly. Two years ago I was making, oh, lots and lots of lovely money as a radar technician, and I can't even fix this bloody tape recorder. But I think it's in the motor."

"John will come up later tonight if you want him. He's out hustling people into the Prison."

"Shouldn't you be in Prison now, yourself?"

I nodded. "Yes, I left my guitar there. But I prefer being here. I'll get back in awhile."

"All this—" and her voice became a breath out toward the ivory runneled sea "—is so beautiful, has been so beautiful for thousands of years. And yet they say the universe is running down, all moving toward entropy. One day the last wave will come lapping in from the Aegean, leaning toward Faliron, and just not make it. Everything being used up, nothing new coming about, everything running down."

"Didn't I tell you," I said, "about the spontaneous generation of matter?"

"What?"

"Didn't I tell you that the spontaneous generation of completely new matter and energy is going on in the universe all the time?"

"Huh?" She looked mildly and amusedly surprised. "Conservation of . . . Well, I don't even think I should even say it."

"You shouldn't. No, really. I knew a kid from Columbia University, brilliant physicist, about twenty-one, who just came up with a pretty airtight proof that when electromagnetic energy passes through a gravitational field, small bits of new matter [and] new energy are generated literally from twisting the space."

"But that's impossible," she said. "It's science fiction!"

"It was 1965, dear. And this is '66, beautiful, warm, mid-February on the Aegean."

"Ohhhh . . ." because the breeze brushed the cloud of fine hair across her shoulder. She leaned forward and put her chin on her joined fists. "Pigeon?"

"Yes'm?"

"How come you know all the people you do?"

"What people?"

"Well, you're going to bring this English engineer to fix my recorder, and this physicist—and Pigeon, that dinner party at my house!" She looked up at me and blushed in the moonlight. "I really think that's why I left Athens, to get away from the memory of the whole thing!"

I laughed, leaning from my marble pediment. "It was a great party."

She swallowed. "I know but . . . Well, when you said . . . Oh!"

This marvelous girl, you see, had a marvelous hobby. Cooking. When you want a good meal, for you and four or five friends, you all forked up 75 or 100 drachmas (a drachma is 3¢) on Tuesday morning, and Wednesday evening you ate Paella (lobsters, clams, and crabs are just a part of a Paella), or Ten-Boy Curried Octopus (coconut, chives, un-laid duck eggs are just three of the ten boys), with maybe Bananas Chandre Flambé for dessert (and the Flambé is with the best Greek Metaxa, of course), "I'd rather cook than do anything, paint, fix radar sets … anything," and much much very ordinary Retsina, the house and garden wine that's as common as corn flakes here. So I'd asked if I could bring a nice young couple I'd met. The boy was a year my junior, a Greek, and his charming little Danish wife.

"But when you said his name was Constantine, I had no idea … And those policemen that stood outside the door all evening!"

"Constantine and Ann had a very nice time."

"Well … So did I. But I just wasn't prepared for …"

"You were most elegantly prepared."

"But Pigeon, where do you meet people like that?"

"It's just Athens, I think. You're as likely to be having dinner with the King one evening as a bunch of dock-hands the next."

She stood up. "But I don't think it's Athens," she said as we started back the rounded marble blocks, brown water in a depression here, there a warm iron stud holding together a weakened block. "Perhaps it's Anaphiotika. Let's go back."

We walked down through the arched port of Zeus.

Anaphiotika?

That's a neighborhood in Athens; it's much more. When you get to Athens, you probably won't find it, even though it's very real, and, by the time you finish this book I will have taken you there by the hand, led you a trillion light years away, and brought you back again. Athens. There are parks in Athens that are as lovely in their greener way as the Luxembourg Gardens. There is a place that looks like Times Square six hours before New Year's Eve every night of the week. There are streets nearly identical to the shopping center of Newark, New Jersey, only more crowded. There are tenements of old Venetian mansions converted to boarding houses; there are wide, sunny avenues of houses and stone luxury apartments, and a subway system where the people are polite; but Madrid has that. Ruins? Well, you can't see quite as spectacular ones anywhere else, but if you go through Rome you'll at least know what a ruin is. Anaphiotika? Only Athens has it. It's only here. And she keeps it a secret. It's in the center of the city, between the entertainment area of Plaka, nestled on the southeastern wall of the Acropolis. The superhighway of Leoforos Sofias arcs away on the right. Stadiou Street, the Fifth Avenue of Athens, is a three minute walk to the left. But you can't get there in a car or taxi. I know two people who attempted it on a motor scooter. One has a broken spine. The other's dead.

This marvelous girl and I were heading back there now. Let me tell you how I first got there. Start off, be born black in the USA. Add a private, very progressive elementary school education, secondary school training aimed at being a nuclear physicist. By the middle of college the contradictions explode. Work shrimp boats off the Gulf Coast awhile. Write a half dozen books over which there is a minor critical debate (more ferocious in England than America) about whether they are poetry or prose. For awhile run an illegal hustling service for middle-age executives, which when you mention it the first time to people they looked very shocked, and then about an hour later start bugging you for all the morbid details. And when you find yourself broke in some strange city you've never been in before, take out your guitar and start singing: which is what I did—now playing in a Plaka nightclub called the Golden Prison. And there you might meet a Greek poet (with a Harvard degree, and another from the University of Haifa) who decides you're different enough not from other Americans but just from the world at large to take you up those steps, between those hedges of cypress, where a few thousand years vanish. After you've been led there a few times, you may be able to find it yourself. And if I sound rather mystic and mythic, believe me, all I am doing is talking about the physical difficulties of getting to the place. Greece is like that. Athens is more like that. Και το λοιρα, Anaphiotika.

"I wonder about that, Pigeon," she said. Black cats streaked across the roofs—lengths shingled with rounded terracotta—circled, cried and disappeared down stone steps.

"What are you wondering."

Water dripped across the stone siding like veins of glass. She reached to touch one with her finger. "Whether it's the place, or you in the place. You said to me before that you always used to know a lot of interesting people, but even more is the way you're always bringing them together. It's a talent."

I paused halfway down the wooden ladder to the street below. "It is, in a way."

"Just as much as playing the guitar or writing."

I waited for her to reach the bottom, helped her down and we made our way down the alley so narrow you had to walk sideways. "I thought that too, once or twice. But it's a talent I don't know what to do with yet, at least not the way I know how to use the others." Her shoes sounded on the verdigris of the spiral stairway. I followed her up, and Athens on one side and the stone mountain wall on the other, turned about me.

"It's a shame," she said. "One hates to see talent wasted. Maybe you should be a diplomat." She pushed open the wrought iron gateway. "Well come in, have some stuffed mushrooms, and listen to my tapes. If you hear anything you like, you might learn it and sing it in Prison."

"Fine idea."

She turned on the light which went crazy on the pastel creation she had chalked, like Michelangelo, on the white walls and ceilings. Landscapes flamed away into seas. Women with gold hair and red scales battled pulsing monsters with Bosch-like weapons, and a beautiful man cried as he held up a dead swan on the volcano's rim. "Mushrooms are there. You know how to run the coffee machine. That's retsina in the raffia jug. Make yourself at home." I did, while she unsnapped her rucksack.

The black and silver Uher sat on the table and tongues of tape lisped the tiles as she checked one and the next. "Here!" she said. "Try this."

"Try this," I said, handing her a cup of Turkish coffee. "Here."

The Uher hissed on the tile table and she sat down beside me on the navy cushions. And kept hissing. After a few moments, she frowned at me.

"Maybe you didn't use that band?" I suggested.

She looked at the recorder, sipped at her coffee. "But I had four tapes and used all eight bands. I played them all through just before I got on the plane."

Silence hummed in the speakers.

"Maybe that part you broke in the desert?" I suggested.

"No. The playback is working."

+ + +

"Wolf"

I must write this damned book if it kills me—and maybe two or three other people beside.

To re-outline things:

Prologue, New York
Part One, Martha's Vineyard
Part Two, Venice
Part Three, Texas
Part Four, Athens, Islands, Athens
Epilogue, Paris

The Branning family

Leontyne Branning—Arthur Branning—Mildred

    Arthur Branning   Catherine Branning

This is a book of limits. Three sentences is the maximum amount of background about anyone save Wolf, Arthur, or Catherine—and one of those sentences must relate the background to the manner in which Wolf perceived it.

Catherine's dialogue—should some speech affectations distinguish her?

For economy's sake, we must meet first Wolf, then Catherine, then Arthur, probably all through Anton Corbelli, at least in the Prologue.

+ + +

"Freedom or death"

Captain Lorq, a pirate in space, who raids on the colony worlds. Meets Ell, and they fall in love, after which the Tains imprison her mind, and he rampages through the galaxy, collecting monsters and upsetting the Princes

A twelve inch scar . . . of bronze. When he walked into the Opal, two hopper-bums who were arguing at the bar and close to a fight quieted and moved further down the counter. A woman who no one knew raised her goblet and regarded him through the distorting curves and amber liquid. And the Rat grinned. "Y, Lorq! Port bio I mort?"

"Y." Lord answered. "Port auto-me." He laughed and swung the silver thing up under his arm on its leather strap. "Port music." His hands were banded with cracked corn on the ham and at the base of the fingers from what work the Rat did not want to guess. The blunt fingertips had the same yellow calluses, from playing the electronic harp that hung on his chest. He swung the silver thing up before him.

"D qu' world port music, th' now?"

"D polly astra, d polly world," silver quivered soundlessly under his striking palm. "As th'all-chron."

"Sp'play," Rat said softly, leaning over the counter, his filed teeth like blades behind grinning lips. "Sp'play, Lorq!"

"D bio i d mort?"

"D all'chron^2, all're^2!"

Lorq's lips answered the smile with a soft word that made everyone in the bar raise their eyes attentively: "D erotik[3]." And his hands struck at the harp through the whisper and silver blossomed into light and sound. The instrument was a beautiful one with a full tone ranging through all five senses, and harmonics that echoed in the sixth and seventh. The woman put her glass down. The hopper-bum stopped with his hand on his companion's shoulder and watched (and listened, and smelled, and tasted, and felt) as Lorq sp'played d erotik[3].

[sequence continues]

+ + +

Discovered Gregory Corso was in Athens

These mythical passings
in the Greek city with light and smoke and rain
are the loves of my young ages.
go, Gregory, called ugly in stone castings
This is not only pain,
Gerry, this is something that rages
Never saw anything except a picture of you
on a book's back, over which I rubbed off when I was sixteen
Here you come to the house
that a day later I have come to
in lighteneen. Athens is not clean
but the blonde girl who met you douse-
es rags at the sink and
sitting in another tiled room you fill my hand

—Athens, Anaphiotika
March, 1966

+ + +

Dear you,

Here I am in Istanbul. It's raining and once more I have fallen in love with a new city. I've been here perhaps three hours, acquired a Turkish vocabulary of twenty-five words, made arrangements with a charming high school girl named Gül ("Rose" in Turkish) to exchange English lessons for Turkish lessons, which will at least give me something to do for the week I'm here. The blue mosque is large and lovely. Istanbul is a parody of itself with little boys running up to you to change money. The tea is as strong as pot, and the hash is as strong as mescaline. I am very high. Hitch-hiked up from Thessaloniki with Jerry. Got a ride all the way into Istanbul with strange pair of 20-year-old newlyweds, German boy, American girl, 1950 Volkswagen with one headlight. Turks are infinitely more sophisticated than Greeks. Staying at a semi-youth hostel well located. Hope it stops raining so I can walk around the city. Have some addresses to look up. Mosques & minarets all over the place.

+ + +

The Basilica Cistern

Trickling halls under the brown Byzantine brick with these columns, waterlines above & below my head, the long vaults shimmer, and the mud floor shivers. I perched on the porch rail, read the near column where the tourists have scratched their names in the green stone. I read the far columns solid in shifting water.

March 20th, 1966
Istanbul

+ + +

Let's think about *Nova*. First of all I want a massive book, with a thick, real, experienced hero, Lorq. His foil is Ratt. Lorq is experienced in the physical, but learns in the physical, [experienced] in the artistic (his s'harp) but learns in the artistic, experienced in the social, but learns there as well. Thirteen chapters, but good thick ones. He commences with a failure—failure to save the Nizerine's life. Background on Lorq is the body of Chapter II, with circling sections from the enemies' point of view. Symmetrically chapter 12.

major failure
primary background
artistic
social
physical
primary battle fought
major success

problem encountered and backed off from
educational experience sought out and undergone
problem encountered and worked through

+   +   +

Parenthetical question. Is thinking about the S-F in such formal terms a waste of time? I have the feeling I must do something formal. Perhaps the answer is to work on novel *Wolf* and to exorcise this formal passion with poetry. Here I sit in a noisy Istanbul tea-house writing on a green table whose corners are freckled with cigarette burns. Jerry, quiet and pensive these last few days, is reading *Alpha Yes, Terra No*. It's warm here, I've eaten, and the world looks rather odd through the Istanbul mud and rain. Wonder how G. Corso is doing in Athens. This seems to be a month for poetry in me. But it comes very disquietly, and is to fill the big love-hole in my stomach. (Perhaps it's a little lower down.) Our absences are stifling. Obscenity is wearing thin. The hole in the gut? Rather the shape not there when I grasp my wrist with my hand. I empathize with that great cistern where I poemed this afternoon. The water level is going down, going down. I cannot get up any enthusiasm either on *Wolf, Fabulous Formless Darkness*, or *Nova*. *Wolf* is the easiest to write, and goes the slowest, because it also engenders the most guilt. I wish John Hetland were here. I keep on coming back to the incredibly meaningless fact, as I lean into my 24th year, [that] he is the only person I ever really felt safe with. God, the danger in this unloving world (the danger in me, stretched like a trampoline, catapulting me from city to city—the knowledge of the working of my tongue (how it licks the eye, tickles the ear) is a brass kettle over my head. I wish I could take it off.)

+   +   +

ANOTHER TEAHOUSE

Closer to the Grand Bazaar than Sultanahmet
there are no foreigners here. The Turks
dicing over black and maroon tavli
lick their fingers. The cataracted waiter
squashing his heels would be beautiful if his vision were
binocular. The windows drool
with rain and evening. On another

mud street, girls squat over chai and cigarettes
while memories stoop the crowds
staring by the bars at breasts and black panties.
Here, restricted love is tepid as my bellying
glass of red dorchi.

+　+　+

What do I know about the short story? There were three conflicts, and a short story dealt with one: man vs. man, nature, himself. Characters should be limited, it should revolve about one incident, limited number of characters. Three is a lot for a short story. Theodore Sturgeon's "rule," posit a character with one or more specific personality traits and a situation that blocks the expression of one of them, then watch the story develop. While we're at it, let's think about Lorq, & *Nova*. Let's posit a society, a world, galactic in scope, its economics, its workings, with much space for rambling, as well, a grand design. There will be short stories in it, illustrating pertinent themes. Posit at least a galactic society, not at war, but bordering on it. Novelettes also, but I want something that achieves what *The Fall of the Towers* set out to do. Cut out the nonsense about death. The […] in society is too pat.

+　+　+

Just as a test, can you reconstruct the contents of *Voyage Orestes?*

Prologue

The Road
The Bridge
Margaret Mourning: Night Study
The City

In Praise of Limestone
Summer
The Scorpion Girt by Fire
Snake by Moonlight: Night Studies
Why I have Tyme and Space
O Elektra
The Roads of Night

Nor this behooves me
The Bright Season
The High Hall of Night
Margaret at Dawn
This then My Voice

Epilogue

+ + +

"Languages of the worlds"

The history of a language is [the] history of the people who speak the language. The history of *T'tongue*—the Trading Tongue that is the sole communication element for 89 percent of today's interstellar society—is the history of the growth of interstellar commerce. Only the ruling Imperia still speak High English with any proficiency—H'English as it is usually called, by its T'tongue name. At the beginning of interplanetary travel, many scientific and technical lingos, jargons, and argots had sprung up, many incomprehensible to one another. Most of them were clumsy, based on decayed metaphor (e.g. "a small segment of the population," viz. a few people) or tautological (e.g. "the female human organism," viz. a woman), took more space to write and energy to sound than their simple English equivalents. But the life of the early traders demanded a precise yet economic, technical yet domestic language. When the superfluities of 20th and 21st century techniquese fell away, the basic vocabulary and grammar of T'tongue was laid. The formal distinctions of nouns and verbs disappeared. Informative ornaments—accents and melody systems—that had rested only in Chinese and other Oriental languages came back into universal use, with the emergence of Oriental Earth as a power in the space age, though most of the word roots go back to the early Latin, Greek, and Germanic technical vocabularies. The nine-level melody system which establishes chronological positions of words and word clusters is difficult to hear, but easy to notate, with numerical superscripts. (E.g. Loc man^{+4}—a man will be here. Loc man (sometimes written Loc man^{0})—a man is here. Loc man^{-4}—a man was here. Loc—from the English: Location.) The other superscripts denote various moods and tenses. Though this can get complicated in the combined tenses, expressing numerous shades of subjunctive, optative, conditional, imperative, [and] infinitive, the general idea is that as the tone runs from −4 to o to +4, the temporal condition changes from past to future. (A few complex examples. House^4 red^{-4} Monday—By next Monday the house will have been painted red for quite awhile. House end^{-1}—the house has just been completed.) The place-holding accents give T'tongue the flexibility that has been lost since the inflectional tongues of Latin and Greek. Thus one could speak of the táll trée, a grëen bïrd, blînd cât in that order, or as the táll grëen blînd trée bïrd cât. This is all very prosaic, but when literature began to develop, and poets like Harwell or Wu-sing began to write in the demotic speech of the trading lanes, then began the annealing process through which language becomes. Object clusters baffle the non-T'tongue speaker. I-thou give, for example: it is impossible really to tell who gives and who receives. But this is a minor fault of an otherwise very exact language, and the ambiguity can be cleared by temporally distinguishing "I^2 thou^3 give," which informs us that the giving affected "I" before it affected "Thou," and in all probability I gave thou, rather than the other way around. An incredible sense of democracy pervades the language. "Y," the common greeting word, is intimate enough for a lover to greet a lover in the dark, yet dignified enough for any half-illiterate trade-scab to greet the highest member of the Imperium. The infrequency of conjunctions—there is usually only "i"—or, "n"—and, the "if then" implication "syn," and negative accent represented by ≈ in front of the word or words negated—also makes the T'tongue seem dreadfully limited to someone used to the over personalized nuances of H'English, but yet what other way could Wu, at the peak of Mount Klaert on Kroger, have described the way his thoughts drifted back to the seashore of his youth as he waits for the smoking crevice to erupt.

Röck now loc mist^{-1} lïst-over I-thou tell n mist^{-2} i crevices^{+2} at my feet blâck fïll syn memories mist^{-3} y! under a sky-day delve my sloped^{-3} sànds y light^0 mïst n spray^{-4}

+ + +

SF works published or on the way.

The Jewels of Aptor
Captives of the Flame
The Towers of Toron
City of a Thousand Suns
The Ballad of Beta-2

Babel-17
Empire Star
The Ends of Time (Dog, Çiron, Star-Pit)
*Nova—in progress
*A Fabulous, Formless Darkness—in progress

Novels in general:

Those Spared by Fire
Voyage, Orestes
Afterlon
Scavengers
Lost Stars
The Flames of the Warthog
The Lovers
The Assassination
Cycle for Toby

+   +   +

Things to include in *Nova*

    A wedding. A birth with some indications as to what will happen to the kid. A funeral. A city invaded by war. The warehouses with the men working. The plantation owner for dragons. The prostitutes' quarter. The Imperia. The war. The Imperia wedding, the customs the same as the out-laws.

    The five deaths.

    Once a great creature much stronger than him. Once a thing much weaker.

He was an old man.

He was a strong man.

Jommy looked up from the corner table as the codger lurched into the bar. He came straight forward, banging a table with his hip, striking a chair with his bare foot; his leather vest flapped over matted white hair. Old, strong. The third thing Jommy realized: he's blind.

He stopped in front of Jommy's table. Then he leaned forward and his yellow nailed hand swung up Jommy's cheek like a spider. "You, boy—"

Jommy stared into pearls behind rough, blinking lids. "What ...?"

"You boy, do you know what it was like?"

He must be blind, thought Jommy. He moves like blind men move. The other hand flapped out, landed on the back of a chair. Chair feet rasped. The codger sat down. "Do you know what it looked like, felt life, smelt like—do you, boy?"

Jommy shook his head, making the fingers tap his cheek.

[sequence continues]

+ + +

Dear Theodore Sturgeon,

The first draft of this letter was planned and patterned on the C-shaped island of Milos in the South Eastern Aegean. Later I put all the thoughts into a different coat over three long beers in the flower passage just off crowded Istiklal in Istanbul. Now, months later I am re-sewing and re-stitching by the North Entrance of Putney Bridge in London. The message is: thank you. Alone for 2 months in hills with donkey paths walled in shoulder high with pink marble under a mild Hellenic November, I found myself with time to ask myself what had formed me—for better or worse— into who I was; what had given me pleasure, which makes a person trustful and honest, and pain, which makes a person kind and quiet (I think what makes people cruel is inconsistency, confusion and illogic, whether it comes pleasurably or painfully). Over the past fifteen years, you are one of the half dozen people who has given me my largest measure of pleasure. I read my first Sturgeon story when I was nine. Since then stories and novels of yours have been fixing me to my eyes, my hands—have made it so much easier for me to touch and see my own world. They have been a major factor in the equation I had to form to prove that my world touched, overlapped, was congruent to the world of other men; the equation whose solution explodes the solipsistic shell of childhood, and lets us touch maturity. Tolstoy says that if he could have written a book that would irrefutably solve all philosophical problems, he would not devote an hour to it; but if he could write a book that would make people laugh and cry and thrill to life twenty years hence, he would give this book his entire life. Such an artless statement encloses the whole mechanic of art. Your stories have shown me fascinating mechanations turning within the enclosure.

(As your stories have given me pleasure, your comparative silence during the past few years has been painful. But if I am correct in the last statement of my first paragraph, then certainly you know that statement bears no recrimination.)

Several years ago a little girl (named Ana Perez) came to visit you in Woodstock with a guitar and played and sang for you. Some of her singing you liked enough to tape record; among the songs was one to which I had written the music. (It was called "Tom O'Bedlam.") She later told me this, and I was very proud. The words to the song were of course traditional; so my first communication with you was via this most abstract way of music. I like that.

Though the impulse is to say thank you, when the first sound stutters out from under my palate, flooding after it comes the rush. All the images composing my remembered life rise after it; I want to give you the whole of it. That's trust, and distance is *not* the main reason. Your writing has meant to me—more, defined how meaning means for me. I think it must have done the same thing for many people. But it took two solitary, windy months on a stony island digging for myself in Hellenistic ruins, searching out myself in long, terraced mountains before I was compelled to acknowledge my thanks. If more people have not done so, it is because they were not so lucky to have the peace to explore those places where you strike. Your spirit is simple, bright, and it digs to places many people would rather not acknowledge. But I know how firm it must be lodged.

Since writing the music for "Tom O'Bedlam," I have also published some seven novels. Two more are working. I should like to make the thanks official and dedicate one of them to you,

This book
is for T.S.
with thanks.

I am not trying to imply to readers any nonexistent personal relation between us, which is why I use initials. My feeling has nothing of presumption in it (though its expression may). A book, which is called *Nova*, was begun at the same time as the first thoughts of the letter, though it is only as the book, seven months later, draws to conclusion (as does the drafting of this letter) that I think of dedicating to you. The idea of dedication is original with this third London draft.

+ + +

Outline for *Nova*

Part one completed

Part two: the world of ice, from the girl's point of view, the queen of the Ice World for whom Lorq is getting the "fire." The men, the queen, the men, the queen, the men.

Part three: Miscellaneous adventures with a villain.

Part four: Adventures of a smuggleress who has plotted to steal the "fire" from Lorq.

Part five: The Nova, catastrophe, in which the albino is "blinded" instead of the Mouse. They carry the "fire" back and Lorq is "killed" by the smuggleress. They bring the living body[;] they all arrive at "hell" on the Moon of Uranus. They leave the albino there.

Part six:
  Istanbul:

+ + +

John Brunner
Mike Moorcock
John Witten-Doris
Paula Osius

+ + +

Dear M. M.:

Henry M. doesn't *seem* to be mad. (I transmit a shrug across the Atlantic which means, I'm still not exactly sure what's going on.) And I don't think it's as hysterical as we thought. I mean: he's still in business. He's moved to a more expensive office. And he's had to stop taking new clients purely out of being busy. His first question to me, upon learning that I'd just been in London was: "*What* is going *on* over there?" He tells me he sent you contracts twice, and sent you some six letters over the past two months. The contracts that finally came from Silverberg, Morrison gave Silverberg to send. Apparently there was a two month period when a lot of his foreign mail—noticeably to South America—didn't get through. Showed me a bunch that came back. Though the mail he sent you never was returned. I also learned that Fred P. had brought *The Star-Pit* a week before I returned. That hurts. H. M. sent you two letters about that; first and second thoughts. I hope something comes out that's acceptable.

His comment about the last letters he's sent you: "Well, if he doesn't get these, I suppose I could always kill myself."

That would be sad. I hope this letter doesn't cause more confusion, for it is only intended to clear a bit of the transatlantic fog that, between distance and boat strikes, seems to have settled. My regards to beautiful Hillary.

Sincerely
Chip Delany

P.S. Hello Langdon. Judith Merril said something nice about you in her review of Ballard's "Crystal World." But she's there, isn't she. My regards to her if she's still in London.

+ + +

Dear Paula and Chris:

Hitch-hiked for two days in steady rain from Paris to Luxembourg. Got to Lux at four. Bus left for the airport at five. And: here I am in New York. Many thanks for forwarding my letter (it contained $20.00). London is fascinating; you made it warm and friendly as well. Many thanks. My agent has poured a summer of hard work on my head; I won't be able to breathe till the end of August. Oh well; deep breath, and ready to plunge.

My love to you both,

Chip

+ + +

Epigraphs for *A Fabulous Formless Darkness*

In pity for man's darkening thought
He walked that room and issued thence
in Galilean turbulence;
The Babylonian starlight brought
a fabulous, formless darkness in.
      —W. B. Yeats

The modern artist needs gigantic assimilative capacities, emotion—and the greatest of all—vision ... It is to the pulse of a greater dynamism that my work must resolve. Something terribly fierce and yet gentle.
      —Hart Crane, letter to Gorham B. Munson

There are none here except madmen; and few there are who know this world, and who know that he who tries to act in the ways of others never does anything, because men never have the same opinions. These do not know that he who is thought wise by day will never be held crazy by night.
      —Niccolò Machiavelli, letter to Francesco Vittori

I have heard that you will give $1000 for my body which as I understand, it means as a witness ... If it was so as I could appear in court, I would give the desired information, but I have indictments against me for things that happened in the Lincoln County War, and am afraid to give myself up because my enemies would kill me.
      —William H. Bonney (Billy the Kid), Letter to governor Lew Wallace

My trouble is, such a subject cannot be seriously looked at without intensifying itself toward a center which is beyond what I, or anyone else, is capable of writing of ... Trying to write it in terms of moral

problems alone is more than I can possibly do. My main hope is to state the central subject and my ignorance from the start ...
    —James Agee, letter to Father Flye

What, then, is noble abstraction? It is taking first the essential elements of the thing to be represented, then the rest in the order of importance (so that wherever we pause we shall always have obtained more than we leave behind) and using any expedient to impress what we want upon the mind without caring about the mere literal accuracy of such expedient.
    —John Ruskin; *The Stones of Venice*

Harlow? Christ, Orpheus, Billy the Kid—the other three I can see. But what's a young spade writer like you doing all caught up with the Great White Bitch—Oh, but then it's pretty marvelously obvious, isn't it.
    —Gregory Corso, in conversation

But I have *this* against thee, that thou didst leave thy first love.
    —The Revelation of John 2:4

Quotes from *Psychedelic Review*
Where is this country? How does one get there? If one is a born lover with an innate philosophic bent, one will get there.
    —Plotinus, The Intelligence, the Idea, and Being

Throughout most of the history of man the importance of ritual has been clearly recognized, for it is through the ritual acts that man establishes his identity with the restorative powers of nature or marks and helps effect his passage onto higher stages of personal development and experience.
    —R. E. Masters and Jean Huston, *The Varieties of Psychedelic Experience*

+ + +

As we passed beneath the black wood of the Academia—it had grown cold—I tried to assimilate the flowers, the vicious animals, and the story of Lobey's adventures. They all apply somehow. Above, Orion straddled the water. Below, lights from the shore shook in the water as we passed beneath dripping stones of the Rialto.
    —Author's Journal, Venice, October '65

Slipped from the night waters of the Adriatic and now we skirt down the streets toward Piraeus. At the horizon, right and left, monstrously beautiful mountains gnaw the sky. The ship is easy on the morning. The ship's speaker gives up French, English and Greek rock n' roll. Sun silvers the hosed deck, burns above the smokestack. Bought deck passage. Big and bold, last night I walked into a first class cabin, and slept beautifully. Back on the deck now this morning, I wonder what the effect of Greece will be on *Fabulous Formless Darkness*. The central subject of the book is myth. This music is such an appropriate art form for this world. I was aware how well it fitted the capsulated life of N.Y. It seems even more congruent with the rest of the world. How can I take Lobey into the center of the bright chaos that glitters in this music? Drank late with Greek sailors last night, and in bad Italian and worse Greek we talked about myths. Taiki learned the story of Orpheus, not from school or reading, but from his aunt in Eleusis. Where shall I go to learn it? The younger sailors, my age, wanted to hear pop English and French music on the portable. The older ones wanted to listen to the traditional Greek songs. "The traditional songs!" exclaimed Monoles, "all the young men in them want to die as soon as possible because love has treated them badly!"

"Not so with Orpheus," Taiki said, a little mysteriously.

Did Orpheus want to live after he lost Eurydice? He had a very modern choice to make.

—Author's Journal, S.S. Kypros, November 1966

Came back to the house early. They have brought wine for New Year's. There were musicians in the white stone city. I remember a year and a half ago, when I finished *The Fall of the Towers*, saying to myself, you are twenty-one years old, going on twenty-two; you are too old to get by on being a child prodigy. You must get by on your own merit. Still, the nightmare images of youth are still plaguing me, Chatterton, Radiguet, Greenberg. By the end of this book I hope to have excised them. Billy the Kid is still the last to go. He staggers through this abstracted novel like one of the mad children in the Krete hills. My story is abstract; what is the essence of abstraction? We'll hunt you down, Billy, and find out. Tomorrow, weather permitting, I will return back to Delos to explore the ruins around the Throne of Death in the island's center that faces the necropolis across the water on Rhenia.

—Author's Journal, Mykonos, December 31, 1966

This morning I took refuge from the thin rain in a tea house with the dock workers. Yellow clouds moiled outside above the Bosporus. Found one man who spoke French and two more who spoke Greek. We talked about voyages and warmed our fingers on glasses of tea. Between the four of us we'd girdled the globe. The radio over the stove alternated repetitive Turkish modulations with Aznavour, the Beatles, and Sylvie Vartan. Lobey starts the last leg of his journey. That's one I can't follow him through. When the rain stopped, I walked along the waterfront through the fish market, where the silver fish had their gills pulled out and locked over their jaws so that each head became a bloody flower. A street of wooden houses wound up the hill into the city. A fire had recently raged up the street. Few houses had actually burned down, but rising (around the children playing with orange peels in the mud) slabs of glittering carbon leaned over cobbles. Ahead of me I saw a redheaded boy chased by two other children. His face was wet, he tripped in the mud, and then fled before me—his heels had been cut off his shoes—up the hill. Perhaps on a re-writing, I shall change Kid's hair from black to red. Followed the wall beside Topkapi palace, kicking away wet leaves from the pavement. At Sultan Ahmet, I stopped inside the mosque. The blue designs rose on the dome. It was restful. In a week, another birthday. I can start the meticulous process of overlaying another filigree across the palimpsest of *Fabulous Formless Darkness*. The stones were cold under my bare feet. The designs kept going, taking your eyes up and out of yourself. Outside I put on my boots, and started across the wet courtyard. In the second-floor tea-house across the park, I sat in the corner way from the stove and tried to wrestle my characters into their endings. Soon I start again. Endings to be fruitful must be inconclusive.
    —Author's Journal, March, Istanbul

+ + +

New Wor(l)ds / Many Inventions

It was an aural escape from complete silence, the rich man's rock and roll, played at parties so no one would trip over the silences in conversation.

Historically, chamber music—the string quartet and trios—began as light music, to be played while people ate, talked, wandered around the room and did everything but listen. Who could take seriously such a limited form? Since then, the chamber piece has become the proving ground for a composer. "It is like writing music naked," one composer told me. "It is all music, and you can't disguise any of your mistakes with noise, the way you can in a symphonic work." It is the repository for some of the greatest musical statements of Bartok, Haydn, Beethoven, and Vivaldi.

Turned out quickly and hurriedly and in great amounts, for any social occasion, [it was] one of the few ways a competent musician could make a living.

The Jupiter symphony of Mozart is in four movements, the opening movement in loose sonata form, the subsequent ones more informal in their structure. It takes approximately thirty-five minutes to listen to.

The 13th Bartok Quartet in G Major has the same four movements, the first movement in loose sonata form, the following three presenting some interesting parallels with the Jupiter symphony—which might be [a] subject for another essay.

One, however, has all the variation in tone, texture, dynamics, sound quality and emotional coloring that can be given by a full orchestra. The other is scored for three different instruments (two violins, viola, and cello); the texture of the tone between the cello's lowest C and the violin's second harmonic is much less than, say, the difference between a note on the drum and one on the flute, to take two instruments from the orchestra. Surely through the variation and amount of sound available, the string quartet is a more limited form than the symphony.

Yet no musician could suggest that the G Major Quartet was a less valid musical experience than the Jupiter. Both take the same time and concentration to appreciate; both bear up to the same analysis, with the same critical vocabulary. And both are so abundant in musically and emotionally productive material, that if a critic feels called upon, even when comparing them, to mention the "limitations" of the "string quartet" in other than precursory [dismissal], I am warned that his criticism is on a "young people's guide to the orchestra" level, or, he's simply missing the musical point.

Both in and out of print over the last year, writers, editors, and fans have all heard demand[s for] a critical vocabulary for science fiction that carries with it the seriousness accorded mainstream fiction. Dating from the days of *Weird Tales*, the few who look have seen there is too much going on in the field to dismiss it with, "a good, fast paced adventure story set in the far/near future." Fifteen and twenty years ago there were stories by Sturgeon and Bester with such highly wrought surfaces, that accomplish their effects with such bravura, that we are first tempted to ask why should we analyze them, they seem so perfect. But then we discover that they have more than the flash of simply an effect brought off. The light lingers, and we look back, and back again. More recently, there are the stories and novels of Ballard and Cordwainer Smith, not so clear in their intended effect, not so easily comprehended, sometimes because the effect is difficult to conceive, or because the technique to achieve it has not been fully realized, but occasionally because both the effect and the technique are doing something very different from anything that the previous writers have prepared us for. Still more recently there are writers, like Disch and Zelazny, who in whatever landscapes they build themselves, are concerned, respectively, with Evil and Beauty. Zelazny with a near hallucinated language, Disch by bludgeoning the reader with oddly understated violence, work these concepts into producing overtones and reverberation I cannot find elsewhere in literature. Then the analytical thing, the searching thing, the human, say "How? Why? Take it apart and talk about the method of its meaning."

In Theodore Sturgeon's story "The Other Celia," a very ordinary rooming house is evoked as intensely as any setting I have come across in mainstream or SF before, as well as the ordinary hero who, admittedly, suffers from extraordinary curiosity about the other occupants. There is *no* point to this story. Rather, there is as much point and of the same sort as some of Ballard's latest prose poem constructions. The hero more or less accidentally causes the destruction of an alien thing masquerading as a girl; but there is no sentimental or moralizing digest as to whether it was right or wrong. The remains are dumped in a garbage can and the hero moves to a new house. The alien represents all that the S-F convention allows: something so totally different that we can not judge it by *any* of the standards we judge ourselves by, kindness or cruelty, good or evil. At the end of the story, the alien has done nothing "good" or "bad"—and, even though he has destroyed it, neither has the hero. Yet the significance of this vivid world only comes the moment it is illuminated by [the] flaring light of the incinerating . . . thing. The story defies a thematic digest: it is not a tale about fear or distrust of the strange. It makes a terribly immediate statement inchoately joined to the modern world. Those who have decided not to consider S-F seriously will be unable to consider this statement. SF is the only way it could be made.

Yet there was nobody around willing to talk about content, structure, thematic development. It was embarrassing to deal so analytically with material of such limited form. The limitation is a fact of speculative fiction. Limiting is not the same as stifling. The conventions of S-F, not just the technical barrage of faster-than-light drives and hydroponics, super cities and computers, but the conventional attitude of the S-F writer to his material, can be productive, can lead the SF writer, and reader, into a cohesive, valid world with the sympathetic resonance of everyday life that makes meaningful art. Whether a character climbs into a "rocket ship," "teleports" himself, or uses an "ornithopter," the writer is using a convention as established as any baroque trill, grace note, or appoggiatura. It means basically, "This character is traveling between two places that, on the social, economic, or psychological spectrum are different from any two places you could travel between by car, plane, or bus." Rocket, Teleport, or Ornithopter are all the same convention, but the writers most closely connected with the latter two, Alfred Bester in his *The Stars My Destination* and Cordwainer Smith in his stories of the Instrumentality, have used it as an aesthetic statement; Bester, by his employment of teleportation within his novel, Smith purely by the linkage of the organic and the mechanical in a linguistic bond. Any writer still using the first is, in all likelihood, employing it with as much aesthetic significance as the majority of conventional musical ornamentation. But to the writer of S-F who wishes to write material worthy of serious criticism, as well as the critic, the answer is not to throw away the conventions, to make the S-F appear as much like mainstream fiction as possible, but to realize what these conventions indicate: in the case of the "rocket," the world left, the world arrived at, and the person making the journeying between. Even the many stories that take place totally within cabins of rocket ships—and there are many fine ones—that would seem to tell us only about the people, are telling us about the world at both ends of the journey by what it reveals of the people in this conventional "microcosm." At this point the convention may be dispensed with, varied, or retained.

Science fiction is more limited than mainstream fiction. To argue here is the sort of quibbling which will prevent a new vocabulary from ever forming. The novel *The Naked and the Dead*, through fictional methods, makes both an internally cohesive aesthetic statement that is concerned with only its own form, as well as a real statement about a real war that was fought. The novel *Starship Troopers*, through fictional methods, makes an internally cohesive aesthetic statement concerned with only its own form, and an abstract statement about the theory behind war. I may or may not want to look for faults in the formal setup of each book, dissect those fictional methods, comment on the conception and development of the characters; in *The Naked and the Dead* I can make no comment on its statement about the war it discusses. That belongs to the real. I could argue for hours about the theory of war explored in *Starship Troopers*, because it belongs to theory.

Apologists always say, well each form has its advantages, each its disadvantages. To say that both symphony and quartet have their advantages, has some truth; yes, each covers its own ground particularly well. The quartet is still the more limited form, if only because in the symphony the composer can simply turn most of the orchestra off and let a small concertante of soloists do the delicate things a quartet can do for a few notes, or a whole movement, while a quartet simply cannot end a movement with crashing chords; the few attempts, by even a notable composer such as Brahms, sound silly and pretentious.

Stendhal's *Charterhouse of Parma* is basically an adventure, but along with much action, escape from towers, assignations missed and kept, gives a brilliant portrait of decadent Italian society during the late 18th century. Bester's *Demolished Man* gives brilliant vignettes of an upper middle class telepathic society, and the glittering party sequence in Zelazny's *This Immortal*, just after the idyllic opening on the isle of Kos, gives a cuttingly real picture of the high strung, the dispossessed, and the amoral aristocracy of a dying earth receiving a Vegan celebrity. The writing in all three is witty, brilliantly evocative; and to a modern reader, the familiar elements in the parties of Zelazny and Bester are closer to him than Stendhal's scenes. Still, Stendhal's have the purely external reverberation of reality, if not as it is, at least as it once was. Zelazny and Bester, because of their conventional distortions (telepathy and aliens are conventions as much as rocket ships, each with their valid meaning), their statement is made about the working of social theory. To say that such a statement (apart from the individual handling by [the] author) is intrinsically more or less valid, is rather like saying a melody played by quartet is intrinsically less valid than the same melody played with the tonal variation that an orchestra can give. Most S-F conventions are a way of introducing absolutes into literature; and when something is extended to an absolute, we are left with theoretical statements, both in terms of extensions, and limits. Telepathy often represents an absolute in communication; the alien is just that, a living being whose experiences have been different from yours. The S-F writer uses aliens and telepathy rather than Anatolian farm girls, or good friends who have known each other for years, because he *doesn't* want to make a statement about "differences" in theory, "communication" in theory.

Though I have often heard music that has disturbed my emotions, bringing up joy, sadness, rage, or tenderness, I can count the times on one hand (without using my thumb) when instrumental music has made me cry. A performance of the Beethoven Quartet in A Minor did so once. The proximity of melodic motifs and harmonics was able to shape out a silence in me that held as much resignation and bravery, as [much] suffering and outrage against it that I could bear.

The limits of science fiction are not emotional ones; they do not restrict the humanity of any given character or situation.

SF critics, seeking a new vocabulary, have come up with a term that has been critically fruitful for the reader predisposed to SF, but distracting for the non-disposed reader: "the wonderful invention." Often in the introductions to the intelligent anthologies of Judith Merril and Groff Conklin, for example, you will find this idea very accurately discussed in an attempt to distinguish SF from mainstream fiction. But "wonderful invention" is a concept only useful in defining a convention (and conventions, as I pointed out earlier, are conveniences rather than necessities, so there are many fine S-F stories, especially recently, that just don't have them) that appertains to the limits of S-F, rather than any good critical tool for analyzing its productive center. Also this is one of the things that leads the non-S-F reader to say, "But S-F is writing about things, not about people." Now to dismiss a story or novel that takes place in a spaceship, unread, because it must be *about* a spaceship, instead of people, is as silly as dismissing a Conrad or a Melville novel that takes place on a boat because it's about boats. The wonderful invention of any significant SF story exists only to tell you something about the world that produced both it and the characters involved. And the S-F story that posits the totally "real" world with a single wonderful gadget and of perplexities this foists on the characters, ninety-nine times out of a hundred dooms the story at best as a humorous conceit, unless we can see people (and by implication their world) traversing true, human changes that would go along with such an invention *were* it real. Often, especially in novels, the whole world and setting of a story is the wonderful invention itself. To say that "Teleportation," or "PyrE" is the wonderful invention of *The Stars My Destination* is to miss the point gloriously. The same would be true of anyone who tried to center their interest on a Cordwainer Smith story on Ornithopters, Planoforms, "Underpeople," or the "golden ship" that hovers over them all. The miasmal, dying worlds of Ballard's novels, almost devoid of any technological effects, have significance[,] as the glittering world[s] of his stories—[the] super cities, the Besteresque artist's colony of Vermilion Sands—are all places where people are learning to accept death or rebel toward life. And these worlds are meaningful in terms of the real world because their worlds force the characters to this rebellion or acceptance through the same mechanics that ours forces us to the decision. There is no [way] that such a clear statement, not distorted by reference to a particular real situation, solely about the quality of these mechanics, can be made, other than through SF.

The reactions of Conrad Nomikos to his dead and dying earth, to his wife lost in the Aegean, are not real. But Zelazny's writing makes them moving, and through the identification, Zelazny's dying world lights ours, not in spite of its mutants and spiderbats, its mythical and neo-mythical beasts, but *with* them.

In the heart of the world-engulfing plant, humanity creeps in its petty way toward extinction. The pettiness is human. Because of it the plant becomes a symbol, in Thomas M. Disch's *The Genocides*. People have talked of SF supplying a modern mythology. Again, I think that is asking it to go beyond its limitations. To become mythic, a symbol needs time, most of all, must be sieved from a great amount of reality weighed, strained, and weighed again. Babbitts, Uriah Heaps, Gullivers, Candides, Bovaries and Huckleberry Finns, are more needed to symbolize modern predicaments than Big Brothers. The sort of symbolism SF provides is the bright, metallic one akin to the language inventions of the Early French Moderns, perhaps the surrealists, where a symbol flares for the length of a single poem, story, or book, and then dies—must die—to fill its purpose.

The aesthetic statement of any art, music, poetry, painting, or fiction, is basically a discussion of form, balance, proportioning; the vocabulary that is employed varies from medium to medium. Music is one medium. Fiction is another. Whether the music is a symphony or a quartet, the vocabulary is pretty much the same; the difference is more in the tacit acceptance of the extent or limitations of each type of music.

The critical vocabulary of fiction involves characters, environment, style, etc. The distinction between the criticism of mainstream and SF is basically a matter of the critic accepting the limitation of [the] mode of fiction he is criticizing before he begins. The critic who blames a quartet for not being a symphony is going to miss the beauty of clean linear development in the "smaller" work.

+ + +

Note:

In 1942 Robert Heinlein published "Waldo," in retrospect a major event in S-F; for the wonderful invention of that story, a set of mechanical hands, which through ratio mechanics could move mountains—large hunks of mountains, anyway—or operate the tiny valves in the three chambered heart of a robin, a few years later became reality as well; they kept the nickname that their envisioner gave them. That same year, much more incidentally to the course of S-F, I was born; just short of two dozen years later I found myself in a truck garage in Butler N.J. helping a truck driver and two mechanics (none of whom had heard of Heinlein, a situation I hope I corrected) tear down the rear-end transmission of GM four-banger, with the incidental help of a couple of waldoes; and I got the idea for the following story. Since 1942, S-F (and me) have done a lot of growing up. Growing up is what the story's about; I thought you might find it interesting to know where I got the idea and, incidentally, the waldoes.

+ + +

All that I have, is the life that I have.
All that I have, is the life that I have.
And the life that I have
All that I have is the life that I have
And the life that I have is yours
The life that I have and the love
That I have shall be yours &
Yours & yours
The sleep that I have and the rest
That I have, though death is
But a pause
And all our life in the long
Green grass
Shall be yours & yours & yours.

Hey Hey Chip what do you know.

+ + +

Let's think about *Nova*. At the end of part one, Lorq is on his way to destruction and collects the crew which consists of Rayy, the sense harpist,

Night, the Gemini, the twins who can psych things out, Blacky of course, Mouse, Galahad, the Witch.

Lorq, Night, Rayy, Gemini I and II, Mouse, Galahad, the Witch, Blacky.

The general pattern should go this way:

The Group starts off, Lorq gets captured, horrible things are done to him (A), the group saves him (B) they return en masse and beat the daylights out of them (C) at which point part or parcel of the group is captured (D) and Lorq saves them (E) and more horrible things are done to the enemy (F). If this entire six part pattern is carried through three times, plus a good size prologue and epilogue, you should have a fairly lengthy and exciting novel.

Some locations: Megapolis, the underworld and overworld
A mining planet
A prison ship
A society ball to auction Art Works
Slave workers somewhere or other
A Stellar War
Gladiators for some decadent aristocracy
An assassination
Cave of Illusions—where he finds Nova
The Mansion of Izinon

+   +   +

Mike Moorcock
87A Ladbroke Grove
London, W11

+   +   +

Next three sections of *Nova*.

Orgy-ish section with the crew, Ratt playing syrynx's with the girls from the other ship, Jommy tries to tell Ratt about Dan. Ratt won't listen, or doesn't hear.

On the lip of Hell Three Lorq Von Ray and Dan have a confrontation.

9

....

Changing Scenes

....

When Delany returned to New York on April 15, 1966, he and Hacker attempted to live together again. However, after a few days it became clear that this arrangement would not work and Hacker relocated to a building on Hester Street to which her friend, the painter Bill McNeill—introduced to Hacker by Delany shortly before leaving for Europe—had recently moved.[1] Delany, meanwhile, began an affair with a young actor, Ron Bowman, and soon moved in with him.[2]

During this restless movement among homes and relationships, Delany and Hacker remained friends. Hacker introduced Delany to a number of people associated with the Spicer circle who had recently arrived in New York City. McNeill was part of this circle, along with Russell and Dora Fitzgerald, Link Martin, and Pat and Helen Adam. (Ron Bowman appeared in the New York production of Adam's *San Francisco's Burning*, at the Judson Poets Theater.)[3]

Between the spring of 1966 and early spring 1967 Delany put finishing touches on *The Einstein Intersection* and submitted it to Ace. He also continued to work on *Nova* and the "Faust" novel, and wrote a number of stories that would appear in the *Driftglass* collection, including "Driftglass," "Corona," and "The Star-Pit"—the last of which, like *The Einstein Intersection*, was already substantially complete by this time.[4] Meanwhile, also in 1967, *Babel-17* won the Nebula Award for best science fiction novel of the previous year.

Throughout this period Delany became increasingly involved with various science fiction communities. In the fall of 1966 Delany traveled to Cleveland to attend his first SF convention, Tricon.[5] Shortly afterward he participated in the Milford Writers' Conference, a workshop run by Damon Knight and Kate Wilhelm. There he met Joanna Russ, had his story "Corona" workshopped by the other participants, and, over a span of just three days, wrote and typed three drafts of "Aye, and Gomorrah," which would appear in Harlan Ellison's *Dangerous Visions* anthology in 1967 and win the Nebula Award for best short story of that year.[6] As Notebook 83 indicates, during the 1966–67 holiday season Delany returned to London to visit his British and American colleagues. In addition to seeing Moorcock, Brunner, and Merril, during his stay he also met Thomas M. Disch, Pamela Zoline, and Christopher Priest.[7]

The sole entry in the final notebook, Notebook 69, consists of an early cast list for Delany's radio adaptation of his novella "The Star-Pit" for WBAI-FM—a project that consumed Delany's attention for the remainder of the summer of 1967.[8]

NOTES

1. K. Leslie Steiner [Samuel R. Delany], "Anatomy of a Nova" (unpublished essay, 1997), 20; Samuel R. Delany, *The Motion of Light in Water: Sex and Science Fiction Writing in the East Village* (1988; reprint, Minneapolis: University of Minnesota Press, 2004), 562, 566–67.

2. Steiner [Delany], "Anatomy of a Nova," 20; Samuel R. Delany, "Chronology" (unpublished personal document, 2014), 12.

3. Steiner [Delany], "Anatomy of a Nova," 20; Delany, "Chronology," 12, 14.

4. Steiner [Delany], "Anatomy of a Nova," 22; Delany, "Chronology," 12.

5. Steiner [Delany], "Anatomy of a Nova," 22; Delany, "Chronology," 12.

6. Steiner [Delany], "Anatomy of a Nova," 24–26.

7. Steiner [Delany], "Anatomy of a Nova," 36.

8. Steiner [Delany], "Anatomy of a Nova," 37–38.

Shall we try one good fast swashbuckler to go as a long side to *World Without Form* (*FFD*) to be written in twenty days.

Hero is Mak.

Two heroines, Laya the criminal heroine, seductress, double-crosser, generally interesting female character.

Then we have Ruby, the goody-goody heroine, all sweetness and light.

The Buddy. What will we do here. The Buddy must be small, dark, young. Buddy.

The villain; he captures Minel for his wife. And he rapes Laya. Among other things. Devill

We need somebody to end up with Liza. Some young Prince or other who should have her, really. (Prince is his name.)

Incidents.

Escapes from mountain prison.

Fights wild beast with a whip.

Swims out of stormy water.

Fire in the wreck of rocket ship.

The hall of mirrors, with psychic overtones.

For a science fiction novel, the hero must call on technological experts (so must the villain)

Technological Experts.

Madam Duclos, the Genet type madam of illusion, caters to men's passions.

The Psychic Twins, who gamble and read minds.

The computer, who can be asked anything.

Magicians who deal in occult.

You must postulate a world situation and then postulate your main characters as somehow coming out of that situation. We also have to have some social division, and see how the different elements of society react to the social distinction.

The hero dies for a while, and is reborn as a machine. Then is returned to his body.

+ + +

Re-plotting *Nova*

Open with Mak's childhood on the island. Politics must be clear.
The colonies have Illyrion, the polarizing element, and are gaining a distorted power fast, but they have very poor and very rich, whereas the Old Order has a more egalitarian setup.
In school, Lorq goes to play with a bunch of refugees from the skirmishes, gets into a fight, and gets his face laid open, but he is looking for light. It's in a musty cellar where they hold the fight, by a sweet blonde youth named Devill.

+ + +

Nova

Lorq our hero. He has to be lower middle class in origin.

Lorq, Leah   Devill
             The Mouse
             Ruby

The structure

As a young child, he watches the various elements of society gather for a cockfight. As a young man he gets in a cockfight with Divall.

The Prince comes to visit Lorq in the first scene with the cockfight.
Second scene: Lorq goes to visit Prince.
They sneak down to where the migrants are and Lorq gets in a fight with a boy named Divall, who lays open his face, cheerily. At a ball where Leya is.

+ + +

Seven stories
The Singer on the boat
The Tourists
The Future of L.D.

We are going to do, now, seven short stories, between 6 and 8 thousand words that are—chronological, deal with one, two, or three characters, center around a single incident, dwell on the motivation, and change. If they have more than one location, then the locations are concurrent, joined via some unity. Make all the settings near future ones rather than far, more or less singular viewpoints, with an essential conflict.

Connect up the prison incident with the future.

"The prison was established in 1947, and we ain't never had one escape; so we've played it safe, we run it just the way they ran it when it was built. And we ain't gonna change it till we have to."

Connect up the Big Foot's atrocity with this future society. He applied for a position as spiritual advisor to a colonial expedition, was laughed out of the office.

When Buddy came to New York, he first applied for a colonial. But the colonies had stabilized, and suddenly a great deal was made do over his jail record and his application was refused. So he took a job at Kennedy.

What does the music mean to Lee

"It means life to me, not a life where there's no pain, but pain given form so at least I can bear it."

+ + +

Then they sent me my sales report which said 85,000 copies. And I was very young.

The Jewels of Aptor, my first book, was created from 14 nights of nightmares and my determination to have fun with them. But there was this piece of paper saying that 85,000 people were listening. I had no illusions that this was particularly high sales for a paperback novel. But it was a sobering figure. I decided if that many people were listening, I had an obligation to say something.

So, strolling along the Brooklyn Bridge with my wife, I conceived of the *Fall of the Towers* trilogy. The idea that came first: I wanted the first and last chapter to set each other's images in reverse. Then the overall idea: a country surviving alone in a radioactive world, has finally reached the psychological, sociological, and economic condition where it must have a war. But there is no one left [to] have a war with. So they invent an imaginary enemy. Dealing with all economic and social levels I wanted [to] web a group of characters together in complex, reflective dances.

In the first volume I would set up the economic and social situation; in the second, the war would be fought. In the final volume, the imaginary enemy would triumph.

Toss a mirror in the sun above a crowd: it spins. Reflected? Soldiers and statesmen, acrobats and street urchins, doctors and duchesses, thieves and teachers, poets and princes, criminals and con men.

Thus I peopled my story. I further divided my cast evolutionarily. There was a race of future humans and a race of primitives in this country. Then, for commentary's sake, I formed two super races to watch the whole affair. And comment.

My main story was to show a man from this country learning to deal with freedom—that is the only story there is.

I begin with my main character then, escaping from prison. In each section, I recounted his escape from a different viewpoint. First from a more or less omniscient position; then from the point of view of one of the guards who tried to catch him; and finally from the point of view of one of the prisoners left behind. Each was to deepen and broaden the significance of his escape. The story of my main character must end when, coming to terms with his family and fate, this freedom is accepted. The other stories must all demonstrate, contrapuntally, characters either succeeding or failing at the same task, thwarted either by inner or outer circumstances, represented by the Random Game that provides one of the focuses of the work.

I had just turned twenty when the trilogy was begun. It was finished a bit before my twenty-second birthday. And the two years were two years in which I learned and learned and learned. And artistic indecision caused a great deal of my intention to go foggy. What I have given you is the bright concept of the bridge.

The problems that came up? This was the primary one: how discrete should I make each volume? I conceived the work as a whole. I know now the solution was simply, be faithful to your concept.

But there were several themes and characters that I knew would not reach their climax until the third volume. I knew where the foreshadowing should go in the first volume—particularly of Vol Nonik, and the City of a Thousand Suns, and four or five other things—but they would seem fabulous and unresolved if the first volume were read alone.

My major mistake, in the second, was to give the enemy a name, some android ambassadors and a few other ornamentations. I did it because I was unsure how the book would stand by itself. But naming the enemy vitiates the symbolic impact of its unreality. I was wrong. This was the conclusion I had come to before I finished the final volume, with which, at least structurally, I am satisfied.

I can talk about them now with equanimity because a British edition is being considered and I have had a chance to correct my mistakes and do what I originally knew should be done; and strengthen the places were my own insecurities had made me waiver. As well I could pick over the style (poke poke, pick-pick, cut-cut-cut) and do the things that a romp through the typewriter will do if you have blue pencils for eyes. I am passionately concerned with writing: it eases the pain growing from one's own natural reticence. (All writing I suppose comes from *l'esprit d'escalier.*) I would like to make people see and touch as I do, and feel as my characters feel, as well as order those sights and sounds into a significant form. The best writing lays foundations from which the reader may erect a grander frame of consciousness. Such construction is the greatest of all entertainments. And so would I wish to entertain.

+ + +

There are certain things each of us must do.

As a moth must chase light, or a man race toward a star, so the Mouse must strike his syrynx.

+ + +

The Bloi triplets.
The extent of the Destruction.
The Attack in the Woods.
Flight into the Source Cave.
To find their way out. He goes to the Computer's message.

In the Kage in Branning

Entrance. Search among the Madmen. Almost sees Friza, [hears] her talking to him, and starts to lead her out.

A little organization now, if you please.

Marilyn has moved out. I hope it is for the best. We are still friends—as if we could ever be less close than touching—but my life has exploded since her departure to the five room cavern on Henry Street. Ron Bowman, a blond bearded pick-up, has filled up this last week as SF conventions and conference filled up the previous ones—in much the same way.

Pause. Joe Soley and I are taking the truck—great half block of aluminum caterpillar shaking and shaking up through night and the mountains—to Endicott N.Y. Morning bruises the night above the eastern clouds. We pass above valleys filled with sky. I've had more sex in the past week (real sex, not binge sex) than in any other comparable week, and it's left me a little shaken.

+ + +

Samuel R. Delany was born on April Fools' Day in 1942. He grew up in New York City's Harlem and variously considered becoming a physicist, a mathematician, and a composer. He attended Dalton Elementary School, the Bronx High School of Science, and City College where he was poetry editor of *The Promethean* for a term. His first SF novel, *The Jewels of Aptor*, was written when he was nineteen. His subsequent trilogy *The Fall of the Towers* was completed while he was still twenty-one. Last year his novel *Babel-17* was nominated for the Science Fiction Writers of America Nebula Award for best SF novel of 1966. *FFD* was a written mostly during a year of travel in England, France, Italy, Greece and Turkey. He is 24, married and lives on the Lower East Side.

+ + +

Prefatory Note

The author begs anyone who considers the rather stiffly epigraphed chapter headings pretentious to ignore them. They comment not on the book's plot but on its method of construction. They define a net of human values and morals in which a few readers might enjoy swinging the decidedly unhuman amoral values of this book, either to test the weight of the one or the tensile strength of the other.

+ + +

Get your stories straightened out. What's your schedule now that Ron has come erupting into the center of your psyche, being male and there, primarily, secondarily a fine, intelligent, if mildly tortured man—though basically independent as hell. Question Mark. *Nova* should not be rushed, though the section should be finished. Then there are the stories.

My titles:

Driftglass, Susanna in Babylon
Silence, Water, Someone Saying My Name
He Stands and Thunders on the Hill

Let us plot out "Driftglass," à la Zelazny method, just to see if it works. Characters location and conflict. Characters: a bunch of Interplanetary J.D.'s, starting out with their escape from the prison. A beautiful woman, and a deformed ex-spaceman, writer, composer, mathematician.

Cal, the deformed narrator of the story, who goes down to the beach to collect driftglass, where he sees the girl beat up the old man, and learns she is the bridge for the psychic escape.

The children's escape, from which she Ariel escapes.

Scene One—Escape from the Reform School.
Scene Two—On the beach, with Tony collecting driftglass in the city's shadow.

+ + +

To make the final action significant, either Catherine, Corbelli, or Wolf must be responsible for the terminating catastrophe. It means nothing if Wolf's lover kills her. So, after rape, Catherine flees to Corbelli's shop for protection, but is hysterical, begins to break the instruments. Corbelli hurts her while trying to stop her. Heshy, who has gone there to effect some sort of confrontation, sees this and comes back and tells Wolf, who then sics the gang on Corbelli's shop.

She shouldn't be a writer.

Self-destructive, novelist

Wolf, Catherine, writes
Wolf, quietly amoral, She, wild and moral

The psychologically doomed are the focus of tragedies. The sociologically redeemable people comedies. And a compassionate vision may bridge them both. Hence Lee and Buddy in one story. Both were inspired by one person, a blonde boy from the woods of Alabama, unable to write his last name or read mine, who'd spent most of his adolescence in grown-up prison. During the two weeks he stayed with me, he played pop music constantly, while narrating the templates for most of the incidents here, including a bizarre series of pre-puberty suicide attempts. Somewhere he picked up enough math to integrate for the area of $x^4 + y^4 = k^4$. That is not easy. Why deal with all this in science fiction terms? The medium is the best for clear delineation and integration of the more confusing technical elements of the modern consciousness. It really is.

+ + +

What goes into an SF story? This SF story? An affluent month in Paris; a summer of shrimp fishing on the Texas coast. Another month flat broke in Istanbul; and in some other city, I heard two women at a cocktail party discussing the latest astronaut:

"He's so antiseptic, so inhuman, almost asexual."

"Oh, no; he's perfectly gorgeous!"

Why put all this in SF? I sincerely believe the medium is the best in which to clearly integrate the disparate and technical with the desperate and human. Someone asked me about this particular story, But what can they do with one another? The answer is

+ + +

Me

Jo: Wanted More
John:—
Anne:—
Carol: Sentimental.

Piers: Discontinuity.

Blish: Overlong. (Extra-length in prison scene.) Histories contain irrelevant information. The girl's speeches. The iodine. Three or four stitches— and iodine.

K. Anderson: Nits. Cutting.

J. Bova: Buddy's deformities. The build-up needs work.

Spinrad: Jail scene.

Knight: Why Sf fiction? Avoid background story.

Laumer:

Ellison:

Kate:

Bok: Story

Brunner:

Ted: Good scenes: lead nowhere.

+ + +

Pertinent Questions for Henry

Those Spared by Fire—wha happen?

What has happened to
    They Fly at Çiron

(Try resubmitting "Dog in Net" to *Playboy*, perhaps.)

Short stories:
    Dog in F.N.
    Corona
    They Fly at Çiron
    In the Ruins
    Ad Owhmia
    Aye, and Gomorrah
    The Star-Pit

V.O. What happen?

Call Ted White

Call Henry M.

Call Fred Pohl

+ + +

Reflection the day after the Nebula Awards banquet: lying in bed, contemplating last evening, it occurs to me there are probably a fair number of people at any given instant "thinking" about me. This fact hits me in a way that has never occurred about my family. How many days pass when I do not at all think about Rimbaud, Dostoevsky, Zelazny, Nabokov—etc. and the order not important.

There are Ibsen's life-lies. Then there are the social-lies. I do not feel I have a life-lie, but I do feel I have webbed myself in social lies and I must stop: telling Daniel Keyes that I have read *Flowers for Algernon* in the novel version when in truth I just got around to reading the short story version a few weeks ago. Telling Eric Anderson that I once lost $300 to make him feel better about losing $80.

+ + +

Notes for *Nova*, god damn it.

Katin: how much trouble a man living five hundred years ago would have navigating today. Cleanliness becomes superfluous.

About novel—changing his name.

+ + +

"Mandala"

Opening:

Synopsis: Jimmy as he moves closer and closer to home reviews his relation with his parents & family and friends.

His father is dying of cancer, but neither Jimmy [nor] his family can really accept it.

The one person [Jimmy] can go to [to] discuss [it] is a young man named Geo Keller, a poet of twenty-one, a friend of Jimmy's from childhood. Geo, through a series of coincidences and accidents that has nothing to do with his work, has gained quite a bit of notoriety despite his age. He is being turned into one of those super-young, pop/mythical figures that our society insists on creating. But he maintains his humanity despite this.

Jimmy finally arrives home to confront his mother, his dying father, and his sister Margaret, as well as his friend Geo Keller.

The Bridge
The City

Synopsis

The middle section of the book throws Jimmy and Geo and the deaf-mute Snake together again in a search for Geo's wife, Laile. During the search, the powers and circumstances that have been crystallizing the Myth of Geo Keller work and machinate. There is a riot at a poetry reading at Harvard. It is learned that the waif Snake whom they have picked up is a homosexual prostitute who has been hopelessly involved with the gangs and underworld of New York, and because of the publicity attendant on Geo, this nearly gets them into serious trouble several times. Geo's marital troubles are picked up to be splattered about newspapers and magazines; which often comes close to destroying both Geo & his wife.

Jimmy, during this wild flight [from] level of reality to level of reality has met and made love to a young singer named Ann, and has been reaching for his own maturity.

Toward the end of the hectic flight, Geo and Jimmy abandon one another several times. Once Jimmy is left in a small upstate New York town.

The Roads of Night
Nor This Behooves Me
The Bright Season

Jimmy has been greatly wounded by the character revelations about Geo, and himself. The healing process is a difficult one, during which he must regain his belief in his own personality. Meanwhile the catastrophic forces that whirl about him with him as the focus constrict: there are the criminal elements that center around Snake

The High Halls of Night
This Then My Voice (incomplete—)

Jimmy meets and faces his mother and his sister. He arrives at some resolution of his own personal problems. But he returns to the city to get a job and live on his own. He has one last encounter with Snake.

Then to the epilogue, where Jimmy details the final culmination of the myth.

+ + +

Mandala, though a long and leisurely first-person narrative, is a tightly structured account of young people in their late teens and twenties dealing with the problems, ontological, sexual, racial, artistic, [that] this particular age and society has defined for them. It opens with a quote from Rilke ...

Nova—

Outline and notes on the Party Sequence in Paris—the climax of this must be when Lorq receives the scar, and falls in love with Ruby, and the source of Illyrion is discussed.

Lorq must wake up to his father's true occupation. Brian represents the blond, blue-eyed articulation of Lusunna's rather narrow minded middle-class view, there is no culture, there is no significant anything going on. Dan represents a lower-class view of the upper, or something like that— perhaps a worker's opinion as opposed to a security player's.

The Party:
They land, Brian is upset about clothing, Lorq is oblivious to problem. Dan just doesn't care if he can get drunk. Prince runs up to rescue a damsel in distress in a tower on Mars. Cliff hanging.
The Party.
The outlining. The fight on the banks of the Seine.

+ + +

Time is the great myth. We believe we live in time. But time lives in us.

+ + +

Outline of the scene in the Commons Room.

Captain and Mouse and Katin, Sebastian and Tyÿ.
Captain: how does that work—Mouse's syrynx.
Katin: How are we supposed to get the Illyrion.
Tyÿ volunteers to read the Tarot on the whole business.
The Mouse cries superstition, and Katin explains the reality behind the Tarot.
Captain interrupts—sends Tyÿ and Sebastian back to watch. Lynceos and Idas come out.

+ + +

Write: John & Marjorie Brunner, Mike Moorcock, Roger Zelazny. John Witten-Doris. Judy Merril. Piers Anthony.

+ + +

For the "Array of Characters"

Pig-meat Miller, a night watchman to one of these factory building housing printing shops, things of such nature.

Buddy—the southern truck driver who has come to New York, rapist, and murderer, beautiful.

Juan—the grubby Puerto Rican, fifteen years old, hoodlum and hustler, becomes Buddy's boy.

Heshy—the twenty-year-old, bohunk kid, apish and sensitive, who is with Pig-meat a while.

Wolf/Mike—small, hard, twenty-three, works in a fish store, must be totally degraded in sex, bullish and belligerent otherwise.

Tony—the dark Italian retarded kid who masturbates in book stores.

Toni—the brilliant Negro girl who is fascinated by these people, writes poems, and is finally raped and killed by Buddy.

+ + +

Things to have in this book.

Three chapters getting Buddy further and further north.

Chapter I
   Buddy and the fishermen, we see the child's opening masochism.
Chapter II
   Buddy, now nineteen, rapes and murders the girl, and his reaction to getting away with it. Decides to go north.
Chapter III
   Pig-meat and Tony in New York, and they meet Buddy, age twenty-seven on the pier, and the other Toni.
Chapter IV
   Pig-meat, Tony, Buddy and Jose.

+ + +

I don't know whether you enjoy science-fiction, but perhaps your children do. If so, pass my book on to them.

The "science" this particular book deals with is verbal communication, and the hero is, naturally, a poet—which is why I thought you might find it interesting how a technical mind views the *craft* of poetry—I also hope I got a bit of insight into the art as well. In another book somewhere I threw out the idea that: "The most important elements in any society are the artistic and the criminal, because they alone are the elements that can force the rest of the society to change." This book is an examination of that idea—though not an affirmation. I still don't know whether it's true or not.

The book is one of the nominees for best sf novel of 1966, incidentally, a small distinction, but ego boosting.

Best to you and your wife.

Sincerely

Chip

Samuel R. Delany

+ + +

Man and machine have settled their differences, and a man may be part of a machine or a machine may be part of a man.

The story moves on this canvas.

The thirty-first century; the stellar society of the galaxy has broken up into the Draco Sector, with Sol, and specifically Earth as its capital, and the Pleiades Federation, with the world Ark as its capital. As well a new group of stars is just moving into political prominence, the Outer Colonies, where the power source Illyrion is mined. The appearance of this third political entity is upsetting the stable economic and social relations of Draco and the Pleiades. It is a time of changing values, ways of life, vast migrations of people from one side of the universe to the other.

The story itself moves.

Though he is intimate with the slums of a dozen cities of earth—Istanbul, Melbourne, Athens, Bombay—the gypsy boy Mouse is inexperienced and provincial by the standards of interstellar society. But he plays a rare and marvelous instrument, the sensory-syrynx, a machine that projects sound and light and smell, creating abstract or real images. He has come to the outer moon of Uranus. In his wanderlust, he wants to see the rest of the universe; he has worked on interplanetary ships before; now he wants to crew on a job on his first star-ship.

After two dejected weeks of playing around the star port, he is approached by Lorq Von Ray, a scarred giant of a man, to crew on his ship, the *Roc*, on an at first seemingly impossible mission to a Nova, to retrieve seven tons of the power-material Illyrion from the very heart of the exploding sun—they will be racing for their goal against Prince Red, Von Ray tells his crew.

With the Mouse on the crew are Katin, a young intellectual from Earth's moon, who is making endless notes on an as yet unbegun novel.

Lynceos and Idas, two brothers out of a set of triplets from the Outer Colonies; their third brother, Tobias, is still in an Illyrion mine, on the world of Tubman. Huge, shy fellows, their ancestors were African; Idas is black, and Lynceos is an albino.

Sebastian and Tyÿ are a husband and wife from the Pleiades. Tyÿ is a quiet, slight woman who gives Tarot readings. As the symbols on Tarot cards have survived over the past 12 hundred years unchanged, so they survive the next 12 hundred. But the future interpretation of symbols—

Sebastian, her husband, is a squat, yellow haired oriental who enjoys a good fight, and keeps a half dozen vicious black bat-like creatures for pets.

Just before the trip begins, an ex-crewmen of the *Roc*, under Von Ray, kills himself by throwing himself in the huge volcanic chasm of Hell[3] that winds over the surface of Uranus's moon. He was a broken old man who had been blinded and deafened by an accident on Von Ray's last expedition.

With this evil omen, the trip begins.

Pooling their knowledge of the various worlds that they come from, the crew realizes that Von Ray is not just an ordinary freighter captain. He is the scion of perhaps the wealthiest family of the Pleiades Federation on Ark.

Prince Red, against whom they are racing, is the heir to the incredibly powerful industrial family from Draco, Red Shift Ltd., which produces almost all the space drives for the galaxy.

Now Lorq Von Ray reviews the history of the conflict between them. It began when they were just boys of seven at a weekend party together with their families. Prince, who has a prosthetic arm, and is hopelessly overprotected by his father, has become completely neurotic about his deformity. The decadent aristocrats attend a "cockfight" with the lower-class

Illyrion minors. The children sneak in to watch, where the conflict erupts between them.

In late adolescence, Lorq, who has become an up and coming space-yacht racer, attends a wild "jet set" party on Earth in Paris given by Prince Red. The enmity between the two boys erupts in a fight at the party over Prince's sister, Ruby. In the fight, Lorq receives the scar that will mar his face for the rest of his life.

Meanwhile the political economic situation has changed such that only one of the families can survive, and the outcome will ultimately be determined by who gets his hands on enough Illyrion, which will bring the galactic market price down.

The crew has joined Captain Von Ray for the last battle between himself and Prince. As the story continues, it becomes obvious that only one man, Prince or Lorq, will survive; only one family will triumph, the Von Rays, or the Reds; ultimately only one stellar nation will be able to retain its power, Draco or the Pleiades.

The *Roc* must first stop at the Alkane Institute of Arts and Sciences on the world of Vorpis—

Set high in the temperate mountains of a mist-flooded world where "fishermen" in flying nets ply the chasms for "fish"-like creatures that hide in the mists scarfing the rocks.

The Institute is as big as a fair sized city—a museum that is at once a combination of Munich's Deutsches Museum and the Louvre, taken into the 31st century.

In this tomb of man's history, Prince tries to trap Captain Von Ray. He is rescued by the Mouse and the crew who invades the museum with a group of fishermen. One of the fishermen, Leo, is the same man who taught the Mouse to play the sensory syrynx years ago on the docks of Istanbul. With their information, they flee Vorpis just in time.

They must wait a week for the Nova, which is in the Outer Colonies. They take refuge on one of the charred planets in the Pleiades, circling the Dim Dead Sister, the home of Tyÿ and Sebastian.

Prince, desperate to destroy Von Ray, confronts Von Ray in person, in a burning building.

Von Ray, using the mouse's syrynx as a weapon by turning up the intensity beyond the danger point, blinds him, deafens, blots out his smell. Prince is rescued by his sister, Ruby.

Later, Ruby and Lorq confront each other; she shows him the "living corpse" of her brother, now only a malevolent brain controlling a whole medusa of prosthetic devices.

Von Ray decides to leave, collects his crew and they take off.

Half-way into the Outer Colonies when they are shanghaied by a ship running miners to a world of a sun only a few light months away from the star to which they are going.

They are imprisoned in the icy underwater mines, where they work in ice-caves.

Captain Von Ray, as a one-time foreman of a mine, and Lynceos and Idas as former miners hold up fairly well. But the Mouse, Katin, Tyÿ and even the burly Sebastian have simply had no experience and almost succumb to the incredible undersea condition. Lynceos and Idas discover their third triplet Tobias, who is now an overseer in the mine.

Prince, with malevolent curiosity, comes to see them—he still is not exactly sure what and how Lorq was going to accomplish what he set out.

With the help of Tobias, bliss, and an all out free for all, they take over his ship, turn him off and imprison his sister, and take off toward the Nova, in his best racing style.

During the trip Ruby escapes, nearly wrecks them. She and Lorq have a fight just as the ship reaches the Nova.

Lands briefly on a moon of one of the sun's planets.

They take off into the nova. There is danger from the moon which follows the ship, and from Prince. Katin's knowledge of moons, plus the Mouse's heroism—in which he has to actually look at the nova—save the situation.

(The technique for retrieving the Illyrion, for dealing with the gravity, the heat, and why the moon does not disintegrate in the nova—when we get down to the nitty-gritty of describing the event—is dealt with in hard SF terms, based on last year's work by Dr. Lloyd Motz and Frederick Kantor on the propagation of gravity through space; and the propagation of electromagnetic waves—heat in particular.)

The outcome of the conflict I won't reveal, even to you.

Katin and Von Ray, back on the mining planet several months later, discuss Katin's novel under the light of the nova which has finally reached the mining planet. Katin has finally decided on the subject of his novel:

the subject is this final trip of the *Roc*. The closing words of the book, which Katin records for the opening of his novel, from Captain Von Ray:

"There are certain things each of us must do. As the moth must seek light, or a man plunge toward a star, the Mouse must strike his syrynx—"

+   +   +

Dear Andy,

I have looked over my blood, guts, and gore stories, and I'm afraid these are the only two that are salvageable:

"They Fly at Çiron" and

"In the Ruins."

Following those two is a 20,000 word novelette which must be completely recast to be even readable, in which Rahm and Clikit arrive in Calvicon, become friends forming a big-black-haired-giant-and-his-[...] wiry-little-blonde-buddy team à la Fafhrd & Mouser.

They enter the services of Lord Wyatt of Calvicon, and, disguised as highwaymen, they have a grand old time wheedling their way into Myetra, battling the science and sorcery of the eastern menace.

There is another encounter with Kire and with Naä, and a whole host of strange, mutant beings.

The title is "The Claws of Kirke."

And finally there is a 500 words vignette called "Vigil" in which Rahm, a rich, old Lord, comes back to Çiron and re-encounters Vortcir.

I'd send it along, but it's a little meaningless without the intervening novelette.

In all the stories, however, I completely avoid any explanation of the why and wherefore of my world, and at the same time keep close grip on either a moral or mythic focus.

+   +   +

22,000	"Star-Pit"
12,000	"They Fly at Çiron"
9000	"Corona"
8000	"Driftglass"
10,000	"Dog in a Fisherman's Net"
2500	"In the Ruins"
63,500	

+ + +

Tonight   Paula
Wed.   Marjory & John.
Thursday: Jimmy Ballard.
Friday: John's Agent's Party
Saturday: Elston-Othello
Sunday: afternoon with Judy
Monday: Brian's, 5–6
Tuesday: John & M's dinner

+ + +

Insert scene at the bar between Dan and Lorq—help establish relationship.

+ + +

Dear Miss Pinkerton,

At *New Worlds*, we appreciate constructive criticism, and were delighted to get your letter. When someone understands what we try to do, and tells us, it makes us feel that all the turmoil is worth it. From our older readers—you say that you're fifteen—we don't get much encouragement. Their cry seems to be: return to the good old days. But when some[one] writes how entertaining as well as intellectually stimulating she finds our magazine, we can only say thank you, and try to keep it up. I shall pass on your letter to Mr. Ballard; he will be glad to hear how much you liked his story.

Faithfully,

M

+ + +

Sebastian spits in the mouth of his pets.

+ + +

Architectural study

Dune: "It comes down to this. *Bene disserer est finis logicis*, a Latin translation of a Greek assumption: if you agree with it, basically *Dune* is a good novel; if you don't, then it isn't."

Style: "The man has style? So has the lady." (Judith Merril)

The comparison of the editing of the first few pages of mag. vs. book version of "Conrad."

"Style forces the reader to supply the ugly parts of the sentence."

The Jack Spicer "color blind" example.

(New Year's in Mykonos) Crete—Istanbul—New York. (New Year's in London)

The search for solid light—and finding it not in Greece, but in the British Museum in the Mogul miniatures with T. Disch. Pamela making masks for NY's party. Description of same. *Time* magazine's article on being under 25. (J.B.'s comment—you're not going to be 25 forever.)

Pamela's gift & the inscription therein.

McLuhan—the economy—the relation of images. The wish to inform my writing with the same light.

+   +   +

I am very interested in science fiction as serious literature, but the canons of aesthetics all spring basically from the canon on entertainment.

What do you like in Sf?

Humanity? Science? Writing?

Why do you think science-fiction is as popular as it is?

What is the prejudice against science fiction; does it have to do with the general prejudice against science?

What don't you like in modern sci.-fi.

Whom do you like & read.

Do you read mainstream literature for entertainment.

(Perhaps go into *This Immortal* if that comes up.)

+   +   +

Things to Do:

Get Henry to send "Dog" to M. Moorcock.

Get copy of "Star-Pit" to Judy.

Finish reading *Dune*.

Write article: show to Terry.

+   +   +

Let's see what image I can fall in love with now:

(Three holiday weeks spanning the nexus of 1966 & 67 in London. Return to N.Y. and just saw Helen Adam's *San Francisco's Burning*—the first modern work I have seen that attempts to deal with the mythic focus of death through the texture of life, from the whores of the "hanged man's house" to the intrigues of Nob Hill.)

Roach is missing a tooth.

He got an earring an' a motorcycle and 27 years bumming, and a knife, and black hair, scrawny over his belly, thick round his root which humps his left leg like a ten-inch grave.

A dirty sweatshirt with sleeves torn off. A jean jacket (also sleeveless) over that. On his forearm a dragon, an eagle on his bicep in four colors of ink.

He wears one boot, and one sandal and he doesn't wash. His toenails are long and black. And the feet & hands are grimy. Thumbs thick, the first points blunted by the gnawing. Each nail is a grease crescented ruin sunk in the wide nubs.

+ + +

The year is the letters of James Sallis, who from Iowa pinions the flow of these months since the Tricon to the structure of solid time.

+ + +

Here we go. Time to take literary stock of me-self. I am working toward a goal I thought I wanted four years back. What I've learned has, of course, been valid. Was there a sacrifice? I find myself at a point where the future, which should be defining itself for me, shatters over the points of possibilities. *Nova* is a novel I sincerely want to finish. But there is no reason, now, for me to write anything I don't want to write. I think here and now I should abandon the idea of "The Claw of Kirke" unless I am really seized with an inspiration for it. My writing, focused through the distortion of my life, has sent me bouncing around the world, has given me the fulcrum on which to liven away my set complacencies. By some sort of faith that is almost religious seeming I know I am strong enough to deal with the confusion below. But deal with it is one thing, ordering with the strength of art is another. Has the formation of a craftsman [...] obscured the formation of an artist? In these last years, I have learned how to live. That is not good. One cannot unlearn. But as art deals with truth, I have been much too close to and tempted by corruption. I must again make of art a method of dealing with that which I don't understand. That is the biggest problem now—this must go into Katin's character in *Nova* if I am ever to write anything after that. One lies not only out of envy (I watch poor Tanto—the 19-year-old girl who stays here with her husband Keith, the 17-year-old B.H.S. graduate—talking about her 180 W.P.M. as a typist.) One lies to simplify one's own image and make it easier to deal with. I was rather surprised at myself how little I was upset by J. Brunner's note when he discovered I had clap. [...] The person I feel verbally closest to, of all the people I spent time with in England, was Judy Merril. And she, like me, seems to be going through the greatest problems in creating of them all. People seem to find me a nice person; loneliness is the biggest cause of that, and loneliness is what causes the lies—the social lies, the lies that try to distort the truth in a non-artistic milieu that makes the loneliness/truth more apparent. There are three lies in particular; I wonder what they mean? There is the lie that comes out of that story "The Torture Garden" written back when I was 15 or so, that I once did such violence to a friend, even told to M. and has now progressed to murder. (That's all that incredible hostility—yes, Dr. Grossman.) Then there is the lie about the method of composition for *F.F.D.* It was written as any other book of mine was written—why the need to imply all this psychological delving. I cannot write without psychological delving for images. Why the necessity of these mythical notebooks on the bottom of the Aegean? There is none really. I think I must retitle Terry's essay "An Architectural Fiction with 365 Supports." Writing all this makes my stomach hurt. The last persistent falsehood is the need to compliment other writers on their bad writing. [...] I am really incredibly lonely for someone who knows as much about writing as I do. This is why I am furious at Marilyn for turning herself off to me. And I suppose that's what it boils down to.

Have been sick, throwing up, unable to enjoy eating, and, till now, incapable of writing these last three days. Slept most of the time away. (Or it could "boil down" to that; which is probably what M. would say.)

Georgia, country, with blue eyes like circles cut in morning, he had one broken tooth, and a scar through the heavy gold of his eyebrow. Hands? The hair on the heavily veined backs was like brass. His thumb was broad and blonde, and not much nail left from biting. He was spading his balls around in his greasy jeans. "Hiya, there, boy." He grinned at me when he caught me looking from across the dock, and hooked his thumbs now over his studded belt. The lumps of his shoulders were freckled and there was a line of sunburn before the leather vest (the laces trailing on his matted chest hair). He wore one, black, scuffed boot, with his cup jammed in. His other foot, bare, rested on its yellow heel with the sole black and cracked, bare.

"Hey," I said from the barge. "What you doin'?"

He glanced over his shoulder where the smoke curled between the buildings against the dawn. (There was a blue swastika tattooed on his arm, and again on his right hand between thumb and forefinger.) "Came to get away from the fire. Most of them as gonna leave the city done left already. What about you?"

"My barge stays anchored here," I told him. I was holding onto the cabin doorway, leaning out to smell the smoky morning. The dock was warm under my toes. "I guess with the fire there [won't] be any papers coming. On the water I guess I'm safe."

"Say," he gestured with his thumb, "you always wake up with a hard on like that, nigger?"

I looked down. "Just about every time I go to sleep."

That made him laugh. "Dreamin' about getting it into some white cunt?"

"Get it into anything I can."

He got up from the pile, came to the dock's edge, and squatted.

"Back when I had my old lady livin' with me, I used to go out every night and hunt up the biggest, blackest son of a bitch I could find, take him home for her. She was a pretty thing, too. I'm one of those guys who writes things on john walls, come here at 7:30 if you want to fuck my wife. Sometimes I'd get five or six blacks in there together, and a case o' beer, and man, we'd go to town on that little bitch." He licked a back tooth, waiting for me to say something.

I asked, "What happened to her?"

He shrugged. "She ran off with somebody who worked in the office at a college. Then she left him, and came back to me for one weekend. I was living with a guy who was one of them civil rights Negroes. We all got drunk, and, man—" The smile left. "Anyway, then she ran off again."

His fingers cupped his crotch. "I sure wish she could've gotten a cunt full of that." And he thumbed toward me.

I went over to the cabin and took it out to pee. From the deck he sucked his lips.

With a hardon it takes a long time, and when I was a kid I couldn't take a leak at all with someone watching.

"Hey," he said, "you got any coffee? I'll go make up a pot."

Pee struck the tar paper wall, tongued down to puddle my feet.

In the cabin, he was lighting the benzene stove under the coffee pot. He was taller than me by the mass of blonde hair; not as broad.

"You live in the city?" I asked.

"Got there when I was eighteen."

"So you been here since the fire began."

"That's right."

I put my bare foot on top of his, and he shifted his toes under mine, but didn't take his foot away.

"What was it like?" I asked. "The fire."

He [shrugged]. "You can't see it." Gauze of flame over the burned metal. "I mean you can't get close to any part of the city that's really burning. But you can walk through the burned out parts. I got my motorcycle, and sometimes I ride through the streets where it's still smoking. That's what I was doing all last night. And the moon came up at four in the morning and everything was lit up till sunrise." Outside, across the rail, the light beaded and flowed on the water. "Most everyone's left. Only people 'round are cooks like me," he drawled, and glanced at me, grinning over his broken tooth. "What's your name?"

"Sam," I said.

"Hey!" He laughed, "Sambo? Geez—" He stuck his hand down on my crotch and felt around for it. "Wish I'd gotten that dingus of yours up my ol' lady's cunt. Juicy, boy! I'd a given my right ball to watch you fuck."

I sat down on the mattress in the corner. He turned. His heavy, wet lips broke on his yellow teeth again. He plowed his thumb through the matted gold of his belly. "You wanna see my pecker?" He undid the big double ring buckle, and his zipper rasped. The balls fell out like red peaches. On the side of the veined length was another blue tattooed swastika. He fisted the limp thickness, and the foreskin peeled. On the wet, red, plum sized head was a bumblebee. "How'd you like that to stick you?" He laughed, and shoved himself back into the jangling flaps of his jeans. "Got almost as much as you, you black bastard." His face tightened a little: he was a few years older than I thought at first. "Don't I?"

"Yeah."

He grinned again. "I guess you think you're safe from the fire down here." He looked around the cabin. "Uptown the fire got down to the docks." He shook his head. "Hey!" He saw the pile of comic books on top of the milk crates I'd set up for shelves in the corner. "You read these?" He flipped through the top half dozen. "Don't you got no war ones? Those are the kind I like." He got another bunch and started flipping.

"I don't got none of those," I said.

"Oh." But he still kept flipping. "What you gonna do, nigger, when fire gets down here to the docks?"

"Watch it burn."

He put down the books, and walked over to the mattress, his thumbs in his pockets. "You been in to see the city?"

I shook my head. His hands were dirty. He smelled. I put my foot on top of his again.

"You wanna go?"

I nodded. "You wanna show me around?"

"That's why I asked." He looked down where my foot lapped his. I felt him flatten his toes and spread them beneath mine. "You know," and then he squatted, his hand falling to flap his groin, "I remember . . ." For a moment his voice lost its blatancy, and the blue eyes fell unsteadily. "Back when it was the first time." He waited for me to respond. I just nodded. He put his hand on my knee and grinned. "My old man had a farm in the red earth, and a still. After the 18th kid, Ma kicked off, Pa sat on the porch with his bottle and drank, sometimes rubbed the dirt between his toes, and laughed."

[sequence continues]

+ + +

Lorq's tarot:

*—The World
1—Three of Pentacles
    (skill, mastery of trade) nobility, glory. Construction, material increase.
2—Page of Swords—reversed.
    An active, dark [haired] boy, spying for either good or evil—reversed: impostor likely to be defeated.
3—Page of Pentacles
    Gold, prosperity, wealth. Ecstasy, bliss.
4—Nine of Pentacles
    Solitary enjoyment of the good things of life. Success, accomplishment.
5—The Tower—reversed
    Imprisonment.
6—Two of Swords—reversed
    False love, instability; too violent passion
7—King of Swords
    A dark man: he has the power of life & death. It may be a very wise man—who will teach you something.
8—Three of Wands—reversed
    Beware of help offered. There may be treachery or disappointment
9—The Devil Reversed—(good both ways)
    The beginning of spiritual understanding
    A physical (or mental) healing has started—violence, revolution, bond to the material, extraordinary effort.
10—Queen of Swords
    A dark woman—widowhood—sterility, privation, separation, acquaintance with sadness.

+ + +

Yet more notes on *Nova*
—and what to do with it.

Sebastian's pets—describe as mad leaves.

Brian's remark about Prince's arm, comes to fruition.

The psychological effects of the sockets—
    The extension of man into a tool—how this has injured the Mouse,

Prince, and Dan. (The extended tool is not always the most efficient, but they have become psychologically dependent on them)

The section under the Dim Dead Sister—Venice

Change speech pattern of the dwellers of the Pleiades Federation.

+ + +

The torpor swallowing all my actions this February makes me feel like a character in a J. G. Ballard story. I have been making an attempt to clean the house: the next step is to cleanse the house of a few of the noisier people.

+ + +

Dialogue for the Pleiades Federation speakers.

Perhaps it was built nine hundred years ago. But that's just a guess.

Subject is distinguished by introducing subject with the subscript $_a$. Predicate by $_b$. Object by $_c$. Indirect object by $_d$.

"$_a$It $_b$was built' nine hundred' ago' perhaps.' But $_a$that'$_b$'s just a 'guess.'"

"Hey, Mouse. $_c$What $_a$you $_b$got?"

"$_b$Are $_a$you' sure.' Where $_b$did—"

"Where $_b$did' $_a$you find' $_c$this?"

"$_a$I $_b$didn't know $_c$that there $_b$were $_a$any on Earth, much less here."

"Give these^2 $_d$gentlemen^2 their' $_c$lunch'."

+ + +

Should I fix this time?

What sort of mind turns to words in times of strain, positive or negative?

Yesterday, a half-dozen advance copies of *The Einstein Intersection* arrived. By today I had given them all away, the last one going to Lew Warsh.

Came out of 34 St. Marks, saw him across the street, in his window, putting on his shirt. He waved, and I bounded across the street and rang his bell. Quickly I inquired after Anne's cold—she had been indisposed with a strep throat at John Wiener's reading a few days back—and finding she had recovered, I gave him the book.

Damon Knight sent me a letter telling me that I had received the Nebula for best novel of the year. It was a slightly hysterical reminder to *be* at the banquet. I've had a bad cold all this week, but have been forced not to take care of it. The confirmation of the award flung me into hours of fantasy— the sort that can only be relieved by disciplining them toward writing. And I did not feel well enough to write.

Stalking up and down Ron's apartment, I envisioned possible reactions to the presentation. I walked over to the O.R. and told Jamey. Thence to Russell's womb-like studio. Corey Martin (whose stud powers I have been hearing about for years from Ana Perez, though I never met him) was there. Russell was sketching his hand, making a study for one of his blazing allegories.

On the black stage at the studio's [back], the gutted horse flames on burning money. The bloody couple iridesce among livid ribs. Russell's work astounds me and tends to make me inarticulate before him. Later I came uptown to Mother's to eat. Spent the night unable to sleep, my mind exploding on mythical cadences resolved.

+   +   +

Going mad again

It has its humour.
The distance from the object
becomes more important than the object.
Fear is real.

+   +   +

The small pain on my skull's
cap has been with me a week. It chills
before beer. The book
that had been working on me this year has a strange look.
Sometimes I break out and scream.
I dream of Barbara and Russell and John, and each dream
happens on the surface of sleep.

I have difficulty reading. Letters keep
coming to take the place of poems
coming. I go feed my cats; there are cans
all over the floor. I have no home.
There are no lights or gas. I can
not eat at home. And the windows glitter.
Mornings my mouth is bitter.
It is sad I am a man.
One goes
on binges of sex to prove oneself alive.
There is the old urge to go barefoot again
and feel shit in my toes.
It is sad that with so much crisp health in the slow lift of April
pain thrives.

April 4, 1967

+ + +

I like the clearness being hungry gives.
—A bit of humour is involved in having it happen a second time.

+ + +

Dear Damon,

Thank you very much for the Xerox copies of Jim Sallis' stories "The History Makers" and "A Few Last Words." I'm giving a talk at the Lunacon April 29th; in the line of giving *Orbit* some publicity I wanted to use some quotes from Jim's stories to make a point or two.

Thanks also for letting me know about the nomination of *The Star-Pit*. A full list of proofreading corrections would run to a couple of typed pages (I've made such a list a couple of times for people), but of the significant "radishes/ravishing" variety here are a couple:

For "you're sweet, affectionate, and a good businesswoman"

Read "you're sweet, you're fun in bed, and a good businesswoman"

For Teehalt read Ratlit throughout.

To avoid an accidental republication of names between this and a Jack Vance story (the sort of thing that gives fan nightmares) a character who had originally been called Teehalt had his name changed throughout the manuscript to Ratlit—in all but three places.

For "snap" read "nap"

There are lots more, but they are, I'm afraid, just some of those maddening little impedimenta to the perfect life I'll have to live with till the next edition.

Best to you and Kate.

Till the 12th Annual

Writer Con.

+   +   +

Outline for Sex Novel

Basically, young kid, fifteen, arrives as a dirty cabin boy on a ship to an African port.

He watches the sailor masturbate.

They go off the ship, where the African port is in revolution. At the Tavern he meets and is raped by the Black Leader. Fight.

He's passed on to the two white Lieutenants who fuck him up. Another fight.

He's then gang-banged by the whole platoon of black sailors.

+   +   +

Notes on finale of this section.

Lorq's finish—no, we're not leaving immediately. We're waiting for another message.

Then we go to the Pleiades, but we wait at the shore.

The Mouse—Gabe is well—talks to Leo who wants to go home. Katin comes in; briefly recounts what happened. Mouse doesn't care about that, but if Captain is going back to the Pleiades, would he mind taking Leo back? Katin: *Huh!?*—Well, maybe. M: let's ask him, cause this is important.

Lorq: Yes, I'll take him; they go.

Lorq and Ruby. (The subject is the conflict between them—as in note at top of page 6—& its significance.)

Katin, drunk, explains his theory of history to Mouse in the dark net house with Leo insisting that the Mouse play till Idas comes to tell them the Captain says to go.

CHANGING SCENES [409]

+ + +

Jim, I've been living with your stories this week. "The History Makers" and "A Few Last Words" have been read in toto perhaps five times — in section much more. "Letter to a Young Poet" just arrived this morning. I've read it twice. When I go through it a few more times I'll give comments on it. Feel odd.

I could so easily praise these stories. There is so much in them, about them to praise. They are rich, rich tales. I will try not to give you the easy praise that will come from other people — has probably already started coming — at least from Damon. (Conceited mother-f that I am) [I] ask you to accept my critical attention as a compliment.

If I read these stories and they had been signed J. G. Ballard, I would breathe a sigh of relief, and tell everyone I know, "I take it all back. J. G. Ballard can write after all. These are definitely his best stories."

You said your work stands (or falls) by itself. It's lovely to talk with someone inexperienced with your published work. Your work stands beside everything else the reader has ever read. Ultimately

+ + +

Where are we going?

I suddenly realize I am living without a home.

My own house, without lights or cooking facilities, has been taken over by Janet, the children & Andy. Ron's apartment is in chaos: he is transversing indeed, a time of chaos in which I am just a factor in the confusion.

But I'm nearing a time when I need a home to work in. *Nova* has stalled — and just at the point where I thought the structure would begin to proliferate towards its own conclusion. So to the park, then, to take the sun and relax. It is perhaps ten in the morning. My diurnal rhythms have been shattered as though I'd flown a third of the way 'round the world. I sleep nights, days, evenings, mornings. The spring is filthy, and all the buildings wear dusty coronas.

Perhaps I will wander through the wild dogs that mass & turn in the park and go down to see Russell. When *Nova* is finished, I think I will start a desultory journal again, to impose some life on the fantasy of my "fictional existence" as Ballard calls it.

+ + +

Voices in SF

or

A Talk Talk

or

Silence; Water; Someone Saying My Name

Introduction

Speech is the most common way of communicating information from one person to the other, the way we feel (*"Was* that party really last night? Christ have I got a head!"), warnings of danger ("Bridge is out ahead. You better drive round Pottsville.") and relate facts ("Young lad, you'll find the book you want in the back shelves under Sex."). From speech developed song, poetry, and ultimately writing, which allowed us to record speech and to communicate much more sophisticated patterns of information—it developed as man's greatest social tool—

At which point I say stop, and forget what I've been saying. What I've just been outlining is the traditional view of the development of speech held firmly up till twenty years [ago]. Now it's only beginning to be broken down.

The new ideas have not been fully codified, but from recent experiments psychologists are beginning to admit the probability that this development followed a totally different pattern.

Speech seems to fulfill an internal psychological need in the human mind. A few cases where children have been raised without hearing human speech—hearing children in societies of deaf mutes, for example—as well as a few more bizarre cases—they develop their own private, verbal language—a primitive one, but usually has elements of a grammar, and is used to communicate with himself. Language's main function seems to be communicating within the mind. Apparently a good deal of the communication that takes place within the brain, from one part to the other, is done in the language that the person speaks. Anthropological evidence would seem to indicate that the first use of language was in social chanting—well before words took on their specific denotative meaning. Those specific elements of poetry, in other words, developed before the denotative communicative elements of talking. Rhythm and song, again, very possibly developed before the exact denotative element of speech was codified. Dr. Suzanne Langer of Harvard has examined the area of aesthetic communication and more or less found it to be a preverbal matrix of information, rather than a super-sophisticated distillate of the verbal process. And anthropologists have finally begun to face the fact that all cultures, no matter how primitive, develop *an* art, *a* music, and *a* poetry *before* they develop *any*thing else. The will to order seems to be—along with the need to socialize—a basic human need, out of which speech grew. The use of speech to warn, to discuss, and to inform is apparently a secondary function that grew out of its major, individually internal one.

It is only in the light of the more primitive function of language, to invest with meaning an entire area of non-verbal formalism, that much of what is happening in modern writing, particularly in poetry, and particularly in modern science fiction, [is] comprehensible.

I'm going to talk about Voice in modern SF this afternoon. But I do not want to talk about it in terms of the socially functional aspect of speech, warning, expression, informing—but rather its more primitive power to invest with significance what it circumscribes.

There are three voices in modern SF that I would like to deal with. One I call the Alien Voice, the other I call the Objective Voice; the third I called the Subjective Voice.

The Alien Voice is the one that I think is unique to SF. It is the one that mainstream does not have: I'm not talking about stories that deal with aliens: I am talking about the places in stories and novels where the language chooses to deal with alienness. Historically, this was brought into focus by Hal Clement's books like *Mission of Gravity* and *Cycle of Fire*.

I want to use a modern example, however, because among SF writers there is more facility in relating this voice to the other two—and I think ultimately it is the harmonizing of all three that produces the great work.

This is a quote from Roger Z's *This Immortal*. "The alien" speaks with Diane.

[Quote]

The fact that an SF "alien" is talking just makes this a particularly clear example. But it is the voice that invests this totally alien experience not only with reality, but with significance.

The objective voice on the other hand deals with that part of the fictional experience that tries to capture an approach to fictional reality. This is the whole workaday voice of SF. I won't give an example. You can find examples in any good science fiction stories.

The particular purpose of the objective voice in SF is to objectify an object or situation, often to take an unreal object or situation and invest it with reality. But I'm aware that this—in a broader way—is what three quarters of all fiction does. But when the two voices harmonize, we get the valid beginnings of aesthetic tensions in SF. The third voice I want to talk about, the subjective voice, is one that we have comparatively little of in science fiction. It is the voice that tries to define the internal objects of sensibilities.

It is the voice used to invest with significance not perceptions or thoughts, but a state of mind or an outlook.

For an example I want to use a quote from a story by James Sallis, "The History Makers" that will be appearing in one of Damon Knight's forthcoming *Orbit*.

[Quote]

To summarize, these are the three voices that, whether used well or badly, most SF, especially modern SF, speaks to us in—Alien, Objective and Subjective.

Not too long ago I read a series of critical essays by Robbe-Grillet on the New Novel. They were basically discussions of the "new" objective style. He was decrying the use of pat phrases, the use of clichés, but they were couched in such critical claptrap that I was halfway through the book before I realized, he was simply talking about "good" writing versus "bad." He had rediscovered it for himself, in the way, I suppose, that, ultimately, every writer must re-invent the language. But nevertheless, that's what all the furor was: write well, clearly, precisely, with linguistic vitality instead of vaguely, and with worn-out language.

Similarly, last week I listened to a recorded interview with J. G. Ballard done on the BBC. He made the point that man lives in a world of intersecting fictional planes. The first is the historical fiction of the latest shot at Cape Kennedy, or the assassination of some political figure.

The second plane is the fiction of our day to day lives, our jobs, [our] homes.

The third is the inner reality, in that each of us is a figment in our own fantasy.

Where these planes intersect, there the modern writer finds his material.

After listening to this, I was suddenly thrown back to the whole theory of the Victorian novel—the novel that tries to take its incidents as they are affected [by] the historical moment—the economy & changing social structure—as well as the personal events—also, the psychology of the characters.

Ballard has managed to re-invent the novel in the same way that Grillet has reinvented the canons of good writing.

Rather than distrust this, I would think this is the only sort of aesthetics I trust: one that begins to make its way—in the vocabulary of its own time—back to these verities that have existed through epochs of art. I have a feeling my discussion of Voice is heading in the same direction. But since you are getting [it] in the formulative stage, I have not yet seen it through to the end.

The third title of this talk will perhaps illuminate some of the more difficult parts of this discussion. In an old bunch of papers, I discovered a list by a girl I've never met headed: Things I like.

The list contains some hundreds of entries; I read through it, trying to reconstruct the personality of the girl who had composed it. Often I was caught up in the rhythm of noun after noun so that I would pass down five entries and not know what I'd read except that they all contained the letter "p." Another selection, and my mind would start compiling my own list, till again my attention would suddenly snap back.

One picture would begin to form, and another entry would contradict. Indeed, many of the entries were outright contradictions, which, admittedly suggested breadth of character—

("Do I contradict myself? Very well, then, I contradict myself. I contain multitudes"—is what Walt Whitman said.)

—but still, no limits. Then, among the hundreds, I came on:

silence; water; someone saying my name

and suddenly a person, whom I had never known before, but whom I always suspected the existence of, was invested with presence, and definition.

It was a totally personal reaction. Possibly—not the same for you. But this process, however it works, is the process I want to analyze: not to kill, not even to imitate it, but because this is the process which is Voice speaking to a listener.

SF speaks from realms where that which is to be—not communicated, but invested with the immediacy of aesthetically validated experience—is the most vital area of information left the modern writer.

Chapter Six

Outline:

On the *Roc*
The Tarot Game, embodying the notes with bit about the novel should be about relations—the establishment of character through the three types of action—the three concerns of fiction: historical, objective, subjective. Who is playing the game:
    Idas, Leo, Sebastian and Tyÿ.

+ + +

Note for Katin—to be expressed or demonstrated sometime soon in the novel:
"Mouse, here we are, you and I, essentially good people, with concerns outside ourselves, but also leading rather aimless lives. The Captain's obsession has imposed an order here—or perhaps a more meaningful chaos. Products of this confused age, we are supremely thankful, are we not?"
The Mouse shrugged. "I'd go nuts if I spent as much time as you in all that thinking."
"Ah, Mouse. I go nuts if I spent as little time at it as you."

(—Omit? Or perhaps not till much later.)

—Perhaps after the big encounter with Prince.

+ + +

Voices in SF:
    The Alien Voice
    The Human Voice
    The Inner Voice of the Mechanism

+ + +

I used to think I could envision eternity, and this was one of the glories of the human mind; till I realized what I was envisioning were only the limits of my own consciousness.

+ + +

There is no reason for the sexually healthy to have any rigorous morality. Perverts of one sort or another are the only ones who, through force of experience, develop a just ethical system.

+   +   +

It's new notebook time!

Sitting here in agent's office, everything newly decorated, including me, all white dress turtleneck, mouton vest, and Henry has a long-haired zebra throw over his parka. Time perhaps, while Henry wheels on the phone, to take

Re-plotting for the City of Dreadful Night section.

One: On the strip, and they call Setsumi
    Katin #1: Character through action

Two: At the Villa; the reaction of the crew, the Captain; the Twins want bliss. The Mouse plays.
    Katin #2: if I worked that hard ...

Three: Mouse & Captain go for bliss, return
    Katin: At the Villa: The Great Minds of the Past—interrupted suddenly by the advent of Prince. (Something dramatic—like the recorder playing while Prince walks about the room.)

Four: The return of Lorq, and the scalding of Prince; the release of the crew. They flee.
    Katin #4 (you have to think about this one): The incomplete Grail legends & quest tales. (Not recorded? Yes: Think that's best.)

Five: Shanghaied to the mine.

Followed by:
    The Tarot game in which one of the twins is called away (they know where they're going, and figure that's Prince's ironic punishment) because he's worked in a mine. The Mouse is all upset about the use of his syrynx (?). Think about how to work that in—possibly earlier—to shut Katin up about Tarot & incomplete Galahad tales.

+   +   +

Outline again:

On the strip—
    #1—Katin's notes on the way to Taafite

At the Villa:

Reactions of the crew. The Captain's reaction, but growing nervousness. The twins think about bliss. The Mouse starts to play.

#2—Katin and Mouse's exchange. About "working hard." The captain decides to get some bliss.

The Mouse and the Captain go for bliss, Leo leaves, with his goodbyes.

The Mouse leaves his syrynx behind. Deprived of the instrument, he delivers the beginning of monologue.

They couldn't contact the Man. The Captain tells about the people who are shanghaied to the mine.

The Mouse does his monologue—if only I could play it—ends with bit about being shanghaied would be so bad. Captain says yes it would: you'd die. The twins & I would survive & the rest of you would die. They get the bliss and start back.

At the Villa—#3—Katin is watching the others have a good time. They're dancing, while Katin is talking of "the great minds of the past" speech into the recorder. Tyÿ asks him to dance. He starts when there is an interruption. Prince and Ruby walk in.

Lorq and the Mouse return. Confrontation between Lorq and Prince. The cockfight—how the thing that upset them was Aaron enjoying it. Prince is going to kill them with bare hands. Lord snatches up syrynx. There is a fight in which they break the wall. The scalding. They flee.

Take-off skipped.

The Tarot game, through which Katin is musing on the quest and the incomplete grail legends. The Mouse interrupts him, and we realize how much he has been shaken up by the evil in the whole encounter.

Katin asks the Captain whether he ever reported Dan's death.

+ + +

This book springs from a peripatetic and virtually homeless year for me, and was written at the indulgence of people incredibly generous with spare bedrooms, living room couches, dinner invitations, loaned typewriters, and the like: Heidi Mueller (and her Pharaoh under the Greek sea), John Witten-Doris, DeLys Robinson in Athens, Chris Gosling, Paula Osius, Norman Allen, John & Marjorie Brunner in London, Damon and Kate Knight in Milford, Russell and Dora Fitzgerald, Dick and Alice Entin, Paul Caruso, Joseph Soley, and Marilyn Hacker in New York; and Ron Bowman.

+ + +

Think about the structure of shorter works, hinging on a single scene, a single confrontation, developed in terms of an idea: try and make it a new idea as well.

Isis Descending

Silence; Water; Someone Saying My Name

Fire in the City

+ + +

This morning a bit after six, I woke up in a total panic that my heart would stop. I must've catapulted from the deepest sleep because I was exhausted. After I was awake a moment my heart began to pound and I began to sweat. I tried to return to sleep, but this obsession rode my mind like a bronco rider. I lay there holding my pulse, trying to discover other places where I could feel it. Each natural change would terrify me. I knew it was all ridiculous anxiety, yet I was completely convinced. Half a dozen times I began to fall into tingly, nervous sleep, and pulled myself awake. I knew this anxiety must be generating from the confusion around me. Ron is leaving in June, and we treat the business as though it is the end of the relationship. My mother just left for her vacation in Greece, and her worries were all about leaving me alone. As I write this, I feel my anxiety rising, and yet I can't follow the connections. I was obsessed with the idea of speaking to Marilyn. But there is no money in the house to call. I think the whole business was sparked last night when Linda Sampson came over to see Ron, quietly hysterical. I had put in my first good day of work in weeks. Ron & Linda talked in the other room. She was having one of those negative female adolescent epiphanies: she was alone and terrified and wanted Ron to go away with her. She verged over into tears a couple of times. I felt sympathetic. I also hated her for being weak—there was perhaps just the faintest bit of jealousy that Ron paid so much attention to her, but even more I was terribly envious of her for being able to feel like that. A few more years have passed and I have not cried. I hate every-body who can: I suppose that especially means women who do it so easily. It sits like a ball in the back of my throat, wanting to get out. I remember Dr. de la Vega telling Dick he was afraid to drink water because he would cry. There is so much rage inside me: I don't know how to deal with it at all. I am still so totally furious with Marilyn, for never being home when she was needed. On the one hand I know she is truly weak and incapable of it, and quite miserable because of it. But these four years have made me almost incapable of demanding anyone reach out to me. She wants to get and somehow thinks that not giving is a positive act. She somehow has got it in her head that "not questioning," "not challenging," "not probing" is a favor that can be bought. I am very alone because of that. The part of me that says good things can't last, is rather anxious for Ron to go away. But there is much of me that wants him to stay. It is the first time my feelings toward anybody have had the *scope* of love. So that when I tell him I love him, I at least know my statement lies in the general area of the truth.

I suddenly begin to understand just a bit of the whole masculine matrix as I have tried to avoid it. There are two different ways to be alone: one requires that you tell someone what to do to cure it. The other requires that you be told. I have never thought enough of myself to think I had any right to tell people what to do. I more or less developed an ethic that said people should not want to be told what to do. I really think that part of M's problem is that she never thought she was capable of carrying out what she was told. Both require self confidence. The anxiety is still in a knot in my stomach. It eases, then comes back. There is still that dichotomous urge to look at my naked self and cry. The self defacement bit stops that too: how could anything like you even be worth crying about. I don't want to look among the clichés current for a phrase to categorize my problems: "I can't touch," "I can't communicate." Silly. But there are certain areas, of both rage and pity, that are blocked. I am exhausted. The panic attack in the morning was just the last of many interruptions. Before that, Ana rang the bell at 5:00 or thereabouts, needing someone to talk to, & again Ron went off with her. Do I feel rejected? I really don't think so. Except perhaps on that infantile plane where connections make and break and we are unaware. I am afraid of living alone. That is the anxiety again. The only way I could tolerate it is with pen & notebook, meticulously mapping my course through madness. I want to have a wife and children I suppose. I sincerely wonder what children would do to Marilyn. That's fear on my part. Girls still terrify me—in terms of what they are capable of demanding. My foot is still in pain.

I just took my medicine (with vague hints of "Maybe it will hurt me— I'll suddenly develop an allergy to it"). The exhaustion is almost total. The combination of it and the anxiety is too much, really.

It is odd; I am getting to the scene in *Nova* where the rage of the main character must break out full force. Is that what frightens me, I wonder.

Time to re-read now. And try to sleep again.

Just re-read. It seems clearly written but I am too tired to delve its meaning. My foot really hurts. I got up, shaved, and made an attempt to walk outside—to go see M, and perhaps talk to her about this—but got only to the corner before the pain made me turn back. (Was it more than that?) Anyway, it was then that I decided to write all this down and try to work through it this way.

+ + +

BROADWAY, 9:40 A.M.

I had three hours sleep. I have to kill
twenty minutes here among Greeks and formica.
Things that artists cannot give away:
the dead mornings, the long mornings, the turnings away.
I watched them fondle her a while, then beat
retreat and fucked some spade on Clinton Street
who stood inside the gate with open fly
waiting for the youngsters passing by.
Pretending to be five years dumber than
I was, I stayed to pat his shoulder when
he mumbled, "See you ..." Somehow youth excuses
what dawn and horn and loneliness abuses.
Alexei who is white and brash and virgin
shies at the rigorous life. He'll be on time
wanting to buy books and the new Beatles.
He will say, "You look tired," and contrive
not to mention he's two years older than I.
Between ten and twenty age is an annoyance
to those who live on it, prostitutes
and prodigies; between twenty and
thirty it annoys those who didn't.
Malaka'!
The Greeks apocopate their S's. She
is new here and talkative. I have a head.
St. George's strikes. There. Twenty minutes dead.

June 3, '67

+ + +

Reflections of the short story, the single idea, the direct form. Two characters, whose conflict hinges about a single incident. The "classic" rules come back to me now from my 7th grade English teacher Mrs. T. The conflict of the short story is either man against man, man against nature, or man against himself. What must I do still from "Isis Descending."

Who is Isis and what is the basic change in the characters?

The fascination with crime, and who and why.

+   +   +

Notes for the untitled novelette.

It starts with Mike—the fifteen-year-old, grubby Irish kid; it also has Louis, the cracker truck driver; it has Spike, the Nazi motorcyclist; and all the Negro sailors and fishermen.

Starts out with Mike and black sailor, ends with his rape by all the sailors and fishermen.

Anyway, you have to finish all the parts first.

+   +   +

During the odd months I lived among the Greek islands, John Brunner in a letter which discussed form in SF, proposed the following revolution: a science fiction story or novel which begins as a perfectly naturalistic tale that, as images proliferate among themselves and create resonances and overtones, expands into a science fiction story, rather than the standard form in which the S-F postulates are defined in the exposition and then used to control the development. This sort of story could only be written in a world which accepts both "real" and "S-F" stories on the same level; the only analogous situation in the arts exists in pop music, where Baroque configurations on a harpsichord can be used to introduce the farthest out pop melodic and rhythmic variations of electric guitar, drum, and voice. John himself has attempted this sort of thing in his novel "The Productions of Time," and far more successfully in his novel "Quicksand" to be released soon from Doubleday. The idea fascinated me enough to try the following short story. A naturalistic tale then: Milos, the island on which I spent the most time, is the largest of the North West Cyclades. It has clay and obsidian mines that have functioned on and off for the past four thousand years. During the winter, it is also the least touristed of the islands, and is only visited once a week by the boat that comes from Piraeus to Syros, which, though a smaller island, is the thriving metropolitan center of trade in the Cyclades. In the island's mountains there are brown haired herders; on the shore, black haired fishermen. And once, thousands of years ago—But that doesn't come into the story till much later.

(This has nothing to do with the gimmick story where the bad guys (or the good's) turn out to be men from Mars on the last page.)

+   +   +

It's dues paying time.

I just wish I knew what the fuck I was paying them for. Probably for having lived such an emotionally safe life. I've internalized all the dangers, and they're trying to kill me. I don't want to die. But I'm afraid of it. I must live, really live, and that means meaningful relations. How to mean is the problem.

+   +   +

Dear Judy,

Much forgiveness I ask for being so hard to get hold of. The day you came knocking on my door, I had just been informed (that morning) that I had a kidney infection (nobody at the house knew yet) and in desperation I scooted home to mother where I collapsed for the next couple of weeks. Meanwhile the young couple who owned the apartment on St. Mark's returned from their two year stay in Europe, unexpectedly, and everyone was asked to vacate. I had let the lights and gas go in the 739 E. 6th Street studio (you remember climbing up all those stairs?) and I had just moved back the day I got your note to call Ed Ferman. That's the brief explanation of what I meant by "evicted." I've been staying at the lightless studio only when necessary. There's still $60 odd bucks owed Con. Ed. which should get paid next week sometime. All this time, you see, I was trying to complete *Nova*. I did. It goes to Larry Monday.

The Star-Pit   Reading for WBAI

Characters:

Adult
Me—Narrator
Bai Searles—Announcer
Joe Dicostanzo—Sandy
Bai Searles—The Other Pilot
Bai Searles—The Golden laughing
Joseph (?)
Bai Searles—News tapes
Bai Searles—Reporters

Child
Christopher—Antony
Ratlit
Androcles

Female
Anthony's ma—Marilyn
Little Girl—Judy Ratner
Vyme's mother—Marilyn
The Lady Golden—Marilyn
Allegra—Judy Ratner
Poloscki—Barbara
Grandmotherly—Marilyn

Characters—17, requiring 4 men, 2 children, 3 women

Bai Searles: Announcer, News Tapes, Reporter, The Other Pilot, The Golden, The Other Golden, The Sailor in Bar
Joe Dicostanzo: Sandy

Me: Narrator
Chris Taborne: Antoni
?: Ratlit
?: Androcles
Marilyn: Antoni's Ma, Vyme's Ma, The Lady Golden, The Portapix Voice
Judy Ratner: Allegra
Barbara Randal: Poloscki

10

Prism, Mirror, Lens and Other Projects

Having finished *Nova* and sold it to Doubleday, Delany began to outline an ambitious project: a five-volume science fiction series collectively titled *Prism, Mirror, Lens*, which would tell the story of a solar system–wide political revolution. (As various entries indicate, the title of the series would go through several permutations before settling on its final form.) Delany signed a contract for the project with Avon Books and produced extensive outline material, as well as several scenes and sequences, for the series.[1] As the entries dealing with the series make clear, this project would supply key story elements, as well as a chapter title, for *Dhalgren* (1975).

Delany's development of *Prism, Mirror, Lens* provided the backdrop for numerous other projects from this period. One of these would become his first published pornographic novel, *Equinox*—most of the first draft of which can be found in Notebook 88, and notes and scenes for which are scattered through other notebooks from this time. (Delany occasionally refers to this novel as *Faust*, which is consistent with his use of elements from the "Faust" project for this new book.) During this time Delany also worked on "Time Considered as a Helix of Semi-precious Stones" and completed the novella "Lines of Power," which would eventually appear in the *Magazine of Fantasy & Science Fiction*—with a cover painting by Delany's friend Russell Fitzgerald—and eventually in the *Driftglass* collection under the title "We, in Some Strange Power's Employ, Move on a Rigorous Line." Delany also continued corresponding with members of the SF community; Notebooks 33 and 35 contain fragments of drafts of correspondence with the *Australian Science Fiction Review*, an SF fanzine with an intellectual bent.

In the midst of these projects Delany cofounded the rock band Heavenly Breakfast, which soon metamorphosed into an urban commune of the same name.[2] Hacker, meanwhile, had become involved with Link Martin, who was part of the Spicer circle; later in 1967 Link returned to San Francisco with a standing invitation to Hacker to join him.[3] Delany and Hacker moved in temporarily with the gay couple Paul Caruso and Joe Soley, after which Hacker headed to the West Coast and Delany moved in with the commune.[4] A little over a decade later Delany would publish a memoir, *Heavenly Breakfast* (1979), recounting his experiences in the commune.

In the spring of '68 the commune disbanded and Delany moved into a new apartment on Seventh Street.[5] During the same period, *The Einstein Intersection* and "Aye, and Gomorrah" won Nebulas, and *Nova* was published.[6] Over the summer Delany wrote articles for the rock magazine *Crawdaddy!*, taught a course at the Clarion Workshops with Judith Merril, and again attended the Milford conference. He also briefly took a new lover, Joe Dicostanzo, and wrote a short story destined eventually for the *Driftglass* collection, "Night and the Loves of Joe Dicostanzo."[7]

During this time Delany also wrote critical essays on science fiction, including "Faust and Archimedes" and "Alyx." These two essays focused on the three science fiction writers of Delany's generation with whom he has claimed the most affinity: Thomas M. Disch, Roger Zelazny, and Joanna Russ.[8] Just after Christmas, Delany presented a lecture on science fiction at the Modern Language Association, which would be revised and expanded into the essay "About 5,750 Words."[9]

At the end of 1968, on New Year's Eve, Delany flew to San Francisco to reunite with Hacker.[10]

NOTES

1. Samuel R. Delany, "Chronology" (unpublished personal document, 2014), 16.

2. K. Leslie Steiner [Samuel R. Delany], "Anatomy of a Nova" (unpublished essay, 1997), 37.

3. Delany, "Chronology," 14.

4. Ibid., 14–15.

5. Samuel R. Delany, *Heavenly Breakfast* (1979; reprint, Flint, MI: Bamberger Books, 1997), 113.

6. Steiner [Delany], "Anatomy of a Nova," 47.

7. Delany, "Chronology," 16.

8. Steiner [Delany], "Anatomy of a Nova," 25.

9. Delany, "Chronology," 16.

10. Ibid.

YOU THERE!

Yes?

YOU HAVE GOT TO PULL YOURSELF TOGETHER!!!!

Yes, sir; I know, sir; I was aware of that, sir.

WELL?

Well, sir. Just the other day I was saying to myself, you've got to pull your-self together. Only I couldn't really think of any way to accomplish that I really couldn't.

AT ONE TIME SO I HAVE HEARD YOU WERE A <u>WRITER</u>?

Well, yes, I have been known to put a few words on paper now and then.

SO WHY THE FLYING <u>FUCK</u> DON'T YOU WRITE SOMETHING?

What would you suppose I write?

WELL ...

Well?

+   +   +

Mirror and Lens

One:
Ian starts to run away from his home in Mars city but is turned back by Joaquim Faust, the mystic. He falls in love with Lanya, a girl from the fas-cist state on Triton. They are married, she becomes pregnant; as the revo-

lution begins she is called back to Triton. They arrive in time for their son to be born. The war is threatening, but Lanya's family believes there is security within the home.

Two:

Marshal Yen, one of the leaders of the revolution, is a friend of Lanya's family, and although the family is opposed to his politics, they pride themselves that they allow him in their home to argue. Ian listens to him one evening, goes with him and becomes involved with the revolutionary activities. This the family cannot take, and after several incidents, Lanya herself asks him to make a decision. He decides on the revolution. There is a large battle in which many people are killed. Ian is shipped to a socialist state on Ganymede where the revolution is going more peacefully. He meets Rill, a girl who is an artist on Ganymede, she helps him recover, and it looks like the beginning of a romance. Ian learns that Lanya and his son [are] on Ganymede. He meets with them, in an attempt to reestablish their relationship. Ian is much shaken up. He finds he cannot go back with Rill either, and [becomes] depressed. Completely disillusioned, he wanders away.

Three:

The asteroids are a hiding place for smugglers and "pirates." Ian ends up here, and the book begins with another argument between [him and] Joaquim Faust who accuses him of running away again. This time Ian is persistent. Ian becomes an outlaw, preying upon the capitalistic worlds of Earth and Mars. Ian starts a career as a mercenary and a smuggler. He becomes quite successful, but in the middle of the book causes great damage to his father's career. He has a confrontation with his father, who tells Ian that he wouldn't mind if his son were on one side or the other, but his indecision is disgraceful. Ian only redoubles his efforts at wreaking chaos on the establishment. He is enlisted by the side of the established government, only to betray them, finally, to allow a shipment of Rill's sculptures to go to a museum. He turns revolutionaries and establishment away. This volume closes with another argument between Joaquim and Ian in which he threatens to try and become dictator.

Four:

Rill finds Ian half crazed. She is living among the revolutionaries on Earth, where the revolution has almost reached its truce. The establishment is trying [to] blackmail Ian in[to] returning to a life of crime by holding his son in an orphanage. The book deals with Ian's attempts to get his son. He has him three times, but loses him twice. Finally there is a confrontation with his father again and the General Sabor of the governmental establishment. Because of the truce, Ian is allowed his son back.

Five:

Ian has settled with Rill and his son, as Lanya has remarried. His varied background has given him a remarkable informational grasp, and he has been working as a synthesizer. Through the problems his son has growing up, and the problems his wife has as an artist, he begins to realize the human problems implicit in this new way of life when his son runs away from home. He also realizes he can deal with them, and regains much of his faith in himself. He finally decides to move his family, make peace with his father, and they set off for a new world. He ends up, waiting to leave, talking to Joaquim, and discovers that Joaquim had a hand in sending his son back to him, as Joaquim sent him back to his own father in the first volume.

I have always enjoyed the way new notebooks become old. The process has usually gotten markedly underway before ten pages are actually covered with text.

+ + +

Odd; the note at the head of this page, I recall, was written the first day I purchased this notebook from the little toy store on the west side of Ave C between 5th and 6th Street across from all the vegetable pushcarts. This note, now, as I look through the book for free pages. All the rest have been filled with notes, pornography, other graphy.

Wish I had a pack of Tarot cards.

Invent now:

Tarot Solitaire: "Seven Seventeen"

78 Cards.

The fool is wild. A pack of 13 cards laid face up on the table. A hand of seven cards, held as if there were another player.

+ + +

Night

I woke with his hand over my face. I looked up at him between his wide fingers, callus of forefinger on forehead, second & thumb on the sides of my eyes, third & fourth on the right of my jaw. There were leaves shaled green by the mercury lights behind his face. Then, rich darkness. Purple.

I caught his wrist with both hands, sat up on the bench, looked. Big. Twice as big as mine. Rough knuckled. Dirty. The nails gnawed back on the horny nubs. He grins down at me. One side tooth was broken. The face was freckled and then sun-tanned almost dark enough to hide them. His blue eyes between the white gold lashes were brilliant. "What's a kid like you sleepin' on a park bench?"

"No place to go." I shrugged sleepily.

His hair was red, brush short.

Gold wire snarled around and between his nipples, thick on his belly above the brown leather belt. His shirt was open, the sleeves torn off. I looked down.

His bare foot, horny & grime-caked: the long toes were on my sneaker.

With his free hand he tugged at the crotch of his jeans. "Christ, this fuckin' muggy weather. I keep half a hardon all day."

I let go of his wrist. He mauled the great thing around under the black canvas cloth, then sat beside me. "What's your name?"

"Joe," I told him.

"My name's Red Faust." He stuck his hand over, grinning.

I shook it. Then without letting go, he let them fall on his lap. He moved the back of my hand over something like half a policeman's nightstick. "See what I mean?" He smelled of alcohol. He looked up and down the walk. "You like that?"

I blinked.

"Come on," he said. "I seen you hanging around the john across the park there in the afternoon." He pressed my hand into his crotch again. His tone had started toward belligerence. It gentled again. "You're a good lookin' kid. I sure would like to see your face working down between my legs." The hand that was on the bench behind me came to massage the back of my neck. "How old are you, kid?"

"Seventeen."

"Shit." He kept rubbing. "By the time I was seventeen I had two kids and they're both older'n you now." He looked up and down the walk again. "Come on. Nobody's comin'." He nodded toward his fly. "You can take it out. Play with it." He let go of my hand. I felt the shape that made a tent along his thigh.

He hooked his thumb in the zipper and pulled it down. "Go on." He nodded again, spread his legs, and put his arms out along the back of the bench.

I reached between the runners. Hot, wet. I tugged the

+   +   +

Journal entry

Tuesday Night, July 11th '67—I have been working very hard, almost as a way of getting away with my—I started to write "from my" but I indulged in what I am sure was a dreadfully revealing slip of the pen—nervousness. I have been trying to put together my marriage and a singing group. I cannot really yet judge the success of either. As well, IAMC—Interval Artists

Music Co—has been handed over to me; at my own request. The music group consists of myself, Sue Schweers—a tall, somewhat gawky, but extremely engaging and brilliant girl of 21 with much musical and human incisiveness at her command. Then there is Steve, who has a good strong voice, a fine layman's capacity for musical understanding, and the ability to work hard. And since we began, he has demonstrated this ability well.

The last two days of rehearsals have been somewhat abortive. I have a cold, and have been tired, for one thing. As well, there have been a few personal crises between myself and M.—resolved, but still a bit taxing.

This afternoon Sue & I came out to Sea Cliff N.Y. to Sue's parents' home—in the cellar bedroom of which I write this. Spent the evening at a high school rehearsal of *The Music Man.* Sue was playing flute in the "Summer Band" which was rehearsing at the same time.

Very revealing about small town psychology and the mechanics of the great world. We discussed this coming back through the thin fog along the highway to Sue's home.

Late supper: Lamb in a *very* impromptu béchamel sauce, on toast. Many cooking stories from me till mother got in from work at 11:30 at night. Wonder what she does?

+ + +

thick thing out of his pants.

"Ahhhh—" he grimaced as it came out. "Take my balls."

I lifted them out. They filled my hand, like hairy peaches. He held my own hand holding them and made me squeeze, hard. He grinned. His fingers slipped to the shaft. It was shaggy, thick, and roped with big veins. He fisted back the loose hood that wrinkled over the great punctured helmet. "Go down on that, boy," he whispered. He pushed my head toward it. His fist began to move up and down. "You want it, don't you. It ain't the biggest you've ever had in your face. But it ain't the smallest either. Go one, kiss it for daddy. Ohhhh—" he moaned when my lips broke on the head and thrust into my face. "Cocksucker!" Smell of him, gamey, rich. "Oh, suck me, baby. Suck it hard, you two bit little bastard. Eat all the junk out from under the hood. Lousy cocksucker. No good cocksucker. Work on it, you dirty son of a bitch." I kneeled between his legs, clutching his hips. He filled my mouth, my head. His beating fist battered me. Was gone. And the piston plungered me.

He thrust his bare foot between my legs. I hugged his thigh and dog rubbed myself there, while my face bobbed on his lap. Then the under-shaft thickened on my tongue.

"... gonna shoot your brains out, cocksucker," he whispered hoarsely. "Here it comes ..."

Salt juice spurted, filled, flooded my mouth. Urgently I drank him.

His hips relaxed.

My pants were wet between my legs and getting wetter. He rubbed my hair, as I lay my head in his crotch, tonguing the wilting shaft.

"Hey," he said suddenly. "What the fuck are you doin'? Pissing in your pants?"

I nodded.

"Hey," he laughed. "That feels good all down my leg."

He lifted me off his dick by the hair.

"When I come, I always piss. It's like a supper long coming."

"Yeah?" he asked. "I can feel it running all over my foot." But he didn't push me away.

"You ever try that?"

"I will next time you suck me off," he laughed and let me nuzzle the sweaty flesh of his groin gleaming with my spit. "Hey, come on. Let's go." He stood, suddenly.

"Why?"

"Yeah. Come with me."

He left his hand on my shoulder as we walked out of the park. He'd put himself back in his pants but he didn't close his fly.

"Where we going?"

He looked down at me. "You don't got no place to stay. I figured you'd come up to my place. You can do me a couple of more times if you want. Anyway, it would be a place to stay for the night. Maybe even a few days." We turned out of the park. "What do you say?"

"Okay."

He squeezed my shoulder, then his hand dropped to his crotch again. "Jesus, I'm all hot again. I'll come five or six times a day, you know. When I was your age, I bet my dick used to get calluses, I pulled on it so much. Now—" He pursed his lips. "I gotta beat my own off maybe once, twice a day. That's all. I always seem to have enough ass around me, you know?"

Suddenly he thumbed his pecker out again. It sloped out.

"Hey—" I said. "There's somebody—"

"See. He's turning the corner." Red laughed. "Ain't nobody care about my cock except you." He was moving closer to the wall as we walked. He stopped and leaned against the brick. "Why don't you get down and work on that some more." It was stuck up now. "I just got an inkling of what you was like. Now I want to really see you hauling my juice on your knees."

He gave his stick a few long, slow strokes with his cradled fingers. "Go on, sucker. Nobody's comin'." His hand went in, and his balls came out. "A little air feels good down there. A

+ + +

She said:

"When you're in a forest, if you really want to see what's around you, you have to look at the space between the leaves."

Hours later, when we were standing beside the car, oaks and maples vaulting the road, the Delaware River and evening through one side and ferns and saplings and much mountain on the other, I realized what she meant. At once what had been a patterned screen gained depths and levels, and estimable distances. I am city, but all my summers and a handful of winters have been spent in green. I go camping, and have a fair command of which plant is which. Still, a revelation: for the length of my life I have misobserved an essential part of the world.

Joachim sat on the fender. His hair is shoulder length. He has pimples, and dresses in paisley and mattress ticking. "Oh, man." He sniffed. "What a hell of a place for a flat. Does anybody have any aspirin?"

Boots, bald and bearded, looks up from the hubcap. Another bolt careens around the rim, then centers. "Well, you'll have to hold on till we get there. Micah, how far do we have to go?"

Peggy answers for her, "It said twelve miles on the sign." Her southern accent is rich and sits well in all this afternoon greenery. And she, the tallest of the three girls,

+ + +

man needs to let his tools cool off. Stick that into your face again, son. You let your teeth tickle it just the way I like it."

I remembered the smell of him.

I remembered the taste.

I kneeled in front of him, took it, and he leaned into my face. "I'm gonna try that pissin' bit." And leaned again. This time catching the back of my head. "You don't mind a little piss? A butch little stud like you? It's the queens who get prissy. You'd probably lick my ass out if I let you." He laughed & locked his fingers in my hair. "Suck on it, kid. I'm gettin' it all ready. Baby, that feels good." Somebody walked by. They didn't see, maybe, because Red just turned a little to the wall. I didn't care. He buried himself in me. I felt it thicken. "You're really goin' wild down there. Oh, give it to me, cocksucker! You love that, huh? Bet ten men couldn't drag you off my rod." They couldn't have. "Oh, here it comes, you two bit bastard. Here—" The thickness erupted—"Ohhhhhhh—" and kept going. My mouth filled. And filled. Filled. I tried to swallow the bitter salts. Piss burst my lips, ran his pants, my face. He clutched my head, ground my face into his lap with bent knees: "Oh, man!" The shaft slipped from me, and he got his hand in there and massaged his crotch while he pee'd all over himself and rubbed my face against his streaming pork. At last he stood panting, wet hands on my shoulders. I rose from the pool around his feet, my knees soaked.

"Man!" He put his wet hand on the back of my neck. "That was a bitch." He looked down at himself, then pushed his works back into his fly. He fooled with his zipper, but couldn't get it together. "Fuck it." So we started walking. "Might as well leave it opened. I'm gonna get you down there again before the sun comes up." I put my hand into the waist of his pants, holding to his belt. The muscle of his flank worked on my knuckles as we walked. "Jesus," he said. "I gotta do that more often." He hefted his soaking crotch. "You know a couple of times a week I get so drunk I wake up in some doorway and I done pissed all over myself. If I'm gonna pull that sort of shit, I might as well enjoy it."

"I guess so."

"Hey," he shook my shoulder. "You know, I like you, kid."

"Why," I said. I didn't ask.

He shrugged.

"You swing on my tool like you like that. And that's what I like." After a moment he said, "You really like to suck, huh?"

"Yeah."

He nodded. "And there's two things in this world I dig: my mouth sucking on a bottle, and somebody else's mouth sucking on me."

The street sloped down to the river, and between the houses I could see water, lights, and Queens.

"I'm right in here." We turned into a warehouse fronting the docks. "I got the top floor." He was invisible before me: he was the sound of bare feet padding.

Light cracked the door.

The street lamps below flooded the girdered ceiling through huge windows. And I caught my breath.

The place was filled with great abstract sculptures. Stone.

Welded metal.

Wood.

"This is my shit," Faust said. "What I make."

I gazed around the forms. "Yeah?"

Plastic.

Wire forms.

Plaster.

Shapes hung from the ceiling.

Shapes sat on the floor.

Somebody was sleeping on the mattress in the corner; he rolled awake now, a big man lumbering to his feet full dressed in the half light, then lumbering in his boots towards us, fisting at his eyes. "Hey there, Red. What you been out doin'?"

"Hi, Bull." Which would have been my name for him too: a big bellied bronze haired galoot with a studded belt and tufts of hair coming through his denim jacket. He hooked a thumb in his pocket and glanced at me.

Red, long & angular, hefted his balls. "Joe here has been doin' me up somethin' fine."

"Oh yeah?" The big hand swung between his legs and got things into place. "I picked up that stone in the truck for you. It's downstairs. We'll bring it up when you want it." He looked at me again. "Cute kid."

Red nodded. "I'm gonna keep him here awhile. What you been doin'?"

Bull let a low slow grin twist his heavy mouth. "That little bitch of yourn' came up here a while ago."

"Yeah? You get any?"

"She fed me pussy for an hour," Bull drawled. "Before she got in the door and hello how are you, I had my hand under her dress." He made a fist with middle finger up. "She danced on that like a monkey on a stick. And then—" Bull stuck his tongue out & waggled it.

"Did you get your dick in it?"

Bull made a face. "You know I ain't interested in none of that shit. Long as you got a few cute kids around like him—" He winked at me.

Red grinned at me. "Bull's [been] eatin' pussy all day and probably ain't got his rocks off yet. You wanna swing on his meat for awhile?"

"Hey," Bull said, "the kid don't even know me—"

Red reached between Bull's legs and caught the crotch.

"Hey—" But he came forward.

Red pushed me. "I want to see you chew on that awhile. Bull's got a good stud on him and I want to see it stuck in your face."

Bull put his hand in my hair and pulled me down. His big, callused fingers fumbled the brass buttons on his fly. He groped out his mango sized nuts and the stubby red club flopped after it. It was thick as my wrist and the round head pushed from wrinkled skin.

"Give it to him wet and sloppy," Red said.

"Yeah?"

"Real wet," Red drawled.

Bull laughed. I was goin' for it when it spurted. I went back under the piss. Red caught me. He had a hardon too. Bull just laughed and pissed while I went after his balls. He bent his knees and ground it into my face; Red kept me from falling over. He was laughing too.

Red kept putting his hand around and trying to feel in my mouth where the head was giving and I nearly drowned twice. But finally Bull's bladder was empty and I was just workin' easy on stiff swollen tool. Red would

+ + +

Mirror and Lens

A series of five novels following the life and times of Ian Scorda during the Solar Revolution. Each volume will be between 70 & 80 [thousand] words. Actually it is a continuous work which at present I estimate will run between 375 and 400 thousand words.

In 2184, there are humans living throughout the solar system. The major concentration of the population is on Earth, Mars, and the Jovian Moon Ganymede, and [the] Neptunian moon Triton. The nearest stars have been explored as well as their planets, but interstellar travel is rare. A few people have returned, but having undergone some ineffable experience during the trip to the stars, they have become mystic wanderers on the worlds of our sun. They serve as a "chorus" for *Mirror and Lens*. It begins and ends with a dialogue between Ian and the wanderer, Joachim Faust; but the story concentrates on humanity.

Through the solar system there are many governments, communist, capitalist, monarchies of various strengths, fascist states, oligarchies. A new socio/politico/economic system has been proposed, and through spontaneous revolutions, it gains popularity and advocates through the worlds of the solar federation. It is an informed-anarchy, that is, an a-governmental system of life checked from becoming chaos by the fantastically efficient information dispersal that the technology allows. It is rather like Marshall McLuhan's concept of the "world-wide tribe"— although in this case it is a "worlds-wide tribe." *Mirror and Lens* tries to dramatize the technology capable of bringing it off, keeping it functioning and developing.

In collective societies, the Revolution takes place bloodlessly, but with personal tragedies for many. The changeover is a bit more prickly in capitalistic countries. In monarchies, the court intrigues range from comic to brutal; in fascistic states, the revolution breaks out into open war.

Over the fifteen odd years covered by *Mirror and Lens*, Scorda observes all of these changes from the inside, outside, as well as interesting places on the periphery. He himself vacillates between both sides, for a while tries to stay uncommitted, but eventually comes to side with the Revolution.

Mirror and Lens takes Scorda, the adopted son of a minor Martian government official, from his late teens into his early thirties, through his first marriage, separation, and into his second; the children of both are characters. The majority of the drama takes place in family structures, and the conflicts are between parents and children—first between Scorda and his own parents, finally between Scorda and his own fourteen-year-old son.

The machinating figures of the actual revolution move to the foreground or fade with news reports and word of mouth. In volumes two and four they become personally involved in the story. The progress of the revolution, however, governs everyone's lives. The characters come from all levels of society, bohemian, educated, illiterate, workers, middle class, entertainers, artists, scientists, academicians, as well as the political, military, and aristocrats that people most S-F novels.

The fifteen years of *Mirror and Lens* follows the Revolution from its inception to its conclusion; no side is awarded a total victory, but a truce is finally decreed during which there is a double society, the two existing intertwined with one another, but with the strong implication that another generation will see an almost total switch to the new system.

Like my previous trilogy, *The Fall of the Towers* (*Out of the Dead City, The Towers of Toron*, and *City of a Thousand Suns*), *Babel-17*, and *Nova*, the story rises out [of] the characters set against a series of baroque locations (in *Mirror and Lens*, it should go without saying that I want to plumb to far greater depths an entire interrelated panoply of ideas and psychological states—a depth commensurate with the scope). Here is [a] list of a dozen locations that will support some of the action of *Mirror and Lens*:

London

Mykonos

Ceylon

Mars City

The Gladiatorial School on the shore of the Martian Dust Sea

The Capital of Ganymede, Methrine

The David Glaciers of Triton

The Cave of the Winds in the caverns of frozen methane on Jupiter

The Royal Way, a strip of pirate dens, and the center of underworld smugglers among the asteroids

The gutted ruins of Kahrmon on Luna

The Space-field at Mars City

During the great New York fire

Due to the general popularity of series, I am asking $2000 per volume, $10,000 for the entire work. That is to be paid out as a $2500 advance on acceptance of this outline (and sample chapter), the rest to be paid $1500 on the acceptance of each of the complete manuscripts.

I feel I can reasonably have the work completed in 2 and a half years; so, to facilitate scheduling and avoid confusion, I will ask for a 3 year deadline. (Reminder: *Nova* was completed 6 months ahead of deadline. By and large, this is the way I like to work. After the publication of nine books, I feel it's safe to say this seems to be my pattern.)

+ + +

Mirror and Lens

Chapter one

The need for SF rose from the clash of levels of reality.

The juxtaposition of ideas: social SF.

The juxtaposition of objects: *Dune* et al.

The juxtaposition of words (objects)

The subject of SF is a particular perception of the world's texture, akin to what the French symbolists were trying to do, which so far has not been done in English.

Chapter two
Harness and *The Paradox Men*, and the attempt to develop the redupli-
cated plot.

Chapter three
More Than Human: setting the standards by which a life must be looked
at, in its intensity, et al.

Chapter four
Bester's attempt in *The Stars My Destination* to weld the two, texture
and form.

Chapter five
Attempts to forge the poem: Vance Aandahl, Bradbury, Katherine Mac-
Lean.

Chapter six
Attempts through material: Ballard—*Vermilion Sands*, the novels, the
New Thing.

Chapter seven
Some of the *New Worlds* writers in general, and what *New Worlds* has
meant to SF.

Chapter eight
The American exponents of the New Thing: Kurt Vonnegut; Cordwainer Smith; R. A. Lafferty.

Chapter nine
Zelazny and the double coin—suicide and immortality.

Chapter ten
Tom Disch's *Camp C*

+   +   +

stick a few big fingers in my mouth to get them wet and then work them
under Bull's balls. Bull moaned and shoved and thickened.
"Hey, Spade!"
I think I remember footsteps.

"Whyn't you hose that bastard too."

I heard a big laugh.

The sound of runners.

"Take dat bitch-buster in yo' han', Bull." The words came out like rock falling in chalk dust.

Just then Bull came, first spurt deep, slipped out, still coming on my cheek, and Red caught it and shoved it back in. Bull clutched my head; and the stream hit. I turned.

Bull was holding a black dick and playin' it in my face.

Jeans stuffed in the tops of scuffed boots, three inches of studded leather looped low around his black belly, naked except for a black captain's cap, the nigger grinned down at me with a hippopotamus' mouth full of big, yellow teeth. Thumbs in his pockets, he let Bull hose me down.

Red stuck his foot between my legs, and rubbed my own pecker with his foot. "Little son of the bitch is hung like a horse!" he exclaimed.

"Drink dis nigger's fuckin' piss," Spade drawled, reached out, grabbed my hair, and pulled me onto his dick while he got his balls out. He buried the black stake in my throat, sank himself into me again and again. "Eat dat thing! Eat me, cocksucker."

"Watchin' that little bastard work on Spade's fuck stick is gettin' me hot all over again." I heard Red say. "You suppose I could get into that ass of his?"

"You want some ass, you jam my shit hole," Bull said. "Nazi is gonna be here soon, and you know how he gets."

Spade plunged and plunged. Red rubbed my face, and tickled Spade's balls, then stuck his dirty hands in my mouth along with Spade's dick.

He rubbed his crotch—cock all stiff again—on the back of my head.

"Suck on the black bastard, boy. He looks good down there, swingin' on that nigger's bolt. You like that, nigger? You like that little white face down there on your black cock." Spade got real excited, now. Panting, he forced a long drink of come down my throat. Then he pulled out, his great shiny black rod still stiff.

"Man," Spade said, reaching for Bull's ass. "I heard you talkin' about getting your shit hole jammed." Spade grinned, pulled at Bull's belt. "Wrap your ass around my rod, boy. This black bastard's just getting' started."

Bull grinned and undid his belt.

Red cuffed the back of my head. "Come on. Let 'em fuck each other," he grinned, and we walked across the room. Red had his hand around my shoulder. I held onto his callused thumb.

We sat on the mattress, all warm and wet with pee. I nuzzle Red's gamey armpit.

"What you like best?" he whispered hoarsely, then his tongue ground my ear. "You like Bull piss, nigger piss, or mine?"

"Yours."

"Good," he laughed. "Cause you gonna get a whole lot of it before you get out of here." He licked my wet cheek.

"I suck off anybody you tell me to."

He pulled me closer. "Yeah. I thought you liked that. You're a good lookin' little guy. I dig seeing your face down there between some stud's legs, working on some nigger's great big black pecker, or getting a face full of piss. I know a lot of niggers with dicks big as Spade's." Red dug in his nose with his thumb, then sucked the snot off. "We gonna get along real good." He dug in his nose again. "You want some of my snot? You drink my piss, I bet you'd eat my snot." He shoved his fingers in my mouth. I sucked the salty coating from the blunt nub with its bitten nail. "Go on. Feed me."

I dug some stuff out of my nose and he sucked my finger. Then he took my hand in his and looked at it:

"You bite your nails bad as I do. You know, the first time I saw you, this afternoon in the park, you were in the little hall in front of the piss-house, diggin' in your nose and eatin' it. You didn't think no one was watchin'."

+ + +

Notes on *Nova*

Insert
　　Encounter with the patrolman outside of the "dope den" in the City of Dreadful Night.
　　Confrontation speech between Lorq and Prince

Things that could possibly be cut for *Cavalier*
　　Leo
　　Ashton Clark and explanations in general
　　The Tarot

+ + +

"I didn't care."

Red leaned over me with his mouth opened and stuck his tongue into my mouth. He filled up my mouth with his, pulling me to and lots of spit followed his tongue, which got me all hot again, and I rubbed my prick against his belly.

Red got his hand in my pants and rubbed my dick up and tickled my balls a while. He stopped taunting me long enough to whisper, "Hung like a fuckin' mule."

"Ain't as big as you."

"Ain't many people are."

He let me suck his tongue deep into my throat. He went back and pulled down my pants and let me rub off on his hairy belly. He stuck his hand in and made me come all over it; then he took his stick out and jerked himself off with my come. I watched his face.

His eyes closed, real tight.

His lips pulled back.

And shaking with the beating of his fist.

"... you want it? Suck on it now you little cock-sucker." And he pushed the back of my neck to make me go down.

I caught his fist against my mouth half a dozen times. Then he just held me there and fucked my face and filled my mouth with gout after gout of come. And I was swallowing: and the bitter went salt and began to flow.

So I let go my own bladder. And lay there sucking from his dick and peeing all over his chest. He laughed, "Pissed all over by a fuckin' horse."

Then we lay together and he held me tight and I held him tight and he panted into my neck with his dick up my leg and fingers digging my buttocks. And then we relaxed and he held my face in his hands and we licked each other's tongues and laughed, and lazied our tongues in each other's mouths till the horse reared and I clutched him and he held me and rocked me in his arms and gave me all of his big tongue in my throat.

+ + +

Historical background

The French poet Paul Verlaine had gained his reputation as France's most promising poet by his early thirties. At that time he married a sixteen-year-old girl named Mathilde, daughter of wealthy French parents. Even a successful poet is seldom rich, and most of their married life they lived at Verlaine's in-laws, whom he openly despised and often quarreled with.

In 1871 Verlaine received the first of Rimbaud's letters from Charleville, containing poems that were eventually to overshadow Verlaine's, "Les Poètes de sept ans," "Le Bateau Ivre." Verlaine invited Rimbaud to Paris, introduced the seventeen-year-old genius to his literary friends, including Victor Hugo. Rimbaud scandalized Verlaine's in-laws even more than they had been before. Eventually, after Verlaine & Rimbaud spent the winter together in London, Rimbaud, now 18, returned to Charleville, and Verlaine effected a reconciliation with his wife.

About a year later, after Rimbaud had written his long prose and verse series *Une Saison en Enfer*, Rimbaud once more wrote to Verlaine.

Mathilde's parents were on a trip, and Mathilde and Verlaine were alone in Mathilde's parents' house. No one knows exactly what transpired that afternoon, but after the three were alone for about an hour, Verlaine attempted to shoot Rimbaud in the wrist, for which he subsequently spent a year in prison. Mathilde finally severed the marriage, and Rimbaud left for Germany and eventually Africa, and never wrote again.

+ + +

Stories begun that *must* be finished

> Isis Descending
> Lines of Power
> The Girl in the Woods
> The Sadist

+ + +

Hell! Editorial introduction

Aldous Huxley makes the point in his introduction to the young Radiguet's *Devil in the Flesh* that, whereas musical prodigies are almost the rule, literary prodigies are comparatively rare. One area of literature in which this is not the case is speculative fiction. Isaac Asimov's first story appeared when he was 18; John Brunner's first novel when he was 17; Theodore Sturgeon's first story when he was 20. The list of SF writers who were in print before they could vote is impressive. *The Jewels of Aptor* was written when the author was 19. Though the age is not necessarily remarkable, such control of style and structure is rare at any age.* Due to the Ace format, from considerations of length, we were obliged to cut the book by a third at its original publication six years ago. We are happy to be able at last to reissue the book in its complete form.

*After *The Jewels of Aptor*, over the next two years Delany was to write the *Fall of the Towers* trilogy, and a year later, *Babel-17*, which won the Nebula Award of the Science Fiction Writers of America for best novel of the year, *The Einstein Intersection*, and most recently, *Nova*. Over half of his short stories have received anthology merit. Delany grew up in New York City's Harlem; he attended the Dalton Elementary School, the Bronx High School of Science, then City College where he was poetry editor of *The Promethean* for a term. He traveled for a year in Europe (where *The Einstein Intersection* was written). He is married to the poet Marilyn Hacker, who wrote many of the spells and inscriptions in *The Jewels of Aptor*.

+ + +

October 23rd, 1967

Just finished "Lines of Power"—a feeling of dissatisfaction there. From the commercial point of view, the story is over orchestrated, and hence—though all is necessary for the total statement—the opening movements are too slow. From the artistic point, the voice is too facile so it cannot deal with these at first extraneous seeming sections with the intensity that would illuminate them enough to compensate for the leisurely structure. I usually try to avoid a dichotomy between "artistic" and "commercial." Esthetic canons are esthetic canons and they apply in all cases, governing "entertainment" as strictly as they govern "art," but today I am intensely aware of at least the expediency of the distinction.

After I finished preparing "Lines" I went through the chapter of *Voyage, Orestes* that Doubleday had returned to me for reworking. At a four year distance, I was amazed that I had come as close to success as many times as I did. It was exhilarating to move back into the realm of a work with as much scope as *Voyage, Orestes*. The movement was so clear in my mind that the awkwardnesses fairly corrected themselves. I begin to see— well, I always saw, but now I have regained a sympathy with—what Tom Disch meant by aesthetic purpose. The chapter "In Praise of Limestone" was basically a transition chapter, and so presents difficulty in judging in itself. The only scenes whose focus resolved by the focus of an emotional statement are those with the mother, because they are the termination— or at least a suspension—of certain themes in the work; and the scenes with Snake in the village and in the pigeon store, because they introduce a new set of thematic concerns in the form of mysteries. All else in the chapter, including the "literary" sections, is transitional, having its beginnings earlier on in the book, nor does it reach a conclusion until later—I must inform Doubleday of this and hope that they take it into account when they pass judgment. Even so, I hope I've been able to rid the chapter of those surface annoyances that blurred [the] fine work of the finish. I hope I can maintain this enthusiasm. It will be the first thing I have done in a depressingly long time for which I will be able to have full aesthetic respect.

+ + +

People to contact:

Judy Merril
Bernie Kay
Virginia Kidd
Stewey Bernstein
Alex Panshin
Ted White
Joanna Russ
Ginny Carew
John Brunner
Bill Stribling

+ + +

Ars Poetica

One of the things Marshall McLuhan has brought back to us: the rules [of] the proper esthetic handling of any medium spring from the inchoate properties of the medium itself. Let us talk about the medium of written prose.

A creative writing class:

"We're going to talk about the problems of written communication. But first we need a common writing experience to examine. Take out your pencil and paper. For the rest of the period you may say anything you want to your friends—correction: You may write anything you want. Pass notes—gossip, question each other, offer answers. You can discuss anything you want, as long as you write down what you have to say; either personal, or of general interest. You may get up and move around to pass your notes."

The first ten minutes of the class were slow. But somebody at last passed a note. Somebody laughed. And more notes began to circulate. Somebody got up to write a suggestion on the blackboard. By the halfway point the class was writing away. Two or three times I had to chide them for breaking out in spoken words. By and large the class went politely and well.

At the next session:

"Now, what seem to be some of the specific problems of writing to communicate as opposed to speaking? Did our last session give you any thoughts on the nature of writing and how it differs from speech?"

Here is a digest of the points made by the class . . .

*   *   *

The two most powerful positive literary emotions I have gotten from literature: the emotional response to somebody breaking out of old strictures, perceptions, and mental poses (realizing the absolute spiritual necessity for such a break), to new insight. The other: a person tentatively tries to make human contact and finds it works.

+   +   +

Dear Roger,

Marilyn wants to use your story for the (hopefully) February issue of *City*. I've given a story to *F&SF* (the title is "Lines of Power") that, rather in the spirit of your pastiche of Cordwainer Smith, "The Furies," attempts a pastiche of your own work. I distinguish it from a parody, one) because it's an essentially a serious story, and two) because I tried to give the story inchoate merit so that the pastiche element is only ornamentation. The plot concerns a sort of future Hell's Angel named Roger . . . His last name is, well, something unpronounceable and Polish beginning with Z and ending with Y. The villain and narrator is an eccentric Negro demon just promoted to devil named Blacky who lives in a Gila Monster when he's not out doing dastardly things. The story is built about images from Spencer, Milton, and Pound, with a bit of heraldry. My motivations are, all & total, respect, admiration, affection, love for you; and a mild ironical intent to that critical fannish blather in which we are always turning up in the same paragraph. Though, with the publishing lag, the story probably won't appear for five or six months, but I thought I'd let you know. If the story ever appears in a collection, I promise to dedicate it to you.

+   +   +

Three letters to write:

John Brunner—general apology
Mike Moorcock—general query
Virginia Kidd—general niceness
Joanna Russ—oh, yes!

+ + +

The Journal—Milford SF con. 1967

There are days when I am very happy to discover who I am. Have been ill three days, in bed at Virginia Kidd's (in her bed, the hastily ordered chaos of her office around me) and kept having fever sweats even today. But by and large, I have been well. (I was so sick, it was, apparently, too tiring for me to manufacture the small neuroticisms I usually use to impel/impede day movement. I had first anger surge this morning when Katherine MacLean (and is there a writer here this year whose work I admire more) had the brass-assed chutzpah to wake me up at 8:00 AM to suggest I EXERCISE. Still, I want to write. How delightful. I am almost ready to go home from the conf. just to return to work. What a lovely, healthy impulse, it seems so right, I will probably be able to enjoy it even if I don't act on it.

+ + +

September 27, 1967

Here I am in Rifton, New York, staying with Jack and Phoebe Gaughan (hunting back through journal for a clean page to write on, since I don't want to interrupt the flow of "Lines of Power" any more than necessary). I've been writing well the week. This evening the Lupoffs are coming over for a Mexican dinner and all last night and day, I made chili, beans from scratch, the whole shmear in a great black plot that I am reheating now. [...]

This all started out to be a list of things to do for this evening since dinner seems to be my affair.

Rinse & marinate artichoke hearts
Make shrimp dip

Do something with the mushrooms
Grate Muenster cheese
Prod Phoebe into tortillas
Cut celery
Olives out
Grate cheese and shredded lettuce & douse with lime juice
Chill glasses for margaritas

+ + +

Draft of a Letter to "Lydia Stephenou"

Dear Miss Stephenou,

I was *ecstatic* to hear from you!

To many people, many times, I have said that I would like to get in touch with you. But I did not know DeLys had actually written you. My "message" to you has gone from mouth to ear to mouth to ear enough times to have gotten a bit garbled.

Let me clarify.

Just before I left Greece, the July before last, I spent an afternoon with Phil and Sarah during which I read your long narrative poem, "The Life, Times, and Topology of Yk" (do I have the title wrong? My apologies—it has been over a year). I read the literal translation you had made for Phil. I read about 10 pages of Phil's translations. The next afternoon I returned and for an hour or so I compared the Greek text & your translation (and Phil's).

I have been seldom so impressed by a work of art, and anything I can do to help get your work published and circulated, I do gladly.

The magazine that my wife edits is called *City*. Alas it is very small, with a circulation of about a thousand, and we cannot pay for manuscripts we publish, as most of the printing costs come out of our own pockets. If you would like to give us some of your shorter works, *City* would be very happy.

Much more important, however, I think there is a very good chance for your publishing "Yk" in full in an English magazine whose editor, Michael Moorcock, I have talked to at great length about the poem.

During [the] time I was with Phil & Sarah, I made notes on the poem—actually copied out the opening section of your translation.

+ + +

More structural notes:

Three visits to The Pit (call it something from out of Dante's *Paradiso*—maybe just call it Haven, or High Haven; somewhere work in Angels on High).

The first he meets [are] Vulcan and Fidessa (didn't occur to me that Mabel is Mab). Fidessa lures Blacky up for visit, during Walpurgisnacht, during which Sue gets raped by Vulcan (and Blacky makes the comparison between himself and Zal and Sue and Pit, about ages) during this visit.

III—First visit to Haven, meets Vulcan & Fidessa, almost falls in love with Fidessa. Discusses the incoming cable. There must be a certain amount of power [per] person. Don't want it.

IV—Mabel has already started laying the lines. Blacky is a little pissed. Argument begins. I told you we'd argue, says Mabel. Resolution, they don't have to use the power. Blacky: Well, okay.

V—Visit first from Pit & Vulcan. Sue & Pit hit it off with the throwing blade. Blacky watches the work from the balcony.
     Mab, maybe you were right.
     Visit from Fidessa that evening. Come up and watch the party. Bring a girl. He takes Sue.

VI—At the Walpurgis Nacht at High Haven. The chase among the clouds on the Bikes. The argument with Zal about the power lines, You have the power; I would fight, but I'm not crazy. Sometimes I feel crazy. Fidessa & Blacky. Zal discovers them. Zal & Blacky discuss "Burning." Vulk tries to rape Sue. Thence back to Gila Monster.

VII—The work continues. Description (set piece) of the Gila Monster at work.

VIII—Visit from Vulc and Pitt; they want to escape. Blacky says yes. Mabel says no. Blacky lets them stay. Argument with Mabel as the work goes on. We have the power; how the hell do you delegate rank & power?
     That evening the warning by Fidessa. Followed by

IX—An attack on the open cable. Zal & Blacky have discussed burnings in VI. Zal rides down the open cable—they've killed one person already. Mabel threatens to turn on current but Blacky runs out on the cable to do battle. Mabel says: I'll turn it on anyway. Stan agrees. Blacky jumps off. Zal goes up.

Up at High Haven. He confronts Fidessa. "When angels fall, hell is always waiting to catch them." The others will go into society. Picks up the ring back at the cable as the Gila Monster is filling in the trough.

X—Final paragraph. He was assigned to another Gila Monster. Maybe a conversation with Mabel, or/and a poetic evocation of the Gila Monster scouring the nets, and his eyes filled with the fires of burning men & women.

Final argument with Fidessa:
Doesn't Zal's death make you want to change your life.
Did your wife's death.
Sometimes I wonder if I'm on the side of the Angels.

+   +   +

Tuesday 11th
Wednesday 12th   Come back from Sea Cliff
                   Rehearse
Thursday 13th   Record at Ivan's
Friday 14th   Write in the morning
                   Rehearse in afternoon
                   Pick up arrangements in the evening
Saturday 15th   Write in morning
                   Music in afternoon
Sunday 16th   The same.
Monday 17   Monday—9–12—I work out arrangements
                   1–5 We work out arrangements
                   6—We record—work with Donna.
Tuesday 18—   Have hunted up musicians
Wednesday—   Get together with them
Thursday—   Record voice and music of whole production to show
                   Bernie

+ + +

Songs
of
the
HEAVENLY BREAKFAST

Da-da
My Uncle Used to Love Me But She Died
Sapphires
Dawn Passage
Jamie

English Biography

Samuel R. Delany was born in New York City on April Fools' Day nineteen-forty-two. He grew up in New York City's Harlem. His early interests included mathematics and music. But during high school he won over half a dozen writing awards. His first speculative novel *The Jewels of Aptor* was written when he was nineteen. At City College he was poetry editor of *The Promethean* for a term. Over the next two years he wrote the *Fall of the Towers* trilogy. A month after his 23rd birthday he began *Babel-17*. "The first page of part two was in the typewriter when I decided to take off for Texas. I hitched around the American South, worked for a while on shrimp boats on the West Gulf Coast. At the end of the summer, I came back, finished the book, and in October took off for Europe with a friend I'd made in Texas." For a year he wandered around Europe "from Paris to London by way of Istanbul," supporting himself by playing and singing American folk music in cafés and nightclubs. During this time he wrote *The Einstein Intersection*. He returned to the States to find *Babel-17* nominated for the coveted SFWA Nebula Award. It won. Soon after, *The Einstein Intersection* appeared to rave reviews. His most recent full-length novel, *Nova*, will be issued in the States in the fall of '68. Mr. Delany is also the author of several distinguished novelettes and short stories, among them *Empire Star*, "Driftglass," *The Star-Pit*, and the controversial "Aye, and Gomorrah." He is married to the American poet Marilyn Hacker. They live in the East Village.

+ + +

Seven Reasons Why I Should Be Pope.

I think that [I] would be a better pope than Robert Silverberg.

1) If Robert Silverberg can be pope, why can't I?
2) Joan has already established a precedent.

3) So I could establish an order of dancing nuns who would work their way from Iowa to the Vatican like Ruby Keeler.

4) There's always the Manichaean and the Arian heresies.

5) M would not miss any ecumenical council meetings because of prostate trouble.

6) The sixth one is obscene that has to do with that funny chair they use during the coronation ceremony.

7) So I could make Joe, Edwin, Harry, Russell and Link cardinals.

+ + +

Write something.

My head feels like half my brain has been pickled.

We are staying, Marilyn and I, in Joe Soley's back room. A cluttered, overheated apartment. I want to be somewhere else. The people are delightful & friendly. My mother lives a block away. I see very few people outside business. I am not really writing—hence this.

Last night we went down to Mr. Keyes where Judy was having a small party—Kit Reed and husband, an actor from *The Edge of Night* & wife, as well as Gene Stockman, who revealed in the middle of things that he used to be Blakesley of London on *Captain Video*, which made the evening. A delightful blonde dancer who didn't really start to open up until he had his coat on, but then began to talk. Mark Heighfli, sans sleep for five days, came up and Marilyn has decided he isn't so bad. He isn't. I get points for not asking him about what's happening with my Doubleday novel.

+ + +

Jason Scorda, Xero Stoan
Aluvia Scorda, Jane Scorda
Lanya Monos and Family
Wren Baines
Ty Yen is there, as the leader of the opposition. Rank is expected but never arrives.
Talk of "Gus" and Ana Marie among the young.
(The painting of the Pearl Thief.)

Hang the night with the walls of Scorda.

These high windows look over the parks, across to where they are building.

"The plans—" rasps, and comes up out of it, laughing, "—must be laid before you start to construct." And they turn and laugh on the terrace.

"What kind of building will it be, Xero?"

"I want a building that's—I call it organic. One of the things the plans include is possibility of change any time during the construction. And even after it's finished. Now we can include the random in a project of such dimension."

+   +   +

Having rounded page 50, it's time to do some work on the structuring of *Faust*.

Chapter One: Riders of the Scorpion: Write in the girl looking in the portal. The dog returns with the girl's wallet in which is her picture and Faust's.
Chapter Two: Hall of Mirrors: Write in the encounter with the young Southerner who just got into town and can't get no pussy. Write in a second encounter with the young man when the Captain leaves the Labyrinth.
Chapter Three: Faust in Italy: simply adjust to fit what's gone so far.
Chapter Four: Homunculus: same as above. Lift speech from Sambo in V and place here.
Chapter Five: The Stones of Saint Mark: Write in the encounter between Nig & Dove, and the Southern boy who can't get no pussy.
* * * Finish Benny's tale: followed by Faust's speech. Followed by a lyric passage from Kirsten's point of view in which she has Gunner, perhaps in the church balcony.
Chapter Six: *Walpurgisnacht*: the Southern boy breaks into Faust's studio, takes drugs, and goes through a distorted surreal nightmare where the characters of the book perform [in] the great church.
Chapter Seven: The Scorpion at Sea: Faust comes back, with Catherine, kicks the young man out. He meets the Captain, who promises him Kirsten and Gunner, and a job. The young man walks around, meets Nazi, whom he talks to about what's coming. Nazi kills him, goes to the boat, and takes his place. "You'd rather have me?"

+   +   +

The warm surge up through the belly and down the thighs as you start to piss.

As opposed to the much more intense relaxation that rolls the body, following much the same paths but going so much further and wreaking a havoc of tremors and tension releases when you come.

+   +   +

1

The color of bell metal.

Longer than a big man's foot, thick as a woman's wrist. Veins make vines in low relief, below the wrinkled hood. Dark fingers climb the shaft, drop to the dark hair like steel wool, move beneath the canvas to gouge the wrinkled sack that spills his palm (and it is a big hand) climb the shaft again.

There is little light.

What's there comes in gold bars through shutters. Water lisps and whispers outside. The cabin sways, falls, rises. There is a wind out to sea, that means. But here at port it is a clear evening. The dog on the floor scrapes the planks with his claws.

+   +   +

Template for "Faust"

Chapter One:

The devil (never named, but I'll call him Sam) comes seven times with Kirsten and Gunner.

The dog brings in Faust's wallet. They look through to find the two pictures of the woman. There is a hundred and fifty dollars.

Leontyne & Catherine.

They return the wallet.

Faust requisitions him to destroy the two women to end his impotency.

The museum, with Leontyne.

Faust studio—the acid trip.

Small orgy.

The Museum

The Church

Faust's Studio

+ + +

1   The Boat
2   The Cave
3   Faust's Studio
4   The Cave
5   The Museum
6   Catherine
7   The Chinese Girl
8   The Acid Head (Night's opening)
9   The Sirens—Kirsten, Leontyne, the Chinese Girl
10   The Gang
11   Faust's studio (Faust and Leontyne)
12   The Church
13   Faust's Studio destroyed
15   The Boat

+ + +

The Inn

The name of the tavern is the Labyrinth. It's the hangout of a den of criminals, headed by Bull.

Hall of Mirrors

Discussion between Sam and Bull

The story of Bull & his men.
The story of Faust's youth.
The story of Faust & Helen
The story of Faust & Catherine
The story of Sam & the children.

"Belongs to a guy who used to come in here a lot. Faust—you ever heard of him? (The privacy that notoriety affords.) People used to come and ask for him, a couple of times photographers from magazines. They didn't like the place much. Too many mirrors."

+ + +

Faust studio—

The seduction of "what's happening" is that it blinds you to "what has happened," which is what has caused "what's happening" to "happen." He who understands what has happened has total control over of the phantasmagoria of today.

The progress of the corruption of wisdom.

I began as a medical doctor. Something of an academic prodigy, I went into college at fifteen, graduated at eighteen, and went into medical school. I did well, but by the time the prospect of interning arose, I knew that the human part of doctoring was beyond me. I say it glibly. The realization came to me with great pain, a great feeling of failure, and it was perhaps the first time that I really doubted myself. At any rate, I retreated back to college, and picked up my academic career.

> I leave you free to choose whatever lie you think worthiest to be the truth.
>
> —Valéry / *My Faust*

+   +   +

Faust's studio

Leontyne and Faust

It is the fact that we don't lose either will or consciousness during orgasm that makes us gods.

Evil is self-conscious ignorance.
Good is self-conscious wisdom.
Good is always fascinated by evil because it represents another choice.

+   +   +

Your friends will judge you by the intention of your best work and the achievement of your worst.

+   +   +

Baird Searles, director of drama and literature at WBAI-FM, is producing a series of dramatic readings of modern science fiction stories, designed to show the literary merits of s-f. The series began with Theodore Sturgeon's "The Skills of Xanadu" followed by Roger Zelazny's "The Doors of His Face, the Lamps of His Mouth." These programs will include Arthur C. Clarke's "The Star" and Mervyn Peake's "Titus" stories. Currently in preparation is Samuel R. Delany's *The Star-Pit*, directed by Daniel Landau, with Randa Haines, George Harris, Jerry Matz, and Phoebe Wray. This radio adaptation will be broadcast in February, [and] will be narrated by the author.

+ + +

Background for the whole business. 22nd century, Solar society. Cities on Mars. Cities on Earth.

New York, Bellona, Triton 1, Triton 2, Triton 3

New York 1, Triton 2, Bellona 3, London 4, Mars Desert 5, Triton 6, Mykonos 7

Rock & Roll group, the fortune teller
The Sadist
A Circus.
The Jewel thieves—a society of thieves of which Arthur is a part, whose password is a jewel.

Jasper
1   Maud and Arthur
       New York

Three major locations: Entertainment Area.
The Cloisters, only it is now a museum of comparative religions.
Slum area of the city with pack of pickers from Mars.
Sutton place, with the city aglitter in the glass tower.
The sadist from Mars. A collector

+ + +

Table of Contents for

We, in Some Strange Power's Employ, Move on a Rigorous Line
1. "Corona"
2. "Driftglass"

3. "The Star-Pit"
4. "Dog in a Fisherman's Net"
5. "We, in Some Strange Power's Employ, Move on a Rigorous Line"

<u>Notes</u>

(Lines/Power) Written for, inspired by, would not have been written had he not written, and is dedicated, with reverence, to Roger Zelazny.

(Driftglass) This was written during a stretch I lived on St. Mark's Place while the start of the summer influx of hippies swarmed to the East Village. Never been to Brazil. But I'd like to go.

(Cage of Brass) was a cover story, done for Fred Pohl's *If*. I suppose every writer faced with a cover to form a tale around, has the initial reaction that his cover is just the most uninspiring bleakness imaginable. Mine was an exquisite pop art rendering of a lot of rocks, a black sky, stars, mist, with something mustard colored and vaguely obscene growing beyond the horizon. Conflict, action, and imbalance, which are, alas, the stuff of stories, were just not to be seen. Faced with such a landscape, I decided to write a story about the most colorful city I know.

(Corona) The psychologically doomed are the focus of tragedies. The sociologically redeemable people comedies. A compassionate vision may encompass both. Hence Lee and Buddy in one story. Both were inspired by one person, a blonde boy from Alabama, unable to write his last name or read mine, who'd spent most of his adolescent years in prisons and mental hospitals. (My own experience with both can be measured in months.) During the two weeks he stayed with me, he played pop music constantly while narrating the template for the incidents here, including the bizarre series of prepubescent suicide attempts. Why put all this in an SF story? The medium is the best for integrating and delineating the technical and human, so meshed today.

(Dog in a Fisherman's Net) The largest of the South Western Cyclades, where I passed much of the winter '65–'66, is also one of the least populated. It has a military airfield, but the Greek soldiers are only allowed in town five at the time. At the tip of the C shaped island, at Polonia, are clay and obsidian mines that have been functioning—on and off—for the past four thousand years. January saw me moved to Mykonos, an island famous for its international colony. I'd started the story on Milos, I finished it with the nostalgia (for what had happened the week before) and distance of another island.

(The Star-Pit) In 1942, Robert Heinlein published "Waldo." The story has become a classic example of S-f become reality. Much less conspicuously, that year, I was born. Two short of a couple of dozen years later, I was in a garage in Butler, New Jersey helping tear apart the rear end transmission of a GM diesel truck. Tracking across the ceiling were two mechanical claws that raised & lowered on cables. The fourteen-year-old red headed grease monkey called them waldoes. He had never heard of the Heinlein story. I began the following story that evening.

(They Fly at Çiron) The hero of this tale, of course, owes its inspiration to the creations of Robert E. Howard. The plot was lifted from an incident in the first volume of Merejkowski's *Christ and Antichrist* in which a soldier assigned the execution of the pretender to the Eastern Roman Empire recognizes his prisoner.

Jasper
Agate
Opal
Garnet
Topaz
Beryl
Tourmaline

Three major locations:
      Entertainment Area
      The Cloisters — the museum of comparative religion
      Hell's Kitchen with the pack of knives, of Arthur

The Sadist

Agate
      Begins with Henrietta, Countess of Effingham
      The Honorable Clyde Effingham

+   +   +

Dear *Australian Science Fiction Review,*

It's good to see such a collection of criticism, and it is certainly heartening to hear the positive reactions to the *ASFR* that occasionally come past on this side of the equator and the I.D.L. An editorial problem you do have is, that while the critical intent is always high, alas, the performances don't always [pass] muster. I suppose one learns the particular eccentricities of the reviewers after a bit. I have, sadly, only seen some seven issues. But occasionally I am three quarters of the way through a review or critical piece before I am aware just where up and down on the critical scale the reviewer is sitting as he declaims his praise or damnation. Occasionally, I feel the standard introductory paragraph of a review [should] be able to précis to the form, "This is a good (or bad) book because—" and the quality of what follows the "because" lets the reader know where the reviewer is at in relation to the book, e.g. "... because I read it all the way through in an hour and a half," defines one kind of "goodness" while, "... because the cogent analogy of the story with the current plight of the migrant fruit pickers of Southern France was both moving and incisive," defines another, as "... because, while he has nothing new in the line of ideas, the author's facility with language and storytelling was a delight"—defines still another. No matter how subjective the review becomes from there on, the reader knows at which level the reviewer has chosen to climb into the work. This sort of clarity is the kind of thing an editor can push for without (hopefully) stepping on the individual analytical talents of his reviewers.

I wish you all the best. The review is managing to become one of the more fascinating forces in the dialogue of current SF.

Sincerely,

Samuel R. Delany

+ + +

Everybody's problems can usually be put in the form:

Here I am, __ years old, and I haven't done __.

I don't understand human relationships.

And: Perhaps my parents were right ...

+ + +

Perusing *ASFR*, I find in the brain box odd hairs laying themselves anent the porcelain floor of my mind beneath harsh light, ready to be split.

Reviewing and criticism—if they are "arts," where is the art in them? One of the few times in my life when arguing with somebody ever changed a mind: a young author was preparing the manuscript of his first book, a book length critical study of a much older and established writer, recipient of many awards, a writer who had made an undeniable contribution to his field of literature, but had also been the focus of much adverse commentary, by people who thought they detected unpopular political ideas in an essentially fictional *oeuvre*. The young author freely admitted that the subject of his book had afforded him personally much pleasure, as entertainment, as well as intellectual stimulation, and had been a shaper of his own philosophy. I was quite anxious to see the book because the material and the context would appear to offer a critical field day for the author. What I found, when I read the manuscript, after an introductory chapter of primarily biographical content, [was that] the book consisted of a careful plot summation of every story the subject had written, in chronological order, followed by what, in our critic's opinion, were the structural flaws in the plots. Then a concluding chapter with some rather dismal predictions about what he thought the author's next book would be.

All of which brings me to question: Why write it? Why read it? The particular question that this incident raised, was: Why write a book-length piece of criticism?

The answer I came to after what seemed days of discussion with said author, was: the purpose of criticism is that the reader can go (or return) to the work being criticized with more enjoyment than he would have if he had not read the criticism.

Granted a

+ + +

Thanks muchly for the space you've devoted to me.

Reading a review of one's own work is an extremely odd experience. The time between writing and reviewing for myself has never been less than a year and a half—that record for promptness, by the by, was set with Foyster's review of "Driftglass" in number #— and the lapse has been as much as four years. The effect is rather like someone running up to you and earnestly beginning to tell you about something particularly witty, or absurdly gauche, you said at last year's New Year's Eve party. You know you did it, but for the life of you, you can't remember this fellow being there.

By and large the distance is a good thing. Both extravagant praise and damnation seem unreal, irrelevant, and ultimately make little impression. What does hit home is when a critic says "the author does such and such," or "such and such is in this book," and, yes, it is something I did try to do or put there. Then there is a great surge of pride and a feeling of success. Conversely, when the reviewer sees something that I expressly wanted to avoid, or thinks I'm trying to do one thing when I wanted to do another, there is a feeling of failure, I find myself depressed by the review, even at a distance years from the work under examination. After all, writing is essentially communication; and successful writing communicates what the writer had in mind.

The most useful review—and of course I am biased toward that review which helps my work on whatever I am writing at the time I read it—is the thoughtfully considered one that more or less follows the form, "the author is trying to do __ in this book, but he fails (or succeeds) because __." It is helpful to me as a writer when it is said about my own work; it is helpful when I am selecting what I want to read when it is said about others. (Though, of course, part of this is because I read as a writer interested in the way other writers have handled the inextricably meshed problems of art and entertainment.) This is, alas, the hardest type of review to write, and there will probably always be too few of them. But I am thankful for each one that comes along.

For a quick example: "The author is trying to tell a good, swift, colorful adventure. But the *actions* of the characters have so little psychological consistency that the reader must constantly stop to reform his picture of the characters with the result that the flow and the pace of the adventure are seriously slowed." There are many many writers whose aim is to write adventure and who would take such a review to heart. Such a review, presented sincerely and without posing, does everybody good.

+   +   +

Note on the science in S-f.

Note a heading over a review of Jack Vance, "The Science in S-f." An interesting subject that recently netted me what must be by now a classic experience for the S-f writer. In May of '67 I finished a novel that, among other things, discussed a series of stable elements with atomic numbers well over 100. I postulated that stability (which almost totally breaks down at number 99) would recommence near about atomic number 300. My theory was based on a very non-rigorous perusal of "hyperon" data, some of which went back to 1959. Particle physics is a field notorious for completely revising itself about once a month. So I should have known my data would be outdated by '67; still: at the NYcon this Sept I was discussing said theory with Harvard physics instructor Sid Coleman. Sid allowed as how the idea of high number stables was interesting but demonstrated pretty quickly that my idea of hyperon nuclear-energy transference just wouldn't hold up. Two months later out came the news of the synthesis of high-stable (well, comparatively stable) 256. (I searched the article for mention of hyperon nuclear bonding, but Sid was right; the great lump of the nucleus was glued together with pions, just like you and me.) Now to revise the book (which will not appear from Doubleday until August '68) I would have to rewrite perhaps five sentences to bring the matter up to date with the information available—say two months ago. I don't intend to do it.

The reason is a bit complicated:

Even the most "poetic" S-f writer is probably a good deal more scientifically informed than the average man on the street. One of the historical uses that S-F will be put to, I'm sure, is a way of measuring the progress of the dispersal of scientific knowledge among the intellectually informed. How exciting it would be if we had as much S-F from the time of, say, Roger Bacon, as future historians will have from the time of Bertrand Russell! How much light it would throw on the intellectual tenor of the times, telling us what the ordinary intellectual considered probable, considered possible. For this reason, I think the composition date (always dutifully placed on all my manuscripts and dutifully removed by all editors) is important rather than publication date.

Larry Niven has a similar anecdote about his first published story written in June '64, "The Coldest Place," that has a sort of a twist having to do with the fact that the coldest place in the solar system is not the frigid wastes of Pluto, which is large enough to have the faintest atmosphere and hence keep a respectable number of degrees above zero Kelvin, but rather the dark side of Mercury, the planet closest to the sun; Mercury being too tiny to have any atmosphere at all—or so it was feasible to think up till August '64, when it was discovered Mercury did have just the slightest gaseous envelope after all. The story was published in December. The point, however, is that, though the story is "obsolete," it is not invalidated. "The Coldest Place" essentially asks the question, "What is a man?" in a way redolent with poetic irony. And I respond to it even with all of its (now) outdated science. A scientifically "inaccurate" (as opposed to scientifically illiterate or merely totally unbelievable, which is something else) story as soon as it's written simply becomes an historic document in man's progress from ignorance to knowledge.

One of the attitudes I've always personally deplored in S-F is the cliché, "technological progress means dehumanization and loss of freedom." Misuse of technology is what causes dehumanization, the same way that the misuse of politics, economic force, or any social force causes it. For this reason I always try for reasonable accuracy in the science of my stories; and I've never put any hard science in a book or tale without checking on it first.

The "science" section in *Babel-17* that John Foyster got so upset about was a dramatization of Frederick Kantor's rather brilliant solution to what was considered a classically unsolvable problem—up until 1965; the solely internal determination of location from within a free falling system. It's a problem that classical relativity maintains it is impossible to solve. 22-year-old Kantor discovered his ingenious & much lauded solution (particularly beautiful because it uses nothing more complicated than the math a high school senior might expect to learn in his first month of solid geometry) two months before I wrote the section. Within physics circles concerned with such things, it was quite hot news at the time. But that was '65. The book wasn't published, if I remember, until April '66. Even so, months after publication, I was receiving congratulatory letters from physicists, who, upon recognizing the rather well known problem, assumed the solution was mine! That, I suppose, merely comments on the dispersal speed of scientific information through this country. (I'll grit my teeth and say nothing of the time it takes for such information to get to Mr. Foyster. Well, he says he only skimmed the book.)

Hey, am I doing something in as bad taste as bridling at a review? Oh well. My apologies. Passing thoughts.

+ + +

Ideas for "Quest."
A tarot deck, in which four players play a simplified game of tarot Whist with the trumps always trumps.
The board is set up with four mirrors.
The highest card played gets that number of moves. Whoever plays a trump gets to pick a fortune card, declaring whether he will read it right side up or in the mirror.
He who *lead*[s] trumps gets to declare fool's high or low (as opposed to who first trumps a trick).
To take with a page means ten ahead.
Put someone back 1, 2, 3, 4.

+ + +

Warsh
Wakoski
Waldman
Kyger
Hacker

Berrigan
Clayton Eshleman
Tom Veitch
Ron Padgett

+   +   +

The hero, a young orphaned juvenile delinquent—
The background.
Society of thieves
Guild of singers
Jonathan Faust

+   +   +

Prism and Lens
   Prism, Lens, Mirror
   Mirror, Prism, Lens

Ian Scorda

The First Solar Revolution:

2373   it begins.

Vol I   73–78   –18
Vol II   78–81
Vol III   81–84
Vol IV   84–87
Vol V   87–90   –35

First of all postulate some historical events.
What do you need?

Monarchy
Communists
Fascist
Republic
Oligarchy

Mars—the oligarchs of Mars
The Terran Republic
Ganymede, Monarchy
Triton, Fascist
The Moon, Luna, and
the artificial worlds of Demos & Phobos, and China

+ + +

The Federation of Martian Oligarchies. The Polis of Bellona. The Polis of New Canberra, the Polis of Glaise.

Bellona: an urban complex.
Part of the Communist complex—the Triplanetary Collective [with no one there] with a base on Mars
Aries is the
The playground on the outskirts of Bellona.

The foundation of building that is completed in the third volume, and destroyed in the last.

(To use the painting of R. Pious' "The Thief"—which Ian is younger than in the beginning, and slowly ages around it)

For "Stoan"—"The plans must be laid before you start building."

The brilliant young man to Ian, "Their lives are about each other."

+ + +

Prism, Mirror, Lens

The problem now is to outline the 500,000 words of the book.
The Colosseum, in its foundations
Ian Scorda over 17 years and the solar revolution.

Vol. I
The foundation of the Colosseum
Meets Rank at the party given by his father, Jason
The birth of Sam

Vol. II
He enlists in the forces with Rank
Disillusioned with Rank he goes completely illegal

Vol. III
He picks up the pack.
Some big deal after which he decides to show up his father

Vol. IV
The completed Colosseum
Rank and [Ty Yen] both demand his help

Vol. V
First problems with Sam
The Colosseum is demolished
Possible solution of problems with Sam

Ian's four lovers.
    Rena—intellectual, alive, rebellious
    Saline—very much a thing of expediency, whom he treats abysmally, uses much as an object.
    Denny—a boyfriend gradually aces out Saline.
    Quilla—the artist whom he moved out from Denny's on

+   +   +

to isolate a fragment from the infinite and eternal.

+   +   +

That the mind starts to die quietly in the head at about twenty-five. But habit keeps the consciousless body going.

+   +   +

Wound the autumnal city.

Beyond port, tower, and parks and museums, throngs from late theatres across Sovereign Plaza, beyond the Cage, shot with markets, Ian ambled with the divergence of Bellona's lights deviling his green eyes. Through a puddle: mud tongued the red grit dusting his boots. The wire fence by the torn earth meshed night. (This youngster's aloneness is a huge thing in from his eyes ...)

A brown boy, and the brown burned red. Eighteen and the veins were already heavy over arms and big hands. Gold nests of hair on wrists and chest: on his head, brown and tightly curled. A broad face with ramped cheek bones, hints of epicanthi. A solid neck. He tried to move easy; and moved primitive. Ian played his hand on the wire and gazed in the quarter mile tear: rusty rock. Water. Three bulldozers. Two beds of concrete, one here, one way over there. The foundation diggings for the Bellona Colosseum: a wound widening. Ian thought about the cold. Windless, the evening had seemed mild even though breath clouded. He'd left the battery medallion off his jacket. The cloth would be enough ... Later, the temperature/time lights on the bank had blinked 35°/10:33. Both informations astounded him. So cold and so late ... Now that he had walked half an hour, the cold had blades in. If you relax, blood flows freer than if you scrunch. He tried to let his shoulders hang.

Hey. Steps here, leading into the dig. The gate was ajar. He left off his trivial questioning of reality, gazing.

Across was another stairway up. Part of his mind's adolescent burble, seeking symmetries and testing imbalances, wondered if the other gate were open. He had never walked that side of the foundation. He did not want home.

So, sideways, through, and started the steps. The first dozen: rough cement. Second: a jerry-rigged metal stairway—the rail broken from the bottom newels. Iron dirt beat his heels; the crosswalk lit back the rhythm of doubt and ponder. (The unexamined life is not worth living. Yeah ... But it won't stay still for me long enough to see anything, even. What am I doing here? I mean, is any of this real, the way an idea begins and forks and shoots and bends too fast like branches on the frozen water.) Third: a wooden ladder that felt more solid than the steel; grabbed to steady; and the rungs were colder.

Ian was halfway across when they came.

Suddenly he grew a shadow. And it grew longer. He turned. The light pulled harsh laces of pain across his face. Fear was big as his heartbeat. No; I'm not going to run, because those are only news stories and people's hysterical stories—

They dropped, burning.

Then he whirled, ran. Trying to stop: Fascination turned him back, dancing. His boot heels clicked the concrete and they were burning: two.

His mouth was filled with something [that] wouldn't let him cry out. It was his tongue.

[sequence continues]

+ + +

Wednesday 12:30 at Avon

+ + +

I   *Capricorn in Ascendance*
II   *Archer*
III   *High Aries*
IV   *Gemini*
V   *The House of the Crab*

Locations
   The Oligarchs of Mars
   Polises of Bellona, New Canberra, Glaise
   The Terran Republics
   Ganymede—monarchy
   Triton Fascist
   The Socialist Satellites
        Moon, Phoebus, Demos, & China

Capricorn in Ascendance '76
1 The Foundation of the Colosseum—(Joachim Faust)
2 The Party (Lenya and family—Rank expected—Rill—Ty Yen)
3 Courtship of Lanya
4 Meets Ty Yen at last
5 Marriage (move to Triton)
6
7 First mixed idyl
8
9
10
11
12
13
14
15 Pass by the asteroids, but Lanya won't let them stop.
16
17

18

19

20 The birth of Sam on Triton

21

22

23

24

25

Archer '79

1

2

3

4 Enlists with Ty Yen

5 Lenya & Ian break up

6 Illegality—Selene

7 Ian transferred from Fascist to Socialist State.

8

9 Seline—illegality

10

11, 12, 13 Rill—with discussions on Art-Politics, his unfaithfulness to Seline

14

15

16

17

18 Seline and the leader of the pack

19 Breaks with Ty Yen

20 Goes completely illegal. Attempts to re-est with Lenya now that family
is dead. She says no.

21

22

23

24

25

High Aries '81

1 Into the asteroids

2 With Seline

3

4

5 Joaquim Faust, run into by accident.

6 Preys off Earth & Mars.

7

8

9

10

11 Fist fight with Dark and wins Denny.

12 Denny enters

13 Quick news of Rill's successes in the "flower world"

14

15 The scheme that causes his father disgrace

16

17

18

19 The foundations of the Colosseum—the building complete.

20 Confrontation with his father; rage and fury—it is his uncommitted-
ness that hurts Jason

21 Rank demands that Ian put his power at their disposal. He betrays them
too. Rank should look very sympathetic in this encounter.

22

23

24 Saline fights by self.

25 Ian raging.

Gemini '84

1 Rill and Ian on Earth

2

3

4 Saline, Denny: Sam returns just then.

5 On Earth Rank tries [to] induce him back to the Pack.

6 Sam and Rill and Ian

7

8 Officially made Agent.

9

10

11

12

13 Exit Denny with first bit of doom prophecy.

14

15

16

17

18

19

20 With Lanya, who has remarried, is content for son to go with him.

21

22

23 Truce on Earth return of son.

24

25

The House of the Crab '87

1 The family of Agent Ian Scorda trying to track things down

2

3

4

5

6

7

8 He dons the light again to fight and vanquish his old enemy Dark and wins.

9

10 He meets his father on the moon.

11

12

13

14

15 The Colosseum is blown up.

16

17

18 Letter from his father.

19

20 Reconciliation with Ty Yen, revealing the existence of the bomb planted there 15 years ago.

21

22 He gets back his son.

23
24
25

Subplots

Capricorn—Basically a jet set sort of novel, the figures whom they try to model themselves after are the child count and countess from Ganymede aristocracy, are often in their part scooting around the system. Several times the royal couple are attacked. The child of the couple is born almost at the same time as

Archer—In the opening movement, the count & countess, comes the news, have been attacked by the people in light, and the countess and the baby killed.

Aries—When he goes to see the Colosseum, he meets the mad count.

Gemini—When Lanya remarries it is to the count. Rill makes the point— "Were you any less mad than he was?"

Basically, *Gemini* and *House of the Crab* deal (with humor and lightness) with the problems of being married to a brilliant but dizzy [...]

In *Archer* he has to be introduced to the "flower people" who are grubby imitations of the set he ran with. There is not the same desire to imitate since he has seen the real thing.

In *High Aries*, the light pack, Rill uses them to "clear the street" for a "flower world reading"

At the end of each volume a good healthy selection of journal entries.

The architect for the Colosseum appears briefly at the party. Major figure in volumes two & three, and equally brief party sequence volume five. Xero Stoan

A transportation strike
A power blackout

A political assassination
A race riot
A 300,000 people march

The commune and who & why.

+ + +

Jan 1, 1968 — 12:00 and a few seconds
  Looking over my old journals — it is New Year's just seconds ago — with the snow a-swirl, I discovered the preposterously brash entry of December 6, '61 when M. went to visit Auden. I read it to Marilyn, who announced:
  "All nineteen year olds are absurd. That is their tragedy. No twenty-nine year olds are. That is theirs."

+ + +

  New Year's Day: The snow beyond the window checkers the green. Bare trees, bright lights between the lobby doors. Dawn will slip down across Columbia in less than an hour. The first few pages of text, and arrays of notes. Charts of movement, attempts at synopsis of the tones and ranges of the various volumes. W-Fu-Man-Chu FM from Upsala is asking people to call. Countering the depersonalization that the computerized and mass communications media can produce when misused is the sense of immediacy and inter-involvement they *force* when used correctly. *Prism, Mirror, and Lens* — think about views and ways of viewing.

+ + +

Should Xero Stoan & Joachim Faust be combined into one person? No. Joachim very definitely makes nothing, is pragmatically useless to society because he *has* no personal possessions.

+ + +

Dear Bay,

  The Star-Pit has taken much too much time, from you, from the studio. Only this by way of consolation: when Sue, Ed, and myself have said of any fragment of tape, "Well, that's finished," that particular piece has been everything that I, at any rate, hoped it would. I am only anxious that you feel the same way when you hear the whole thing, hope that it will repay the concern that these delays must have cost you. You must have wanted to wash your hands of the whole thing half a dozen times. Thank you for being as patient as you have. If it helps, I knew it was strained. And you have not heard the results; for me, each piece we have done has surpassed what were, before all this, the maxima I let myself hope for. We are now at the final dubbing, and Ed projects there is three hours more work to be done.

The biggest reason is the simplest. Neither Danny, Sue, nor myself have ever done anything vaguely similar to this before. And according to Ed, he has never tried anything of this complexity either. We were learning all the way. The things that went smoothly and the things that took time were not at all what I would have expected. The three track overdubbing and mixing, for example, went as smoothly and expeditiously as anything we did. What doubled the time was the use of electronic distortion on the instruments. It took a session and a half for all three of us to finally agree this technique was just too complicated—after we had, indeed, found a way to get what we wanted. But the mixing, syncing, and underlay went like soft butter over hot toast. For future reference, the multiple track score is quite feasible, as long as the tracks are recorded with nothing more complicated electronically than a bit of echo.

Another problem that stretched half a session's work over two full days and added another ten hours of rehearsal outside studio time: because the score has to be recorded in non sequential fragments, if the musician(s) have only rehearsed the piece linearly, all hell will pop up in the studio. The musician(s) must spend their time learning what the overall shape of the score is, rather than concentrating on how to get from one section to the next. That is done on the tape editor. The musicians must know the score as a set of fragments; otherwise when they first encounter the dislocated sections, they lose confidence, want to re-write, and this—in the midst of a recording session—is the way to total insanity.

One problem that I know is administratively insoluble, but, Lord, how it would expedite matters. With all our problems, delays, mistakes, there is no five days' work that could not [have] been done in three [if] those three days could have come consecutively. If studio time could be booked in blocks of even two and three consecutive days at a time for complicated productions, how much faster things would go. Four to eight days between work periods completely destroys any sense of rhythm; so much time must be spent repeating things, trying to recall what was done. Meticulous notes, which we took from the second session on, facilitate things, but not nearly enough. During the past 40 days, I've spent fifteen at the studio.

Two blocks of five days, and we would have been finished assuming we made every single mistake and false start that we did.

Having been through *The Star-Pit*, I feel that I could be of invaluable assistance to anyone in the planning stages of another production. There are half a dozen effects that we stumbled on by accident, that are both impressive and relatively simple. There are the half dozen more that we could warn people away from. I only wish somebody who had been through a previous production had sat us down and gone over the technical limitations and extent in detail. A half an hour with a technician just before taping time just isn't sufficient for anything approaching this in complexity. An hour and a half, spent with a technician, going over the script and all the effects, coordinating the whole business in advance (and for god's sake, the same engineer for the *whole* production!) would lop days from the production schedule.

As it stands now, *The Star-Pit* has been done without a producer, and when all the performers are totally unfamiliar with the medium—well, praise be to Ed and Neil, especially Neil: without him we might have all torn one another's throats out.

With what I know now, had I the chance to reschedule production on *Star-Pit*, it would go:

Two days to record dialogue (instead of 1)
Three days to record music (instead of 5)
Two days to edit dialog (instead of 3)
Three days to edit music (instead of 6)
10 days total   instead of 15

The producers should have three long planning sessions in which:

First: he goes over the entire script with the director.
Second: he goes over entire script with the musician (this being after the musician and the director have both been over it together).
Third: with the director, musician, and technician.

If the planning is done properly, I really feel that one to two hour productions as complicated, and more complicated than *The Star-Pit* could be fit into this ten day production schedule with ease.

Final thoughts: as soon as the complexity of a production rises above the accompanying dialogue (it must be true for both SF and non SF), the techie *is* the production. Sue suggested at the end of our last session that the credits read: music composed, arranged, and performed by Ed Woodard and Sue Schweers. There is much truth here. This is why it is essential the techie be intimately involved in the planning stage. Complement to Ed: he is an intelligent, sensitive, and consummately craftsman like worker. I am terribly impressed by all his judgments as to the effectiveness of various ideas, and his incredible ability to explain patiently (and when explanation balks over technical vocabularies, to demonstrate) to us just what we ourselves are thinking. It is absolutely ridiculous/insulting and a waste to throw the engineer into the project like someone come to sweep up the floor. Again the extent to which this happened in the beginning was my fault: I just didn't know. If there were moments of strain between us, especially at the beginning, it was because I did not see what he was doing. Now that we [are] near the end, I'm mortified when I remember some of my original presumptions.

Again, I hope you are as pleased with the results of all this as I am. Very, very seldom in this world is an artist given laissez-faire to do whatever he wants, whatever it is. That is, in effect, what you have given Danny, Sue, and myself. There is no way to say how much I prize that.

Respectfully,

Chip

NOTEBOOK 35 — 1968

[Early Spring 1968]

Dear Roger,

Thank you & Judy for making "my" convent. as fun as it was. Once more we
missed a chance to really talk. But . . . oh, well. All my selfishness comes
pouring out here; I have so much enjoyed your writing, that I desperately
want to elicit as much of it from you as I can.

+ + +

Dear Kate and Damon,

I have owed you a letter and many thank-yous now for the longest time.
The excuse I was making to myself this week: no access to a typewriter.
Well. I have this notebook, see—

One of the things I must thank you for is the delightful weekend Marilyn and I had at the Anchorage with Jim and Jane Sallis.

Jim's and my collaboration has hit a temporary snag, which is all my
fault, I'm afraid. But soon we shall be back at it.

Kate, the enclosed ten dollars is a belated something toward the "Vietnam" advertisement that was run in the magazines. Thanks again for your
patience.

My love to both of you.

Give my best to Dick, who really gave us an enjoyable weekend while
you were in New York.

The best,

Chip Delany

+ + +

Orchestration for Ian Skorda—opening party.

Maureen and Aluvia alone in the ballroom.
Conversation about Rank and Ty Yen between the two.
They receive the first guests in the autumn garden.

Incident, where the party is going—having to do with Scorpions.
The winter garden

* * *

The spring garden

* * *

The summer [Ian and Lenya]

* * *

The autumn garden [Ian and Rilla]

* * *

The winter garden—Ian alone, looking for Lenya.
Maureen and Aluvia alone, discussing the party and the fact only Rank came

+ + +

Right after the Trilogy there was about a year period at that point when I decided to find out what the inside of a mental hospital looked like, didn't do an amazing amount of writing. Some time during that period *The Ballad of Beta-Two* came out. (I was in Texas, I remember, working on shrimp boats. For the longest time I could hardly recall having written the book and the "on publication check" went to bail a friend of mine, Bob Folsom, out of jail.) It was started sometime between volume two & three of the trilogy, and the last fifteen pages were written right afterwards, I guess April or May of sixty-five.

Later that autumn, back in New York, I finished up *Babel-17* in July '65. Sept of the same year I wrote *Empire Star* & *The Star-Pit*.

I started the first notes [for] *The Einstein Intersection* just before I left for Europe in October '65, and it wasn't completed until I was back in New York, September '66.

Jan '66, "Dog [in] a Fisherman's Net" was written on Mykonos. (To be published in Ted White's *Stellar*)

+ + +

There's a chapter missing from the Ace version of *The Einstein Intersection*, did you know? The chapter was three short sentences long, while the epigraphs filled up the rest of the page. It was there, first, to balance the forty-page chapter containing the minotaur sequence. And also to let readers know my tongue was just the lightest bit in my cheek with all those quotes. It got misplaced.

+ + +

By and large a paperback S-F writer doesn't get much consideration. This is why it is such a pleasure to have anything to do with editor/writers like Moorcock and Merril. You get used to running around, breaking your tail to make things easier on editors ("Well, yeah . . . I suppose you can look over the galleys to check for mistakes. But can you have them back to us by nine tomorrow morning. We've got twelve books to bring out this month, you know . . ."). Then you get something to do with *New Worlds*, or the *Year's Best* anthology (where *The Star-Pit*, unmutilated, will finally appear) and suddenly here are two people (I once made a list of mistakes in the "Worlds of Tomorrow Version"—it ran two pages, single spaced!) asking if there's anything, anything at *all*, they can do to make it easier on you! Hesitatingly you start to *think* something—and it's done! It's all rather dazzling. Any editor has a right to turn down anything submitted to him, on whatever grounds. Both Mike & Judy have turned thumbs down on work of mine. But with their acceptance goes their full respect. Pardon me if I wax rhapsodic. I've been in this business for years, & the experience is still rare enough to rhapsodize over.

+ + +

Dear John,

Thanks for your very well informed note appended to John B's letter. I do appreciate it. I'd hoped that the key word in

"I've always tried for reasonable scientific accuracy"

was "reasonable." Although, on consideration the whole thing may be one of those meaningless phrases like ". . . slightly unique . . ." In matters of scientific accuracy, something either is or is not accuracy.

I've spent the afternoon trying to find out where to refer you to Kantor. The article that I first saw it mentioned in wasn't by Kantor, it was about him. The publication was about the size of *F&SF*; it was blue; alas that doesn't help you much, does it . . .

Do I expect you to take my science "seriously"? Of course not. I'm at best an informed listener in any scientific discussion. If the section about the great circles in *Babel-17* is really that confusing, then . . . Well, what can I say. I would be curious—quite pragmatically so I'd know to watch out for it if I want to do the same thing in another book—if the people you know who have read it find it impenetrable also.

The Sigma / Sigma Prime binary in *The Star-Pit* is imaginary. In a galaxy-wide society, however, where *no* star is more than two days away from any other (as no place on earth is more than two days away from any other) distance just isn't the prime factor in "the trade routes." "Five days" and "a long time on that one" refer to the amount of time Vyme spent *working*, not traveling.

I also appreciate your concern for my feelings in giving your corrections in a personal letter. Thank you.

Alas, John, if I goof on a fact, I goof. Please: mention it anywhere you like, and make as much of it as you think it warrants. ("the red giant Tau Ceti"! ... dear me, I did do that, didn't I ...)

As far as inaccuracies, I can list you some that I think are even more important than the ones you've caught. In just the opening scene of *Babel-17*, for example: voiced and unvoiced *th* are not allophones in American English (the language the book was written in) because of the minimal pair "either / ether."

As well there are not "two types of codes"—there are codes and ciphers. And toward the end of the book: Jebel Tarik, in most cases should be Tarik Jebel, since Jebel is the Moorish for mountain (or, more accurately, cognate with the Moorish for mountain) and Tarik was the name of the old Moorish chieftain!

On the other hand, things like "corelate" in *Out of the Dead City* (as well as the consistent misspelling of Gödel (Goedel!?!?!) throughout *The Einstein Intersection*) is the copy editor's fault, not mine. Being only a lowly paperback SF writer, I am not, as a rule, shown galleys, or given a chance to check copy editing. Although recently I've been making myself a pest at the Ace Books office to do just that.

I happened to be in the office last year when the galleys of *TEI* came in. I proofread the first hundred pages, got ill, left the office, and was in bed two days. Mistakes numbered over 160. (The book is still, through a pure oversight, *missing* a chapter; comes between page 106 and page 107 of the new edition.) Is there any information you might need for your article?

By 1969 there will be accurate versions of about half my stuff around. The Gollancz hardcover version of *TEI* has that chapter restored, and mistakes corrected. (Although their version of *Babel-17* is even worse than Ace's, which is horrendous.) The Sphere Books edition will more or less be the final one. Ace is releasing, next week, an "enlarged and completely revised" version of *The Jewels of Aptor*. For "enlarged" read "uncut." Because Ace used to have a policy (now dropped) of not publishing first novels of more than 50,000 words, I had to excise about 25,000 for the original edition. I.e. chopped off as much as I could intelligently; finally I closed my eyes and just plucked out random pages, then wrote the last sentence on the previous page into the first sentence on the next page. The whole business stands out in my mind as one of the nightmares that ended my adolescence. ("Revised" means I took the tattered carbon of the original home with me, read it with a blue pencil in my teeth, and dropped out a whole lot of adjectives and dangling prepositional phrases—hopefully the sort of thing I would have done if I had been allowed the distance of galley proofs.)

For an unmutilated version of *The Star-Pit*, you have to wait for Judith Merril's 12th Annual. I once sent somebody a list of the mistakes in *The Worlds of Tomorrow*—runs two typed pages single spaced. (I don't know who Teehalt is either.)

The Fall of the Towers is just going into production with Sphere Books in England. You may have seen the article in Andy P's *Algol* which was written at the first proposal of the idea two years ago.

John B said he wants to publish a bibliography along with your article, with dates of composition. The following dates are those on which the last page came out of the typewriter.

I am terribly flattered by all this attention (both the negative and the positive). I am quite eager to read your article, more because it's by you than because it is about me. Again, if there is anything I can do to help, please let me know.

+ + +

Dear Roger,

I can't tell you how much I enjoyed a dinner with you, Judy, and Dr. Rossman that evening at Danny's. The entire "Baltimore Experience" was a complete delight. I *will* contrive to see you again *before* the next convention . . .

However, till then, a letter. I mentioned "Damnation Alley" to you. One thing we began to talk about was the difference between representational and conceptual art; the difference between writing for the eye and for the ear. If I can enlarge. By writing for the eye, I, of course, don't mean writing visual descriptions—I mean writing so that the eye can take in whatever information you're dealing most easily. Because the eye takes in information faster (by a factor of five I believe it tests at) and can retain it longer, the "eye" is happiest when it is being utilized fully. Most words in most people's writing are noise words, sounds that in speech are stuck in to give the comparatively slow ear time to catch up to the meaning, underline information that really could be deduced from what is already there. More than deduced—known immediately upon reading. E.g.:

> "The tires made a crunching noise as they passed over the gravel that lay scattered over the road."

The only necessary information in that sentence is:

> "The tires crunched the gravel."

From that we *know* the car is "passing over" (but isn't it really passing on, or down—but not quite . . . visual confusion) and from the context situation, we know the car is on the road. Where else, then, might the gravel be, than lying scattered over it.

It is the way you manage to have only necessary information (word for word) in most of your stories (he suggested fearfully) that makes them as intense and immediate as they are. Any of those gorgeous descriptions in "Mortal Mountain," back to "Rose" could be made the most limp and flabby over-writing by the addition of a few "seemed like"s, "began to"s, "suddenly"s, and those host of noise words and phrases that do all the indicating for the reader. I pass on to you the opening pages of "Damnation Alley" from *Galaxy* with all that pen scratching most humbly. Really I do.

+ + +

The time has come, Delany, to write another journal entry, to try, to define, to put things in places (theirs). The whole purpose of verbal literature is to free people from language—to create a structure that suddenly the observer realizes contains something that is ineffable.

But nouns, verbs, situations. There I am (I'd like to say here I am. Somehow it doesn't work that way) in this Second Street commune with a rock group, passionately (on one level or the other) in love with all three other members. (Passion—it's rather ameliorated by phrases like on one level or the other but that on one level or the other is the point.) More (or less) made Bert last night who is sitting on the floor across a Go board from Ann:

his voice is like a well modulated machine gun. His hands are grubby. One wants to hold him and listen to him pant on one's neck. Sigh. The back room is lit with a red bulb, is filled with people and hash smoke. I cannot sleep. Sue reassures me with warm angles and mental lights and responses beyond what I'm used to asking for. Fucks like a flipping gazelle. Thinks like the definitions of sanity. One could be very happy with that. Why won't I be happy. (You ought to know about questions like that)

+ + +

When we talk of possibilities and probabilities, even when we give them mathematical expression, we are talking about and giving measurements to our own ignorances, not our knowledge.

+ + +

Consciousness is a function of time. The universe, its shape and development, is an object in space-time.

Three ideas:

1) The past is firmly fixed, while the present is like a ring slipping along the infinite diversities of the future and binding them into place.

2) The past and future are fixed, and the idea of randomness is a manifestation of what we don't know.

3) Both the past and the future are infinitely changeable, and the present is merely a point of the five dimensional object of the universe where many pasts merge before becoming many futures and the faultiness of our ability to know accurately what *has* happened as well as our inability to tell what will happen (on any micro-macro scale) actually defines the divergence of both the variable past & future.

Number one is the most commonly held view of the temporal mechanics of the universe, and is also the easiest to prove inadequate. The second is the view that the world of Newtonian physics ultimately implied, and that Einsteinian physics began to break down. If the third view is true, then although probability is a study of ignorance, at least the edges of that ignorance define wisdom.

+ + +

Everything is finite
Everything is finite
See how they run
See how they run

They all took after a Möbius strip
Who sent them all off on an acid trip
Did you ever try to encompass it
Everything is finite

    Joshua Scott
    Bert Lee

+   +   +

Refute:

Ludwig Wittgenstein's discussion of meaning: "Fetch me a red flower from the meadow."

+   +   +

Note for Bill.

"Just once I'd like to know what a room looks like before I walk into it."

Capricorn in Ascendance

I

to wound the autumnal city.

Beyond flies' eyes, blown big as buildings, port, tower, and parks and museums, throngs from late theatres across Sovereign Plaza, beyond the Cage, shot with markets, Ian ambled with the divergence of Bellona's lights deviling his eyes.

Through a puddle: mud tongued the grit dusting his boots. The wire fence by the torn earth meshed night. (This youngster's aloneness is such a huge thing from in his eyes ...)

A dark boy, and the darkness burned a bit. Eighteen and the veins already heavy over arms and big hands. Nests of hair on wrists and chest: on his head, tightly curled and dark again. A broad face with ramped bones, hints of epicanth, a solid neck—he tried to move easy.

He moved primitive.

Ian played his hand on the wire and gazed in the quarter mile tear: rusty rock, water, three bulldozers, two beds of concrete (one here, one way over there), first shafts.

The foundation diggings for

Bellona Colosseum

Xero Stoan, Architect

a wound widening. Ian thought about the cold. Windless, the evening had seemed mild, even though breath clouded. He'd left the battery medallion off his jacket. Just cloth would be enough ... later the temperature/time lights on the bank blinked 35°/10:33. Both informations astounded. Now that he had walked half an hour, the cold had blades on. If you relax, blood flows freer ... He tried to dangle a shoulder.

Hey. Steps here, into the digs. The gate was ajar. He left off his trivial questionings, gazing.

Across, steps up. Part of his mind's adolescent burble, seeking symmetries and testing imbalances, wondered if the other gate were opened. He had never walked that side of the foundation. He did not want home.

So, sideways through; he started the rungs. First dozen: cement. Second: a jerry rigged metal—the rail broke from the bottom newels. Framed with earth, frost ferns struck in the puddle crusts. (What am I doing here? Iron dirt beat his soles; the cross-walk let back the rhythm of doubt and ponder (The unexamined life is not worth living. Yeah … but it won't stay still for me long enough to see any small thing). I mean, is this real, the way an idea begins and forks and shoots and bends too fast like branched cracks in the frozen.) Third: a wooden ladder, colder, that felt more solid than steel; grabbed to steady. The rungs were colder.

Ian was halfway across when they came.

He grew afraid and a shadow. The shadow grew longer. Ian spun and the light pulled harsh laces of pain across his face. Fear was as big as his heartbeat. No; I'm not going to run, because those are only news reports and people's hysterical stories—

They dropped, burning.

Then he was trying to stop running. Fascination turned him back, dancing the concrete, and they were burning: two.

His tongue stuffed his mouth so he couldn't let cry.

[sequence continues]

+   +   +

Dear Judy,

Had a chance to read your "love letter" with a normal temperature (I had a fever yesterday) and though there is nothing in it that could possibly offend me, I do, very humbly, beg one or two smallnesses, if you would.

Could you leave out the "at 26" and the "at 15"? It's been something that I've been plagued with since I was 17. And once one is twenty-five, I don't think there is anything "amazing" or even "interesting" about whatever you happen to be doing.

The "Heavenly Breakfast" at present consists of 4 voices, 3 guitars, and an incredible variety of flutes.

+   +   +

Dear Sirs,

I am writing you about the forthcoming Sphere Books edition of my trilogy, *The Fall of the Towers*. I'm very excited about the project, because (among other things) the Sphere edition will be the only completely accurate one in existence.

I have a suggestion which I hope will come in time to avoid possible problems. I do not know where you are (or if you are) in production, but if there is time, I have the following proposal.

Once the typescript has been copyedited, Xerox it (for a safeguard), and return the copy-edited manuscript to me by airmail. I will check it thoroughly, and return it to you. (It will be in my hands no more than 72 hours before it goes back into the mail to you.) This way you can assure yourself that galley corrections will be at a minimum. After eight books, I have had final bound copies handed to me with upwards of 150 errors in them (the Gollancz hardcover edition of *Babel-17* is a case in point—which is why I sent you my own setting copy). I recently went through a new edition of my first novel with Ace Books here, re-set from the manuscript where I was allowed to check copy editing. Galley corrections, including "littorals," were under 24; and that's not bad for a hundred and sixty page book, and it's a book I can say is as I wrote it. (On the other hand, I just returned Gollancz the galleys of *The Einstein Intersection* which were in much better shape than *Babel-17*, and assuming they follow my corrections, it should be perfectly satisfactory to set from.)

You'll have noticed that I have included two pieces of art work. They're both by the American artist Russell Fitzgerald. The color print is a cover proof for the May '68 issue of the *Magazine of Fantasy & Science Fiction* which features a novelette of mine. He has also done the cover for my forthcoming Doubleday novel *Nova*, and I have been more than delighted with both. To my mind, they converge with a certain quality of my work in a way that the dozen odd illustrators I have had in the past have never achieved to my satisfaction. I mentioned to him recently your forthcoming edition of the trilogy, and he explained he would like to do three related cover illustrations, and that he was already familiar with the books in their American editions. I told him I would pass on his offer to you with my heartiest endorsement. In our discussion I pointed out the disparity between British and American prices. He said he was well aware of this, and that the desire to do the series of covers came from his regard for the works themselves. If this suggestion is amenable to you, then I would be very happy if you could write

> Russell Fitzgerald
> 68 East 3rd Street
> New York, NY 10009

giving particulars as to size, dimensions (I'm assuming you use four-color covers; if you use "graphic" covers, I believe he would still be interested), and so forth. You might even send him some sample covers of your recent books—this assuming, of course, the suggestion meets with your approval. If you have made other plans, or do not feel the use of an American artist to be feasible, please let me know, writing me in care of my agent Henry Morrison.

+ + +

AN ALBUM

1	Da-da	—FAST ODD	4 min.
2	This Way	—FAST	3 min.
3	Big White Marshmallow	—FAST	20 sec.
4	Dawn Passage	—FAST	2 min.
5	Sapphires	—SLOW	3 30
6	Blue Locomotive	—SLOW	4 min.
7	Here We Are	—SLOW	3 min.
8	Rain	—ROCK & ROLL	2 min. 30
9	Bring Help Along the Way	—E. A. SLOW	3 min.
10	The Big Complexed Song (Needle Nose)	—FAST	2 30
11	Olive Lord	—SLOW	3
12	Winter in New York	—FAST	2
			35–37 min.

One Side
    This Way
    Blue Locomotive
    Big White Marsh ...
    Dawn Passage
    Bring Help
    The B.C.S.

Another Side
    Here We Are
    Winter in New York
    Sapphires
    Olive Lord
    Rain
    Dada

+   +   +

Somebody questioning me if I was going to add another book to the Toromon trilogy, when I said "No," suddenly asked, "Whenever you write another book, do you have to create a completely different future?"

The answer I gave surprised me too, because it articulated something that had been clinging to the underside of my brain in the shadows a long time: "A science fiction writer doesn't create futures. He creates different presents."

I have never sat down and systematically tried to figure out what the world would be like in a given number of years. I could. As a fairly intelligent person, my predictions stand the chance of being as accurate as anybody's here. But if I worked the whole thing out with rigorous logic, I could very easily see myself writing no more science fiction, or at any rate, only writing one more work, absolutely chock-full of social message—then sitting around for a long time waiting for my mind to change.

April 4—4:00 A.M. Thursday—morning of the premiere of *2001: A Space Odyssey*

Beauty results from the tensions of an object and an environment.

Picked up Baird Searles (of the golden earring and bronze beard) at WBAI–FM radio station. Sandra Ley (Willy Ley's daughter). Bai has white turtleneck with black trim ruffles. Choice of two jackets.

Sandra, in the yellow mini gown and mink jacket (Sue is down to the floor in black and I am up to the chin in silver) all agree on the second. "What time do you think we should arrive—for maximum effect?" Baird.

Sandra, who knows about such things, suggests we try for ten after eight. The conversation scintillates till ten of; then to Madison for a cab. We have to walk all the way up to 42 before we get one. The cab pulls up around Fifty First. The crowds clot the street to the corner in both directions. Police: blue. Police barricade: gray. Two spotlights (Bai, who is a dancer and tall, could lie spread eagle on the glass face and not touch the rim) have yellow fires in their polished bowls and pillars of white light lean over Broadway.

"That's right," I tell the driver, "that's where we're going."

We are let between the barricade—lost in the welter of formal wear and cameras. Sandra & Bai are in the orchestra. Sue & I are in the mezzanine. The escalator: people are sitting along the lobby in their ties and gowns. No one is actually fanning himself with his program, but many look as though they want to.

Our seat is on the absolute edge of the theater. Listening [to] the conversation above and below, we discover we are surrounded by the board of managers of MGM who are quietly furious that they have been placed off to the side.

"... Next time I want to see a film I'll have my own screening ..."

"... Imagine, putting the director of the board ..."

"... There're beatniks (sic) down there, look, sitting down there ..." which I can only guess is the reference to the number of men in formal turtleneck.

—Picture of Stanley Kubrick carefully selecting the seats that are to be assigned to each member of the board.

Intermission: we go downstairs to look for Bai & Sandra among the satin and marble & brocade. No luck. Back upstairs, we're having a couple of cokes and sitting on the sidelines looking like we should be fanning ourselves with our own programs, when Bai arrives. So we go down and talk to Sandra.

"Who have you seen …"

"Paul Newman …"

"Well, there's Keir Dullea. But I've got to get close enough to see if his eyes are really that pale …"

"Would you believe the board of directors for MGM …"

"Liza Minnelli …"

"I haven't seen anybody." That's me talking. "You're tripping over [them] everywhere you turn."

Back upstairs, in the mezzanine, Sue leaves her velvet cape on the chair (black outside—an op-art pattern of white & black satin inside) inside out on her chair to go for water. She returns and is in black, with a beaten silver necklace of huge links on her bare skin. And everyone watches [her] come back to her op-art throne, including the Board of Directors for MGM whose conversations stop … in fact it is the only thing that stops them talking throughout the entire preview, including the picture.

I go for water.

Coming from the men's room, an elderly man with a brush of white hair: we catch each other with an eye hook. Hands are seized.

"Dr. Clarke …" I, exclamation.

"Chip …? Delany!" He, declarative. "But you had a beard last time I saw you. Do you like the film?"

"It's … wonderful!" Which is all I can get out. "It's wonderful, Dr. Clarke."

The foghorn they have in place of a bell sounds. "Oh, you better get back. You don't want to miss the beginning of the next part."

I flee.

"Hey! Let's play who did you see. You know who I just saw …!"

Afterwards, and downstairs, and shattered, Bai and Sandra and Sue & I [reconnoiter] among broken sentences.

Leaving, we pass Keir Dullea going through the intriguingly delicate situation of introducing a young starlet to a young star.

"Hey!" Baird says. "His eyes really are that pale."

And then April gives us bright cold Broadway, and we stroll to the corner among the darker suits and bright gowns (moving to drinks & the O.R. and Judy Merril, where all this becomes real and the night dies). Broadway is all the young men in tuxes—too warm for coats—and Sandra says, passing a store-window full of Peter Max posters: "That's funny; they seemed so bright when I saw them this afternoon."

The next night, while Sue & I are having dinner at Bunches, looking over the stills from the program-booklet, Lamar and Lionel burst into the restaurant with the news that Martin Luther King has been assassinated.

There are burning candles in Tompkins Square and a small group of people, white & black, gather to talk quietly in the light rain. Passing back through the park a few hours later, the half-dozen candles set on the lip of the band shell are still burning.

Someone has propped up the Daily News with the headline

Martin Luther

King Shot

and the people passing through stop to look, and walk on. The rain has stopped. Joe Koenig and I, who are on our way back from Russell's, where we had gone to look at the magnificent triptych of jewel-like paintings Russell had nearly completed for the British edition of *The Fall the Towers*, stop for a while, then return to 7th Street.

+   +   +

Igor Stravinsky was once hired by MGM (or one of its ilk) to write the music for one of the bigger spectaculars and it was felt that the composer's name would bring a note of culture to the credits. And apparently Stravinsky had been intrigued by the possibilities of the medium to accept the commission. The director was introducing him to the cast and the more important people of the technical crew when he finally got to one gentleman: "Oh, and this, Mr. Stravinsky, will be your arranger."

"I beg your pardon," was Stravinsky's reply. Then he turned around, left the studio, and never came back.

It is surprising how long it has taken "pop" music to learn one of the simplest musical facts of life: the arranger makes the song, and I use the verb connotatively and denotatively.

When one artist decides to do another's song, it takes the utmost musical sensitivity to decide how much of the arrangement is part of the song, how much can the tempo be violated, what shifts can be made in back-grounds and harmony.

And nine times out of ten the artist who tries to reproduce the tempo and arrangement as exactly as possible is the most successful (one thinks of Nielsen's "She's Leaving Home," the Mamas and the Papas' "Dancing in the Streets," Big Brother and the Holding Company's "Piece of my Heart" as exemplars of one group doing another's material).

We have only seen [Randy] Newman as a composer and arranger. Along with Van Dyke Parks and Brian Wilson, he is responsible for a "new sound" that recently I heard referred to as "South C. salon rock." His songs are to be heard by artists as varied as Judy Collins, Harper's Bizarre (where you can hear some [of] them in Newman's own fire and filigree arrangements) and Tony Randall (!).

Now we have a reprise album of Randy Newman performing his own songs in his own arrangements.

+ + +

Things that Must Be Done

Cover Story for Fred.
New Worlds Story
Helen Adam
Marilyn Hacker
Prism, Mirror, Lens

Now: order of Real priority.

Prism, Mirror, Lens
Poems of M. Hacker
Helen ish
New Worlds story
Fred's story

+ + +

Thoughts on the development of *P.M.L.*

Ian passes time as a social observer, time as an outlaw leader, time as a mystic, time as a family man, having to call on all.

+ + +

The bureaucratic satire.
The three of them are all dead—
The reduplication of images.
When man really comes across a superior intelligence it will be as incomprehensible as this.
The twisted [allegory].
The Dawn of Man.
Insert of subtitles
The cutting
Physical disorientation
Three audiences who wouldn't watch the film

When man comes up against a truly superior intelligence, the encounter will be at once totally involving, and yet as incomprehensible—well, as some people have claimed the ending of *2001* is.

Actually the film is totally open. The bulk of the plot concerns six people, three of whom are asleep, three of whom might as well be—without sensitivity or human reactions—locked together on a nine-month voyage to Jupiter. One of them is a computer. They kill each other, brutally, slowly, and finally. The film says, if anything, that even this man can be reborn.

+ + +

The budget of most paperback book companies—and most hardcover ones—simply does not allow enough money to do extensive advertising. Even in a field as allegedly cohesive as S-f, the 2 S-f books a month that Doubleday issues, or the eight S-f titles a month that Ace releases—these are all very different products, and for maximum distribution, meetings would have to be held about each book, decisions would have to be made about where to place a book, which periodicals in which to take advertising, and what sort, whether to distribute it through general bookstores, college bookstores, or newsstands, what cover and copy to put on it that is likely to intrigue people of the particular type and interests that the book inside

+ + +

"I love you."
"So do I."
The humor here, and the deeper ambiguity so masked, lies in the con-

fusion of an objective semantic statement with a subjective semantic statement.

So = thus.

Do = performance of any predicate.

I = the speaker.

+ + +

Dear John,

Your letter was a brightness on this grey morning in the city of late-prison-Gothic architecture. I just sustained (if that's the proper word) a robbery last week, lost my typewriter, and my other shirt; so please forgive the handwriting.

Glad of the rain.

Re: *Empire Star* and definitive Delany: (Picture puzzled writer scratching his ear, frowning, turning your letter over and around to see if there's a bomb in it, or something, or maybe two or three words he skimmed over that change the whole meaning) I don't know (more accurately "I dunno," which, like Strine, loses something in translation). Between nineteen and twenty-six one does a lot of changing. Both *Babel-17* and *Empire Star* are the work of a rather eccentric twenty-three-year-old, and one whom I doubt muchly if I'd get along too well with were I to meet him today. Definitive Delany for me, of course, has to be what I'm working on at the moment.

Please don't take this as a pose; it's just a matter of preserving sanity, something on which my grip is not all that strong at the best of times: I can only look at my canvases from the back, I see all the knots, the underpainting, the sizing and the glue. I will never be able to know, firsthand, what it's like to pick up a Delany novel and read it through for the first time. Reports from the most well wishing people have been so contradictory, that the only way I can look at them is to make a sort of "double-think" adjustment and pretend they are all talking about somebody I will simply never have a chance to read. That's not to say that I don't find them interesting, informative, even usefully instructive. But to try and enter the discussion myself in terms of intended meaning (as opposed to intended effect) is impossible.

I can give you a bit of information about "how" *Empire Star* was written. You (or Mr. Broderick) will have to decide whether the method had any effect on the "definitiveness." I really offer this most humbly.

It's a little difficult to talk about *Empire Star* without mentioning "the noisy number" (as one fan called it) because the shorter book grew directly out of the longer. *Babel-17* was about nine/ten months in the writing. I was pretty sure Ace would use it as a longer half of a double. There used to be a special royalty consideration for authors if they wrote both sides of the double, so I decided to do a short novel that would fill out the double length. As well, I had just had a whole series of as yet "un-grokked" experiences, hitch-hiking around the American South, working for a summer on shrimp boats along the Texas Gulf, had found a lot of patterns in the world, similarities, differences among people; all this, on top of just having terminated a brief stay in a mental hospital, lingering over from which were still more loose ends of life to be tied up. I decided to deal with them all by writing *Empire Star*, and writing it in a way I had never written a book before (nor have I since). Every day for two weeks, I sat down and thought about the book for four hours (I made notes, did no other writing). An hour for lunch; then I came back and actually wrote for four hours more. Two weeks later: *Empire Star*.

Actually, that process was only carried on for eleven days. At which point, I'd finished the first draft. Then about a week later I put it through the typewriter again, which took another three/four days—so two weeks is a good estimate on the length of time it took.

I'd never written a novel in two weeks before, and I never want to again. I think, by and large, the ratio of planning to writing is a lot higher in everything else I've ever written. But the planning was never done in such a concentrated form before.

Babel-17 (like *Nova*) was written in a fairly relaxed (well, comparatively relaxed) manner, planning, writing, rewriting, with lots of time out to do other things, which for me is mainly a way to keep up enthusiasm. *The Einstein Intersection* was another sort of experiment in methodical intensity, but of a different type.

Of course, in typical Ace fashion, the company decided not to put *Babel-17* and *Empire Star* back-to-back for mysterious reasons of their own. I believe *Empire Star* was published first; then *Babel-17* was issued as a single a few months later. Well, such are the vagaries of the publishing world.

Don't take the "revision[s]" on *The Jewels of Aptor* too seriously. They entailed my reading over the carbon copy of the original uncut and uncopyedited manuscript two hours before I had to deliver it to the Ace office. I blue penciled out about two pages worth of adjectives. I had to cut the original manuscript by a third (a perfectly impossible job: toward the end,

I simply was pulling pages at random, then writing the end of the page before into the page after) at which point creative copy editors took over, managed to reverse all the dialogue of the two major characters past chapter five, changed mother and daughter to mother and sister, etc. etc. etc. The whole incident stands out as one of the more unpleasant nightmares that concluded my adolescence.

By Terry Carr's rather generous estimate, the "revised" edition differs from the original MS as submitted by perhaps fifteen hundred words (all of them missing rather than added). The "un-revised" differs from the original MS as submitted by about twenty-five thousand—altogether, a chunk substantially longer than *The Star-Pit*.

But Ace thought it would sell more copies . . .

                      *   *   *

About eight/ten years ago, *Das Glasperlenspiel* was the center of a pseudo-intellectual cult here in the States only slightly smaller than the recent Tolkien craze. Alas, it didn't penetrate into S-f circles, but there was a four year period where literally everyone with any intellectual pretensions had a copy, was trying to lend it to you, was trying to borrow it from you. When I read it in high school, I must say I found it vastly entertaining. But looking back on it (perhaps I'm biased by the intellectual atmosphere that ultimately generated about the book), I find it, and most of Hesse's work, philosophically shallow. There is great surface ingenuity, and one goes through it under the impression that one is being given a great deal to think about. And one is. But when one starts to examine the depth with which he deals with his ideas, one hits the bottom awfully fast. If one hasn't encountered that sort of intellectual matrixing of ideas before, then it's a very exciting book; and I think it's a great book for bright adolescents. But if one comes to it as a mature reader, familiar with what others have done with these ideas, and then looks to Hesse to see where he takes them . . . well, as one German woman I knew who had just gotten her degree in philosophy from the University of Munich (no small feat at twenty-three) said, "It's rather like instant plastic philosophy; it's very bright and pretty, but it cracks too easily and the flavor doesn't last." Really, I have nothing against the book. It gives me great pleasure, as I said; I'm just reacting to all that's been made of it over here, I suppose.

The Campbell book, on the other hand, I actively dislike. I find it uninformed, sloppy, and pernicious. In the guise of a scholar, assembling a mythography to illuminate the mechanics of narrative, he shamefully maneuvers a mythography to support whole handfuls of modern literary prejudices. What I suppose I find most distasteful, is his complete lack of respect for the incredibly powerful resonances of the material he deals with ... a failing he shares with Jung and which I find equally abhorrent in both. I much prefer Graves' *The White Goddess*; I think it is a far more valid work.

To do this sort of thing with any rigour, one again and again must face great areas of one's self and the universe that are patently unknown: at which point one must throw up one's hands, scream, cry, laugh, or have some other human reaction.

Graves, at least, laughs.

Campbell, with bright and shining face, closes his eyes and slogs on, pulling irrelevancy after inaccuracy from here and there that mean nothing, rather like a Victorian spinster who accidentally enters a whorehouse and sits there for hours, having tea, commenting on the lovely sofas and the red plush drapes, and simply refusing to see that anything out of the ordinary is going on.

Campbell is also, often, wrong. But that's forgivable. The attitude isn't. Graves presents his book as an intellectual plaything, a scholarly joke, that is ultimately a profound speculation on just the sort of literary process Campbell is incapable of even conceiving. Campbell presents his book in all seriousness and comes off having done a ludicrously inadequate job on what could have been a very exciting and meaningful subject.

Even Velikovsky, admittedly a crackpot, has more respect for the power of his methodology.

And of course, it goes without saying, all these mythographies pale before Frazer's *Golden Bough*, which I had the overpowering experience of reading (all thirteen volumes) during my lunch hours back when I was working in the cellar stacks of Barnes & Noble, just after I dropped out of college (about age 18). The only really relevant modern thing that really gets down to the subject is Tolkien's essay on fairy tales, which I guess boils down to: There are certain wizened little gray men and old women sitting around with golden apples, and if you take their advice, and are good, kind, and respect both the known and the unknowable, you at least have a chance of getting out alive, ... oh, well.

By the way, Campbell's other major work (of which he is co-author), *A Skeleton Key to Finnegans Wake*, is as absurd as its title is in bad taste.

Much thanks for your nice words on "Corona."

Also, thanks for the idea about the universe as an open sphere. While you're right in general about the uselessness of readers' suggestions, this one arrives at a propitious time; with your permission, I'll use it to get me over a rather ticklish situation. It's a perfect analogy to describe the mental state of one of my characters—and then the mental state becomes an analogy for another character who is in the physical situation of being near the boundary of the "open sphere" of the universe (or rather "was" some years before the novel begins). All very neat. It's a very long book. (I described it to one editor as, "Oh, say, about *Dune*-and-a-half size.") And it's got at least another year's work to go. Working title: *Prism, Mirror, Lens*.

I don't know if you are planning to do any re-reading for the article, but in case you are, here is a list of the accurate editions:

The Jewels of Aptor (Ace "expanded and revised" edition is O.K.)

The Trilogy (Either Sedgwick and Jackson (British) in hard-cover, or Sphere Books (British) in soft-cover. The Ace edition is nearly as hopeless as the original Ace edition of *Aptor.*)

Babel 17 (Sphere Books O.K.—Ace is poor, the Gollancz hardcover is worse.)

The Einstein Intersection (Gollancz hardcover is O.K. The Ace edition, besides being poor, managed by accident (!) to leave out a chapter.)

Empire Star and *Ballad of Beta-2* (Ace versions are pretty accurate. No more than two dozen proof-reading errors in either. Which is amazingly good.)

The Star-Pit (*The Worlds of Tomorrow* version is a wreck. Judith Merril's *12th Annual* contains the novelette as written.)

"Driftglass" (*If* version almost a wreck. Reprinted properly, save one amazing, but obvious typo, in Ace's *World's Best: 1968.*)

"Corona" (*F&SF* is adequate.)

"Lines of Power" (*F&SF* version has been cut by about 10%, but proper version will have to wait for a collected stories.)

"Cage of Brass" (*If* version, save for my spelling mistakes the copy editor missed, is surprisingly good. One "your" should be "you.")

Nova—the Doubleday edition waits to be seen.

I missed *LORE*, but I'm looking forward to your zine when it arrives.

+ + +

Thing[s] to do tomorrow. Get nail clip, worm-pills, and meat, a pig skillet, get check up to Henry, get review typed for Blish.

+   +   +

Everybody has an aspiration to leave something behind them, whether it's a suicide note or a novel.

—Bob

... For the *Crawdaddy* article

The validity of a given effect becomes ultimately a question of intent. Or perhaps that is conversely true. That is to say, if the effects are timed right, the point will be made sharply and accurately, and there will be no question of why those particular devices were used.

Were we given a song to arrange, lyrics perhaps about the confusion of modern life (as many are), we might work out an instrumental composed of tapes doctored, horns and computer sounds structured to simulate a massive traffic tie-up, the song presented as a nearly subliminal newscast (from a car radio with rolled up windows), the actual details being lost in bursts of static.

Gimmickry employed thusly as if to make you say "O, I know how they're doing that." But is that the right response to anything that pretends to art. For art is artificial, the art object pretends to be only itself, the vastest presumption.

+ + +

Language disguises thought. So much so that from the outward form of the clothing it is impossible to infer the form of the thought beneath it, [...] because the outward form of the clothing is not designed to reveal the form of the body, but for entirely different purposes.

The famous Proposition 7 from Wittgenstein's *Tractatus*:
"That which we cannot speak of, we must pass over in silence,"
leads us to reflect:
"Just what can be spoken of?"
Horace, in his epistle to Pisos, more generally known as *Ars Poetica*, opens with the following dicta:

> Should a painter join a human head and horse's neck, add limbs from every beast, and cover them with multicolored feathers, so that a lovely woman at the top ends in a black and ugly fish's tail, when you saw this, my friends, wouldn't you laugh? Believe me, Pisos, such will a book where idle fancies, like a sick man's dreams, are fashioned without unity of head or foot.

Science fiction—in particular modern SF—stands in direct opposition to these classical parameters of order.

+ + +

The first thing to say about "The New Thing" in S-f is that there isn't one. This includes Ballard's fragmented condensed novels, the latest Disch stories, the new stylized creations of Zelazny such as *Lord of Light* and *Creatures of Light & Darkness*, and certainly everything of my own. What there has been is an incredible marshaling of literary technique from all facets of literature, some experimentation with forms not usually found in S-f writing styles. It is the sort of thing that very often presages the birth of a "new thing," but so far, on all fronts, this is only the arraying of the arsenal.* We still have to see if any of this arsenal will fire.

*Some people have mistaken the advent of the technical freedom for the accomplishing itself, and have hailed this as glorious for the genre, and there's a lot in it that is glorious. Some have seen it as threatening to what was science fiction, and it is threatening, rather the way the talking picture threatened the silent movie. I think, for the first time in S-f history, we are a couple of years, or possibly even months away from a "New Thing"—

I am cast back to Wittgenstein's justly famous Proposition Seven from the *Tractatus*: "That which we cannot speak about, we must pass over in silence." Wittgenstein was not talking about the morality of a subject, whether it was appropriate to speak about; actually he was referring to that whole area of human experience that is simply nonverbal, but as he himself finally realized the whole purpose of literature—poetry and fiction—is to create a form that could—if only momentarily—free us from the verbal experience. The purpose of writing a story or poem, rather than an essay, was to make something happen inside us that was not an answer, not a response in words. In short, its purpose is to present, to study, and to examine those things we can't speak of.

And the development of art, again and again, has been a movement from one area to yet another area of the unspeakable.

The preoccupation of fiction (drama and poetry included), from classical times through the 19th century, was with those human problems that sprang from the passions. Science fiction certainly didn't invent—but just as certainly brought into focus—those human problems that spring from the intellect. *The* science-fiction sensibility that probably had most to do with the forming of the modern science-fiction mind was—I'd like to suggest—not H. G. Wells, but rather George Bernard Shaw, and I don't mean Shaw of *Back to Methuselah*, but the Shaw of *Man and Superman*—which is S-f not only because of the Don Juan in Hell fantasia, but also because of the way the motorcar is handled and Shaw's ability to relate the advent of the internal combustion engine (then a bit behind where space travel is today) to the sensibilities of a whole social range of characters. Besides the fact that the Shavian comedy willed Heinlein et al. their entire didactic method.

Hopefully we won't take three thousand years to get to the next step. Ballard, who is probably the most articulate theoretician, if not practitioner with these new techniques, has coined the phrase "interspace," pointing inward as the next unknown to explore.

To re-phrase: What are the human problems caused by what has been called "the spirit," or to use a more current term, "man's state of consciousness." But this is essentially a "mystical" problem. I don't think it is odd to look for this in S-f. The most popular work of the writers most lauded as "hard-core" science fiction writers, Heinlein's *Stranger in a Strange Land*, Clarke's *Childhood's End*, Blish's *Case of Conscience*, are all essentially mystical. Don Allen, last night at dinner, spoke of the thing that attracted him to science fiction as the epic sense enlarged to a totally cosmic scale, where writers from Stapledon to Asimov have seriously pondered on the fate of the entire universe. Again, a basically mystical concern. It's also very primitive mysticism. And mysticism grows up as soon as one realizes that worrying about the fate of the universe is basically a sublimation, albeit an interesting and occasionally productive one, of one's worry about one's own fate—a problem no less mystical because of its immediacy.

I don't think that the most powerful artistic exploration of these problems—the human problems man's consciousness creates for him—will come from writers oriented through organized religion, because no matter how socially involved a person, organized religion still entails a renunciation of the material world that is social and condoned. Alienation is the mystical problem, but though alienation may be the impetus for the religious renunciation, as soon as soon as alienation *is* socially condoned, it becomes something else.

One reason the exploration of these problems may come through S-f is that they grow directly out of our technical environment; the multiple worlds we live in, inner, outer, and worlds both bigger and smaller than both, clash on one another, and we are wounded.

Hopefully the New Thing will be a large vision that encompasses all of these worlds and explores the overlap between them. But the exciting thing about it is that it will make articulable things, which in the Wittgensteinean sense, now we cannot speak of. To try [and] figure out what it's going to be, or even look like when it gets here is a waste of time. I'm painfully aware that I should be writing rather than talking. But there is enough excitement to have some left over for the conference. Which hopefully goes to prove how exciting it is.

+   +   +

Evil as a corruption of good.
Alas, good can also be a corruption of evil—and a whole man must know both.

+   +   +

A letter reviewing *Warhoon*?
Mmmmm.

Dick:

A fine zine. Word hungry to the end, my favorite in the issue was Bank's McBane letter. Jesuitical argumentations have always been a favorite pastime of mine, so Atheling was a delight. I want to take him up on just about every other point, but *Warhoon* isn't a religion symposium: I'll content myself outlining one theologic dilemma that he still hasn't managed to resolve; and if he could (he tries in *Black Easter*—my favorite of the three—but doesn't quite make it): Genesis aside, it is not that knowledge in itself is a form of evil. Evil ultimately must be measured in terms of evil actions, (or potentially evil action, or, more sophisticatedly, in terms of thoughts that may lead to evil action: for evil, read that which will cause pain and death). The ethical problem contained in the statement that knowledge is evil is actually this: the acquisition of knowledge is of necessity going to entail many evil actions. Watch: ignorance is basically unawareness of the consequences of what one does. The only way to attain knowledge is to go out (either mentally or physically) and do things, then watch the results. Since ignorance is the state in which the actions were performed, probability has it that a percentage of them will cause pain and death. Hence, once knowledge is attained, the "good man" (at least the medieval "good man") set up the equivocation between inaction and good, and conversely between action and evil.

The existentialists through the last half of the nineteenth century and the first half of the twentieth pointed out forcefully that if the world is to continue (and it seems to be) there is no ethicality left in opposing passive good to active evil. Active evil always wins. And since some actions *are* good (even to the point of actions that have side effects of pain and death), then action is defensible—even unto totally evil action, especially when opposed to none at all.

Theologically, this is a complicated way of resurrecting the Arian heresy: God is good; God created both good and evil. Therefore evil is good.

We are going through an ethical revolution, of the sort that takes a century or two to complete. But at present this action/evil on the one hand and virtue/good has been the ethical breaking point of almost every expression of man's thought from Wittgenstein's *Tractatus* (*Was sich überhaupt sagen lässt, lässt sich klar sagen; und wovon man nicht reden kann, darüber muss man schweigen*, to which the modern artist opposes: Why? And why can't I try, even if it means battering my head bloody in the attempt? And if I don't, how are these limits to be changed? And if they don't change, we'll die.) to films like *Hud* (where the choice is between a wise, ethical, and impotent old man who cannot maneuver his situation and a brash, nasty, totally unlikable "Snopes" of a young man who happens to achieve practical ends that, on the largest scale, ultimately cause the least pain, the least death). It is the failing point for all three volumes of *After Such Knowledge*, a flaw that is implicit in every Faust story and invalidates the ultimate point of modern retellings from Gaddis' *Recognitions* to Disch's *Camp Concentration*.

It's probably the basis of all generational conflicts as well (even unto waves old and new breaking on one another amidst much critical foam & froth).

To wait with bated breath for the next *Warhoon* would be tantamount to suffocation. Still I enjoyed 23 more than enough to have me hoping for 24.

Best,

Samuel "J" Delany

+ + +

Landscapes

He meets the people he will love all in the first volume:
The strange masochistic aristocratic girl who finally cuts him loose. The stupid girl he uses and at the same time the hoodlum boy. The girl who rescues him from the monastery. Lanya (1st), Quill (last), Selena, The Hawk.

The Architect, and Scorda Halls, and Scorda Halls blown up. The Mad Count and Countess. The delinquents, the Scorpions with their light armour. The monastery. An amusement park. A frozen waste of mountains. The [...] city at night. The Labyrinth, and the lady psychiatrist and the Architect.

The dock clubhouse for the Scorpions. The Scordas who hire Ian to do something for them.

Ian Dorkk spends time in a reform school. He also had the tutelage of a good family whom he protects.

The daughter of the Scordas who can see the future.

Ian has a diary going.

The Singers of the city—the Hawk, whom he protects in a bar battle.

There has to be some driving line.

It's another family than Scorda that has the daughter who can read the future. The other Scorda son becomes a singer.

The theatre production with the crime committed there.

The Count insane in the palace.

Ian, black haired, handsome, with ugly hands, the Hawk—the blonde seventeen-year-old poet.

+   +   +

Time to do some serious thinking and revising of the whole flow and structure of the book. The point is, it should be an adventure. It should exist outside society and work into it, rather than existing in it and working out. There is something very American about Huckleberry ... alas. The things that work for me are the Scorpions, the Monastery, and afterwards. Physically I like my hero. Perhaps the answer is to define him in terms of active personality traits rather than passive ones.

+   +   +

Character—that's the question. I've almost killed this book with outlining and questioning. I have Ian, whom I like as a body, but who palls on the background against which I've set him. We'll lift his name and give it to a black haired, thin boy with black eyes, and muscles struck sharply under dark skin. Large hands with wide fingers that quickly turn the inside of clocks. He has a passion to know, is brilliant and diabolical.

+   +   +

to wound the autumnal city.

Blade these streets, prowling the markets and parks of my city, riding on the highway, looking down on the storehouses, the homes at Rift's edge, the long graveyard. What purpose, or all the passion of wandering in the cold? Beyond a city of flies' eyes blown big as buildings, port, tower, and parks and museums, throng from the late theatres across Sovereign Plaza, Ian stalked with the divergence of Bellona's light deviling his eyes.

+   +   +

What is the desire?

The atmosphere is of obsession and heavy baroque landscapes—but not the sophistication of *Nova* and *Babel-17*.

Ian, some sort of criminal. An all-purpose adventure, feeling outside society. A dark man, tall. The face was classically handsome, dark eyes below black hair that often fell loose. The hands, much too big, frightened many people. Veins bound craggy knuckles and high ligaments together. The wide, callused fingers ended in gnawed wrecks.

+ + +

The great Halls of Scorda, combed with secret passages, uncompleted, magnificent, with movable gardens and mystic pools, and in the garden of the equinox, the Sky Globe.

Black Jason, with his harem of wives, sons and daughters. His architect Xeno Rank.

The Monastery

The lair of the Scorpions, by the old docks near the sea.

The labyrinth.

+ + +

Ian's childhood: three bouts with insanity, twice through his training. Earth as not the center of the universe.

+ + +

The party of Scorda Halls
1   The Three Wives
2   George & the Baines arrive
3   Ian passes Rill on the stairs
4   Ian Franx, Stinky, the Guyers
5   Ian & Lanya (with F. S. & the Guyers)
6   General Rank
7
8
.
.
.
.
21
22

23 The Two Wives, Jane and Marlene
24 Ian alone

1   Three Wives
2   George and the arrival of the Baines
3   Ian passes Rill on the steps
4   The children and the Guyers
5   Lanya
6   The General
7   Allen en Famille
8   The General and the Scordas
9   Ian and Lanya
10 Aluvia and Rill
11 The Scorpions arrive in place of Ty Yen
12 The General and Stoan
13 Ian and the Scorpions
14 Lanya and her parents
15 Ian and Rill
16 Stoan and Scorpions
17 Aluvia and Jason, commenting on the party
18 General & the children with Rill
19 Lanya alone
20 The Guyers completely charmed by Scorpions
21 The Baines and Lanya's parents
22 Dr. Himlek, the Guyers, and Stoan
23 Denny alone
24 The Young Scordas and the Older Ones
25 Previous joined by Baron Crawford and Franx
26 The Scorpions break them up
27 Rill alone
28 Massive description of the Party—Ian and Lanya again
29 Jane & Jason
30 Ian & the Scorpions, as they go
31 Jason & the Baines complimenting him on his family
32 Ian looking at Allen et al., & wanting to go
33 The children taking their leaves (& Allen & Ian & Stoan)
34 Jane and Marlene alone
25 Peggy and Tonni ushering out the Guyers
36 Ian alone

Lanya & Ian. Politics, their dissatisfaction with Triton and Mars.
The Caprice of Chinese marriages.

+ + +

All public mistakes come from assuming the rest of the world is different from you. All private ones, from assuming it's the same.

+ + +

The understanding Rill comes to, the faults of one gen. are exactly what
threatens the next, artistically—
like Hemingway's sex and art usage,
—because these faults are what causes the hangups of the next gen.
You need exceptional indiv. or 2 gen's, to appreciate anyone.

She hates Stoan's work, comes to accept it.

+ + +

Poul asks a question:
"In the most precise terms possible, what would you like to see us—
including yourselves—do that we aren't doing now?"
This is not Poul's entire question; what he wants to know is really a very
complicated query that generates, unstated, from his whole letter. And it
is the same thing that Brian is probing in the letter (Brian and Harry's)
and (B & H) critical excerpt that provoked Poul's responses. I attempt to
answer, aware of the resonances with the larger question.
But I can't give specifics without some generalities: no one is asking any
more than that you (we) be the best writers possible. That statement is still
safe for everybody because "writer" is undefined; and I have specified the
parameters of "possible."
Next generality: S-F, as a genre of which I consider myself very much a
part, is deplorable. Considering the probable average I.Q. of its practition-
ers, the discrepancy between the intellect/sensitivity available and the
worth of its production is paralleled, maybe, by the Hollywood film (which
for a while claimed the I.Q. acme of the country among its writers, of all
professions). I don't say this as someone buried under the 95% detritus of
Sturgeon's Law. I am talking about the median, generously illuminated by
the indisputable excellences of Bester, Sturgeon himself, Heinlein, et al.
Last generality: what I would like to see is some vast changes in attitude
toward what you (we) are doing so that a question like Poul's doesn't come

off like a complete absurdity, rather like (absurdly shocking hyperbole chosen to shock absurdly) Goebbels asking "Well, what specific changes would you like to see made in our method of government?"

+   +   +

Note in the final volume: they (Ian) meets the writer who takes the journals and realizes by inserting the party sequence, he can make it a novel.
Ian refuses—the contradiction is left unresolved.

+   +   +

Rill at a premiere, black dress, silver chain, "Committed the unforgivable crime of being twenty three."

+   +   +

Structure for *P. M. L.*

Begins with journals of Ian
The Party—done in objective prose
Followed by journals of Ian again.

+   +   +

The first principle of organization is selection. Some is, and some isn't.
All organization springs from this. When I place this in my frame, you consider it. I place it in relation to the other objects in the frame so you can consider the relations.
Now—aesthetic problems arise when you place an object in relation and other relations arise as well which you *don't* want considered.

+   +   +

From the beginnings of the Industrial Revolution through World War II, fiction writers have mainly dealt—albeit using a variety of techniques—with the tensions between the individual and his environment. For this assumption to work, "environment" is almost always basically bigger than man, partaking of "great cosmic" forces, at best something that man can realize is there; at worst, something completely beyond his comprehension.
Through the information revolutions that have come about in the last 25 to thirty years, there is a girdle of urban oriented humanity about the globe who sees environment quite differently. Environment is seen today

almost as a projection of man, his will or his caprice—often his stupidity or ignorance, but always his responsibility. In America, it is very difficult to walk through our great forests and not be aware that they are "national parks." The feeling that you are standing where no man has ever stood before, for most of civilized man is a poetic anachronism. Space exploration may ultimately revive this. But to date, the number of people who have orbited the earth in space satellites could not fill out the roster for Columbus' three ships.

If we err today in assessing our environment, it is because we assign to man what is *not* his. But it is the same process which caused writers like Zola, George Eliot, Frank Norris, or even D. H. Lawrence to see such denotatively human institutions as railroads, factories, even cities as reflections of natural forces.

To see the world as basically a projection of our collective consciousness does not make it any more safe. This shift in vision took place in the light of the discoveries of psychoanalysis. If anything, knowing these psychological dangers makes us more accurately aware of what our grandparents meant by "forces of nature."

It is very much from this current consciousness, however clumsily, that my own work comes.

My first novel, *The Jewels of Aptor*, was written when I was nineteen and living in a lower East Side tenement whose halls were roamed in winter by packs of wild dogs. It was inspired by a series of extremely vivid nightmares that left me with terribly [clear] visualizations that I could not articulate to my wife; so therefore tried to organize into a tale for her. It has all the faults of enthusiasm and youth. If it has any redeeming worth as entertainment, it is because my wife was an editor at the time for a publishing house that specialized in speculative fiction (and who eventually published the novel) and would come home excruciatingly aware of the most common flaws of the genre; I had to avoid them out of embarrassment. But the landscapes through which the protagonists and villains amble and machinate are quite nakedly dream stuffs to which I tried to give only the barest external cohesion.

In my next three books, *The Fall of the Towers*, I wanted to deal directly with the idea of man's environment as a projection of himself. In '63 & '64 the atrocities of Vietnam were making those Americans of sensitivity completely revise their opinions of themselves and their country. The first Kennedy assassination (I was delivering a manuscript to a publisher that afternoon; when I walked into the elevator of the office building ignorant of the Dallas disaster incident, I walked out of the elevator able to announce to the staff of Meredith Press, "He's dead." Thus our consciousness is shifted by an elevator man with a transistor radio.)

On the one hand, there is no American who was not shocked by this assassination. On the other hand, no American who was in touch with the tenor of his country could honestly have been surprised. These are the incidents that were happening around the writing of the trilogy and are reflected in it. Robert Heinlein had recently published an extremely popular novel called *Starship Troopers* which is basically a defense of war as a civilized practice. More frightening than his thesis, which is assumed rather cavalierly as an intellectual conceit, is [the] cogency of his logic (if you accept his basically absurd premise: that the enemy is not human, by any definition).

The *Towers* were planned in direct response to Heinlein's book. Its referent is "war." But its major character never is in battle. The textual elements of the books are gleaned from the occurrences happening at the time of writing:

One country, alone in a world of radioactive wastes, has managed through technological development, to reach the point of economic excess and socio/psychological tensions where it must have a war. Since there is no one left to fight with, it invents an imaginary enemy and funnels its population and technological excesses into a frantic mock battle that the populace does not know is a projection of its own collective nightmares. When the situation is revealed to the populace, a "truce" is declared. But the "imaginary" will not accept it and moves on to destroy the country.

The plot weaves characters together from all social classes, with— artists, scientists, beggars, tradesmen, aristocrats, and soldiers. The central question of these books is: what is the meaning of "freedom" within such a society?

If I had answered it to my own satisfaction, I should have written no more novels.

The next two years I drafted three novelettes (*The Ballad of Beta-2, Empire Star, The Star-Pit*) and a full-length novel, *Babel-17*. All of them in one way or another show characters coming to terms with their own projected realities, against landscapes that are, in turn, my own personal projections.

At the completion of the last of these, I was able to trade the static poverty of a New York freelance writer for the mobile poverty of a free-lance writer roaming Europe. During that peripatetic year in Greece and Turkey and Italy, I did much of the work on *The Einstein Intersection*.

Some months after I returned to New York from London, a number of things happened with propitious coincidence. *Babel-17* tied for the Nebula Award of the Science Fiction Writers of America for best novel of the year in the same week that *The Einstein Intersection* was published. Shortly thereafter a controversy that I have seen the beginnings of in London, the various merits of "New" and "Old Wave" science fiction, broke on our shore. Both factions seem[ed] to find enough to praise and damn in my work to keep the critical [dialogue] going for another year, whereupon *The Einstein Intersection* and a short story "Aye, and Gomorrah" both won Nebula Awards as best novel and best short story.

If there is anything "new" in *The Einstein Intersection* it is that the projected reality is all mine and the protagonists do not so much try to come to terms with it as live with it, navigate through it, do the things it demands of them—but they do not strike out at its basic nature, as, for instance, does the heroine in *Babel-17*, or the heroes of ever so many other S-f novels.

Nova, my most recent book, though different in texture and structure from *The Einstein Intersection*, shares this. I find myself, since *The Einstein Intersection*, less and less interested in telepathy and time travel, and more concerned with internal psychology and time as both historical and psychological projection.

I am currently finishing a novella, "Time Considered as a Helix of Semi-precious Stones," which is something of a prologue to a larger work currently under the working title *Prism, Mirror and Lens*, a very long novel in which I hope to explore this fully. As the field is deployed today my sympathies are with the growing number of writers who see the boundary between S-f and that which is not S-f breaking down. There is as much pressure from outside the field as inside to bring this about. I feel that it is happening through no more effort than that which the writers expend at the typewriter. Most of the commercial S-f writers are quite frank about not being interested in the aesthetic of writing beyond that which directly bear[s] on the tale of adventure set against an imaginary background, which is a more accurate description of what the genre S-f really is.

+ + +

People to send *Nova* to

Robert Duncan
Gary Snyder
John Ciardi
Tom Veitch
X. J. Kennedy
Robert D. Cohen
Lew & Ann
David Hartwell
James Sallis
Marie Ponsot

+   +   +

Lay axes on the circle of the century and cut me a quadrant. Third quadrant if you please.

Editorial note

Two winters ago I was given the Scorda notes for publication. I had judged six months ample for assembling the five volumes. Two years and three complete sets of galleys later I am still not satisfied. The historical interest in these notes is manifestly evident. Ian Scorda lived through the most fascinating decades of the past two centuries; scholars, looking for analogs from the classical period, when earth was home, always search out a comparison at this point. But the truth is simply that a single world could not produce an analog. Imagine Hitler and Napoleon alive and operating at the same time, then contemplate the journal of a young man who spent time as a close friend of both, from his adolescence through his manhood, who had a chance to view the turmoil, the glories and the evils both men generated about them, was mobile enough to move through several different points of view. The editorial problems have been those of bringing the incidents of historical interest into historical focus. Ian Scorda was not writing history when he began these eccentric reminiscences at age eighteen. Nor was he particularly interested in noting biographical information about the two colossi who shattered the twenty-third century and who implemented, from either side, the Revolution. When he began these notes, both men already had established political reputations, but it is fairly obvious from the first pages, that Scorda was concerned, first, in chronicling his own shifting consciousness, and second, in describing the people and objects that impinged on that consciousness—i.e., what he saw around him. Both giants so impinged, and he described them as they did so. But as time progressed, when it must have become evident to Scorda that indeed what he was writing (or recording; a good third of these notes were dictated in a portable recorder; we are publishing the transcriptions) was history, it is exactly at these times that he explicitly claims himself uninterested in the public, often taking refuge in the totally ambiguous.

But Ty Yen and General Tomlin Rank dominated the last quarter of the 23rd century. It would be fairly inconceivable that any diary from this period, if it touched the public world at all, would not reflect these giants.

With all of Scorda's attempts to retreat from their influences ("retreat" is the word some commentators have used to describe his actions), it is fair to say that they dominate these notes as they dominated their times. There are perhaps fifty or seventy-five people who could have met both Ty Yen and Rank. But the partisan split between them[1] was such that the people who left records of those meetings were liable to make much of one and as purposefully ignore the other. For much of his life Scorda set himself the stated aim of ignoring the historical; he managed to ignore the partisanship. Therefore his notes remain the only [first] person account of a relation with both figures.

But I have been detailing the elements that make these journals interesting today.

The difficulties that I have encountered as an editor are the following. First, the particular disaffection, self-involvement, and general over-indulgence of those admittedly extant, but avowedly morbid centers in the personality (while there is a good argument to be made that it is the disaffection that allows them their bipartisan observations which is their major value to us today) that are indicative of an intellectual pose with which we have little sympathy. Ian Scorda was from a wealthy and powerful family. Indeed, this is the only way that he could have been in the position of observation that he was. But he had the vision if not to analyze, to intuit the social discrepancies between the wealth, the power, and the uses of that wealth and power in the world around him. Hence the vague feelings of discomfort and disaffection that plague these pages from first to last, the masochistic preoccupations with violence, physical and psychological, the onanistic sexuality that informs his ponderings, even his relationships, most of them psychological debacles for all concerned.

The notes open with unrealized rebellion against his family structure; they close with them, as they have to if this edition is to have any of the feel of the disorganized sheaves of script that were delivered into my hands. But this *is* a popular edition and the editorial decision to be made is between deleting these morbidly reflective sections that contribute nothing

---

1. Case in point are the Himlers *père* and *fils*, who are responsible for the definitive biography of Ty Yen and the extremely useful, if not definitive, biography of general Rank. Since we know for a fact (from Scorda's notes if from nowhere else) that both Dr. George Himler and his son Franx were in a position to meet both men, it is amazing in all that survives of both men's writing there is no mention of General Rank in the work of the elder George and no mention of [Ty Yen] in the younger Franx.

to the historical portrait for which most of our readers will be turning to these volumes. Or, discovering some way of deploying them through the edition so that they, one) are not so intrusive, two) are not too far away from a chronological order, and three) where possible, to place them where they highlighted some incident previously described (or in several situations anticipated something about to happen) as to provide resonances and unity. The latter choice, was (of course) my decision. Hence two years rather than six months. The other major editorial decision concerns another of the two-faced aspects of the work. The characteristic accompaniment to the malaise claimed by Scorda is a dilettantish (and usually completely romanticized) concern for the arts. Again, through his social origins, he had the exposure to the best art available in his day, and through temperament he sought out a number of the artists whose work we do turn to today for an expression of the times. Indeed his relation with the sculptress Rill Di Quema is what first made him the subject of scholarly inquiry and which first unearthed the existence of these journals. But it must be remembered that his mother Aluvia Scorda was the center of a very vital group of artists: those who enjoy the particularly textural approach to sonic structuring characteristic of the music for a fifty year [period] before and during the revolution consider the most successful of her compositions equal to the classical music of the one world period.

Ian Scorda considered himself a failed artist—a failed novelist to be exact. Among the notes there are a number of attempts at fictionalization of the incidents described. None of them are complete. It is doubtful that he showed them to anybody. He is a failed novelist. The most fully realized is the first attempted. After the age of 27 they cease entirely. The inspirations for these attempts seem to be the moments when he could actually be enthused about the "historicity" of the events he had lived through—usually a few months after they had occurred. In such a mood he attempted the fictionalization of the party given by his parents for the architect Xero Stoan. I have placed it as the second sequence. It was written perhaps a year after the notes that open the book, which were composed the night the party actually occurred (the first half of the first page has been torn away, hence the notes beginning in the middle of a sentence). The editorial decision here is a classic one; how much fictionalization has occurred. From the manuscript one would hazard very little. Most of the characters are given their real names (including Ty Yen and Rank). The names that have been changed are disguised with the thinnest of camouflages. Franks Himler for Franx Himler; and the families Hynes and Foyer are fairly recognizable as Baines and Guyer; at least this is the editorial position I have taken. Although he caricatures them so heavily they might well be composite portraits. The reasons this might possibly be the wrong editorial decision [are] equally apparent. When Scorda fictionalized, the majority of the time is spent reconstructing things he was not physically present at. Of the minuet-like conversations, encounters and cross-encounters that make up the party sequence, Ian is only present in nine out of forty.[2]

Although the only people he treats subjectively are members of his family, where perhaps he had reason for feeling he could project their psychologies, the reader should bear firmly in mind, while perusing these pages, that as these notes move into the objective narrative, they are actually at their most subjective, are most completely a projection of Ian Scorda's inner world, rather than any representation of the historical reality of events. In the light of this, the thing that I, as an editor, found the most distasteful, is the interminable aesthetic theorizing and agonizing over the narrative craft by a writer who never produced even one completed short story—who, indeed, there is more reason to judge[, was] the most reprehensible and execrable of criminals.[3] Indeed, it is only circumstance that makes his logorrheic outpouring relevant to us today. I deplore the hagiographic tone which a number of commentators have adopted when dealing with the fragments of this oeuvre that have been published over the last 25 years. I equally deplore the absolutely archaic and self-righteous tone other commentators have assumed in attempting to vilify him (to borrow a classical image: they have only betrayed the presence of his grave by the dirt they have heaped thereon). We live in a much more emancipated time than Ian Scorda, morally, sexually, economically, spiritually; this no one will deny. There was a revolution 200 years ago: suppression—moral, sexual, economic, spiritual—is the fire that ignited it. That is simply an unavoidable historical truth.

My final editorial pronouncement, then, and the one that implies a decision that all editors before me have shirked: this five volume edition contains every word that has come down to us from Ian Scorda. Torn

2. During which time he is always a third person character (even in the diary proper he often refers to himself in the third person, part of the dilettantish affectation of his time).

3. Such metaphysical concerns are doubly reprehensible from a man in the middle of a revolution when all situations around him are demanding a personal commitment.

pages, references, notebooks we do not possess assure us that this is not every word he wrote. Conceivably, if some of these lost pages reappear, we might alter our conception of the man. At any rate, this is the first edition that can claim to contain every passage extant, if not in the order in which it was written or transcribed.

I feel safe in saying that the one thing this edition does, is to hold up to us in a way that no abridgment could accomplish, the man in his times for us to view in the light of our liberality.

His hagiographers cannot bring themselves to admit that as a saint, there is no concrete thing, there is no action of his we can point out which had consequences in the way that we can point to the actions of half a dozen people he describes; Ty Yen and General Rank are only the most obvious examples.

Even his journals and incomplete fictional attempts have no aesthetic weight without extensive editorial rearrangement. His vilifiers, hopefully, at the appearance of this edition will have to come to terms with some of the facts that they have heretofore passed over. One understands why they have. Our "liberality" is such that, at two centuries' distance, it is astoundingly easy to romanticize his most "reprehensible characteristics out of all proportion." Because they are true and sincere vilifiers, they avoid even mentioning these, for fear they will inaugurate the process unintentionally. Still, facts cannot be avoided. Not only by the constricted morality of his own time, but by the far more enlightened standards of ours, Ian Scorda was a sexual deviate in the profoundest sense. As well, for all his agonizing over the unachievable perfection of a nonexistent aesthetic form, he was an assassin, a mass murderer; he died in his bed, having fathered a dozen-odd children, and from these pages one gathers he felt only the most peremptory guilt for having done either.

George Ernstbarger
New York
January 2889

+   +   +

Dear Tom,

Vital statistics; these are all my sold short stories to date with these three exceptions: "High Weir," "The Power of the Nail" (a collaboration with Harlan Ellison) and "Helix," the story I finished at your home in Milford a few weeks ago. But for all practical purposes, between age twenty-three and twenty-five this is my complete short fiction.

The major concern beyond the game of aesthetics which is, of course, my passionate preoccupation, is in the area of social and economic density: eating, sleeping, and earning a living; how people who do it one way spend their leisure time (most adventures happen in what is basically one's spare time, and only become significant as they resonate with eating, sleeping, etc.), and secondarily, how people who do it one way react, communicate, or fail to communicate with people who do it another.

Looking over these tales, I suppose they are all my more or less bungling attempts to deal with the "eternal verities." Oh, well. If you could say something about them, it would be most appreciated.

I have ordered them as they proceed into the "future," which with one exception, means in the order that they were written: exception is *The Star-Pit*, which was written first and which I place last to preserve some unity.

+ + +

What is hap:

SF presaged this change
Now it doesn't—

There are people [...] workin' in the idiom of the field

The scientific predictions influenced scientists
The method of thinking has distilled out

Looking for new values to replace the values which were criticized only in S-F

The problems of living in a synthetic environment

Romantic-realism

Mutation—informed sources—Vonnegut—Sturgeon—Leiber—Ballard

The environment—humanity in terms of the world we are living [in] & the world into which we are moving

The conventions of lit. create a certain optimism—even with black humor

An interest in color, adventure, that certainly makes reading more interesting

Aim of anthology—select work that has optimum combination of experimental thinking & contemporary writing

SF-12. Haven't pushed as hard for ex. techniques, & experiments aren't obviously successful

I do subscribe to the old idea, that reading should be entertaining, esp. reading that calls itself fiction

+   +   +

WOW!

To travel.

Overwhelmed by what is going on in a small segment of academia:

Somewhere between the descent for kicks and the decree for life—there is beginning to be an intense interest in thinking & learning.

Milwaukee—the professors' interdisciplinary com. on different levels is happening—and increasing.

Clarion—set up by a prof.—But the students. The intensity they brought. The first accredited college course in fantasy writing. A resident course. All the students are in one dormitory building.

Reactions to *2001*—discussion lasted several days.

The 3 BBC tapes.

Fiction has fallen far behind the graphic arts & music.

Harlan bought four stories for his anthology.

¾ could become selling writers.

+ + +

Deployment of forces, landscape, and characters to further a conceptual understanding on the part of the author of chapter seven, "The Scorpion in Harbor," of his novel "Faust."

1

> The waterfront is blanketed by fog. The Captain and Kirsten sit on the wheel house and talk about Faust, begin to make love, wonder where Gunner is. They want to take off before dawn.

2

> Gunner
> Replotting of the last chapter.
> First Kirsten with Sambo, Nig, and Dove, a rather idyllic gang-bang. The Gunner with Donnie, Bull, and Nazi, which gets more and more violent, and stops when Nazi takes out his knife.
> The captain on the boat, has decided not to wait for the kids. Sandy comes looking for a job. "I'll do anything for you, Captain. Anything." They sail into the foggy night.

+ + +

My mother is music. My father is politics. The verbal arts are a language game by which we can win back time.

+ + +

August 12, 1968

Once again you have let the confusion level get too high. What is to be done—

This morning heard the news from C.V.J.A. when I called up *Crawdaddy* that Don McNeal had drowned up at Trina's summer home. Very upsetting. I had only met him two weeks ago, when Paul W. brought him over at 3:00 in the morning. They stayed around till five and we had much pleasant conversation and taped a rap and I very much wanted him to come back. A gentle, grimy, and articulate young man. How the patterns break up.

Mailed off my essay on Joanna Russ to Richard Patt in Baltimore.

Later on Bill Meyers dropped by, a neighbor who wants to work for *Crawdaddy*—he'd been down there this morning—who had read some of my books and article. Large, absurdly healthy, very affable, thick blond hair and black framed glasses. We had coffee, talked about a mutual acquaintance, Karen Dalton, and then he hurried tactfully away. A big, freckle-handed young man; hope he gets the job. I like him.

The question: to organize the schedule of my writing. As things stand, everything juts and flies. Nothing comes to rest.

Things to be done:

Article for *Crawdaddy!* But it requires research.

The pornographic novel—if I work on that anymore my dick will fall off.

Zodiac—but I seem completely unable to hold the characters in my mind. I must sit and force myself to read the MS. from beginning to end, and then define the major traits of the two main families.

Who is Lanya? Who is her father, her mother? There must be more polymorphous families—at present, Scorda's is the only one. Otherwise, it won't make the contrast between the insularity of Lanya's seem strong enough.

+ + +

Harbour of the Scorpion

Structural notes: Gunner and Kirstin are back. The Captain gets up, walks up the dock, turns down by the hall of mirrors, discovers the cellar window is open. At the church Niger joins him silently, he stops before Faust's studio, begins to go in, but hears Faust whistling happily. Goes back. Finds Robby waking up, anxious and eager; sends him to get something in the town. As soon as he goes, he wakes Gunner and Kirstin and sets sail before Robby gets back.

+ + +

Restructuring (yet again) for Faust

Chapter Five

... The rape of Mary Ann, followed by Robby, finding her; she runs to the church. Faust's speech, with a call to gather the Demons: because that is the only way he can fulfill his fantasy, and Catherine is all that can tempt the devil at this point.

Nig, Dove, Dommy, & Nazi (transferred to the Hall of Mirrors basement)
Kim & Bull on Colson Hill, to get the drugs.

Benny's tale when Gunner asks about Dommy.

Further speech by Faust (?) interrupted by a phone call from the church to inform Bull about the rape of Mary-Ann.

+   +   +

The theme of *M.P. & L.*

The (sociological) descent from the haut bourgeois that does not lose one access to the h.b. *because* of the media revolution.

The great theme through which all must be focused.

Ian's resignation of the h.b. which does not lose him their advantages—a sour grapes novel that works because the world is not the same as it was—five, ten years ago.

+   +   +

Now, let us look at "Alchemica" a little more closely than we have been. (Here it is, past midnight at the Déjà Vu, days before the autumn equinox, which is my deadline for the completion of *Faust*.)

Possible structures.

A long introduction in which Nazi finds Nig & Dove—no, no, it already feels wrong.

As they all gather behind the *Hall of Mirrors*, Gunner asks who that man in the basement is. A scientist who invented a strange drug that is passed through the system. Bull is going to release him, but Benny runs in and tells that father Michael is there. People begin to take their pills.

The interview between Bull & Father Michael. "She is like a daughter to me ..."

Bull goes to the back: explains he has to go, and that Catherine is alone in the church. Who did it? Father Michael thinks it's a drifter who's just come into town.

The Captain: Naw. It wasn't him.

Bull: Sure?

The Captain nodded.

+   +   +

Thomas M. Disch

Am bed ridden with grand malaise. Beg your forgiveness.

Chip

NOTEBOOK 79 — [WINTER 1968]

In this strange field of speculative fiction, where the blurbs and bio-graphical squibs so frequently offer the amount published as an indi-cation of the writer's competency and craft ("... has over three hundred stories and articles in the country's leading magazines ..." I see on the cover flap of a book currently on my desk), I can give only the most mea-ger list of fictional works. Seven years of publishing stories and novels leaves me with well under two dozen titles. I have published substantially less non-fiction; the four available pieces that relate to speculative fiction I would allow for consideration are a biographical piece appearing in the fanzine *Lighthouse* in 1967, "A Fictional Architecture with 365 Supports that Manages Not Once to Mention Harlan Ellison," an article in the sub-sequent issue, *Lighthouse* 1969, "Faust and Archimedes," a discussion of the work of Thomas Disch and Roger Zelazny; there is also a guest edi-torial in *New Worlds* #173, for 1966, "Sketch for Two-Part Invention" and "The Five Sided Mirror," which will shortly appear in Langdon Jones's an-thology "————" published in England by Hutchinson, a collection of notes on the speculative novel. Rather than exhaustive bibliography, indulge me by letting [me] give not first publications, but rather the most accu-rate publications. Speculative fiction remains a commercial field which almost guarantees some butchering in the initial appearance. The lists are in order of composition.

Shorter fictions

The Star-Pit	*S-F 12*, Judith Merril (ed), 1968
"Dog in a Fisherman's Net"	*Nova*, Harry Harrison (ed), 1969
"Corona"	*Best from F&SF*, Ed Ferman (ed), 1968
"Aye, and Gomorrah"	*Nebula Award Stories*, Roger Zelazny (ed), 1969
"Driftglass"	*World's Best SF*, Terry Carr (ed), 1968
"We, in Some Strange Power's Employ, Move on a Rigorous Line"	*F&S-F*, Ed Ferman (ed), April, 1968

"Cage of Brass"	*If,* Fred. Pohl (ed), May, 1968
"High Weir"	*If,* Fred. Pohl (ed), October, 1968
"Time Considered as a Helix of Semiprecious Stones"	*New Worlds,* #185, Michael Moorcock (ed), 1968
"Night and the Loves of Joe Dicostanzo"	"————," Anne McCaffrey (ed), 1969

Novels

The Jewels of Aptor	Ace Books, 1968
The Fall of the Towers:	
Out of the Dead City	
The Towers of Toron	
City of a Thousand Suns	Sphere Books, 1968 (Great Britain)
The Ballad of Beta-2	Ace Books, 1965
Babel-17	Ace Books, 1968
Empire Star	Ace Books, 1966
The Einstein Intersection	Gollancz, 1968 (Great Britain)
Nova	Doubleday, 1968

+ + +

Image rules.

1) Never answer a reviewer back on a criticism—either in print or in person.

2) Never give a literary example of anything from your own work.

3) Never refer to a specific problem you have had with a publisher; always generalize.

4) Never apologize for any piece of your own work.

5) Never talk about specific influences—where you stole the necessary things you stole.

6) Only response to a reviewer if response is called for is to thank him for the time he took.

+ + +

The bridge:

Include the synopsis of the tirade on "Modern Woman," or think about it.

Insert: p. 11

Geo began a philippic on the problems of Modern Women. It held me by its wit. I goaded him, taking everything he offered as revolutionary and pointing out how old-fashioned it was. Goad him it did. We amused ourselves like this for blocks, till it struck me that the inspiration for all this wit was sitting alone back in his apartment. The whole business suddenly seemed rather empty.

+ + +

Love

When we are in it—everything describes it. Leaves on the sidewalk, bird flights, children's movements on a playground. Just out of it, we only know how indescribable it is, and the attempts of others seem painfully banal. But later (when there is hope, need, anticipation) we grow easy with the poems and proselytizing.

Love cycles between "joy" (the word is inadequate to that elation and contentment); "pain" (how "pain" brutalizes those exquisite anguishments). The young search it out with passionate diligence; those a few years older fend it off with wit.

In its straits, the young grow older and wittier, and [the] old mellow under years of it, growing wise and sincere.

+ + +

Works in 1968:

3	"Cage of Brass"
4	"High Weir"
16	"Time Considered as a Helix of Semi-Precious Stones"
37	*Equinox*
_7_	"Night and the Loves of Joe Dicostanzo"
75	

7	"Faust and Archimedes"
7	"The Five-Sided Mirror"
5	*2001*: Film Review Plus Music Reviews
5	*Charley* " "

5   *Barbarella* "   "
5   *Black Easter*

16,000 Criticism
75,000 Fiction

Jrrnal.

In Search of
Silence

"I want to declare that I am a traitor
to the human race."
— Henry Miller

Make me a mandrake, so I may groan here,
Or a stone fountain weeping out my year.
— John Donne

... that strange craving for sea-sickness
children have.... But certainly I felt this
strange need, even more than they. I liked to
feel my heart beat irregularly and fast. The
spectacle before me, so rich in poetry, satisfied
me more.
— Raymond Radiguet

First page of "In Search of Silence" (Notebook 2 – January 1959).
Courtesy of the Howard Gotlieb Archival Research Center.

I

In the search for the things I can not say
I move through the crevices in the city, the
streets, the littered alley-ways of winter. I
was born in autumn, though my birthday
in in April, and my road travels through
an icey, January sun. I want to prologue
what I have seen with something that
opens me up, something that tears apart
my face and lets you look behind my eyes.
They say that thought is an inversion
of experience; what is experience, then:
an extroversion of thought?

I am strangled with words, suddenly,
and the things which need to be said — t
don't even know what they are. That's
why I cry so poignently at times; and the
poignance is not because my situation calls
so much for pity, but because something
is locked in my gut was screams for love,
and so this something makes me effect
poignance; for pathos is a subject I am
well studied in. There was brilliance I
once wanted to to achieve, an ebullience
of style and subject, but I don't have
it — it was never mine to exercise. Why
does language suddenly burst forth for some
— sometimes for me — and rocket the hearer
and the heards so far that — that —
and here the metaphor fails, language fail,
words become depleted to bags of breath
and sighs, and I can find no semblance
of meaning in any thing.

This incalculable emptiness that is as

Second page of "In Search of Silence." Courtesy of
the Howard Gotlieb Archival Research Center.

much inside me as out —

— When I had worked my way to the back of the bus — No!

It was hot with people, and in the bus you have to strain ~~away~~ to reach over old lady's sholders so that you can ~~reach~~ prob reach the ~~strap~~, and when you finally get back where there ~~are~~ are not enough people to be uncomfortably crowded ~~I~~ and too many to feel free (and my coat was for the brittle winter air outside, not the ephlufia of body heat that bloats up a crowded bus) you can reach a fair sort of ballance between agony and simple displesure. ~~In the back seat was a~~ The back seat of the bus runs from one side to the other, ~~and~~ The rest are placed either in rows along the side or, (in those places just over the wheels) with the seat backs to the wall so that the people in them must ~~either~~ stare straight across the aisle into the dull faces of those people perched above the other wheel who are staring back.

There was a boy in the back seat, with a blue zipper jacket on — he was near fourteen. He had ~~a~~ good hands; I remember that's what first made me look at him. Then suddenly he turned away ~~the~~ behind the sholder of a bigger boy who was sitting next to him and spit up a handfull of brownish fluid into ~~his~~ palm. He must have been trying to hold it in, but he couldn't, and he

Third page of "In Search of Silence." Courtesy of the Howard Gotlieb Archival Research Center.

vomitted again, this time all over the ~~sleu~~ sholder of the boy next to him. He got out his handkerchief and tried to wipe his hand, and wipe off the ~~boy's~~ sholder. The boy ~~and he~~ turned around and ~~saw~~ saw what was happening, ~~He~~ and gave the kid another handkerchief ~~and then he sat forward in the seat and put his and~~ Then he tapped the knee of a young guy who was sitting on the ~~other side~~ of the kid. The guy was probably asleep, ~~but~~ and the boy had to hit him hard, but when he woke up, he looked and then moved to a seat infront of the back seat, and he tried to tell the poor kid to relax. The kid sat there with his hands filthy and all wrapped up in the dirty hankerchiefs. ~~Then s~~ He was embarrased as hell, and when he ~~tried~~ had to spit up again, he looked around and tried to do it ~~behind the~~ in the seat behind the first boy, only it ran all down his blue zippered jacket. The first boy had moved foward in his seat and now he rested his ~~head on~~ arms on the back of the chair behind him ~~and put~~ his head down on his arms. The guy who had moved was patting the kid on the knee and telling him to relax and there were tears streaked across the kids face, not from crying but from the effort of trying to keep it back. The kid just sat there with his ~~jacket dirty on~~ streaked and his hands and pants messy. ~~You~~ I could smell it now.
One ~~middle aged~~ ~~old~~ man in a brown coat ~~g~~, clutchin

Pete makes face masks through
the blanket, in the sand.
"Here," he says, "Feel it."
I put my hand in. (His arm
is sun dark, but his sholder
is white.)
"You can feel the eyes, the
nose the chin."
We have been in the water +
dry now (on a red blanket in
the sun).
Something I remember brings
me to the point of all this.
While I was walking to the boat,
I reached back to adjust the capo
on the guitare. I pricked my
tumb on a loose string, and
sucking it, a drop of blood, when
I looked, glazed thin through
saliva over the whirls of my tumb
print. I sucked it, and then
it stopped. For a moment then,
I wondered I would be able to
play if I was called. But I
didn't hurt, so I forgot
about it, until just a few
moments ago. I didn't record it,

Excerpt from *Journaux d'Orphée* (Notebook 12–July 1960).
Courtesy of the Howard Gotlieb Archival Research Center.

— almost. But these journals are not to remember the things I record, but for all the things that pass ~~noticed~~ un-written, and forgotten. That is far the majority of the trip. For all the single drops of blood at Newport, or anyplace. For shadow configurations on the sand, to Pete's wet hair, dark and filimental, to all the things — the million un-recorded thoughts I have over Eurydice. That's what these journals are for.

Pete digs beside the blant un lifts out handfulls of wet sand, only a few inches down. I relax + watch. ▮ (close to 6:00, Pete says.)

Bongos down the beach.

Recorder replaces Bongos.

Pete looks for faces in a stone. Now he tosses rocks in a bean can. The sea csound behind.

An occassional gull: black dots skimming over clear blue glass.

Excerpt from *Journaux d'Orphée* (Notebook 12–July 1960), continued.
Courtesy of the Howard Gotlieb Archival Research Center.

It's a port city.

Fumes have rusted the sky ~~here~~, the General thought. Layers of industrial gasses flushed the evening with oranges, salmons, purples that ~~were~~ too ~~red~~ ~~with a reddish hue~~. ~~To the~~ the West, the ~~pale~~ ~~cloud~~ ~~were~~ lascerated again and again the clouds ~~by~~ (descending ~~and~~ ascending transports ~~com~~ shuttling cargoes from the ~~inter~~ Stellar-Centers and the inner satelites.) It's a rotten-poor city, thought the General, ~~He~~ turned the corner by a garbage-~~strewn~~ ~~clutted~~ curb. Since the invasion there had been six ~~mino~~ ruinous embargoes ~~so~~ ~~strange~~ that for months a piece had ~~and~~ strangled ~~this~~ this ~~sprawling~~ metropolis whose life line ~~pul~~ must pulse with intersteller commerce to survive. How could a city like this, ~~support itself~~ sequestered, exist? Six times in twenty years he had asked himself that question, each time with increasing panic. After the first time, the answer was obvious. It can't.

Panic, riots, burnings, ~~twice~~ ~~canabo~~ migrations, twice canabalism —

flies eyes, blown ~~tags~~ as building
~~and~~ ~~buildings like flies eyes~~
Wound the autumnal city.
Beyond ~~the glittering slabs of~~ building, ~~beyond~~
~~the ports~~ ~~sort, tower~~ ~~and the towers~~, ~~pass~~ and ~~the~~ parks, and ~~the~~ museums,
~~the~~ throngs ~~drifting~~ from ~~the~~ late ~~shows~~ theatres across Sovereign
Plaza, beyond the ~~slab~~ the Cage, shot ~~through~~ with
markets, I an ~~came~~ unblemsd with the divergence of ~~two~~
~~moonlight on~~ Bellona's lights devilling ~~his~~ green
eyes. ~~The sting strut was~~ puddled ~~his~~ ~~made a the~~
~~walked~~ Through a puddle; ~~and the w which licked~~
~~muddy tongue on~~ the red ~~dust~~ grit dusting his
boots. ~~I~~ The wire fence ~~by~~ by the torn earth
~~with~~ ~~meshes~~ of night ~~space~~. (This youngster aloneness ~~locks~~ ~~in~~ a huge thing ~~from seen~~ from ~~his~~
his eyes...)
A brown boy, and the brown burned red. ~~Eighteen~~ E
and the veins were ~~already~~ heavy over ~~his~~ arms and
big hands. Gold nests of hair on ~~arms~~ wrist and chest:
~~brown~~ on his head, brown and tightly curled. A broad
face with ~~flaring~~ ramped cheekbones, hints of epicanthi
at the ~~long eyes~~. A soled neck. ~~A heavy, grapled~~
~~body.~~ He ~~tried~~ tried to ~~move~~ ~~of~~ easy; ~~ordk movement~~;
its effect was primative ~~fine~~. He played his
hand ~~along~~ on the wire and gazed ~~into~~ in the ~~tear~~
~~quarter tear a~~ mile tear; ~~in the~~ rusty rock. Water.
Three buldozers. Two beds of concrete, one
here, one way over there. ~~beneath shovel~~.
The foundation diggings for [the Bellona
Coloseum]: a wound ~~as the~~ widening. I an

Opening scene from *Prism, Mirror, Lens* (Notebook 33–December
1967 [December 1967–January 1968]). Courtesy of the Howard Gotlieb
Archival Research Center.

11

....

To San Francisco

....

Upon his arrival in San Francisco on New Year's Eve, Delany was met at the airport by Hacker, Bill Brodecky, Paul Caruso, and Joe Cox. That night, the five made the rounds of New Year's Eve parties. Delany moved in with Hacker on Natoma Street; Caruso was their roommate.[1]

Delany continued to work on *Prism, Mirror, Lens*, but the work stalled in the early months of the year.[2] He began reconceiving the project, retaining its far future scenario but focusing more closely on the urban landscape of a futuristic San Francisco. But he remained dissatisfied, and his subsequent decision to reconceive the project signaled the beginning of the writing of *Dhalgren* proper.[3] The fallout from this decision, coupled with the new prominence of San Francisco during this period, marks a new phase in Delany's journals—which will be presented in the next volume.

NOTES

1. Samuel R. Delany, "Chronology" (unpublished personal document, 2014), 16.

2. Samuel R. Delany, "The Making of *Hogg*," in *Shorter Views: Queer Thoughts and the Politics of the Paraliterary* (Middletown, CT: Wesleyan University Press, 1999), 300.

3. Delany, "Chronology," 17.

Reconstruction of the lost MLA seminar

Introduction:
   The difficulty of the internal description
   Wittgenstein's prop.
   Ballard despairs of the future.
   The number of books and writers.
Body
   Zelazny
   Disch
   Russ
   The development of consciousness (natural in the decade that has made psychedelic its catchphrase)
Conclusion:
   Why is it science fiction. The distancing process changes.
   The difference in the order of subjunctivity

+ + +

RÉSUMÉ

Samuel R. Delany
1067 Natoma Street
San Francisco, Cal.
94103
Phone. 415–626–9142

BIRTH:
I was born April 1, 1942, in New York City, and grew up in Harlem, the city's black ghetto.

MARITAL:
My wife is Marilyn Hacker (*The Terrible Children*, Ravich Press 1967, *Be-*

fore the War, The Communication Co. 1969), poet and currently editor of the poetry quarterly *City*. We were married in Detroit, August 24, 1961.

MILITARY:
I was declared 4-F in 1966 through a combination of medical reasons including insufficient control of eye muscles resulting in lack of depth perception and an adolescent history of ulcers.

EDUCATION:
I attended kindergarten at the Horace Mann Lincoln School. From my fifth year through the eighth grade, I was a pupil at the Dalton School, from nineteen [forty-seven] to fifty-six.

I graduated from the Bronx High School of Science in 1960, having been an editor and contributor to the school literary magazine, *Dynamo*, for three years, and a feature columnist for the school newspaper.

I attended City College for two years from 1960 to 62, completing one and a half years without declaring a major. During my last term I was poetry editor of the school literary magazine, *The Promethean*. My first novel, *The Jewels of Aptor*, appeared while I was still a student, and I left school to devote myself full time to writing.

Subsequent History
During the next two years—Summer 1962–[Spring 1964]—in New York, I completed a trilogy of novels, *The Fall of the Towers*, followed by various shorter pieces, including the novellas *The Ballad of Beta-2*, *Empire Star*, and *The Star-Pit*. My next full length novel was *Babel-17*, a novelistic exploration of the limits of language.

Autumn 1965–Autumn 1966—I traveled a year in Europe. Spending eight months in Greece, the rest of my stay was divided among Paris, London, Venice, and Istanbul. *The Einstein Intersection* was written during my travels, a novel that deals with the resonances between ancient and current ("pop" if you will) mythology.

Autumn 66–Winter 68—Again in New York, (with a brief visit to London for the '66 holidays), I finished my most recently published novel, *Nova*. During the winter of 67, WBAI-FM of the educational Pacifica Radio Network, selected *The Star-Pit* for dramatization. I did the adaptation and worked closely with the technical crew (original music, electronic and otherwise, was composed for the production). The drama and literature director of the station, Baird Searles, informs me sometime later that the two-hour production had drawn twice as much mail as any previous dramatic presentation in the station's quite substantial history—a warming revelation indeed.

In May 68, I was asked to take part in the "Secondary Universe" conference at the University of Wisconsin where I spoke on the panel, "New Directions in Speculative Fiction."

In July I took part informally in the Clarion College [Workshop] of Imaginative Writing, directed by Prof. Robin Scott, which entailed reading and criticizing of student manuscripts, and informal lecturing at the morning sessions.

Thomas Clarisson asked me to deliver a seminar at the Modern Language Association convention in New York on "New Directions in Speculative Fiction." The paper, "Here and Now and Speculative Fiction," was read on December 27, 1968.

1968—Immediately following the MLA conference, I moved to San Francisco. My wife and I intend to reside here while I complete work on my current novel.

Publication:

Novels

The Jewels of Aptor (pub. 1962)
The Fall of the Towers (a trilogy):
   Out of the Dead City (1963)
   The Towers of Toron (1964)
   City of a Thousand Suns (1965)

Babel-17 (1966)
The Einstein Intersection (1967)
Nova (1968)

Novellas

The Ballad of Beta Two (1965)
Empire Star (1966)
The Star-Pit (1967)
We, in Some Strange Power's Employ, Move on a Rigorous Line (1968)
Time Considered as a Helix of Semiprecious Stones (1968)

Short stories

"Corona" (1966)
"Aye, and Gomorrah" (1967)
"Driftglass" (1967)
"Kage of Brass" (1968)
"High Weir" (1968)
"Night and the Loves of Joe Dicostanzo" (1969)
"Dog in a Fisherman's Net" (1969)
"The State of Kings" (1968)

Awards

Undergraduate

National Scholastic First Prize, in Short-Short Story, 1958
National Scholastic Third Prize, in informal essay, 1958
New York University Prose Writers Contest, First Prize, Short Story, 1959

Professional

Scholarship for the Bread Loaf Writers Conference from Harcourt, Brace
    for a novel submitted in 1959
Science fiction Writers of America Nebula Award, for best speculative
    novel of 1966 (*Babel-17*)
Science fiction Writers of America Nebula Award for best speculative
    novel of 1967 (*The Einstein Intersection*)
Science fiction Writers of America Nebula Award for best speculative
    short story of 1967 ("Aye, and Gomorrah")

+ + +

MYKONOS '65, LONDON '66,
NEW YORK '67, SAN FRANCISCO '68;
NEW YEAR'S EVES

> *There are some cities you*
> *must be dying to visit.*

A bit north there is another city,
Anó Merá, where we do not go in

this world with no winter. The wine-shops
        closing early make the fishermen
despair as much as the internationals.

But John will stay
up as long as I will
and talk by the cistern
        we can hear our voices come back from
the cistern. We can watch

the moon through cactus paddles
while we try to define:
that the worst of them are
        awful and the best indifferent
is the easy way. Rather

it is as hard to admit
what you have done as what
you have not. This is
        a place we do not usually go, and
certainly not on holiday.

She said, in London, "I've
been up since four. Come
in and teach me your old
        family recipe for egg-nog.
Let's have a wild party."

Here, time allows me winter. In Camden Town
there was another party to which
(she said) I certainly couldn't go.
        Pamela brought homemade masks and Tom
wore full dress among the jeans and paisley.

I wondered what the old
family would do if it could see
me now. "Now is specious," I explained
        to someone with a violet shirt and acne.
"This year we admit the violence in our faces.

"This year; and we have learned to bear
what is cleared by proximity,
blurred by temporal distance."
        Next year no one in my family
made egg-nog. In my mother's

beige and green rooms, I got the feeling
there was some place I should go.
Looked through the picture window at
        New York's winter rain. Midnight over
I stayed up till four, with my wife, reading our old journals.

Let's admit just because we have
or have not is no reason not to want to go.
Tell me, can you bear another city?
        Sure, if I survive the year. Rumours
Come back from places we never visit.

Some don't survive; that some run crying
into the bone cage, into the night's socket,
claw up the rugs and eat the tufts
        from the carpet tacks, outraged
by all that has no definition, dying

when their names are mispronounced. "Let's have a party!"
The basement of the Stanford Court apartments
looks like a ship. In the elevator
        Turn out the light and watch the sky
come at you in the hatch. The court-

ings and counter-courtings, from the Nob Hill roof,
lend the city definition. (but every one of us here
is basically an Indian giver.) At
        a Haight Street party I sat in black light
and watched a tall girl dancing in the corner,

watched a corner redefine a dance. "I admit
there simply are some places in the city
no one in his rightful mind would go

after dark." Behind the Christmas tree
The bay window is black. "Basically though

it's just a lovely city. At the airports
this afternoon at four? ... Oh. Do you intend
to stay?" but there are more here to talk to,
      even when they have to ask your name,
asking only you allow their voices to
bring back more than messages from their family,
fixing the city to the year this year.

Jan 3, 1969
San Francisco

+   +   +

PROSODIA

First, can it be taught. If
it cannot be taught, is
there any way to keep from going mad?

The choice, as of early January: shall I take eight thou a year to teach a new
experimental course
      in creative writing at Penn, or
ten thou to teach Afro-American lit. upstate?
A stipulation with A-a-1 is freshman English.
      Can it be taught? Brodecky says
      good art makes excellent art
      look better, the human that allows
      a community of art. Of age, I know
      that community. What kills the adolescent
      prodigy is the sureness that no community is possible. No warm one.
How do you tell someone in love not with the sound of his own voice, but
the very muscularity in the tongue shaping other men's words that he has
something to say that cannot be said in anything other than his own voice.
Then, assuming this is learned, how do you tell someone to follow a canon
of thirty thousand years that pre-ordains each chip of the chisel, brush-
stroke, or word. And assuming that has been learned, how do you explain
it has to be if this is all forgotten each time the pen comes from the paper,

the brush halts in the impasto. And
must be learned all over at motion's commencement
and that the gauge of difficulty
though inaccurate, is the only one that even hints.
That it is a process, not a thing,
 That it is a process
which makes things bearable. Well,
  at least it can be taught.
  What will we do with our
  re-assurance of sanity? How do you
  explain that the noun in English can bear
  no more than one adjective, despite
  Hardy; that a prepositional phrase
  weights the end of a sentence
  and drowns the meaning despite
  Marlowe; that poetry is information
  of a specific order, but
  repetition of information is one) boring,
  two) insulting whether it be from
  poem to poem, even word to word,
  and no one likes to be told what
  he already knows, sanely.
That the aesthetics of a rose window from inside the cathedral this evening parallel the placards above the cross-town passengers.
That the mother screaming at the four-year-old in the Hyde Street
Market is the reason for both yet has nothing to do with either.
  This simplicity: a poem is a particular
  person talking about a particular
  situation about which he feels a particular
  way. This complexity, practically all
  work is to clarify
  person, situation, work, way.
  A painting is a particular
  person looking at a particular
  situation (often no more than a configuration
  of paint) from a particular
  direction.
  Person, situation, of paint, direction.
Doing it is ultimately a matter of sanity, and

explains all of Mr. Duncan's Wednesday Evening Service,
as well as Mr. Donne's and Mr. Taylor's. To say
that it should not mean but be is a lie
by misdirection. It relates to the world.
It is what propels past the lip, laughter
or the hiss.

+   +   +

There is no way to escape pain, suffering, ennui, or death. But pleasure, the most terrifying, a few of us can elude.

+   +   +

The process by which public speech becomes private. The process by which private speech becomes public. Took half a dozen novels learning communication wasn't just a socially useful inevitability of the process. Certain shapes called poems hold meanings, but the poet is the maker of shapes (with words), the person who knows in the heels of his hands, poems come before communication. A poem about poetry is a poem about the season's changing. If you start by writing love poems, you will go on to write poems on how poetry works.

+   +   +

You learn art looking at it.
Craft you learn trying to make something that looks like it and why doesn't
it?
Look at it.
Communication is something that always happens when you achieve art.
Art does not always happen when you achieve communication.

Give the word.
We will inform the word.
(We will tell it what we want it to mean?)
The problem is to forge and purify the voice
   before we forge we heat
   before we purify we clarify

A poem is always about how much the words can tell you about what the poem is about.

+ + +

I was born in 1942, & grew up in New York City's Harlem. My first novel, *The Jewels of Aptor*, [was] published when I was still a student at the College of the City of New York, whereupon I left school to devote myself full time to professional writing. Since then I have been winner of the Science Fiction Writers of America Nebula Award for best novel of the year twice, and once for best short story. This past Christmas, I was invited to deliver a seminar "New Directions in Speculative Fiction" before the Modern Language Association.

In all areas of writing there are elements of craft and art. The one can be taught; the other, if it cannot be taught, can at least be encouraged. The ability to articulate what we think, express vividly what we feel, and recount accurately what we have seen makes us more responsive to our lives on all its levels, as well as more responsive to what we read.

+ + +

A poem is sketched here between retort and forge
make gold in the mouth all moving
turn in this, maunder in that
while we blow the morning fatigue—
    What is this moment's coming
    essence, and what moors it to the falling moon?

Feb 7, 1969
San Fran.

+ + +

I am not likely to believe it unless it has something of passion.
Even if it's about boredom, alienation, or the one we can't name that [we] examine.

+ + +

The purifying of the voice
The forging of the voice

Time and narrative:
    Microscopic narrative.
    Macroscopic narrative.

Isomorphic narrative. Linear representation of a moving pano-
rama.

The dynamic moment—
Present behavior is the resolution between an ever changing picture of
the world and an ever changing picture of the self.

NOTEBOOK 37—APRIL 1969

[February–April 1969]

On reading yet another biography of Byron and Shelley

> I fall upon the thorns of life! I scrape
> my knee and bind it with adhesive tape.
>
> —Marilyn Hacker
> February 21, 1969

+ + +

> I live with lust, I live with death.
> I cannot live, except in lust.
> My worth from heaven, (my faults from myself)
> from my chosen actions, which is stolen.
>
> My freedom his servant, my divinity mortal
> to me. Oh unhappy state.
> What misery, to what a life I am given.
>
> —Michelangelo
> after Gerald Langston Fabian's translation in 1969

+ + +

My library specialized.

Poems of Keats, Letters of Keats, paperback. Trilling editing is really incredible—or maybe the paperback editor is to blame.
Selected poems of Byron   Leslie Marchand—editor
Evil Companions by Michael Perkins. This is the point where pornography and poetry join. No, George Bataille already achieved that (not to mention Cleland).

+ + +

Notes for *Prism, Mirror, Lens.*

Eventually have Hogg read over the first scene with himself (when they're stranded someplace) and be very dissatisfied with it.

The last notebook should be stolen too.

Audrey, at the end of this one turns into a tree. The tree turns back into Audrey in the beginning of Book 3.

+ + +

The loss (misplacement?) of a notebook impels this:

Structure:

Hogg, already clear as a stricture of bone and callus, muscle and hair. Hands and cock roped in the same thick veins.

Jerk-off, discs of plastic on the spatulas of his fingers, his smile and his ignorance supporting him through indulgent labor.

Angel, just that, too young & too depraved & too strong. Black hair, soft mouth, seventeen, and no childhood.

Night, often trying to be Hogg's alter ego, and yet is the intersection of some funky smells, a dialect, and a job. He endures in me, a bit. That's what I seek.

+ + +

One writes; and that's knowing how to do something. One lives; and that's knowing how to do something else. But the time spent are sides of a single surface. Is it real?

—April 9, 1969, San Fran

+ + +

Childhood / Joaquin Faust
(party)
poet
thief
(Faust's death
his own child)
king
mystic
(nature idyll)
old age

as a child he spares an old man
as a thief he spares a poet

as a king he spares a thief
as a mystic he spares a king
as an old man he helps a child

as a poet, he hates his childhood
as a thief, he puts down his poetry and wants to recapture his childhood
as a king, he forgets his childhood. New intellectual rebels put down his poetry. Others idolize his thefts.
As a mystic, he realizes that if the society needs the myth of a poet who was a thief, they will use it. If it needs the myth of the thief who became a king, they will use it. If they need a king who became a saint they will use that. He puts down his kingship but occasionally pines for the days of being a thief. The absolutions, near the end of each period, help him go on to the next.

+ + +

to wound the autumnal city.

Must tell the story.

But there, while I got up to pace and ponder (in this room where Bill painted a mural a year ago in sloppy lavenders and greens, and in the room beside it, the sides of the heater bell) I look back and see that some-one has already stolen the first notebook.

Probably Taq.

Probably Chayn.

They are crouching now, I bet, in the corrugated walls of the San Francisco Gear Works, burning my spiral notebook (160 narrow lined pages) leaf by leaf. Taq holds the match, and snickers. The light gets lost in all his hair, red as a polished penny, blurs and flashes on Chayn's leather and zippers (with maybe a glitter on the gold sand of his stubble). Start all over? Tell you who I am again? Why they helped me when they helped me? Why they hindered me when they did? Why they sneaked in here to steal all that (what Chayn was doing with the key in the first place)? And why I'm going on?

I'm fired, and I'm exhausted.

To go on, and too much so to go back.

No, I'll go back again to tell you about the girl with no name. And again if I have to. And again.

[sequence continues]

The problem is the five-part novel for Avon. The whole work, primarily—what happens. There is a revolution. The major point of view is a disaffected Ian Scorda. But I don't like disaffected characters. You want to write an inner landscape novel, a dark book of madness and internalized sensibilities.

12

Appendixes

Although Notebook 89 has been given no date in the catalog, internal and external evidence strongly suggests that it precedes Notebook 1 and is chronologically the earliest notebook in the collection. First, using a numbering system he applied to most of his Bronx Science notebooks, Delany had written "Vol. I" on the cover of this notebook and "Vol. II" on the cover of what the Gotlieb archive designates as Notebook 1. Second, the "Howard Pease" story in Notebook 89—the opening of which is excerpted here—is briefly continued in Notebook 6, where Delany designates it as having begun in "V. I." Third, the people named in the outline at the beginning of the notebook are all friends from Science, rather than from NYU.

I have placed Notebook 89 in an appendix for several reasons. Most crucially, its juxtaposition with the fuller version of Notebook 1 in the second appendix highlights important structural relationships between the two notebooks. Furthermore, having traversed the volume the reader will recognize numerous relationships between the material in Notebook 89 and various earlier entries; placed here, Notebook 89 invites the reader to reconsider that earlier material. Finally, separating Notebook 89 from the chronological continuum of the volume, highlights the fact that the Delany archives are a work in progress: undated material forms an important part of their contents, and further archival work remains to be done.

Outline for "Great American Novel"

Section One

Part one — Satisfaction of Readers;
1) Love seekers.
2) Cleanliness seekers.
3) Human seekers.
4) Escape seekers.
5) Reality seekers.

Part two — Weaving of Themes.
1) Love & Escape — method; similarity
2) Cleanliness & Reality — method; contrast.
3) Victorian Myth & Human — method; absurdity.

Part three — Frustration
1) Victorian myth — Pseudo-human
2) Pseudo-escapists
3) Pseudo-realists
4) Pseudo-cleanliness
5) Pseudo-humanist
6) Pseudo-love seeker.

———

Section Two

Part one — Episodic character study
1) M. Hacker
2) Cary Reinstein
3) Jean-Pierre Schachter.
4) Stuart Byron — (Shelley and Lord Byron)
5) Chico Ramez — (National Geographic, Sputnik)
7) Louise Steiner.

1) Part Two—plot. (I, the innocent bystander)

2) Tragedy of J-P. Schachter; M. Hacker.

3) Tragedy of M. Hacker; Cary Reinstein

4) (her father's death)

5) The anthology incident—(Plot intro-

6) -duction of S. Byron)

7) Tragedy of C.R. and M.H.; Louise Steiner (and Flip-

8) Chico Ramez)

9) Marilyn Hacker & Me.

10) Tragedy of Stuart Byron. (figure out some-

11) -thing)

12) Chico, Louise; Marilyn, me.

———

Section Three

Part One

1) Satisfaction of Reality seekers.

    a) Negro bourgeoisie spree.

    b) White-black love clash which doesn't quite make it.

    c) Bohemian white and black uncomfortable mix up; Nany's party, you know …

2) Satisfaction of Escape seekers

    (A little adventure of some sort with Chico, me, and characters of Section One)

3) Satisfaction of Cleanliness seekers.

    a) Snow with Chico

    b) I meet the happy love seekers, Bobbi & Joe.

4) Satisfaction of Human seekers.

    After the incident with Bobbi & Joe. "They went too far; he had to marry her that February. That was sad too; nice people; and maybe it was wonderful. I hope so. Hope, I do hope."

5) Satisfaction of the Love seekers.

    a) Cary & Louise once & he tries hard but doesn't make it.

    b) Chico & I come up with Marilyn from the night.

+ + +

The Place of The Individual In Society

Of the 2.5 billion people on this earth, every one of them capable of thinking must have performed this catechism at one time or another:

Who am i?
What am i?
Why am i?
I have no answer.

———

Society is the necessary outgrowth of man upon the earth. It manifests itself in two forms: where in one, the wishes of individuals determine the movement of the group, or two where the group determines its own movement.

———

We live in a horribly complex matrix of socio-psycho-(group & individual) pressures, and tensions. In this matrix the individual locomotes; he locomotes within the boundaries set up by these pressures; when these boundaries inhibit the wishes of the individual, he may do one or more of several things. 1) He may accept the inhibition as it stands. 2) He may not accept the inhibition, deny its existence and move as though it were not there. 3) He may try to find the cause and source of the inhibition and try to remove it.

Many times 2 & 3 turn out to be identical. The inhibition is there simply because people acknowledge its existence. In order to remove this inhibition we need only to deny its existence, or as in this case acknowledge it as a non-entity. Whether or not an inhibition can be denied successfully is determined by several factors. The first I shall discuss is that of cause. A pressure can generate from either an individual or a group. Because of the physical aspect that an individual is more mobile than a group, it is more dangerous to cross, e.g. children playing in a vacant lot. If the lot is owned by a man (with a shotgun) who is there to protect it from children who appear to have difficulty reading "No Trespassing" signs, then the lot will probably remain, for the most part, relatively free of pests. On the other hand, same lot, same sign, this time owned by the Board of Education (incidentally, same children), we will find that come hell or high water, the brats will be scrambling around like mice. This example showing the mobility of the group as opposed to the mobility of the individual, has several interesting connotations. The one which probably comes to mind first is, why doesn't the Board of Education hire a guard? In nine out of ten cases, this is what happens; we then have the concept of an individual enforcing the ideas of a group which is the basis for government.

Who is a member of society?

Those who may influence or be influenced by the bonds it sets up. The most pertinent factor here is probably geographic location. Next, and closely linked, is communication.

Who—individual or group—generates the bonds which holds the members? This too is a factor in seeing whether or not a bond can or cannot be broken by tracing it to the source. Previously we have mentioned, 1) Inhibitions generated from an individual, 2) Inhibitions generated from a group. (I may remind the reader that in this case, when the bond is denied, there is little the group can do—that is, a group which is accustomed to functioning intellectually; I was not referring to mob violence which is a very interesting facet which will be taken up later) and 3) we mentioned bonds generated by a group, and enforced by an individual. So far I have been referring to physical rebellion against mentally generated inhibitions. May I point out that this is the only kind of rebellion [with] which society is concerned. No matter how much you wish to differ, you can think about *anything*—I reiterate Anything under the sun, and until this thought manifests itself in some physical form, even such as writing it down, you can't experience any social inhibitions.

+   +   +

Peter Salaff

To grow with a musical instrument is a wonderful thing; Peter honestly could not recall when he had not played the violin. He grew up with sort of an extra mouth with gut and steel vocal cords. Technique was something which he really sat back and laughed at. Maybe he wasn't a great violinist yet—greatness in music is beyond technique—but he could talk with the violin just as he could with his mouth. He had as much to say as any fourteen-year-old had to say, and being fourteen myself it was enough for me. I remember once we were listening to one of the Brandenburg concerti. He had the score right there and was just sort of sitting playing along with the record, only he was jumping from part to part following the melody. That was the first time I knew what the melody was supposed to be.

You wouldn't believe it, I guess, but I've only seen him twice in my life, but he made quite an impression. The first time was when a very bohemian type girl gave this party out in Croton; it was one of those all night things were everybody sleeps on the floor, and nobody ever gets to sleep. Peter happened to live in Croton and was invited. He was as shy as hell and he didn't have his violin (which someone remarked to me in passing that he played very well). I have two assets, and two faults. The faults are one) I wear glasses, I guess I'm just pretty ugly in general, two) I have a violent superiority complex which as usual is a shield for a pretty poignant inferiority complex. My assets are one) I play the guitar, two) I have an almost inexhaustible supply of folksongs when I feel like coughing them up. Well the assets were outshining the bad points and pretty soon we were all sitting around singing songs; it was then that I became aware of Peter.

* * *

Beginning of Howard Pease Adventure Story:

Black Watch and Treasure.

I—<u>Flight in the Night</u>.

The sea swelled heavily by the shore line waterfront of the M'mbay, tugging at the worried boats with the tide call of "To sea, to sea!" The land was black with fog pierced occasionally by a street lamp feebly glowing against the night. Numerous little side streets passed in and out of obscurity, and from one of these streets came a man. Tall and fascinatingly snakelike. He walked under a dimly glowing lamp and his features shone out broad and black; he was a Negro, tall, slender, ebon skinned and his smooth teak like skull covered with a well shorn pate of close cropped bristly wool. He wore a black turtleneck sweater, black pants, and shiny leather boots. His black hands had their strong thumbs hooked over black leather belt; he was completely swathed in night, skin and clothes, save for a silver buckle. Unobtrusively decorated with intricate scrollwork, at his waist. He carried himself with the elegance of a king, ears alert, ivory eyes slicing the fog.

There was a sound in the night and a figure came pummeling out of the inky fog. His hands reached out and caught the boy by the shoulders.

Just before those incalculably strong hands grasped him from his flight, Larry had been running as fast as his bare feet on the ill cobbled street would take him. He was panting heavily, his frayed jeans flapping around his legs. A penniless American youth can get into quite a fix in an unknown port in Africa. He had come as cabin boy when his father had died, in search of adventure. But that was what seemed like years ago; he had found no adventure, only hard work, and he wanted no adventure, he wanted to get back to the States. But the States were far from his mind now. He was running for his life now. Two huge burly blacks chased him with death in their minds and hands. He had stolen some food from them, a piece of meat which he clung to now, scared as a chicken. It had been lying wrapped in blood soaked paper beside them while they dozed half naked in a night dimmed doorway. The messman who was his only friend on the boat, would fix it for him and he would feast. The ship's food, even for a friend of the mess, was putrid, and the crew never passed up an opportunity to swipe food when in port. So he ran with the blacks hot behind him. Then suddenly he was jerked violently under a lamp light and he was staring up into the calm eyes of a tall slender black.

Immediately Larry saw this was no common nigger of the ports. The black looked down at the white boy's face, bronzed by work on the ship's deck, the ill-kempt blonde hair and frightened eyes. He glanced down at the package to which the boy hung as if it were gold.

"They're ... after me ..." panted Larry in complete despair. He heard the sound of feet running behind him. He jerked away and crouched beside [the] man like a dog seeking protection from its master. The two Negroes lumbered into view under the glow of the street lamp. They stopped when they saw the tall slender Negro, and stood there, arms dangling like two apes. Bare footed and bare-chested, rag-shaggy pants wrapped around their middle with filthy ships-rope. Larry saw that they were looking at the man beside him, they seem to have forgotten about the meat; he was about to turn and run when the black beside him spoke. It was a strange language tinted with the accent of the jungle. The voice played forth like the low register of an oboe. The sound was so strong that Larry stood there transfixed. The other men mumbled something and pointed to Larry. The man's long hand shot down and retrieved the blood soaked package from Larry's arms and tossed it to the waiting darkies who slunk off into the night again with their treasure returned.

"Gee—" said Larry, "Thanks, mister."

"Who are you?" asked the man in strangely accented English.

Larry was surprised. This man who conversed in the tongue of the bestial savages of the jungle, was now talking to him.

[*sequence continues*]

+   +   +

The Lost Generation

And so we too arose from tumult of the stark and raging night and are the lost generation. *Who we are* runs amok in hysterical pandemonium, torn between Dostoevsky, Hemingway, and Pamela Moore; and Ginsberg Howls; and the eternal Françoise Sagan—are of the lost; who we are. Those who are snared by an all too complexed society and drowned amid the inhibiting, censoring bonds of a sick civilization, are we.

Let's pause for a minute and figure out a Christmas list. Inside the family there is: Daddy, I mean:

1st
Daddy
Mom
Peggy
Grandma

2nd
Dorothy
Boyd
Barbara
Betty and Julian

3rd
Tante
Sweetheart
Uncle Myles
Uncle Lenny

Burton
& Sylvia
Sonny
& Barbara

Edward
Nany
Bill
Aunt Laura and Uncle Ed

+ + +

Lost Generation (continued)

I read of people like myself who found that they were swarmed about
not so much by sheer ignorance but rather ignorant society which left us
stranded without roots or handhold where we too might find a place to
stay as man was meant to be.

And then I wondered just who really were the lost. Though I do find
myself amidst a swarm of crumbling, crass, tradition. Flinging out with
lewd, archaic morals-symphonies, perhaps it is not I who am the lost—(I
reach my hand from out the muddy rubble in search of understanding of
three great billion circled souls)—rather it is those who so inundate themselves with broad rococo newel posts on which they languid rest in abject
luxury and say with lips of tepid coloring and cheeks spat upon by waxen
petaled yellow roses; "I stand alone!"

———

Character beginning

He grinned slightly as he moved forward facelessly. He brought his
arm up across his chest, then swung it out full force, bringing the back
of his hand, curved slightly to extend the muscles, slashing down across
the jaw of the other boy's face. The blow cracked out like a rifle shot. He
let the backlash come on bringing the palm—hard—up across the face
still coming forward. And down—knuckled once more opening a slash
along the boy's cheekbone—crack—up once more, and the head snapped
around and went down slowly; the backlash ripped up again knocking the
mouth lopsided and limb muscles cracked it back into place, and forth,
and back, and forth, and back, following the slowly crumbling figure to
the floor until he was kneeling over the boy with his hand walloping the
lolling head left and right like a relentless perpetual pendulum. Panting
through the grin, he stopped. Then he stopped grinning. Very seriously he
stood up, breathing hard.

+ + +

Planning out a narrative.

The first thing to do is pick a point, or rather first pick a subject and
about the subject, a point to make. All that the reader is interested in is
"what people do."

What did I do.

I woke up in [an] infant world of white.

Short Story.

In the November of the city—so diametric to the November of the country—he walked with a deceivingly purposeful expression on his face which was meant to tell the numerous people whom he passed—I have a destination! I am going someplace! And I will arrive!—which was of course an out and out lie; nobody paid attention anyway. Down the busy fairway of humanity parading itself on the carnival [...].

And cars.

Inevitably cars, roaring silently along, their horns stilled by the inculcated fear of the law which towered over the slaves of the gasoline-circulatory systemed vehicles, threatening monstrous twenty five dollar fines for illegal disturbance of the great peace of Broadway.

And people.

Incessantly people who roared silently too with Madison Avenue twenty five dollar junior executive attaché cases. A lady with the eternal bundle of packages brushed by him. He looked at her hands as he saw them disappear behind him—they both continued seemingly oblivious to each other—they were rather slim, he reflected. The veins showed only slightly beneath well padded skin. He observed that he could conjure up no recollection of her face.

[sequence continues]

+ + +

Book Collection

The Rule of the Pagbeasts (The Fittest)	—J. T. McIntosh	(SF)
The Bright Phoenix	—Harold Mead	(SF)
Cycle of Fire	—Hal Clement	
The Power	—Frank M. Robinson	
Fahrenheit 451	—Ray Bradbury	(3 stories)
The Martian Chronicles	" "	(short S.)
The Circus of Dr. Lao	" "	(ed.) (SS)
The Illustrated Man (SS)	" "	(SS)

The October Country (SS)	" "	(SS)
The Golden Apples of the Sun	" "	(SS)
Childhood's End	—Arthur C. Clarke	(SS)
Prelude to Space	" " "	(SS)
Reach for Tomorrow	" " "	(SS)
Expedition to Earth	" " "	(SS)
The Synthetic Man	—Theodore Sturgeon	
A Way Home	" "	(SS)
I, Libertine	(Frederick R. Ewing)	
E Pluribus Unicorn	" " "	(SS)
The Revolt of the Triffids	—John Wyndham	
(Day of the Triffids)		
Out of the Deep	" "	
Sometime, Never	—William Golding	(SS)
	Mervyn Peake	
	John Wyndham	
Rebirth	" "	
Tales of gooseflesh and laughter	" "	(SS)
The forgotten planet	—Murray Leinster	
Contraband Rocket	—Lee Corey	
City Under the Sea	—Kenneth Bulmer	
Star Waves	—Poul Anderson	
The Transposed Man	—Dwight V. Swan	
One in 300	—J. T. Macintosh	

+ + +

People fascinate me. It's a shame; my latest fixation which has been running on for a month now is a kid with a cleft palate.

I still have to get rid of Ellen. Ellen is a standby. She's a minor character who always keeps popping up with that gorgeous red hair of hers. After I write a novel about her, then I will probably be satisfied. Oh well. Ellen, Ellen, Ellen.

God help me if I'm falling in love with her! I haven't written more than a line about Marilyn. That's a shame; but Marilyn is too unbelievable. Then there's Vicky! Eternal Vicky. We need more of these socialist type women around. They know how to be good women. To hell with intellectual women. Yes! I am a misogynist at heart. I mean, I was in love with Marilyn for about three hours; but Vicky and Ellen know how to be and act like women. (good good good)

Remember to get to work tomorrow on Lewis Tassoff's portrait!!!

What's wrong with me? I'm in a slump! The only time I ever finish what I write is when I'm in a slump. Tragedy is always mistaken for pathos. I run the riot down in town: millions of Indian peasants dashing around in circles; get the connection; riot; *ryots?* ha, ha, ha. (Spanish) *ja, ja, ja!*

Why get rid of Ellen at all? She lends a note of intangibility

What follows is a more complete transcript of material from Notebook 1. The personal entries are now accompanied by the creative work surrounding them, which includes short stories, poems, story fragments, a play script, and a dance scenario.

This fuller transcript of Notebook 1, juxtaposed with Notebook 89 in the preceding appendix, reveals two significant relationships. First, we see that the earliest entry in Notebook 1—which begins in mid-sentence with the word "to," and is written on a set of pages that have come loose from their spiral binding—is actually a direct continuation of the final entry from Notebook 89, which ends in mid-sentence. (The fortuitous resemblance of all this to the opening and closing passages of *Dhalgren* will not escape the reader; in a sense my manner of presenting this material can be considered a "reading" of *Dhalgren*.) This means that the loose pages that hold the first entry, the story "The Torture Garden" that follows it, the acronym "R.U.R.," and the author list actually came from Notebook 89; at some point in the archiving process, the pages had been displaced from one notebook to the other. Under closer scrutiny, then, even the notion of the "notebook" as a stable, discrete unit is open to revision and correction.

Second, inspection of the loose pages shows that the first page of "The Torture Garden" is on the reverse side of the page containing the "opening" entry; that is, the beginning of the story is directly adjacent to that entry. When the entry is re-joined with the closing entry of Notebook 89 and the resulting entry is read in full, part of the context of "The Torture Garden" becomes clear: among other things, it is directly contiguous to young Delany's consideration of what he has identified as his own misogyny, his own sexism. This connection exemplifies the dialogical relationship between journal entries and creative work—a relationship often hinted at, but as often elided, by the selections that have been made for this volume. Again, context expands infinitely.

to every thing. That's it: my writing—at times—captures the intangible. Good for me! (Conceited bastard that you are!) And it is almost always when I write about Ellen! I must stop being so analytical when I read; and be more so when I write. I have lost more effect from the greatest works of literature than anybody in the world!—I bet. That's it! I'm too chemical. I know too much about what is being done with the words and themes. Although I can whip the words into place myself; I can see the scars on the backs of the words whipped by other writers. That analytical frame of mind is hell. I write creatively as though I were writing a math textbook, and damn it, it comes out just as good. I know what humor is, I know what suspense is. Someday I will know what tragedy is. I do not want to know; then I will be static completely. The hell of it is, when I don't understand the construction, I don't get the effect; or rather, I block out the effect. Oddly, in my contemporaries this is not true; I can read their writing and achieve the effect and not be so scathingly analytical. I hope it continues.

+ + +

The Torture Garden

She said softly, "Go to hell." And stood there quivering with her eyes closed and her lips parted slightly.

It would be very esthetic to say I was shocked dumb, hurt beyond words, broken into mute silence; but I wasn't. I told her what type of girl she was—and she wasn't that type at all—I yelled it hot to her, and she simply existed there, eyes closed, and trembling. She cries like that. I hated her; I wanted to hurt her with the most exquisite torture imaginable for her equally exquisite body. So I told her; I wanted to whip the words into place with a scathing Shavian tongue, but they came out thick and loud, crass, and messy with the gutter. The gutter is always there when your mind is numbed beyond the intellect.

Then I went away.

The air was rotten. I saw Jommy standing across the way. He asked me what I was doing.

"Nothing," I said.

"Doing anything tonight?"

"No," I said.

"Maybe you wanna go see a movie?"

"No," I said again.

We had started walking along toward some unknown place. We moved purposelessly along in one direction which changed to another as the surrounding objects dictated. I didn't like Jommy.

"What's wrong?" he said.

"Nothing." It seemed like my conversation had gone on a negation binge.

He was silent. Quite suddenly he moved off into another direction; soon I stopped looking after him.

I kept on drifting over the place in a sort of fog. Then I saw Pete. It occurred to me that maybe an hour had passed since that time when I had last seen her. So here was Pete. He had on this black leather jacket. He's the only person I know who really has one. I sat down as he walked up. He stopped in front of me. I never know what Pete is thinking; he moves like that, stiff and every once in a while he gives the impression of a blonde cadaver.

"You seen Jommy?" he asked.

"Yeah," I said.

His head went over to the side and he said sort of strangely, "Oh."

"Why?" I asked. I didn't want to know, really; it was sort of an automatic response.

But he didn't answer, anyway.

I was waiting for him to ask me what had happened.

"Where did you see him?"

"I don't remember." And I didn't.

"When?"

"'bout an hour ago."

"Oh," he said.

"Why?" I asked again.

"Too many questions," he muttered.

His jacket pulled in on an already thin waist. I was sitting so that I could only see about from above his knees to the bottom of his chest proper. He was only standing about two feet away from me.

"Yeah," I said.

He moved away and stood there blinking gray eyes at surroundings which looked quite as gray.

"What are you gonna do?" I asked him.

"What d'you mean?"

"I don't know." I felt bored and irritated and rubbed the wrong way and maybe even sick. It was a sort of intangible sickness.

"What d'you mean?" he asked again.

"Nothing." Mumbled.

"No—I mean, I wanna know what—"

"Goddamn you, shut up," I said.

"Aw, frig you," he said.

He sat down, too.

"Who are we?" I asked.

My questions aren't the kind you ask after that kind of conversation. There is a circle of people who note me only from my dabbling in the field of esoterica.

"You heard me that time, didn't you?"

He sat with his shoulders hunched forward, and swung his head up at me and leered.

I burst out laughing.

"You stink," he said.

"Yeah," I said.

"That's stupid."

I didn't want to argue; maybe it is stupid.

"What's with Jommy?" I asked.

"Huh?"

"Why'd you wanna know if I seen him?"

He sounded a word which I have a feeling means "I don't know" in at least three languages, probably more.

Suddenly I started saying things, just repeating them, verbatim, from the time I had said them to her. I didn't realize they had made such an impression on me. The words came out like I was reading a speech or something. Pete sat there listening quietly, and when I was finished, he said her name, which made me know he understood.

The wind came from noplace and moved his hair.

"I shouldn't have told you that," I told him.

He swung his head up at me again. He was staring at me.

"Stop it," I told him.

"No," he said.

I waited while he just looked. I wanted to get up and walk away, but I didn't.

Jommy said: "Hello, Pete."

Where the hell did he come from, I thought, and looked up at him.

He was standing there with a sort of miserable dignity. Pete got up and they drifted away together.

I said "I'm sorry" softly just to see how it would sound. It sounded like sandpaper over my teeth. Well bless her goddamn perfidy, I thought. She looked too innocent. Goddamn her.

A girl moved next to me from someplace (after about two days had passed).

This time, her name was Maureen. I asked her for a date, then she stood me up; then, she said she was sorry, and I said, hell, that's all right.

So went out the next evening—and we walked, and I kissed her—I mean—a couple of times, that's all. So she didn't really pull me down into it like before. I'd even maybe learned a lesson. And maybe I am a misogynist at heart, now.

It was boring as hell.

The world waved on with a million characters passing by: I caught Pete on the down way once; I grabbed his arm; "Hey; what is all this going on, anyway."

"You think I know?" he said.

"It's running out too fast," I said.

"You know it too?"

"Man, we gotta catch up to it; get back up to it."

"We were never with it to start with," he told me.

"It pulled away from you the day you were born," he said.

Then he drifted away. Sometimes it worries you and scares you even; it's like trying to think up close on dying. Maureen was a pain all of a sudden. But she thought I was a pain too by now, so it was all terminated nice and quickly.

Pete asked me—on the last day—if I minded him moving in.

I told him, hell, no, and that I didn't know what the hell he was talking about.

"I mean—I remember about her," he said.

If he had said any more, I would have gotten mad. After standing there for five seconds, I said; "I didn't even know you knew Maureen." Then I said, "But I mean it's all right. I mean—go on."

He looked at me strangely, then he laughed.

"What are you laughing about?" I asked.

He stopped. "I was thinking about what you asked me."

"When?" I asked.

"About it all running out too fast, when you grabbed me, remember?"

"Oh, yeah. What about it?"

He was smiling down at me.

"You're young, man," he said. "We're young."

"What the hell are you talking about?" I asked.

Then he really started laughing.

I called him a name: he was Jewish, and I wasn't.

"You didn't mean that," he said evenly.

"No," I said; he was a confirmed atheist and I knew it would get him on edge that he should be chagrined over a name that kicked at the religion he had abandoned.

"Then why did you say it?"

"I thought you didn't believe in God?" I said. "Why does it bother you?"

He stood there and said, "Man, you really got it bad."

My eyes were burning behind my head. "You shouldn't have laughed," I said slowly.

Then he smiled again and I felt like heat. I said: "Goddamn you." Then I said it again, and again. He kept on smiling like that and I wasn't there anymore. I put my right hand on my left shoulder and massaged it sort of. Then I swung out and cracked the back of my hand across his face.

"Jesus Chrisss—" he mumbled and moved backwards falteringly. I hit him again so hard that every muscle from my waist to my head twisted out of proportion and my mouth opened with pain in my hand.

He didn't fight back. He couldn't, I guess. I don't know—I didn't know anything anymore.

He kept on mumbling "Jesus Chris'"—he couldn't say the "t," and soon the "s"es got all tangled up with "h"es.

I didn't feel anything when I walked away.

The air was gray now, and the sky was the top of a cave. We moved through the fog; with such a limited space, I knew it had to happen.

I saw her, and suddenly I was 17 feet tall; motionless like a damn fool. She didn't want to see me—and, God, I didn't know what I wanted.

"Hello," I said.

She looked at me.

"What you been doing?" I asked.

"Hello," she said.

"Christ, it's been so long," I said.

"What?" she asked.

"I said, 'What have you been doing while I was gone?'" It was too weak.

"What?" she asked again.

"Oh—I mean—how have you been?"

"Oh—" she said, indicating that she had been doing many things. Then she giggled. I must have been grinning suddenly from ear to ear.

"You want a soda?" I asked. The soda fountain is the most important thing man has ever invented.

We were talking—or half talking. It's so easy to talk about what was said—and I was so wrapped up in what I was trying to say, I couldn't hear her. Then quite suddenly it was finished—the hemming and hawing—and I was talking with her, like before.

"I didn't like him," she said finally.

"Hell, if you don't wanna talk about it."

"No," she said. "No." But she didn't say anything about it after she thought a little while.

"Hello," Jommy said.

I turned. "Hey," I said.

"Have you seen Pete?" He looked sort of afraid. Everybody knew about what I'd done.

"No," I said, "Why?"

"Nothing," he said. "Nothing." He moved off.

"I don't like him," I told her.

"He's nice," she said.

"Maybe," I said. "Maybe."

What probably happened was this:

Jommy left, looking for Pete. When he found him, he said, "Hello."

"Hello!" said Pete.

"How's Maureen?" asked Jommy slowly.

Pete turned and left. He told me that he walked by the river. He looked at the ice floes, swelling up and down around the piles.

Pete and I were walking along that night. It had been one of those double dates. We had dropped the girls off. Funny; believe it or not, Pete was my best friend even after all that. As we moved along in the false night of the city, he began to speak.

"I kissed Maureen, tonight," he said. "That's good isn't it?" The question wasn't mine. Then he continued. "The other guys never knew about Jommy and me, did they? That's funny."

"What about?" I asked.

"Just funny. The guys never knew, and now it doesn't matter. That's through," he said. "Have you ever wondered how that starts? Maybe a year ago—maybe—and two boys start fooling around, and suddenly it's done. You don't even realize it. It's all got to do with images, it's a replacement of the father image, maybe. Hey, it sounds like I know what I'm talking about. Maybe I do; I hated my father. Sounds like one of those stupid things on that questionnaire Louis dreamed up for neurotics. 'Do you hate your father? If not, why not?'" he quoted from a practical joke dreamed up by a couple of refugees from the plains of schizophrenia. "And I never knew why. So Jommy was a father image. That's funny." He laughed. "And I was a father image too, for Jommy. That's even funnier." He didn't laugh. "You convince yourself that it's good. No, that's not quite true; you don't convince yourself. It's the only thing you know so you have to think it's good. Fathers; great fathers of ages. Then it's over, suddenly. That's good. Maybe you feel free. So now everything is all right. I hate my mother now, and everything is all right." He laughed. "It's hard to talk about seriously. 'Mysterious Convention has deemed [it] unprintable,'" he quoted again. I was surprised I recognized it. "And something even more mysterious has deemed thoughts, real thoughts, unspeakable," he went on. "It's part of the Matriarchy in which we live," he said. "So man, get with [it], before—" he stopped. "But then," he said, "it never had you. The time is running out, you told me. You were right. And I told you to get with it. Do you feel that way now?" he asked.

"No," I said.

"That's her," he said. "You know that, don't you?"

"Yeah, sure," I said. "I guess so."

"So do I." It was from a lowered head now as we walked. "The matriarchy," he said, "rules the country."

I wasn't quite sure I knew what he was talking about.

"They destroy and twist the world around their little fingers."

So I asked him, "What the hell are you talking about women for? You didn't seem to be so much against them tonight with Maureen."

"Yeah," he said, "Yeah, man. But you have to keep them in place."

"Sure," I laughed. "Sure."

I looked at him; he was right of course; from his point he was right, and from his point he would always be.

Then I knew what was going on.

We went on through the night, false with night light, and street lights in interminable rows of red and green.

Poor Jommy.

+ + +

R.U.R.

+ + +

Dickens
George [Eliot]—Mill on the Floss
Hawthorne
Thackeray
Victor Hugo—Les Misérables
Cooper
Melville

+ + +

Feb. 6, 1960—after CEEB

They came
Beneath the intransient mist among
The lame,
The blind, the mutilated, they who sung
Strange songs
Of stranger monsters who could not condemn
Their wrongs
But only drifted by and followed them.

They moved
Along the orbit of the vampire, their flight
in smooth
And rounded curves encircling light

+ + +

I waited for you down at the steamer pier. We begged some coins off the boat and dove for them. But then you didn't show up so I quit and left the other guys there.

+ + +

Blue Denim Jazz

The stage is bare except for a series of outcropping platforms of different heights and overlapping one another. Enter Peter; he goes over to the
top platform and sits on a small bench and looks offstage. The orchestra
brings in the sound of sea music with an occasional foghorn permeating
the atmosphere.

Enter Joe. He munches a hot dog and goes[,] not seeing Pete[,] up to the
level below him. Sound of a tug boat coming by.

Joe:	Hey, look at that one.
Pete:	Yeah. (He turns to Joe) Hello?
Joe:	Hi. What you doing here, huh?
Pete:	Me? Just looking.
Joe:	You down here at the docks much?
Pete:	Naw. I just came this time.
Joe:	You like boats, huh?
Pete:	Yeah—I mean—I guess so.
Joe:	I do. I think—hell—I guess I'm crazy about them. That's funny, huh?
Pete:	What do [you] mean?
Joe:	No, I mean you wouldn't think a guy like me would like to just come and watch boats, would you.
Pete:	Hell, I don't know, I mean what's wrong with watchin' boats?
Joe:	I dunno. They just move around out there and swing back and forth through the water.
Pete:	You ever seen really blue water?
Joe:	Huh?
Pete:	I mean—hell—water's suppose to be blue, ain't it?
Joe:	Sure, I guess. I mean—hell—I don't know. I don't think so.
Pete:	(Sings) Blue—
Joe:	This old river is always green—or black maybe (Sings) Blue—
Pete:	Moving blue—through—the water—
Joe:	Whatta you do?
Pete:	Blue—
Joe:	Ya' gotta be blue—
Pete:	Ya' gotta stay blue
J & P:	And this is what they call, the blue movement.

Pete: Movement in blue!
          I made it out blue
               And it stayed out
                    dragged out, blue
          I knocked it down blue,
               And it stayed down
                    Watch it fade down
                         Into blue, —
          Into a movement in blue.
Joe: Like—I mean, waddaya do—Just sitting here; that doesn't get
          you anyplace.
Pete: And that's why it's blue.
Joe: But you gotta keep it slow,
          Keep it on the go
          But go slow.
Pete: Doin' anything now?
Joe: I'm just a Joe,
          Who goes slow.
Pete: Then c'mon, huh; let's make it out some place; I mean here is
          nowhere.
Joe: Sure, c'mon.

They trot down from the platform.

Enter: Pops.

Pete: Hi, Pops. (To Joe) You wanna stay for dinner maybe? (To Pops)
          Can Joe stay for dinner—oh—Pop, this is Joe. Joe Fineberg.

Pop wears a white apron; he is a grocer.

Joe: Hello, sir.

Pops remains silent.

Pete: C'mon, Joe.

They exeunt.
Pops sits down and sings.

Pops: Years ago, years ago
And the time she goes so slow
—So slow now, since Maria died
But that's years ago.
And Maria's dead.
A vacant vanity
And half an empty double bed
Got no place to go
Since Maria's dead.
And that's so long ago
And I got a son what's no good,
Don't I know it,
Everything he does, shows it.
And Maria, she's dead
So long ago.

He gets up. An imaginary customer comes.

Pops: (Speaking) What's that? (He turns and takes some imaginary boxes and puts them on the counter) Something else, ma'am?—One milk, right here. (He brings the imaginary milk. He shakes out a non-existent paper bag, and packs the goods in. He takes a pencil and scribbles the total on the bag—mumbling) 39¢, 26¢, and—17¢—that'll be 82¢ ma'am. (he takes the money and plunks it into an imaginary cash register which rings) (he hands her the change) Thank you ma'am. (he watches the phantom exit. Then he sits down again and sings:)
        Years going by
        Too quick, they go too fast
        Watching time fly
        Everything going past
And Maria,
        She's dead.
Oh, Maria
        She's dead,
And it's no good
        living here
With a son

What's no good
    and I fear
All the time
    Which passes, passes, passing.

Blackout.

A spot light comes on and shows Betty standing on one of the middle platforms. She is leaning on one of the other platforms. She sings:

Betty: I saw a robber
              And he saw me
          And we were moving through the sun
              together
          And then that Robber
              Sang of the land and the sea,
          Of the rain and of sunny weather.

          And we moved through—
              the blue—
          Together—
              Take it
          And Make it, Escape,

          When you want to make it out
          Make it out of here
          Hurry up and take it
          Take it and get clear

Pete & Joe come out on the upper platform and a spot picks them up.

Pete: You ever been to the planetarium.
Joe: Yeah; once we went there in school.
Pete: I used to come out here and try to pick out the stars like they
         do there—Christ—I never could get past the Big Dipper.
Joe: Yeah; them pictures that the stars are suppose to make is a lot
         of bull.
Pete: You know it too? Stars, stars in my hair.
Betty: (Sings) Stars in my hair.

	Stars, stars in my hair.
Joe:	(Points down to Betty:) Hey, speaking of stars.
Pete:	Huh; what do you—(he sees)—oh man.
Joe:	(Sings) I see a star
	Moving through the blue
	Moving out on far
	Moving me and you
Betty:	(sings) Stars in my hair
	Great clouds of stars in my hair,
Pete:	Yeah man!
P & J & B:	Stars; stars, all stars in my hair.
	I saw a star
	And (He/She) saw me
	And we were moving through—
	—the blue
Together.	
Joe:	(Nudges Pete) Ain't she a peach.
	(Sings:) Ain't she a peach?
Pete:	Yeah, man.
Pete:	(calling to her) Hey, you down there.

Betty looks up.

Betty:	Hello?

J & P nudge each other knowingly. They suddenly realize they have nothing to say.

Joe:	(calls) Hello!
Pete:	(Joe nudges him—his brain sort of numb, he calls again:) Hello.
[Betty]:	(Laughing slightly […], calls back) Hello!

They all laugh. Joe's turn to think of something.

Joe:	(calls) How are you?
Betty:	(playing along with the joke—I mean, this is not the kind of conversation one carries on at 10:00 at night, yelling from the roof to the street—) I'm fine; and you?

Joe: What did you say?

Betty: I said "how are you."

Joe nudges Pete to speak—

Pete: I'm fine and you?

Betty: I'm fine.

Pete: That's good!

They laugh. There is an orchestral swell. The orchestra settles down.

In the dark the chorus sings:
            Stars, Stars, great clouds of stars,
            I'm dreaming of great clouds of stars
    (Betty & Pete:)
            Stars, stars in my hair.

The lights begin to dim.

Pete: Hey, can you come up on the roof?

Betty: I've got to go in now.

She steps out of the light and the lights go completely out.

They go on again on part of stage with a slight blue overcast.

In this spot stand two boys, the place is a drug store; they are looking at a row of pocket books. One of them takes out one.

1st Boy: Hey, look at this.

2nd Boy: Gee; I'll still be around then!

1st Boy: I know I will!

The lights get brighter to reveal Pops behind an imaginary counter.

1st Boy: Hey, Pops, you know where Pete is?

Pops answers unconcernedly.

Pops: I ain't seen him.

Enter Pete.

Pete: Hey; Hi Pops! (He seats himself on the stool next to the boys.)
1st Boy: Pete?
Pete: Yeah?
1st Boy: You seen that girl?
Pete: What girl.
1st

+ + +

——————————*Amerika*

The air stopped its breathing of the wet, damp pellets of rain and Karl
Rossman emerged from the cabin of the great ship to see the fabulously
beautiful New York skyline. The sun came down into the moist air and
glowed momentarily on the young boy's shining face; then he retreated
once more into the cabin. He walked quickly down the hall that led to
the lower decks of the crew's quarters. In these passages, the intriguing
bowels of the ship, Karl had wandered for hours listening to the obscene
and profane exploits of the numerous sailors; a passing phrase when two
sweat-hulking giants lurched by him in [the] passage—"Man, I jus' stood
there and said, woman; then I yanked at that there flimsy peace of shit
she had on; and she didn't even have a bra"—quickly Karl turned to follow
them—"and petted each one of them; jus' rubbin' 'em up an' gettin' her hot:
then I stepped back and downed my pants, see—and then I pulled out the
old log and started to jerk it off a little—the old dog just barking for her.
Then I rammed it in: hell, I nearly pinned her to the wall!" And they disappeared through a corridor in timpani rolls of bass guffaws. It was little
episodes like this that gave Karl a little lift to an already hectic trip. Karl's
living habits followed a rather erratic pattern; he suddenly decided to find
someone to talk to: That was easy enough. He descended one more level
and looked around at the base of the spiral stairway. There was a cabin he
had never entered; he made toward the [. . .] door and pushed it open. It
was small little cubby with a double-decker bed, on the top berth of which
was an inky black

+ + +

Ballet Scenario.

After weird introduction based on a dissonant sinking theme, a spotlight picks up a boy in blue-jeans crouched in fear on a platform in the middle of the stage; 6 hands come into the light, and weird lighting and dramatic, but equally weird music follow a dance, in which three furies try to capture the boy. He is trying to escape and they want to [...] keep him, and capture him. The stage is designed in many levels and the dancers move throughout the entire platform. At last they all leap on him and drag him down from the top level, and finally roll him the rest of the way down. He lands in a broken heap at the bottom of the stage. The furies fade away.

A girl comes out from the darkness. She sees him. A sailor swaggers out of the darkness and tries to make her go with him. She tries to make the sailor go away. He goes, and she picks [up] the boy and drags him out. There is a bizarre theme and children, teenagers, in street clothes, appear. They dance through the street activities of a night, going to, returning from a party, necking, a fist fight, an evening at a jazz place, wandering lonely without friends, or with a friend. The cops, sailors and drunks move among them. This scene ends in a gang war which the cops break up. From somewhere, somebody is practicing the trumpet.

Scene Two

+   +   +

Try to think up a situation involving kids. What types of characters: Ellen; a shy girl. Reserved: Vinni; Shy as hell. Tito; he is an all around type of person. Other; confused. Vivian, all around. Phyllis is out & out glamour girl type. Ruben; he will do whatever is demanded of him. Paul is an inhibited younger brother type. Whom should I pair Ellen up with? Not Paul. Who's taller then Ellen? Joe! Not for Ellen. Tito! That's who! All right. How? Vinni & Butch. Ruben with Vivian. What about Mildred? Mildred is indispensable as a character. Analyze Mildred: Nice. Shy. Likes to pretend. No! That is not right for Ellen. Characters: A Dreamer! That's right, a crazy mixed up kid. That is Ellen. Punchinello! That's Butch. But that's cruel. So what. Forget about the actors. That's hard. Let's see. I like the dreamer. And I like Ellen in the C.M.K. role. What about the boys. I like the juvenile delinquent kick. What to do with it. Tito is the hero type, he is more dynamic then Vinni. Vinni is tragic type. Vinni, he can be the juvenile delinquent with his friend. Tito wants to grow up. Growing up. There is a conflict, man—or boy, against society. What will be the symbol for adulthood. The dreamer, her symbol is the tree. The tree! That's it. It's all falling into place. Good. Tito and Mildred are brother & sister. The tree—I see her throwing herself at the tree. Ellen makes a play for him. Vinni is sort of in love with Ellen. Vinni kills Paul. Oh, that's fun. Butch, what & where is she? She wants to help Mildred. What is her problem. Vinni! That's her problem. Vinni & Tito are friends. (What about Other? Forget about him!) So far so good. What to do about Paul. I don't know! Where do we stick him in. I have this feeling we should start off with Paul. No. Yes, I don't know. I have to get a first scene. How I like the back alley. All right. The back alley. What do we do with it? I've got to get—I've got it. Mildred & Paul. Mildred to see the tree. And Paul teases her. Then Tito to chase Paul away with Vinni. Mildred—

Write it, stupid. Don't just talk about it. Write it out!

This appendix contains three examples of creative work Delany produced at Bronx Science and shortly after graduation. They were excluded
from the main body of the text for various reasons: length, absence of a
fair copy in the pages of the notebooks, lack of balance when juxtaposed
with other entries, not fitting selection criteria, or a combination of these.

The first is a short short story Delany wrote in the spring of 1959 for
students in a remedial reading class he taught at the community center of
the General Grant Houses. "Mike" and "Jesus" are based on real students
in the class. As the reader will surmise, Delany's intention was to present
a story using simple language and a limited vocabulary.[1]

The second work is a translation of the Song of Songs, which Delany
completed during his early months at City College.[2] A draft of the translation appears in the opening pages of Notebook 11 but was not included
among the selections from that notebook because of its length. The end of
the notebook, however, contains a short entry on the Song of Songs, which
has been included in the selections.

The last work is a translation of Rimbaud's poem "Le Bateau ivre." As
its composition date suggests, Delany produced it shortly after translating
Rimbaud's "Voyelles," which appears among the selections from Notebook
15.[3] Both translations were completed soon after his father's death.

NOTES

1. Samuel R. Delany, interview with Kenneth James, August 9, 2014.

2. Samuel R. Delany, *The Motion of Light in Water: Sex and Science Fiction Writing in the East Village* (1988; reprint, Minneapolis: University of Minnesota Press,
2004), 9.

3. Ibid.

THREE SHORT WORKS FROM 1959–1960

Spring 1959

MIKE,
JESUS,
AND
ME

(A Short
Short Story)

by
Samuel Delany

There was a woman who lived in my house; she told me about the Community Center. "Have you ever been there?" she asked me.

"No," I said.

"Why don't you go?" she asked.

"I don't know anybody there," I told her.

"Oh," she said, "you would have a lot of fun if you went."

"I don't know anybody," I said again.

"Come anyway," she said.

* * *

There were a lot of boys and girls sitting in front of the door of the building. They sat on benches and some of them were smoking. It was getting dark. Nobody paid any attention to me so I went in the door.

Inside there was a man sitting at a table. He was checking the names of the people as they came in.

While I stood there, four boys came in and started to go past the man without telling him their names.

He called them back but they didn't come. When he called them a second time, they came. He asked them what their names were, and they stood very still, and then they laughed. Finally he asked each boy, one at a time:

"What is your name?"

"A———a—a—Robert. Robert Harris." The boy began to giggle.

"What is your name?" he asked the next boy.

"My name is Robert Harris too." And then they all started laughing.

"Do you boys belong to the center?" the man asked.

"Robert Harris belongs to the center," the third boy said. Then they laughed again.

While the man was talking to them—I think he knew that they were just kidding and did not belong to the center—I walked by the table and down the stairs. He didn't see me.

In the basement there were many closed doors. Some of them said
MEN

or

WOMEN

so I knew they were bathrooms. There was a strange noise from one of the rooms; it was like metal clanging or cement or something.

I walked toward that door—it was at the end of the hall—when suddenly it opened and a boy in an undershirt and blue jeans came out. He walked past me and went to the water cooler. He took a drink and then started back inside. Another boy came out of the room and the two of them talked for a minute in Spanish. Then they went in the door again.

When they opened the door, I saw that there were a lot of people inside and they were working with dumbbells and barbells. I wanted to go inside and try them but I didn't know what I would do after I went in; whom would I get the weights from? What would I do with them after I got them? I had never lifted weights before.

I went into one of the other rooms. There was a woman in this room who asked me what I wanted to do.

"I don't know," I said.

"Do you want to paint?"

"Yes," I said. I didn't really want to, but I had nothing else to do.

She gave me some paints and a piece of cardboard.

"Do you want to paint on this?" she asked.

I didn't really care but I said "Yes" anyway.

I sat down and began to fool around with the paints. I painted a picture of a man on a dark desert at night. He was all by himself. Even if there are people, you might as well live in a desert if you don't know any of them.

An old woman came up to me and asked (without looking at the picture), "What are you painting?"

"Nothing much," I said. She never did look; she just walked away.

I painted some more and pretty soon a bunch of boys came in. One of them came and looked over my shoulder. "Hey," he called to another boy across the room, "come here!"

The boy came. They were the two boys who had come out in the hall from the weight lifting room.

"Did you paint that?" the first boy asked me.

"Yes," I told him.

"There are no people in that picture," he said.

"Yes there is," the other boy said. "There's one. But he's alone."

"Yeh," said the other boy.

"You paint a lot?" The first boy asked me.

"No," I said (which was true).

"Oh," he said; and then they watched a little while longer.

"Were you in the weight lifting room?" I asked.

"Yeh," one of them said.

"Can anyone come in?" I asked.

"Yeh, sure," said one of them. "Just come in. You ever weight lift before?"

"A little," I said (which was not the truth).

"You've got to start with a little at a time," he said.

"Do you live in the projects?" I asked.

"Yeh," he said. "Do you?"

"Yes. I live in 80 LaSalle."

"I live in 76 LaSalle," said the first boy. "That's right across the street."

Just then, the woman who had given me the paints called: "It's time to clean up, everybody."

I started to put the paints away. I took them over to the shelf. When I came back, the boys had gotten sponges and were wiping off the table.

"Thanks," I said. "You don't have to do that."

I gave the woman my picture.

When we were all finished, we went outside in the hall.

"Say, what's your name?" I asked; he was the shorter one of them.

"Mike," he said. "Some people call me Micky. Some people call me Mike."

"My name is Chip," I told him. Mike went over to the water cooler to take a drink. When he finished, he took out a comb and combed his hair.

"Which building do you live in?" I asked the other boy. We were walking up the stairs.

"I live on the corner of Broadway and LaSalle," he said.

Micky came up behind us. "His name is Jesus, but we call him Chu."

"Oh," I said.

"Do you play basketball?" Micky said.

"Not very well," I said.

"Do you want to play with us tomorrow?" he asked.

"O.K." I said, "but I don't play too well."

"That's O.K." said Chu.

"Yeh," Mike said. "But you come anyway."

When we went outside the center, the sky was very black but the lights from across the street made everything look bright.

"I guess we'll see you tomorrow then?" Micky said.

"Yeh," I said. "So long."

"So long," they said and I watched them as they crossed the street, shoulder to shoulder.

Spring 1960

Ch. i

This was her song of songs which is Solomon's:

Oh, that you would kiss me with your mouth
for all your loving is better than wine;
for the savor of all your sweetness,
and the taste of your name like poured perfumes,
the virgins cluster about you.
Go quickly, and I shall come after,
for when your kingship calls me to his chamber,
while memory flowers in my skull
I shall know you are loved by good men's straight arms.
> And though I am onyx-skinned and comely
> as the drapery upon the poles of Kedar's tent
> or your curtains, Solomon, I will say
> to Jerusalem's women who stare at my darkness:
> "I took grapes at my brother's vineyards,
> so my own are wild and torpid."
And, King, where have you pastured your flocks,
beneath what shadows did you slumber at noon-tide?
Did you dream of me, and not of your handsome men?
> > *Wouldst thou know beneath what shadows*
> > *I take the noon in my hands*
> > *And scarf it 'round my neck like a golden chain,*
> > *Let its sheer folds drift jewels across thy cheek?*
> > *Then walk by the footsteps of the flock*
> > *And feed the young goat in the shadow of the shepherd's tent.*
> > *Thou art a mare in the chariot of Pharaoh*
> > *And thy harness shall be tender with gold.*
When my King sits upon his couch,
then I undo the little bag of myrrh
that I have hung for fragrance between my breasts
and let him smell of its scent,
then revolve the images of flowers and green foliage
among the memories of his face
and I hold him within me:

a cluster of camphor from the vineyards of Engedi.

> *Thou art fair, my love, and thine eyes*
> *Have the look of longing doves.*

You are fair, my love
and lovely, and sweet cedar
and soft smelling fir roofs over
our green bed.

Ch. ii

Am I the flower of the parched and heated plain
and the blossom dipping above the valley stream, at one?

> *As the bloom among the thorns*
> *Art thou among these women.*

As the fruit-tree among the trees of the wood
are you among all these men. And I
sit in your shadow—languidly, and
your fruit is sweet in my mouth.
We have walked to the wine-shop together
and heard the rustlings of the banners hung above the door
each murmuring the single, simple syllable, "Love!"
Give me raisins to eat, and sweet quince, and love,
and love, for I am ill of love.
Beneath my head I felt your left hand
and on my body you moved your right.

> To Jerusalem's women I will charge
> by the wood's hart and the field hind
> that they chain passion till he breaks them.

If I watched you all the time, would I see you
bestriding mountains and hills to come to me, like a roe,
like the young deer; and if my eyes could pierce
this blank wall, what would I see through
this window, through this lattice.
Would you have said, "Rise up ..."

> *Rise up, thou fair formed lover,*
> *And walk where winter has deserted*
> *With spring rains. The flowers appear on the earth*
> *And it is the time of the singing of birds;*
> *The land is filled with the voice of the turtle.*

> *The fig-tree gives good fruit and puts out green twigs,*
> *And thy wild grapes, they give of a good smell. Rise up,*
> *Thou fair formed lover. That bird*
> *Hidden in the crevice of the third stone step*
> *Of the palace sings not. He has by heart, sweeter*
> *Than thy comely body. Take us up then the foxes,*
> *The little foxes that devour the tenderer fruit.*

You are my love and I your lover
and you graze all the fields of my body,
for when morning comes and the shadows mist away,
turn, and be like a roe, or a young deer.

Ch. iii

I fear the night, for once
I sought you in the shadows of the dream
within my bed; I did not find you.
"I must get up," I said, "and go about the city streets
and in the broad-ways quench the love I have for you with whom I find
   there."
And I could not find you.
While I walked by the tower, I saw a watchman and I asked,
"Where has my soul's love gone?" But then
at the fall of the towers
when the shadows of the dream crumbled, I woke
and found you beside me,
and you laughed because I held you
until your mouth moved on the hills of my breasts
and you came straight into the valley of my womb.
   Oh, I will charge Jerusalem's women
   by the wood's hart and the field find
   that they wake not passion till he calls them.
I saw you come like a column risen in smoke,
perfumed with my breasts' myrrh, and frankincense,
and all the powders that the merchants vend in the market;
and there were sixty soldiers of Israel
bearing your bed. They too feared the night
and held their swords against their thighs,
and while they bore your palanquin, silver pillared,

pedestaled with gold, and looped with purple drapery,
paved with ivory, ebony, or love,
    I said to the women,
    "Oh, Jerusalem's women, go out," and today
    they will see you, Solomon,
    with the crown relinquished from your mother's hand
    in the afternoon of your gladness.

Ch. iv

> *Behold, thou fair formed lover of love*
> *With the longing eyes of the turtle,*
> *Hair like the dark herd*
> *Couched upon Mount Gilead,*
> *Teeth like the white herd*
> *From their washing, stately, identical, and continually processioned.*
> *Thy lips are a scarlet cord, and thy mouth*
> *Well spoken; I see the dark crimson pomegranates*
> *Behind thy veil.*
> *Thy neck is the Tower of David,*
> *An armory on which that necklace of flat beads becomes*
> *Like a thousand bucklers hung thereon,*
> *Shields of the great men you have conquered;*
> *Thy breasts, twin fawns, grazing the anemones.*
> *Until morning, I sucked among the hills of myrrh and the mists of*
>   *frankincense.*
> *Fair and unblemished art thou.*
> *Come thou out of Lebanon, my bride.*
> *Come thou out and look from the top of Amana, from*
> *Senir, Hermon—where the lion lurks with the leopard.*
> *Thou hast ravished my heart, my sister in love,*
> *Thou hast ravished my heart with the looks of thine eyes*
> *And thy heart, beating in thy throat.*
> *How fine is thy loving, my sister in love, oh thy loving is better*
>   *than wine,*
> *And the scent of my body boasts all the spices.*
> *Thy lips are freshets of honey; honey and milk are under thy tongue*
> *And thy robes are redolent with the breezes of Lebanon.*
> *Be my cool, sealed cistern, my fresh fountain, a stifled spring.*

> *Thy flowers are those of the luscious pomegranate,*
> *Henna, rose, camphor, spikenard, and saffron,*
> *Sweet calamus, and bitter cinnamon, all spices.*
> *Thou art a fountain of water cascaded from the hills of Lebanon.*

I asked the north winds to rise for you
and came the south, blowing softly through the garden,
wafting the scent of myrrh. You may come and take your fruit.

Ch. v

> *I am come into thy garden,*
> *My sister in love, it is the garden of myrrh*
> *And thy sweeter spices, and I lick the honey from your comb,*
> *And thy sweet wine is mixed with my milk.*
> *I drink from thy body all the joys of thy love.*

I slept with my heart opened, and within the silver shadows of the dream
I heard you say, "Let me ..."

> *Let me come into thee, soft*
> *As a dove's breast against me,*
> *For I touched thee, and my hand returned hot with dew*
> *And my locks hang heavy with the night's damp.*

I had disrobed. Why should I dress again.
My feet had been washed. Should I have soiled them.
And when you put your hand between the grill-work of the lattice,
my bowels set to aching in my loins for you.
I rose to let you in, with scents upon my hands;
but before I could open the door, you had turned away
and gone; my soul dissolved within the presence of your absent voice.
I called you but you did not answer.
While I walked by the shattered tower, I saw three watchmen looking at
   me.
Then the strongest one approached me and hit me.
One pulled my mantle off, these night wanderers of the wall.
I called to Jerusalem's women that they would tell you how this loving
   made me faint.
The remnants of the dream shattered, and rising from the well of sleep
I saw what makes you lover and men's king.
You are white and ruddy among ten thousand men,

and your face is sun-burned gold beneath the black clusterings of your
    hair.
Your eyes are doves floating upon milk washed pools;
your cheeks are banks of balsam, clefts of sweet odored herbs;
your lips, the scarlet anemones emitting perfumed breath,
and the sun has burnished your hands golden
and tipped each finger with a gem of Tarshish.
Your belly is ivory polished and veined with lapis lazuli
and your legs, two alabaster columns,
and again, the sun has gilded your bare feet.
You are all of Lebanon,
tall and straight as the cedar trees,
tender spoken, yes, altogether lovely, my friend,
and I tell this to Jerusalem's women.

Ch. vi

Where did you go in the shadows of my dreaming,
for am I not a fair woman.
You went into your own place
to visit sweeter spices,
but you are my lover, and I am your love,
though you hold the herbs of your men's garden.
> Be thou lovely, as lovely as Tirzah
> And handsome as all of Jerusalem's women,
> Terrible as a bannered army.
> Take thine eyes off me, for they disturb me deeply.
> Behold, thou fair formed lover of love,
> With the longing eyes of the turtle,
> Here like the dark herd
> Couched upon Mount Gilead,
> Teeth like the white herd
> From their washing, identical, and stately, continuously
>   processioned,
> Thy lips, a scarlet cord, and thy mouth well spoken,
> And I watch the dark crimson pomegranates behind your veil.
> Of queens there are three score,
> Four score of young slaves, and limitless virgins,

And yet, my spotless dove, love of thy mother, love
Of those that bore you thither, and praised by the young slaves
    and queens;
Who art thou, army terrible, moon fair, sun clear, and morning
    fine?

I have gone in the early sun through the nut Garden
to see the vines in bud, and in the sun I saw the pomegranate in bloom
and when the moon had at last come, I had reached
the broad way where eager people watched the dancing girl.
"Turn 'round! Turn 'round, O Shulamite," they cried,
"and let us look at you. Turn 'round!"
I wondered why they laughed and called so loudly,
crying and singing to the little dancing girl as if
they themselves were whirling and dancing as the folk dance
of the two groups. (If I were to whirl and dance like that in my sandaled
feet …)

Ch. vii

How beautiful are thy sandaled feet,
Dark prince's daughter,
The joints of thy thighs are like jewels
In the hands of a cunning workman,
And thy navel, a round goblet, wanting no sweeter wine,
Thy belly, smooth as lily petals, and dark as heaped wheat,
Thy breasts, twin fawns,
And thy neck, like a dark ivory tower.
Thine eyes are like Heshbon's pools by the gates of Bath-rabbin.
Thy fine nose is like Lebanon's tower that looketh to Damascus.
Thy head is filled with thoughts both gold and crimson,
And thy hair is night-shadowed purple,
And, like the shadows of a dream, they have caught a king.
How pleasant are all thy delights;
Thy stature brings to me the swaying of palm trees,
Thy breasts, two dark date clusters,
And I will hold this tree,
And I will pluck this fruit,
And I will breathe the smell of quince in thy breath;
The roof of thy mouth tastes of fine wine

And I am drunk therewith,
    As my sleeping lips awake.
I belong to your desire, and your desire is all mine.
Come then, Love, to the fields,
stopping over at one village until dawn,
for the vineyards may have budded,
and the pomegranate may bloom:
there you will taste my love, beneath them.
Here is the fragrance of mandrake
and other luscious fruit,
both fresh fallen and ripe; and they are yours.

Ch. viii

They would not have veiled their faces in shame
had you been my brother, and I had kissed you as I did
before my door. And had you come to my mother's house more times
she would have served you spiced wine,
and I could have given you my own pomegranate liquor.
    Yet I will say to Jerusalem's women,
    by the wood's hart and the field hind,
      that they loose not passion's chains while he sleeps,
      but free him in the tempest of his roaring.
Hold your left hand under my head,
and embrace me with your right.
I came up wild from the wilderness,
leaning upon you, my lover.
I roused you from your slumber beneath the quince tree once,
and you laughed and said that it was upon this spot that
your mother bore you. Make me
a seal on your heart, upon your arm. Love can challenge death,
if jealousy be cruel as the grave.
Its fire has a vehement flame,
and many waters can not quench it,
neither floods extinguish it, and if a man
must sell his wealth for love
then he is poor indeed.
Our little breastless sister worries about her courtship.
If she be frigid, then more silver shall she have for her dowry.

If she'd be open like wide portals, then shall she be shut up
behind sweet cedar gates.
I can be cold, my breasts, fortresses against your attack,
but for you, I am a warm haven.

> *I, Solomon, have a vineyard at Ba'al Hamon.*
> *I let my vineyard unto keepers.*
> *Each one brought a thousand pieces of silver for the fruit.*
> *I need not a thousand, nor two hundred, nor any silver.*
> *My own vineyard can I keep myself,*
> *And about who dwellest therein,*
> *This is thy song—*

"Be like the wood's hart, or the field hind,
Amid the hills and the perfumes of the valley."

The
Drunken
Ship

(1870 or 1871)

by
Arthur Rimbaud

I ran down rivers that they could not run
And found my hawsmen gone, for where I passed
Shrill Indians, seeking targets, went and nailed
Their naked bodies to the painted masts

And I, insouciant of all my crew
(I carried Flemish wheat and English cloth),
With my hawsmen strangled by their own screams
I drifted freely on the river-froth

Last winter in the fury of the tide
Mistaken as a deaf-child's sound delusion
I sped! And no peninsula washed loose
Has ever known a more supreme confusion

The tempest consecrated my awakening
I danced on waves, lighter than cork I seemed
(Some call those waves the tumblers of corpses)
Ten nights I did not miss the light-house gleam

Sweeter than tart apples to a child was
The green water which soaked my hull of pine
And washed me of the wine stains and the bile
Then broke my rudder, cut my anchor line

From that time I was bathed within a poem
Of Sea, fed on stars, with white milk-drinks drunk,
Gorged on blue-greens; the flotsam was a wan
Pale pensive corpse, who, on occasions, sunk

Then, coloring the blue, deliriums;
Languid rhythms which the day had bled,
Stronger than alcohol, or our singing,
Ferment the sea of love to russet-red

Skies split by lightning into day and night,
Waves, whirlpools, a race of sea-bird dovelings,
I saw at times what men thought they have seen
And I have knowledge of the evening

And in those evenings, horror stained the sun
With long and violet clouds. Like ancient mimes
The waves move in a stately ancient drama
Or close and open like Venetian blinds

My dreams were filled with snow that kissed the sea,
Her breasts, her eyes, her arms. While I was dreaming
Among those currents, flowing like strange saps,
I heard the music of the phosphors' singing

For months I watched the sea beat at the reefs,
Intense, fierce, exploding on the shore,
Unmindful that three Marys could rise up,
Could calm her panting voice, could stop her roar

I passed Floridas, and panther eyes
Viewed me from the flowers; rim to rim
Taut rainbows stretched across the pallid skies
And on the water brilliant sea-birds skimmed

Weirs where a half decayed Leviathan
Lolled in the marsh weeds, and a crumbling pall
Of falling streams a little further on
Crashed and cascaded down a water-fall

Glaciers, waves, suns of silver, burning skies,
Dim wrecks below; dropping on the waters
From the trees, the giant coiled snakes, leaving
Vapours and dark thick olid odors

I wanted to show those fish to a child,
The blue dolphin, or the gold; the frail weeds
At times would consecrate my days and nights
At other times the wind would give me speed

At times, I wearied of the zones and poles
A martyr, I, and, eased with sobbing seas,
Lost in the shadow-flower of the waves
Where, like a woman, I fell on my knees,

I was a chunk of dissoluted earths
Pierced by bird shrieks. Upon the sea I burned
With brightness. In my wild tattered rigging
The drowned and sleeping corpses swung and turned

Now, through the storm of Maenad locks, I hurled
To birdless voids, and soon I was sea-daft
And thought my hulk much better to be drowned
Than salvaged by some Hanseatic craft

My freedom smoking with a violet mist
Transfixed red heaven, and I smelled the one
Spice no living poet can resist:
Blue slime shifts on the lichen of the sun

The waves were run with sharp electric crescents
The frail sea-horses hovered at my sides
And like a cudgel the heat of July
Crashes up against the ultramarine skies

The gaping throats of Maelstroms and Behemoths
Tremble in the wind, and yawn, and glower
As I move through the shimmering blue stasis
I long for Europe with her ancient towers

I saw sidereal archipelagoes
And isles with raving skies where sailors go
And in this depthless night, are you golden
Birds exiled, who, with new strength fly low

But I have cried too long! The new dawn cracks
On the horizon of my heart. And we
Feel the agony of sun and moon. Oh,
Explode my keel, and let me go to sea!

If I want Europe's waters, I want just
A black puddle under a shard of sky
Where a child can launch a paper boat
As frail and harmless as a butterfly

Oh, waves, I can no longer roll with you
Nor cross the sea-paths where the vessels dip
And rise, where pennants flap against the skies,
Nor pass by windows of cold prison ships

Translation:
Samuel R. Delany
New York,
November, 1960

ACKNOWLEDGMENTS

I am deeply grateful to Suzanna Tamminen at Wesleyan University Press for giving me the opportunity to gather and present this selection. I am also grateful to Parker Smathers at Wesleyan, Glenn E. Novak, and Susan A. Abel at UPNE for giving such intelligent editorial attention to a very complex manuscript. I also wish to thank the anonymous readers of an earlier draft of the manuscript for astute suggestions regarding the clarification of some aspects of this material.

I extend heartfelt gratitude to Samuel R. Delany for his support throughout the long gestation of this project, one of the pleasures and privileges of which was the opportunity to spend many hours reviewing the manuscript with him and discussing his recollections of the events recorded within. My sincere thanks to Marilyn Hacker for permission to reproduce her writing in this volume, as well as for her graciousness and candor. Thanks also to Henry Morrison for patience, clarification, and invaluable assistance, and to Andrew I. Porter for the use of his photograph of Delany at the 1966 World Science Fiction Convention.

My deepest thanks to the staff of the Gotlieb Archival Research Center at Boston University, and in particular to Sean Noel and Jennifer Pino, for their generous responses to my numerous queries and requests; it has been a pleasure working with them. More general thanks to the director of the Gotlieb Center, Vita Paladino.

I carried out this project while teaching and engaging in other research at the University at Buffalo, Villa Maria College, Niagara University, and the Squeaky Wheel Film & Media Arts Center; I wish to give general thanks to these institutions for the opportunities they have afforded me.

For long-term support, new friendship, and crucial assistance and suggestions just when I needed them, I thank friends, colleagues, and family: Christine Liddie, Eryq Dorfman, Deborah Stearns, Jud Caswell, Megan Faragher, Ric Best, Ron Drummond, David Schmid, Victoria Brockmeier, Patrick Robbins, Melissa Smith, Heather Ellsworth, and my brother, Tim James.

For their generous hospitality during my visits to the Gotlieb Center in Boston I give warm thanks to the Trudell family: Travis, Diana, Matilda, and Joaquin.

Finally, I extend thanks and love across the universe to my dear departed father, Roland James, for being an attentive and patient host and witness as I herded this manuscript through to completion. "I have gone up to Maine ... "

NOTES

1. BRONX SCIENCE AND OTHER NEW YORK SCENES
Notebook 1—January–February 1958

3   **"to every thing"**: Although Delany may have intended the word "every-thing," the words "every" and "thing" are clearly separated on the page. In early entries Delany sometimes splits compound words; this is an example of the sort of stylistic idiosyncrasy I have tried to preserve for this volume.

3   **Ellen:** Probably Ellen Krevett, a Bronx Science student who participated with Delany in the Hunter College Dramatic Workshop for Young People (Samuel R. Delany, *The Motion of Light in Water: Sex and Science Fiction Writing in the East Village* [1988; reprint, Minneapolis: University of Minnesota Press, 2004], 98). A partial draft of a script Delany wrote for the workshop can be found in the more complete transcript of Notebook 1 in the second appendix to this volume.

3   **R.U.R.:** 1920 play by the Czech writer Karel Čapek; the title is an acronym for the play's subtitle, *Rossum's Universal Robots*.

3   **"Try to think up a situation involving kids"**: The "kids" mentioned in this entry are fictional, although some are named after Delany's friends. In conversation, Delany has said that these notes, most likely for a play, were probably instigated by his recognition that his proper focus as a young writer ought to be on the lives of the young. This insight was prompted by his attending of plays that featured well-developed youthful characters, including James Leo Herlihy's *Blue Denim*, which opened on Broadway in February 1958, and Lillian Hellman's *Watch on the Rhine* (1941) (Samuel R. Delany, interview with Kenneth James, August 9, 2014).

Notebook 3—January 1959

5   **"TRUE, BUT I DON'T *KNOW* THE WORD"**: Marginal comment inserted by Hacker, written in capital letters in the original and, as with all entries in Hacker's handwriting, indicated in the text with bold type.

6   **"Bruitto half drowsily"**: This entry appears in its entirety, as do all entries not otherwise accompanied by editorial comments in brackets.

Notebook 7—1959 [March–April 1959]

8   **"The Talking Inverted Blues"**: Humorous verse jointly written by Delany and Hacker (Delany, interview with James, August 9, 2014).

10   **"I know a [centered] man"**: In the notebook, the word is "centaured." Upon reviewing this entry, Delany suspected "centaured" to be a dyslexic misspelling of "centered" (Delany, interview with James, August 9, 2014).

Notebook 6—1959 [April 1959]

11   **"H.P. continued from Vol. I":** A continuation of the "Howard Pease" story begun in Notebook 89, and from which an excerpt is presented in appendix 1. "Vol. I" refers to a numbering system young Delany used for his earliest notebooks. He alludes to this system in Notebook 2.

       The traces of the system in the notebooks present an incomplete and contradictory story. On the covers of the notebooks he produced at Bronx Science, Delany wrote "Vol. I," "Vol. II," "Vol. III," and so on, in two locations: center and lower right. He used different writing implements, pencil and pen, at each location, suggesting two separate attempts to designate a proper chronological order for the notebooks. When Notebook 89—"Vol. I"—is placed in this series, the pairs of volume numbers for the first three notebooks are consistent both with one another and with the internal evidence of the notebooks themselves, though they differ from the order suggested by the archival labels they have been given.

       After the first three notebooks, however, the numbers on the covers begin to disagree both with one another and with the internal evidence. This divergence suggests a change of mind on Delany's part about the proper order of whichever of the two series of numbers came first (which cannot itself be determined from the available evidence). There are also two repetitions of "Vol. IV" in one of the number series. For these reasons the volume numbers on the covers have not been taken as reliable guides to proper notebook order.

12   **Bruno Callabro:** Name of a character from one of Delany's early novels, *Those Spared by Fire*. As Delany recounts in *The Motion of Light in Water*, "Bruno Callabro" became the pen name under which he submitted his science fantasy novel *The Jewels of Aptor* to Donald Wollheim at Ace Books (Delany, *Motion*, 181–82).

Notebook 4—April–May 1959

13   **Ruben:** Bronx Science student (Delany, *Motion*, 98).

13   **"Quotes":** In her junior year at Bronx Science, Marilyn Hacker had been admitted to NYU at age fifteen on a creative writing scholarship (Delany, *Motion*, 95). Through her social network at NYU Delany made new friends and acquaintances. In Hacker's comments in the entry for April 29, "M" is Marilyn and "J"/"Judy" is Judy Ratner, a close friend of Marilyn's from NYU (Delany, *Motion*, 98–99).

14   **Paul, Polly:** NYU students.

16   **Pierre:** Pierre Kyria, a French graduate student who would shortly publish *Manhattan Blues* (1961), the first of several novels (Delany, interview with James, March 27, 2016).

17   **Linda, Jane:** Linda and Jane Anderson, acquaintances of Delany's from Jack and Jill of America, a social club for middle-class African American families (Delany, interview with James, March 27, 2016).

18   **"Passacaglia with Death in the Higher Voices":** Short story (Delany, *Motion*, 90).

18   **"those lesser known—to a few—areas of the park":** Specifically, the Ramble – a popular cruising area (Delany, interview with James, March 27, 2016).

19   **Bob:** Bob Aarenburg, a friend of Delany's at Morningside Gardens. Delany moved in with Bob a few months after starting City College, shortly after his father's death (Delany, *Motion*, 8, 108).

20   *Florida Review*: In conversation Delany has said he has no memory of the circumstances of his mention of the "forthcoming literary magazine" (presumably the *New Ark*, which he mentions a few paragraphs later) in which he claims a story of his is about to be published. Possibly this was wishful thinking in anticipation of a publication that never came about (Delany, interview with James, August 9, 2014).

20   **Dr. Allen and Farrow:** Delany knew Farrow through Jack and Jill of America (Delany, *Motion*, 87–88).

20   **Karin:** Karin Anderelli (Delany, interview with James, March 27, 2016).

20   **Gwendolyn Davis:** Delany's former art teacher at Dalton. Delany recounts the circumstances around Davis's remark on "shape, line, and color" in his essay "Eric, Gwen, and the Esthetics of Unrectified Feeling," from *Atlantis: Three Tales* (Middletown, CT: Wesleyan University Press, 1995, 134–42).

21   **"first and second prize":** The works in question were the short story "The Gravedigger" and the essay "Portrait of the Artist as Six Characters in Search of Tea and Sympathy" (Michael S. Peplow and Robert S. Bravard, eds., *Samuel R. Delany: A Primary and Secondary Bibliography, 1962–1979* [Boston: G. K. Hall, 1980], 16).

21   **Gale:** Gale Emeus, another close friend of Hacker's at NYU. The entry Delany mentions having written in Gale's notebook is an account of a cruising experience that began at a movie palace on Forty-Second Street, now called the New Amsterdam Theatre (Delany, "Coming/Out," in *Shorter Views: Queer Thoughts and the Politics of the Paraliterary* [Middletown, CT: Wesleyan University Press, 1999], 83–84).

23   *Dynamo*: Literary magazine for Bronx Science (Delany, *Motion*, 54).

23   **"And I ... am no more than a prostitute":** Another reference to the New Amsterdam Theatre experience. In conversation Delany has said that the emotional turmoil implied by this passage is an overdramatization of his frustration at what had been, for him, a disappointing introduction to public sex (Delany, interview with James, August 9, 2014). In his essay "Coming/Out" Delany alludes to the "stock phrases of despair and disgust" he'd found himself using in his note to Gale describing the experience; this passage seems to draw from the same stock (Delany, "Coming/Out," 84). It furnishes an example of the problem of using "the public language you've been given" to "talk about something openly for the first time," which Delany examines in relation to his discussion of his homosexuality

with his therapy group at Mount Sinai Hospital, an episode he recounts in *The Motion of Light in Water* (Delany, *Motion*, 405).

24   **Murray:** Murray Wasserman, a student at Bronx Science (Delany, interview with James, August 9, 2014).

24   *"Turn over"*: According to Delany, the situation implied here is a dramatic inflation of what had been an undramatic situation: Gale had simply been engaging in horseplay (Delany, interview with James, August 9, 2014).

24   **The Ascolis:** Peter Ascoli was a former Dalton student whose father, Max Ascoli, edited and published the *Reporter*, a New York City–based news magazine. "S.A." is *Scientific American*, to which the Ascolis had given Delany a ten-year subscription as a gift while he was still at Dalton. Delany became a faithful reader of the magazine (Delany, *Motion*, 33, 93; Delany, interview with James, March 27, 2016).

Notebook 5—1959 [Summer–Autumn 1959]

26   **"What is the matter":** The doggerel in the first entry is written on the margins of school notes. "S.S." was late-'50s slang for "Social Studies" (Delany, interview with James, March 27, 2016).

28   **"Another trilogy":** Outline notes for *Cycle for Toby*. The story "Salt" won Delany the NYU Prose Scholarship, the same scholarship Hacker had won two years earlier (Peplow and Bravard, *Samuel R. Delany*, 18). However, Delany chose to forgo NYU in favor of City College.

28   **Victor:** Victor Arwas, a graduate student at NYU (Delany, *Motion*, 107; Delany, interview with James, October 30, 2011).

2. IN SEARCH OF SILENCE
Notebook 2—January 1959 [January–February 1960]

31   *In Search of Silence*: This is the first of Delany's attempts at exhaustive journal-keeping; the second is the *Journaux d'Orphée* in Notebook 12. Although the archival date of this notebook is January 1959, in the notebook itself Delany directly states his age as seventeen and nine months, which places the entry in January 1960. The young people described here hail from both Bronx Science and NYU. (See Delany, *Motion*, 107–8, for a discussion of the circumstances of Delany's contact with Lloyd, Stuey, Paul, and others.)

35   **"even the minor cross-references in Camus suddenly illuminate whole series of works":** Delany is reacting to a scene in *L'Étranger* in which Meursault, in prison, reads a newspaper article whose contents mirror the plot of Camus's play *Le Malentendu* (Delany, interview with James, March 27, 2016).

35   **Ian:** Ian Stogle, a Bronx Science student with whom Delany shared a writing class (Delany, interview with James, October 30, 2011).

35   **L.M., Marty, Jennifer:** L.M. is Lloyd Mac Low, an NYU student, as is Marty (last name unknown). Jennifer was a friend of Lloyd's (Delany, interview with James, October 30, 2011).

35   **Stuey:** Stuart Israel, a book clerk at the 8th Street Book Shop. In *Motion* he is referred to as "Stewy" (Delany, interview with James, October 30, 2011; *Motion*, 108).

35   **Paul:** Paul Israel, Stuart Israel's cousin (Delany, interview with James, October 30, 2011).

36   **Elly:** Probably Eleanor (last name unknown), another friend of Lloyd's at NYU. Unlike the others in this group, most of whom, as Delany has said in conversation and as the passage suggests, smoked pot, Eleanor used harder drugs (Delany, interview with James, October 30, 2011). It is interesting to read the tone of Delany's characterization of Elly in relation to his critique of similar rhetoric regarding Judy in *Heavenly Breakfast* (Samuel R. Delany, *Heavenly Breakfast: An Essay on the Winter of Love* [1979; reprint, Flint, MI: Bamberger Books, 1997], 83–84, 92–93).

37   **J. P. Schachter, José:** Schachter is a Bronx Science graduate who had gone on to NYU, and José is a young professor of French at NYU (Delany, interview with James, October 30, 2011).

38   **"Silent Monologue for Lefty":** Short story. It and "A Prose Thing" were published in *Dynamo* (Peplow and Bravard, *Samuel R. Delany*, 154; Delany, *Motion*, 109).

38   **Reinstein:** Cary Reinstein, a Bronx Science student discussed at some length by Delany in *The Motion of Light in Water*. Near the end of his time at Bronx Science, Reinstein produced a set of drawings titled *The Fall of the Towers*, which Delany later appropriated as the collective title of his SF trilogy (Delany, *Motion*, 197–99).

38   **"twelve volumes":** This refers to the notebooks with volume numbers inscribed on their covers. If Delany's count here is correct, then at least three additional notebooks from the Bronx Science years have been either misplaced or lost, as only eight notebooks with volume numbers on their covers are extant in the section of the archive devoted to Delany's journals.

38   **Louise:** Louis Steiner, a poet in Hacker's writing class at Bronx Science (Delany, interview with James, October 30, 2011).

38–39   **Lew, Vicki, Erik Felderman, Johnny Lipsky:** Bronx Science students. Lew is Lewis Warsh, who, already writing poetry at this time, would go on to a distinguished career as a writer, editor, and teacher (Delany, *Motion*, 197).

39   **"Elizabeth Drew's book":** *Poetry: A Modern Guide to Its Understanding and Enjoyment* (New York: Dell, 1959).

40   **Mr. Glicksman:** Senior English instructor at Bronx Science (Delany, interview with James, March 27, 2016).

40   **Dr. Gordon:** College AP English instructor at Bronx Science (Delany, interview with James, October 30, 2011).

40   **Mike O'Hare:** Bronx Science student, already known to Delany through Camp Woodland (Delany, *Motion*, 70).

40   **Dr. Krim:** Delany's therapist during his time at Bronx Science (Delany, interview with James, October 30, 2011).

41　**"Song of My Hands":** Pro-labor song by Bernie Asbel (Delany, interview with James, March 27, 2016).

42　**Marie:** The poet Marie Ponsot, Delany's mentor and friend during this period (Delany, *Motion*, 96). Ponsot had been a friend of one of Hacker's instructors at NYU; Delany met Ponsot at a Halloween party on the NYU campus, and she invited him to visit her in Queens (*Motion*, 8–9). This led to regular visits for about a year and a half, after which Ponsot became close friends with Hacker (Delany, interview with James, October 30, 2011).

42　**John Kronenberger:** A friend of Delany's from Dalton (Delany, *Motion*, 155).

44　**"Pimply skin will never become a criterion for beauty…":** At this time Delany was beginning to notice his attraction to men whose skin was cratered from acne scarring (Delany, interview with James, March 27, 2016).

52　**"an UNSMOKED pipe full of shit":** Upon reviewing this passage, Delany speculated that while the term "shit" would seem to refer to hash, its lack of availability in New York City at this time, the usual practices of Lloyd's crowd, and Delany's emphasis in the passage that the pipe had gone unsmoked all suggest that he had been referring to pot (Delany, interview with James, March 27, 2016).

52　**D. Ephraim:** David Ephraim, part of Lloyd's circle (Delany, interview with James, October 30, 2011).

53　**The Lambeth Singers:** A misstatement; the performers in question were Lambert, Hendricks, & Ross, a vocal trio (Delany, interview with James, October 30, 2011).

54　**"Boyd, my well-meaning cousin":** Boyd Savoy. A few months after this episode, Boyd would accompany Delany to a performance of Allan Kaprow's "Eighteen Happenings in Six Parts" (*Motion* 200–208).

54　**"In Grant's—":** Fast-food establishment on the corner of Forty-Second and Broadway (Delany, interview with James, October 30, 2011).

55　**"Silver," "Salt":** Stories from *Cycle for Toby* (Delany, interview with James, March 27, 2016).

56　**"The boat house," etc.:** Outline material for *Cycle for Toby*.

57　**Otto, "J. Rivers (Erik)":** Bronx Science students. In conversation Delany has said that J. Rivers (Jimmy Rivers) was a nail-biter, and became the model for Erik Torrent, the protagonist of Delany's first attempt at a novel, *Lost Stars* (Delany, interview with James, October 30, 2011; *Motion*, 76–77).

58　**"Trouble in Mind," etc.:** Performance set, either for Delany as a solo performer or for the Harbor Singers (Delany, interview with James, October 30, 2011).

Notebook 8—March 1960

61　**"This Place, Rumoured to Have Been Sodom—":** Outline material for a portion of the novel *Those Spared by Fire*. The title refers to the Robert Duncan poem, "This Place Rumord to Have Been Sodom." A character mentioned in the outline, Paul Bherens, is the "young white man" in the passage read by William Sloane at the Bread Loaf Writers' Conference, which Delany attended in the summer of 1960 (Delany, *Times Square Red, Times Square Blue* [New York: NYU Press, 1999], 131–32; Delany, interview with James, March 27, 2016).

61 **"How People React to Various Emotions":** This entry records an incident that took place at Delany's maternal grandmother's apartment at 80 LaSalle Street. Delany had just received a call announcing the death of his grandmother's best friend since childhood, Hardenia Mahood (Delany, interview with James, October 30, 2011).

62 **Gramp:** Delany's maternal grandfather, Samuel Hugo Boyd. Boyd's cousin was Margaret White (Delany, interview with James, October 30, 2011).

62 **"So I sat there and then I got up and went out ... ":** An example of Delany censoring himself. At the moment of the blackout, young Delany had been in mid-bowel movement; with discomfort, he'd clenched the stool back inside before getting off the toilet (Delany, interview with James, March 27, 2016).

Notebook 11—Spring 1960 [Spring–Summer 1960]

63 **"Epigraph for *Afterlon"* and outline material:** *Afterlon* was another non-SF novel Delany produced during this period (Delany, *Motion*, 99).

64 ***Nation and Rebirth*:** The two "studies" under this title are early versions of what would become the prologue for Delany's most ambitious non-SF project of the '60s, the novel *Voyage, Orestes*, whose ultimate fate is discussed in *The Motion of Light in Water* (Delany, *Motion*, 327–30).

65 **Edna Silem:** This exchange is likely an insert for the novel *Voyage, Orestes*, in which Edna Silem was a major character. As mentioned in the introduction, Edna Silem, an inversion of Mélisande, was a nickname Marilyn Hacker had chosen for herself.

66 **"The Song of Songs":** The placement of this entry is a good example of a pattern found in many notebooks in this volume. The opening of the notebook (when read in conventional front-to-back direction) contains Delany's translation of the biblical Song of Songs—one of many translations he did during this period, as indicated in his table of contents for *Portraits of the Immature Mind*—while the closing of the notebook features this brief critical comment. In many notebooks, creative work advances front-to-back and critical work back-to-front; this suggests that the writing of the translation and the writing of the comment were probably not widely separated events.

3. *JOURNAUX D'ORPHÉE*
Notebook 12—Inclusive to July 1960

69 **Pete:** Peter Horn was a gifted banjo player and Woodland alumnus two years Delany's senior. He lived two floors down from Delany's family's apartment at Morningside Gardens (Delany, *Motion*, 7; interview with James, October 30, 2011).

73 **Gerry:** Identity unknown; possibly a fiction or composite created for the purposes of the piece (Delany, interview with James, August 9, 2014).

74 **Danny, Susan:** Delany's classmates at Bronx Science (Delany, interview with James, October 30, 2011).

74, 77, 86 **George Auerbach, Johnny Lipsky, Dicky Bellman & girlfriend, Mike Michaels:** A circle of friends from Queens and Brooklyn. Michaels had been another friend of Delany's at Woodland and taught Delany to play the guitar. Auerbach was probably also known to Delany through Woodland (Delany, interview with James, October 30, 2011).

75 **Eurydice:** Nickname for Hacker and occasionally for other female friends as well. There is thus some ambiguity in Delany's use of the name here and elsewhere (Delany, interview with James, August 9, 2014).

76 **The Gittelmans:** Morningside Gardens residents Martin and Rochelle Gittelman; both were psychologists (Delany, interview with James, October 30, 2011).

80 **Erik Darling:** Darling was Pete Seeger's replacement after Seeger left the Weavers (Delany, interview with James, March 27, 2016).

81 **"It is _____":** In the notebook Delany has drawn a straight line to convey the flat calm of the sea.

83 **"Ana's Travelin'":** A song by Ana Perez of the Harbor Singers.

84 **Ewan MacColl:** British singer-songwriter and popularizer of traditional British folk music (Colin Larkin, ed., *The Encyclopedia of Popular Music*, 4th ed. [Oxford: Oxford University Press, 2006], 5:403–4).

84 **Fred Hellerman:** Singer-songwriter and member of the Weavers (Larkin, *Encyclopedia of Popular Music*, 8:557).

84 **Sabicas:** Virtuoso flamenco guitarist of Romani origin (Stanley Sadie, ed., *The New Grove Dictionary of Music and Musicians*, 2nd ed. [London: Macmillan, 2001], 22:65–66).

84 **Olatunji:** Nigerian drummer Babatunde Olatunji, whose albums for Columbia Records influenced many Western performers (Larkin, *Encyclopedia of Popular Music*, 6:295–96).

86 **"Advice to a Guitarist":** A poem Delany had read in *Dynamo*. Its author, Peter S. Beagle, had attended Bronx Science a few years ahead of Delany. Beagle, like Delany, published his first novel (*A Fine and Private Place* [1960]) at the age of twenty and became a highly regarded fantasy author (John Clute, "Peter S. Beagle," *The Encyclopedia of Fantasy*, ed. John Clute and John Grant [New York: St. Martin's Press, 1997], 94–95).

86 **Oscar Brand:** Canadian-born singer-songwriter and host of the long-lasting radio show *Folksong Festival* (Larkin, *Encyclopedia of Popular Music*, 1:808–9).

88 ***Sing Out!:*** Important folk music publication (Ronald D. Cohen, introduction to *"Wasn't That a Time!" Firsthand Accounts of the Folk Music Revival* [Lanham, MD: Scarecrow Press, 1995], 7).

90 **The New Lost City Ramblers:** A folk band that focused on reproducing

traditional arrangements and performance styles (Larkin, *Encyclopedia of Popular Music*, 6:166).

90   **Cisco Houston:** Gilbert Vandine "Cisco" Houston, a singer-songwriter who performed and recorded extensively with Woody Guthrie (Larkin, *Encyclopedia of Popular Music*, 4:382–83).

90   **Odetta:** Odetta Holmes, African American folksinger who incorporated a range of styles into her repertoire, including blues, jazz, and gospel (Larkin, *Encyclopedia of Popular Music*, 6:278).

91   **John Jacob Niles:** Singer-songwriter as well as collector and popularizer of traditional folk songs (Ronald D. Cohen, *Rainbow Quest: The Folk Music Revival and American Society, 1940–1970* [Amherst: University of Massachusetts Press, 2002], 53).

92   **Alan Mills:** Canadian singer-songwriter (Cohen, *Rainbow Quest*, 89).

92   **Abyssinian Baptist Chorus:** The chorus of the Abyssinian Baptist Church in Harlem, a longtime center for gospel music and community activism (James A. Miller, "We've Come This Far: A History of the Abyssinian Baptist Church," in *The Abyssinian Baptist Church: A Photographic Journal*, by Robert L. Gore Jr. [New York: Harry N. Abrams, 2001], 24).

92   **Bob Gibson:** Highly influential but lesser known singer-songwriter in the folk revival (Larkin, *Encyclopedia of Popular Music*, 3:741).

92   **Frank Warner:** Like John Jacob Niles, a collector and performer of traditional folk songs (Larkin, *Encyclopedia of Popular Music*, 8:514–15).

92   **The Gateways:** The Gateway Singers, a short-lived folk group, very popular in the late '50s and early '60s (Larkin, *Encyclopedia of Popular Music*, 3:694).

92   **Theodore Bikel:** Well-known screen and stage actor as well as folksinger; one of the co-organizers of the Newport Folk Festival and a popularizer of global folk traditions (Larkin, *Encyclopedia of Popular Music*, 1:606–7).

94   **"The Glass Negro":** The title of this project is a play on Norman Mailer's essay "The White Negro" (Delany, interview with Jones, October 30, 2011).

4. CITY COLLEGE
Notebook 13—September 1960

99   **Gibran:** Kahlil Gibran, a Lebanese American poet best known in the United States for *The Prophet* (1923). Danny Auerbach, a friend of Delany's at Bronx Science, was a Gibran fan and introduced Delany to his work (Delany, interview with James, October 30, 2011).

99   ***The Flames of the Warthog:*** One of three short novels Delany wrote in quick succession during the time spanning his graduation from Bronx Science and his early months at City College. The other two were *The Assassination* and *The Lovers* (Delany, *Motion*, 12).

100   **"Prism & Lens":** Poem by Hacker, which, with several others mentioned in this entry, appears in Hacker's second book, *Separations* (1976). A portion of "Prism and Lens" and excerpts from other poems by Hacker serve as epigraphs for Delany's science fiction novel *Babel-17*.

100 **"A—":** Auden (Delany, interview with James, March 27, 2016).

100 **"Chapter One / To the Ship":** Chapter titles for *The Jewels of Aptor*. Since Delany did not start conceiving *The Jewels of Aptor* until after he and Hacker were married—a year after the bulk of this notebook was filled— these notes are apparently an instance of Delany using blank pages from an earlier notebook to develop later material.

102 **Bruce:** A hustler in his late twenties or early thirties who was part of Bernard Kay's circle (Delany, interview with James, October 30, 2011).

Notebook 14—Autumn 1960

103 **"Marlin Night-Bound":** Delany's attendance at the Bread Loaf conference was supported by a work scholarship that required him to wait tables at the conference facilities. Marlin, one year younger than Delany, worked in the kitchen. (Delany, interview with James, October 30, 2011).

104 **"On the dying of the poet's Father by cancer":** Delany's father died on the afternoon of October 6, 1960. That evening, Delany wandered barefoot around Grant's Tomb and produced the first draft of this poem (Delany, *Motion*, 5).

105 **"Water-Logue":** Delany produced several translations during this period (Delany, *Motion*, 9).

106 **"Advice to an even younger writer":** Possibly verse by Hacker. "Little brother" was the nickname of a lover of Delany's from City College (Delany, *Motion*, 9). "Arthur" is Arthur Rimbaud (Delany, interview with James, March 27, 2016).

Notebook 9—Winter 1960

107 **The Fall of the Towers:** This refers not to Delany's SF trilogy, but to an earlier work Delany considered designating with Cary Reinstein's title.

110 **The Harbor Singers:** A folk group Delany formed with Ana Perez, Judy Leibowitz, and David Litwin—all friends from Bronx Science—as well as Laura Hunt, one of Delany's neighbors in Harlem (Delany, *Motion*, 10). Ana continued performing and recorded albums in San Francisco (Delany, interview with James, October 30, 2011).

110 **Richard & Shit:** Upon reviewing these notes for *The Assassination*, Delany was interested to learn that as far back as 1960 he'd thought to name a character "Shit." Having forgotten this first usage, he used the name for one of the two principal characters of *Through the Valley of the Nest of Spiders* (Delany, interview with James, March 27, 2016).

112 **"xi":** Probably qi or chi, the traditional Chinese concept of life energy.

113 **"Auberon":** During their trip to Detroit in the summer of '61, Delany and Hacker collaborated on a comic novella titled *Auberon*. However, as this entry indicates, they had first conceived the idea for *Auberon* well before the trip (Delany, interview with James, March 27, 2016).

Notebook 10—Spring 1960 [Spring 1961]

115 **"Lateday sadness":** Delany's copy of a section of "Soliloquy for a Sunset," an unpublished poem by Hacker. Delany quotes and discusses this poem in *The Motion of Light in Water* (Delany, *Motion*, 74–76, 571).

116 *The Flames of the Warthog:* The title of this short novel is adapted from a line in the poem "Song from an Allegorical Play" by John Ciardi (*Motion*, 196; Delany, interview with James, March 27, 2016).

Notebook 16—Spring, Summer 1961

119 **"the rejection of a manuscript":** The manuscript in question is probably *Those Spared by Fire* (Delany, interview with James, October 30, 2011).

122 *Portraits from the Immature Mind:* A projected collection of Delany's significant work up to this point. The list of titles gives a sense of the volume and range of his output from this period. "The King of Harlem" and "Murdered by Heaven" were translations of originals by Federico García Lorca. "Nine Square Inches" was a response to John Cage's *4'33"*; the text consisted of a sheet of blank paper. "Επιθαλαμια" romanized is Epithalamia—nuptial songs. (Delany, interview with James, October 30, 2011).

126, 127 **"Geo's Poems," "Fragment for Geo":** "Geo" is Geo Keller, a major character in *Voyage, Orestes*, the long novel that capped Delany's non-genre work of the '60s.

Notebook 17—Summer 1961

136 **M. Davis and T. Monk:** Miles Davis and Thelonious Monk.

138 **Robert Green Trio:** Identity unknown (Delany, interview with James, August 9, 2014).

139 **James Baldwin:** Delany's aunt Mary, wife of his paternal uncle William, had long wanted to get young Delany in touch with Baldwin. Mary taught at St. Augustine's and was a friend of a number of black writers, including Baldwin; she and Baldwin were both members of the Harlem Writers Guild. Delany describes his eventual abortive phone conversation with Baldwin in *The Motion of Light in Water* (563).

139 **"I have run narcotics ... even made pornographic films":** According to Delany, these are romanticized descriptions of what are more accurately characterized as carrying a nickel bag from one friend to another, and assisting with the lighting of a friend's nude photography project (Delany, interview with James, August 9, 2014).

139–40 **Robert Frost, John Ciardi, Allen Drury:** Delany had met these writers at Bread Loaf. Frost was a poet, Ciardi a poet and translator as well as director of the Bread Loaf Conference, and Drury a mainstream novelist (Delany, *Motion*, 7–8).

140 **"The Prologue to this silly novel":** *Voyage, Orestes*.

141 **"The 'Jo' poems and *The Terrible Children*":** The 'Jo' Poems are described in the passage; "The Terrible Children" was a chapbook contain-

ing poems by Hacker and Delany (Delany, interview with James, August 9, 2014).

142 **Bill Sloane:** William Sloane was a prominent publisher Delany had met at Bread Loaf (Delany, *Times Square Red, Times Square Blue* 131–32; Delany, interview with James, October 11, 2011).

5. MARRIED LIFE IN THE EAST VILLAGE
Notebook 18—August 1961

This notebook accompanied Delany and Hacker on their trip to Detroit to be married. It contains the text of *Auberon*, the comic novella on which Delany and Hacker collaborated during the trip. The beginning of the novella alternates between Delany's and Hacker's handwriting; while Hacker's handwriting ceases after a few pages, she continued to dictate to Delany and produced half the overall text.

The list of authors at the opening of the notebook is for the "work of literary criticism" mentioned in Notebook 15.

Section § 3 of *Auberon*, which consists of just one sentence, was intended to be an extended chapter describing how Martha got hold of Auberon. The chapter was also to introduce the character of George, whom Martha would meet wandering in the field.

The two entries after the main text are imaginary author biographies and cover matter for the book; the final entry consists of notes Delany kept during the writing of the novella (Delany, interview with James, October 30, 2011).

Notebook 15—September–October 1961
[October 1960 / September–October 1961]

Although the archival label for this notebook correctly designates the time of inscription for the entries treating Delany and Hacker's marriage and Hacker's subsequent miscarriage as September–October 1961, the original contents of the notebook—consisting mainly of school notes and some poems—date from Fall 1960. The entries from 1961 were, as Delany states, written on the margins of the 1960 notebook (Delany, interview with James, October 30, 2011).

162 **Mike and Virginia:** The identity of Mike is unknown; Virginia was Delany's maternal aunt (Delany, interview with James, October 30, 2011).

162 **David:** David Litwin, a friend from Bronx Science and one of the original Harbor Singers (Delany, *Motion*, 10).

162 **Sharon Rohm:** Bronx Science student and wife of Mickey Ruskin, founder of Max's Kansas City, a restaurant and nightclub that became a significant gathering place for New York City artists and celebrities (Delany, *Motion*, 13).

163 **Randy Mueller:** Friend of David Logan (Delany, interview with James, October 30, 2011).

163 **David and Claudi, Paul Elitzik:** David and Claudi Logan, who roomed

in the back of Kay's home. David Logan was an NYU student with whom Hacker had shared a class. It was through being introduced to Logan by Hacker that Delany met Kay. Paul was a Bronx Science student and mentee of Kay (Delany, interview with James, October 30, 2011).

164   **"my book of poems"**: The "Jo" poems.

164   **"my uncle Myles"**: Myles Paige, husband of Delany's mother's sister, Dorothy. Myles, like Delany's father's older brother Hubert, was a judge; both men were prominent civil rights figures in New York City prior to the 1960s (Delany, interview with James, October 30, 2011; Martha Biondi, *To Stand and Fight: The Struggle for Postwar Civil Rights in New York City* [Cambridge, MA: Harvard University Press, 2003], 39–40, 216–17).

164   **Greenwood Lake:** A popular upstate summer destination for well-connected black families, artists, and intellectuals; Myles owned a summer house there (Delany, *Motion*, 27).

166   **"Sonnet After Rimbaud":** As the date of inscription indicates, and as Delany mentions in *Motion*, this translation was produced during Delany's early months at City College (Delany, *Motion*, 9).

166   **"For poetry I say to the unwary":** Delany's transcription of a couplet by Hacker (Delany, interview with James, October 30, 2011).

Notebook 19—November 1961–June 1962

167   **"Life is too serious":** Verses Delany and Hacker wrote to one another during the early months of their marriage. The first half, by Hacker, has been transcribed by Delany; the second half breaks off as indicated in the text.

169   **"December 6, 1961":** The anticipated visit from W. H. Auden and Chester Kallman mentioned here is described in detail in *The Motion of Light in Water* (Delany, *Motion*, 164–71).

169   **"Tired hysterical Jewess that you are!":** Refers to a line in Lawrence Durrell's novel *Justine* from the Alexandria Quartet (Delany, interview with James, October 30, 2011).

169   **"Pierre ... has published a novel":** Pierre Kyria, *Manhattan Blues* (1961) (Delany, interview with James, March 30, 2016).

172   *I Come for to Sing*: A version of the rejected *Seventeen* article on folk music (Delany, interview with James, October 30, 2011). "We Come for to Sing" was a folk song written by Delany himself (Delany, interview with James, March 30, 2016).

173–74   **Laura, Pete, Tony, Ann:** Members of the Harbor Singers: Laura Hunt, probably Peter Horn, and Ana Perez (Delany is lightly fictionalizing here) (Delany, interview with James, October 30, 2011). "Tony" is wholly fictional (Delany, interview with James, March 31, 2016).

Notebook 21—Spring 1962 [January 1962]

178   **"Precocious genius":** In this passage, Delany misremembers the name of the Brontë sisters' childhood home; it is Haworth.

Notebook 20—Spring 1962 [March 1962]

179 **"Geo leaned"**: Scene insert for *The Jewels of Aptor*.

180 **L.H.**: Identity unknown (Delany, interview with James, October 30, 2011).

6. THE FALL OF THE TOWERS AND VOYAGE, ORESTES
Notebook 22—Summer 1962

183 **Notes [on] trilogy**: Sequence from opening chapter of the first volume of the *Fall of the Towers* trilogy.

184 **"Last summer"**: A draft of the prologue to *Voyage, Orestes*.

184 *Cities of the Flames*: Original working title for *The Fall of the Towers* (Delany, interview with James, October 30, 2011).

188 **Baird**: Baird Robinson, an artist Delany and Hacker had met through Ana Perez. His wife, also an artist, was Margie Robinson (Delany, *Motion*, 236).

Notebook 23—November 1962 [October–November 1962]

189 **Ray Trilogy**: The three films Delany discusses—*Pather Panchali* (1955), *Aparajito* (1956), and *Apur Sansar* (1959)—are usually referred to as the Apu trilogy. They were directed by Satyajit Ray.

Notebook 25—Inclusive through March 1963
[Autumn 1962–Spring 1963]

195 **Hilda, Aunt Yetta**: Hacker's mother and aunt (Delany, *Motion*, 25, 28–29; Delany, interview with James, October 30, 2011).

195 **B. and Evelyn**: Aunt Yetta's son Burton and his wife (Delany, interview with James, October 30, 2011).

195 **Tante, Dorothy**: Delany's maternal aunt, Virginia Savoy, and her daughter (Delany, interview with James, October 30, 2011).

195 **Dick & Alice**: Dick and Alice Entin, friends of Delany's (Delany, interview with James, March 30, 2016).

195 **John Hetland, Rose Marion**: Friends Delany had made while all three were coworkers at Barnes & Noble (Delany, interview with James, October 30, 2011).

195 **Mr. Luria, Dr. Gordon**: Teachers of, respectively, creative writing and A.P. English at Bronx Science (Delany, interview with James, October 30, 2011).

195 **Cade Ware**: Young editor at the Bobbs-Merrill Company who had shown a strong interest in *Voyage, Orestes* (Delany, interview with James, October 30, 2011).

195 **Mrs. Bruning**: Baird Robinson's mother (Delany, interview with James, March 30, 2016).

195 **Thelma Watson**: Identity unknown (Delany, interview with James, March 30, 2016).

195 **Jesse Jackson**: Downstairs neighbor at Morningside (Delany, *Motion*, 96).

196 **"The Black Comet"**: A projected space opera series. Upon reviewing this entry, Delany noted that while writing *The Mad Man*, which mentions an

imaginary series of SF short stories collectively titled "The Black Comet," he had forgotten that he'd already used the title for a tentative SF series back in '63 (Delany, interview with James, August 9, 2014).

196 **Simon Kestenbaum:** In his late twenties or early thirties at the time of Delany's entry describing him, Kestenbaum had, by his mid-twenties, established himself as a successful painter. Kestenbaum, himself gay, had told Delany about the cruising area among the trucks on the Christopher Street waterfront, which Delany describes in *The Motion of Light in Water* (Delany, *Motion*, 215–16, 225–27).

197 **Mike:** The first person to take Delany to the St. Mark's bathhouse. Delany's initial experiences at the trucks and the bathhouse fell within the same six-week period (Delany, *Motion*, 290–95; Delany, interview with James, October 30, 2011).

198 **Susan Sholley:** NYU student. Sholley met Delany at Barnes & Noble and moved in with Delany and Hacker for a time (Delany, *Motion*, 277–78).

199 **Appleton-Century-Crofts:** A publishing company.

199 **Bobs Pinkerton:** An editor at the Bobbs-Merrill Company (Delany, *Motion*, 283).

199 **Donald Wollheim:** Science fiction writer, editor, and publisher. Well known as the editor-in-chief of Ace Books and creator of the Ace Doubles format, a venue for the career debuts of several prominent science fiction authors, including Delany, Philip K. Dick, Thomas M. Disch, and Ursula K. LeGuin (John Clute and Peter Nicholls, *The Encyclopedia of Science Fiction* [New York: St. Martin's Griffin, 1995], 1341).

199 **Jack Gaughan:** SF illustrator associated with Ace Books who painted the covers of the first editions of *The Jewels of Aptor*, *Captives of the Flame* (*Out of the Dead City*), *City of a Thousand Suns*, and *The Einstein Intersection* (Clute and Nicholls, *Encyclopedia of Science Fiction*, 477; Delany, interview with James, March 30, 2016).

200 **Guy:** Guy Henderson, a former Bronx Science student and John Hetland's lover (Delany, interview with James, October 30, 2011).

201 **"Half of man's problems would be solved if the human body smelled of perspiration … ":** Delany had recently recognized, after a one-night stand, his liking for the smell of male sweat (Delany, interview with James, March 30, 2016).

Notebook 24—Inclusive to January–February 1963

203 **Outline for "Tel" novelette:** Refers to a subplot in the second volume of the trilogy (Delany, interview with James, October 30, 2011).

204 **Miss Bernheimer:** A local supporter of the Bread Loaf conference who made a point of befriending participants (Delany, interview with James, October 30, 2011).

205 **Randy and Donya:** Randy Nieburg was David Litwin's roommate and probably another Bronx Science student; the identity of Donya is unknown (Delany, interview with James, October 30, 2011).

Notebook 75—[Spring–Summer 1963]

207 **"Notes on 'What Dreams May Come'":** Outline for a science fiction project.

208 **"Outline for the historical novel":** Further commentary on this project can be found in Notebook 68.

209 **"Small comment [on]** *The Ballad of Beta-2***":** Taking a break from his struggles with volume 2 of the *Fall of the Towers* trilogy, Delany began working on the short novel *The Ballad of Beta-2* (Delany, *Motion*, 216, 300, 319–20).

212 **"Ending of O Elektra":** Insert for *Voyage, Orestes*. The speaker is Geo.

216 **Sonny:** An ex-convict Delany took as a lover while Hacker was away in Mexico taking art classes (Delany, *Motion*, 218–25, 232–35).

217 *Les faux-monnayeurs*: As the reader will infer from the outline material in the notebooks from this period, the content and structure of André Gide's 1925 novel influenced *Voyage, Orestes*. Traces of this influence appear to have carried over to *Prism, Mirror, Lens*, and from there to *Dhalgren*.

218 *The Corn King and the Spring Queen*: A feminist historical fantasy by Naomi Mitchison, published in 1931.

219 **"If you are angle":** This stanza from Hacker's poem "The Terrible Children" (1960) eventually served as an epigraph for *The Motion of Light in Water* (*Motion*, 18).

221 **"Then came one to the city":** Lyrics to the titular ballad of *The Ballad of Beta-2* (Delany, *The Ballad of Beta-2* [1965; reprint, New York: Bantam, 1982], 6–8).

Notebook 68—[October 1963]

226 **"This book is more or less reserved":** Commentary and notes for the historical novel outlined in Notebook 75.

229 **"I am a Rat Fink. / I shall write a novel":** This entry refers to Delany's reneging on his decision to devote his energy exclusively to music (Delany, interview with James, March 30, 2016).

230 **"Black pants—":** This entry discusses details from dreams described in entries that follow it: an example of Delany writing entries from the back of a notebook to the front.

230 **"Acrophobia":** This entry refers to the increasingly frequent episodes of anxiety and compulsive behavior that would ultimately lead Delany to seek psychiatric help at the Mount Sinai Day/Night program (Delany, *Motion*, 330–33).

233 **"Spearing my buttock":** Delany describes this incident in *Motion* (187).

234 **"Peter Hutchinson":** A man with whom Delany had had a one-night stand (Delany, interview with James, March 30, 2016).

235 **"Tony Calon":** A young man who lived at Bernard Kay's (Delany, interview with James, March 30, 2016).

Notebook 71—[Winter 1963]

239 *The Assassination*: Title of a short novel Delany had completed near the start of his time at City College; in this notebook he appears to be reusing the title for a new project.

240 **"Growth of Legend"**: Outline material for *Voyage, Orestes*.

240 **"Carmina Catulli"**: This title of a work by Geo is a reference to Carl Orff's cantata that set the poems of Catullus to music (Delany, interview with James, August 9, 2014).

241 **"Phaedra"**: Either a translation or a retelling of Jean Racine's play *Phèdre* (Delany, interview with James, August 9, 2014).

243 **"Diachronic," etc.**: The first appearance of terms from structural linguistics in Delany's journals. Delany was introduced to the terms and concepts by a fellow student in a Greek class at City College (Delany, interview with James, March 31, 2016). Structuralism and semiotics would become important theoretical foundations for Delany's fiction and criticism in the '70s and '80s.

243 **"Ananstha, Anatha"**: Delany may be intending to refer to Anat, Inanna, and/or Athena.

245 **"Blues Jumped the Rabbit," etc.**: Part of Delany's folk performance set (Delany, interview with James, August 9, 2014).

245 **"Opening Scene for Novel"**: This marks the first appearance of notes for the "Faust" project, which Delany would develop intermittently for many years. In conversation Delany has said that the project grew from his early one-act play *The Night Alone*, which focuses on the relationship between Arthur Rimbaud, Paul Verlaine, and Verlaine's wife Mathilde Mauté. This evolved into a five-act play about a poet who resembled Rimbaud, which then led to the "Faust" project (Delany, interview with James, August 9, 2014). Some elements from this project found their way into Delany's first pornographic novel, *Equinox* (1973).

251 **Dr. Gabriel de la Vega**: Therapist of Delany's friend Dick Entin. Entin arranged an appointment for Delany with Dr. de la Vega, who arranged for his entry into the Mount Sinai Day/Night program (Delany, *Motion*, 334).

Notebook 92—[Spring 1964]

252 *"Those Spared by Fire"*: Revisitation of a novel from Delany's Science years.

254 **New York Psychoanalytic Institute, etc.**: Programs Delany was considering for treatment of his psychological problems (Delany, interview with James, August 9, 2014).

7. *BABEL-17* AND BEYOND
Notebook 26—June–July 1964

259 **"Insight about anger → sex"**: This is the first of several entries that focus on Delany's experiences while undergoing therapy at Mount Sinai. Delany

discusses these experiences at length in *The Motion of Light in Water* (325–411).

259   **Dr. Grossman:** Delany's primary psychiatrist at Mount Sinai (Delany, *Motion*, 336).

260   **"Let's see if we can take the pornography a little further than usual.":** Delany let off anxiety during his treatment at Mount Sinai by writing pornography (Delany, interview with James, March 30, 2016).

262   **"Outline for yet another science-fiction novelette":** Delany is here re-outlining his "Çiron" stories in another attempt to unify them as a novel (Delany, interview with James, March 30, 2016).

265   **Terry:** A Puerto Rican woman who was part of Delany's therapy group (Delany, *Motion*, 401).

265   **Dick:** Another patient in the therapy group, who, as Delany recounts in *Motion*, was obsessed with his own stomach (Delany, *Motion*, 401).

265   **Mike Kraft:** "Hank" in *Motion* (402–5, 432–33).

265   **Mrs. Gilbert:** An older patient at Mount Sinai whose husband removed her from the program well before she'd made meaningful progress (Delany, interview with James, October 30, 2011). In conversation, Delany has commented that recalling her desperation and powerlessness could still make him cry, five decades on (Delany, interview with James, March 30, 2016).

267   **Esterson:** Dr. Esterson, Delany's psychiatrist while he attended Bronx Science (Delany, interview with James, October 30, 2011).

268   **"Camping on Bear Mountain":** Refers to a trip upstate taken by Delany and Hacker shortly before their trip to Detroit to be married (Delany, interview with James, October 30, 2011).

268   **"m (inclusive = t / exclusive = l)":** Notes on the artificial language Delany and Hacker developed during their camping trip. Further work on the language can be found in Notebook 27. The notion of a semantically and syntactically compressed artificial language would become the central science fictional premise of Delany's novel *Babel-17*.

270   **"Passing thoughts on Deirdre's suicide":** Deirdre's suicide by hanging, mentioned in *Motion*, served as the model for a major episode in Delany's novel *Dark Reflections* (Delany, *Motion*, 401; Delany, *Dark Reflections* [New York: Carroll & Graf, 2007], 171–72).

270   **P.I.:** New York Psychoanalytic Institute. Delany was here considering the possibility of attending school while simultaneously being a patient in a mental hospital. "All that Bernie says about psychiatry" refers to Bernard Kay's recommendation that Delany try to move on with his life in a more autonomous fashion (Delany, interview with James, March 30, 2016).

271   **Heshy:** Character based on a Bronx Science schoolmate (Delany, interview with James, March 30, 2016).

Notebook 27—August 15, 1964

Notebook 27 is pocket-sized. Delany treats different subject matter on the verso and recto faces of the notebook pages, and sometimes between upper and lower halves of pages; hence the rapid cross-cutting between small sections of text.

274 **"Verb Endings," etc.:** Further development of the artificial language that first appears in Notebook 26.

282 **Hart Crane Biography:** Philip Horton, *Hart Crane: The Life of an American Poet* (New York: W. W. Norton, 1937). (Delany, interview with James, March 30, 2016.)

282 **"Bruce":** This poem refers to the hustler who was an acquaintance of Bernard Kay (see note for Notebook 13).

283 **Cary:** Cary Reinstein.

283 **"—ask Mom about the Roosevelt story":** This refers to a family story Delany had been told as a child. According to the story, Franklin Delano Roosevelt, walking in a cavalcade through Harlem, had stopped to look into a carriage in which the infant Samuel Delany lay. When Delany later recounted the story to Marie Ponsot, she said it sounded impossible, as Roosevelt's polio would have prevented him from walking up the street. Ultimately, Delany did not follow through and ask his mother about the story (Delany, interview with James, October 30, 2011).

283 **T.S.:** T. S. Eliot (Delany, interview with James, March 30, 2016).

283 **"For The Dynamic Moment":** "The Dynamic Moment" was an essay Delany was planning to write, exploring a theme articulated in *The Jewels of Aptor*—that human actions always require at least two forces or motivations. Delany envisioned the piece as a book-length essay modeled after Camus's *The Rebel* (Delany, interview with James, October 30, 2011).

Notebook 28—September 1964–January 1965

294 **"Thoughts of Time & Death":** The opening entry refers to the suicide of Deirdre, one of the patients at Mount Sinai. "He" refers to Delany, while the "kid" is a student one year ahead of Delany at Bronx Science who was also a patient at Mount Sinai (Delany, interview with James, October 30, 2011).

297 **K. Sassel, Steve:** The identity of K. Sassel is unknown. "Steve" is Steve Greenbaum, who became the lead singer of the Heavenly Breakfast band; in *Heavenly Breakfast* he is referred to as "Dave" (Delany, *Heavenly Breakfast*, 5).

Notebook 87—[Early Spring 1965]

298 **Mr. Wright:** An acquaintance of Delany's mother who worked at City College and facilitated Delany's return to school (Delany, interview with James, August 9, 2014).

299 **"We began it on the way back from a camping trip":** Refers to Delany and Hacker's trip to Bear Mountain. Note that Delany lightly fictionalizes

here, claiming the trip had occurred "this summer," i.e., the summer of 1964, rather than several summers earlier.

299 **"transcribing the manuscripts of Samuel Greenberg":** Delany may be exaggerating here. In conversation Delany has said that transcribing Greenberg was something he had wanted to do at the time but does not recall carrying out before he was a professor at the University of Massachusetts at Amherst, when he worked on the short novel *Atlantis: Model 1924* and the extended essay "Atlantis Rose . . ." (Delany, interview with James, August 9, 2014).

300 **Ben Laforge:** LaForge was an editor at New American Library (Delany, interview with James, August 9, 2014).

300 **"Bernie was not in with *Ballad of Beta-Two*":** Delany had briefly enlisted Bernard Kay's help in cowriting *Ballad*. Kay wrote a few pages of material, which Delany ultimately discarded in completing the story. In this entry Delany is referring to an attempt to retrieve the manuscript from Kay (Delany, *Motion*, 319–20).

300 **Steve:** Steve Greenbaum.

303 **David Chote:** An acquaintance of a friend of Hacker's at Bronx Science. Chote had told Delany and Hacker of an experience of running naked to Central Park (Delany, interview with James, August 9, 2014).

Notebook 82 — [Summer 1964–Spring 1965]

305 **"this accursed book":** Delany is referring to the "Faust" novel.

306 **"J.D.":** juvenile delinquent.

307 **"'Where are you going?' said Wystan to Chester":** Delany's transcriptions of verses by Hacker. The first is a parody of Auden's "O Where Are You Going?"; the second was written on the occasion of Hacker's visiting Auden, which led to Auden and Kallman's visit to Delany and Hacker's apartment, as described in *Motion*.

308 **"Rejected from New American Library":** The rejected manuscript in question is *Voyage, Orestes*.

308 **"Autumn struck the city":** A draft of the opening scene for the "Faust" novel. The first lines seem to anticipate the opening of *Dhalgren*. Kip's exuberant toss of his newly published book echoes Delany's own response to the publication of *The Jewels of Aptor*, which he describes in *Motion* (Delany, *Motion*, 270).

309 **"Notes for Space Opera":** *Babel-17*.

310 **"Three dreams":** The two sets of dream descriptions in this entry are evidence of Delany's starting private therapy with Dr. Grossman during this time, a year after his stay at Mount Sinai (Delany, interview with James, April 1, 2016).

310 **Steve Johnson:** Identity unknown (Delany, interview with James, August 9, 2014).

310 **Miss Newby:** Delany's math teacher at Dalton (Delany, interview with James, August 9, 2014).

310 **Johnny Nields, Priscilla:** Fellow Dalton students (Delany, interview with James, August 9, 2014).

310 **J.L.B.:** Identity unknown (Delany, interview with James, August 9, 2014).

311 **"you":** The person addressed in the first dream description is most likely Hacker (Delany, interview with James, August 9, 2014).

311 **Evelyn:** Hacker's cousin (Delany, interview with James, August 9, 2014).

311 **David:** David Logan (Delany, interview with James, August 9, 2014).

Notebook 81—[Late Spring 1965]

313 **"Plot of S-F Novel":** This notebook contains outline material for *Babel-17*, as well as a draft of the novel's opening sequence.

313 **Marie:** Marie Ponsot. At this time Delany was visiting Ponsot once a week to socialize, and had also begun tutoring her son Antoine in math. Delany shortly called off the math lessons, and young Antoine speculated that this was because Delany was writing another novel. In his dedication for the second volume of the *Fall of the Towers* trilogy, Delany confirms this (Samuel R. Delany, *The Fall of the Towers* [1970; reprint, New York: Vintage, 2004], 149.)

Notebook 29—June–July 1965

317 **"Having returned from Texas":** In the spring and summer of 1965, Delany hitchhiked to the Texas coast and crewed on shrimp boats with Bob Folsom (Delany, *Motion*, 474).

318 **"orbis," etc.:** The multilingual list of words for "sphere" was compiled for a sequence from *Babel-17*, in which the protagonist, Rydra Wong, navigates her starship without the use of computers, by utilizing the concept of the great circle (Samuel R. Delany, *Babel-17* [1966; reprint, New York: Vintage, 2001], 65–68).

318 **"Muels Aranlyde":** Muels Aranlyde, an anagram for Samuel R. Delany, is a character in both *Empire Star* and *Babel-17*. Delany conceived the two novels as potentially being publishable together as an "Ace Doubles" paperback. (An "Ace Doubles" book contained two novels and had two "front" covers; upon finishing the first novel the reader flipped the book over and began the second. The Vintage reprint of *Babel-17* and *Empire Star* replicates this format.) In *Empire Star* Muels Aranlyde is a writer who has his consciousness uploaded into a computer and becomes the character Lump (one of Hacker's nicknames for Delany). In *Babel-17* Aranlyde is a friend of Rydra Wong and the author of a novel titled *Empire Star*— which implies that *Empire Star* is an artifact from the universe of *Babel-17* (Samuel R. Delany, *Empire Star* [1966; reprint, New York: Vintage, 2001], 65; Delany, *Babel-17*, 95).

322 **"Being set on the idea / Of getting to Atlantis":** An excerpt from W. H. Auden's poem "Atlantis," used as an epigraph for *Empire Star*.

322 **"Simplex / Complex / Multiplex":** Modes of thought delineated in *Empire Star*.

323 **"San Severina," etc.:** Characters and episodes from *Empire Star*.

323 **Bobby Riccioti:** Steve Greenbaum's best friend from childhood, who lived on the top floor of Joe Soley and Paul Caruso's building (Delany, interview with James, August 9, 2014).

323 **"Dear Sir":** Draft of a letter of introduction to Henry Morrison. After returning from Texas, Delany began to plan a trip to Europe and decided to hire an agent who could represent him while he was out of the country. After hearing about Morrison through Bobs Pinkerton, Delany visited Morrison's office. Morrison was not in, so Delany sent him a letter. Morrison took Delany on as a client, thus beginning a lifelong professional relationship (Delany, interview with James, August 9, 2014.)

324 *Prism:* This story was eventually published as "Prismatica" (Delany, interview with James, August 9, 2014).

325 **"Discover wounded Golden":** Notes for the novella "The Star-Pit."

327 **"Have You Spoken to Bob":** Bob Folsom. Delany had met Folsom through Bernard Kay; Folsom moved in with Delany and Hacker in February 1965 and stayed with them through the spring. Delany describes the relationship between the three in detail in *The Motion of Light in Water* (416–18, 429–549). Shortly after Delany left Texas, Folsom was arrested for disorderly conduct; Delany wrote these notes to Hacker while she was on the phone with Folsom's lawyer (Delany, interview with James, March 30, 2016).

330 **"Dear Heart":** Mentioned in this letter to Hacker are Mr. Flood, Folsom's lawyer, and Darlene, Folsom's wife (Delany, *Motion*, 543; Delany, interview with James, August 9, 2014).

332 **"Actions derive their value ... ":** Notes for a critical study of science fiction.

8. TRAVELS IN EUROPE
Notebook 67—Autumn 1965–Summer 1966

337 **"Here in the highest spot in Athens":** During his stay in Athens, Delany lived halfway up Mount Lykavittos, which gave the highest vantage in the city. (Note that here, as elsewhere, dates and other internal evidence suggest that some entries were not written in conventional front-to-back order.) (Delany, interview with James, August 9, 2014.)

337 **Ron:** Ron Helstrom, whom Delany had befriended during his stint in Texas (K. Leslie Steiner [Samuel R. Delany], "Anatomy of a Nova" [unpublished essay, 1997], 11).

339 **Bill:** Bill Balousiak, a Canadian whom Delany and Helstrom had met on their flight to Europe (Steiner [Delany], "Anatomy of a Nova," 12).

341 **"Blair Faust":** Notes for Delany's short story "Corona." In the final version of the story, "Blair Faust" became "Bryan Faust."

341 **"having been in shuttley London for a bit over a week now":** This entry postdates entries in subsequent notebooks, which suggests that

during this period of travel Delany used earlier notebooks to record later material.

Notebook 96—[Autumn 1965]

343 **"Minor interruption of 'Shadows'":** "Shadows" was a story Delany worked on during his stay in Greece (Delany, interview with James, August 9, 2014).

344 **"Spyros asks Dr. Gautier about his Greek":** Notes for "Dog in a Fisherman's Net."

Notebook 31—March 1966 [February–March 1966]

346 **"Performing and working together on songs":** A schedule and song list for the Harbor Singers (Delany, interview with James, October 30, 2011).

346 **"DeLys, loves to cook":** DeLys Robinson, the woman described in this entry and the one to follow, rented her apartment to Delany while she traveled to London. This was his residence during the events recounted in "Citre et Trans." The "illegal hustling service" Delany mentions refers to the period when Bob Folsom lived with Delany and Hacker; during this time Folsom supported himself through hustling, as, occasionally, did Delany (Delany, *Motion*, 452; Delany, interview with James, March 31, 2016).

349 **"Constantine":** The implication is that this was Constantine II, the king of Greece. This incident, while fictional, was inspired by an actual event. Delany had been wandering in a school library, probably at the University of Athens. At the same time, and unbeknownst to him, the campus was cleared to make way for a visit by Constantine's spouse, Anne-Marie, formerly Princess of Denmark. Making his way to the library cafeteria, Delany found himself in the vicinity of Anne-Marie, unaware that she was the queen of Greece (Delany, interview with James, April 1, 2016).

353 **"Discovered Gregory Corso was in Athens":** Delany had met Corso at a café at the bottom of Plaka, the neighborhood on the northeastern slope of the Acropolis. Corso invited Delany to lunch, and the two of them explored Athens for the day. It was during this time that Corso made the remark about Delany's novel in progress, *The Einstein Intersection*, which eventually became an epigraph for that book (Delany, *Motion*, 170).

353 **"Dear you":** The addressee is Hacker (Delany, interview with James, October 30, 2011).

354 **Jerry:** Delany's hitchhiking companion to Istanbul ("Citre et Trans," 181–82). *Alpha Yes, Terra No!* (Emil Pataja, 1965) was published with *The Ballad of Beta-2* as an Ace Double (Delany, interview with James, March 27, 2016).

Notebook 30—December 1965 [Spring 1966]

360 **"He was an old man":** Opening scene of *Nova*. In this early draft, the character later named Katin is here called Jommy, and it is Jommy, not Mouse,

who is first approached by Dan in the bar. "Jommy" had been the name of the protagonist of A. E. Van Vogt's *Slan* (1946); Delany, having read *Slan* but at the time unaware of its importance within the genre, appropriated the name for this draft. (See appendix 2 for another appearance of the name "Jommy.") (Delany, interview with James, March 31, 2016.)

360   **"Dear Theodore Sturgeon":** Theodore Sturgeon and Alfred Bester were the SF writers of the previous generation who had had arguably the greatest impact on Delany's own work. Although Delany neither sent the letter drafted here nor ultimately included Sturgeon in the dedication to *Nova*, a character in that book, the would-be novelist Katin Crawford, mentions Sturgeon as a twentieth-century writer who had inspired him. In conversation Delany has said that his first direct contact with Sturgeon occurred shortly after the publication of *Dhalgren* in 1975. During a public reading and signing of the novel at the Science Fiction Book Shop in New York City, Sturgeon phoned to congratulate Delany and thank him for the mention in *Nova*, which had greatly touched him (Delany, interview with James, October 30, 2011).

362   **John Brunner:** A British SF writer Delany met and befriended while in England. Shortly after this time Brunner would produce the novels for which he is arguably best known: *Stand on Zanzibar* (1968), *The Sheep Look Up* (1972), and *The Shockwave Rider* (1975).

362   **Mike Moorcock:** Michael Moorcock was a prolific and influential SF and fantasy author who had recently taken over the editorship of the SF magazine *New Worlds*, using it as a platform for the publication of innovative genre fiction by UK writers like J. G. Ballard, Brian Aldiss, and Barrington Bayley, and U.S. writers like Thomas M. Disch, John Sladek, Pamela Zoline, and Delany. *New Worlds* became the center of what would come to be called New Wave science fiction, characterized by an interest in literary experimentation as well as a heightened attention to the so-called soft sciences and politically relevant near-future scenarios (Clute and Nicholls, *Encyclopedia of Science Fiction*, 822–25).

362   **John Witten-Doris:** A British expatriate whom Delany had met on Mykonos. Witten-Doris is "John" in Delany's essay-memoir "A Fictional Architecture Which Manages Only with Great Difficulty Not Once to Mention Harlan Ellison," and "English John" in Delany's later memoir "Citre et Trans" (Steiner [Delany], "Anatomy of a Nova," 14).

362   **Paula Osius:** At Witten-Doris's suggestion, once in London Delany contacted Witten-Doris's friend Paula Osius and her boyfriend Chris, and stayed with them for several days (Delany, interview with James, October 30, 2011).

363   **"Dear M. M.":** Letter to Michael Moorcock. "Henry M." is Henry Morrison; "Silverberg" and "Fred P." are SF writers Robert Silverberg and Frederik Pohl, and "Langdon" is Langdon Jones, associate editor of *New Worlds*. Judith Merril, from the mid-'50s to the late '60s, edited the influential *Year's Best* science fiction anthology series, which showcased many

writers associated with the New Wave (Clute and Nicholls, *Encyclopedia of Science Fiction*, 799).

363   **"Dear Paula and Chris"**: Paula Osius and her boyfriend Chris (Delany, interview with James, October 30, 2011).

364–67   **Epigraphs for *A Fabulous Formless Darkness*, "Author's Journal" entries:** This collection of texts makes up the material that heads the chapters of *The Einstein Intersection*. As the reader will infer, while the "Author's Journal" entries describe real incidents, most were apparently written not on the immediate occasion of the events they recount, but shortly afterward and with their role in the novel already in mind (Delany, interview with James, March 30, 2016).

367   **"New Wor(l)ds / Many Inventions"**: Delany had been invited to write an editorial for the last digest edition of Moorcock's *New Worlds*. This text, trimmed and retitled "Sketch for Two-Part Invention," became Delany's first piece of published SF criticism (Steiner [Delany], "Anatomy of a Nova," 17–18).

368   **"The 13th Bartok Quartet in G Major"**: This is an error, as Bartok composed only six quartets. Delany likely meant the String Quartet no. 13 in G major by Dvořák.

374   **"Note"**: This is a critical-autobiographical blurb for "The Star-Pit."

374   ***"All that I have, is the life that I have"***: The handwriting here is neither Delany's nor Hacker's. Possible authors include Ana Perez, Steve Guilden (an artist Delany had met at Mount Sinai), and Guilden's girlfriend, Fran Wiseman (Delany, interview with James, October 30, 2011).

9. CHANGING SCENES
Notebook 80—[Spring 1966]

379   ***"World Without Form (FFD)"***: FFD = *A Fabulous, Formless Darkness*. Working titles for the novel eventually published as *The Einstein Intersection*.

381   **"Then they sent me my sales report"**: Michael Moorcock had suggested to Delany that the British publisher Sphere Books might be interested in publishing *The Fall of the Towers*. This may be a draft of a cover letter to Sphere, though it may also be an instance of Delany simply working through some ideas about his writing (Delany, interview with James, August 9, 2014).

383   ***"The Bloi triplets"***: These notes refer to *The Einstein Intersection*.

384   **"A little organization now, if you please"**: Shortly after Delany returned from England, Hacker moved in with a mutual friend, Bill McNeill, to whom Delany had introduced Hacker shortly before leaving for Europe (Delany, *Motion*, 557–62). McNeill was one of a number of individuals now living in New York City who had been associated with the Spicer circle on the West Coast. Others from this group mentioned in the journals are Helen Adam, Russell Fitzgerald, and Link Martin (Luther T. Cupp) (Steiner [Delany], "Anatomy of a Nova," 20; Lewis Ellingham and Kevin

Killian, *Poet Be Like God: Jack Spicer and the San Francisco Renaissance* [Middletown, CT: Wesleyan University Press, 1998], 352; Delany, interview with James, August 9, 2014).

384 **Ron Bowman:** Delany had first met Ron Bowman outside Bowman's apartment on St. Mark's Place, which was across the street from the home of Delany's former Bronx Science colleague, Lew Warsh. When Delany's friend DeLys Robinson—who had let him stay at her home in Athens while she traveled—arrived in New York City, Delany loaned her his own apartment and moved in with Bowman (Delany, interview with James, August 9, 2014). An actor and singer, Bowman had appeared in Helen Adam's New York production of *San Francisco's Burning* and would eventually appear in Delany's short film *The Orchid* as the young man with the microphone (Delany, interview with James, August 9, 2014; Delany, "Chronology" [unpublished personal document, 2014], 12). Delany stayed with Bowman through the publication of *The Einstein Intersection*. Toward the end of 1966, Michael Moorcock invited Delany back to London for the holidays; upon returning from that two-week visit Delany learned that Bowman had started an affair with a writer associated with Andy Warhol's circle. Delany has said that Bowman had desired the sort of social stimulation that could be found around Warhol; by contrast, Delany's round-the-clock writing held little allure (Delany, interview with James, August 9, 2014; Delany, "Chronology," 13).

384 **"Samuel R. Delany was born on April Fools' Day ... ":** Author's biography for *The Einstein Intersection* (here still titled *A Fabulous, Formless Darkness*) (Delany, interview with James, March 31, 2016).

385 **"Let us plot out 'Driftglass,' à la Zelazny method ...":** "Driftglass" is a short SF story whose title became that of Delany's first short story collection (1971). The "Zelazny method" of developing a story was to talk it through until one was ready to write it (Delany, interview with James, March 31, 2016).

Notebook 91—[Fall 1966]

386 **"The psychologically doomed":** Blurb for Delany's short story "Corona."

386 **"Both were inspired by one person":** In fact, they were inspired by two. The principal person in question is Laford Mott. Delany and Hacker had met Mott at the Old Reliable and attempted to create a *ménage à trois* with Mott similar to their earlier trio with Bob Folsom, without success. (Delany's claim that Mott is from Alabama is mistaken: he was from Baton Rouge.) The "suicide attempts" mentioned here and dramatized in "Corona" were originally recounted to Delany by Mott (Steiner [Delany], "Anatomy of a Nova," 20; Delany, interview with James, August 9, 2014). Mott's ability "to integrate for the area of $x^4 + y^4 = k^4$" was actually an achievement of a precocious camp-mate at Woodland (Delany, *Motion*, 60–61; Delany, interview with James, August 9, 2014).

386 **"What goes into an SF story?":** A draft of the afterword for "Aye, and

Gomorrah," which appeared in Harlan Ellison's *Dangerous Visions* anthology (Harlan Ellison, ed., *Dangerous Visions* [Garden City, NY: Doubleday, 1967], 544).

386 **"Me":** Notes on reader feedback for Delany's short story "Corona," from a workshop session at Milford. "Jo" is likely Joanna Russ, "Anne" Anne McCaffrey, "Carol" Carol Emshwiller, and "Ted" Theodore Cogswell.

387 **"Ad Owhmia":** A story of Çiron (Delany, interview with James, August 9, 2014).

388 **"Mandala":** Alternative working title for *Voyage, Orestes*. The episode synopsized at the beginning of the outline is based on Delany's own experience: Jimmy's return home to his dying father corresponds to Delany's return home from the Bread Loaf conference (Delany, interview with James, August 9, 2014).

Notebook 83—[December 1966–January 1967]

393 **"I don't know whether you enjoy science-fiction":** The addressee here is a young man who had recently interviewed Delany for a periodical; his name and the periodical are unknown (Delany, interview with James, August 9, 2014).

393 **"Man and machine have settled their differences":** This detailed synopsis of *Nova*, which includes episodes dropped from the final draft, was possibly penned as part of an attempt to sell the book, or episodes from the book, for magazine publication; the book already had a hardcover publisher by this point (Delany, interview with James, August 9, 2014).

397 **"Dear Andy":** Andrew I. Porter was the publisher of the fanzine *Algol*, which printed "In the Ruins," another story of Çiron, in 1968 (Peplow and Bravard, *Samuel R. Delany*, 71).

398 **"Dear Miss Pinkerton":** This appears to be a draft of a letter Delany ghostwrote for Michael Moorcock at *New Worlds*.

398 **"Architectural Study":** These are notes for Delany's essay-memoir "A Fictional Architecture Which Manages Only with Great Difficulty Not Once to Mention Harlan Ellison." The essay first appeared in Terry Carr's influential fanzine *Lighthouse* in 1967 and was eventually collected in *The Jewel-Hinged Jaw* (Steiner [Delany], "Anatomy of a Nova," 48).

399 **"I am very interested in science fiction as serious literature":** These are probably prompts Delany wrote for himself as a moderator for an SF convention panel (Delany, interview with James, August 9, 2014).

400 **James Sallis:** Sallis, who was to become a highly regarded writer of crime fiction, poetry, and criticism, had begun a correspondence with Delany. The two eventually met at the Milford workshop, where Sallis was working as Virginia Kidd's assistant. He went on to become the assistant editor of *New Worlds* in London (Clute and Nicholls, *Encyclopedia of Science Fiction*, 1046–47). Sallis also edited the first collection of Delany criticism, *Ash of Stars: On the Writing of Samuel R. Delany* (Jackson: University Press of Mississippi, 1996).

400 **"The Claw of Kirke":** Earlier title for *They Fly at Çiron* (Delany, interview with James, August 9, 2014).

401 **Tanto, Keith:** Identities unknown. The situation referred to involves Tanto lying on her résumé about her abilities as a typist (Delany, interview with James, August 9, 2014).

401 **"J. Brunner's note when he discovered I had clap":** This refers to an episode in which Delany, staying with the Brunners in London, had sought pinworm medication. He shortly discovered that in England, unlike the United States, this medication could not be obtained over the counter; eventually he was able to obtain it at an STD clinic. At the clinic, he was asked to provide an address and gave the Brunners'. After Delany left England, the clinic sent a notification to that address, causing the Brunners some startlement (Delany, interview with James, August 9, 2014).

401 **"There is the lie that comes out of that story 'The Torture Garden'":** A draft of "The Torture Garden" can be found in appendix 2 of this volume. In Delany's recollection, the "lie" in question was a response to Hacker's asking him, upon reading the story back at Bronx Science, if an episode in it—presumably the moment when the protagonist strikes another character—had been based on a real experience. At the time, Delany had claimed that it had (Delany, interview with James, August 9, 2014).

401 **"There is the lie about the method of composition for *F.F.D.*":** Here Delany is referring to a passage from the essay-memoir "A Fictional Architecture . . ." that describes him producing passages from *The Einstein Intersection* by flinging scraps of writing into the sea and then retrieving them (Samuel R. Delany, *The Jewel-Hinged Jaw* [1977; reprint, Middletown, CT: Wesleyan University Press, 2009], 313). Delany may also be thinking of the deliberately planned aspects of the "Author's Journal" entries from that novel, as indicated in the working notes in Notebook 30 (Delany, interview with James, March 30, 2016).

Notebook 84—[February–April 1967]

402 **"Georgia, country":** Pornographic fantasy with a "burning city" scenario that anticipates *Dhalgren*. That scenario is not developed beyond what is quoted here; with the transition to the story of "my old man," the narrative heads in another direction.

406 **"The torpor swallowing all my actions":** Delany is still living with Ron Bowman; the "noisy people" Delany mentions are various of Bowman's friends (Delany, interview with James, August 9, 2014).

407 **"Damon Knight sent me a letter telling me that I had received the Nebula for best novel of the year":** Knight was a science fiction writer and editor who was very active in the SF community. He cofounded the Milford Writers' Conference, which he headed for two decades with his wife, the SF and mystery writer Kate Wilhelm (Clute and Nicholls, *Encyclopedia of Science Fiction*, 673). The novel in question is *Babel-17*, which had tied with Daniel Keyes's *Flowers for Algernon* for the Nebula.

407 **O.R.:** A number of people who figure in this period were regulars at the Old Reliable, a bar that catered to both gay and straight clientele and served as a social hub for downtown artists. "Jamey," one of these regulars, was a mutual friend of Delany and Hacker. Corey Martin was a friend of Ana Perez (Delany, interview with James, August 9, 2014).

407 **"Thence to Russell's womb-like studio":** Russell Fitzgerald was a painter to whom Delany had been introduced by Hacker a few days after his return from London. (On the same occasion Delany had met Helen Adam, the director of *San Francisco's Burning*. Adam served as a model for the character of Edna Silem in "Time Considered as a Helix of Semi-precious Stones.") Fitzgerald painted the covers for the British Sphere editions of *The Fall of the Towers* volumes, as well as the cover of the Doubleday first edition of *Nova* (Steiner [Delany], "Anatomy of a Nova," 20; Delany, interview with James, August 9, 2014).

407 **"I dream of Barbara and Russell and John":** Russell is Russell Fitzgerald; the identities of Barbara and John are unknown (Delany, interview with James, August 9, 2014).

410 **"My own house ... has been taken over by Janet, the children & Andy":** Janet Japin was the former girlfriend of Steve Greenbaum. The reference to "the children & Andy" is an anomaly, as Andy was himself one of Janet's children (Delany, interview with James, August 9, 2014).

411 **"Silence; Water; Someone Saying My Name":** This phrase will later appear in *Dhalgren* (29).

412, 413 **"(Quote)," "[Quote]":** As the context suggests, these were placeholders for passages by Roger Zelazny and James Sallis.

Notebook 76—[Spring–Summer 1967]

418 **"This book springs from":** This is a tentative dedication paragraph for *Nova*; only a few of the names listed here appear in the published dedication.

418 **Heidi Mueller:** Mueller appears in Delany's memoir-essay "Citre et Trans." Like John Witten-Doris, Mueller was part of the international expatriate/tourist population of Athens, which, Delany has said in conversation, was fairly small in the mid-'60s (Steiner [Delany], "Anatomy of a Nova," 16; Delany, interview with James, August 9, 2014).

419 **"This morning a bit after six":** Delany is still living with Ron Bowman.

419 **Linda Sampson:** A friend of Bowman's; further details unknown (Delany, interview with James, August 9, 2014).

419 **Dick:** Dick Entin (Delany, interview with James, August 9, 2014).

421 **Alexei:** Identity unknown; possibly he was a habitué of the Old Reliable (Delany, interview with James, August 9, 2014).

422 **"During the odd months I lived among the Greek islands":** This entry discusses the genesis of Delany's story "Dog in a Fisherman's Net."

423 **Judy:** Judith Merril.

423   **Ed Ferman:** Editor of the *Magazine of Fantasy & Science Fiction* (Clute and
       Nicholls, *Encyclopedia of Science Fiction*, 425).

423   **Larry:** Larry Ashmead, editor at Doubleday (Steiner [Delany], "Anatomy
       of a Nova," 45).

Notebook 69—[Summer 1967]

This "notebook" is a small booklet of music staff paper. Its only contents
are the notes transcribed here, which date from an early phase in the development of the radio adaptation of "The Star-Pit" for WBAI-FM. Originally Delany had planned to direct the program himself, and Judy Ratner,
Hacker's close friend and then Baird Searles's assistant, had wanted to
play Allegra, the Golden junky. Eventually Delany decided that directing
and playing the lead were too much to handle at once, and Danny Landau
stepped in as director. Landau in turn enlisted Randa Haynes to play Allegra (Delany, "Notes on *The Star-Pit*" [unpublished essay, 2005], 2).

10. *PRISM, MIRROR, LENS* AND OTHER PROJECTS
Notebook 86—[Summer 1967]

429   **"YOU THERE!":** In the original notebook, this entry is a playful experi-
       ment with handwriting; the interrogator's lines are written in large, ex-
       pressive letters and the interrogatee's in diminutive ones.

429   ***"Mirror and Lens":*** The multivolume science fiction series outlined here
       marks the beginning of the project that would eventually evolve into *Dhal-
       gren*. In the outline readers will recognize names eventually used in that
       novel. The title of the series and its variants allude to Hacker's poem *Prism
       and Lens* (Delany, interview with James, April 1, 2016).

Notebook 32—July–October 1967

433   **"Journal entry":** This entry describes life in Heavenly Breakfast, the rock
       band and commune Delany cofounded in 1967. Sue Schweers, mentioned
       in the entry, was a member; Schweers also assisted in the production of
       the *Star-Pit* radio play (Delany, "Notes on *The Star-Pit*," 6). "Steve" was a
       friend of Schweers; Delany and he later became friends. Interval Artists
       Music Co. was one of Bernard Kay's companies (Delany, interview with
       James, October 30, 2011).

436   **"She said:":** "She" is Sue Schweers. A version of this episode can be found
       in Samuel R. Delany, *Heavenly Breakfast: An Essay on the Winter of Love*
       (1979; reprint, Flint, MI: Bamberger Books, 1997), 49.

436   **Joachim:** A young truck driver, real name unknown; Delany gave him
       this designation for the purposes of the passage (Delany, interview with
       James, October 30, 2011).

436   **Micah, Peggy:** Identities unknown (Delany, interview with James, Octo-
       ber 30, 2011).

439   ***"Mirror and Lens":*** An editor at Avon Books, George Ernstberger, had
       been impressed with *Nova* and was now courting Delany. Delany's agent,

Henry Morrison, felt Avon was a good prospect and encouraged Delany to write a proposal, of which this is a first draft (Delany, "Chronology," 16; Delany, interview with James, October 30, 2011).

441 *"Mirror and Lens"* **(second appearance):** Here Delany uses the title *Mirror and Lens* for a hypothetical book of criticism. In the original notebook, just preceding this outline is another for the same project, headed with the title *The Dynamic Moment.*

444 **"Notes on *Nova*":** Mentioned in this entry is *Cavalier*, a men's magazine that frequently featured work by SF writers, including Ray Bradbury, Theodore Sturgeon, Isaac Asimov, William Tenn, and others (Delany, interview with James, October 30, 2011).

445 **"Historical background":** Possibly this passage refers to *The Night Alone*, Delany's one-act play on Rimbaud and Verlaine (Delany, interview with James, October 30, 2011).

446 **"Hell! Editorial introduction":** Hypothetical front matter for a new edition of *The Jewels of Aptor.*

447 **"Just finished 'Lines of Power'":** "Lines of Power" was the working title for the short story "We, in Some Strange Power's Employ, Move on a Rigorous Line," published in *Fantasy & Science Fiction* in 1968 and collected in *Driftglass.* Note the appearance of outline material for "Lines of Power" later in the same notebook; this order of entries is an example of working notes and commentary advancing backward through a notebook.

448 **Virginia Kidd:** SF writer, editor, and literary agent (Clute and Nicholls, *Encyclopedia of Science Fiction*, 664). Delany had met Kidd at the Milford conference (Delany, interview with James, October 30, 2011).

448 **Joanna Russ:** Very influential writer of feminist SF, whom Delany had met at the Milford conference (Clute and Nicholls, *Encyclopedia of Science Fiction*, 1035–36). Delany has claimed that he had considered Russ, Roger Zelazny, Thomas M. Disch, and himself to constitute "a kind of quartet" whose work was in mutual dialogue (Delany, *Silent Interviews* [Middletown, CT: Wesleyan University Press, 1994], 69).

448 **Ginny Carew:** An academic interested in SF (Delany, interview with James, October 30, 2011).

448 **Bill Stribling:** Possibly Phil Stribling (Delany, interview with James, October 30, 2011).

449 **Roger:** Roger Zelazny, an American science fiction writer associated with the New Wave (Clute and Nicholls, *Encyclopedia of Science Fiction*, 1365–66).

450 **Katherine MacLean:** American science fiction writer (Clute and Nicholls, *Encyclopedia of Science Fiction*, 760).

450 **Jack and Phoebe Gaughan:** Jack Gaughan was a science fiction illustrator; Phoebe was his wife (Clute and Nicholls, *Encyclopedia of Science Fiction*, 477).

450 **"The Lupoffs":** Dick Lupoff is an American science fiction author (Clute and Nicholls, *Encyclopedia of Science Fiction*, 741–42).

451 **Lydia Stephenou, Phil, Sarah:** Delany had met Stephenou through Phil (an American writer Delany had met while traveling in Greece) and his wife Sarah (Delany, interview with James, October 30, 2011).

452 **"More structural notes":** For "Lines of Power."

453 **"Come back from Sea Cliff":** Sea Cliff, New York, was Sue Schweers's place of residence. The schedule listed in this entry is for the production of a demo tape by Heavenly Breakfast (Delany, interview with James, October 30, 2011).

453 **Ivan:** A friend of Schweers's who owned recording equipment (Delany, interview with James, October 30, 2011).

453 **Donna:** identity unknown (Delany, interview with James, October 30, 2011).

Notebook 88—[Autumn 1967]

455 **"Seven Reasons Why I Should Be Pope":** The "I" in question is Hacker; the material that follows is hers, with Delany taking dictation. The passage was written after a meeting with Robert Silverberg at his home in Westchester. The identities of "Joe," "Edwin," and "Harry" are unknown (Delany, interview with James, August 9, 2014).

456 **"Mr. Keyes":** Daniel Keyes, author of *Flowers for Algernon*, which tied with *Babel-17* for the 1965 Nebula.

456 **Mark Heighfli:** A young editor for Doubleday under Larry Ashmead and the in-house editor for *Nova*; he served as a model for the character of James in *Dark Reflections* (Delany, interview with James, August 9, 2014).

457 **"Having rounded page 50":** This project, which Delany refers to in this and a subsequent entry as *Faust*, will eventually be retitled *Equinox*.

458 **"The color of bell metal":** Opening lines of *Equinox*.

460 **"Baird Searles, director of drama and literature at WBAI-FM":** This is likely a press release for a radio programming guide. WBAI produced Delany's adaptation of "The Star Pit" (Delany, "Notes on *The Star-Pit*," 1.)

461 **"Background for the whole business":** Outline material for "Time Considered as a Helix of Semi-precious Stones."

461 **"Table of Contents for":** Blurbs for stories that would, with the exception of "They Fly at Çiron," appear in the *Driftglass* collection.

Notebook 33—December 1967 [December 1967–January 1968]

464 **"Jasper":** This entry consists of notes for Delany's short story "Time Considered as a Helix of Semi-precious Stones."

464 **"Dear *Australian Science Fiction Review*":** This and the following related entries eventually became one long letter that was sent to the *ASFR*. Delany had found a copy of *ASFR* at Milford and was excited by the amateur criticism he found there (Clute and Nicholls, *Encyclopedia of Science Fiction*, 72–73).

469 **Warsh, Wakoski, etc.:** Prominent young poets of the '60s.

470 **Tom Veitch:** The brother of comic book artist Rick Veitch. While Delany

was in San Francisco, he and Veitch collaborated on three short stories, but these were not ultimately published (Delany, interview with James, October 30, 2011).

470 **"The hero, a young orphaned juvenile delinquent"**: Notes for "Time Considered as a Helix of Semi-precious Stones."

472 **"Wound the autumnal city"**: Draft of the opening scene of the first book in the *Prism, Mirror, Lens* series. The first line will eventually evolve into the opening line of *Dhalgren*.

474 **"Wednesday 12:30 at Avon"**: Lunch appointment with George Ernstberger, editor at Avon, to discuss the *Prism, Mirror, Lens* project.

479 **"Dear Bay"**: Baird Searles (Delany, "Notes on *The Star-Pit*," 1).

480 **Danny:** Danny Landau, director of the *Star-Pit* production.

Notebook 35—1968 [Early Spring 1968]

483 **"Dear Roger"**: Zelazny. "Judy" was Zelazny's wife.

483 **"Dear Kate and Damon"**: Kate Wilhelm and Damon Knight.

483 **"Jim's and my collaboration"**: The collaboration Delany speaks of is a short-story project Delany intended to develop with James Sallis but eventually carried forward on his own, which became "Time Considered as a Helix of Semi-precious Stones" (Delany, interview with James, October 30, 2011).

485 **"Dear John"**: John Foyster, at the *Australian Science Fiction Review*. Foyster was a computer programmer who, along with Joanna Russ, carried out an extensive correspondence with Delany after Delany moved to San Francisco (Delany, interview with James, October 30, 2011).

487 **Danny's:** A restaurant (Delany, interview with James, October 30, 2011).

488 **"The time has come"**: Entry on the Heavenly Breakfast commune.

488 **Bert:** Bert Lee, member of the Heavenly Breakfast.

490 **"Note for Bill"**: Bill Brodecky was a painter who was part of the social circle surrounding Jack Spicer, as well as a longtime friend of Link Martin. Hacker befriended Brodecky upon moving to San Francisco with Link, and discussed him in her communications with Delany from the West Coast. On New Year's Eve of 1968, when Delany flew to San Francisco to reunite with Hacker, he met Brodecky—who, with Paul Caruso and Joe Cox, had accompanied Hacker to the airport. (The five of them subsequently visited a string of New Year's Eve parties in San Francisco.) Several months later Brodecky performed with Hacker and Jerry Sabian in a production of Genet's *Les Bonnes*, directed by Delany and eventually broadcast by the Bay Area Pacifica station, KPFA (Delany, "Chronology," 16, 17; Delany, interview with James, October 30, 2011; K. Leslie Steiner [Delany], "Samuel R. Delany," *Pseudopodium*, Ray Davis, 7).

Notebook 77—[Early Spring 1968]

492 **"Dear Judy"**: Draft of a note to Judith Merril responding to a draft of her introduction to "The Star-Pit," which was to appear in Merril's *World's Best*

SF #12 (Judith Merril, afterword to "The Star-Pit," in *SF 12* [New York: Delacorte Press, 1968], 381–82).

493 **"Dear Sirs":** Letter to the editors at the British publisher Sphere Books.

494 **"AN ALBUM":** Track list for projected Heavenly Breakfast album.

Notebook 85—[Spring–Summer 1968]

496 **Sandra Ley:** Willy Ley was a writer of popular introductions to space-flight, first for German audiences and then, after fleeing Nazi Germany, U.S. audiences. His daughter Sandra was, with Baird Searles and Sue Schweers, a co-owner of the Science Fiction Book Shop (Clute and Nicholls, *Encyclopedia of Science Fiction*, 718; Delany, interview with James, August 9, 2014).

497 **Keir Dullea:** Lead actor of *2001*.

497 **Dr. Clarke:** Arthur C. Clarke, the co-writer (with Stanley Kubrick) of *2001: A Space Odyssey* (Clute and Nicholls, *Encyclopedia of Science Fiction*, 229–32)

497 **"Coming from the men's room":** An example of Delany's strategic distortion of material related to homosexuality. In the entry Delany describes spotting Clarke as Clarke emerged from the men's lavatory into the lobby; in fact, Delany had run into Clarke in the lavatory itself. In conversation Delany has said that although there was nothing sexual in the encounter—the exchange between them went as described in the entry—he had been aware that Clarke was gay and might wish to keep this fact out of general public awareness. To head off a reading that could misconstrue the meaning of the encounter, Delany represented it in the entry as taking place in the lobby (Delany, interview with James, August 9, 2014).

498 **Lamar, Lionel:** Actors. Lionel appears in Delany's film *The Orchid*, and a character based on Lamar appears in Delany's novel *Dark Reflections* (Delany, *Dark Reflections*, 24–25, 32; Delany, interview with James, August 9, 2014).

498 **Joe Koenig:** A neighbor in Delany's building (Delany, interview with James, August 9, 2014).

500 **"The bureaucratic satire":** Notes for Delany's review of *2001*, which appeared in the *Magazine of Fantasy & Science* Fiction in August 1968 (Samuel R. Delany, "Stanley Kubrick's *2001: A Space Odyssey*," *Magazine of Fantasy & Science Fiction* 35, August 1968, 61–62).

501 **"Dear John":** Probably John Foyster (Delany, interview with James, August 9, 2014).

503 ***Das Glasperlenspiel:*** 1943 novel by Herman Hesse, translated as *The Glass Bead Game*. Delany had read only fifteen to twenty pages of the book at this point (Delany, interview with James, March 31, 2016).

503 **"The Campbell book":** Joseph Campbell's *The Hero with a Thousand Faces*.

505 ***LORE:*** Likely a fanzine.

506   **"worm-pills":** Pinworm medication. (Delany, interview with James, March 31, 2016).

506   **Bob:** Identity unknown; possibly another frequenter of the Old Reliable whose remark Delany had overheard and recorded (Delany, interview with James, August 9, 2014).

Notebook 90—[Summer 1968]

Most of the pages in this notebook are blank. The notes that remain are either illegible (written hastily in thick marker) or fragmentary, save for the notes included here.

Notebook 78—[Summer–Autumn 1968]

508   **"The first thing to say about 'The New Thing'":** This is a draft of a response to an article on the "New Thing" (later called the New Wave) by Judith Merril. Delany's piece was never published (Delany, interview with James, August 9, 2014).

510   **"Warhoon":** Fanzine edited by Richard Lupoff (addressed as "Dick" in the salutation that follows).

512   **Samuel "J" Delany:** Delany is probably pointing out an error in Dick Lupoff's original letter (Delany, interview with James, August 9, 2014).

516   **"Poul asks a question":** This is a response to a letter posted by science fiction writer Poul Anderson in *Science Fiction Forum*, a monthly "letter zine" compiled by the Science Fiction Writers of America (Delany, interview with James, August 9, 2014).

516   **Brian, Harry:** Brian Aldiss and Harry Harrison, British and American science fiction writers respectively, who, as cofounders of the journal *SF Horizons* and editors of a series of SF anthologies, worked to improve the level of critical discourse within the genre (Clute and Nicholls, *Encyclopedia of Science Fiction*, 12–13, 546).

521   **"People to send *Nova* to":** In addition to the already familiar names, Robert Duncan and Gary Snyder were West Coast–based poets, and David Hartwell was to become an important editor of SF and a major supporter of Delany's work. (For instance, Harper's small press, Draper Press, published Delany's first three collections of critical essays: *The Jewel-Hinged Jaw*, *The American Shore*, and *Starboard Wine*.)

521   **"Lay axes":** Draft of the opening line of "Time Considered as a Helix of Semi-precious Stones."

Notebook 34—August 1968 [August–September 1968]

522   **"Editorial note":** Around the same time Delany began this notebook, he signed a contract with Avon for the *Prism, Mirror, Lens* series. This entry is a draft of the faux-scholarly introduction to that series. The fictive editor's name, "George Ernstbarger," is a nod to the Avon editor, George Ernstberger (Delany, interview with James, October 30, 2011).

526 **Tom:** Thomas M. Disch, science fiction writer, critic, and poet (Clute and Nicholls, *Encyclopedia of Science Fiction*, 339–40).

527 **"What is hap":** Preliminary notes for a talk given at a science fiction convention (Delany, interview with James, October 30, 2011).

529 **"C.V.J.A.":** Chester V. J. Anderson, a science fiction writer (Clute and Nicholls, *Encyclopedia of Science Fiction*, 29).

529 **Trina:** Trina Robbins, a cartoonist, clothing designer, and, at the time, girlfriend of Paul Williams. Williams was the founding editor of *Crawdaddy!* (Delany, interview with James, October 30, 2011).

530 **Karen Dalton:** Influential folksinger who had met Delany and Hacker at a downtown performance venue. The three became casual friends. In conversation, Delany has recalled Dalton visiting Hacker, Folsom, and himself in their apartment, and the four of them singing together (Delany, interview with James, October 30, 2011).

530 **"my dick will fall off":** Delany had decided to draft *Equinox* only while holding an erection (Samuel R. Delany, "Pornography and Censorship," in *Shorter Views: Queer Thoughts and the Politics of the Paraliterary* [Middletown, CT: Wesleyan University Press, 1999], 295).

530 **Zodiac:** Alternative title for *Prism, Mirror, Lens* (Delany, interview with James, October 30, 2011).

531 **"Alchemica":** Chapter from *Equinox*, here again called *Faust*.

Notebook 79—[Winter 1968]

532 **"Langdon Jones's anthology '——'":** This as-yet-untitled anthology did not ultimately see publication (Delany, interview with James, October 30, 2011).

533 **"'——,' Anne McCaffrey (ed.), 1969:** The untitled McCaffrey anthology was eventually published as *Alchemy and Academe* (1970) (Delany, interview with James, October 30, 2011).

11. TO SAN FRANCISCO
Notebook 36—January–February 1969

539 **"Reconstruction of the lost MLA seminar":** Originally titled "Speculative Fiction," this talk was an early version of "About 5,750 Words," which eventually appeared in *The Jewel-Hinged Jaw* (1–15).

542 **"The State of Kings":** Part of *Those Spared by Fire* (Delany, interview with James, March 30, 2016).

543 **John:** John Witten-Doris.

543 **"I've been up since four":** The speaker is Judith Merril (Delany, interview with James, October 30, 2011).

543 **"Pamela brought homemade masks and Tom / wore full dress":** Pamela Zoline and Thomas M. Disch (Delany, interview with James, October 30, 2011).

545 **"shall I take eight thou a year":** These were actual teaching opportuni-

ties Delany had been considering, but chose to forgo with his move to San Francisco (Delany, interview with James, October 30, 2011).

Notebook 37—April 1969 [February–April 1969]

This is the single instance in which I have presented entries in the reverse of the order in which they appear in the original notebook. When the dated entries are read in conventional front-to-back order, they appear to advance backward in time, which implies that, like entries in other notebooks, they were inscribed from the back of the notebook to the front. With their order reversed here, the entries show both correct chronological order and a clear conceptual progression. However, I invite the reader to read these entries the other way around, which is consistent with how I have presented the entries in the rest of the volume. Contrariwise, I also encourage the reader to experiment with reading entries in other notebooks in reverse order as well.

550 ***"Evil Companions* by Michael Perkins":** In his introduction to the Masquerade edition of *Evil Companions* (1968; reprint, New York: Masquerade Books, 1992, 8), Delany describes his first encounter with Perkins in the Earley by the Park bookstore in the spring of 1968. Several weeks later, in early summer, both men gave a public reading at that bookstore; Delany read from *Nova* and Perkins from *Evil Companions* (11). Perkins's novel greatly impressed Delany, and shortly before departing for San Francisco, he met with Perkins to discuss his pornographic novel *Equinox* (Delany, *Silent Interviews*, 245). Delany has said in conversation that Perkins encouraged him to move beyond the fragmented structure of *Equinox* and explore the possibilities of writing a fully cohesive pornographic novel (Delany, interview with James, August 9, 2014). This advice was a major impetus for Delany's writing of *Hogg*, which he dedicated to Perkins (Rob Stephenson, introduction to *Hogg*, by Samuel R. Delany [1995; reprint, Normal, IL: FC2, 2004], 5).

551 **"The loss (misplacement?) of a notebook impels this":** Preliminary notes for the story that would evolve into *Hogg*, which, while substantially completed in 1969 and reworked over the next several years, would not see publication until 1995 (Stephenson, introduction to *Hogg*, 8).

APPENDIX 1
Notebook 89 [Winter 1957–January 1958]

558 **Chico Ramez:** Probably an amalgam of several of Delany's Latino friends (Delany, interview with James, August 9, 2014).

558 **Stuart Byron:** Student in the creative writing class at Bronx Science attended by Marilyn Hacker (Delany, interview with James, August 9, 2014).

561 **Peter Salaff:** A young violinist Delany had met only once at a party thrown by one of his friends from Camp Woodland. Young Delany was instantly smitten with Salaff; he later wrote a violin concerto for him, and made him

one of the dedicatees of the first volume of *The Fall of the Towers* (Delany, *Motion*, 92).

562 **"Beginning of Howard Pease Adventure Story":** This is the opening of the "H.P." story mentioned in Notebook 6. As a boy Delany had been captivated by Pease's novel *Bound for Singapore* and desired to write a similar story (Delany, interview with James, August 9, 2014). Anticipating his transgressive fiction to come, Delany's draft of the opening chapters of *Black Watch and Treasure*—written when he was no more than fifteen—is a racially charged, pornographic pastiche of Pease.

564 **Christmas list:**
> **Daddy**—Samuel R. Delany Sr.
> **Mom**—Margaret Carey Boyd Delany.
> **Peggy**—Sara Boyd Delany, Delany's younger sister.
> **Grandma**—Sara Ophelia Fitzgerald Boyd, maternal grandmother.
> **Dorothy**—Dorothy Savoy, maternal cousin.
> **Boyd**—Boyd Savoy, Dorothy's older brother.
> **Barbara**—Barbara Paige Randel, maternal cousin.
> **Betty and Julian**—Barbara's younger sister and her husband.
> **Tante**—Virginia Boyd Savoy, maternal aunt.
> **Sweetheart**—Dorothy Boyd Paige, maternal aunt, mother of Barbara and Betty.
> **Uncle Myles**—Myles Paige.
> **Uncle Lenny**—Leonard D. Savoy, husband of Tante.
> **Burton**—Delany's father's assistant at the funeral parlor.
> **Sylvia**—Burton's wife.
> **Sonny**—Harry Delany, adopted son of Delany's paternal uncle Hubert T. Delany.
> **Barbara**—Sonny's wife.
> **Edward, Nany, Bill**—Delany's first cousins, the children of Aunt Laura and Uncle Ed.
> **Aunt Laura and Uncle Ed**—Delany's father's next older sister and her husband (Delany, interview with James, August 9, 2014).

APPENDIX 2

Notebook 1—January–February 1958

577 **"Feb. 6, 1960—after CEEB":** The meaning of "CEEB" is unknown. The date is an anomaly, as the other material in the notebook points toward the archival date of January–February 1958. Either the date of the poem is itself a fiction, or, more likely, it indicates that the poem was simply written at a later date and inscribed in the pages of this earlier notebook (Delany, interview with James, August 9, 2014).

578 **"Blue Denim Jazz":** A partial draft of a script Delany wrote for the Hunter College Dramatic Workshop for Young People. The title is an allusion to James Leo Herlihy's play *Blue Denim* (Delany, interview with James, August 9, 2014).

BIBLIOGRAPHY

Biondi, Martha. *To Stand and Fight: The Struggle for Postwar Civil Rights in New York City*. Cambridge, MA: Harvard University Press, 2003.

Clute, John, and John Grant. *The Encyclopedia of Fantasy*. New York: St. Martin's, 1997.

Clute, John, and Peter Nicholls. *The Encyclopedia of Science Fiction*. New York: St. Martin's Griffin, 1995.

Cohen, Ronald D. *Rainbow Quest: The Folk Music Revival and American Society, 1940–1970*. Amherst: University of Massachusetts Press, 2002.

———, ed. *"Wasn't That a Time!" Firsthand Accounts of the Folk Music Revival*. Lanham, MD: Scarecrow Press, 1995.

Delany, Samuel R. "And Janis Joplin." *Crawdaddy!* 19, October 1968, 28–30.

———. *Atlantis: Three Tales*. Middletown, CT: Wesleyan University Press, 1995.

———. *Aye, and Gomorrah: Stories*. New York: Vintage, 2003.

———. *Babel-17*. 1966. Reprint, New York: Vintage, 2001.

———. *The Ballad of Beta-2*. 1965. Reprint, New York: Bantam, 1982.

———. *Bread and Wine: An Erotic Tale of New York*. New York: Juno Books, 1997.

———. "Chronology." Unpublished personal document, 2014.

———. *Conversations with Samuel R. Delany*. Edited by Carl Freedman. Jackson: University Press of Mississippi, 2009.

———. *Dark Reflections*. New York: Carroll & Graf, 2007.

———. *Dhalgren*. 1975. Reprint, New York: Vintage, 2001.

———. *Driftglass*. 1971. Reprint, New York: New American Library, 1971.

———. *The Einstein Intersection*. 1967. Reprint, Middletown, CT: Wesleyan University Press, 1998.

———. *Empire Star*. 1966. Reprint, New York: Vintage, 2001.

———. *Equinox*. 1973. Reprint, New York: Masquerade Books, 1994.

———. *The Fall of the Towers*. 1970. Reprint, New York: Vintage, 2004.

———. *Flight from Nevèrÿon*. 1985. Reprint, Middletown, CT: Wesleyan University Press, 1994.

———. *Heavenly Breakfast: An Essay on the Winter of Love*. 1979. Reprint, Flint, MI: Bamberger Books, 1997.

———. *Hogg*. 1995. Reprint, Normal, IL: FC2, 2004.

———. *The Jewel-Hinged Jaw*. 1977. Reprint, Middletown, CT: Wesleyan University Press, 2009.

———. *The Jewels of Aptor*. 1962. Reprint, New York: Bantam, 1982.

———. *The Mad Man*. 1994. Reprint, Rutherford, NJ: Voyant, 2002.

———. "The Mirror and the Maze." *American Literary History* 24, no. 4 (Winter 2012): 768–74.

———. *The Motion of Light in Water: Sex and Science Fiction Writing in the East Village*. 1988. Reprint, Minneapolis: University of Minneapolis Press, 2004.

———. "Notes on *The Star-Pit*." Unpublished essay, 2005.

———. *Nova*. 1968. Reprint, New York: Vintage, 2002.

———. *Phallos*. 2004. Reprint, Middletown, CT: Wesleyan University Press, 2013.

———. Preface to *Evil Companions*, by Michael Perkins, 5–16. New York: Masquerade Books, 1992.

———. The Samuel R. Delany Collection. The Gotlieb Archival Research Center, Mugar Memorial Library, Boston University, Boston.

———. *Shorter Views: Queer Thoughts and the Politics of the Paraliterary*. Middletown, CT: Wesleyan University Press, 1999.

———. *Silent Interviews*. Middletown, CT: Wesleyan University Press, 1994.

———. "Stanley Kubrick's *2001: A Space Odyssey*." *Magazine of Fantasy & Science Fiction* 35, August 1968, 61–62.

———. *Starboard Wine*. 1984. Reprint, Pleasantville, NY: Dragon Press, 1984.

———. *Stars in My Pocket Like Grains of Sand*. 1984. Reprint, Middletown, CT: Wesleyan University Press, 2004.

———. *The Straits of Messina*. Seattle: Serconia Press, 1989.

———. *Tales of Nevèrÿon*. 1979. Reprint, Middletown, CT: Wesleyan University Press, 1994.

———. *Through the Valley of the Nest of Spiders*. New York: Magnus Books, 2012.

———. *Times Square Red, Times Square Blue*. New York: NYU Press, 1999.

Delany, Samuel R. *See* Steiner, K. Leslie.

Delany, Sarah Louise, Annie Elizabeth Delany, and Amy Hill Hearth. *Having Our Say: The Delany Sisters' First 100 Years*. New York: Dell, 1993.

Ellingham, Lewis, and Kevin Killian. *Poet Be Like God: Jack Spicer and the San Francisco Renaissance*. Middletown, CT: Wesleyan University Press, 1998.

Ellison, Harlan, ed. *Dangerous Visions*. Garden City, NY: Doubleday, 1967.

Foucault, Michel. "What Is an Author?" In *Aesthetics, Method, and Epistemology: Essential Works of Foucault, 1954–1984*, edited by James Faubion, 205–22. London: Penguin, 2000.

Frazier, E. Franklin. *Black Bourgeoisie: The Book That Brought the Shock of Self-Revelation to Middle-Class Blacks in America*. New York: Free Press, 1957.

Galison, Peter. "Trading Zone: Coordinating Actions and Belief." In *The Science Studies Reader*, edited by Mario Biagioli, 137–60. New York: Routledge, 1999.

Gide, André. *The Journals of André Gide*. Vol. 1, *1889–1924*. Translated by Justin O'Brien. New York: Vintage, 1947.

Gore, Robert L. *The Abyssinian Baptist Church: A Photographic Journal*. New York: Harry N. Abrams, 2001.

Hacker, Marilyn. *Presentation Piece*. New York: Viking Press, 1974.

———. *Separations*. New York: Alfred A. Knopf, 1976.

———. *Winter Numbers*. New York: W. W. Norton, 1994.

Jarrett, Gene Andrew, ed. *The Wiley Blackwell Anthology of African American*

Literature. Vol. 2, *1920 to the Present*. Chichester, West Sussex, UK: Wiley-Blackwell, 2014.

Larkin, Colin, ed. *The Encyclopedia of Popular Music*. 4th ed. Oxford: Oxford University Press, 2006.

McLemee, Scott. "Derrida, a Pioneer of Literary Theory, Dies." *Chronicle of Higher Education* 51, no. 9 (2004): par. 11. http://chronicle.com.gate.lib. buffalo.edu/ article/Derrida-a-Pioneer-of-Literary/30791/.

Merril, Judith, ed. *SF 12*. New York: Delacorte Press, 1968.

Peplow, Michael S., and Robert S. Bravard, eds. *Samuel R. Delany: A Primary and Secondary Bibliography, 1962–1979*. Boston: G. K. Hall, 1980.

Sadie, Stanley, ed. *The New Grove Dictionary of Music and Musicians*. 2nd ed. London: Macmillan, 2001.

Sallis, James, ed. *Ash of Stars: On the Writing of Samuel R. Delany*. Jackson: University Press of Mississippi, 1996.

Smith, Evans Lansing. *Ricorso and Revolution: An Archetypal Poetics of Modernism*. Columbia, SC: Camden House, 1995.

Sontag, Susan. *Reborn: Journals and Notebooks, 1947–1963*. Edited by David Rieff. New York: Picador, 2008.

Steiner, K. Leslie [Samuel R. Delany]. "Anatomy of a Nova." Unpublished essay, 1997.

———. "Samuel R. Delany." *Pseudopodium*. Ray Davis. http://www .pseudopodium.org/ repress/KLeslieSteiner-SamuelRDelany.html.

Stephenson, Rob. Introduction to *Hogg*, by Samuel R. Delany. 1995. Reprint, Normal, IL: FC2, 2004), 5.

INDEX

Aarenburg, Bob, 19, 96, 609

"About 5,750 Words," 428, 539, 642

Abyssinian Baptist Chorus, 92, 615

Ace Books, 243, 486, 502–3, 518

Adam, Helen, xxi, xxii, 377, 631, 632.
  See also *San Francisco's Burning*

Adams, Léonie, 171

Afterlon, 29, 63–64, 126, 129, 131, 214,
  223, 246, 613

Agee, James, 39, 220, 364–65

Aldiss, Brian, 516, 641

Allen, Farrow, 20, 609

"Alyx," 428

"Ana's Travelin'." *See* Harbor Singers

Anderson, Linda and Jane, 17, 608

Anderson, Poul, 516, 567, 641

Appleton-Century-Crofts, 199, 216,
  238, 324, 621

"Apu" film trilogy, xxiv–xxv, 181, 189–
  94, 620

Aranlyde, Muels, 318, 627

art, 45–46, 119–20, 120–21, 196–98,
  283, 517

artists, social role of, 42–48, 119–20

Arwas, Victor, 28, 610

Ascoli family, 24, 610

Asimov, Isaac, 446, 510

The Assassination, 95, 110–12, 117–18,
  122, 126, 132, 133–34, 239–40, 241,
  616, 623

Atheling, William. *See* Blish, James

Atlantis: Model 1924, xxxii, 626

Auberon (novella), xxvi, 96, 143, 616,
  618; full text, 149–60; notes, 113,
  148, 160–61, 163

Auden, W. H., xxiii, 143, 146, 169,
  170, 307, 619, 626, 627; "Atlantis"
  excerpt, 322, 627

Austen, Jane, 127, 244

Australian Science Fiction Review
  (correspondence), 427, 464–69,
  485–87, 638

Avon Books, 427, 474, 553, 634, 636,
  639

"Aye, and Gomorrah," 377, 428;
  afterword for *Dangerous Visions*
  anthology, 386–87, 632–33; Nebula
  Award, 428, 520, 542

Babel-17, xxi, 255–57, 377; artificial
  language lexicons for, 255–56,
  268–70, 274–80, 299, 624, 625;
  discussion following writing, 440,
  455, 469, 484, 485–86, 493, 502,
  519; language research for, 318–19,
  627; Nebula Award, 377, 455, 520,
  634, 638; opening lines, 314–15;
  working notes, 296, 309–10, 313,
  314, 315–16, 317–22, 626, 627

Baez, Joan, 74, 80, 134, 638

Baldwin, James, xxiii, 139, 140, 229,
  617; *Another Country*, 242, 244–45

The Ballad of Beta-2, xxi, xxxii,
  181; "Ballad" lyrics—221–22, 622;
  discussion during writing, 241,
  300, 626; discussion following
  writing, 484, 519; working notes,
  209, 235, 620

Ballard, J. G., 369, 406, 410, 413, 508,
  509; *Vermilion Sands*, 372–73, 442

ballet, 24–25, 26–28

Balousiak, Bill, 257, 335, 339, 343, 628

Bataille, Georges, 550

Baudelaire, Charles, 146, 170

Beagle, Peter S., 86, 614

Bear Mountain, 255–56, 268, 299, 624,

625–26. *See also* "Camping on Bear Mountain"

The Beasts, 223

Beauvoir, Simone de, 10

Beckett, Samuel, 59, 148

"A Bend in the Road," 335

Benjamin, Walter, xiii

Bester, Alfred, xxiii, 332, 368, 370, 371, 372–73, 628; *The Demolished Man*, 332; *The Stars My Destination*, 332, 370, 372, 442

Bikel, Theodore, 92–93, 615

Biondi, Martha, xvi

"Black Comet" notes, 196, 620–21

"Black Watch and Treasure," 11, 557, 562–63, 608, 644

Blake, William, 170

Blish, James, 506, 510, 511

Blue Denim, 607, 644

"Blue Denim Jazz," 578–84, 644

blurbs, xiv–xv; for published work, 206, 252–53, 381–83, 384, 446–47, 462–63, 532; for unpublished work, 100, 128–34, 141–42, 179, 214

Bobbs-Merrill, 324

Bogan, Louise, 171

Bowman, Ron, xx, 377, 384, 385, 407, 410, 418, 419–20, 632, 634, 635

Boyd, Samuel Hugo ("Gramp"; maternal grandfather), 62, 613

Boyd, Sara ("Grandma"; maternal grandmother), 61–62, 564, 613, 644

Bradbury, Ray, 332, 566–67

Brand, Oscar, 86, 614

Brecht, Bertolt, 105–6, 139

Brodecky, Bill, 490, 537, 545, 639

Brontë sisters, 148, 178, 619

Bronx High School of Science. *See* Delany, Samuel R.

Brown v. Board of Education, xvi

Bruce, 102, 282, 616, 625

Brunner, John, xxiii, 336, 362, 378, 418, 422, 446, 630, 634

Burroughs, Williams S. See *Naked Lunch*

Byron, George Gordon (Lord), 141, 142, 145, 171, 347

"Cage of Brass," 462, 534

Callabro, Bruno, 12, 61, 144, 608

Cambridge Book Company, 57–58

Campbell, Joseph, 503–4, 640

"Camping on Bear Mountain," 255–56, 268

Camp Woodland, xviii–xix, xx, xxxv, 21, 67, 176, 265, 611, 613, 614, 632, 643

Camus, Albert, 37, 147, 168, 296

Carr, Terry, 503

Caruso, Paul, 67, 257, 418, 428, 537, 639

Cavalier magazine, 444, 637

The Charterhouse of Parma, 371

Chatterton, Thomas, xxiii, 29, 35, 139–40, 141, 178, 366

Chaucer, Geoffrey, 94

Ciardi, John, xxi, 29, 139–40, 147, 617

"Citre et Trans," 335, 629, 635

City College. *See* Delany, Samuel R.

City of Night, 244–45

Clarion Workshop, xxi, 428, 541

Clarke, Arthur C., 461, 567; at *2001* premiere, 497, 640

Clement, Hal, 412, 566

Cocteau, Jean, xxiii, 34, 224

Cogswell, Theodore, 387, 633

"The Coldest Place," 468

Coleridge, Hartley, 178

"Coming / Out," xviii, xx, 609

Conan, Neil, 481

Conrad, Joseph, 372

Constantine II of Greece, 348–49, 629

The Corn King and the Spring Queen, 218, 622

"Corona," 377; blurbs, 386, 462, 632, 633; Milford workshop notes, 386–87; working notes, 341, 381, 628

correspondence drafts, 57–58, 93–94, 215, 298–300, 323–25, 330–31, 360–62, 363–64, 393, 397, 408–9, 449,

464–65, 465–69, 479–82, 483, 485–88, 492, 493–94, 501–5, 526–27

Corso, Gregory, 355, 629; epigraph for *The Einstein Intersection*, 365; subject of Delany's verse, 353

Cox, Joe, 537, 639

Crane, Hart, xxiii, 41–42, 281–82, 364

Crane, Stephen, 227

Crawdaddy! magazine, 428, 507, 529–30, 638, 642

creative writing by Delany in journals: collaborative, with Hacker, 8–10, 143, 167–68, 235–36, 237, 607, 618; song lyrics, 83, 614; translations, 105–6, 166, 550, 587, 592–600, 601–4, 616, 619; verse, 6, 7, 8, 10, 21–22, 23, 26, 60–61, 103, 104–5, 119, 128, 148, 268, 282, 344–45, 353, 355–56, 407–8, 421, 542–47, 548, 577, 607, 610, 616, 625, 629, 642–43, 644

Cuban missile crisis, 194

Cycle for Toby, 1, 29, 56, 67, 122, 126, 129, 130, 199, 214, 612

Dalton, Karen, 530, 642

Dalton School. *See* Delany, Samuel R.

Dark Reflections, 255, 624, 640

Davis, Gwendolyn, 20, 609

Davis, Miles, 136, 617

Deirdre, 255, 270, 294, 624

Delany, Elizabeth ("Bessie"; aunt), xvi

Delany, Henry Beard (grandfather), xv–xvi

Delany, Hubert T. (uncle), xvi

Delany, Margaret Carey Boyd (mother), xviii, 283, 419, 423, 456, 564, 625, 644

Delany, Samuel R.: acrophobia and anxiety attacks, 182, 230–31, 232, 622; Bread Loaf conference, xx–xxi, xxii, 29–30, 64, 67, 103, 129, 133, 140, 204, 206, 211, 323, 616, 617; Bronx High School of Science,

xi–xii, xvii–xviii, xx, xxiv, 1–2, 21, 23, 29, 39–41, 43, 48, 56–57, 67, 96, 206, 231, 256, 557, 607, 608, 609, 610, 611, 612, 614, 615, 616, 620, 621, 623, 624; City College, first stint, xi, 95–97, 107, 206, 256, 615; City College, second stint, 294–95, 297, 298–300, 301, 308, 313, 623, 625; Dalton School, xvi–xvii, xx, 20, 206, 234, 310, 609, 626, 627; Detroit trip and marriage, xxxi, 148–49, 162–63, 164, 255, 618, 624 (see also *Auberon*); family, general notes, xv–xviii, xix, xxxvi, 29, 40, 61–62, 64, 612, 613, 644; folk performance, xi, xii, xviii–xix, xxxvi, 29, 41,81, 83, 85, 86, 90, 134, 172–77, 182, 225, 245, 335, 614, 619, 622 (*see also* folk music revival; Harbor Singers); Harlem home, xi, xii, xv, xvi, xviii, xix, 62, 64, 69, 140; Heavenly Breakfast experiences (*see* Heavenly Breakfast band and commune); hospitalization from pneumonia, 182, 223–25; Mount Sinai experiences, 182, 255–56, 259–60, 265–67, 270–71, 294, 502, 622, 623–24; move to San Francisco, xii, xiii, xxi, 428, 537, 541, 542–45, 548, 551, 643; National Scholastic prizes, xx, 1, 21, 23; Newport Folk Festival, xix, xxxv, 67, 69–93, 613–15; NYU scholarship, 67, 93–94, 130, 610; open marriage and Delany's homosexuality, 167–68, 619; relationship with Bob Folsom (*see* Folsom, Bob); relationship with Ron Bowman (*see* Bowman, Ron); relationship with Sonny, 216–17, 622; teaching remedial reading, xix, 234, 299–300, 588–91; Texas trip, 256–57, 317, 338, 350, 484, 502, 625, 627; travels in Europe (*see* Europe, Delany's travels in)

Delany, Samuel Ray, Sr. (father), xv, xviii, 104–5, 260, 564, 644; illness and death, xviii, 29, 95, 104–5, 587, 616

Delany, Sara Boyd ("Peggy"; sister), 62, 564, 644

Delany, Sarah Louise ("Sadie"; aunt), xvi

Derrida, Jacques, xxv

Dhalgren, xii, xiii–xiv, xxi, xxiii, xxvi, xxxi, xxxii, 427, 537, 626, 630, 634, 635, 639

Dickinson, Emily, 42, 170, 338

Dicostanzo, Joe, 424, 428

Disch, Thomas M., 144, 369, 373, 378, 399, 428, 447, 526–27, 531, 532, 543, 637, 642; *Camp Concentration*, 442, 512; *The Genocides*, 373

discourse, xxv–xxvi, xxviii, xxix, xxxii–xxxiii

"Dog in a Fisherman's Net," 335, 635; composition, 484; discussion, 422, 462–63; notes, 344, 484, 629

Donne, John, 113

Dostoyevsky, Fyodor, 47

Doubleday, 500, 636

Dr. Faustus, 204–5, 245–46

"Driftglass" (short story), 377, 385, 632

Driftglass (story collection), xxi, 377, 427, 428, 461–62, 637

Drury, Allen, xxi, 29, 140, 617

Dullea, Keir, 497, 640

Dune, 398, 399, 441

Durrell, Lawrence, 121, 147, 619

Dylan, Bob, 301, 338

"The Dynamic Moment," 283–84, 625, 637

Dynamo, 1, 23, 25, 58, 611

The Einstein Intersection, xxi, xxiv, xxxii, 257, 335–36, 377, 428; author's journal passages, 337–39, 365–67, 628–29; discussion during writing, 337–38, 355, 379, 629, 631; discussion following writing, 396, 455, 484, 493, 520, 540, 502; epigraphs, 364–65, 627, 628; Nebula Award, 428, 520, 542; publication, 520, 401–2, 493, 630; working notes, 328–30, 364–67, 383, 384, 629

Eliot, T. S., xxiii, 38, 42, 59, 146, 171, 283, 295–96

Ellison, Harlan, 378; *Dangerous Visions*, 632–23

Elly (Eleanor), 36–38, 611

Emeus, Gale, xx, 2, 21–23, 24, 35, 50, 52, 609

Empire Star, xxi, 257, 627; discussion following writing, 501–2, 519; epigraph, 322, 627; working notes, 322–23, 326, 331. *See also* Auden, W. H.

Equinox, xxii, 182, 427; discussion during writing, 457, 530, 639; opening sequence, 458, 636; working notes, 457–60, 529, 530–31, 638, 642

Ernstberger, George, 636, 641

Europe, Delany's travels in: xii, xxi, xxxi, 95, 256, 257, 335–36, 628; Athens, 337, 342, 346–51, 353, 628, 635; Istanbul, 336, 353–54, 355–56, 360, 367; London, 336, 341, 360, 378, 401; Milos, 337, 343, 344, 360, 422; Mykonos, 344, 366; Syros, 343–44, 422; Venice, 339

Eurydice, xxiii, xxxv, 73, 75, 82–83, 84–85, 86, 87, 92, 614

Evil Companions, 550, 643

existentialism, 37, 45–46, 168, 511

Fabian, Gerald Langston, 550

"The Fall of the Towers" (pre-trilogy), 96, 107, 115, 123

The Fall of the Towers, xxi, xxii, 181–82; blurbs, 252–53; British publication, 631, 635; conception on Brooklyn Bridge, 181, 198, 381–

83; discussion during writing, 187, 198–200, 225, 241; discussion following writing, 206, 215, 299, 300, 315, 356, 381–83, 440–41, 455, 518–19; excerpt, 183; general working notes, 184, 620; working notes for *City of a Thousand Suns*, 203–4, 211, 212–13, 247–48, 250, 253; working notes for *Out of the Dead City*, 183, 185–86, 215; working notes for *The Towers of Toron*, 186–87, 203, 207, 621; and the Vietnam War, 518–19

Faulkner, William, 28, 35, 47, 127, 147

"Faust and Archimedes," 428, 532

Faust myth, 245–46, 249

"Faust" project, 181–82, 377, 427, 623; discussion during writing, 355; excerpt, 308–9, 626; working notes, 245–46, 249–50, 251, 259, 271–72, 280, 296, 301–2, 304, 305–7, 333–34, 339–41, 351–52

"A Fictional Architecture which Manages Only with Great Difficulty Not Once to Mention Harlan Ellison," 335, 398–99, 532, 630, 633, 634

fiction writing: novel, 117–18, 120, 127; short story, 356, 421–22

film criticism, 189–94, 500

Fitzgerald, Russell, xxi, 377, 407, 410, 418, 427, 493–94, 498, 631, 635

The Flames of the Warthog, 95, 99, 108–10, 116–17, 122, 126, 128–29, 131, 133, 142, 223, 615

Flaubert, Gustave, 206

"Flesh and Roses," 60–61

Flight from Nevèrÿon, xxxii

Florida Review, 20, 609

folk music revival, xviii–xix, 176; history of folk music, 175–76; Newport Folk Festival, xix, xxxv, 83, 85, 86, 90, 132, 214, 265, 266. *See also* Harbor Singers

Folsom, Bob, 256–57, 327, 330–31, 484, 627, 628, 632

Foucault, Michel, xxv–xxvi

Foyster, John, 466, 469, 485–87, 501–5, 637

Frazer, James, xxiii. *See also The Golden Bough*

Freud, Sigmund, 41, 42, 49. *See also* psychoanalysis; psychology

Frost, Robert, xxi, 29, 139, 211, 617

Gaddis, William, 244–45, 512

Galison, Peter, xxx

Gateway Singers, 92, 615

Gaughan, Jack, 199, 450, 621, 637

gender: masculinity, 420; misogyny, 241–42, 567, 569, 570, 573

General Grant Houses, xix, 587

"Geo's Poems," see *Voyage, Orestes*

Gibran, Khalil, 99, 615

Gibson, Bob, 92, 615

Gide, André, xiii, xxiii, 9, 29, 34, 38, 59, 147, 235–36; *The Counterfeiters* (*Les faux-monnayeurs*), xxiii, 217, 239, 281, 622

Das Glasperlenspiel, 503, 640

"The Glass Negro," 94, 123, 615

Goethe, Johann Wolfgang von, 147

The Golden Bough, 41, 130, 504

Gordon, Dr., 40, 43, 48, 611, 620

"The Gravedigger," xx, 1, 132, 609

Graves, Robert, xxiii, 147, 170, 504

Greenbaum, Steve, 297, 625

Greenberg, Samuel, xxiii, 145, 299, 366, 626

Greenwood Lake, xvi, 164, 619

Grossman, Dr., 255, 259–60, 267, 270–71, 311–12, 401, 624

Grove Press, 323, 324

"The Gryphon Has Two Heads," 49, 52, 56–57, 126, 132

Guthrie, Woody, 85, 90

Hacker, Marilyn, xi–xii, xvii, xviii, xx, xxi, xxii–xxiii, xxvi, xxxi, 1,

2, 29, 67, 95, 96, 97, 143–44, 181, 182, 255, 256–57, 377, 428, 537; at Bronx Science, xvii, 558–59, 643; correspondence with Delany on Bob Folsom, 256–57, 330–31; Delany's comments on her poetry, 95, 100, 107, 141–42, 224, 338, 615, 617–18; Detroit trip and marriage to Delany (*see* Delany, Samuel R.); editor at Ace Books, 144, 518; miscarriage, 164–65, 618; moves, 323, 384, 631; move to San Francisco, 428, 537, 639; at NYU, xvii, 1, 14–17, 29, 67, 96, 609, 611, 617; pregnancy, 96–97, 162; relationship with Link Martin, 428, 639; scholarship to NYU, 67, 608, 609, 610; at Soley and Caruso's home, 456; and Spicer circle, 428, 631–32, 639; trip to Mexico, 182, 223, 224, 622; visits to Auden's home, 143, 169, 307, 619, 626

Hacker's writing in Delany's journals: collaborative, with Delany, 8–10, 143, 167–68, 235–36, 237, 607, 618 (*see also Auberon*); epigraphs, 321–22; handwritten comments, xvii, xxxii–xxxiii, 2, 5, 13–14, 25, 60–61, 149–50, 151, 331, 607, 608; transcribed comments, 455–56; transcribed verse, 115, 166, 167, 168, 170, 219–20, 224, 307, 321–22, 550, 616, 619, 626

"Half of Blindness," 55, 57

Harbor Singers, xix, 29, 143, 612, 616, 619; "Ana's Travelin'," 58, 83, 125, 614; "I Come for to Sing" (article), 172–77, 619; song lists, 58, 110, 346, 629

Harcourt, Brace, 55, 323, 324

Hardy, Thomas, 127

Harness, Charles, 442

Harrison, Harry, 516, 641

Hartwell, David, 521, 641

Heavenly Breakfast (memoir), 428, 610, 634

Heavenly Breakfast band and commune, 427–28, 433–34, 436, 453, 454, 488–89, 492, 494–95, 636, 638

Heighfli, Mark, 456, 638

Heinlein, Robert, xxiii, 509; *Starship Troopers*, 370–71, 519; *Stranger in a Strange Land*, 510; "Waldo," 374, 463

Hellerman, Fred, 84, 614

Helstrom, Ron, 257, 335, 337–39, 343–44, 628

Hemingway, Ernest, 135, 147

Herbert, Frank, xxiii. See also *Dune*

Hesse, Herman, 503, 640

"High Weir," 526, 534

"Historical Novel," 208–9, 226–29, 622

Hogg, 551, 643

Holiday, Billie, 37, 53

Holmes, Odetta, 90–91, 92, 615

homosexuality, xii, xx, xxiii, xxvii; cruising, xx, 2, 22–23, 259–60, 421, 609–10; and discourse, xx, xxvii–xviii; and literature, xxiii, 8–10, 145, 245; and morality, 416; and patriarchy, 260; Sappho as lesbian poet, 46. *See also* sexuality

Horn, Peter, xxxv, 67, 69–71, 75, 77, 79, 83, 84, 87–89, 214, 613

Houston, Cisco, 90, 615

Howard, Robert E., 463

Howard Gotlieb Archival Research Center, xi, xiv, xxix–xxxi

Hugo Award, xi, xxii

Hunter College Dramatic Program for Young People, xxxvi, 1, 20, 607, 644

"I Come for to Sing" (article). *See* Harbor Singers

"In the Ruins." See *They Fly at Çiron*

In Search of Silence (journal), 29, 31–57, 610

Israel, Paul, 35, 37, 51–52
Israel, Stuart, 35, 52–55

Jack and Jill of America, xvi, 608, 609
Jackson, Shirley, 222
James, Henry, 59, 145
The Jewel-Hinged Jaw, xxii, 641
The Jewels of Aptor, xxi, xxii–xxiii,
   xxxii, 95–96, 144, 181, 616, 625;
   blurb, 446–47, 637; discussion
   following writing, 189, 206, 228,
   381, 455, 518; excerpts, 101–2,
   179, 620; Hacker's contributions
   to, 447; publication, 195, 381,
   624; trimming for publication,
   446, 486–87, 502–3; in *Voyage,
   Orestes*, 199–200, 202, 209, 210, 217;
   working notes, 100–101, 177, 616
"Jo" poems, 141–42, 200, 617, 619; "The
   Ballad of Wandering Jo," 107, 123,
   134, 141
José, 5, 37, 611
journal writing, commentary on, 18,
   37, 38, 48, 49, 50, 139, 162, 265–66,
   416, 420–21, 432, 471, 479, 608, 611
Journaux d'Orphée, xxxv, 67, 69–93,
   610, 613–15; discussion following
   writing, 94, 132, 214, 265, 266
Joyce, James, xxiii, 28, 94, 118, 147, 301,
   341
Jung, Carl, 41, 504

Kafka, Franz, 16, 38, 147, 584
Kallman, Chester, 143, 169, 170, 626
Kay, Bernard, 96, 122, 140, 162, 163,
   164, 216, 233–35, 238, 243, 256, 271,
   300, 311, 331, 453, 624, 625
Kay, Iva, 96
Keats, John, 141, 171, 550
Kennedy, John F. (assassination), 182,
   243, 518–19
Kestenbaum, Simon, xx, 196–98, 199,
   621
Keyes, Daniel, 456, 634, 638
Kidd, Virginia, 448, 450, 637

King, Martin Luther (assassination),
   498
The King Must Die, 343
Knight, Damon, xxi, 377, 407, 408–9,
   410, 413, 418, 483, 634
Krevett, Ellen, 3–4, 13, 567–68, 570,
   607
Krim, Dr., 40, 48, 611
Kronenberger, John, 42, 122, 612
Kyria, Pierre, 16–18, 23, 608

Landau, Danny, 480, 482, 639
Langer, Suzanne, 411–12
language: and society, 112–13;
   artificial, 255–56, 624, 625 (see
   also *Babel-17*; *Nova*); Greek, 337,
   338, 342; and speech, 411–12; and
   thought, 507
"The Last Hour of Night," 107–8
Le Guin, Ursula K., 144
Lenin, Vladimir, 47–48
Ley, Sandra, 496–98, 640
Ley, Willy, 496, 640
Liadain, 100, 168–69
"Lines of Power." *See* "We, in Some
   Strange Power's Employ, Walk on
   a Rigorous Line"
"Lion Cubs," 7, 124, 135
Lipsky, Johnny, 39, 74, 611
Litwin, David, 163, 200, 205, 238, 616,
   618, 621
Logan, David, 96, 163, 311, 618–19
Lost Stars, 1, 57, 122, 126, 131–32, 223,
   612
The Lovers, 95, 122, 126, 132–33, 142,
   615
"Love-Tide," 38
Lowell, Amy, 170–71, 178
Lupoff, Dick, 511–12, 641

MacColl, Ewan, 84, 614
MacLean, Katherine, 450
MacLow, Lloyd, 35–37, 50–55
The Mad Man, xv, xxxii, 620–21
Madame Bovary, 206

Mailer, Norman, 147, 229; *The Naked and the Dead*, 370–71
Makeba, Miriam, 110
Mann, Thomas. See *Dr. Faustus*
"Marlin Night-Bound," 103, 616
Martin, Link, xxi, 377, 428, 639
Marxism, xxxiii
McCaffrey, Anne, 386, 533, 642
McCarthy, Mary, 229
McGinley, Phyllis, 172
McLuhan, Marshall, 440, 448
McNeill, William, xxi, 377, 631
Melville, Herman, 3, 16, 146, 147, 307, 372, 577
Merejkowski, Dmitry, 463
Merril, Judith, xxi, 336, 363, 372, 378, 399, 401, 428, 485, 492, 543, 630, 639–40, 641, 642
Michaels, Mike, 86, 614
"Mike, Jesus, and Me," 132, 587, 588–91
Milford Writers' Conference, xxi, 377, 418, 428, 450, 633, 635, 637
Miller, Henry, 31, 38, 49, 147, 211
Mills, Alan, 92, 615
Modern Language Association, 428, 539, 541, 642
Monk, Thelonius, 136, 617
Moorcock, Michael, xxi, 336, 362, 363, 375, 378, 398, 451, 485, 630, 631, 632, 633
Moore, Marianne, 171, 212
Morningside Gardens, xix, 96
Morrison, Henry, 256, 257, 323–25, 363, 416, 494, 506, 628
The Motion of Light in Water, xi–xii, xviii–xix, xx, xxii, xxxiii–xxxiv, 95, 96, 143, 144, 181, 182, 255, 256, 257, 609–10, 613, 617, 621, 622, 624, 626
Mott, Laford, 632
Mozart, Wolfgang, 368
Mueller, Heidi, 335, 418, 635
myth, 41, 63, 128, 135, 195, 243, 284, 286–94, 324, 503–4, 540; classical mythology and drama, 287–93; Faust myth, 245–46, 249; Goddess myth, 285–86; literary myth, 195–96, 240–41; and sexuality, 264–65, 285–86

Naked Lunch, 147, 244
Nation and Rebirth. See *Voyage, Orestes*
Nebula Award, xi, xxi, 378, 428, 634. *See also* "Aye, and Gomorrah"; *Babel-17*; *The Einstein Intersection*
New American Library, 300, 301, 308, 323–24, 626
New Lost City Ramblers, 90, 614–15
New Wave science fiction, 508–10, 520, 630, 641
"New Wor(l)ds, Many Inventions," 336, 367–73, 532, 631
New Worlds, xxi, 398, 442, 485, 628, 629, 632
Newport Folk Festival. See folk music revival
Newport Jazz Festival, 97, 132, 136–39
New York University (NYU). *See* Delany, Samuel R.; Hacker, Marilyn
Nietzsche, Friedrich, 15, 48, 113, 147
"Night and the Lives of Joe Dicostanzo," 428, 534
Niles, John Jacob, 91–92, 615
Niven, Larry, 468
Nova, xxi, 335, 336, 377, 427, 629, 630, 637, 635, 636, 641; discussion during composition, 355, 362, 385, 400, 410, 420, 423, 502; discussion following composition, 440, 441, 467–68, 493, 502, 520, 521; imaginary languages for, 352–53, 357–58, 406; opening lines, 360, 629–30; synopsis, 393–97, 633; working notes, 341–42, 354–55, 356, 359, 362, 374–75, 380, 383, 388, 405–6, 409, 415, 444, 635, 637

O'Hare, Michael, 40, 611

Olatunji, Babatunde, 84, 614

"On the Dying of the Poet's Father by Cancer," 95, 104–5, 107, 616

"On the Unspeakable," xxxii

Orbit, 408

The Orchid, 632, 640

Orpheus, 71, 86, 93

Osius, Paula, 362, 363–64, 630

Paige, Myles (uncle), xvi, 164, 564, 619, 644

"Passacaglia," 18, 57, 126, 132

patriarchy, 260, 285, 287–90, 292–93

Peake, Mervyn, 461, 567

Pease, Howard. *See* "Black Watch and Treasure"

Peirce, Charles Sanders, xxx

Peplow, Michael, and Robert S. Bravard, xxiv, xxx

Perez, Ana, 83, 174–75, 177, 361, 407, 420, 616, 631

Perkins, Michael, 550, 643

Phallos, xxxii

Pinkerton, Bobs, 199, 218–19, 225, 238, 242–43, 300, 621

poetry, craft of, 5, 38–39, 41–42, 113, 119, 128, 170–72

Pohl, Frederik, 363, 630

"Pomegranate," 28, 56–57

Ponsot, Marie, 29, 42, 97, 122, 140, 217, 313, 612, 625, 627

pornographic writings, xiii, xx, xxvii–xxviii, xxxiii, 634; outlines, 392, 409, 422, 551; passages, 6, 11, 60–61, 260–62, 267, 273, 280–83, 325–28, 399–400, 402–4, 432–39, 442–45, 458, 584

Porter, Andrew, 397, 633

"Portrait of the Artist as Two Characters in Search of Tea and Sympathy," xx, 1, 609

Portraits from the Immature Mind, xxii, 95, 613, 617; blurbs, 128–34;

contents, 122–27; discussion, 129, 139, 142, 200, 214, 223

Pound, Ezra, xxiii, 42, 59, 148, 171

precociousness and prodigies, xii, xxiii, 35, 38, 130, 131–32, 133, 141, 142, 145, 148, 178, 240, 366, 446, 492

Prism. See "Prismatica"

"Prism & Glass," 238

"Prism & Lens," 95, 100, 615

"Prismatica," 324

Prism, Mirror, Lens, xxiii, 427, 537, 636–37; discussion during writing, 505, 513, 520, 530, 553, 639; editor's introduction, 522–26, 641; opening scene (drafts), 472–73, 491–92, 513, 552, 639; synopses, 429–31, 439–41, 636–37; working notes, 456–57, 470–72, 474–79, 483–84, 499, 512–16, 517, 531, 550–51, 551–52

"A Prose Thing," 126, 132, 611

Proust, Marcel, 9–10, 28, 58, 117–18, 127, 147, 265, 303, 341

psychoanalysis, xxxiii. *See also* Freud, Sigmund; psychology

psychology: of artist, 46, 47, 49, 266; and culture, 42–43, 44; general remarks, 99, 102, 170, 264–65, 283–84, 300–301; and science fiction, 517–20; and sexuality, 259–60, 265. *See also* Freud, Sigmund; psychoanalysis

"Quicksilver," 28

Quiñones, Jesus, 234, 587

race, xii, xv–xvii, xviii, 20, 94, 229, 324, 559, 617

Radiguet, Raymond, xxiii, 29, 31, 34, 145, 366, 446

Ramez, Chico, 558–59, 643

Random House, 47, 142

Ratner, Judy, 13–19, 21–22, 122, 424, 425, 608

Ray, Satyajit. *See* "Apu" film trilogy

Rechy, John, xxiii, 244–45
The Recognitions, 244–45, 512
The Red Badge of Courage, 227
Reinstein, Cary, 38, 96, 283, 558–59, 611, 625
Renault, Mary. See *The King Must Die*
Return to Nevèrÿon tetralogy, xxxii
Richards, I. A., xxiii, 134
Rickett, Dennis, xxxiv
Rilke, Rainer Maria, 48, 148
Rimbaud, Arthur, xxiii, 9, 94, 100, 106, 133, 139, 143, 145, 170, 445–46, 587, 616, 623; Delany translations, 166, 601–4, 619
Rivers, J. (Jimmy), 57, 612
Robbe-Grillet, Alain, 59, 413
Robbins, Trina, 529, 642
Robinson, Baird, 188, 620
Robinson, DeLys, 335, 346–51, 418, 451, 629, 632
Rohm, Sharon, 162, 618
Ruben (Bronx Science student), 13, 608
Rukeyser, Muriel, 171
R.U.R. (Rossum's Universal Robots), 3, 577, 607
Ruskin, John, 365
Russ, Joanna, 377, 386, 412, 428, 448, 529, 633, 637

Sabicas, 84, 614
Salaff, Peter, 561–62, 643–44
Sallis, James, 67, 400, 408, 410, 413, 483, 633, 635, 639
"Salt," 28, 55, 67, 610
"Sand," 39
San Francisco's Burning, 377, 399–400, 632
Sappho 46, 170, 172
Sartre, Jean-Paul, 37, 45, 147
Saussure, Ferdinand de. *See* structuralism
Scavengers, 1, 122, 126, 131, 223
Schachter, J. P., 37, 558–59, 611

Schweers, Sue, 434, 636, 638
science fiction: criticism, 341, 367–73, 411–14, 422–23, 441–42, 464–69, 495, 508–10, 516–17, 527–28, 539; editing, 485, 486–87, 493; landscape as projection of psychology, 517–20; New Wave, 508–10; publishing, 500; relation between SF and non-SF work by Delany, 199–200, 355; science in, 467–69, 485–86
Scientific American, 24, 610
Searles, Baird, 460–61, 638, 639; Delany correspondence with, 479–82. *See also* "The Star-Pit"; WBAI-FM
Seeger, Pete, xix, 85, 614
Separations, 95, 615
Seventeen magazine, 97
sexuality, 206, 457–58. *See also* homosexuality
"Shadows," xviii
Shakespeare, William, 46–47, 141
Sholley, Susan, 198, 621
Silem, Edna, xxii–xxiii; character in *Voyage, Orestes*, 65; Hacker nickname, 133–34, 142, 198, 199
"Silence, Water, Someone Saying My Name," 385, 411–14, 419
"Silent Monologue for Lefty," 23, 38, 126, 611
"Silver," 39, 55
Silverberg, Robert, 363, 455, 630, 638
Sing Out!, 85, 88, 614
Sloane, William, 29, 142, 618
Smith, Cordwainer, 369, 370, 372, 442, 449
Soley, Joe, 67, 257, 384, 418, 428, 456
"Song of Songs," 587; note, 65, 613; translation, 592–600
Sonny, 182, 216–17, 622
Sphere Books, 486, 487, 493–94, 631
Spicer, Jack, xxi, 377, 399, 631–32, 639
Stapledon, Olaf, 510

"The Star-Pit," 257, 336, 377; blurb, 374, 631; discussion after writing, 363, 463, 519, 408, 484, 485, 486, 487, 492, 519, 527, 639–40; radio adaptation, 378, 424–25, 460–61, 479–82, 540–41, 633, 636 (*see also* Searles, Baird; WBAI-FM); working notes, 325, 328, 628

Stars in My Pocket Like Grains of Sand, xxxii

"State of Kings." See *Those Spared By Fire*

Steiner, K. Leslie (Samuel R. Delany), xxiv

Steiner, Louise, 38, 558–59, 611

Stendhal, 371

Stephenou, Lydia, 451, 638

structuralism, 243, 623

Sturgeon, Theodore, xxiii, 220, 356, 360–62, 368–69, 446, 461, 567, 630; *More Than Human*, 332, 442; "The Other Celia," 369; Sturgeon's Law, 516

tarot cards, 432, 469; in *Nova*, 394, 415, 417, 418, 444

"The Terrible Children," 141, 197, 617–18

Thackeray, William Makepeace, 127

They Fly at Çiron, xxii, 262–64, 387, 397, 400, 624, 633, 634

"This Place, Rumoured to Have Been Sodom." See *Those Spared by Fire*

Thomas, Dylan, 113, 171

Those Spared by Fire, 1, 29, 61, 119, 144, 252, 612–13, 617, 623, 642

"Three, Two, One, Contact: Times Square Red," xxxii

"Time Considered as a Helix of Semiprecious Stones," xxii, 427; discussion, 483, 520, 526–27, 534, 638; working notes, 461, 464, 470, 521, 638, 639

"Time-Tide," 38

"To Read *The Dispossessed*," xviii

"The Torture Garden," 132, 401, 570–77, 634

Tricon, 377, 400

Trilling, Lionel, 141, 550

Trotsky, Leon, 47–48

2001: A Space Odyssey: New York premiere, 496–98; notes for review, 500, 640

Vega, Gabriel de la, 251, 419, 623

Veitch, Tom, 470, 638–39

Verlaine, Paul, 9, 171, 445–46, 623, 637

Vidal, Gore, 24

Vietnam War, 518–19

Voyage, Orestes, xxii, xxiii, xxiv, 29–30, 95, 181, 182, 613, 617; discussion during writing, 133, 140, 142, 197, 198–200, 216–18, 218–19, 222–23, 225, 239, 242–43, 447–48; excerpts, 127, 212, 241, 533–34, 622; "Geo's Poems," 134–35, 126, 197, 617; prologue (drafts), 29–30, 64, 184, 613, 620; publication difficulties, 300, 301, 308, 324, 626; working notes, 102, 195–96, 202–3, 205–6, 209–11, 214–15, 217–18, 219–21, 225, 229–30, 236–37, 238, 239, 240–41, 281, 282, 283, 307, 356–57, 388–90, 622, 633

"A Walk in the Country," 57

Ware, Cade, 195, 216, 620

Warhoon, 510–12, 638

Warner, Frank, 92, 615

Warsh, Lew, 38–39, 406–7, 611, 632

"Water-Logue," 105–6, 107, 125, 135, 616

WBAI-FM, 378, 424–25, 460–61, 636, 639

"We, in Some Strange Power's Employ, Move on a Rigorous Line," 67, 427; discussion during writing, 446, 450, 637; discussion following writing, 447, 462, 637; letter to Roger Zelazny concerning, 449; working notes, 452–53, 638

Weavers, the, 80, 92

Wells, H. G., 219, 509

Western genre, 45–46

"What Dreams May Come," 207–8, 238, 622

Wilde, Oscar, xxviii, 121, 266

Wilhelm, Kate, 377, 409, 418, 483, 634, 639

Williams, Paul, 529, 642

Witten-Doris, John, 335, 347, 348, 362, 418, 543, 630

Wittgenstein, Ludwig, xxx, 490; *Tractatus Logico-Philosophicus*, 508, 509, 511–12

Wolfe, Thomas, 59, 147

Wollheim, Donald, xxi, 144, 199, 215, 300, 301, 621

World War II, 62, 64

Wright, Mr., 256, 298–300, 625

writer's craft, 3, 5, 35, 41, 121, 122, 128–34, 227–28, 246, 270, 302–3, 400, 413, 447–449, 487–88, 509, 545–47, 548. *See also* fiction writing; poetry, craft of

Year's Best SF, 485, 492

Yeats, William Butler, 63, 146, 171, 364

Zelazny, Roger, xxi, 144, 369, 371, 373, 385, 412, 428, 442, 461, 635; *Creatures of Light and Darkness*, 508; "Damnation Alley," 487–88; Delany correspondence with, 449, 483, 487–88, 637; "The Doors of His Face, the Lamps of His Mouth," 461; *Lord of Light*, 508

Zoline, Pamela, 378, 399, 543, 642

SAMUEL R. DELANY is an acclaimed novelist and critic who taught English and creative writing at Temple University and lives in Philadelphia. He is the author of works of criticism, fiction, and science fiction, most recently his novel *Through the Valley of the Nest of Spiders*. In 2013, Delany was named the 31st Damon Knight Memorial Foundation Grand Master by the Science Fiction and Fantasy Writers of America.

KENNETH R. JAMES graduated *summa cum laude* from Cornell University and holds an MFA in film and media arts from Temple University as well as a PhD in English from SUNY Buffalo. He has written several essays on Delany's work, including the introductions to *1984: Selected Letters* and *Longer Views* and a contribution to the critical edition of *Phallos*, the latter two books published by Wesleyan University Press.